A History of German Business

Toshio Yamazaki

A History of German Business

In Global Context from the late 19th Century until the End of the Second World War

Springer

Toshio Yamazaki
Faculty of Business Administration
Ritsumeikan University
Ibaraki City, Osaka, Japan

ISBN 978-981-96-8475-5 ISBN 978-981-96-8476-2 (eBook)
https://doi.org/10.1007/978-981-96-8476-2

This Springer imprint is published by the registered company Springer Nature Singapore Pte Ltd.
The registered company address is: 152 Beach Road, #21-01/04 Gateway East, Singapore 189721, Singapore

For my wife, Naomi and son, Tomotaka

Preface

Regarding the internationality and nationality of capital, determining how each country maintains and develops its life power in globalization is vital. Globalism is the principle of competition over acquiring the global hegemony to create more advantageous foundations for corporate behavior, economic development, and the governance as issue of building order. It is important to clarify the special characteristics of capitalism of the country concerned, the generality of capitalistic accumulation, and the power of the life of capital by considering the historical conditions and the processes of birth and development of capitalism in each country. How has German capital maintained its life by exhibiting national characteristics and changing limitations to restrictions under the pursuit of its globalism and the pressure of countries with hegemony in each period? How can the development of German capitalism and business management be understood from this perspective?

This book examines the history of business management in Germany during the shift to monopolistic capitalism that began at the end of the 19th century through the end of World War II from the perspective of comparative management studies. This book elucidates Germany's specific development through analysis from the viewpoints of the historical context of the global economy and German capitalism as well as international economic relations, as seen in the world linkages in aspects of market and capital. The original processes and characteristics determined by each country's unique cultivation of capitalism and the commonalities among various countries can be observed throughout the history of business management. Although the United Kingdom defeated Germany in developing a capitalist economy, Germany promptly realized the shift to monopolistic capitalism at the beginning of the 20th century (as did the United States). It became one of the mother countries presiding over the emergence of business administration as a scientific field (*Betriebswirtschaftslehre*).

Before the end of World War II, German capitalism experienced distinctive development, as evidenced by the early birth of monopolistic capitalism, the birth of the Weimar Republic as the first typical democratic nation in history, and the emergence of National Socialism as one of the most reactionary ideologies adopted by nations. How did this typical development of German capitalism influence the developmental process of the business management field? While influenced by American management methodology, what original development processes did German enterprises undergo, and how were such unconventional characteristics of business management established? What is "German-style management"? What significance did these developments have, and what results did such processes precipitate in the social economy? How did business management's unique evolutionary process affect the development of German capitalism? How were business management practices until the end of the World War II succeeded by new processes after the war? This book examines the late 19th century to the end of World War II from two comparative perspectives: identifying the differences between industrial sectors and those between enterprises. It attempts to identify the characteristics, significance, and limitations of methodological changes in business management through this approach.

This analysis covers a few periods through the end of World War II (the Second Reich, the Weimar Republic, and National Socialism) without limitation to a specific period or historical view. We broadly consider various essential characteristics of business management, such as enterprise concentration, management philosophy, management system, production systems, organizational structure, and business strategy, without limiting the analysis to any specific field. Through such analysis, this book attempts to clarify the overall structure of business management in Germany before the end of World War II and the interrelationships between management systems in each field. This book considers the following four main themes: (1) the concentration of enterprises and its corresponding system of industrial concentration; (2) the labor management system and the deployment of the Taylor system; (3) the deployment of the Ford system and the transformation toward mass production; and (4) changes in the enterprise and organizational structures. This book explores these themes using many original historical materials, such as internal documents of representative enterprises in various significant industries and primary source materials maintained by the Federal Archives in Germany and the National Archives in Washington D. C., as well as numerous books, articles, and annual reports of representative enterprises in major industries.

This book introduces the following six main viewpoints to analyze the history of German business management.

First, the interrelationships between the determinative factors prompting business management transformation, the actual conditions of such changes, and the significance of these phenomena are clarified in relation to the historical conditions of global and German capitalism during each period. The management measures performed by each enterprise are independently established and implemented by top executives and managers; however, their decision-making is influenced and determined by objective economic conditions. Therefore, changes in business management in each period are considered in the historical context.

Second, this book offers a multifactorial analysis of business management through the author's original analytical framework, "total system of business management." This approach refers to a structural framework for conditions that define the established business management methods within the characteristics of capitalism as they are practiced in a specific country. This book analyzes business management concerning German capitalism's structures and the cooperative, interdependent structures that arose from industry coordination. A unique understanding of business management and capitalism in Germany is possible by applying the author's original framework to this analysis.

Third, this book attempts to grasp German capitalism and business management in the history of globalism as the principle for competition over acquiring global hegemony and establishing a world order. It clarifies how Germany was incorporated into the globalism of a country with hegemony in each period, how Germany coped with such movements by pursuing its own globalism, and which trends are seen in Germany's capitalistic accumulation and development of business management from this viewpoint.

Fourth, this book considers business management in Germany in the context of European regional conditions in the period before the end of World War II compared with those in the postwar period. After World War II, Germany promoted the construction of a system of European integration that ultimately evolved into today's European Union and the pursuit of more favorable commercial, industrial, and economic development of the European region. In contrast, before the end of World War II, Germany was not able to establish an accumulation and reproduction structure of capital based on Europe, even though the country's share of exports to this region totaled approximately 70% or more (Statistisches Reichssamt 1902; S.139; Statistisches Reichsamt 1915, S.253-254; Statistisches Reichssamt 1931; S.236-239; Statistisches Reichssamt 1935; S.228-229; Statistisches Reichsamt 1943, S.322-323). How were the differences between these two periods created? This book investigates this research problem relative to the internal structure of business management from a comparative historical perspective and the perspectives of the economic and business environments.

Fifth, German business management is explored relative to the deployment of American management methods from an internationally comparative perspective. Historically, four waves of American management processes can be identified to understand their deployment and implementation as a model of "Americanization." The first wave began at the beginning of the 20th century and ended with the outbreak of the World War I, and the primary occurrence was the deployment of the Taylor system. In the second wave, during the 1920s, the Taylor system diffused, and the Ford system emerged. The third and fourth waves occurred during two periods of economic growth after World War II, through the early 1970s and the 1990s, respectively. This present analysis focuses on the changes in business management during the first and second waves.

Sixth, this book analyzes "continuity" in business management before the end of World War II and after the war and its significance. The significance and limitations of business management are determined by examining how changes before the end of the World War II succeeded after the war and by identifying the points to be evaluated concerning postwar development.

The structure of this book is as follows. Chapter 1 introduces the book's purpose and significance by explaining the various issues covered and its analytical framework. It considers international trends in business management and business history studies, identifies research topics, and reviews prior research and ensuing issues. It also explains the analytical framework and clarifies the division of the periods until the end of World War II and the primary business management issues in each period.

In Part I, the history of the globalism of hegemonic nations and its influences on other nations, and the total business management system in Germany as the structural framework defining a country's management style are considered applying the author's original framework. Part I clarifies the fundamental basis for developing business management and corporate expansion at both global and domestic levels. Chapter 2 examines how countries with hegemony pursued their globalism and the influences they exercised on other countries. Chapter 3 considers the total system of business management in Germany in three periods before the end of World War II compared with the period after the war.

In Part II, the business management changes that characterized the shift to monopolistic capitalism from the end of the 19th century through the end of the World War I are considered. Chapter 4 analyzes enterprise concentration, the birth of monopolistic capitalism, business management problems stemming from Germany's shift to monopolistic capitalism, the actual conditions and characteristics of concentration, and the functions of such measures in business management. Chapter 5 examines the transformation of the labor management system. Management changes are explored by analyzing the original goal of increasing efficiency and deploying the Taylor system. Chapter 6 explores the birth of the modern business enterprise that integrated multiple functions such as production, sales, and purchasing and that featured a managerial hierarchy, as well as the appearance of a managerial enterprise run by salaried managers.

Part III considers the development of business management during the Weimar era relative to the rationalization movement in the 1920s. Chapter 7 examines the concentration of enterprises in the form of trusts and their function, considering the reorganization of the division of labor in production within the giant trusts resulting from mergers. Chapter 8 analyzes the diffusion of the Taylor system and changes in the labor management system represented by the emergence of the uniquely German management system REFA (Reichsausschuß für Arbeitszeitermittlung) system[1]. Chapter 9 explores the deployment of the Ford system using case studies of representative enterprises in the processing and assembly sectors, such as the electrical engineering, automobile, and machinery industries. This chapter elucidates the actual conditions of implementing the Ford system, the characteristics of the German-style deployment, and the economic effects of mass production. In Chapter 10, based on the case of IG Farben, changes in organizational structure resulting from rationalization and business diversification are examined comparatively through the case of Du Pont, a corporate pioneer who adopted a divisional structure in the 1920s.

---

[1] REFA was founded in 1924 as the *Reichsausschuß für Arbeitszeitermittlung* (Reich Committee for Working Time Determination) (Pechhold 1974, S.56; Mommerz 1987, S.142). During the Nazi era, it was known as the *Reichsausschuß für Arbeitsstudien* (Reich Committee for Labour Studies) (Hachtmann 1989, S.180; Winkel 1938, S.505; Maschinenbau 1936, S.215).

Part IV analyzes business management during the Nazi era in the context of the economic system under National Socialism, changes in market conditions brought about by the militarization of the economy and the shift to a war economy, and the rationalization movement led by the state. Chapter 11 considers the further progress in implementing the REFA system and changes in labor management on the basis of various case studies of industrial sectors such as the electrical engineering, automobile, machine, iron and steel, mining, and chemical industries. Chapter 12 examines the deployment of the Ford system and the progress of mass production based on the tremendous expansion of the munitions market. It elucidates the significance and limitations of the deployment of the Ford system. It attempts to clarify an economic structure based on mass production relative to the unique character of the munitions market as distinct from that of private demand by comparing it to developments in the post-World War II period.

Part V considers the history of Germany's globalism and regionalism and the development of German capitalism and corporate expansion before the end of World War II. Chapter 13 examines the history of Germany's globalism and regionalism from the late nineteenth century to the present. Chapter 14 clarifies the unique character of German capitalist development and corporate expansion during the period before the end of World War II in connection with the historical context of each period, regional conditions in Europe, and the relationships between German and US capital.

Building on this discussion, Chapter 15 explains the implications of this book in its concluding remarks. It clarifies the characteristics of business management changes in Germany until the end of World War II in terms of (1) enterprise concentration, (2) labor management system, (3) development of the Ford System and mass production, and (4) corporate and organizational structure. Furthermore, the significance of business management during this period is explained by an in-depth examination of how various elements of business management developed after World War II, focusing on "continuity" and "discontinuity" before and after the war. Moreover, this chapter clarifies the origins of enterprise as "a social community" by examining the pursuit of economic rationality in Germany from a comparative perspective with the United States.

I am grateful to those who have supported me while writing this book. Prof. Masaki Nakata, emeritus professor at Ritsumeikan University, Japan advised me to work on this study. He also provided many invaluable instructions for me. Without them, it would not be able to complete this book. I express my gratitude to the late Professor Toni Pierenkemper of the University of Cologne and Professor Christian Kleinschmidt of the University of Marburg. They invited me to their universities as a visiting researcher. I pray for the repose of Professor Pierenkemper's soul. I also thank my family: my wife, Naomi, who encouraged me and supported my research life, and our son, Tomotaka, who gave me the strength to complete my research.

Without their support and understanding, this book would not have been possible. I dedicate this book to my wife and son.

Osaka, Japan Toshio Yamazaki

References

Hachtmann R (1989) Industriearbeit im 》Dritten Reich《. Untersuchungen zu den Lohn- und Arbeitsbedingungen in Deutschland 1933–1945. Vandenhoeck & Ruprecht, Göttingen

Maschinenbau (1936) Refa=Reichsausschuβ für Arbeitsstudien. Maschinenbau 15(7/8):215

Mommertz KH (1987) Böhren, Drehen und Fräsen: Geschichte der Werkzeugmaschinen. Rowohlt Taschenbuch-Verlag, Hamburg

Pechhold E (1974) 50 Jahre REFA. Beuth, Berlin, Köln, Frankfurt am Main

Statistisches Reichssamt (1902) Statistisches Jahrbuch für das Deutsche Reich 1901. Puttkammer & Mühlbrecht, Berlin

Statistisches Reichsamt (1915) Statistisches Jahrbuch für das Deutsche Reich 1914. Puttkammer & Mühlbrecht, Berlin

Statistisches Reichssamt (1931) Statistisches Jahrbuch für das Deutsche Reich 1930. Verlag von Reimar Hobbing, Berlin

Statistisches Reichsamt (1935) Statistisches Jahrbuch für das Deutsche Reich 1934. Verlag von Reimar Hobbing, Berlin

Statistisches Reichsamt (1943) Statistisches Jahrbuch für das Deutsche Reich 1941–42. Verlag für Sozialpolitik, Wirtschaft und Statistik, Berlin

Winkel A (1938) Die Auswirkung der Refa-Arbeit im Unternehmen. Maschinenbau 17(19/20):505–506

Contents

About the Author

Toshio Yamazaki, Dr. in Business Administration, Ritsumeikan University, is Professor at the College of Business Administration, Ritsumeikan University. He previously held the positions of Assistant Professor, Lecturer, and Associate Professor at the Faculty of Humanities and Economics, Kochi University; Associate Professor at the College of Business Administration, Ritsumeikan University; and Visiting Scholar at Free University of Berlin, University of Cologne, University of Marburg, Goethe University Frankfurt, and Humboldt University of Berlin.

Professor Yamazaki's areas of expertise include management studies and comparative business history. His research focuses on the history of business management and interfirm relationships. He served as director of the Japan Association for the Comparative Studies of Management of Japan from 2011 to 2017. He is the editor of the "Journal of Business Management" (edited by the Japan Association of Business Management, language: Japanese). Professor Yamazaki has published numerous monographs and articles, including "German Business Management" (Springer, 2013), "Relationships between Industry and Bank in Germany" (Springer Nature, 2024), and "Japanese and German Enterprises" (Springer Nature, 2024). He has also received an academic award from the Japan Association for the Comparative Studies of Management (*German Business Management: A Japanese Perspective on Regional Development Factors*, Springer, 2013).

List of Figures

List of Tables

Chapter 1
Introduction: Research Topics and Analytical Framework

Abstract This chapter elaborates on the purpose and significance of this book, first reviewing international trends in business management studies and examining business history. This book explores the findings of previous research based on related topics and ensuing issues. We identify research topics by examining major issues in German capitalism and business management before the end of World War II (the focal topic of this book's analysis), focusing on the period from the monopolistic capital transformation to the end of World War II. The analytical framework is explained, and this chapter presents a division of the periods before the end of World War II and the characteristics of business management in each of the three periods: (1) the Second Reich Era (1871–1918), (2) the Weimar Era (1918–1933), and (3) the Nazi Era (1933–1945). This chapter considers the primary factors that determined changes in business management in each period.

Keywords Americanization · Business management · Concentration of enterprise · Fordism · German capitalism · Globalism · Governance · Mass production · Rationalization · Regionalism

The establishment of mass production based on the Ford system created and developed by the Ford Motor Corporation in the United States (US) symbolizes the capitalistic accumulation mode in the twentieth century. A capitalistic accumulation system based on mass production called "Fordism" prevailed globally after World War II; however, development in each country differs, determined by the socioeconomic and market conditions and development pass of each capitalistic country, namely path dependency. Analyzing nationality (historical determining conditions and the foundation for birth and development) in each capitalistic nation clarifies the specialty of developing a country's capitalism and the generality of capitalistic accumulation. Therefore, the unique characteristics of capitalism in the concerned country, the generality of capitalistic accumulation, and the life of capital's power must be clarified by considering the historical conditions and the processes of birth and development of capitalism in each nation (Taguchi 2018, pp.139, 146). This approach is indispensable for understanding the special characteristics of the concerned country's capitalistic

T. Yamazaki, *A History of German Business*,
https://doi.org/10.1007/978-981-96-8476-2_1

development to elucidate how capital in each country maintains its life by exhibiting nationality and changing limitations to restrictions by examining enterprise business management changes as a central behavioral agent.

Examining the internationality and nationality of capital reveals how each country's capitalism maintains and develops its life power through globalization. Each country is deeply concerned with globalism as the principle for competition over acquiring global hegemony to create more advantageous foundations for corporate behavior and economic development and establish the world order. At the same time, globalization is a process in which global interdependence in both aspects of markets and productive forces strengthens. Globalism means the principle, norm, and doctrine of setting an institutional framework and rules for acquiring global hegemony and building a world order. This situation contributes to the concerned country's development and can be restrictive conditions for activities to pursue its national interest. In the case of other countries grasping hegemony, other countries are forced to follow rules set by nations that build a hegemony nation. Therefore, in this book, changes in business management and development of German enterprises are considered concerning how the globalism of countries with hegemony has changed the global development of economic activities. We examine the position of Germany in such phenomena, the pursuit of Germany's globalism, and the historical context of German capitalism and world capitalism in each period until the end of World War II.

German capitalism underwent distinctive development, evident in the early building of monopolistic capitalism, the birth of the Weimar Republic as the first democratic country in history, and the emergence of National Socialism as one of the most reactionary ideologies adopted by nations. Germany experienced defeats in two world wars and failed to achieve its hegemony in building the world order. How can capitalistic expansion and business management development in Germany be understood from the perspective of attempts to pursue the power of life of German capitalism? Moreover, how can the development of German capitalism and business management be understood from this perspective?

This book aims to provide insights regarding business management and corporate expansion in Germany from the late nineteenth century until the end of World War II (comprising the Second Reich, the Weimar Republic, and National Socialism) from the perspective of comparative management studies. This study analyzes the influences of the typical development of German capitalism and American management methods on business management to clarify the characteristics, significance, and limitations of changes in business management. This research elucidates Germany's specific development and its commonalities with development in the US through analysis from the historical context of the global economy and German capitalism and the international economic relations in both market and capital linkages.

First, Sect. 1.1 reviews international trends in business management and business history studies. Next, Sect. 1.2 presents research topics to be clarified in this book. Section 1.3 explores previous research findings on related topics, and Sect. 1.4 explains the analytical framework. Finally, Sect. 1.5 presents the division of the periods before the end of World War II, elucidating the main issues in business management changes in each period and the historical and socioeconomic backgrounds of such changes.

1.1 International Trends in Management and Organization Studies and Business History

1.1.1 International Trends in Management Studies: A Historical Turn in Management and Organization Studies

First, considering international trends in business management and business history studies, one prominent characteristic can be seen in the rise of interest in the analysis approach, focusing on the historical viewpoint and including historical phenomena in management and organization studies called the "historic turn."

Üsdiken and Kipping (2020, p. 79) indicated that the growing call for "more history" in management and organization studies was due to the implicit assumption that history had only a negligible presence in the extant literature. As Godfrey et al. (2006, p. 591) suggested, the historic turn in organization studies began with a set of influential articles by Alfred Kieser and Mayer Zald (Godfrey et al. 2016, p. 591). Zald insisted in 1993 that although "there was not much of a conversation between historians of organizations and other social scientists interested in organizations" (Zald 1993, p. 519), "the time is right to re-examine our fundamental assumptions about the nature of the field" and the links of organizational theory with history is necessary (Zald 1993, p. 513). In addition, Kieser points out "historical analyses teach us to interpret existing organization structures not as determined by laws but as the result of decisions in past choice opportunities" (Kieser 1994, p. 611). Üsdiken and Kipping (2020) stresses "the scientization of management research since the 1950s played an important, if not decisive, role" and that historical perspectives and approaches were removed from the new mainstream (Üsdiken and Kipping 2020, p. 10). Rowlinson and Hassard (2014) examines "the implications of the cultural turn for business history and organization studies, and the prospects for a rapprochement between these neighboring fields brokered by cultural theory" (Rowlinson and Hassard 2014, p. 148). Rowlinson and Procter insist that "the conventions at various levels of organizational culture studies prevent them from becoming more historical, and the conventions of business history make it difficult to engage with the concepts of culture." They stress that "a more historical approach in organizational culture studies and a more reflexive engagement with the concept of culture in business history would facilitate the deconstruction of founder-centred narratives of corporate culture" (Rowlinson and Procter 1999, p. 369).

The special issues regarding the historical turn and new direction of studies were published in multiple leading journals. The most representative include "Moving forward by looking backward: Business history and management studies" in the

"*Journal of Management Studies*" (2010), "History and organization studies" in "*The Academy of Management Review*" (2016), "Use of the past" in "*Organization Science*" (2016), and "History and strategy research: Opening up the black box" in "*Strategic Management Journal*" (2020). Furthermore, a book titled "*The Routledge companion to management*" generalized some important arguing points regarding "the historic turn" in management and organization studies and was published in 2015. This book comprises 29 chapters and was written by 37 researchers (Wilson et al. 2017).

In this way, "historic turn" has become a more economically passing term that refers to bringing history to organization studies (Decker 2016, p. 364). Godfrey et al. (2016) point out "following the 'historic turn,' organizational history has developed as a subfield of organization studies" (Godfrey et al. 2016, p. 590). In contrast, Wim Van Lent and Gabrielle Durepos (2019, p. 435) indicated that "the theoretical fruits of the historical turn seem to remain limited" in empirical attempts to connect history and management and organization studies (Van Lent and Gabrielle 2019, p. 435). Moreover, the historic turn does not successfully engage in a large-scale transformation of management and organization studies (Van Lent and Gabrielle 2019, p. 430).

1.1.2 International Trends in Business History Studies: Response to New Trends in Management and Organization Studies

New trends have also appeared in business history studies, where Alfred D. Chandler, Jr. (1962, 1977, 1990) attempted to offer a theory of the firm and the firm's organization (Chandler 1962, 1977, 1990); however, the orientation toward theory building did not progress. Significant changes have occurred due to trends in new management and organization studies. Institutionalization and systematization of business history studies have been pursued, and some important books have been published, including "*Business History around the World*" edited by Franco Amatori and Geoffery Jones in 2003, and "*The Oxford Handbook of Business History*" edited by Geoffery Jones and Jonathan Zeitlin in 2007. The former comprises three parts: Part I regarding general issues, open questions, and controversies; Part II regarding area patterns; and Part III regarding comparative business history (Amatori and Jones 2003). The latter comprises four parts: Part I, related to approaches and debates; Part II, related to forms of business organization; Part III, related to functions of enterprise; and Part IV, related to enterprise and society (Jones and Zeitlin 2007). Furthermore, "*The Routledge Companion to Business History*," edited by John Wilson, Steven Toms, Abe de Jong, and Emily Buchnea, was published in 2017. This book comprises five parts: (1) the discipline of business history, (2) business ownership, (3) international varieties of capitalism, (4) institutions, and (5) management and ethics (Wilson et al. 2017).

The reaction of business history to the movement toward a historic turn in management and organization studies has progressed. For example, in 2004, a special issue regarding historical interests in organization studies was published in the journal "*Business History*." Following the introduction, "History in organization studies" by B. Üsdiken and A. Kieser (editor of this special issue) (Üsdiken and Kieser 2004), five articles were printed, including a paper regarding interaction between organization history and organization theory by H. Leblebici and N. Shah (2004) and Clark and Rowlinson's (2004) article of which title include the term "historic turn" (Clark and Rowlinson 2004). Furthermore, the new journal "*Management and Organizational History*" appeared in 2006 by researchers on both sides of organization and business history study. This journal represents the "historic turn" in organization studies and has characteristics related to business history. In the first issue of this journal, Booth and Rowlinson (2006) indicated a 10-point agenda including the "historic turn" in organization theory, historical methods and styles of writing, the philosophy of history and historical theorists, organization history, and business history and theory as the targets of this journal (Booth and Rowlinson 2006). As they point out, "the historic turn in management and organization theory raises questions about methods and appropriate styles of writing for more historically oriented research" (Booth and Rowlinson 2006, p. 8). They also stress that "in parallel with the historic turn in management and organization theory, business history has become more open to an engagement with theory from sociology and cultural studies" (Booth and Rowlinson 2006, p. 21). Special issues were published thereafter in this journal as well. Such cases can be observed in "Doing Historical Research in Management and Organizational Studies" in 2013 and "Re-visiting the Historic Turn 10 Years" in 2016. In the journal "*Business History Review*," a special issue titled "Debating Methodology in Business History" was published in 2017. Maclean et al. (2017, p. 479) argued that a "fruitful synthesis between history and organization studies" should be promoted (Maclean et al. 2017, p. 479).

Moreover, a prominent book titled "*Organization in Time. History, Theory, Method*" edited by Marcelo Bucheli and Daniel Wadhwani, was published in 2014, focusing on results like those in the session regarding "the historic turn" in organization studies by associations related to business history in Europe and North America. It comprises 13 chapters written by 19 people, including 12 researchers in organization studies and 7 in business history (Bucheli and Wadhwani 2014). At the same time, interchanges between management and organization studies and business history studies have progressed, and the trend toward pursuing social scientific studies and interdisciplinary studies is evident. In a preface in the journal "*Business History*" in 2007, orientation toward social science was worked out, as seen in promoting and welcoming the submission of articles directly dealing with the central theme of social science (Harvey and Wilson 2007, pp. 2, 6). In the preface of its 2011 publication, the "*Business History Review*" regards the field of business history "not as a subdiscipline of history, but as a multidisciplinary field on its own," highlighting the importance of "a wide range of methodological approach, including those from other social sciences" (Friedman and Jones 2011, p. 2). In 2015, the journal "*Business History*" published a special issue regarding "new business history." As editors of this special issue, A. de Jong and Higgins (2015, p. 2) emphasize the need to complement case study analysis with social scientific approaches based on theory development and hypothesis testing despite the recognition of the importance of case study (de Jong and Higgins 2015, p. 2; de Jong et al. 2015, p. 24). A. de Jong et al. (2015, pp. 12–13) stress that new business history orients toward experience and theory and can make business history study more scientific by the loop of theory and actual proof comprising (1) case observation, (2) case analysis, (3) theory and domain, and (4) presentation of hypotheses (de Jong et al. 2015, pp. 12–13). This special issue published many papers with approaches different from the orientation toward economics and actual proof based on hypotheses testing, indicating various directions in business history studies. Decker (2015, p. 31) insists that "it is more appropriate to speak of and foster the development of a variety of reflective methodologies in business historical research," and the title "new business histories" as the plural form is appropriate for indicating a new trend in this field (Decker et al. 2015, p. 31). It also points out that "the designation 'new business histories' suggests a more productive and fruitful dialogue about the multiple ways to understand and study the past" (Decker et al. 2015, p. 36). Meanwhile, an attempt to rebuild the study field of business history as an entirely new business history in collaboration with the neighboring social sciences also appeared (Scranton and Friedenson 2013).

1.1.3 Dialogue Between Management and Organization Studies and Business History Studies and Its Difficulties

Attempts at dialogue between management and organization studies and business history studies have tended to advance under the abovementioned trends in both fields.

Rowlinson et al. (2014, pp. 250, 252–259, 269) published an article in the journal "*Academy of Management Review*" in 2014, insisting on the necessity and importance of a historical approach and dialogue between business history and organization theory. They discuss three epistemological dualisms of (1) explanation (narrative and analysis), (2) evidence (source and data), and (3) temporality (periodization and chronology) (Rowlinson et al. 2014, pp. 250, 252–259, 269). Furthermore, in the abovementioned special issue of the same journal in 2016, a study aimed at exploring "the potentialities for a creative synthesis between history and organization studies as endeavors that share common ground" (Maclean et al. 2016, p. 609; Godfrey et al. 2016) and a paper attempting to use three historical approaches of realist history, interpretive history, and poststructuralist history for further understanding of "the historical embeddedness of strategic processes and practices" (Vaara and Lamberg 2016, pp. 633–635, 651) were published. Research results in the boundary fields of management and organization studies and business history increased with the aforementioned special issues in each leading journal as momentum. Godfrey et al. (2016, p. 592) noted, "There is now a well-established dialogue between organization theory and business history." They cited a book titled "*Organization in Time: History, Theory, Methods*" edited by Bucheli and Wadhwani (2014) as its exemplification (Godfrey et al. 2016, p. 592).

Conversely, the dialogue across both disciplines is insufficient and sparse (Álvaro-Moyap and Donzé 2016, p. 126). Wilson et al. (2022) also point out "no consensus has emerged about how to reconcile the epistemological and ontological differences between business history and management and organizational sciences" (Wilson et al. 2022, p. 94. regarding similar indication, see pp. 50, 94). Interdisciplinary dialogues increasingly require methodological transparency (Maclean et al. 2017, p. 459). Organization scholars and historians continue to debate historical reasoning and its relevance to organizations, the ambiguity of historical methods, and the separation of business historians and organization scholars into distinct intellectual communities (Wadhwani and Bucheli 2014, p. 5). Maclean (2016, p. 610) suggests that it is a challenge to integrate history and theory by overcoming the antipathy to the theory of historians and neglecting the historical process by organization theorists (Maclean et al. 2016, p. 610). Leblebici (2014) also stresses that the eventual integration is much more complex. It points out that "what organization theory scholars may consider as history friendly research might simply look like highly flimsy historical research to historians" and "while historians may use the term 'theory' in their papers, they may mean something substantively and rhetorically different in its usage" (Leblebici 2014, p. 57). As seen in the differences in the publication genres preferred by history and organization studies (book or journal), "the institutionalization of disciplinary boundaries and professional practices creates obstacles for the incorporation of history into management and organization studies" (Wadhwani and Bucheli 2014, p. 23). Regarding publication genres (such as quantitative management research), qualitative management studies always aim at journal publication, and organization scholars apparently prefer journal publication to book publication. In contrast, researchers in history tend to view the book as a preferable publication genre. As Yates points out, "books are viewed by historians as providing a more detailed and better supported argument concerning change over time, while articles are typically seen as isolating one piece of a more involved argument" (Yates 2014, pp. 276–280).

Furthermore, the dialogue between management and business history studies is complicated because the former orients toward theoretical generalization and the latter toward historical strictness. Fruitful collaboration depends on dual integrity as it meets the requirements of theory development in organization studies and historical veracity in business history studies. Dual integrity is "the overarching principle in the synthesis of organizational and historical for scholarship" (Maclean et al. 2016, pp. 609, 616). Leblebici emphasizes the basic dilemma for interdisciplinary discussion: "One discipline becomes the driver of the research agenda, making the other discipline a secondary contributor" (Leblebici 2014, p. 78). Wadhwani et al. (2018) point out that "while organization scholars have focused on the micro-processes and temporal structures of historical interpretation in organizations, historians have been primarily concerned with the contexts within which this occurs and the struggles between firms and other actors to define the past" (Wadhwani et al. 2018, p. 1677).

Even under such conditions, Godfrey (2016) states "whereas organization theory that engages with historiography would represent theory-with-history," "academic business history that incorporates organization theory could be seen as a manifestation of history-with-theory" (Godfrey 2016, p. 592). Furthermore, Üsdinken and Kipping (2020, pp. 272–273) explain three possibilities of dialogue between management and organization studies and business history studies. These possibilities include (1) dispatch from historians and their participation in discussions in management and organization studies, (2) a research program called "use of the past," and (3) attempts called "historical cognizance" as an approach in which history is considered "a kind of boundary condition," which enables scholars to create theory more contingent on context (Üsdinken and Kipping 2020, pp. 272–273).

1.1.4 Significance of Noticing History in Management and Organization Studies

Observing history and attempts to incorporate it into management and organization research can be divided into the study of historical backgrounds (historical contexts) of management phenomena and the historical narrative. In the former, "historical context and contestation in determining how institutions are shaped and reshaped over time" must be clarified. Meanwhile, the latter focuses on "how the development of ideas by historically situated actors shapes when and how 'social problems' emerge of institutions and why they have consequences for institutions and organizations" (Wadhwani 2018, pp. 551–552). Suddaby et al. (2014) propose the term "historical institutionalism" to deepen the understanding of institutions as a continuous historical process (Suddaby et al. 2014, p. 118).

Setting the historical period is important in studying the historical background or context. Regarding the period, diachronic and synchronicity periods can be seen. Sewell (2005) indicates that the term "historical" actually has two quite distinct meanings in contemporary speech: (1) "the obvious adjectival meaning derived from its root 'history'" designating "happenings that take place over time" and (2) meaning "'in the past' standing at a distance from the contemporary world." At the same time, "history as transformation" is the synchronic face of history, and "history as transformation" is the diachronic face. "'Synchronic' means that different times are present in a continuous moment." "History as temporal context is historical in the sense that it is placed in some past era, but it is concerned not with the process of change during the time." Sewell stresses "a proper appreciation of synchrony is the secret ingredient of effective diachronic history" (Sewell 2005, pp. 182–184). Therefore, it is important to grasp phenomena by focusing on a certain age and stage, namely the synchronic period, and to understand the dynamism of phenomena in the development of time, emphasizing diachronic changes. As seen in some studies such as Yates (2014), which examines historical methods in organization studies by comparing quantitative, qualitative, and historical methods, and Decker et al.

(2015, pp. 34–35), who insists on the advantages of methodological variety (Decker et al. 2015, pp. 34–35), movements to attempt to clarify historical methodology have become prominent. For instance, Kipping et al. (2014, pp. 312, 325) took up (1) source criticism, (2) triangulation, and (3) hermeneutics as historical methods and explained their effectiveness (Kipping et al. 2014, pp. 312, 325). Furthermore, Hodge and Costa (2021, p. 747) insist, "oral history allows for several paths for management to actually incorporate the historic turn" (Hodge and Costa 2021, p. 747).

Meanwhile, the study of historical narrative has its characteristics in that actors intentionally talk about and construct organizational history. The "use of the past" approach investigates "how organizational actors produce and use history for purposes in the present." In this approach, the past is "a source of social symbolic resources available for a wide variety of creative uses" (Wadhwani et al. 2008, p. 1664). Jonathan Zeitlin points out that "the capacity of economic agents to imagine and weigh alternative courses of action connecting the present with both the future and the past through narratives that constitute their identities and interests" is crucial to the process of strategic reflection (Zeitlin 2003, p. 65). As Maclean et al. (2018, p. 1735) pointed out, a long-established organization with a rich history can be considered an effective competitive resource (Maclean et al. 2018, p. 1735). Suddaby et al. stress that "history is a persuasive interpretation of the past" (Suddaby et al. 2010, p. 152). Using the term "rhetorical history" is effective as history can be an effective managerial means within an organization. Strategic use of the past is "a persuasive strategy to manage key stakeholders of the firm" (Suddaby et al. 2010, p. 157). Rhetoric history is important as "a competitive organizational resource" (Suddaby et al. 2010, p. 167). The strategic value of rhetoric history lies in its flexible capacity to integrate and align multiple and often contradictory interests (Suddaby et al. 2010, p. 165). The major short-term change can be legitimized by indicating continuity from a long-term viewpoint. Olof Brunninge (2009, pp. 22–24) points out that "the organizational use of history is an interesting and fruitful perspective for understanding organizations in general and organizational stability and change in particular" and "organizational members in various ways refer to the past and sometimes purposefully use organizational history to influence change process" (Brunning 2009, pp. 22–24).

Regarding the significance of the historical narrative, its authority is the authority of reality itself. As Hayden White stressed, "the historical account endows this reality with form and thereby makes it desirable, imposing upon its processes the formal coherency that only stories possess" (White 1980, p. 23). A historical narrative of a social problem conveys why it is a problem, what brought it to develop, what might be done regarding it, and that a problem has arisen. Actors outside and within organizations may use history for social problems "in ways that have consequences for the de-legitimation of some institutions and the construction of new ones" (Wadhwani 2018, p. 551). Historical narratives can be regarded as "resources managers use to achieve specific organizational goals" and "important organizational resources that can be strategically mobilized to accomplish corporate goals" (Foster et al. 2017, p. 1191). Wadhwani et al. (2018) also define history as "the mobilization of the past" and stress that "the 'uses of the past' approach examines how organizational actors themselves produce and use history for purpose in the present" (Wadhwani et al. 2018, pp. 1664, 1666). Therefore, history in studies of historical narrative is subjective. Whether a past narrated by actors can be history and regarded as fact is an important problem; in essence, history is based on accumulating objective facts.

This book emphasizes the perspective of clarifying the historical backgrounds (contexts) of phenomena. It is important to elucidate when, why, and how a particular management phenomenon occurred concerning the historical contexts of the world economy and capitalism in each country and the characteristics of each industry. In studying historical background, it is significant to clarify phenomena that occur with the progress of time, paying attention to diachronicity as the flow of time. Such a study can be regarded as an "explanation of dynamism." It is also important to clarify what phenomena appeared, emphasizing the influences of a certain age and actual conditions, namely the synchronic period rather than the flow of time as the background. This study style is called "clarifying of evens" (Sakai and Izawa 2022, p. 11).

Under the abovementioned international trends in management and organization studies and business history studies, how these research results are used is significant. This book emphasizes the following classifications raised by Üsdinken and Kipping (2020): (1) "history to theory," in which "the past is employed as a source of data or evidence with the purpose of developing, testing, refining or elaborating theory"; and (2) "history in theory," in which history is incorporated into theory to capture the effects of past conditions or processes. While the former uses history to develop and test theory, the latter uses history as a component of the theory model. As a methodology, this classification holds for each quantitative and qualitative study. Regarding qualitative studies, "history to theory" emphasizes history as a traditional theory study or a source of qualitative evidence and data. In contrast, analytically structured history is important in "history in theory." Üsdinken and Kipping (2020) point out that in "history in theory," imprinting and path dependency are prime examples; however, resource-based view, dynamic capabilities, and co-evaluation are also noticeable perspectives (Üsdinken and Kipping 2020, pp. 16–17, 94–94, 196, 220, 240, 246, 272–275, 282, 288).

Regarding theoretical generalization, "theory building in historical context" is important (Yates 2014, p. 279). At the same time, two directions can be significant: (1) pursuing theoretical generalization through considering historical phenomena and (2) "historical cognizance" as writings where theories are seen as "subject to boundary conditions derived from particular historical contexts" not as universally applicable theories. "Historical cognizance" is an attempt at theorization by considering historical contexts, namely "contextualized theorizing" (Üsdinken and Kipping 2020, pp. 272–275, 282, 288). Theorization emphasizing age division must consider business circumstances peculiar to a specific period (Kikkawa 2009, pp. 8–9; Kikkawa 2018, pp. 24–25). Regarding each period of German business history, this book emphasizes contextualized contingent theorizing that emphasizes historical contexts peculiar to the period by grasping factors determining the occurrence of major phenomena and their contents and characteristics, as well as the significance of changes.

1.1.5 Trends in the Business History Study in Germany

In addition to international trends in business management and business history studies, this section considers trends in research on business history in Germany. Outstanding and highly eminent general historians committed to business history during the 1990s (Schröter 2003, p. 170). Nonetheless, the increase in studies entrusted to historians by companies and the progress of opening company archives for external research led to "a further spurt in the quantity and quality of writing business history" (Schröter 2003, pp. 181–184. Regarding the increase of entrusted research by enterprises, see Schanetzky 2018). After around 2000, disputes over the object and methodology of business history studies became active.

Toni Pierenkemper (2000a, b) raised important research issues regarding the object and methodology of business history study. He pointed out that it is difficult to answer the object of business history (Pierenkemper 2000a, S. 14), and understanding entrepreneur decision-making and determining factors of economic success is possible only or exclusively based on empirical-historical research (Pierenkemper 2000a, S. 71). However, scientific analysis is lacking (Pierenkemper 2000a, S. 65) and this discipline does not use a definite paradigm (Pierenkemper 2000a, S. 281). He stresses the necessity of study based on scientific theories and methods (Pierenkemper 2000b, S. 158). Hans Jaegers also points out that a weak structural point of business history lies in its inability to build theory (Jaeger 1992, S. 127). Triebel and Seidl (2001) discuss an analytical framework for the subject of business history and indicate a framework as a graphically visualized model that shows the business enterprise in the center of the network and its interrelations (Triebel and Seidl 2001).

Business history in Germany tends to orient toward American business history (Pierenkemper 2000a, S. 74), and the influence of American business history is substantial. Pierenkemper (1999, 2000a, b) emphasized the importance of concentrating the analysis on the issues of the economic core (Pierenkemper 1999, S. 20, 31; Pierenkemper 2000b, S. 166). He stressed the necessity of emphasizing individuals and groups in a company and using research results in neighboring disciplines such as economic and social history and historical sciences. The development of enterprise theory is a universal project that is spreading to other related disciplines. Although strategic behavior in a company is a core of modern business history, issues of politics, society, and culture must be incorporated into the analysis (Pierenkemper 2000a, S. 281–284, 2000b, S. 158). He pointed out that economic action follows proper logic that needs a unique analytical tool, which holds for business history (Pierenkemper 1999, S. 19). According to Pierenkemper (2000a, b), it is important to rely on methods of economics and developments in the field of economic history for clarifying an enterprise's inner economic logic and dedicating further dimension to its action (Pierenkemper 1999, S. 21, 31; Pierenkemper 2000b, S. 162, S. 166); case studies are especially suitable for such analysis (Pierenkemper 2000b, S. 164). As Pierenkemper pointed out, the relationship between business history and general economic history as a discipline is not apparent (Pierenkemopoer 2000a, S. 73; see also Schröter 2003, p. 180). The trend in which business history tends to be studied with a deep relation with economic history in Germany is because lectureships of economic and social history dominate in German universities and colleges (Kleinschmidt 2019, S. 276–267; Jaeger 1992, S. 130; Schröter 2003, pp. 172–173, 180). Conversely, Harm G. Schröter (2018) points out that business history tends to have typically played a minor role in economic history institutes in Europe, including Germany (Schröter 2018, p. 309).

Manfred Pohl (1999) stresses that "actual German business history no longer gloss over difficult periods and themes" and the necessity of "a broader rather than a pure economic approach" (Pohl 1999, S. 150). He suggests that the inner economic logic of corporate behavior that Pierenkemper raised could not be definitively clarified, and it is important to make efforts to explain decisive relations in which core persons, such as entrepreneurs, managers, and workers or politicians, exist (Pohl 1999, S. 153–154). Pohl (1999) insists that business history is a vital discipline to entrust with only economic historians (Pohl 1999, S. 160). The theme "enterprises in the Nazis" brought about a research boom including important research issues, such as the roles of enterprises in the Nazi regime (Pierenkemper 2000b, S. 164; Werghoff 2004, S. 139); however, the phenomenon of enterprises should not be exclusively identified with "enterprise in the Nazis" (Pohl 1999, S. 158).

Regarding the need for studies based on scientific theories and scientific methods, many researchers point out the effectiveness of methodologies of economics, such as Neo-institutionalism economics and other schools in business history (Plumpe 2006, 72–75; Berghoff 2004, S. 141–142; Nieberding and Wischermann 1998; Borscheid 2001, S. 7–9). These studies stress the significance of the concepts of the principal–agent problem and the transaction cost theory. Based on the transaction cost approach, Nieberding and Wischermann (1998) clarified that the better the building of trust, the lower the transaction cost created in the cooperative process is (Nieberding and Wischermann 1998, S. 41). Moreover, trust as a cultural foundation of the behavioral capability of the enterprise factor of success can be more cost advantageous than control (Nieberding and Wischermann 1998, S. 40, 44).

However, snares and problems in adopting analytical methods of this economics also occur. Plumpe (2006) stresses that they can explain the existence of a company; however, they cannot clarify how a company develops (Plumpe 2006, S. 66, 76–77), and the concept of Neo-institutionalism economics is too static and narrow for grasping complex historical transformation phenomena in industrial organization (Plumpe 2006, S. 87). Hartmut Berghoff (2004) also points out the risks of an economic-reductionism (Berghoff 2004, S. 142). Plumpe (2006) insists that the theoretical clarification of the decision-making process in a company is important (Plumpe 2006, S. 77). Moreover, the application of evolutional economics to explain issues regarding how an enterprise develops and emphasizes the effectiveness of combining the organization and decision-making theory on the one hand with the evolutional economics as an analytical tool on business history on the other (Plumpe 2006, S. 72–73, 76, 83, 87). Kleinschmidt (2019) also points out that using Neo-institutionalism and evolutional economics theories provides a great possibility of clarification for culture-oriented business history (Kleinschmidt 2019, S. 289). Conversely, Plumpe (2006, 2018) stresses the lack of a general description of

German business history that satisfies the demands of integrated analyses of micro- and microeconomic perspectives (Plumpe 2006, S. 87, 2018, S. 100). Hans Jaeger (1992) also stresses that the interaction of macro- and microeconomic phenomena opens a new dimension of analysis (Jaeger 1992, S. 120). Kleinschmidt (2019) also indicates that methodological and theoretical research is stagnant or their innovation has been brocaded until now (Kleinschmidt 2019, S. 290).

Furthermore, regarding the research boom, in "Business in the Third Reich," Tim Schanetzky (2018) points out a fatal restriction in writing German business history, stressing that new interpretations or methodological innovations have not occurred. Moreover, these studies lack discussion at the relevant social scientific research level (Schanetzky 2018, S. 24–25, 30–31). Christian Kleinschmidt (2019) posits a similar view regarding the evaluation of some publications on German companies in the Nazi period—including issues of labor and forced labor from methodological and theoretical points (Kleinschmidt 2019, S. 287–288).

New books on modern business history have also been published in Germany. Examples include Berghof's (2016) second edition, which focuses on theme and theory, and a book that discusses new perspectives of business history, including various related fields of historical science such as economic and social history, culture history, and political history (Kleinröder et al. 2024a). Kleinröder et al. (2024b) aim to promote interaction between business history and historical science, understand the usual possibilities of each methodological tool, and open new related research fields in an essayistic way (Kleinröder et al. 2024b, S. VIII).

Clarifying the decision-making process by managers and entrepreneurs is very important in analyzing corporate development; however, this book focuses on grasping objective changes in business management in German enterprises due to corporate behaviors in the peculiar historical context of each period and their significance. For example, regarding the National Socialism period, this book does not consider corporate behaviors and their results, such as seen in anti-social phenomena of German enterprises at the time, such as compulsive work, holocaust, and involvement in war crimes. Instead, this book focuses on changes in management systems or methods as research topics to clarify business management changes. The primary object of this analysis is the historical development of business management until the end of World War II; this book is not research in the field of historical science (business history as such discipline) or wholly based on international trends and the abovementioned German movement in research. This book intends to develop an analysis of business management and corporate expansion in Germany to understand the characteristics of capitalistic development.

1.2 Research Topics

Next, this section clarifies research topics in this book. Regarding the post-World War II development of Germany and Japan, even under the strong globalism and the global strategy of the US, both countries (as defeated nations in World War II) received significant American leadership, assistance, and support after the war. They developed their enterprises, industries, and economies by deploying and adapting technology and management methods from the United States while establishing their own systems of industrial concentration. By these means, both nations became major trading countries. However, their developmental processes differed greatly.

The American influence on Japanese business is still quite strong in trade. Japan could not, and still cannot, establish a complementary relationship with American industrial sectors and their products in the American market. Furthermore, a common market structure like the European Union (EU) does not exist in Asia. In contrast to Japan, Germany has developed independently of American influence and become part of a well-integrated regional economy. This trend can be regarded as "Europeanization." What were the driving forces that precipitated these distinctions? Differences in business management development and industrial concentration systems were deeply intertwined with the different paths of Germany and Japan.

In examining the regional conditions regarding corporate and economic development, shortly after the war, Japan did not have nearby markets as did Germany in Europe; this is primarily because many Asian countries were previously colonies. Therefore, Japan's development of productive forces could sufficiently absorb only the expansion of its domestic markets and exports to the US, causing them to develop a stronger reliance on America. Later, in the 1970s and 1980s, Japanese corporations strengthened their competitiveness in the processing and assembly industries, particularly, the automobile industry, by using low cost and high quality (as measured by minimum defects) as weapons to intensify the Japanese production system. This strategy resulted in an even greater number of exports to the US. However, because the industries in which Japan built international competitiveness were also key industries for the US, it could not build complementary relationships with American producers and industries in the American market and therefore had to maintain a competitive relationship with the US. Under these conditions, Japan's independent development became somewhat complicated. Since the 1980s, Japanese enterprises have pursued a shift to the Asian region in terms of both production as well as their sales market, particularly after the 1990s. However, even today, Asia has not formed any regional economic integration comparable to that of the EU, leaving Japan vulnerable to fluctuations in the yen–dollar exchange rate because its economy relies on exports to the US.

In contrast, Germany evidently had the capacity to develop independently. Although German corporations experienced an Americanization of their business management, they could be further developed by modifying and adapting productive forces and industrial structures in line with European market structures and competition. In addition, they were able to develop diversified quality production (for example see Abelshauser 2003; Streeck 1992, 1997), relying on skilled workers, market structures, and characteristics focusing on quality and functionality. German corporations consistently expanded with European conditions and markets. They developed a production system that enabled product differentiation in quality and functionality that relied on the specialized experience and skill of their workers rather than US-style mass production based on standardization principles or Japanese workers' multi-processing skills. German product quality focuses on functionality and durability and the German production system differentiates on the basis of quality, not price. German corporations have developed on the foundation of a German strategy that builds competitiveness through quality differentiation. As a result, Germany has become internationally competitive in durable consumer goods, investment goods, and capital goods and has built foreign trade patterns that complemented products in the European region on the basis of differences in the industrial structures of other European nations. In doing so, Germany has developed corporate and economic independence without having to follow the American global strategy.

However, this type of development, i.e., one that focuses on quality and functionality, was particularly effective because of European market conditions. Thus, Germany sought to form and reinforce a European reproduction structure and progressed with European integration, leading to the formation of today's EU, to build a foundation conforming to that strategy. This movement toward European integration, which enabled development rooted in the integrated region of Europe, was created at the business management level. Germany has strengthened the Europeanization of business management and economic expansion based on an enlarged European region and Europeanization as a deepening of the regional economic sphere, while the world faced the globalization process (Yamazaki 2013).

Germany realized corporate expansion and economic development based on the European region after World War II; however, conditions until the war's end differed significantly from the postwar situation. Germany before the war was not able to realize the establishment of accumulation and capital reproduction structures based on Europe despite the fact that the ratios of exports to this region to all exports had reached approximately 70% or more(1). Under very difficult market conditions determined by the characteristics of the birth and development of German capitalism, enterprises in this country attempted to modernize business management while building their own industrial concentration systems such as those seen in a "high level of organization of monopolistic capital" to expand exports. Conservative trade policy and industrial policy that permitted the establishment and maintenance of cartels were important foundations of such movements. Large, powerful enterprises combined in cartels and syndicate dominated their industrial sectors such as coal, iron and steel, chemicals, electrical products, and transportation. "The structured, protected, collective capitalism" that characterized the German business system in this period was "a further manifestation of a process that had been underway since the 1880s" (McNabb 2016, p. 87).

However, such development was forced to face limitations in the reproduction structures of German capitalism and, as a result of such limitations, Germany brought about the World War I. Such an attempt failed due to defeat and the Weimar Republic as a democratic state was born. In Germany, the rationalization movement that began in 1924 was an important measure in reinstating and developing enterprises, industry, and the economy. However, there was no condition in which the expansion of the domestic market and exports by increasing efficiency and reducing costs could be realized under the economic burden caused by defeat in the war and the revolution of November 1918. The German economy was forced to be involved in the world economic crisis, which started in 1929, and National Socialism emerged in 1933 as the most reactionary national response, subsequently causing the World War II.

How were German capitalism and business management in the globalism of countries with hegemony and the governance system led by hegemonic countries? How did the peculiar development of German capitalism influence the process of business management development? While being influenced by American management methods, how did German enterprises formulate original developmental processes and create original characteristics of German business management? Which specific management style was created in Germany? What was the significance of these business management changes? How did the special evolutionary process of business management affect the development of German capitalism? Regarding the "continuity" and "discontinuity" of business management in Germany before and after World War II, while market conditions and competition structure considerably changed, how did the changes in business management until the end of World War II influence and contribute to postwar development? How can the significance and limitations of the European region as a core market for German capitalism and enterprises be understood? This book attempts to clarify the characteristics, significance, and limitations of changes in business management during the period until the end of World War II in a global context, giving attention to regional environments in Europe and the world economy, including the influence of the globalism of hegemonic countries, Germany's pursuit of globalism, and international economic relations with the US[(2)]. In this book, some periods through the end of the World War II are covered without limitation to a specific period and the historical perspective for the period before the end of the war will be indicated. This book considers German capitalism and business management from the perspective of globalism and governance, examining German monopolistic enterprises' behavior and business management changes under the economic order on the world scale and domestic level of Germany.

This book clarifies these research topics by examining four main themes: (1) the concentration of enterprises and its corresponding system of industrial concentration, (2) the labor management system and the deployment of the Taylor system, (3) the deployment of the Ford system and the transformation toward mass production, and (4) changes in the structure of the enterprise and organizational structure. This book aims at elucidating the overall view of business management, process of corporate expansion, capitalistic development through the growth of companies in Germany from the 1870s to the end of World War II and presents instructive view of this period.

Regarding continuity of business management before and after World War II, the analysis in this book seeks to understand the development and changes that occurred after the war. What factors determined the differences between the pre- and postwar periods? How were the prewar limitations overcome and the remarkable postwar development of enterprises and the economy in Germany possible? How did business management success in postwar Germany contribute to the process of development and building international competitiveness after the war? Such an analytical perspective is important for examining the process after World War II.

When considering the history of the deployment of American management methods, four waves of Americanization are evident in business management: (1)

the period from the beginning of the twentieth century to the outbreak of World War I; (2) the period after World War I, especially the 1920s; (3) the period after World War II to the 1970s (see Yamazaki 2024, Part III); and (4) the period after the 1990s (Yamazaki 2024, Chapter 14).

The major issue in the first wave was the deploy of the Taylor system. In the second wave, prevailing of the Taylor system that was not be broadly adopted and the Ford system as mass production method were major issues[(3)]. The primary characteristics of US management methods deployed in the third wave were (1) management and production systems (human relations, industrial engineering, statistical quality control, and the Ford system); (2) management education methods; (3) measures for responding to markets coinciding with advancements in mass production (marketing, public relations, and operations research); and (4) the divisional structure (Yamazaki 2013; Kleinschmidt 2002). In contrast, in the fourth wave, Americanization can be seen in the transformation toward shareholder value-oriented management and capital market-oriented corporate governance system emphasizing the company's short-term interests and investors' returns under influence and pressure on business management by the capital market with the US-led "financialization" and the globalization of finance.

Most of the American management methods and techniques that were deployed in the first, second, and third waves reflected the management principles and behavioral mechanisms of companies, as seen in the "improvement of efficiency" and the pragmatic management climate of the United States. Meanwhile, in the fourth wave, the introduction and transfer of the American conception of companies and the ideology that regards companies as a "nexus of contracts" (with the objective of buying/selling and increasing the American management value) became an important problem. Such a management model can oppose corporate behavior such as efficiency improvement and strategic development in market competition.

The principle of efficiency improvement became an important behavioral mechanism for companies in countries that deployed American management methods. However, the part that reflected such American conditions was based on the pragmatic sense of value, which was not necessarily compatible with Japanese and German circumstances. Although American methods were deployed by modifying their individual elements, American management methods and techniques based on the principle of efficiency improvement were driving forces in not only the expansion of enterprises but also the economic development in both nations. Hence, the Americanization of business management in these three waves had significant meaning for both countries as well as other European countries. Therefore, it is important to clarify the commonalities and differences in deploying American management methods in these three waves from a comparative viewpoint. This book compares issues regarding the pursuit of economic rationality in Germany with that in the United States and clarify the origin of character of German enterprise as a "social community" in relation to specific conditions after World War I.

1.3 Prior Research and Issues Thereafter

In regard to the aforementioned research topics, the findings of previous research on related topics are explored.

Regarding the relevance of these topics to this book's central research topic, few studies based on a unified analytical framework cover the period from the end of the nineteenth century, when Germany shifted to monopolistic capitalism, to the end of World War II. Studies that cover all periods through the end of World War II include Kleinschmidt (2007) and Plumpe (2018), who provide a general view of business history in Germany. They are also helpful as introductory books or textbooks on general cases. For instance, Plumpe (2018) outlines the broad contours of corporate development in Germany at the crossroads of the public and private spheres in the nineteenth and twentieth centuries. The work briefly and individually explains various issues in business history and has encyclopedic characteristics and significance as a textbook primarily for undergraduate students. Nonetheless, the distinguishing characteristics of German business management compared to those of other countries, such as the US, are not always clearly presented. Plumpe's book divides the long term from 1800 to the present day into three periods: (1) 1800–1870, (2) 1870–1970, and (3) since 1970. His book considers enterprise development in each period and German enterprises' responses to market changes, focusing on the heterogeneous German market. Still, the book largely overlooks market peculiarities until the end of World War II and market discontinuity between this period and after the war as an important factor determining changes in business management and corporate expansion in the postwar period. In contrast, this book clarifies the characteristics, significance, and limitations of business management changes in Germany. Our work indicates the historical perspective for the period through the end of the World War II by analyzing changes in business management and corporate development from the perspective of comparing historical context in terms of market structure, institutional framework, and relationships with foreign capital during the Second Reich, the Weimar Republic, and National Socialism periods.

Many studies consider only a specific period or two periods before World War II, at most (von Freyberg 1989; Siegel and von Freyberg 1991; Stollberg 1981; Hinrich and Peter 1976; Schock 1977; Zollitsch 1990). This book provides a comparative analysis of three historical periods until the end of World War II (the period from the 1870s to World War I, the Weimar era, and the Nazi era), paying attention to the historical interrelation between each period.

There are many studies which consider only one field or some fields mutually related to business management or management methods. As to changes in labor management, including the deployment of the Taylor system and the implementation of the REFA (Reichsausschuß für Arbeitszeitermittlung) system, some studies provide interesting research results (Stollberg 1981; Schmiede and Schudlich 1981; Trieba and Mentrup 1983; Spitzley 1980; von Freyberg 1989; Siegel and von Freyberg 1991; Homburg 1991; Hachtmann 1989; Jeidels 1905; Söllheim 1922; Schmidt

1993; Hinrichs 1981; Hinrichs and Peter 1976; Schock 1977; Pechhold 1974; Kleinschmidt 1993; Zollitsch 1990). These studies tend to focus on changes in labor with management reforms. In contrast, this book focuses on changes in the system to control work volume by management and their significance.

Regarding the deployment of the Ford system, several studies analyzed cases in many industrial sectors and clarified German adaptation in the deployment of the Ford system by modification during the interwar period (Stahlmann 1993; Bönig 1993a, b; von Freyberg 1989; Siegel and von Freyberg 1991; Hachtmann 1989; Homburg 1991; Schmidt 1993; Kugler 1985; Thieme 2004; Duvigneau 1932; Mäckbach and Kienzle 1926; Wittke 1996; Feldenkirchen 1995). Above all, Bönig (1993a, b), von Freyberg (1989), Siegel and von Freyberg (1991), Hachtmann (1989), and Homburg (1991) provided research results regarding deploying the flow production system in various industries. A tradition existed wherein "the flexible production concept with an emphasis on quality" was observed in the automobile industry (Stahlmann 1993). Germany companies had attempted various methods of mass production, mainly in the automotive, electrical, and the machinery industries, that aimed to secure a certain level of flexibility for dealing with demand fluctuations between products and to gain some of the benefits of mass production even with a decreased production output under the conditions of market constraints (von Freyberg 1989; Siegel and von Freyberg 1991). Although examining the deployment of the Ford system, it is necessary to consider the aspects of standardization of production and flow production system, studies that clarify actual conditions of these methods in major industrial sectors are very rare. It is also indispensable to clarify the conditions and characteristics of the Ford system deployment by comparing product fields in the same industry and between production processes, such as assembly, metal processing, casting, and forging. Such research is sparse. Furthermore, the economic effect of mass production is an important issue. Examining the munitions market in the period of National Socialism could elucidate the significance of mass production in developing the national economy by transforming it into an economic structure where the expansion of mass production's effects could reach many related industrial sectors; however, this research topic has not been explored.

Furthermore, several studies provide prominent insights concerning the concentration of enterprises (Hennecke 2025; Böse 2018; Fear 2005; Reckendrees 2000; Lasch 1930; Liefmann 1932, 1897; Wagenführ 1931; Bechtold 1986; Arndt 1960; König 1960; Michels 1928; Böllter 1907; Mayer 1959; Isay 1969). Many of these studies focused on the formation of cartels or syndicates and their relations with the characteristics of monopolistic capitalism in Germany. However, regarding the significance and limitations of enterprise concentration, the process of monopolization in Germany has not been grasped concerning the differences in competitive power between Germany (where cartels occupied a dominant position) and the US (where the rationalization function of trust was pursued).

Some studies consider some peculiar themes in business history, such as the role of the business world in the political process and decision-making within corporations. For example, Plumpe (2016) considers German economic and business history, focusing on the circumstances that enabled the comparatively stable business and industrial structure characterizing the economy in this country from the mid-nineteenth century onward. Regarding business history in each period, it examines three different themes or issues: (1) the problem of decision-making within a corporation, (2) changes in companies' behavior and organizational patterns under the transformation of economic policy and political revolution in the late 1960s, and (3) the economic development of the Second Reich. In contrast, this book examines some common subject matters in the major fields of business management in the three stages from the 1870s until the end of World War II. This approach allows us to indicate the overall conditions of Germany's business management until the end of Word War II and the historical view of this period.

Furthermore, Berghoff et al. (2013) focus on the roles that the business world played in the political process and examined the influences of three main ideologies—National Socialism, capitalism, and socialism—on the economy. They examine how political changes impacted business during the late Second Reich and early Weimar period and how well executives adapted to new social and political circumstances. They also explore interactions between business leaders and government policy-makers, focusing on the importance of individuals' decisions and actions. They consider the involvement of some business leaders in issues related to politics significantly influencing the economy; however, they do not clarify changes in business management and the process of corporate expansion. The German management style and its significance in corporate development until the end of World War II are also not explored.

Several notable studies examined changes in organizational structure (Chandler 1990; Kocka 1969a, b, 1971, 1975, 1978, 1979, 1980, 1981a b, 1983; Siegrist 1980; Fear 2005; Feldenkirchen 1982; Tanaka 2023; Bongartz 1984a, b; Feldenkirchen 1987; Feldenkirchen 1995; Plumpe 1990, 1991; Tammen 1978; Schneckenburger 1988; Meer 1952, 1953; Haber 1971; Brady 1933; Hayes 1987; Siegrist 1980; Pohl 1981). These studies clarified changes in the organizational structure of large enterprises in major industrial sectors, and many are based on the model provided by Alfred D. Chandler (Chandler 1962, 1977, 1990). Chandler explains "the largest firm (usually the first to make the three-pronged investment in production, distribution, and management) became the price leader, basing prices on estimates of demand in relation to its own plant capacities and those of its competitors" (Chandler 1990, p. 36). Investment in management included the building of the organizational structure. Chandler emphasizes building organizational capability as an important factor in securing competitive advantage (Chandler 1990). Kocka clarified important changes such as the rise of the modern business enterprise that had multi-business units and managerial hierarchy (Kocka 1980), organizational structures in big businesses, the influence of bureaucracy on changes in organizational structure (Kocka 1980, p. 97; Kocka 1981a, b, pp. 459–461), and establishment of the central office (Kocka 1969a) and committees (Kocka 1969b, S. 436–439).

Furthermore, comparative analytical perspectives between industries and companies are critical. Differences and commonalities in business management between industries or enterprises can be observed in various fields. Such tendencies can be observed during each period considered in this book; however, studies considering business management changes in various industrial sectors from such comparative perspectives are rare. Studies that analyze a specific industry have revealed many prominent research results in several industries, such as the iron and steel industry (Kleinschmidt 1993; Reckendrees 2000; Fear 2005; Marx 2013, Dascher and Kleinschmidt 1992), the electrical industry (Homburg 1991; Feldenkirchen 1995; Wittke 1996; Schmidt 1933), the chemical industry (Plumpe 1990; Abelshauser 2007; Abelshauser et. al 2004; Thiel 2020; Lindner 2005), the automobile industry (Stahlmann 1993; Kugler 1985; Feldenkirchen 2003; von Seherr-Thoss 1979; Pesch 1988; Thieme 2004; Schriften der Hamburger Stiftung für Sozialgeschichte des 20. Jahrhunderts 1987), and the machine industry (Herrmann 1985).

Prior studies do not provide sufficient insight regarding the overall view of business management in Germany, which includes various fields such as enterprise concentration, management system, production system, business strategy, and organizational structure. The extant literature also does not clarify the process of business management changes and capitalistic development based on these changes in Germany during the period from the Second Reich to the end of World War II. In comparison, this book investigates changes in business management and corporate expansion by focusing on the interrelationships between the determinative factors promoting management transformation to clarify the overall structure of business management. It is impossible to sufficiently understand the significance and limitations compared with the period after the war without analyzing all of the significant fields of business management in which important changes occurred and grasping the total conditions of business management. Therefore, this book broadly examines various important business management fields such as enterprise concentration, enterprise structure, management systems, production systems, business strategy, and organizational structure without limitation to a specific field. Through such a comprehensive analysis, this book attempts to clarify the interrelationships between the management systems in each field and and the total structure of business management.

The extant literature has not clarified how the peculiar development of German capitalism influenced business management development or which specific management style was created in Germany. Prior studies have also not sufficiently grasped how German enterprises formulated original developmental processes being influenced by American management methods or how "continuity" and "discontinuity" of business management in Germany were before and after World War II. Finally, previous research has not investigated how the special evolutionary process of business management influenced the development of German capitalism and how German capitalism and business management developed in the globalism of hegemonic countries. Therefore, this book analyzes the history of business management in Germany by comparing old industrial sectors, such as the mining, iron and steel, and machine industries, with new industrial sectors, such as the chemical, electrical, and automobile industries. Furthermore, this book examines business management from a comparative perspective between representative large enterprises. These analyses will make it possible to understand the real-world conditions of business management and the significance of individual changes.

1.4 Analytical Framework

1.4.1 Basic Viewpoint of Analysis of Business Management

Next, this section will attempt to elucidate its analytical framework. In Japan, a school of thought analyzes and understands the dynamics of business management on the basis of mutual relationships between political, industrial, and business economics, which comprise the structure of economics (Yamazaki 2013, 2005; Maekawa 1970, 1993; Kanbayashi 1976; Hayashi 1972). Among these mutual relationships, this school of thought identifies the causes of various problems and the unique styles and characteristics of business management, in particular, those in developed countries. In addition, it discusses the societal significance of objective changes and the relationship between the law of change and development. In this book, going beyond specific corporate-level factors, the economic and industrial factors of business management are thoroughly analyzed and the process of corporate activities creating reproduction and accumulation structures are explained, given a country's capitalistic nature. Using this type of analytical approach, this book attempts to understand German capitalism by considering business management and its connection to the problem of industrial concentration. Thus, this book, by nature, is an analysis of business management as an element of economics.

The management measures that each enterprise implements are independently decided and chosen by top executive and managers. However, their decision-making is influenced and determined by the objective conditions of the capitalistic economy (Yamazaki 2005, Chapter 3). Which management problems to be solved under the conditions of global capitalism and German capitalism during each period, especially market conditions and competitive structures, were determined to increase profit? How were enterprise structures and management systems forced to change as a corresponding measure to historical conditions? What is the significance of such changes in business management? The significance of the management of enterprises as well as their socioeconomic meaning are important issues to be clarified.

Therefore, in this book, the development of business management before the end of the World War II will be examined in relation to the historical conditions of global capitalism and German capitalism in each period, considering the interrelationships between (1) the factors determining business management changes, (2) the actual conditions of business management changes, and (3) the significance of such phenomena for corporate expansion and development of national economy. This book attempts to elucidate the mechanisms of enterprise development, industry, and the economy by investigating the interrelationships between these three areas. Such an analysis will enable the understanding of not only the characteristics of business management changes but also new trends and special characteristics of the capitalistic economic society during each period.

Regarding how each country's unique system and style of business management are determined, this book emphasizes that "structures determine business management phenomena." Here, "structure" is unique to the concerned country and comprises three levels: (a) capitalistic structure, (b) industrial economic structure, and (c) structural factors unique to the enterprise level. Elements are related to the capitalistic structure, such as the structure of productive forces, market structure (commodity, financial, and labor market structures), various institutions (such as the law system and regulations, education system, vocational education system, and labor relations), and the economic culture unique to the country concerned. The industrial economic structure includes factors like industrial concentration and the overall industrial structure; structural factors unique to enterprise-level elements—such as management system, management structure, capital structure, management values, tradition of business management, and company culture—are important. Therefore, this framework is a method for a multifactorial analysis of business management. The concerned country's structure at these three levels is the independent variable, and the concrete management phenomenon is the independent variable. It is important to clarify the mechanism that determines commonality among countries and the unique development of business management in each country by examining the relationships between these two variables. How the system and style of business management peculiar to each country are built is determined by the abovementioned three factors (a, b, and c). Each of these three also comprises some elements and is determined by a combination of sub-elements.

Top executives and managers independently decide and choose each enterprise's management measures; however, their decision-making is influenced and determined by the objective conditions of the capitalistic economy. The significance of the management of enterprises and their socioeconomic significance is an important research topic that must be further examined. This book emphasizes grasping the essential qualities of management phenomena only as a result of behaviors based on the subjective decision-making of actors and the objective determinative relations and the significance of changes.

Regarding industry characteristics, it is important to consider how different industrial sectors can be compared. In terms of industrial structures, particularly those defined by the expansion process of capitalism in each country, the nature of these structures, the characteristics of industrial development, the composition of internationally competitive industrial sectors, and the characteristics of these industries are important research topics. In the analysis that focuses on industrial characteristics, the following are important: (1) technological, (2) market, and (3) product characteristics. Technological characteristics determine product and market characteristics, particularly price changes and the stability of markets in terms of how declining trends appear, the length of the product lifecycle, and competitive factors, such as the establishment condition of product differentiation. Therefore, elements of these industrial characteristics significantly influence the conditions of capital accumulation in enterprises and the development of enterprise concentration as an important means in such an accumulation process. Thus, the differences in industrial characteristics are an important factor in determining the importance of business mergers and in selecting measures to address management issues. Therefore, it is important to clarify the differences between industries based on the types of products to be manufactured, business fields, and the characteristics of each business.

In addition, in terms of the mutual relationship between industrial sectors, for example, the market and price control of raw materials industries through business concentration intend to maintain prices at a higher level and become a factor in increasing the cost of various types of products made with such raw materials. This can restrict the rationalization and cost reduction efforts in the producer goods industries, such as those that manufacture production equipment, which influences the actual development of business and capital accumulation in the mutually related functions of a management phenomenon in a specific industrial sector.

In this book, changes in business management before the end of World War II are considered from both viewpoints of the historical context of global economy and German capitalism and the international economic relations including world linkages of market and capital. Such analytical perspectives are indispensable for understanding peculiar characteristics of business management and corporate expansion in Germany.

1.4.2 *Total System of Business Management as a Framework for Structural Analysis*

While this book applies the abovementioned research methods, it also examines various aspects and situations using a unique analytical framework for a total system of business management, wherein we analyze overall business management. The total system of business management is a structural framework comprising conditions that define the established methods of business management within the confines of capitalism in a specific country. This conceptual framework helps understand the overall relationships and structure of business management in the country. The concept of the total system of business management comprises two parts: first, the external factors in business management, including external environmental factors such as the structure of a country's capitalist system, industrial systems, and labor relations; and second, the internal factors related to corporate structures, including structural factors of management such as the system of industrial relations, management, and organization in corporations and executive management systems such as single- and two-layered structures. The relationship between these two phenomena is influenced by the state of business management and external factors of capitalism, which define the development of business management in a country. This state of management is affected by corporate-level institutional characteristics and mechanisms. Further, internal factors in corporate structures influence external environmental factors, such as the double-layered structure of executive management, thereby defining corporate networks through the supervisory board function. Thus, these two phenomena are interconnected.

When considering overall ties with business management, the "global structure of capitalism" reveals the mutual relationships within the capitalist bloc. However, the leadership and hegemony of leading nations signifies a problem in these relationships, particularly in international markets and capital. Although this global structure of capitalism lies outside the total system of business management, it defines, or at least influences, this system. Under the global structure of capitalism, the total system of business management determines a given country's established methods of business management.

The eight elements comprising these external environmental factors within the total system of business management are the following: (1) state–enterprise relationships, (2) labor relations, (3) industrial systems based on interfirm relationships, (4) financial systems, (5) the structure of productive forces, (6) industrial structures, (7) market structures, and (8) enterprise–market relationships. These eight elements are explained below.

State-enterprise relationships comprise state regulative policies, particularly anti-monopoly, trade, and industrial policies. For example, in Germany, issues with the economic principles of social market economy and anti-monopoly regulations were related to regulative policy. One important goal of trade policy was the integration of West Germany into capitalistic markets and the establishment of a common market through European integration. The issues of investment promotion measures and the state's intervention in the productivity movement were critical components of industrial policy.

The labor relations framework revolved around collective agreements, worker participation in management, and labor unions. In corporate structures, these were external environmental factors and the specific state of industrial relations within corporations was an internal structural factor. In Germany, industries were confronted with codetermination issues at the corporate management level, in addition to the dual system of regional collective agreements and labor relations through codetermination at the plant level. The system of codetermination is of great significance for labor–management relationships, German production and marketing strategies, and the production structure and system that supported these strategies. It is critical to investigate the impact of labor relationships on business management via the codetermination system, as well as the role of social redistribution in the postwar economic order known as the social market economy. When assessing the influence of industrial relations on business management in Japan and Germany, differences of not only the regulating powers of trade unions but also the promotional functions of management must be considered.

In Germany, inter-corporate ownership and control structures, interfirm relationships, industrial systems based on industry–bank relationships, and large corporate group systems are examples of industrial systems based on interfirm relationships or industry-level systems based on collaborative interfirm relationships. In Germany, these industrial systems not merely demonstrate cooperative capitalism with regulative functions and a new approach toward monopolies and industrial concentration, which supported the system of large corporate groups, but also built mechanisms for governance. In contrast, in Japan, big banks played an important role as main banks in the industrial groups that were formed after the war. These points are closely connected with the collaborative industrial (regulatory) system based on industry–bank relationships.

Financial systems had issues with corporate financing and the widespread expansion of international ties in financial markets based on what is now known as information technology networks. The development of an interconnected financial system consolidated the universal banking system, which existed in prewar Germany, the house banks, the role of the big banks within the universal banking system, and the credit and security businesses. This point is closely connected with the collaborative industrial (regulatory) system based on industry–bank relationships.

The historical development of productive forces, labor utilization, the system of vocational education and specialized skills reflected in production all influenced the changes in the structure of productive forces. In addition to the prewar tradition of "flexible quality production," which differed from the US mass production system, Germany had a history of developing mass production systems with production flexibility and scale merit with lower production volume (von Freyberg 1989; Siegel and von Freyberg 1991; Stahlmann 1993). The foundation of a production structure relied on skilled workers that were supported by a system of vocational education and specialized skills, such as the Meister system. Although based on the deployment of US technology and management methods, these factors strongly influenced postwar changes to the structure of productive forces.

Concerning industrial structures, particularly those defined by the expansion process of capitalism in each country, the nature of these structures, the composition of internationally competitive industrial sectors, and the characteristics of these industries were important issues. The issues included the following: the composition of key industrial sectors; industrial characteristics (technological, market, and product characteristics); each company's position within the national economy, demonstrated by their interconnectedness within industrial sectors and within international competition; and their relationship with (i.e., relative degree of reliance upon) the state. Among these issues, changes in German business management were associated with their level of transformation, such as the transition from an industrial structure based on producer goods to one focused on the durable consumer goods sector.

Commodity, labor, and financial markets are all parts of market structures. For Germany's commodity markets, the nature of its target markets, the composition of the regions and export market products, trade policy in export destination countries, and competition structures were all closely related to corporate management behavior. Along with the characteristics of German market, the nature and meaning of the European market played a significant role, and such conditions for a common market were important issues that affected the development of business management. Comparing German market conditions with those of the US, in which standardization was very advanced, differences in market conditions such as a consumer emphasis on quality or functionality are to be noted. These market conditions were inextricably linked to corporate product strategy, marketing activities, and labor utilization. In European markets, complementary relationships in industrial and product areas were based on German industrial structures, with the heavy and chemical industries and processing and assembly industries at their core. In addition, there were strong differences in industrial structures among European nations compared with those of other regions. This situation may be related to the state of German business management, which has adapted to European market conditions. In contrast, Japanese enterprises tended to rely on the domestic market and the US market that have characteristics of emphasizing quality, measured by relatively few defects, and pursued establishing a business management system that was compatible with such market conditions. Therefore, it is imperative to consider business management and corporate expansion in relation to characteristics of market paying attention to the regional composition of the export markets.

In enterprise–market relationships, the impact of German marketization on business management and industrial concentration became a problem. As expressed by the term "coordinated market economy," there existed characteristics of marketization in postwar Germany and a market economy system that integrated measures to deal with the "limits of marketization" (Hall and Soskice 2001; Hall and Soskice 2007, pp. iii–xx). The characteristics of the system can be seen in social redistribution functions through social market economic principles, a framework for labor relations based on the codetermination system and its effects on the labor market, and a system for regulating interests in an industrial system based on the universal banking system and industry–bank relationships. Such characteristics of marketization are deeply integrated with the development of business management. In enterprise–market relationships, the influence of German marketization on business management and industrial concentration became a problem. Enterprise–market relationships are also deeply concerned with issues regarding variety of capitalism.

What were the types of business management changes in the overall structures and relevancies mentioned above and the interconnected factors in eight elements? This book clarifies this very crucial question.

In discussions regarding varieties of capitalism, a country's production regime is deeply connected to institutional factors, the complementarity of education and training systems, labor market regulations and corporate governance, financial systems, and interfirm relationships from the perspective of market competition and technology transfer (Hall and Soskice 2001). The Rhenish capitalism (Albert 1991) or a "coordinated market economy" (Hall and Soskice 2001) best represent capitalism in Germany after World War II. This market economy model differs from the US model in that the latter views the entire spectrum of market principles as the greatest good, whether in the commodity, financial, or labor markets.

Such a type of market economy is deeply concerned with issue regarding the pursuit of economic rationality and characteristic of German companies as a "social community." It is economic prudence centered on the coordination of the interests of various stakeholders, including workers. In such ideologies, the importance of long-term profit rather than short-term profit in business, as well as the nature of enterprise as a "social community," is emphasized (Albert 1990, pp. 105, 137, 231–232, 275). In this book, origins of the nature of enterprises as a "social community" are clarified through examining pursuit of economic rationality in Germany.

1.5 Division of the Periods Before the End of World War II and Business Management Changes in Each Period

When examining the historical division of periods in this book, three important periods before the end of World War II can be recognized: (1) the Second Reich (1871–1918), (2) the Weimar Era (1918–1933), and (3) the period of National Socialism (1933–1945).

This section considers the significant issues in business management changes and the factors that determined them in each period.

1.5.1 Business Management Changes in the Period of the Second Reich

First, in examining the period of the Second Reich, special changes occurred after the 1870s and new methods and systems of business management played an important role. Economic crises brought about by overproduction that remarkably exceeded demand occurred in 1873 in both Germany and the US. They were caused not by the influence of depression in the United Kingdom as observed in the crises during previous periods but by the high level of productive forces in Germany and the US as new developing industrial nations. Furthermore, the trend in which economic crises became chronic phenomena, occurring at about 10-year intervals, made the situation very serious.

Thus, in Germany, as well as in the US, the level of productive forces tended to exceed the scale of the markets. An important change in the structure of capitalism in this period can be observed at this point. Under such difficult conditions, there were two effective methods adopted as countermeasures. One was to maintain prices through regulations and by avoiding competition. Enterprise concentration was an important means and the monopolistic system was built through such concentration. The other was attempting to reduce costs. In this period, labor management system reforms, including the deployment of the Taylor system, became an effective measure for reducing production costs. Efforts to cut sales costs by integrating the sales function in manufacturing enterprises also occurred.

In addition, to understand the condition of the market and respond to changes, the internalization of sales functions within a company became necessary and important instead of a structure that specialized in the production function. The internalization of the sales functions as well as the integration of the purchasing function became effective ways to realize the harmonious flow of business processes and throughput. Thus, vertical, functional integration progressed and the reform of organizational structures became necessary with such movements. As a result, managerial hierarchies composed of top, middle, and lower management were built.

Therefore, regarding problems with business management in this period, three fields including (1) the concentration of enterprises, (2) labor management system reforms, and (3) changes in enterprise and organizational structures are issues to be considered. These themes will be examined in Part II.

1.5.2 Business Management Changes in the Period of the Weimar Republic

Next, in considering the period of the Weimar Republic, various important changes in business management occurred under the tremendous changes in the world economy and German capitalism. The rationalization movement, which began in 1924, was one of the most important factors in determining the new development of business management.

A serious situation was brought about by Germany's defeat in World War I such as the exorbitant burden forced by the Treaty of Versailles, which became a great obstacle for the resurrection of enterprises, industry, and the economy. Germany was forced to pay huge reparations and alienate territory, and it lost all of its colonies. However, maintaining order in the capitalist world became a very important issue for the US, which appeared as the most powerful leader of the capitalist nations, rather than the UK, due to the Russian Revolution in 1917. Under such conditions, the resurrection of Germany was regarded as a key issue for the US and credit was given to Germany by the US in the assistance framework of the Dawes Plan in 1924.

When looking at domestic changes in Germany, the revolution in November 1918 exerted tremendous influence. The Second Empire collapsed and economic concessions such as an eight-hour labor system, recognition of labor unions, and wage agreement systems were given to the laborer class to avoid a transformation to a socialist state. These burdens brought conditions in which wages tended to be maintained at a relatively high level and had difficulty falling. The domestic market became even smaller due to hyperinflation. In addition, the effect of dumping in export markets enabled by the remarkable decline in the exchange rate disappeared with the end of inflation.

Under such serious conditions, Germany was forced to attempt to expand exports by thorough cost reductions. Rationalization was regarded as the only measure to realize such a purpose. Changes in industrial relations promoted cooperation between capital and labor through rationalization. The defeat of revolutionary powers in the fall of 1923 promoted workers' collaboration in economic development. A policy based on "the Economic Democracy Theory" of the Free Labor Union regarded such a collaboration as an important measure for increasing wages and workers' standard of living. Labor believed that rationalization would become an effective means of improving productivity as an important premise for achieving a high-level standard of living, such as was seen in the US at the time (Naphtali 1928; Ohashi 1999, p. 107).

Thus, rationalization, which was itself only addressing problems at the level of individual enterprises, was regarded as indispensable for the German state and the people. Rationalization was promoted and developed as a movement by the strong involvement of the state and a cooperative system between capital and labor (Yamazaki 2001).

The field of rationalization in the 1920s can be observed in three spheres as follows: (1) The rationalization and reorganization of industry using enterprise concentration, (2) rationalization based on the development of technology and techniques (technical rationalization), and (3) rationalization based on the improvement of labor organization and management. The latter two fields were concerned with rationalization at the level of the individual enterprise.

Rationalization at the industrial level based on the enterprise concentration was implemented on the basis of fusions called "trusts." In this process, excess production capacity was reduced and the system for the division of labor for production was reorganized within large trust enterprises created by fusion.

In technical rationalization, various results of technological and technical developments were used. Such progress can be observed in, for instance, the transformation to the individual drive method of machine equipment using the electric motor, the use of the newest machines and equipment, and the introduction and expansion of synthetic production systems into various product fields in the chemical industry. However, trends such as the lack of capital and the large burden of capital costs became factors that restricted the thorough implementation of technical rationalization.

Regarding rationalization in the field of labor organization, the deployment of American management and production methods such as the Taylor and Ford systems became an indispensable problem. Although attempts to deploy the Taylor system already began at the beginning of the twentieth century, such American systems did not reach the condition of diffusion until the outbreak of the World War I. Therefore, the deployment of the Taylor system was pursued after the war and became one of the most important rationalization measures. This American management system was regarded as an effective rationalization means without heavy expenditure under the conditions of a lack of capital and the large burden of capital costs.

The Ford system became a key measure to realize cost reduction and mass production. In the US during the 1920s, mass production based on the Ford system diffused into the processing and assembly industries such as the automobile, electrical engineering, and machine industries, and the economic effects of mass production expanded throughout the whole national economy. Therefore, German enterprises were forced to deploy the Ford system and promote mass production to overcome competition with foreign companies, especially those from the US.

Business management in Germany experienced significant changes in the process of implementing the abovementioned rationalization measures. In addition to these changes, the reform of organizational structures was needed with the development of rationalization and the diversification of business. In large enterprises created by trusts, the manner in which numerous companies, plants, and sales organizations integrated into trust enterprises could be reorganized to effectively manage, control, and coordinate all of the trust's activities; the process of reorganization became an important problem to be solved. In addition, in enterprises that adopted a diversification strategy, management issues inevitably arose under functional structures as diversification advanced. One issue was the difficulty encountered by each department's head manager in keeping pace with basic functions such as the production, sales, and procurement of a department in which multiple, vastly different product lines were managed together. Another was the top management's frustration with making administrative decisions rather than entrepreneurial, executive decisions such as allocating corporate or long-term business resources (Kroos and Gilbert 1972, p. 253). This can be seen in the case of IG Farben, which was a company that underwent diversification and was forced to pursue organizational restructuring to resolve these managerial issues. Such factors led to the reform of organizational structures. In the US, reforms based on restructuring principles found in divisional structures were the norm, as seen in Du Pont. Therefore, the reform of organizational structures is an important issue to consider from the perspective of comparison with experiences in the US.

In this way, regarding business management problems in this period, four fields are to be considered, namely (1) rationalization and reorganization of industry using enterprise concentration, (2) changes in labor management systems through the deployment of the Taylor system, (3) deployment of the Ford system, and (4) changes in organizational structures by means of rationalization and diversification. These themes will be examined in Part III.

1.5.3 Business Management Changes in the Period of National Socialism

In examining the period of National Socialism from 1933 to 1945, as well as the Weimar era, rationalization was an important factor that led to business management changes. Since the latter half of the 1930s, rationalization was driven as a movement with the strong involvement of the Fascist state. Under the Second Four-Year Plan started in 1936, the rationalization movement was driven in the fields of production technology and labor organization (Hachtmann 1989, S. 302). It changed conditions to develop the rationalization and management behavior of enterprises. In particular, the Nazi state's labor policy brought about significant changes in the field of labor relations, which built new foundation for the thorough development of rationalization. During the Weimar period, the process of executing the organized collective influence regarding working conditions and wage costs was recognized by the state, which significantly limited the space for business plans. However, the political regulations that created loopholes in the collective labor right to work after 1930 and the dissolution of trade unions in May 1933 significantly contributed to the removal of obstacles that prevented the use of an enterprise's right regarding "labor factors" that were present in the Weimar era (Homburg 1991, S. 3–4). In addition, during the period of National Socialism, "the managerial community theory" that eliminated class discrimination between capitalists and laborers and "the leader's principle" that viewed both parties as having a relationship between direction and obedience resulted in the negation of the exploitation relation; these processes formed an important theoretical foundation for fascism labor management (Ambrosius and Hubbard 1986, S. 253; Maekawa 1993, pp. 190–191). Regarding such significant changes in the field of labor, based on cases in the automobile industry, M. Stahlmann pointed out that the dissolution of the labor union by the Nazis gave management almost unrestricted freedom to implement labor organizational and technological innovations without obstacle (Stahlmann 1993, S. 84).

One of the important characteristics of rationalization in this period is that the Ministerium for Economy pursued the rationalization policy as a measure of efficiency improvement under the Second Four-Year Plan. Such a policy included two aspects: (1) the rationalization of production in enterprises and (2) the rationalization of management as unifying the cost accounting standard. Standardization and securing rational labor methods occupied a central position in the former (Yanagisawa 2013, pp. 132–133). Rationalization was developed as a technological improvement in production and processes and as a measurement of the cost accounting of commodities and profit calculation (Yanagisawa 2013, p. 155). The rationalization policy of the cartel system was also pursued as state control over the cartel organization itself. Its essence can be seen in the formation of compulsory cartels implemented by the Ministerium for Economy. The purpose of such measures was to use the super cartel led by the state to expand productive forces and administer the distribution system. The rationalization policy of the cartel included two elements: (1) organizing the German association (Reichsvereinigung) and (2) consolidating and integrating cartels and their incorporation into the economic groups (Yanagisawa 2013, pp. 61, 67).

Regarding the socioeconomic backgrounds of the rationalization movement in this period, one of great changes can be observed in the lack of materials and labor force, the strengthening of the controlled economy, and the tremendous expansion of the munitions market. Standardization and autarky were promoted and performed as a means of coping with the lack of material. Standardization was handled as a movement of the state as a whole. Such organized endeavors promoted and contributed to the standardization of production in each enterprise in many industrial sectors. The lack of an adequate labor force made it necessary to use machines and equipment that saved manpower and enabled more effective means of labor management and organization. Although the Taylor system diffused as a typical German system in the 1920s, the emphasis on the REFA system shifted from time studies and labor management methods based on it to work studies including broader fields such as preparation for work, work management, work formation, job design, and job evaluation since

1936 (Schlaich 1974, S. 190). Thus, attempts to strengthen labor management were much stronger than in the Weimar era. Furthermore, the involvement of the state or quasi-national organizations became enlarged (*thyssenkrupp Corporate Archives*, VST/590, Richtlinien für organisatorische Fragen innerhalb der Refa-Ausschüsse, S. 2; *thyssenkrupp Corporate Archives*, VST/590, Verzeichnis der Refa-Gau- und Refa-Ortsausschüsse im Reich; Hachtmann 1989, S. 74, S. 82–83, S. 180, S. 303). This prompted changes in labor management through the complete use of the REFA system.

Demand for munitions was remarkably increased with the militarization of the economy brought about by the Second Four-Year Plan started in 1936 and the shift to a war economy in 1939. Under the striking expansion of markets related to munitions, many industrial sectors experienced notable development. These favorable situations gave enterprises in many industries the possibility to implement the Ford system and pursue mass production. Mass production and the rationalization movement first became possible on the strong foundation of continuous sales under National Socialism, preparation for war, and a policy of armament expansion, and the standardization and typization organizationally promoted by the state (Hachtmann 1989, S. 302–303). Thus, the shift to mass production by implementing the Ford system progressed on the basis of new market conditions based on munitions.

In this way, changes in labor management and organization using the REFA system and attempts at mass production through the implementation of the Ford system were effective means of rationalization in this period. Therefore, in Part IV, reorganization and strengthening labor management by implementing the REFA system and deploying the Ford system based on the munitions market will be analyzed. Regarding the deployment of the Ford system, this book examines the problems of realizing mass production using such management methods considering the characteristics of the munitions market as opposed to those of private demand.

The composition of this book is as follows. First, Part I considers the history of globalism of countries with hegemony and its influences on other countries and Germany's total business management system as the structural framework defining a country's management style, applying the author's original framework. Following the examinations in Part I, business management changes in the three periods are analyzed. Part II explores business management in Germany during the Second Reich. Part III considers the Weimar period, and Part IV analyses the period of National Socialism. Part V considers the history of Germany's globalism and regionalism from the late nineteenth century to the present and the development of German capitalism and corporate expansion before the end of World War II. Based on these discussions, Chapter 15 presents concluding remarks and the implications of this book.

In this book, many original historical materials were used, such as the internal documents of the representative enterprises of major industries, various materials owned by the Federal Archives in Germany, and original materials from the National Archives in Washington D. C.

(1) For example, the ratios of Germany's export to countries in Europe to total amount of export in 1900, 1913, 1928, 1933, and 1938 were 76.9%, 76%, 70.6%, 78%, and 75.9%, respectively (Statistisches Reichsamt 1902; S.139; Statistisches Reichsamt 1915, S. 253–254; Statistisches Reichsamt 1931; S.236–239; Statistisches Reichsamt 1935; S.228–229; Statistisches Reichsamt 1943, S. 322–323).
(2) Although studies from the perspective of global history have increased recently, this book is not intended as a study oriented in this direction.
(3) Regarding the Americanization of business management in Germany during interwar period, Jeferry R. Fear points out Vereinigte Stahlwerke AG was "one of the salient examples of the Americanization of German business in the 1920s." He explains that this company was "one of the first major German firm to revamp its accounting system along with American lines," licensed American technologies, and moved to a version of the multidivisional structure during the great depression that began in 1929 (Fear 2005, pp. 520–521). He insists that "German firms often had more advanced forms of managerial and financial accounting methods than American firms, such as depreciation, overhead cost-allocation methods, and internal transfer pricing" (Fear 2005, p. 723) and German accounting norms did not become a mere copy of American methods due to the web of intellectual and personnel ties and business traditions (Fear 2005, p. 724). However, deployment of the Taylor system and the Ford system were major issues in the Americanization of business management in this period. Fear explains it is possible to speak of the Americanization of German business only in ideas about factory management, especially technical aspects of American manufacturing (Fear 2005, p. 734).

References

Abelshauser W (2003) Kulturkamp. Der deutsche Weg in die neue Wirtschaft und die amerikanische Herausforderung. Kulturverlag Kadmos, Berlin

Abelshauser W (Hrsg) (2007) Die BASF. Eine Unternehmensgeschichte. 3. Auflage, C. H. Beck, München

Abelshauser W, von Hippel W, Johnson JA, Stokes RG (2004) German industry and global enterprise. The History of a Company. Cambridge University Press, Cambridge, BASF

Albert M (1991) Capitalisme contre, Capitalisme. du Seuil, Paris

Álvaro-Moya A, Donzé P-Y (2016) Business history and management studies. In: J Evolut Stud Bus 1(1):122–151

Amatori F, Jones G (2003) Business history around the world. Cambridge University Press, New York

Ambrosius G, Hubbard WH (1986) Sozial- und Wirtschaftsgeschichte Europas im 20. Jahrhundert. C. H. Beck, München

Arndt H (Hrsg) (1960) Die Konzentration in der Wirtschaft. Erster Band, Stand der Konzentration. Duncker & Humblot, Berlin

Bechtold H (1986) Die Kartellierung der deutschen Volkswirtschaft und die sozialdemokratische Theorie-Diskussion vor 1933. Haag + Herchen, Frankfurt am Main

Berghoff H (2004) Wozu Unternehmensgeschichte? Erkenntnisinteressen, Forschungsansätze und Perspektiven. In: Zeitschrift für Unternehmensgeschichte 49(2):131–148
Berghoff H (2016) Moderne Unternehmensgeschichte. Eine Themen- und Theorieoriented Einführung, 2. Auflage, De Gruyter Oldenbourg, Berlin
Berghoff H, Kocka J, Ziegler D (eds) (2013) Business in the age of extremes: essays in modern German and Austrian economic history. Cambridge University Press, Cambridge
Böllter A (1907) Eisenindustrie und Stahlwerksverband. Eine wirtschaftliche Studie zur Kartellfrage. G. Böhme, Leipzig
Bönig J (1993a) Die Einführung von Fließbandarbeit in Deutschland bis 1933. Zur Geschichte einer Sozialinnovation, Teil I. Lit, Münster, Hamnburg
Bönig J (1993b) Die Einführung von Fließbandarbeit in Deutschland bis 1933. Zur Geschichte einer Sozialinnovation, Teil II. Lit, Münster, Hamnburg
Böse C (2018) Kartellpolitik im Kaiserreich. Das Koholensyndikat und die Absatzorganisation im Ruhrbergbau 1893–1919. De Gruyter, Oldenbourg
Bongartz VW (1984a) Unternehmensleitung und Kostenkontrolle in der Rheinische Montanindu strie vor 1914, dargestellt am Beispiele der Firmen Krupp und Gutehofnnungshütte (Teil I). In: Zeitschrift für Unternehmensgeschichte 29(1):33–55
Bongartz VW (1984b) Unternehmensleitung und Kostenkontrolle in der Rheinische Montanindustrie vor 1914, dargestellt am Beispiele der Firmen Krupp und Gutehofnnungshütte (Teil II). In: Zeitschrift für Unternehmensgeschichte 29(II):73–113
Booth C, Rowlinson M (2006) Management and organizational history: prospects. In: Manag Organ Hist 1(1):5–30
Borscheid P (2001) Der ökonomische Kern der Unternehmensgeschichte. In: Zeitschrift für Unternehmensgeschichte 46(1):5–10
Brady RA (1933) The rationalization movement in German industry. A study in the evolution of economic planning. University of California Press, Berkeley, California
Brunninge O (2009) Using history in organizations. How managers make purposeful reference to history in strategic processes. In: J Organ Chang Manag 22:8–26
Bucheli and Wadhwani (eds) (2014) Organization in time: history, theory, methods. Oxford University Press, Oxford
Chandler AD Jr (1962) Strategy and structure: chapters in the history of the industrial enterpreise. MIT Press, Cambridge, Massachusetts
Chandler AD Jr (1977) The visible hand: managerial revolution in American business. Harvard University Press, Cambridge, Massachusetts
Chandler AD Jr (1990) Scale and scope: the dynamics of industrial capitalism. Harvard University Press, Cambridge, Massachusetts
Clark P, Rowlinson M (2004) The treatment of history in organisation studies: towards an 'Historic Turn'? In: Busin Hist 46(3):331–352
Dascher O, Kleinschmidt C (Hrsg) (1992) Die Eisen- und Stahlindustrie im Dortmunder Raum: Wirtschaftliche Entwicklung, soziale Strukturen und technologischer Wandel im 19. und 20. Jahrhundert. Gesellschaft für Westfälische Wirtschaftsgeschichte E.V., Dortmund
de Jong A, Higgins DN (2015) New business history? (Introduction to Special Issue). In: Bus Hist 57(1):1–4
de Jong A, Higgins DN, Driel H van (2015) Towards a new business history? In: Bus Hist 57(1):5–29
Decker S (2016) Paradigms lost: integrating history and organization studies. In: Manag Organ Hist 11(4):364–379
Decker S, Kipping M, Wadhwani RD (2015) New business historical plurality in business history research methods. In: Busin Hist 57(1):30–40
Duvigneau G (1932) Untersuchungen zur Verbreitung der Fließarbeit in der deutschen Industrie. Eine wirtschaftlich-technische Studie. Dissertation, Technische Hochschule Breslau
Fear RF (2005) Organizing control: August Thyssen and the construction of German corporate management. Harvard University Press, Massachusetts, Cambridge

Feldenkirchen W (1982) Die Eisen- und Stahlindustrie des Ruhrgebiets 1879–1914. Wachstum, Finanzierung und Struktur ihrer Groβunternehmen. Steiner, Wiesbaden
Feldenkirchen W (1987) Big business in interwar Germany: organizational innovation at Verenigt Stahlwerke, IG Farben, and Siemens. In: Busin Hist Rev 61(3):417–451
Feldenkirchen W (1995) Siemens 1918–1945. Piper, München
Feldenkirchen W (2003) „Vom Guten das Beste." Band 1, Die ersten 100 Jahre (1883–1983), 1. Aufl., Herbig, München
Foster WM, Caraiola DM, Suddaby R, Kroezen J, Chandler D (2017) The strategic use of historical marratives: a theoretical framework. In: Bus Hist 59(8):1176–1200
Friedman W and Jones G (2011) Business history: time for debate. In: Bus Hist Rev 85(1):1–8
Godfrey PC, Hassard J, O'Connor ES, Rowlinson M, Ruef M (2016) What is organizational history? In: Acad Manag Rev 41(4):590–608
Hachtmann R (1989) Industriearbeit im 》Dritten Reich《. Untersuchungen zu den Lohn- und Arbeitsbedingungen in Deutschland 1933–1945. Vandenhoeck & Ruprecht, Göttingen
Hall PA, Soskice D (eds) (2001) Varieties of capitalism: the institutional foundations of comparative advantage. Oxford University Press, Oxford
Hall PA, Soskice D (2007) Nihongoban eno jyobun. Shihonshugi no tayosei to Nihon (Preface for Japanese edition. Varieties of caitalism and Japan). In: Hall PA, Soskice D (eds) Shihonsyugi no tayousei (Varieties of capitalism). Nakanishiyashuppan, Kyoto, pp ii–xix
Haber LF (1971) The chemical industry, 1900–1930. Oxford University Press, Oxford, International Growth and Technological Change
Harvey C, Wilson J (2007) Redefining business history: an editorial statement. In: Bus Hist 49(1):1–7
Hayashi A (1972) Gendai Doitsu Kigyoron (Modern German Enterprise), Mineruva Shobo, Kyoto
Hayes P (1987) Industry and Ideology. IG Farben in the Nazi Era. Cambridge University Press, Cambridge, Massachusetts
Hennecke R (2025) Wettbewerbsregulierung im Wirtschaftswunder. Die Kartellrechtspraxis in Westdeutschland unter den allierten Dekartelierungsgesetzen, *1947–1957*. De Gruyter, Berlin
Herrmann K (1985) Ackergiganten. Technik, Geschichte und Geschichten. Westermann, Braunschweig
Hinrichs P (1981) Um Seele des Arbeiter. Arbeitspsychologie, Industrie- und Betriebssoziologie in Deutchland 1871–1945. Pahl-Rugenstein, Köln
Hinrichs P, Peter L (1976) Industrieller Friede? Arbeitswissenschaft und Rationalisierung in der Weimarer Republik, Pahl-Rugenstein, Köln
Hodge PA, Costa AdSMd (2021) Oral history and organizational research: challenges of building knowledge about the past. In: Organizações Sociedade 28(99):722–756
Homburg H (1991) Rationalisierung und Industriearbeit: Arbeitsmarkt—Management—Arbeiterschaft im Siemens-Konzern Berlin 1900–1939. Haude & Spener, Berlin
Isay R (1955) Die Geschichte der Kartellgesetgebung. W. de Gruyter, Berlin
Jaeger H (1992) Unternehmensgeschichte in Deutschland seit 1945. Schwerpunkte—Tendenzen—Ergebnisse. In: Geschichte und Gesellschaft 18(1):107–132
Jeidels O (1905) Die Methoden der Arbeiterentlöhnung in der rheinisch-westfälischen Eisenindustrie. Duncker und Humblot, Berlin
Jones G, Zeitlin J (eds) (2007) The Oxford handbook of business history. Oxford University Press, Oxford
Kanbayashi T (1976) Keieikeizaigaku・Kigyo riron (Businenn economics・Theory of enterprise*)*. Tokoro shoten, Tokyo
Kieser A (1994) Why organization theory needs historical analysis—and how this should be performed. In: Organ Sci 5(4):608–620
Kikkawa (2009) Jikeiretsu to zettai nendai ni chumoku suru keiei kenkyu (Business management study paying attention to a time series and an absolute age). In: Hitotsubashi daigaku Nihon kigyo kenkyu senta (ed) Nihon kigyo kenkyu no furontia (Frontier of Japanese business studies), Dai 5 go. Yuhikaku, pp.1–14

Kikkawa (2018) Zero kara wakaru Nihon keieishi (Introduction into Japanese business history). Nihon keizai shuppansha, Tokyo

Kipping M, Wadhwani RD, Bucheli M (2014) Analyzing and interpreting historic sources: A basic methodology. In: Bucheli and Wadhwani (eds) Organization in time: History, theory, methods. Oxford University Press, Oxford, pp 305–329

Kleinröder N, Marx C, Gehlen B, Czierpka J (eds) (2024a) Neue Perspektiven der Unternehmensgeschichte. Brill Schöningh, Boston

Kleinröder N, Marx C, Gehlen B, Czierpka J (2024b) Einleitung. In: Kleinröder N, Marx C, Gehlen B, Czierpka J, Neue Perspektiven der Unternehmensgeschichte. Brill Schöningh, Boston, S. VII–XVIII

Kleinschmidt C (1993) Rationalisierung als Unternehmensstrategie. Die Eisen und Stahlindustrie des Ruhrgebiets zwischen Jahrhundertwende und Weltwirtschaftskrise. Klartext, Essen

Kleinschmidt C (2002) Der produktive Blick. Wahrnehmung amerikanischer und japanischer Management- und Produktionsmethoden durch deutsche Unternehmer 1950–1985. Akademie Verlag, Berlin

Kleinschmidt C (2007) Technik und Wirtschaft im 19. und 20. Jahrhundert. R. Oldenbourg, München

Kleinschmidt C (2019) Unternehmensgeschichte als ≪Nebenbeschäftigung≫. Zum Standort der Unternehmensgeschichte—Tendenzen unternehmenshisto-rischer Firschung in Deutschland. In: *Zeitschrift für Unternehmensgeschichte* 64 (2): 274–291

Kocka J (1969a) Industrielles Managemnet: Konzeptionen und Modelle in Deutschland vor 1914. In: Vierteljahrschrift für Sozial- und Wirtschaftsge-Schichte 56(3):332–372

Kocka J (1969b) Unternehmensverwaltung und Angestelltenschaft 1847–1914: Zum Verhältinis von Kapitalisumus in Bürokratie in der deutschen Industrialisierung. Klett, Stuttgart

Kocka J (1971) Family and bureaucracy in German industrial management, 1850–1914, Siemens in comparativ perspective. In: Bus Hist Rev 45(2):133–156

Kocka J (1975) Expansion—Integration—Diversifikation. Wachstumsstrategien industrieller Groβunternehmen in Deutschland vor 1914. In: Winkel H (Hrsg) Vom Kleingewerbe zur Groβindustrie. Quantitätiv-regionale und politischrechtliche Aspekt zur Erforschung der Wirtschafts- und Gesellschaftsstruktur in 19. Jahrhundert. Duncker & Humblot, Berlin

Kocka J (1978) Entrepreneurs and managers in German industrialization. In: Cambridge Econ Hist Europe VII(I):492–589

Kocka J (1979) Familie, Unternehmer und Kapitalismus. An Beispielen aus der frühen deutschen Industrialisierung. In: Zeitschrift für Unternehmensgeschichte 24(3):163–186

Kocka J (1980) The Reise of the modern industrial enterprise in Germany. In: Chandler Jr AD, Daems H (eds) Managerial hierarchies. Comparative Perspectives on the Rise of the Modern Industrial Enterprise. Harvard University Press, Cambridge, Massachusetts, pp 77–116

Kocka J (1981a) Capitalism and bureaucracy in German industrialization before 1914. In: Econ Hist Rev, second series 34(3):453–468

Kocka J (1981b) Groβunternehmen und der Aufstieg der Manager-Kapitalismus im späten 19. und frühen 20.Jahrhundert, Deutschland im internationalen Vergleich. In: Histrische Zeitschrift 232:39–60

Kocka J (1983) Legitimationsprobleme und -strategien der Unternehmer und Manager im 19. und frühen 20. Jahrhundert. In: Pohl H (Hrsg) Legitimation des Management im Wandel. Steiner, Wiesbaden, S 7–21

König H (1960) Kartelle und Konzentration (unter besonderer Berücksichtung der Preis- und Mengenabsprachen). In: Arndt H (Hrsg) Die Konzentration in der Wirtschaft, Erster Band, Stand der Konzentration, Duncker und Humblot, Berlin, S 303–332

Kroos HE, Gilbert C (1972) American business history. Prentice-Hall, Englewood Cliffs, New Jersey

Kugler A (1985) Arbeitsorganisation und Produktionstechnologie der Adam Opel Werke (von 1900 bis 1929). Wissenschaftszentrum, Berlin

Lasch C (1930) Entwicklungstendenzen für die Zusammenschluβformen in der deutschen Groβindustrie seit 1914. Industrie-Verlag und Dr, Düsseldorf

Leblebici H (2014) History and organization theory: potential for a transdiciplinary convergence. In: Bucheli M, Wadhwani RD (eds) Organizations in time: history, theory, methods. Oxford University Press, pp 56-99
Leblebici H, Shah N (2004) The birth, transformation and regeneration of business incubators as new organisational forms' understanding the interplay between organisational history and organisational theory. In: Bus Hist 46(3):353–380
Liefmann R (1932) Cartels, concerns and trusts. Methuen & Co., London
Liefmann R (1897) Unternehmensverbände (Konvention, Kartelle). Ihr Wesen und ihre Bedeutung. J.C.B. Mohr, Leipzig
Lindner SH (2005) Hoechst. Ein I.G. Farben Werk im Dritten Reich. 2. Auflage, C. H. Beck, München
Maclean M, Harvey C, Clegg SR (2016) Conceptualizing historical organization studies. In: Acad Manag Rev 41(4):609–632
Maclean M, Harvey, Clegg SR (2017) Organization theory in business and management theory: present statues and future prospects. In: Bus Hist Rev 91(3):457–481
Maclean M, Harvey C, Sillince JA, Golant BD (2018) Intertextuality, retorical history and the use of the past in organizational transition. In: Organ Stud 39(12):1733–1755
Mäckbach F, Kienzle O (1926) Fliessarbeit. VDI- Verlag, Berlin, Beitrage zu Ihrer Einführung
Maekawa K (1970) Doitsu dokusen kigyo no hatten katei (Development of monopolistic enterpreise in Germany) Mineruva shobo, Kyoto
Maekawa K (1993) Gendai kigyo kenkyu no kiso (Foundation of study of contemporary enterprise). Moriyama shoten, Tokyo
Marx C (2013) Paul Reusch und die Gutehoffnungshütte. Leitung eines deutschen Groβunternehmens. Wallstein Verlag, Göttingen
Maschke E (1969) Outline of the History of German Cartels from 1873 to 1914. In: Crouzet F, Chaloner WH, Stern WM (eds) (1969) Essays in Eropean economic history 1879–1914. Edward Arnold, London
Mayer L (1959) Kartelle, Kartellorganisation und Kartelpolitik. Th. Gabler, Wies-baden
McNabb DE (2016) Converging trends and the future of the global market (A comparative history of commerce and industry, Volum II). Palgrave Macmillan, Basingstoke
Meer F ter (1952) Die I.G.: Ihre Entstehung, ihre Entwickung und Bedeutung. In: Chemische Industrie 4(10):777–806
ter Meer F (1953) Die IG Farbenindustrie Aktiengesellschaft: Ihre Entstehung. Econ Verlag, Düsseldorf, Entwicklung und Bedeutung
Michels RK (1928) Cartels, Combines and Trusts in Post-War Germany. Columbia University Press, New York
Naphtali F (ed) (1928) Wirtschaftsdemokratie: Ihr Wesen, Weg und Ziel, 3, unveränderte. Verlagsgesellschaft des Allgemeinen Deutschen Gewerkschaftsbundes Gmbh, Berlin
Nieberding A, Wischermann C (1998) Unternehmensgeschichte im institutionellen Paradigma. In: Zeitschrift für Unternehmensgeschichte 43(1):35–48
Ohashi S (1999) Doitsu keizai minshushugironshi (German economic democracy). Chuo keizaisha, Tokyo
Pechhold E (1974) 50 Jahre REFA. Beuth, Berlin, Köln, Frankfurt am Main
Pesch M (1988) Struktur und Funktionsweise der Kriegswirtschaft in Deutschland ab 1942—unter besonderer Berücksichtigung des organisatorischen und produktionswirtschaftlichen Wandels in der Fahrzeugindustrie—. Müller Botermann Verlag, Köln
Pierenkemper T (1999) Was kann eine moderne Unternehmensgeschichtsschreibung leisten? Und was sollte sie tunlichst vermeiden. In: Zeitschrift für Unternehmensgeschichte 44(1):15–31
Pierenkemper T (2000a) Unternehmensgechichte. Ein Einführung in ihre Methoden und Ergebnisse. F. Steienr Verlag, Stuttgart
Pierenkemper T (2000b) Sechs Thesen zum gegenwärtigen Stand der deutschen Unternehmensgesschichtsschreibung. In: Zeitschrift für Unternehmensgeschichte 45(2):158–166

Plumpe G (1990) Die I.G. Farbeinindustrie A G: Wirtschaft, Tecknik, Politik 1904–1945. Duncker & Humblot, Berlin
Plumpe G (1991) The political framwork of structural modernization. In: Lee WR (ed) German industry and German industrialization: essays in German economics and business history in the Nineteeth and Twentieth centuries. Routledge, London, New York, pp 220–264
Plumpe W (2006) Unternehmen. In: Ambrosius G, Petzina D, Plumpe W (Hrsg) Moderne Wirtschaftsgeschichte. Eine Einführung für Historiker und Ökonomen, 2., überarbeitete und erweiterte Auflage, R. Oldenbpurg, München, S. 61–94
Plumpe W (2016) German economic and business histrory in the 19th and 20th centuries. Palgrave Macmillan, London
Plumpe W (2018) Unternehmensgeschichte im 19. und 20. Jahrhundert. DeGruyter Oldenbourg, Berlin
Pohl H (1981) Zur Geschichte von Organization und Leitung deutscher Grossunternehmen seit dem 19. Jahrhundert. In: Zeitschrift für Unternehmensgeschichte 26(2):143-178
Pohl M (1999) Zwischen Weihrauch und Wissenschaft? Zum Standort der modernen Unternehmensgeschicte. Eine Replik auf Toni Pierenkemper. In: Zeitschrift für Unternehmensgeschichte 44(2):150–163
Reckendrees A (2000) Das "Stahltrust"-Projekt: Die Gründung der Vereinigte Stahlwerke A.G. und ihre Unternehmensentwicklung 1926–1933/34. C. H. Beck, München
Rowlinson M, Procter S (1999) Organizational culture and business history. In: Organ Stud 20(3):369–396
Rowlinson M, Hassard J (2014) History and the cultural turn in organization studies. In: Bucheli M, Wadhwani RD (eds) Organizations in time: history, theory, methods. Oxford University Press, Oxford, pp 147–165
Rowlinson M, Hassard J, Decker S (2014) Research strategies der organizational history. A dialogue between historical theory and organization theory. In: Acad Manag Rev 39(3):250–274
Ruggie JG (2014) Global governance and "New Governance Theory": lessons from business and human rights. In: Glob Govern 20(1):5–17
Sakai K, Izawa R (2022) Keiei · Sosikiron kenkyu ni okeru rekisiteki tenkai: Sono kiseki to shishin (The trial of the "Historic Turn" in management and organization studies, the path forward). Soshiki kagaku (Organizational Science) 55(4):4–14
Schanetzky T (2018) After the Gold Rush. Ursprünge und Wirkungen der Forschungskonjunkture ≪Unternehmen im Nationalsozialismus≫. In: Zeitschrift für Unternehmensgeschichte 63(1):7–32
Schlaich K (1974) Stand und Weiterentwichklung der REFA-Lehre. In: REFA-Nachrichten 27(3):190–192
Schmidt B (1933) Wege zur Verbesserung der Produktions- und Wettbewerbslage der deutschen Personenkraftwagen-Industrie. Diss. Technische Hochschule Darmstadt, Darmstadt
Schmidt D (1993) Weder Ford noch Taylor. Zu Rhetorik und Praxis der Rationalisierung in den Zwanziger Jahren am Beispiel dreier Siemens Werke. Universität Bremen, Bremen
Schmiede R, Schudlich E (1981) Die Entwicklung der Leistungsentlohnung in Deutschland: Eine historische Untersuchung zum Verhältniss von Lohn und Leistung unter kapitalistischen Produkutionsbedingungen. 4. Auflage, Campus, Frankfurt am Main, New York
Schneckenburger A (1988) Die Geschichte des I.G. Farbenkonzern. Bedeutung und Rolle eines Grossunternehmen. Pahl-Rugenstein, Köln
Schriften der Hamburger Stiftung für Sozialgeschichte des 20. Jahrhunderts (Hrsg) (1987) Das Daimler-Benz Buch. Ein Rüstungskonzern im >Tausendjährigen Reich<. Delphi Politik, Nördlingen
Schock EC (1977) Arbeitslosigkeit und Rationalisierung: Die Lage der Arbeiter und die Kommunistische Gewerkschaftspolitik 1920–28. Campus Verlag, Frankfurt am Main, New York
Schröter HG (2003) Business history in German-speaking states at the end of the century. In: Amatory F, Jones G (eds) Business history around the world. Cambridge University Press, Cambridge, New York, pp 170–191

Schröter HG (2018) Business history in Europe: the vitality of the discipline. In: Zeitschrift für Unternehmensgeschichte 63(2):307–336
Scranton P, Friedenson P (2013) Reimaging business history. The Johns Hopkins University Press, Baltimore
Sewell WH (2005) Logics of history: social theory and social transformation. University of Chicago Press, Chicago
Siegel T, von Freyberg T (1991) Industrielle Rationalisierung unter dem Nationalsozialismus. Campus, Frankfurt am Main, New York
Siegrist H (1980) Deutscher Groβunternehmen vom späten 19. Jahrhundert bis zur Weimarer Republik. In: Geschichte und Gesellschaft 6(1):60–102
Söllheim F (1922) Taylor=System für Deutschland: Grenzen seiner Einführung in deutschen Betriebe. R. Oldenbourg, Berlin
Spitzley H (1980) Wissenschaftliche Betriebsführung. REFA Methodenlehre und Neuorientierung der Arbeitswissenschaft. Bund-Verlag, Köln
Stahlmann M (1993) Die Erste Revolution in der Autoindustrie. Management und Arbeitspolitik von 1900–1940. Campus, Frankfurt am Main, New York
Statistisches Reichssamt (1902) Statistisches Jahrbuch für das Deutsche Reich 1901. Puttkammer & Mühlbrecht, Berlin
Statistisches Reichsamt (1915) Statistisches Jahrbuch für das Deutsche Reich 1914. Puttkammer & Mühlbrecht, Berlin
Statistisches Reichssamt (1931) Statistisches Jahrbuch für das Deutsche Reich 1930. Verlag von Reimar Hobbing, Berlin
Statistisches Reichsamt (1935) Statistisches Jahrbuch für das Deutsche Reich 1934. Verlag von Reimar Hobbing, Berlin
Statistisches Reichsamt (1943) Statistisches Jahrbuch für das Deutsche Reich 1941–42. Verlag für Sozialpolitik, Wirtschaft und Statistik, Berlin
Stollberg G (1981) Die Rationalisierungsdebatte 1908-1933: Freie Gewerkschaften zwischen Mitwirkung und Gegenwehr. Campus, Franfurt am Main, New York
Streeck W (1992) Social institutions and economic performance: studies of industrial relations in advanced capitalist economies. Sage, London
Streeck W (1997) German capitalism: do it exist? Can it survive? In: Crouch C, Streeck W (eds) Political economy of modern capitalism. Mapping convergence and diversity. Sage, London, pp 33–54
Suddaby R, Foster WM, Quinn-Trank C (2010) Rhetorical history of competitive advantage. In: Adv Strat Manag 27:147–173
Suddaby R, Foster WM, Mills AJ (2014) Historical institutionalism. In: Bucheli M, Wadhwani RD (eds) Organizations in time: history. Oxford University Press, Theory, Methods, pp 100–123
Taguchi N (2018) Book review: Kigyo keiei no nichi doku hikaku (Comparison of business management in Japan and Germany, Book review). In: Hikaku Keiie Kenkyu (Journal of the Association for Comparative Studies of Management) 42:139–147
Tammen H (1978) Die I.G. Farbenindustrie Aktiengesellschaft [1925–1933]: Ein Chemiekonzern in der Weimarer Republik. H. Tammen, Berlin
Taylor PJ (2000) Izations of the world: Americanization, modernization and globalization. In: Hay C, Marsh D (eds) Demystifying globalization. Palgrave, Basingstoke, pp 49–70
Thiel C (2020) Entscheidungen und Anpassungspraktiken. Die BASF zwischen 1865 und 1965. Campus, Frankfurt am Main
Thieme C (2004) Daimler-Benz zwischen Anpassungskrise, Verdrängungswettbewerb und Rüstungskonjunktur 1919–1936, 1st edn. Vaihingen/Enz IPa, Stuttgart
Trieba M, Mentrup U (1983) Entwicklung der Arbeiswissenschaft in Deutschland: Rationalisierungspolitik der deutschen Wirtschaft bis zum Faschismus. Minerva, München
Triebel F, Seidl J (2001) Ein Analyserahmen für das Fach Unternehmensgeschichte. In: Zeitschrift für Unternehmensgeschichte 46(1):11–26
Üsdiken B, Kieser A (2004) Introduction: history in organisation studies. In: Bus Hist 46(3):321–330

Üsdinken B, Kipping M (2020) History in management and organization studies: from margin to mainstream. Routledge, New York
Vaara E, Lamberg J-A (2016) Taking historical embeddedness seriously: three historical approaches to advance strategy process and practice research. In: Acad Manag Rev 41(4):633–657
Van Lent W, Durepos G (2019) Nurturing the historic turn: "history as theory" versus "history as method." In: J Manag Hist 25(4):429–443
von Freyberg T (1989) Industrielle Rationalisierung in der Weimarer Republik: Untersucht an Beispielen aud dem Maschinenbau und der Elektroindustrie. Campus, Frankfurt am Main, New York
von Seherr-Thoss HCG (1979) Die deutsche Automobilindustrie. Eine Dokumentation von 1886 bis 1979, 2., korrigierte und erweiterte Auflage, Deutsche Verlags-Anstalt, Stuttgart
Wadhwani RD (2018) Poverty's monument: social problems and organizational field emergence in historical perspective. In: J Manag Stud 55(3):545–577
Wadhwani RD, Bucheli M (2014) The future of the past in management and organization studies. In: Bucheli M, Wadhwani RD (eds) Organizations in time: history, theory, methods. Oxford University Press, Oxford, pp 3–30
Wadhwani RD, Suddaby R, Mordhorst M, Popp A (2018) History as organizing: uses of the past in organization studies. In: Organ Stud 39(12):1663–1683
Wagenführ R (1931) Kartelle in Deutschland. Krische, Nürnberg
White H (1980) The value of narrativity in the representation of reality. In: Crit Inq 7(1):5–27
Wilson J, Toms A, de Jong A, Buchna E (eds) (2017) The Routledge companion to business history. Routledge, Abingdon, New York
Wilson JF, Jones IG, Toms S, Tilba A, Buchnea E, Wong N (2022) Business History. A Research Overview. Routledge, London
Wittke V (1996) Wie entstand industrielle Massenproduktion? Diskontinuierliche Entwicklung der deutschen Elektroindustrie von den Anfängen der „großen Industrie" bis zur Entfaltung des Fordismus (1881–1975). Edition Sigma, Berlin
Wolf M (2005) Why globalization works. Yale University Press, New Haven, London
Yates MN (2014) Understanding historical methods in organization studies. In: Bucheli M, Wadhwani RD (eds) Organizations in time: history, theory, methods. Oxford University Press, Oxford, pp 265–283
Yamazaki T (2001) Vaimaruki Doitsu gorika undo no tenkai (The development of the Rationalization movement in Germany during the Weimar era). Moriyama shoten, Tokyo
Yamazaki T (2005) Gendai keieigaku no saikochiku (*A study of the reconstruction of business management study*). Moriyama shoten, Tokyo
Yamazaki T (2013) German business management: a Japanese perspective on regional development factors. Springer, Tokyo
Yamazaki T (2024) Japanese and German enterprises: Comparison of industrial concentration system and business management. Springer-Nature, Singapore
Yanagisawa O (2013) Nachisu Doitsu to shihonshugi: Nihon no moderu he (Nazis Germany and capitalism: Model for Japan). Nihon Keizai hyoronsha, Tokyo
Yeates N (2001) Globalization and social policy. SAGE, London
Zald MN (1993) Organization studies as a scientific and humanistic enterprise: toward a reconceptualization of the foundations of the field. In: Organ Sci 4(4):513–528
Zeitlin J (2003) Productive alternatives. flexibility, governance, and strategic choice in industrial history. In: Amatori F, Jones G (eds) Business history around the world. Cambridge University Press, Cambridge, pp 62–80
Zollitsch W (1990) Arbeiter zwischen Weltwirtschaftskrise und Nationalsozialismus. Ein Beitrag zur Sozialgeschichte der Jahre 1928 bis 1936. Vandenhoeck & Ruprecht, Göttingen

Part I
History of Globalism and the Total System of Business Management in Germany

Chapter 2
History of the Globalism of Hegemonic Countries and Its Influences

Abstract Following the discussions in Chapter 1, Part I considers the history of globalism of countries with hegemony, its influences on other countries, and the total system of business management in Germany as the structural framework defining a country's management style, applying the author's original framework. In Part 1, the fundamental basis for developing business management and corporate expansion at both global and domestic levels. Chapter 2 revises globalism's history from the late nineteenth century to the present. Which characteristics can be found in the globalism of nations with hegemony? How did such countries display initiative in building the world order and influencing other nations? This chapter considers three periods: (1) the age from the late nineteenth century to the end of World War II, (2) the postwar period, and (3) the period after the 1990s from a comparative viewpoint.

Keywords Globalization · Globalism · Governance · Hegemony · Pax Americana · Pax Britanica · Regionalism · Regionalization

Part I analyzes two themes. The first is the history of the globalism of nations with hegemony and its influences on other countries. The issue of globalism is deeply concerned with the effects on the development of German capitalism and corporate expansion. The second is to present Germany's overall total system of business management in each major period. This approach uses the author's analytical framework for conditions that define the established business management methods within the characteristics of capitalism as implemented in a specific country using the author's analytical framework. The analyses in this chapter clarify the postwar frameworks of German business management.

Chapter 2 considers the history of globalism, focusing on the history of hegemonic nations and their influences. How the capitalism of each country maintains and develops its life power in the process of globalization is deeply concerned with globalism as the principle for competition over acquiring the global hegemony to create the more advantageous foundations for corporate behavior and economic development. Globalization is a process in which global interdependence in both markets and productive forces strengthens, while globalism means the principle, norm, and

T. Yamazaki, *A History of German Business*,
https://doi.org/10.1007/978-981-96-8476-2_2

doctrine of setting an institutional framework and rules for acquiring global hegemony. The latter contributes to the development of the concerned country and can be restrictive conditions for activities to pursue its national interest. In the case of countries grasping hegemony, other countries are forced to follow the rules set by the nations that built a hegemony. Therefore, the chapter considers how the globalism of countries with hegemony has changed the global development of economic activities and the position of Germany in such phenomena.

2.1 Concept of Globalism and Governance

This section first examines the concept of globalism concerning governance. The period after the 1990s is when full-scale globalization progressed, and the pursuit of globalism as a logic of major countries pursuing the realization of national interests (Ikemoto 2001, p.23) is a prominent characteristic. Globalism as an ideology for building hegemony in establishing the global order is deeply concerned with problems regarding governance. Governance and order are interactive phenomena (Rosenau 1992, p.8). Today, international order formation issues are usually called "global governance." "Global governance has been principally defined by notions of inclusion/exclusion that have tended to reflect the prevailing hegemony or dominance of capital and the ruling classes of the most powerful capital states" (Gill 2019, p.376).

Governance means "the sum of laws, norms, policies, and institutions that define, constitute, and mediate relations among citizens, society, market, and the state—the wielders and objects of the exercise of public power" (Weiss and Thakur 2010, pp.5–6). As Alexander King points out, "governance is no longer the monopoly of governments and intergovernmental bodies and its effectiveness will depend on the capacity of leaders to selectively include in their decision making these new actors, which are in fact their partners in governance" (King and Schneider 1991, p.189). The order in which each country pursues the establishment of its hegemony determines the competition among actors; thus, global governance is deeply related to "the complex interlinkage between different societal actors and governmental institutions" (Dingwerth and Pattberg 2006, p.197). States remain one of the leading actors in governance (Weiss 2005, 81; King and Schneider 1991, p.189; Kacowicz 2018, p.62); however, states and intergovernmental organizations are not always the only player or the most important actors on the world stage (Weiss 2005, p.82). The participation of various actors, such as non-governmental organizations, private sector entities, multinational enterprises, the global capital market, and citizen's movements, as well as states and international institutions in global governance (Rosenau 1995, p.14; Weiss and Wilkinson 2015, p.393; Steffek 2006, p.22; The Commission on Global Governance 2005, p.26; Wilkinson 2005a, b, p.3; Acharya 2016, p.454; Rosenau 1992, p.4, Thakur and Langenhove 2006, p.233; Avant et al 2010, p.1) can be considered a countermeasure against the pursuit of globalism by countries with hegemony. Global governance can be understood as "a specific form of multilevel governance" (Zürn 2010, pp.81, 94) and means "world politics as a multilevel system in which local, national, regional, and global political processes are inseparably linked" (Dingwerth and Pattberg 2006, p.192). Under the global multilevel governance system, more competition between institutions to seek and find the best solution to problems can become active (Zürn 2010, p.94). Thus, "the content of global governance embraces the totality of laws, norms, policies, and institutions that define, constitute, and mediate relations between citizens, societies, markets, and states in the international system" (Thakur et al. 2014, p.1). Global governance, an issue and struggle regarding the formation of the global order, has two characteristics: hierarchy and competition among various actors.

What was Germany's position until the end of World War II in the history of globalism? Considering the historical changes of globalization and globalism, which important points of issue can be found regarding the development of German capitalism and business management before the end of World War II? This problem concerns the characteristics of globalism in major countries aiming at building hegemony to create a more advantageous foundation for capitalistic reproduction in each period and considers how globalization has been pursued.

There are various views regarding the history of globalization, such as that it began in the age of discovery or the development of capitalism after 1880, which is the starting point of globalization (Steger 2009; Jones 2005; Ellwood 2001, 1). However, the decisive progress of globalization is due to the reorganization of the world economy by including the socialist countries of Russia and Central and Eastern Europe in the capitalistic economic block and the further progress of the market economy in China and Vietnam. These countries became structural elements of markets in the capitalistic block and strengthened economic interdependent relations in the aspect of trade; they also became elements comprising the productive forces in the capitalistic economy, which indicates qualitatively new characteristics in changes during this period. Under such changes brought about by globalization, new characteristics have appeared in globalism as an ideology for building frameworks and setting institutions and rules, namely the global order enabling the achievement of the purpose of control of world markets to the largest degree.

The high level of globalization after the 1990s—when the internationalization of enterprises and business management and the further interdependence in the markets progressed—was not apparent before World War II and the later Cold War. However, competition over hegemony and globalism among countries and attempts to achieve it have been pursued. In the history of capitalism, the beginning of globalization can be seen in the expansion of exports by the United Kingdom and the reinforcement of its foundation by colonial policy. However, regarding globalism as the fundamental principle and ideology to achieve global hegemony, characteristics can be seen in each period of (1) imperialism until the end of World War II, (2) the Cold War, and (3) after the 1990s.

2.2 Globalism in the Period Before the End of World War II

Next, from the late nineteenth century to the end of World War II, society was built on the basis of the market economy and considered a "market society," represented by the balance-of-power system, the international gold standard system, the self-regulating market, and the liberal state (Polanyi 2001, p.3). World capitalistic powers competed over hegemony in forming the world order. Such competition focused on the interests of building their own economic spheres by acquiring and maintaining colonies under the conditions in which the United Kingdom was centered in hegemony (Pax Britannica). In this period, globalization's fundamental problem seen in the "estrangement between market and governance" was solved by imperialistic colonial policy, partially through force (Rodrik 2011, pp.26, 32–34; Shibayama 2014, p.325). The hegemony of the United Kingdom was grounded in the gold standard system that functioned under the international financial system, in which only London was a central clearing position (Brown 1940, pp.x–xi). The strength and central position of the London market as a financial center was primarily supported by large amounts of commodities and services and a central market for international transactions in goods, services, securities, and insurance (Brown 1940, pp.535–536). The establishment of the gold standard system as an important system to integrate the world economy (Polanyi 2001, p.211) was seen in major countries, including Germany; however, such a system was adopted under the pressure of the United Kingdom as a hegemony nation (Polanyi 2001, p.226). Nonetheless, the currency's collapse means that the relationship with the economy outside the country is cut off (Polanyi 2001, p.238). Economic administration under such institutions became important for Germany, where the narrow domestic market depended heavily on exports.

In the period after World War I, the United Kingdom attempted to manage its balance of payments, protect its Sterling Area leadership, and recapture London's historic position as the global financial center; however, it was forced to rely on financial support from the United States (US) to stabilize the sterling and to adopt the American position on war debts and reparations (Hogan 1987, p.9). The shift of the US from a debtor nation to a creditor nation was an important foundation for the more advantageous competition over hegemony with the United Kingdom. Furthermore, the Dawes Plan, as American aid for Germany, allowed the US to take the initiative to resolve the reparation problem. It was a movement to establish hegemony through the temporary solution of the reparation problem and achieving reform of the currency system in Germany, and overall, was the premise and an important component of America's ground design (Link 1970, S.240). The US aimed to make the US dollar (USD) the core currency in exchange for the British pound (GBP), which was achieved through Germany's return to the gold standard system (Link 1970, S.233–236). Thus, in the competition between the US and the United Kingdom over whether the USD or the GBP acquired the position of core currency (Link 1970, Zweiter Teil, II; Kato 1973, pp.142–143), the US won. In the Dawes Plan, as an assistance measure for the US for Germany, debts were created on political grounds, such as reparation, and loans were provided for partly political reasons (Polanyi 2001, p.240). Thus, under the pressure of the US as a hegemonic country, Germany was forced to pursue its own form of globalism, which was determined by international economic relations.

One of the most important characteristics of this age is the competition over the hegemony that reflected the reproduction structure based on capitalism at the one-country level and colonies and aggressive characteristics under the lack and weakness of international cooperation in the capitalistic world. In this way, globalism was strongly connected to the issue of building a peculiar economic sphere by acquiring and maintaining colonies; however, in this period, globalism without international rule (cooperative linkage) was pursued without an effective institution for international cooperation. The outbreak of two World Wars is deeply concerned with the lack of a framework for international issues.

2.3 Globalism in the Period of the Cold War After World War II

One of the characteristics of globalism during the Cold War was that it was deeply connected with issues regarding establishing hegemony within each block under the correspondence of competition between capitalism and socialism. Within the capitalistic block, the globalism of the US can be seen in the Marshall Plan and the international development of the Productivity Movement to enforce the effects of assistance to each country under the American global strategy. Globalism made many countries accept the US as "a model" through capital aid and technical assistance, providing a more advantageous foundation for learning and deploying American technology and management methods. In the 1950s and the 1960s, technology transfer and the management and realization of a mass consumer society were core issues (Yamazaki 2013). The US military and civilian authorities arrived as occupiers with clear plans to accomplish the profound changes needed in each nation (Stokes 2024, p.276).

The high level of hegemony of the US after World War II began in 1945 with the military defeat of Germany and the end of the financial defeat of the United Kingdom and terminated in 1971 when the Bretton Woods system ended (Taylor 2000, pp.53, 57). The British relied on American financial support to rebuild their economy and protect their leadership of the Commonwealth and the Sterling Area. However, as Hogan stressed, "the terms of this support were often incompatible with their ambitions." "The British agreed to devalue pound sterling and join in plans to liberalize intra-European trade and payments" (Hogan 1987, pp.20–21).

The US was in "a special position to project itself across the spectrum of social relation—political, cultural and economic" (Taylor 2000, p.57). The Bretton Woods system permitted sufficient international discipline to secure active trade and promote trade liberalization. It also reinforced the nation's sovereignty and allowed each government to implement enough policy to cope with its socioeconomic needs

(Rodrik 2011, p.69; Ellwood 2001, p.27). The US created the institutional infrastructure of the international economy to maintain its indisputable hegemony for a long time by setting rules based on indiscriminate principles and multinationalism through international organizations and leaving room for the policy of each nation (Rodrik 2011, p.70). The international currency system was built in which the USD was the key currency and global currency circulation, where the US was a knotting point (Mizuoka 2006, pp.54–55, 77).

The world economic system, where the US was at a core position after World War II, aimed at realizing the economic development of advanced capitalistic countries through the mutual progress of international trade. Such a system did not consider the economic expansion of developing countries (Takemura 2020, p.41). America's initiative in building an international system based on free trade and international currency systems is apparent in the characteristics of international institutions (such as the International Monetary Fund [IMF] and United Nations) for the development of major capitalistic countries led by the US and determined by American interests (Mizuoka 2006, Chapter 2, especially pp.46, 53–56). For Germany, the benefit of such a system was significant. In the first few years of the 1950s, West Germany was the heart of capitalistic rationalization among the countries that received assistance from the Marshall Plan (Thalmann 1956, S 91). The recovery of the European economy had significant meaning for American globalism. Therefore, deploying and transferring American technology and management methods in Germany became an important driving force for US development.

The building of the global order led by the US is deeply concerned with the openness of each country's market. One of the initiatives of the Marshall Plan was realizing the integration of and free trade in Western European countries (Stolper et al. 1964, S 272), aiming to build a multinational order for global trade and payments (Buchheim 1993, p 78). The US compelled Western European governments to open their markets to free trade and international competition (Schröter 2005, p 8; Kudo et al. 2004, p.8), greatly contributing to trade enlargement. "Marshall Planner attempted to absorb Germany into a wider Western European framework and thus reconcile its recovery with the economic and security needs of its neighbors" (Hogan 1987, p.20). Michael J. Hogan (1987, pp.2, 23, 25) stressed that the Marshall Plan was an attempt to establish a new postwar economic and political order, and the US emphasized building a European economic order through its aid (Hogan 1987, pp.2, 23, 25). The Marshall Plan was a starting point for establishing the world order led by the US, which built an important foundation for this country's leading position (Pax Americana).

Fordism was an important foundation for economic development in major capitalistic countries after World War II. It was strengthened and prevailed directly through policy compelled by occupation or indirectly through the Marshall Plan and the direct investment of the US (Harvey 1989, pp.136–137). The international expansion of Fordism (excluding the communist world) meant the formation of global mass markets and the inclusion of the greater part of the global population into new kinds of capitalistic dynamics (Harvey 1989, p.137). Based on America's financial and economic power under the Bretton Woods system, Fordism diffused in various manners (Harvey 1989, p.137), which is the prevalence of Fordism under US globalism during the Cold War. Therefore, it is important to grasp the issues of Fordism until the end of World War II concerning its full-scale development after the war, which is a primary research topic in this book.

The US was unique after World War II in two respects. While the US was "the provider of 'global governance'—through what has tended in the past to be the exercise of 'liberal' hegemony"—it was also a great power that pursued its national interest. America's liberal hegemonic role can be seen in creating a US-led international rule or regime or reaffirming its commitment to collaborative security in East Asia and Europe (Ikenberry 2006, p.14; Ikenberry 2011, p.192). One of the most important characteristics was that the American rule-based and open world order after the war had "characteristics of a stakeholder hegemony that promoted stability and cooperation" (Ikenberry 2006, p.192–193). Ikenberry stresses "United States dominated the order, but the political space created by American Domination was organized partnerships and agree-upon rules and institutions that facilitated restraint, commitment, reciprocity, and legitimacy" (Ikenberry 2011, p.160). The character and logic of the postwar order led by the US differed from anything the world had seen before in terms of hierarchical and loosely rule-based ideas, which were not imperial (Ikenberry 2011, p.162).

2.4 Globalism in the Period After the 1990s to the Present

2.4.1 Characteristics of Globalization After the 1990s

The previous discussion showed that in the periods from the nineteenth century to the end of the Cold War at the beginning of the 1990s, a particular country with hegemony played a significant role in global governance to build the world order, and the influences of its globalism on other countries were significant; however, conditions changed after the 1990s. Unlike the Cold War period, the fundamental characteristics of globalization after the 1990s can be seen in the expansion of the capitalistic economic sphere. This expansion includes the socialistic countries of Russia and Central and Eastern Europe in the capitalistic economic block, the further progress of the market economy in China and Vietnam, and the progress of the integration of the economic zone by information and communication technologies. Globalization is pursuing hegemony, premising the globally expanded economic sphere. It is not a mere process of the overall change but the terminology that prevailed in the transmuting period (Albrow 1996, p.95). "Globalization is not a single, unified process but a set of interactions that may be best approached from different observation points" (Mittelamnn 2001, p.7); it is defined by an increased level of mutual interdependency (Kearney 2001, p.56), which means the rapid expansion of the network of the mutual union and interaction and the interminably increasing density (Tomlinson 1999, p.2; Mittelmann 2001, pp.7–8). Globalization is understood as the integration of economic activities through the market; its driving force is the reduction of costs for transportation and communication and the increase of dependency on market forces (Wolf 2005, p.19). In this way, economic globalization means reinforcing and expanding mutual economic relations across the globe (Steger 2009, p.38).

The most significant development regarding economic globalization after the 1990s can be seen in (1) the internationalization of trade and finance, (2) the increasing power of multinational enterprises, and (3) the expansion of the roles of international economic institutions (IMF, World Bank, and WTO) (Steger 2009, pp.41–42). What globalization brings about, and promoters and the group of such movement, is the worldwide expansion and generalization of market logic (Othman and Kessler 2001, p.134). Ten years after the 1990s, two important changes occurred in the world economy. First, the market became the dominant mode of regulation. Second, countries included in this new system opened to the world economy, which increased the interdependency of the national economy of each country (Chesnais and Plihon 2001, p.34). This situation is also seen in finance, and a set of social institutions and practices regarding international finance indicate characteristics peculiar to this period (Porter 2005, p.30). After the 1980s, the IMF strongly supported the opening of the capital market (Rodrik 2011, p.90). Internationalization of political power includes the concentration of power on institutions between many countries to set global rules and the internationalization of these rules in the policy decisions of each nation (McMichael 1996, p.39). Therefore, globalization's economic and political aspects are deeply connected (Steger 2009, p.64). Roland Axtmann points out that "'globalization' can be used as a replacement term for 'imperialism,' displacing a focus on the domination of developing countries by the overdeveloped ones, or of national and local economies by transnational corporations" (Axtmann 1998, p.1).

In the globalization of the economy that progressed at full scale after the 1990s, a "globalization paradox" phenomenon has appeared (Rodrik 2011, pp.20–21). The Bretton Woods system has integrated the world economy for 30 years (Rodrik 2011, p.69); however, the lack of an institutional framework covering the whole global market and the market tensions between local institutions are essential for understanding the globalization of the economy (Rodrik 2011, pp.20–21). An institution that makes it function smoothly in the global market has not been developed, and the global government that manages the whole does not exist. While trade and finance are expanding beyond borders, the scope of governance remains at the national level (Rodrik 2011, p.xvi; Ruggi 2014, p.5), and market and governance that were harmonious at the national level are alienated globally (Shibayama 2014, p.324). A hegemonic country with the most immense economic and military power among national states must play great roles due to the lack of a unitary world government and world central bank with power and public characteristics (Kaneko 1999, pp.61–62) (Table 2.1).

Table 2.1 History of the globalism of hegemonic nation and the international economic order

The period until the end of World War I	The period from the end of World War I to the end of World War II	The Cold War period after World War II	The period from the 1990s to the present
• The world capitalistic Powers as parties of competition over hegemony in the formation of the world order • Competition among the world capitalistic powers that were deeply concerned with the interests of building their economic spheres through acquiring and maintaining colonies • The world order in which the United Kingdom was centered in hegemony (Pax Britannica) • The gold standard system that functioned under the international financial system in which only London was a central clearing position as the ground of hegemony of the United Kingdom • The strength and central position of the London market as a financial center and a position with large dealing amounts of commodities and services, and a central market for international transactions in goods, services, securities, and insurance • Risk of the collapse of the currency in terms of cutting off from relationships with the economy outside the country for many countries, excluding the United Kingdom	• Decline of power of the United Kingdom due to its reliance on American financial support to stabilize sterling and to adopt the US position on war debts and reparations after World War I • The shift of the United States from a debtor nation to a creditor nation as an important foundation for the more advantageous competition over hegemony with the United Kingdom • The possibility for the United States to take initiative in attempts to resolve the reparation problem by the Dawes Plan as American aid for Germany provided • Realization of the aim of the United States to make the US Dollar the core currency in exchange for the Pound through the return of Germany to the Gold Standard system • The Dawes Plan as America's policy based on political grounds such as the reparation and loans provided due to, in part, political reason • Competition over the hegemony that reflected the reproduction structure based on capitalism at the one country level and colonies and aggressive characteristics under the lack and weakness of international cooperation in the capitalistic world	• Globalism that was deeply connected with issues regarding establishing hegemony within each block under the correspondence with competition between capitalism and socialism • The Marshall Plan and international development of the Productivity movement to enforce the effects of assistance to each country under the American global strategy within the capitalistic block as the globalism of the United States • Globalism in terms of making many countries accept the United States as "a model" through both capital aid and technical assistance • The high level of hegemony of the United States in the postwar period until the beginning of the 1970s with the military defeat of Germany and the end of the financial defeat of the United Kingdom (Pax Americana) • A special position of the United States to project itself across the spectrum of social relations—political, cultural, and economic • Creating the institutional infrastructure of the international economy by the United States to maintain its indisputable hegemony for a long time • Building of the international currency system in which the US Dollar was the key currency and global currency circulation where the United States was a knotting point was built • Characteristics of international institutions (such as IMF and United Nations) for the development of major capitalistic countries led by the United States and determined by the interests of this country • Building of global order led by the United States that was deeply concerned with the openness of the market of each country • Compulsion by the United States via the Marshall Plan to countries receiving US aid to open their markets to free trade, including attempts to absorb Germany into a broader Western European framework • The United States was a unique entity after World War II in two ways: (1) the provider of global governance through "liberal" hegemony and (2) a great power that pursued its own national interest • The postwar order based on the organized partnerships and the agreed-upon rules and institutions led by the United States was different from previous anything in terms of both hierarchical and loosely rule-based system	• The further strengthened privileged position of the international economic institutions such as the IMF, World Bank, and WTO to set and implement rules • American globalism aimed at creating a horizontal competition stage without restriction for its enterprises by expanding the economic system surrounding American corporate behaviors and enterprises on a global scale • Global liberalization of trade, investment, and finance using international organizations as the core of American globalism • Dominant interests and thinking patterns of the financial world in the IMF and those of the commercial world in the WTO • No emphasis on the interests of developing countries in international institutions while focusing on the interests of developed countries • Compulsion by the IMF and World Bank for developing countries to implement "the structural coordination program" as an element of the neoliberal economic policy, which reflects the intentions of creditor nations in exchange for providing finance for developing nations • Expansion of the influence of the shareholder value-oriented management model and corporate governance as an important characteristic of American globalism • American globalism aimed at building the advantageous foundation for reinforcing the competitiveness of monopolistic enterprises such as giants called "GAFAM" as a core of the platform capitalism and competition over such framework between the United States and China • Conflicts and competition over hegemony based on building international economic relations between the United States and China • Regionalism as an ideology to enable building more favorable capital accumulation conditions than nations excluding this area by differentiation of trade conditions and its role as a counterwork to "globalism"

Source This table was compiled by the author, based on discussions in this chapter

2.4.2 *Rise of New Globalism: Neo-Liberalistic Globalism*

2.4.2.1 Globalization and Globalism

Regarding globalization after the 1990s, it is important to distinguish between changes that indicate broad and strong integration into the international economy and changes adumbrating fundamentally different kinds of orders (Hirst et al 2009, p.18). As Steeger (2009, p.99) indicates, globalization is a social process that reinforces global interdependency; however, globalism is an ideology that gives the concept of globalization a specific value and meaning (Steger 2009, p.99). Globalism embodies the logic of major countries aiming to increase their national interest through pursuing globalization (Ikemoto 2001, p.23). Therefore, the study of globalization as a phenomenon of real life must include research on the ideological project that M B. Steeger called "globalism" (Steeger 2002, p.40).

Wherever globalization occurs, there are rules; wherever there are rules, someone compels them (Rodrik 2011, p.9). Globalism can be understood as changes in all rules that prevail in the world by the world markets (Beck 1997, S.195; Beck 2000, p.117). Hegemony means a set of rules supported by authority (and reliance) (Hettne 1999b, p.20). As institutions provide the "rules in the game" for the market (North 1990, pp.3–4), how institutions are designed and whose interests should be protected is important (Rodrik 2011, p.10). One important issue of "globalism" under globalization lies in this point. International economic institutions, such as the IMF, World Bank, and World Trade Organization (WTO), enjoy the privileged position to set and implement the rules of the global economy (Steger 2009, p.54). The IMF influences the interest and thinking patterns of the financial world; in the WTO, those of the commercial world have been dominant in setting rules (Stiglitz 2002, pp.216, 224). These institutions consider the interests of developed countries (and their part) rather than those of developing countries (Stiglitz 2002, p.215). Similarly, "the global public goods debate has been mainly conducted in international arenas from which developing countries are excluded, such as the G7, or within which their influence is limited, such as the Bretton Woods institutions" (Yeates Yates 2014, p.169).

Globalism, at present, is the ideology of controlling the world market, and neoliberalism is the ideology in which imperialism in terms of economic issues has become an important problem. Enterprises acquire the framework enabling them to achieve their purpose to the maximum (Beck 1997, S.26; Beck 2000, p.9). The essence of globalization lies in the embodiment of the national interests of countries with strong economic power. It can be regarded as the setting of the stage pursued by the leading countries at the position of international standardization (Motoyama 2001, p.3; Ikemoto 2001, pp.15–16, 23).

2.4.2.2 Neoliberalism-Oriented Globalism

What distinguishes globalism from the previous market ideology is the believer's innovative attempt to meet the concept of "globalization" in the meaning of neoliberalism. M B. Steger (2002, p.13) distinguishes between (1) globalism as the neoliberalism market ideology that gives globalization a particular norm, value, and meaning and (2) globalization as a social process that is defined and described by various commentators in different and often contradictory ways (Steger 2002, p.13). What attempts to give the concept of "globalism" the norm of a free market and neoliberal meaning is "market-oriented globalism" (Steger 2009, p.99), and it has become the dominant ideology in the present (Steger 2009, p.101). Globalists insist on prevalent ideology to make their political and economic tasks important (Steger 2009, pp.102–103). Ideology is never a virtual concept without a foundation in physical phenomena (Steger 2002, p.13). Globalism can be defined as "programmatic globalization" (Hettne 1999b, p.2).

Globalism as an ideology coincides with the neoliberal doctrine and usually articulates the interest of strong economic actors and the big players in the global market (Hettne 1999b, p.17). The world's top enterprises have become not merely centers of concentrated economic and financial power but also "bearers of the prevailing laissez-faire, globalist ideology." In neoliberal ideology, global laissez-faire is "the optimal way to organize a modern economy" (Kuttner 2000, p.147). Steeger points out that "the central tenets of neoliberalism include the primacy of economic growth; the importance of free trade to stimulate growth; the unrestricted free market; individual choice; the reduction of government regulation; and the advocacy of an evolutionary model of social development" (Steger 2002, p.9; Cliteur 2006, p.26). In this way, economic globalization is "a thoroughly political project involving transnational players, institutions and discourse-coalitions (World bank, WTO, OECD, multinationals, other international organizations) which pursue a neoliberal economic policy" (Beck 2000, p.123). For example, the IMF was greatly strengthened in 20 years from 1998 to 2000 and shifted from a supporter of international payments to the omnipotent leading organization to some degree of "sound" economic policy in neoliberal meaning (George 2001, p.14). Furthermore, the WTO became an institution that plays a leading role in cooperative relations in the world economy, which is quite different from the former (Rodrik 2011, p.76). Unlike a loose General Agreement on Tariffs and Trade, the WTO is a formal international organization (Ellwood 2001, p.32) and aims to pursue hyper-globalization and domestic economic administration to activate international trade and finance (Rodrik 2011, p.76). The IMF and World Bank have required the implementation of "the structural coordination program" that reflects the intentions of creditor nations in exchange for providing finance for developing countries (Steger 2009, p.54). In this way, these international organizations force each country to accept a neoliberal economic policy composed of deregulation, privatization, and decreasing the tariff wall as the global standard (Mizuoka 2006, p.16; Sakata 2015, p.185).

Globalism affects the domestic political balance so that the forces that want more globalism can be favorable and depoliticize issues with inherently political characteristics (Kuttner 2000, p.155). Even as global special integration progresses, states are in the transportation route. To which degree the passage of funds, goods, and labor is permitted on the border is an issue that the sovereign nation managing the border decides by law (Mizuoka 2006, p.43). Originally, the national state typically considered the region as a stage in which national interest could be increased (Hettne 1999a, p.xxiii). Nations and intergovernmental organizations play a role in reinforcing the rules of the global economy and strengthening national competitiveness. Meanwhile, states' powers to shield domestic economies from the negative influences of globalization have decreased (Cox 1996, pp.26–27). Globalism weakens the nation state's ability to regulate labor conditions and pursue policies for high growth and full employment (Kuttner 2000, pp.159–160). Global markets have often undermined the capacities of nations to set their own policy goals and lay the original domestic norm (Steger 2009, p.64). Democratically organized capitalist activities have been controlled by politics and the social state up to this time; however, it became possible for managers and the association of employers to set free the active power of capitalism from restriction and retake it (Beck 1997, S.14), which has been an important factor promoting the pursuit of globalization based on neoliberal ideology.

2.4.3 American Globalism

Current globalization is represented as the emergence of a new empire based on the hegemony of the US, which is regarded as "the only truly global power." The US uses this status by aligning with neoconservative (neoliberal) ideology to establish a world order in its image (Hirst et al 2009, p.6). American neoliberalism makes the most use of foreign conditions to strengthen the competition of US manufacturing firms through global development, activating the American economy by introducing foreign funds into financial markets in this country. Furthermore, the US government's efforts to approach the world using diplomacy, negotiation, and armaments to build more advantageous circumstances for US firms and the economy are core. Such neoliberalism aims at establishing "the global accumulation structure" to rebuild the world so that the interests of the US can be central (Hirano 2023, p.9).

American globalism aims to create a horizontal competition stage without restriction for its enterprises by expanding the economic system surrounding American corporate behaviors and enterprises on a global scale (Nakamoto 2007b, p.1). The current globalization could not progress without strong policies and ideologies to change each country to adapt to American economic and business systems (Nakamoto 2007a, p.iii). Such American globalism is an indispensable driving force for globalization in the present (Motoyama 2001, p.1).

However, it is indispensable for maintaining the US hegemony that depends on the inflow of large amounts of funds to force each country to adopt a financial liberalization policy and open markets on a global scale to create and maintain the mechanism to circulate the USD and constantly flow it back to the US (Kaneko 1999, pp.22–23, 25, 63). Therefore, the core of American globalism is the global liberalization of trade, investment, and finance using international organizations (Nakamoto 2007b, pp.5–6). Unlike the period until the beginning of the 1990s when the concerned nation strictly controlled investment from foreign countries, each country opened its capital account under the continuous pressure of international organizations such as the IMF (Ellwood 2001, p.21). The IMF and the US Financial Ministry have played a significant role in the requirement of the liberalization of financial and capital markets against developing countries (Stiglitz 2001, p.ix). Furthermore, as seen in the Agreement on Trade-Related Investment Measures regarding the liberalization of production and sale of goods, the General Agreement on Trade in Services regarding the liberalization of service trade, and The Agreement on Trade-Related Aspects of Intellectual Property Rights related to the protection of intellectual assets rights, the WTO system can back up the activities of multinational enterprises and banks and the institutional investors that mobilize goods, services, intellectual assets rights, information, and money on the global scale (Nakamoto 2007b, p.9; Takemura 2020, pp.48–51).

As Kent E. Calder points out, American globalism means "an open, rule-based world political-economic order in which the United States exercises preponderant influence through its hegemonic political-military capabilities and related impact on national and corporate political-risk premiums" (Calder 2007, p.257). The capitalistic market economy is increasingly strengthening the American standard under globalism (Motoyama 2001, p.2). Whereas international organizations and the US are the subject of pursuing globalization, developing countries are in a passive position (Kinoshita 2001, pp.201–202, 213, 216), while both are related to the core of the world's hegemony and the subordinate periphery (Mizuoka 2006, p.32). Unlike the postwar period until the end of the 1980s, the opposition by developing and emerging countries to globalism and governance led by the US has dramatically increased, reflecting such situations. Furthermore, various complex and serious problems that a particular hegemonic country cannot solve alone through changing rules and institutions have occurred, and various actors involved in global governance and their claims have increased. However, despite such opposition and the increasing involvement and roles of various actors in global governance, the influence of American globalism on the world order is still significant.

Furthermore, an important characteristic of American globalism is apparent in expanding the influence of the shareholder value-oriented management model and corporate governance based on the consignment relationships and trust of management authority between the shareholders and salaried managers. Management based on a thorough market mechanism is the most suitable under management, strongly emphasizing stockholders' interests, and the prevailing ideology has influenced business management in advanced capitalistic countries.

Moreover, monopolistic enterprises such as giants called "GAFAM" as a core of platform capitalism (Srnicek 2017) are deeply concerned with America's competitive advantage, and the US government is vigorously involved in setting rules for supporting the predominance of business based on such a platform. One of the most important characteristics of American globalism can be observed in this point. Conflicts between the US, as one of the most powerful hegemonic countries, and China, which aims at building its own global economic sphere based on the concept of "One Belt, One Road" and those in the extreme sections, such as information and communication field after the 2010s, indicate an intensification of competition over the hegemony between these two powers.

While China pursues its strategy, such as the Asian Infrastructure Investment Bank founded in 2013 (Wan 2016; Lichtenstein 2018), the plan "One Belt, One Road Initiative" disclosed in 2014 (Freymann 2021), and "Made in China 2025" (MIC2025) initiative launched in 2015 (Li and Branstetter 2024, pp.1–2), the US pursues countermeasures. The Chinese government aims to surround itself with many countries and achieve the transformation and upgrading of manufacturing industries, focusing on the ten most high-tech industries (Yuan and Liu 2024, pp.1, 3; Marcato 2022, p.356; Liu et al 2022, p.1). In response to China's strategies, the Biden government pursued a new type of economic sphere led by the US, strengthening cooperative relationships with confederacies and friendly nations. "Build Back Better World" in 2021 (The White House 2021), the Indo-Pacific Economic Framework in 2022 (The White House 2022), and "Partnership for Global Infrastructure and Investment" in the same year (U. S. Department of Commerce 2022). Competition between the US and China over establishing hegemony for the new global economic order, emphasizing the strategic fields regarding economic security, has become increasingly violent. In this way, an important characteristic of issues regarding globalism can be observed in the increasing importance and significance of economic security.

2.4.4 Development of Regionalization

The development of globalization after the 1990s has involved a shift toward regionalization. The two concepts of globalization and regionalization have acquired a certain preeminence (Hettne 1999b, p.1). Regionalism has characteristics counter to "globalism," such as creating the framework, institution, and rules to control world markets to the maximum degree. The historical significance of regional integration as an attempt to countervail globalism led by the US can be seen in the formation of the European Union (EU) (Motoyama 2001, p.7). Pettman (1999, p.181) points out that dichotomizing regionalism and globalism highlights these two key aspects of global reality (Pettman 1999, p.181).

Regionalization attempts to emphasize a specific region in terms of both market and productive forces and form a more advantageous framework for trade in the area where regional economic integration is realized. Meanwhile, regionalism is an ideology as a behavioral principle and norm that enables the building of more favorable capital accumulation conditions than nations excluding this area by differentiating trade conditions. Regional integration is traditionally regarded as "a harmonization of trade policies" (Hettne 1999a, p.xii). Regionalism is one approach to dealing with various global problems (Hettne 1999a, p.xii) and is still "an important phenomenon in the current global transformation" (Hettne 1999a, p.xxviii). In this meaning, "the dynamics of regionalization must be understood in the context of globalization" (Hettne 1999b, p.11).

The new regionalism after the 1990s is "a reaction to and a modifier of globalization." It is defined as "a multidimensional process of regional integration which includes economic, political, social, and cultural aspects" and goes far beyond the goal of creating region-based free trade regimes or security alliance and beyond the idea of the free trade market. Therefore, it is "a package rather than a single policy" (Hettne 1999b, pp.16–17; Hettne 1999a, p.xvi). Regarding such a movement, the decline of US hegemony and the collapse of the communist subsystem created room for behavior in which this new regionalism could develop (Hettne 1999a, p.xvii).

The differences between the old regionalism until the end of the 1980s and the new regionalism after the 1990s can be explained as follows. (1) "whereas the old regionalism was found in and shaped by a bipolar cold-war context, the new is taking shape in a multipolar world order." (2) "Whereas the old regionalism was created 'from above' (by the superpowers), the new is a more spontaneous process from within the region and also 'from below' in the sense that the constituent states themselves, but increasingly also other actors, are the main proponents for regional integration." (3) "Whereas the old regionalism, as far as economic integration is concerned, was inward-oriented and protectionist, the new is often described as 'open,' and thus compatible with an interdependent world economy." (4) "Whereas the old regionalism was specific with regard to objectives, some organizations being security-oriented and others being economically-oriented, the new is a more comprehensive, multidimensional process." (5) "Whereas the old regionalism only concerned relations between formally sovereign states, the new forms part of a global structural transformation in which non-state actors are active and manifest themselves at several levels of the global system" (Hettne 1999b, pp.7–8; Hettne 1999a, p.xvii).

Although regionalism became prominent after the 1990s, the movements to pursue capitalistic accumulation focusing on a specific region can already be observed before World War II. For instance, in the aspect of trade, even in the period before the war, the ratio of Germany's exports to the European region to all exports reached approximately 70% or more (similar numerical figures in 1928 and 1938 are 70.64% and 75.93%, respectively) (Statistisches Reichsamt 1931; S.236–239; Statistisches Reichsamt 1943, S.322–323). They do not indicate a significant difference compared with figures after World War II when Europe's common market was enlarged (similar numerical values in 1960, 1970, 1980, and 1990 were 67.4%, 73.2%, 74.3%, and 77.7%, respectively) (Statistisches Bundesamt 1962, S.316–317; Statistisches Bundesamt 1972, S.299–300; Statistisches Bundesamt 1982, S.263–265; Statistisches Bundesamt 1993, S.317–319), or when compared with a similar numerical figure in the period after the formation of EU (73.3% in 2000) (Statistisches Bundesamt 2003, S.283–285), and that at the stage in which Eastern enlargement of EU had progressed (68.3% in 2018) (Statistisches Bundesamt 2020, S.429). These figures indicate the significance of European markets for the prewar Germans. Therefore, it is important to understand the problems of regionalization and regionalism in Germany from a historical perspective.

Based on these discussions, the following points can be pointed out as important arguments regarding prewar German capitalism and business management from the viewpoint of the history of globalism. What is the globalism that means "ism" as a fundamental principle and ideology to achieve purpose determined by characteristics of German capitalism until the end of World War II, and which special characteristics can be seen in Germany's globalism? Which characteristics, significance, or limitations are seen in business management in Germany that was developed under global circumstances, with globalism as the principle and "ism" for competition over acquiring the global hegemony in each period? In considering the development of German capitalism and business management concerning the internationality and nationality of capital, such a process indicates how each country's capitalism maintains and develops its life power in globalization. An important analytical viewpoint and method of analyzing capitalism can be seen in this point. This book considers changes in German capitalism and business management as an important foundation for challenges during the Second Reich, the Weimar Republic, and National Socialism compared with the period after World War II. These research topics concern how the relations between Germany's globalism, German capitalism, and business management will be grasp

References

Acharya A (2016) The future of global governance: fragmentation may be inevitable and creative. In: Corporate Govern 22(4):436–460

Albrow M (1996) The global age—state and society beyond modernity. Polity Press, Cambridge

Avant DD, Finnemore M, Sell SK (2010) Who governs the globe? In: Avant DD, Finnemore M, Sell SK (eds) Who governs the globe? Cambridge University Press, Cambridge, pp 1–31

Axtmann R (1998) Globalization, Europe and the State: introductory reflections. In: Axtmann R (ed) Globalization and Europe: theoretical and empirical investigations. Pinter Publications, London, pp 1–22

Beck U (1997) Was ist Globalisierung? Antworten auf Globalisierung. Schurkamp Verlag, Frankfurt am Main

Beck U (2000) What is globalization? Polity Press, Cambridge

Brown WA Jr (1940) The international gold standard reinterpreted, 1914–1934. National Bureay of Economic Research Inc., New York

Buchheim C (1993) Marshall plan and currency reform. In: Diefendorf JM, Frohon A, Rupieper H-J (eds) American policy and the reconstruction of West Germany. Cambridge University Press, Cambridge, New York, pp 1945–1951

Calder KE (2007) Embattled garvisons. Comparative base politics and American globalism. Princeton University Press, Princeton

Chesnais F, Plihon D (2001) The broken engines of growth. In: Houtart PF (ed) The other davos: the globalization of resistance to the world economic system. Zed Books, London, pp 32–37

Cliteur P (2006) Liberal globalism: a defence. In: Nieuwenhuys E (ed) Neo-liberal globalism and social sustainable globalisation. Leiden, Brill, pp 15–38

Cox RW (1996) A perspective on globalization. In: Mittelmann JH (ed) Globalization: critical reflections. Lynne Rienner Publishers, London, pp 21–30

Dingwerth K, Pattberg P (2006) Global governance as a perspective on world politics. In: Glob Govern 12 (2): 185-203
Ellwood W (2001) The no-nonsense guide to globalization. Verso, London
Freymann E (2021) One belt one road. Chinese power meets. Harvard University Asia Center, Cambridge, Mass
George S (2001) A short history of neoliberalism. In: Houtart F, Polet F (eds) The other davos: the globalization of resistance to the world economic system. Zed Books, London, pp 7–16
Gill S (2019) Global governance "As it was, is and ought to be." In: Glob Govern 25(3):371–392
Harvey D (1989) The condition of postmodernity. Basil Blackwell, Oxford
Hettne B (1999a) The new reginalism: a prologue. In: Hettne B, Inotani A, Sunkel O (eds) Globalism and the New Regionalism. Macmillan Press, Basingstoke, Hampshire, pp 15–29
Hettne B (1999b) Globalization and the new regionalism: the second great transformation. In: Hettne B, Inotani A, Sunkel O (eds) Globalism and the new regionalism. Macmillan Press, Basingstoke, Hampshire, pp 1–24
Hirano K (2023) Honsho no taisho to kadai (Object and research topics of this book). In: 21 seiki no Amerika shihonshugi. Gurobaru chikuseki kozo no henyo (Transformation of the global accumulation structure). Otsuki shoten, Tokyo, pp 1–25
Hirst P, Thompson T, Bromley S (2009) Globalization in Question. Polity Press, Cambridge
Hogan MJ (1987) The Marshall plan. America, Britain, and reconstruction of Wester Europe, 1947–1952. Cambridge University Press, New York
Ikemoto K (2001) Keizai grobarizeshon no shin kasetsu (New hypothesis of economic globalization). In: Motoyama Y (ed) Gurobarizumu no shogeki (Shocks of globalism). Toyo keizai shinposha, Tokyo, pp 11–25
Ikenberry GJ (2006) Liberal order and imperial ambition: essay on american power and world politics. Polity Press, Cambridge
Ikenberry GJ (2011) Liberal Leviathan. The origins, crisis, and transformation of the American world order. Princeton University Press, Princeton
Jones G (2005) Multinationals and global capitalism: from the nineteenth to the twenty-first century. Oxford University Press, Oxford
Kacowicz AM (2018) Regional Governance and Global Governance: Links and Explanations. In: Glob Gov 24(1):61–79
Kaneko M (1999) Han-gurobarizumu-shijyo kaikaku no senryakuteki siko (Anti-globalism-strategic thought of market reform-. Iwanami shoten, Tokyo
Kato E (1973) Waimaru taisei no keizai kozo (Economic structure of the Weimar system). Tokyo daigaku shuppankai, Tokyo
Kearney AT (2001) Measuring globalization. In: Foreign Policy 122:56–64
King A, Schneider B (1991) The first global revolution. a report by the Council of the Club of Rome. Pantheon Book, New York
Kinoshita E (2001) Shijyo keizia no tayosei—Gurobarizeshon to kokumin keizai heno Ichi shikaku—(Varieties of market economy—a visual angle of globalization and national economy). In: Motoyama Y (ed) Gurobarizumu no shogeki (Shocks of globalism). Toyo Keizai shinposha, Tokyo, pp 201–217
Kudo A, Kipping M, Schröteret HG (2004) Americanization. Historical and conceptual issues. In: Kudo A, Kipping M, Schröteret HG (eds) German and Japanese business in the boom years: transforming American management and technology models. Routledge, London, New York, pp 1–29
Kuttner R (2000) The role of governments in the global economy. In: Hutton W, Giddens A (eds) Global capitalism. The New Press, New York, pp 147–163
Lichtenstein N (2018) A comparative guide to the asian infrastructure investment bank. Oxford University Press, Oxford
Li G, Branstetter LG (2024) Does "Maid in China 2025" work for China? Evidence from Chinese listed firms. In: Res Policy 53(6):1–14

Link W (1970) Die amerikanische Stabilisierungspolitik in Deutschland, 1921–32. Droste, Düsseldorf
Liu X, Megginson WL, Xia J (2022) Industrial policy and asset prices: evidence from made in China 2025 policy. In: J Bank Finance 142:1–22
Marcato MB (2022) The made in China 2025 aimed hyperglobalization: upgrading, intangible assets, and internationalization strategies. In: Economia e Sociedade 31(2):355–384
McMichael P (1996) Globalization: myths and realities. In: Rural Sociol 61(1):25–55
Mittelmann JH (2001) Globalization. Captors and captives. In: Mittelmann JH, Othman N (eds) Capturing globalization. Routledge, London, pp 1–16
Mizuoka F (2006) Grobarizumu (*Globalism*). Hassakusha, Tokyo
Motoyama Y (2001) Sengo 55 nen (The postwar 55 years). In: Motoyama Y (ed) Gurobarizumu no shogeki (Shocks of globalism). Toyo keizai shinposha, Tokyo, pp 1–8
Nakamoto S (2007a) Hashigaki (Preface). In: Nakamoto S (ed) Amerikan grobarizumu (American globalism). Nihon keizai shinposha, pp iii–viii
Nakamoto S (2007b) Amerikan grobarizumu: Tenkai to tairitsu no kozo (American globalism: structures of development and opposition). In: Nakamoto S (ed) Amerikan grobarizumu (American globalism). Nihon keizai shinposha, pp 1–33
North DC (1990) Institutions, institutional change and economic performance. Cambridge University Press, Cambridge
Othman N, Kessler CS (2001) Capturing globalization. Prospects and projects. In: Mittelmann JH, Othman N (eds) Capturing globalization. Routledge, London, pp 122–139
Pettman R (1999) Globalism and regionalism: the costs of dichotomy. In: Hettne B, Inotani A, Sunkel O (eds) Globalism and the new regionalism. Macmillan Press, Basingstoke, Hampshire, pp 181–202
Polanyi K (2001) The great transformation. The political and economic origins of our time. Beacon Press, Boston
Porter T (2005) Globalization and finance. Polity Press, Cambridge
Rodrik D (2011) The globalization paradox. Why global markets, states, and democracy can't coexist. W. W Norton, New York
Rosenau JN (1992) Governance, order, and change in world politics. In: Rosenau JN, Czempiel E-O (eds) Governance without government: order and changes in world politics. Cambridge University Press, Cambridge, pp 1–29
Rosenau JN (1995) Governance in the Twenty-first century. In: Glob Govern 1(1):13–43
Ruggi JG (2014) Global governance and "New governance theory." Lessons from business and human rights. In: Glob Govern 20 (1): 5–17
Sakata M (2015) Grobarizumu to kokka shihonshugi (Globalism and state capitalism). Ochanomizu shobo, Tokyo
Schröter HG (2005) Americanization of the European economy. A compact survey of American economic influence in Europe since the 1880s. Springer, Dordrecht
Shibayama K (2014) Yakusha Atogaki (Postscript by Translator). In: Rodrik D (translated by Shibayama K, Okawa Y) Grobarizeshon paradokusu (*Globalization paradox*). Hakusuisha, Tokyo, pp 324–329
Srnicek N (2017) Platform Capitalism. Polity Press, Cambridge
Statistisches Bundesamt (1962) Statistisches Jahrbuch für die Bundesrepublik Deutschland 1961. W. Kohlhammer, Stuttgart
Statistisches Bundesamt (1972) Statistisches Jahrbuch für die Bundesrepublik Deutschland 1971. W. Kohlhammer, Stuttgart
Statistisches Bundesamt S (1982) Statistisches Jahrbuch für die Bundesrepublik Deutschland 1981. W. Kohlhammer, Stuttgart
Statistisches Bundesamt (1993) Statistisches Jahrbuch 1992 für die Bundesrepublik Deutschland. Metzler
Statistisches Bundesamt (2003) Statistisches Jahrbuch 2002 für die Bundesrepublik Deutschland. Metzler Poschel, Stuttgar

Statistisches Bundesamt (2020) Statistisches Jahrbuch Deutschland und Internationales 2019. Metzler Poschel, Stuttgart
Statistisches Reichsamt (1931) Statistisches Jahrbuch für das Deutsche Reich 1930. Verlag von Reimar Hobbing, Berlin
Statistisches Reichsamt (1943) Statistisches Jahrbuch für das Deutsche Reich 1941–42. Verlag für Sozialpolitik, Wirtschaft und Statistik, Berlin
Steffek J (2006) Embedded liberalism and its critics. Justifying global governance in the American century. Palgrave Macmillan, Abingdon
Steger MB (2002) Globalism. The new market ideology. Rowman & Littefield Publishing Inc, London
Steger MB (2009) Globalization: a very short introduction. Oxford University Press, Oxford
Stiglitz JE (2001) Foreword. In: Polanyi K (ed) The great transformation. The political and economic origins of our time. Beacon Press, Boston, pp vii–xvii
Stiglitz JE (2002) Globalization and its discontents. W. W. Norton & Company, Inc.
Stokes RG (2024) Ruins to riches. The economic resurgence of German and Japan after 1945. Cambridge Universiuty Press, Cambridge
Stolper G, Häuser K, Borchardt K (1964) Deutsche Wirtschaft seit 1870. J. C. B. Mohr, Tübingen
Takemura M (2020) Kinyu grobarizumu no keizaigaku—Kakusa shakai no keisei to sekai kinyu kiki no boppatsu (Economics of financial globalization—formation of unequal society and the outbreak of financial crisis). Kamogawa shuppan, Kyoto
Taylor PJ (2000) Izations of the world: Americanization, modernization and globalization. In: Hay C, Marsh D (eds) Demystifying globalization. Palgrave, Basingstoke, pp 49–70
Thakur R, Job B, Serrano M, Tussie D (2014) The next phase in the consolidation and expansion of global governance. In: Glob Govern 20(1):1–4
Thakur R, Langenhove LV (2006) Enhancing global governance through regional integration. In: Glob Govern 12(3):233–240
Thalmann H (1956) Durch Rationalisierung ohne Kapital zur verstärkten Ausbeutung der Arbeiterklasse in Westdeutschland. In: Behrens F (Hrsg.) Aktuelle Fragen der Ökonomie und Politik des wiederstandenen deutschen Imperialismus: Festschrift zum zehnjährigen Bestehen des Verlags die Wirtschaft. Verlag der Wirtschaft, Berlin, S 87–114
The Commission on Global Governance (2005a) A new word. In: Wilkinson R (ed) The global governance reader. Routledge, Abingdon, pp 26–44
The White House (2021) FACT SHEET: President Biden and G7 leaders launch build Back Better World (B3w) Partnerships. https://www.whitehouse.gov/briefing-room/statements-releases/2021/06/12/fact-sheet-president-biden-and-g7-leaders-launch-build-back-better-world-b3w-partnership/. Access 20 November 2024
The White House (2024) FACT SHEET: President for global infrastructure and investment at the G7 Summit. https://www.whitehouse.gov/briefing-room/statements-releases/2024/06/13/fact-sheet-partnership-for-global-infrastructure-and-investment-at-the-g7-summit-2/. Access 20 Nov 2024
Tomlinson J (1999) Globalization and culture. Polity Press, Cambridge
U. S. Department of Commerce (2022) Indo-Pacific economic framework for prosperity (2022). https://www.commerce.gov/ipef. Access 20 Nov 2024
Wan M (2016) The Asian infrastructure investment bank: the construction of power and the struggle for the East Asian international order. Palgrave Macmillan, New York
Weiss TG (2005) Governance, good governance and global governance: conceptual and actual challenges. In: Wilkinson R (ed) The global governance reader. Routledge, Abingdon, pp 68–88
Weiss TG, Thakur R (2010) Global governance and the UN: an unified journey. Indiana University Press, Bloomington
Weiss TG, Wilkinson R (2015) Change and continuity in global governance. In: Ethics Int Affairs 29(4):397–406
Wilkinson R (2005b) Introduction: concepts and issues in global governance. In: Wilkinson R (ed) The global governance reader. Routledge, Abingdon, pp 1–22

Wolf M (2005) Why globalization works. Yale University Press, New Haven, London
Yates MN (2014) Understanding historical methods in organization studies. In: Bucheli M, Wadhwani RD (eds) Organizations in time: history, theory, methods. Oxford University Press, Oxford, pp 265–283
Yamazaki T (2013) German business management: a Japanese perspective on regional development factors. Springer, Tokyo
Yuan J, Liu S (2024) A Double machine learning model for measuring the impact of the made in China 2025 strategy on green economic growth. In: Sci Rep 14(1):1–16
Zürn M (2010) Global governance as multi-level governance. In: Enderlein H, Wälti S, Zürn M (eds) Handbook on multi-level governance. Edward Elgar, Nortampton, pp 80–99

Chapter 3
Overview of the Total System of Business Management in Germany: Comparison of Periods of the Second Reich, the Weimar Republic, National Socialism, and the Postwar Era

Abstract Based on discussions regarding the analytical framework in Chapter 1, this chapter considers various aspects and situations wherein we analyze the overall business management. The total system of business management is an analytical method for explaining business management's overall relationships and structure. Of the two parts that comprised the concept of the total system of business management, that is, the external and internal factors in business Management, eight factors regarding the former in Germany are clarified. This chapter examines three periods until the end of World War II: the Second Reich, The Weimar Republic, and National Socialism. It also considers the postwar period for comparison.

Keywords Enterprise-market relationships · Financial system · Industrial system based on interfirm relationships · Industrial structure · Labor relations · Market structure · Productive force structure · State-enterprise relationships · Total system of business management

In this chapter, the overall business management system in Germany as a structural framework for conditions that define the established business management methods within the characteristics of capitalism as implemented in a certain country is considered using the author's analytical framework. This chapter's analyses clarify the prewar frameworks of German business management compared with those after World War II.

When we examine overall ties with business management globally, we find a "world structure of capitalism" that reveals the mutual relationships within the capitalist bloc; however, given the leadership and aid of hegemonic nations, this structure poses a problem in global relationships, particularly those in markets and capital. Although this world structure of capitalism is outside the total business management system, it defines, or at least influences, the system. Under the global structure of capitalism, the total system of business management is a defining factor in a given country's established business management methods.

This chapter explorers the total system of business management. The total system of business management as the author's original analytical framework is an analytical

T. Yamazaki, *A History of German Business*,
https://doi.org/10.1007/978-981-96-8476-2_3

method for explaining the overall relationships and structure of business management. Of the external environmental factors and internal factors in business management as two parts that comprised the concept of the total system of business management, the external factors relating to corporate structures are examined. The eight elements comprising these external environmental factors within the total system of business management are the following: (1) state–enterprise relationships, (2) labor relations, (3) industrial systems based on interfirm relationships, (4) financial systems, (5) the structure of productive forces, (6) industrial structures, (7) market structures, and (8) enterprise–market relationships. The total system of business management is composed of eight factors: These factors define the development of business management.

In terms of the analysis framework for the total system of business management, this chapter provides an overview of the environmental factors of business management based on mutual relations. Sections 2.1, 2.2, and 2.3 examine the overall relevance of the total system of business management in Germany during periods of the Second Reich, the Weimar Republic, and National Socialism, respectively. Based on these discussions, Sect. 2.4 examines the total system of business management in postwar Germany for comparison with the prewar period.

3.1 Overview of the Total System of Business Management in the Period of the Second Reich

First, this section examines conditions in the Second Reich. Regarding the world structure of capitalism, three points can be noted as prominent characteristics. The first is the hegemony of the United Kingdom in the international economic system. Based on the gold standard system at the time, the currency system functioned under the international financial system, in which only London was in a central clearing position (Brown 1940, pp.x–xi). London was a financial center and a central market for international transactions in goods, services, securities, and insurance (Brown 1940, pp.535–536). Thus, the United Kingdom was at the core of building and maintaining the world order. The second is the existence of an economic sphere based on colonies and its restrictive conditions for countries that held few colonies, such as Germany and Japan. The third is the trend in the transformation from free trade to protectionism. These three trends were deeply concerned with the world structure of capitalism in this period and influenced the development of business management and corporate behaviors in each country.

When considering each element of the total business management system, one of the most prominent characteristics (in terms of **state–enterprise relations**) can be seen in the lack of regulation of cartels. This oversight enabled large enterprises to use such monopolistic measures and build cooperative relationships through cartels or syndicates. According to contemporary legal opinion in Germany, cartel agreements were regarded as not contrary to the public interest and lawful from the civil law perspective (Reuter 1967, S.34–35). There was a tendency to regard the cartel as an appropriate means of easing business fluctuations and a passive standpoint against legal regulations (Isay 1955, S.32). The Imperial Supreme Court approved cartel agreements as valid and rejected the view that cartels were contradictory to good customs and therefore invalid (*Bundesarchiv Berlin*, R1501/107163, Denkschrift über das Kartellwesen, Zweite Teil, Vorschriften des inländischen Zivil und Strafrechts unter Berücksichtigung der Rechtsprechung des Reichsgerichts, S.7–9). According to Imperial Supreme Court decisions, duties concluded in cartel agreements were binding (Pohl 1978, S.8; Reuter 1967, S.34; Fear 2005, p.238).

However, the state's policy that proved the existence of cartels functioned by raising the price of imported committees by adopting a conservative trade policy to protect domestic industries (Liefmann 1897, S.66; Liefmann 1923, S.614). The conservative trade policy that began in 1879 was a prerequisite for concentration and building cartels (Bechtold 1986, S.81–82). Thus, both policies were inseparable. Cartels enabled dumping in the export markets based on the possibility of maintaining prices in the domestic market and extra profit (Yanagisawa 2006, pp.162–163) even under circumstances in which prices tended to decline due to excess supply over demand during the period from the late nineteenth century to the beginning of the twentieth century. The German cartel policy made collective monopolies almost completely free, and cartels became dominant (Reuter 1967, S.34, 39). Policies emphasizing conservative trade became important for the rapid development of the key industrial sectors, such as the mining, iron and steel, chemical, and electrical industries; they also functioned as industrial policy.

Monopolistic prices based on cartels or syndicates built an important foundation for dumping in exports, contributing to the increase in exports. However, export dumping could be an important factor restricting the competitiveness of German enterprises due to the possibility for processing companies in foreign countries to manufacture products using materials and semi-finished goods sold at a dumping price (Voelcker 1904, S.515–516). Such a situation became a serious obstacle for exporting products processed in Germany.

Regarding **labor relations**, its fundamental framework was supported by the system and social policy measures provided by Otto von Bismarck, the Minister-president. He attempted to gain support from the worker class by preparing social welfare programs such as health insurance, accident insurance, and old-age and disability insurance. Meanwhile, the Anti-Socialist Law suppressed the socialist parties and significantly restrained the labor movement. The socialist movement that criticized the government's oppressive rule and the labor movement became popular with the progress of industrialization. The Socialist Worker's Party was founded in 1875 under the name "Social Democratic Party" in 1890; it became an important foundation for the labor movement and influenced labor relations during the Second Reich. One of the important characteristics can be seen in the oppositional and despotic labor relations under the power of employers and state policies against workers restricting their rights. The measure prohibiting unity was abolished by the amendment of the Trading Regulations in the north German Federation in 1869, which was applied to the whole Reich. Agricultural workers, domestic laborers, railroad workers, and sailors were excluded from the application of new regulations; however, labor unions and strikes were legalized for workers in industries (Saul 1974, S.211; Müller 1918, S.94–95) and labor union organizations provided a strong foundation for the labor movement (Mottek 1964, S.245). Nonetheless, the development of trade unions was very strictly restricted and regulated (Saul 1974, S.211–213; Müller 1918, S.96; Born 1957, S.101; Erdmann 1957, S.295; Tokunaga 1977, pp.219, 225). The Anti-Socialist Law dissolved many labor unions in 1878, which significantly restricted freedom of labor movement and trade union organization (Lütcke 1978, S.11; Ullmann 1977, S.42). Freedom of solidarity was recognized only at the level of individual freedom (Born 1957, S.103; Saul 1974, S.211).

The state took the opportunity of the massive strike in 1889 and recommended the foundation of the voluntary worker committees as a worker-representative system (Koch 1907, S.34; Teuteberg 1961, S.384–386, 419–421; Kirchhoff 1958, S.106). To correspond to the threat of a strike and prevent strikes, the capitalists instituted the common office regulations (Pieper 1903, S.30–34; Kirchhoff 1958, S.116) and established the strike insurance federation (Kirchhoff 1958, S.116). Meanwhile, the formation of trade unions progressed (Kirchhoff 1958, S.115; Nomura 1980, pp.55, 80, 329). The diffusion of the voluntary worker committees did not progress (Teuteberg 1961, S.386); however, conditions changed in 1905. For example, the Prussian Mining Act was revised after the great strike in the Ruhr mining industry in 1905 as a momentum. The worker committees were compulsorily founded in mines with more than 100 employees to stabilize labor relations, which led to a revision of the autocratic labor relations (Teuteberg 1961, S.436; Rassow and Born 1959, S.259–260; Adelmann 1960, S.355–356, 359–360; Otsuka 1987, p.349; Tokunaga 1977, pp.223–225). Meanwhile, as seen in one of the purposes of the General Association of German Metal Industries (Gesamtverband deutscher Metallindustriellen) founded in 1887, reinforcing solidarity among employers by building their organizations aimed to collectively defend against strikes and restrain-related losses (Kuhlemann 1908, S.83). The number of founding of employer associations increased from 55 between 1883 and 1892 to 168 between 1893 and 1902 (Kessler 1907, S.37). Solidarity regarding disapproval against negotiation and discussion with representatives of workers with lockouts as an offensive countermeasure against strikes enabled employers to build and maintain the antagonistic labor relations (Otsuka 1987, pp.288, 295, 297). In the Second Reich, the legal framework of labor relations admitted freedom of unity only at the level of individual freedom. Individuals were regarded as always subordinated to the state (Bergmann et al. 1975, S.164), which determined a fundamental foundation for corporate behavior. During the Second Reich, the degree to which the overall wage level was determined by strike activities and the organization of class conflict by the threat of lockout increased (Mottek et al. 1975, S.196); however, labor unions did not have the power to regulate working conditions collectively (Nomura 1980, pp.146, 329).

One prominent characteristic of **industrial systems based on interfirm relationships** during the Second Reich is the relationships between industry and banks based on the universal banking system. Regarding financial mechanisms between industrial enterprises and banks, business relationships were not built as individual relationships in credit, securities, and account current businesses. Instead, they were established as the provision of long-term capital credits through liquidating account current credits based on the issuing of securities by industrial enterprises and banks accepting and selling them. According to Jacob Riesser (1971, S.222), the account current business was "the strongest lever for planned industrial policy of bank" (Riesser 1971, S.222). Furthermore, combining this business with the issuance of securities was an important foundation for large companies to raise significant capital and develop a stable credit business for industrial enterprises. In this way, with advance financing of long-term finance performed by combining the debtor in the current calculation that occupied the most short-term credits at the time(1) with the issue of securities(2), the industry–bank relationship was based on financial relations. Such business relations were a premise of personnel ties (Kato 1973, p.214). Under German capitalism's rapid expansion, heavy industries played significant roles, and the capital market was underdeveloped. In this situation, the business development of banks organically combined credit, securities, and accounts of current businesses to collect funds provided by credits; account current credit was an important foundation for unique relationships between industry and banks. On the one hand, the regal form of enterprise as a joint-stock company provided banks with a basis for profitable capital market business (issue of shares and debentures). On the other hand, it created the possibility of systematized relationships between banks and companies through the supervisory board (Dahlem 2009, S.277). Even under such interfirm relationships, the expansion of the account current business as an important point in economic relations premised on the capacity of large banks to lend money and the ability of companies receiving credit to repay through the issue of securities (Tohara 1963, pp.375–376). The personnel connections were built on the basis of business relationships between banks that organically combined credit, securities, and account current businesses and industrial companies. They were essential to guarantee the relationships between banks and industrial enterprises, strengthened through stockholding or capital participation. Thus, interlocking directorates were a unique feature of monopolistic capitalism.

The early twentieth century marked a shift from general capital control to finance capital control (Ленин 1962, p.343). Lenin proposed "Finance capital" as the uniting and knitting of monopolistic capital in industries and the banking sector (Ленин 1962, Chapter 3); its significance indicated important changes at the time. Finance capital refers to the formation of a management entity that works together to accumulate capital through financing, cross-stockholding, accounts of current businesses, and personnel connections (Honma 1984, p.191; regarding the history of the personnel ties based on the interlocking directorates, see Yamazaki, 2024b). The "accumulation" of finance capital is understood as acquiring new profits and reinvestment, which are only possible through knitting industrial and bank monopolies (Honma 1984, p.232).

In Germany, under restrictive conditions, such as underdeveloped financial markets caused by unused money shortages (particularly the security market), the universal banking system and the relationships between industry and banks were vital countermeasures to the rapid development of industries like the heavy and chemical industries. Industry–bank relationships before World War I were based on the financial mechanisms combining credit, securities, and accounts of current businesses; the personnel connections and networks formed through interlocking directorates meant a high level of monopolistic capitalism. Such institutions were important for aligning with restrictive conditions for German capitalism's accumulation and reproduction structure. This structure was defined by the narrowness of the German domestic market, difficulties in export markets, and inferiority to the United States (US) regarding technique and production (Lenin 1953, S.511). Banks became estranged from corporate finance under the excess weight of war financing by credit banks, and the financial relationships between industry and banking became thin (Kato 1973, pp.219, 222). This situation also brought about a significant change in the relationships between industry and banks.

Next, **the financial system** had deep connections with the industrial system based on industry–bank relationships. Examining this system reveals the characteristics of the German system in large universal banks providing commodities and services with the feature of money dealing, such as those in the credit, account current, and securities businesses. Under this financial system, banks' capital participation in industrial enterprises resulted from financial and industrial policies (among other primary financing methods, such as account current credit, the issue and acceptance of securities, capital participation, and personnel connection). Based on the universal banking system, the financial system supported attempts to secure long-term funds by combining short-term credit provided by German big banks and issuing stocks and bonds (Marshall 1970, p.342). However, under the rapid expansion of German industries and the delay in the capital market development, the special financial system peculiar to Germany was forced to build depending on the significant roles of large banks in the way in which these banks not only intermediated issuing of shares but also accepted issued shares, which contributed to the strong and rapid industrial development. The gold standard system adopted in each major capitalistic country under the pressure of the United Kingdom as a hegemony nation (Polanyi 2001, p.226) was an important system to integrate the world economy (Polanyi 2001, p.211) and a vital foundation for the financial system in Germany.

However, a new era for banks began with the outbreak of World War I, and the foundation for financial business lost their previous significance (D.W.I.-Bericht 1961, S.3). The most important business of banks at the time was support in war financing; thus, industrial financing was forced to move backward (Hagemann 1931, S.119–120). The credit, issuing, securities, and account current businesses declined, previously occupying an important position in the bank business from the shift to monopolistic capitalism until World War I (Kato 1973, p.217).

Regarding **the structure of productive forces**, the great expansion of productive forces in heavy industries was an important element related to the characteristics of German capitalism. Additional elements included combining the mining and the iron and steel industries by enlarging production equipment and rapidly developing productive forces using technological developments in the Second Industrial Revolution, such as electrification and methods of synthetic chemical production. Regarding the synthetic chemical production method, attempts to synthesize complex compounds from simple compounds characterized this stage, which became a typical method for modern chemistry in the twentieth century. In this method, the production process was continuously performed (Mottek et al. 1975, S.37). Industries such as chemical and electrical engineering proliferated from the late nineteenth century to the beginning of the twentieth century, and monopolies were formed in these industries. The significance of the fact that Germany and the US led such an industrial revolution was extraordinary. Efforts for further use of these technological results were promoted, emphasizing the field of high-pressure synthesis and driven by the World War I to substitute substances (Plumpe 2022, S.221–223), which were further pursued in the 1920s when the rationalization movement was developed. The development of productive forces during the Second Reich period significantly contributed to the improvement of the international competitiveness of these industrial sectors.

When considering **the industrial structure**, the heavy and chemical industries rapidly developed after the beginning of the Second Reich. During this period, the ratio of the heavy industry (i.e., the mining and the iron and steel industries) to the whole economy (as measured by the amount of production and sale) was substantial. In the electrical industry, the weight of the heavy electric departments, such as the product fields of equipment for power generation and supply, was also significant. Under such industrial development conditions, the producer goods industries dominated the industrial structure. Despite the rapid expansion of new industrial sectors, such as the chemical and electrical industries, the development of consumer goods industries fell behind.

Further, in terms of **market structure**, the fundamental characteristics of the commodity market can be seen in four points: (1) a narrow domestic market, (2) a monopolized market under the approval of a cartel by the state, (3) a protected domestic market by the state's conservative trade policy, and (4) a limited colonial market. The narrow domestic market was one of the most important factors determining the high dependence of German capitalism on the export market. Meanwhile, unlike the US, where the strict anti-monopoly policy was adopted, Germany did not adopt state policies prohibiting cartels; instead, cartels were approved from the perspective of industrial and trade policies. However, without conservative customs setting high prices, cartels could not compete against the lower prices of imported products. The cartelization of Germany's national economy before 1914 resulted from the customs policy (Bechtold 1986, S.114). Furthermore, regarding the colonial market, the ratio of the UK's exports to colonies and dominions to the total exports in 1900 was 32.4% (Board of Trade 1904, pp.120–123). In contrast, Germany's figure was only 0.3% (Statistisches Reichsamt 1902; S.139), and the role of the colonial market was extremely low.

Regarding the labor market, an important characteristic was determined by labor relations, which was insufficiently regulated by labor unions even after the state approved such organizations. Regarding the financial market, the primary characteristics can be seen in the market based on the universal banking system in which large banks provide both credit and securities services and an underdeveloped securities market.

Building upon the previous analysis, examining **enterprise–market relationships** (related to the state of marketization) shows one of the most prominent characteristics: the monopolized market in which cartels or syndicates were formed. Such enterprise–market relationships restricted the function of the market mechanism. Maintaining high prices through cartels or syndicates delayed balancing demand and supply through market mechanisms and prevented market recovery during excess production crises. Thus, monopolistic organizations were forced to face limitations in coordinating productive forces. Furthermore, the market and enterprise–market relationships became an important factor in determining the high-cost structures of German enterprises through maintaining excess production capacity and decreasing operating rates.

Figure 3.1 presents a graphical overview of Germany's total system of business management during the Second Reich, based on our discussions.

3.2 Overview of the Total System of Business Management in the Period of the Weimar Republic

This section considers conditions in the period of the Weimar Republic. In considering the world structure of capitalism, the world order after World War I changed profoundly. The Treaty of Versailles created complicated European problems, necessitating competition and cooperation or opposition and compromise between countries. Furthermore, the beginning of the Soviet Union as the first socialist state needed decisive collaboration among capitalist nations. Under these circumstances, the US acquired hegemony to build the world order due to its strong financial and high economic power. In deepening the global linkage of capital, the US played a significant role and greatly influenced the recovery and development of enterprises, industries, and economies in other major capitalistic countries. The return of each major country to the gold standard system built an important foundation for stabilizing current values, which promoted the global linkage of capital.

Based on the description of changes in the world structure of capitalism, in considering each element of the total business management system in terms of **state–enterprise relations**, the Cartel Ordinance (the Cartel Law) in 1923 first regulated cartels. This situation differed from the period of the Second Reich when cartel agreements were regarded as lawful from the perspectives of trade and industrial policies. However, the Cartel Law did not establish any new legal principles but merely provided a new legal foundation for more intense regulation of the abuses arising from monopolistic combinations [Liefmann 1932, pp.173–174; *Bundesarchiv Berlin*, R/3101/12362, Die Schrift des Reichsrates, Nr.78, Tagung 1922 (29.3.1922), *Bundesarchiv Berlin*, R/3101/12361, Denkschrift betr. Schaffung eines Kartellgesetzes (Oktober 1921), S.2; *Bundesarchiv Berlin*, R43-1/1201, Vortrag des Referenten (30.10.1923); *Bundesarchiv Berlin*, R43-1/1201, Verordnung gegen Mißbrauch wirtschaftlicher Machtstellungen (Oktober 1928)]. The Cartel Ordinance depended

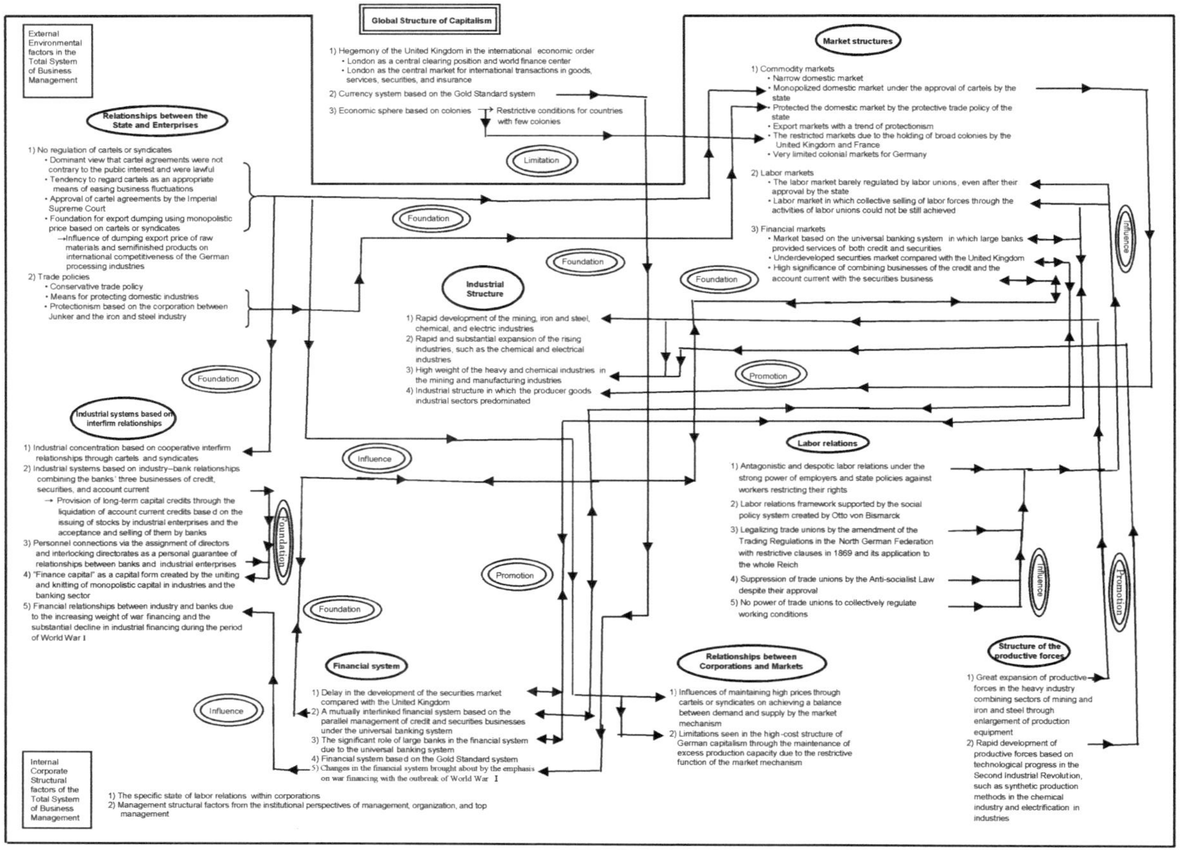

Fig. 3.1 Overview of Germany's total system of business management during the Second Reich
Source This figure was compiled by the author, based on discussions in this chapter

on the Cartel Court assuming the duties assigned to it, and the Court tended not to interfere excessively in the German economy (Liefmann 1932, p.174). Thus, even after the promulgation of the Cartel Ordinance of 1923, economic concentrations emphasizing cartels were maintained under loose regulations against monopolies, representing one of the prominent characteristics of state–enterprise relations in the period of the Weimar Republic.

Other prominent characteristics of state–enterprise relations in the Weimar era included the involvement and roles of the state in the rationalization movement. Such involvement covered (1) involvement in institutions for promoting and aiding rationalization, (2) public investment for promoting rationalization, (3) social policy for driving rationalization more peacefully, and (4) the role of technology policy in promoting rationalization.

Regarding involvement in institutions for promoting and aiding rationalization, promoting the development of rationalization and supporting rationalization significantly contributed to the development of rationalization at all industrial and national levels as "a systematization of rationalization" (Yoshida 1976, p.189). The state's involvement in institutions for promoting and aiding rationalization, such as the National Center for Economic Effectiveness [*Reichskuratorium für Wirtschaftlichkeit* (RKW)], was significant in driving rationalization at the national economy level. The classifications "technical rationalization," "commercial rationalization," and "national economic rationalization" were frequently used for rationalization at the time, as seen in the understanding of the kinds of rationalization in *the Rationalization Handbook* ("*Handbuch der Rationalisierung*" edited by Reichskuratorium für Wirtschaftlichkeit 1930, S.2–5). The state's involvement in institutions that promote and aid rationalization, such as the RKW, was significant in spreading the ideology that drives rationalization. This situation contributed to achieving the true aim of the rationalization movement of gradually depriving workers of the rights they had won up until that point and further increasing labor density covertly (Maekawa and Yamazaki 1995, p.17).

Considering the state's involvement through public investment in promoting rationalization, establishing a base for production by improving the industrial foundations, such as transportation and the harbor, was essential. In the Weimar period, the foundation of many public companies through the state's capital participation was a part of the institutions enabling the substantial capital accumulation of monopolistic large enterprises through establishing an industrial base (Tsukamoto 1964, pp.76–77). Another important point of the state's involvement in rationalization regarding establishing an industrial base was seen in an industrial policy. According to the National Industrial Conference Board in the US in 1931, measures in "the technical rationalization" and "other activities combined with scientific management" ("the labor organizational rationalization") were the deployment of American methods, and nothing new could be observed. In contrast, regarding "the rationalization of the industrial organization" (the rationalization of the industry), Germany indicated a type of industrial policy not developed in other countries. Germany had no legal regulation regarding the rights of individual manufacturers to conclude agreements restricting transactions. The possibility of compelling such agreements by law enabled the development of the "planned economy" system in some of the most important industries. This situation significantly differed from the lack of plans for industrial activities in nations where free competition was still considered indispensable for progress and prosperity (National Industrial Conference Board (1931, pp.5–6).

The state's involvement in the rationalization movement through social policy measures was also significant. During the interim stability from 1924 to 1929, the state's intervention in the labor market expanded. Moreover, social policy was created to address issues unique to this period arising from forced rationalization and several labor legislations created during political disturbance after World War I. The systems of social policy, such as (1) the labor agreement and the mediation system of dispute and (2) systems of job placement and unemployment insurance, took a peculiar form according to the cooperative system in the rationalization of the industry based on labor–capital reconciliation. During this period, the state's interference in the labor market was limited to arranging external terms of the market, such as improving the conditions of price negotiation of labor commodities and maintaining an excess labor force. It did not intervene in the internal labor market by instructing price fixing and increasing demand to address the excess supply of the labor force (Tsukamoto 1964, pp.88–89).

Furthermore, the technology policy was created to measure the imperialistic nation's ability to cope with changes in the historical situation that resulted from World War I and the Russian Revolution in 1917 (Mottek et al. 1975, S.24). The intervention of the power organization in science and technology was pursued according to the level of socialization of the productive forces. This situation meant actively utilizing science and technology to address issues crucial to imperialistic development and increasing monopolistic profit. The state's monopolistic science organization and administration supported the establishment of new scientific fields, such as labor physiology, psychology, and business administration, which were crucial for the exploitation process and intensifying the management of large corporate groups after the start of World War I (Mottek et al. 1975, S.51–52). Regarding the background of such state policy development, the technology policy became significant in Germany from the 1920s to the 1930s because the production relation influenced the development of the productive force as the limiting factor, combined with the concept of capitalistic rationalization in the 1920s. Monopolistic capital attempted to reverse the stagnant trend in production development using state technology policies within the framework of state monopolistic capitalism. Such efforts aimed to overcome the technological delay against or surpass the US (Mottek et al. 1975, S.24; Etzold 1988, S.39). Efforts to increase the productive forces in the industry and reduce production costs using technological and systematic advancement were significant in the type of technology policy (Mottek et al. 1975, S.113); thus, after World War I, technology policy as a constituent element of economic policy became an element of the state's monopolistic regulations and was used mainly in the form of capitalistic rationalization (Mottek et al. 1975, S. 266–267).

Regarding **labor relations**, the revolution in November 1918 was vital in building the fundamental framework. The Second Reich collapsed, and economic concessions, such as an eight-hour labor system, recognition of labor unions, wage agreement systems, and the works council system, were given to the working class to maintain German capitalism and avoid transitioning into a socialist state. These burdens created conditions where wages tended to be relatively high and did not tend to fall. The state reorganized the process of executing the organized collective influence regarding working conditions and wage costs, which significantly limited the space for business plans (Homburg 1991, S.3). The capitalists endeavored to revise the influence of economic concessions on the working class through changes in legislation created during the revolutionary period after World War I; however, the trend of rigidity in wage decline did not fundamentally change (Tokunaga 1977, pp.250–251; Kato 1973, p.363) and was maintained from 1924 to 1929 when the rationalization movement developed.

Meanwhile, the regulating power against management by the works council as an institute for worker participation in management could barely be exercised. Monopolization of the function of job design and the work management by management did not change (Spitzley 1980, S.67). Works councils could not require the introduction of a new work organization or constrain its adoption by the company side (Kaskel 1920, S.205). For example, in the automobile industry, Opel's works council was never able to influence the tempo of the conveyor under the flow production system (Weiss 1926, S.20).

The possibility of shifting to socialism in industrial relations disappeared with the defeat of revolutionary influences in the fall of 1923, promoting the cooperation of labor and capital. The Economic Democratic Theory of the Free Trade Union appeared as an ideology to drive rationalization instead of socialization. It was closely connected with the assertion that workers' economic position could be realized by cooperating in economic development measures, including rationalization. Collaboration in economic development or rationalization occurred under socialization during the revolutionary period after World War I. In contrast, such cooperation was promoted under "democratization" or "economic democratization" during the relatively stable period between 1924 and 1929. This perspective was based on productivity. Among trade union leaders, a high level of productivity was indispensable for realizing a high standard of living, as seen in the US at the time, and rationalization was regarded as the most effective means to achieve their goals (Naphtali 1928; Ohashi 1999, p.107). Thus, the fundamental framework for the labor union's cooperative attitude with the capital side in the development of rationalization was established, and changes in industrial relations promoted cooperation between capital and labor through rationalization.

Industrial systems based on interfirm relationships during the Weimar period were evident in the changes in business relations between industrial enterprises and banks. During the inflationary period after World War I, banks were forced to develop their businesses at lower currency prices. Moreover, the trend toward self-financing of industrial enterprises accelerated due to the enormous profits earned during the war and compensation money for lost factories in the alienated region. Industry–bank relationships significantly changed due to the limited scale of financing of banks and the situation in which a large concentration movement from 1920 to 1921 was developed without bank involvement and influence. Furthermore, the independence of large corporate groups in industry on banking capital increased, and the development of policy of industrial enterprises for banks appeared (Duschnitzky 1927; Hagemann 1931, S.20–21; Lampe 2012, S.370; Wixforth 1995, S.510). Big corporate groups attempted to expand businesses in the banking sector (Duschnitzky 1927, S.227–233). The ratios of 19 large banks of the debtor in the current calculation to total asset accounts decreased from 41% in 1913 to 25.1% in 1920, 30.1% in 1921, and 27.9% in 1923 (Goldschmidt 1928, S.60). As a result, the account current business, which was important in the bank before World War I, changed dramatically. The account current business lost characteristics, such as the fixed capital credit, as seen before World War I (Kato 1973, p.228). The number of securities issued by 19 big banks increased from 750 million gold marks in 1920 to 1,270 million; it then decreased to 185 million in 1922 (Goldschmidt 1928, S.224). The ratio of bills to total asset accounts of 19 large banks significantly decreased from 22.2% in 1922 to 2.5% in 1923 (Goldschmidt 1928, S.60). Thus, banks' liquidity decreased dramatically due to an increase in securities accounts under the inactivity of stock markets after their activity until the beginning of 1922; therefore, banks were forced to restrain the issuing and securities businesses (Kato 1973, p.229). The function of banks' credit businesses almost stopped because the stock issues after 1922 forced them to take charge of roles of credit for distribution rather than bill credit (Kato 1973, p.229).

In the period of relative stability from 1924 to 1929, the general shortage of capital caused industrial enterprises to rely on financial institutions that had funds for lending or intermediate access to the capital market (Hardach 1984, p.217). The rate of bills and debtors in the calculation of the total of asset accounts was high, and that of Berlin's big banks amounted to approximately more than 60%, and financial institutions coped with the capital demands of industrial enterprises through these two credit forms (Kato 1973, pp.232–233). The debtor's increase rate in the current calculation was extremely high, and account current credit was the most common credit extended to industrial enterprises (see Table 3.1). Securities issuing was developed as an axis of corporate finance due to stock price stagnation [share price indicators in the Berlin Stock Exchange (1924: 100) were 25 in 1924 and 27 in 1926. They recovered to 40 in 1927 and 37 in 1928 (Kuczynski 1963, S.67)]. However, it was no longer performed as the long-term financial relationship with industrial companies by organically combining account current credit with securities issuing (Kato 1973, pp.236–237).

Industrial enterprises could not expect funds for rationalization by banks (Chandler 1990, p. 590), and the trend of stronger dependence on US banks and capital was also substantially influenced by changes in the organic relationships between industry and banks (Wixforth and Ziegler 1994, p.113; Wixforth and Ziegler 1995, p.260). This situation refers to the limitation of the organized structure of German finance capital following the establishment of monopolistic capitalism (Kato 1973, p.258). The accumulation of "frozen" debtors in the current calculations intensively

Table 3.1 Ratios of debtors in the current calculation (overdrafts) to total asset accounts in Deutsche Bank, Dresdner Bank, and Commerzbank

	1913	1920	1921	1922	1923	1924	1926	1928	1929
Deutsche bank	28.34	14.33	21.60	19.70	42.26	35.66	43.08	40.63	43.42
Dresdner bank	40.63	22.49	29.13	22.30	37.95	39.33	37.12	37.02	39.94
Commerzbank	38.97	30.33	32.76	33.10	44.02	37.84	40.52	41.72	41.76

Note Each numerical value is presented in percentages
Source This table was compiled by the author based on the annual balance sheets of Deutsche Bank, Dresdner Bank, and Commerzbank

expressed the limping relations between industry and bank (Kato 1973, p.260). As the first movers in industries such as steel, electric equipment, and chemicals became established, organizational capabilities developed, and the structure of these industrial sectors was clearly defined, the role of banks in initial financing and promoting interfirm cooperation declined. At the same time, the significance of formal cooperation increased (Chandler 1990, p.589).

The business relationships between industry and banks changed; however, the numbers of enterprises and mandates in which the three German banks (Deutsche Bank, Dresdner Bank, and Commerzbank) formed interlocking directorates significantly increased during the inflationary period (compared to those established during the period of monopolistic capitalism) (Yamazaki 2024a, b, Chapter 2 and 3). Regarding conditions during the relatively stable period in the 1920s, W. Hagemann (1931, S.82) indicated that the total number of supervisory board positions in industrial enterprises held by banks generally increased more than before World War I (1912). However, the influence of banks showed not an increasing trend but a declining tendency (Hagemann 1931, S.82). Building and maintaining personnel connections with many enterprises in close relationships was critical for large banks during the inflationary period following World War I, and the financial relationships between industry and banks became weaker than before the war. This situation is consistent with the trend of decreasing industrial enterprises' independence from banks in which financial transactions did not occur, which also applied to pursuing cooperation in the management of enterprises through involvement in the supervisory boards with which banks had friendly relations (Berliner Handels-Gesellschaft 1956, S.172). An increase in interlocking directorates was an important countermeasure for banks facing the trend of industrial enterprise independence. It reflected the bank's policy to deal with the need to maintain and strengthen business relationships with many companies as personal guarantees. Increasing the number of people assigned from banks as supervisory board members never strengthened the organic and stable relationships between industries and banks. Instead, it reflected changes in relations between both, such as the destruction of financial relations between industry and bank based on combining account current business with issuing business (Kato 1973, pp.267–268). The characteristics of the financial business relationships between industries and banks were the foundation for personnel connections (Kato 1973, p.263); however, these characteristics changed and were forced to differ from those dispatched to partially large companies, indicating a trend of industrial enterprises' independence from banks in corporate finance (Kato 1973, p.266).

Regarding **the financial system**, Germany was compelled to return to the gold standard system as an indispensable prerequisite condition for receiving funds from the US in the framework of the Dawes Plan (Kato 1973, pp.140–141), bringing an end to the inflation by stabilizing the value of the "Mark." The German state was subject to burdened reparation, and domestic conditions changed depending on the partial charge of payment of reparations by the state as a combined body of government and economic world. Thus, the nation's solidarity was united with the gold standard system due to the supreme duty of maintaining the currency's value against foreign currencies (Polanyi 2001, p.224). For Germany, the currency collapse meant that relationships with the economy outside the country were cut off (Polanyi 2001, p.238). Therefore, the financial system in the relatively stable period was based on the gold standard system. Germany's return to the gold standard system became a restrictive condition for the rationalization movement that should enable the revival and development of German capitalism and corporate expansion and the implementation of economic policy during the great crisis that began in 1929.

Next, considering **the structure of the productive forces**, the following three points show the most prominent characteristics of the Weimar period. The first is an attempt to improve the driving system of production equipment by transforming from group driving by a steam engine or an electric motor to the individual drive method using an electric motor. The second is the complete application of the synthetic production method, which started with dye synthesis during the shift to monopolistic capitalism to other product fields. These production methods were developed and applied fully and extensively, enabling the diversification of the chemical industry. The third is the possibility of increasing the productive forces using the Ford system.

Regarding the improvement of production equipment, the rate of electrification of motive power in German industries and handicrafts increased from 19.7% in 1907 (territory after the Treaty of Versailles) to 65.5% in 1925 and then to 72.6% in 1933 (Wirtschaft und Statistik 1927, S.166; Statistisches Reichsamt 1931, S.33; Statistisches Reichsamt 1936, S.116–117). The horsepower used for power machines in industries and handicrafts increased to 8.69 times from 1907 (territory after the Treaty of Versailles) to 1925 (excluding Saar region) (Statistisches Reichsamt 1931, S.89). The horsepower for the driving of machine tools in these sectors increased by 41.7% from 1925 to 1933 (Statistisches Reichsamt 1936, S.116–117). At the same time, capitalists took a moderate position in transforming to the individual drive method due to the tremendous capital expenditure needed to introduce different types of production using electric power (Mottek et al. 1975, S.33–34; Zygitschko 1970, S.165). This expense is why such innovation did not prevail despite the limitation of the transmission system with an increasing volume of energy needed for production (Mottek et al. 1975, S.28) and the immanent contradictions in the factory system (limitation in the formation of an organization according to the workflows) (Mottek et al. 1975, S.30). The shift from steam-driven working machines to a system driven by an electric motor and then to a system of separate driving of working machines progressed faster after the rationalization boom in 1926–1927. However, the fixation of the separate driving method with the broad foundation was realized in the latter half of the 1930s (Mottek et al. 1975, S.36). Meanwhile, at Ford Motor Co., approximately half of the processing machines were transmission-driven, and the other half were electric individual driving, allowing the company to reduce time in a way unknown in Germany (Witte 1930, Spalte 1860).

Meanwhile, the Ford system enabled mass production primarily in the process and assembly industries represented by the automobile, electrical, and machine industries, as considered in Chapter 9. However, the development of productive forces through the deployment of such an American management method in Germany during the Weimar period encountered significant limitations due to the stringent market conditions, such as seen in the narrow domestic market and difficulties in export markets, which determined the German deployment of the Ford system. The development of modern productive forces, such as that observed in the US then, was not nearly realized.

Peculiar characteristics also occurred in **the industrial structure**. Like the period of the shift to monopolistic capitalism, the ratio of the heavy industry comprising the mining industry and the iron and steel industry to the national economy in Germany was considerable during the Weimar period. Indeed, the relatively active investment in equipment was implemented in the growing industries during this period, such as the chemical, electrical, and automobile industries, compared with the heavy and machine industries, and these sectors expanded substantially. Considering the investment into equipment of the listed corporations with more than one million Reichsmark (RM) of capital, the ratio of the total amount of new investment from 1924 to 1929 to the value of production equipment at the start of 1924 in the heavy industry was 22.1%, below the level of the entire industry (31.6%). In contrast, similar numerical values in the chemical, electrical, and automobile industries were 63.3%, 52.6%, and 81.9%, respectively, significantly exceeding the entire industry's level. Although the value of production equipment in the heavy industry at the start of 1924 (2,460,500,000 RM) was large whereas that in the automobile industry (116,400,000 RM) was small, the relatively active investment in equipment was implemented in the growing industries (Keiser and Benning 1931; Statistisches Reichsamt 1936, S.50; *Wirtschaft und Statistik* 1933, S.594–595). Out of the total production value of the mining and manufacturing industries in 1927–1928, the mining and the iron and steel industries occupied 5.83% and 7.42%, respectively. In contrast, the chemical, electrical, and automobile industries occupied 4.96%, 3.86%, and 1.38%, respectively; the ratio of these rising industries was only 10.2% (Wagenführ 1933, S.57). Despite the rapid expansion of these rising industries, their proportion in the German national economy remained below the mining and iron and steel industries.

In the 1920s, attempts at transition to mass production by deploying the Ford system in the consumer goods industries, such as the automobile and electrical industries, were decisively defeated compared with the US. In Germany, mass production in the automotive industry during this period was only in the first stage of development (Yamazaki 2001a, b, Chapter Part 2). The rapid growth of the new industrial sectors was insufficient to balance the adverse substitution effects, such as the dismissal of the labor force and the cessation of operations of the old production capacity due to rationalization (Mottek et al. 1975, S.270).

In the US, the industrial structure before World War I was based on the relationship between the railroad, iron and steel, and coal mining industries. In the 1920s, the transition to a system based on the relationship between the automobile, iron and steel, and oil and electric power industries progressed (Shiomi et al. 1986, pp.48–49). In contrast, in addition to the narrowness of the domestic market in Germany, mass production in the automobile industry, which could spread economic effects on other related industrial sectors, was not nearly as developed as in the US due to the strict market conditions resulting from the increased sales of American automobiles, and the overwhelming competitiveness of US companies in the German market. This situation significantly influenced the development of other industrial sectors.

The delay in mass production in the automobile industry became a limiting factor for mass production in the machinery industry. It increased the cost of machine production, which also became a limiting factor for rationalization in the electrical and automobile industries. It also reinforced the disparity with other industrial industries, such as the iron and steel industry, which drove the transition to mass production and strengthened dependence on foreign markets (Maekawa and Yamazaki 1995, p.240). Regarding the influence on the iron and steel industry, until 1930, 30% of the total steel production in the US was provided to the automobile industry. In contrast, in Germany, the ratio of steel supplied to this industrial sector to total steel production was only 4% [*Historisches Archiv der Deutschen Bank*, P03204, Sanierung der deutschen Automobilindustrie (8.3.1930)].

Under conditions specific to Germany, the relationship between the industrial sectors fundamentally determined the development and characteristics of the rationalization movement during this period (Maekawa and Yamazaki 1995, p.240). Due to such restrictions on the economic effects of inter-industry relations and the stringent market circumstances, the expansion process was an important limitation for the rationalization movement in Germany during the 1920s. In this process, capital accumulation based on rationalization simultaneously was unable to create demand: the market for more advantageous development could not be realized. In this way, the rationalization in the rising industries could not change the general trend of the entire capital accumulation (Maekawa and Yamazaki 1995, p.240), and the characteristic of the industrial structure during the Second Reich that attached too much importance to the coal mining and iron and steel industries did not fundamentally change.

Regarding **market structure**, the restrictive conditions in the commodity market, such as the narrow and intensely changing domestic market (Siegel and von Freyberg 1991, S.267) and difficulties in export markets, influenced the development of business management and corporate expansion. Germany lost its colonies and the German domestic market narrowed due to inflation, tending to have characteristics of intensely changing markets and the underdeveloped consumer goods markets. Such domestic market conditions remarkably enhanced the importance of the export market. However, in the 1920s, each country could achieve only slight international cooperation and could not prevent the spread of protectionism that hindered world trade due to the preference for economic policy oriented toward national interests in each country (Ambrosius and Hubbard 1986, S.242–243). Furthermore, during the great depression in 1929, building the block economy progressed as countermeasures of major countries like the United Kingdom and France. It limited countries as partners in which free trade was admitted to the extent of core nations (Iwamura 2010, p.103) and promoted more serious economic conditions due to further blockade of markets.

As regards the labor market, the German Revolution in November 1918 tremendously influenced this market. Economic concession to the working class brought about the tendency for wages to fall hard. This situation did not change fundamentally, despite the amendments implemented around the stabilization of the German Mark (Kato 1973, p.363), which was deeply concerned with the characteristics of the labor market.

Significant changes appeared in the financial market as well. The influence of inflation on capital formation was extreme (Prion 1931, S.349), and a shortage of capital was manifested as constant credit shortages (Amamiya 1994, p.295). It caused the development of rationalization with its capital expenditures to be forced within a specific limit due to difficulties in raising capital and the burden of capital costs. The German financial market in the relatively stable period from 1924 to 1929 depended on foreign capital, particularly the US capital, and was a market with a high interest rate.

The market structure heightened the necessity of enterprise rationalization and became an important factor restricting the development of rationalization and its effects. It also influenced business management and corporate behavior.

Next, regarding **enterprise–market relationships**, an important character lay in the appearance of the trend of rigidity in wage decline brought about by labor laws enacted in the revolutionary period after World War I. Indeed, demand–supply relations fundamentally determined the movement of wages. As far as the broad legal rights for workers were maintained, the level of wages was substantially regulated by laws enacted during the German Revolution in 1918.

Figure 3.2 presents a graphical overview of the total system of business management in Germany during the Weimar Republic, based on our discussions.

3.3 Overview of the Total System of Business Management in the Period of National Socialism

This section examines conditions in the period of National Socialism. Regarding the world structure of capitalism, the block economy was built as a countermeasure for major countries like the United Kingdom and France during the great depression, which remained influential after 1933. Therefore, its influence on countries with no colonies, such as Germany, was significant. The trend of protectionism in trade fundamentally continued, which determined the restrictive circumstances until the

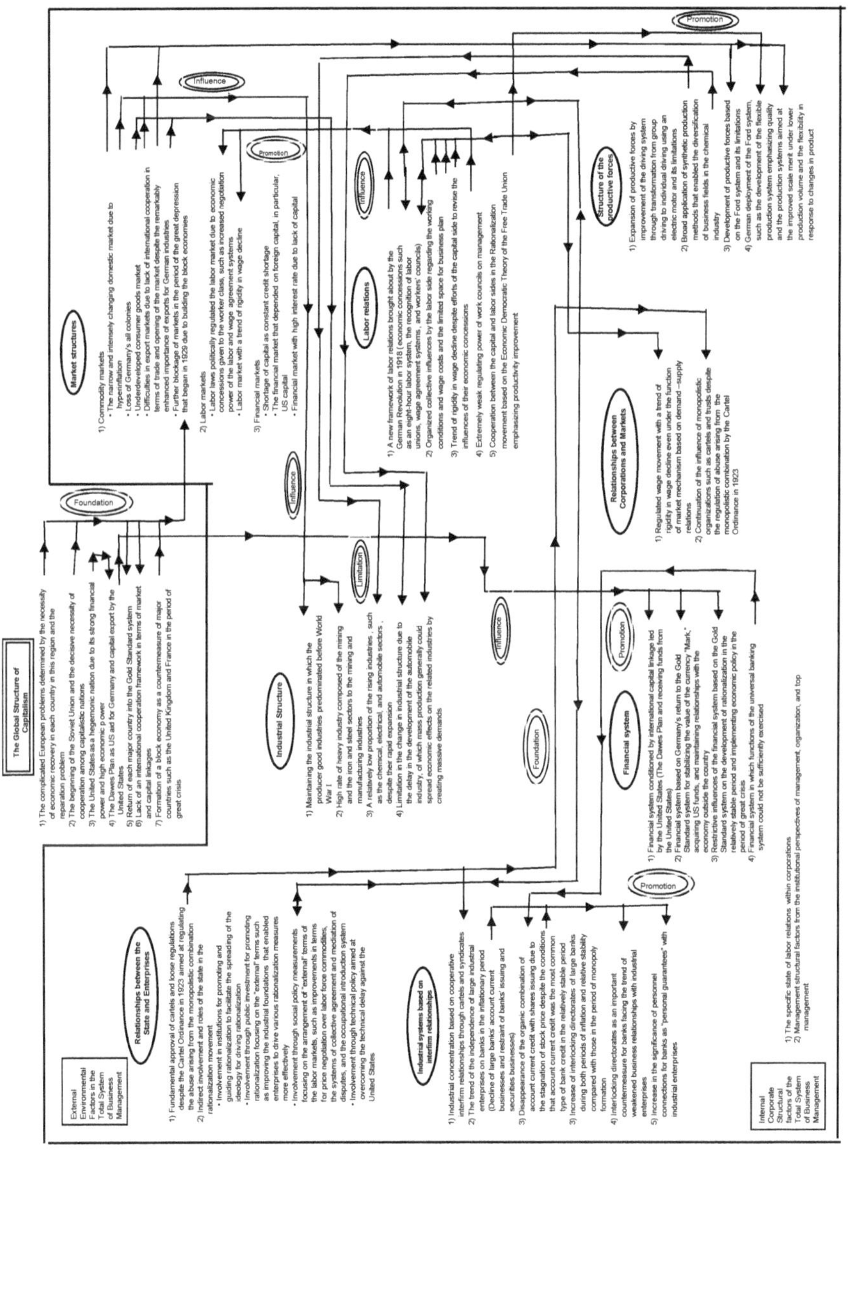

Fig. 3.2 Overview of Germany's total system of business management during the Weimar Republic
Source This figure was compiled by the author, based on discussions in this chapter

outbreak of World War II. In this period, the leading position of the US in the world economic order was essentially maintained. However, the rise of fascist states influenced the global economic system through attempts to create their enlarged economic sphere, such as seen in the "extensive market" ("*Großraumwirtschaft*") by the Nazi state.

In considering each element of the total system of business management, regarding **state–enterprise relations**, one of the most important characteristics can be observed in further reinforcing the state's stand that proved cartel. Such cases can be seen in some laws such as the Law of Change of Cartel-regulation in 1923 (Gesetz zur Aenderung der Kartell-Verordnung von 1923) and the Law of Foundation of Compulsory Cartel (Gesetz über die Errichtung von Zwangkartellen). These cartel laws were based on the government's understanding that the intensification of competition and the formation of uneconomical prices in individual economic departments would collapse important enterprises in the national economy (Die Bank 1934, S.1733). Furthermore, the Order of the Minister for Economy and changes in problems corresponding to cartels under the war economy also indicated the government's policy of strengthening cartels (Die Bank 1937; Die Bank 1940).

The policy of the state for standardization in various industries is another characteristic of state–enterprise relations in the Nazi era. The economic policy of Fascism regarded standardization and reduction of type as new goals due to the benefits of standardization for production, enabling the savings and efficient use of raw materials (Etzold 1988, S.91; RKW-Nachrichten 1935, S.131). The progress of standardization in this period was due to the involvement of the state in promoting technical rationalization in this field under the militarization of the economy (Hachtmann 1989, S.71). With the Second Four-Year Plan in 1936, applying standardization became a primary obligation by order of the Minister of the Economy. Moreover, under the foundation of the "National Committee for Production Increase" in February 1939, standardization activity became a central task in the urgent plan of the Ministry for the Economy in May 1939. Orders to change the number of types and product kinds gave the Minister of the Economy the authority to declare that norms were obligatory. Moreover, appropriate direction by the industrial group concerning standardization, the reduction of type, and cost-cutting was provided on September 28, 1939 (Koehn 1942, S.666; Etzold 1988, S.91–92; Der Vierjahresplan 1941, S.658). Furthermore, the "Committee for Standardization and Reduction of Type," whose chairperson was the head of the German Norm Committee, was organized by the Minister of Armaments on June 24, 1944, to improve the efficiency of standardization activities and increase wartime production. The authority to declare that norms were obligatory was given to the chairman of this new committee. He was responsible for "duties of strict integration and promotion of standardization and the reduction of type" and for the implementation of measures (RKW-Nachrichten 1944, S.72). In this way, the promotion of interfirm rationalization through monopolistic capital organizations (in particular standardization and strengthening the division of labor in production and assembly processes) led the state to emphasize measurements for improving the efficiency of the war economic institution by centralizing state monopolistic regulations (Mottek et al. 1975, S.339).

In addition to the period of the Weimar Republic, one of the prominent characteristics of state–enterprise relations in the Nazi era was the state's involvement and role in the rationalization movement. Three points can be highlighted: (1) changes in the characteristics of public investment and investment control, (2) social policy for driving rationalization, and (3) involvement of the state in enterprise rationalization.

In considering the state's involvement through public investment for promoting rationalization, the 1920s emphasized establishing the base for production by improving the industrial foundations—namely the "external" terms enabling to effectively drive various rationalization measurements (Nitta 1971, p.38). In contrast, direct involvement was developed in the Nazi era. Public investment in this period created direct demand for industries and created the mutual spreading effects of demands within industrial sectors; this type of effectiveness spread as compensations and new investments occurred (Okamoto 1993, p.170). Another noteworthy point concerning the change in the characteristics and role of public investment is that the state implemented investment control to strongly expand investment in industrial sectors related to munitions, which was deeply concerned with the rationalization of technology and technique with capital expenditure. The Second Four-Year Plan was the first attempt at planned control in specific production fields. Such control, mainly composed of prohibition and investment restriction, was implemented primarily in the consumer goods industries (*Der Deutsche* Volkswirt 1937, S.2516). Such control measures enabled government agencies to forbid undesirable investment to secure the needed production capacity for expanding munitions plants and factories, contributing to the purpose of the Second Four-Year Plan (Petzina 1977, S.138). Under the driving force of the militarization of the economy, public investment and investment control by the state significantly and directly influenced the development of technical rationalization through preferred public investment and control of private investment in the industrial sectors related to munitions. Investment control by the state was an attempt to expand munition production and directly promote the accumulation of huge monopolistic capital.

In considering state–enterprise relationship concerning the room of corporate behavior, the authoritarian state changed the framework of the behavior of the enterprise and decision-making so that results in terms of politically desirable armament could be achieved and the routine of daily decisions within the enterprise did not fundamentally change (Abelshause et al. 2003, S.13). The Nazis respected the autonomy of the decision-making of private enterprises on principle (Plumpe 2003, S.251). Although the behavioral room of Germany had become constraint since the outbreak of World War II (Marx 2013, S.508), autonomy in corporate behavior was maintained, and National Socialism hardly influenced the procedures and process of decision-making (Plumpe 2003, S.255, 261).

Regarding the involvement of the state by social policy in driving rationalization, the abolishment of political regulation in the Weimar era and the dissolution of trade unions created a more advantageous foundation for enterprises to pursue rationalization, avoiding the influence of the worker class on management (Homburg 1991, S.3–4). "The managerial community theory" spelled out the class discrimination between capitalists and laborers and built a basis for fascist rationalization without strong conflicts between capital and labor. Under strict labor control, unlike the Weimar period, when the broad legal rights for workers were approved, there was no necessity to develop a social policy to ease problems arising from capitalistic rationalization.

The state led enterprise rationalization and cooperation between the economic world and the RKW. It was based on the Economic Order of November 12, 1936, which required all groups of the industrial economy and committees to perform rationalization in the interest of the military economy. Implementing the specific methods as research results of the RKW was free for enterprises in the Weimar era; however, during the Nazi period, such efforts became an obligation for managers (Etzold 1988, S.44). Efforts to rationalize the German economy came under the protection of the National Committee for Production Increase by the Supreme Order of the Four-Year Plan (Der Deutsche Volkswirt 1939, S.124). This committee was not a new government agency but indicated the integration of parties to rationalization. Its duties were to ensure the smooth implementation of rationalization through common activities among parties, overcome bureaucratic evils, and avoid loss of time (Schmeer 1939, S.846). As mentioned, the promotion and compulsion of standardization and the formation of a compulsive cartel were deeply concerned with rationalization at the company level and changes in business management. Such state involvement in the rationalization of enterprises was also observed primarily in the participation and assistance of the state and quasi-state institutions in Reichsausschuß für Arbeitszeitermittlung (REFA) and its activities (Hachtmann 1989, S.74, 180). In 1920, the state's role in the institution for promoting and aiding rationalization was chiefly in indirect assistance in the aspect of funds, and the involvement of the state in the rationalization process cannot be seen. In contrast, the participation of the state developed to direct involvement in the process of implementing rationalization in the Nazi era.

Furthermore, the rationalization policy as a measure of the efficiency improvement pursued by the Ministerium for Economy under the Second Four-Year Plan included two aspects: (1) rationalization of production in enterprises and (2) rationalization of management as unifying the cost accounting standard. Standardization and securing rational labor methods were considered central issues in the former (Yanagisawa 2013, pp.132–133). The rationalization policy of the cartel system and the formation of compulsory cartels implemented by the Ministerium for Economy (Yanagisawa 2013, pp.61, 67) were deeply related to the state's involvement in enterprise rationalization.

Regarding **labor relations** in the Nazi period, the conditions during the Weimar period completely changed. Laws that regulated labor relations under the Weimar Republic were abolished, including the Works Council Act, the labor agreement, the Dispute Coordination Order, the Coordination System Order, and the Labor Trust Act (Tsukamoto 1964, p.271). Political regulation that restricted functions in the collective labor right after 1930 and organized collective influence over working conditions and labor costs during the Weimar Republic significantly vanished. These measures contributed to removing obstacles that prevented an enterprise from using its rights regarding "labor factors" that were present in the Weimar era. Moreover, the dissolution of trade unions in May 1933 played a significant role in achieving such a goal (Homburg 1991, S.4). Instead of a labor union, the German Labor Front (*Deutsche Arbeitfront*) was an organization for integrating workers.

Moreover, "the managerial community theory" and "the leaders' principle," which considered both parties as relationships between direction and obedience, namely, the negation of the exploitation relation, built an important theoretical foundation for fascist labor management (Maekawa 1993, pp.190–191). The national control institution for the labor market under the fascist system of the Nazi state was built by the National Labor Order Act on January 20, 1934. Under this law, the management of enterprises was regarded as the managerial community composed of management leaders, and the subordinates and capitalists could regally secure the dominant position (Tsukamoto 1993, p.271). Thus, labor relations in the period of the Third Reich can be regarded as one body between capital and labor in a manner of absolute obedience of workers to enterprises.

Regarding **industrial systems based on interfirm relationships** during the Third Reich, credit control significantly impacted banks' credit and security businesses and personnel connections. Various capital-building funds were raised through public means, and the function of bank financing was discontinued. The role of outside funds in raising long-term funds for industries declined, and bank investment credit was effectively excluded from the capital procurement process (Lurié 1947, S.60). The state's promotion of company self-financing was also an important factor influencing the banks' business.

The Nazi state enforced company self-financing and absorbed the profits by issuing war national debts and Mefo bills and allocating such funds to necessary military goods (Yamaguchi 2006, p.7). Companies' self-financing progressed through various economic policies, such as the preferable tax system for equipment investment in 1933, reinforcing monopolies by the Constraint Cartel Law and the Dividend Restrictive Act in 1934 (Neumann 1942, pp.240–241, 261). The Dividend Restrictive Act made the capital market less appealing, which limited capital procurement. Although this law was moderated in 1936, private companies could not access capital markets until 1939, when it was abolished (Neumann 1942, pp.259, 261). Companies used the accumulation of unpaid dividends to expand equipment, capital, and monopolistic control over other companies. The tax laws in the first stage of the rearmament until 1936 also restrained the payment of dividends; thus, self-financing became advantageous by admitting rooms of depreciation in the balance sheet for taxation, allowing the immediate depreciation of nondurable economic goods (Spoerer 1996, S.115). These results show a significant increase in the significance of self-financing in the Third Reich (Spoerer 1996, S.116).

Industrial enterprises expanded their power into almost all other economic activities, including the fields of banks and insurance companies (Neumann 1942, p.264). Despite the possibility of worsening capital raising in free capital markets from 1933 to 1936 and the prohibition on security issuance, customers in industries repaid their borrowings. As a result, banks, an important economic sector, barely functioned (Spoerer 1996, S.114–115). The prevalence of self-financing over loans in monopolistic enterprises indicated an overall decline in the role of bank capital. However,

Neumann (1942, pp.261–262) indicates that the dominant position in finance capitalism shifted from the bank to the industrial enterprise, or what was regarded as the combined body of bank and industrial enterprise (Neumann 1942, pp.261–262).

Furthermore, the Great Economic Crisis that began in 1929, the temporary nationalization of banks, and the impact of bank restructuring were all important factors in the crisis of big banks. The number of supervisory board positions was limited by law as a response to the bank crisis of 1930/31. The 1931 Corporations Act prohibits holding more than 20 mandates on boards (Windolf 2014, p.73; David and Weserhuis 2014, p.16), concerned with the personnel connections between banks and industrial enterprises. Economic policy toward munitions production and the war economy also affected personnel connections. "The trustful network" between industry managers and banks no longer had a decisive meaning in obtaining information and planning strategy and had a definite network with the people in charge of the significance of political decisions (Wixforth 2006, S.893).

In this way, under the Nazi regime, bank credits were not used to strengthen business relationships with industrial enterprises or to increase bank influence. Business relations established through loans and securities issuance deteriorated, resulting in a shift in the foundation for personnel connections through director assignment and the interlocked directorate. With this shift and the increased importance of personnel relations with the people in charge of political decisions, the importance of the interlocking directorate diminished slightly.

The characteristics of **the financial system** in the period of National Socialism are apparent in the financial system based on control over capital allocation by the state. Government finance significantly impacted financial intermediation in the 1930s, and capital markets were reserved for government financing. Private issuance of shares and securities requires special permission (Hardach 1984, p.233). Self-financing promoted by the state for economic advancement and as an integrated component of the superior strategy of resource control in the entire economy built an important foundation for "monopolization of the capital market by state" (Lurié 1947, S.99). The financial system in the Nazi era was an institute to smoothly raise funds for the militarization of the economy and the war economy. At the same time, the system restricted the flow of capital into the private sector by controlling capital and investment and promoting the self-financing of companies.

Examining **the structure of productive forces** shows that the special character of their development in the Nazi period was in the great expansion based on munition markets. Regarding the improvement of the driving system of production equipment (Yamazaki 2001b), Allgemeine Elektricitäts-Gesellschaft (AEG), which provided electric motors, indicated that in the industry in the 1930s, separate driving by an electric motor was more appropriate for the demands of enterprises and replaced the group driving method which had been popular until that point (Allgemeine Elektricitäts-Gesellschaft 1958, S.18). The adoption rate of alternating current (AC) electric motors suitable for the individual driving method to all electric motors for means of labor increased in the 1920s. However, the decision regarding selecting between direct current (DC) and AC was not evident in this period due to the economically disadvantageous results caused by the diversity of types on the producer side

(Siegel and von Freyberg 1991, S.232; von Freyberg 1989, S.85). The situation significantly changed in the 1930s, and the use of AC electric motors came to dominate the field. W. Weigel (1939, S.167) emphasized in 1939 that three-phase AC motors were primarily used in most cases of small and medium machine tools. Moreover, despite cases where DC motors were suitable for small and medium machine tools to make the large coordination scope by electricity as much as possible in the working process, DC motors were chosen only for large machine tools (Weigel 1939, S.167). Mommerz (1981, S.144–145) also stressed that DC motors were popular only in large types of machine tools during the Nazi era, while cheaper AC motors were predominantly used in smaller or medium types of machine tools (Mommerz 1981, S.144–145). Improving production equipment based on the driving system's transformation helped increase the productive forces for munitions. In the transition to the separate driving method of machines, the large-scale fixation of such a driving system with a broad basis progressed in the latter half of the 1930s (Mottek et al. 1975, S.36). However, many enterprises and plants still used transmission apparatus to drive machine tools even in the 1930s (Mommerz 1981, S.136), and some limitations in the diffusion of the separate driving methods occurred.

Meanwhile, in developing productive forces based on the deployment of the Ford system, as examined in Chapter 12, the qualitative characteristics of the munitions market greatly influenced such changes. Indeed, the munitions market was tremendous in scale; however, the kinds of munitions in demand have frequently changed with modifications or fundamental changes in the plans to prepare munitions. Varieties of munitions, the rapidity of technological innovation, and short delivery times were important characteristics of this market. In particular, short-term appointed delivery days made gathering orders of the same types of products difficult for mass production (Siegel and von Freyberg 1991, S.268; Weis 2004, S.21, 25). Such situations made it necessary for German enterprises to implement flow production methods, considering production flexibility to adapt to specific munitions market conditions.

During National Socialism, the increase of productive forces progressed through the further prevalence of synthetic production methods for munitions. Such instances were common in various sectors, such as synthetic rubber, fuel, and fiber. Moreover, the expansion of using such production methods was significant for driving the autarky policy and performing the war by creating various products rather than products made from natural resources. Through the large-scale investment in equipment and R&D, the development of productive forces based on the synthetic production method contributed to achieving the goals of the Second Four-Year Plan.

As regards **the industrial structure**, the state put the producing goods industries over the consumer goods industries, significantly changing the investment structure by increasing the proportion of the producing goods industries to investment in industry (Okamoto 1993, p.173). The rapid expansion of industrial sectors related to munitions under the Second Four-Year Plan brought about great differences in development between such industries and other industries or among the producing goods industries, contributing to munitions production. This situation strengthened the characteristic of the industrial structure in which the producer goods industries dominated while restricting the development of the consumer goods industries. Furthermore, mass production based on the enlargement of the munitions market under the militarization of the economy and the war economy encountered great limitations in developing the national economy. These challenges arose due to the relatively narrow range in which it could generate demands for the related industrial sectors, which did not change the industrial structure led by the producer goods industries until then. A substantial part of automobile production was converted to producing munitions and manufacturing products such as aircraft parts, engines for aircraft and ships, and tanks at a high rate (The United States Strategic Bombing Survey 1947a, p.1; The United States Strategic Bombing Survey 1947b, p.4; British Intelligence Objectives Sub-Committee 1946, p.1); however, the range of industrial sectors related to procuring materials and parts was much narrower than that of automobiles. Thus, the delay in the development of the automobile industry restricted the fundamental change in the industrial structure based on the development of consumer goods, particularly durable consumer goods such as seen in the period after World War II.

Regarding **market structure**, the restrictive conditions that made access to world markets much more difficult for German enterprises were created due to the birth of the Hitler government (Plumpe 2018, S.123). One of the most important characteristics of the commodity market was the expansion of the munitions market and its qualitative nature. The scale of the munitions market was tremendous, and the types of munitions in demand frequently changed with modifications or fundamental changes in the plans to prepare the munition. Varieties of munitions, the rapidity of technological innovation, and short delivery times were important characteristics of this market (Siegel and von Freyberg 1991, S.268, Weis 2004, S.21, 25). These characteristics of the munitions market brought about the limitation of mass production. Furthermore, price control measures such as price stops influenced the commodity market.

The expansion of markets based on the concept of "the extensive market" was pursued by Nazi Germany during World War II. The plan, in which Europe was the arena of war while enlarging munitions and strengthening the Eastern orientation, aimed to build a more advantageous foundation for the reproduction of capital under German rules. In this plan, while "Germany would be the manufacturing heartland of its own area," "the international division of labor would be modified into specialization of function within each area" (Milward 1987, p.9). As well as the system of such division of labor, the exchange rate set in favor of the RM and the bilateral commercial agreement with countries controlled by Germany (Ambrosius and Hubbard 1986, S.262) contributed to a market structure that could support the existence sphere for this country.

In the labor market, labor control was deeply concerned with market characteristics peculiar to Germany in this period. Based on the Law of Labor Trustee (Gesetz über die Treuhänder der Arbeit) in May 1933, the price-fixing of the labor force commodity was regulated by a labor trustee as an officer of the empire state, whom the Minister for Labor appointed. Thus, negotiation over the determination of wages was denied, and the price fixing of wages based on the market price mechanism was replaced with a system done by a third party other than the worker and the capitalist

(Tsukamoto 1964, p.270). Such price control in the labor market needed the control of the allocation of the labor force by the state instead of the labor force's movement according to wage changes, and various control measures were adopted (Tsukamoto 1964, pp.273–275).

In the financial market as well, various control measures were implemented, and the state promoted the monopolization of the capital market (Lurié 1947, S.99). The capital market was the closed condition for private enterprises due to the influences of the Dividend Restrictive Act in 1934, which aimed at the transformation of capital flow into the market of bonds of the state (Neumann 1942, pp.259, 261). Thus, under the emphasis of state financing, the financial market in the Nazi era became special characters unseen in the period of the Weimar Republic.

Based on the previous analysis, in looking at **enterprise–market relationships**, one of their most prominent characteristics can be observed in the state control of the price, the volume to be produced, and the flow of capital. Similar control is also observable in the use of raw materials, development of investment, and determination of wages. Control by state restricted and obstructed functions of market forces based on the demand–supply relation. During National Socialism, the market under the controlled economy greatly influenced corporate behavior.

Figure 3.3 presents a graphical overview of the total system of business management in Germany during the period of National Socialism, based on our discussions.

3.4 Overview of the Total System of Business Management After World War II

Following that, this section considers conditions after World War II. When we examine overall ties with business management, at the global level, we find a "world structure of capitalism" that reveals the mutual relationships within the capitalist bloc. However, given the leadership and aid of victor nations, this structure poses a problem in global relationships, particularly those in markets and capital, which can be seen in the framework for the global structure of capitalism that is centered on the postwar US. The United States led building of postwar world order as the strongest hegemonic nation. US global strategy can be seen in establishing international economic institutions in both aspects of free trade and international monetary systems and the Marshall Plan aiming at rapid rebuilding of economies and opening of markets of European nations (Stolper et al. 1964, S 272; Schröter 2005, p.8; Kudo et al. 2004, p.8). It pursued to create the global linkages of market and capital. Furthermore, efforts to create broader and deeper linkage within some European countries through building common markets also promoted economic integration.

Regarding the total system of business management, in examining **state–enterprise relations**, whereas the Cartel Ordinance of 1923 was based on "abuse regulations" principles, the Restrictive Trade Practices Act passed after World War

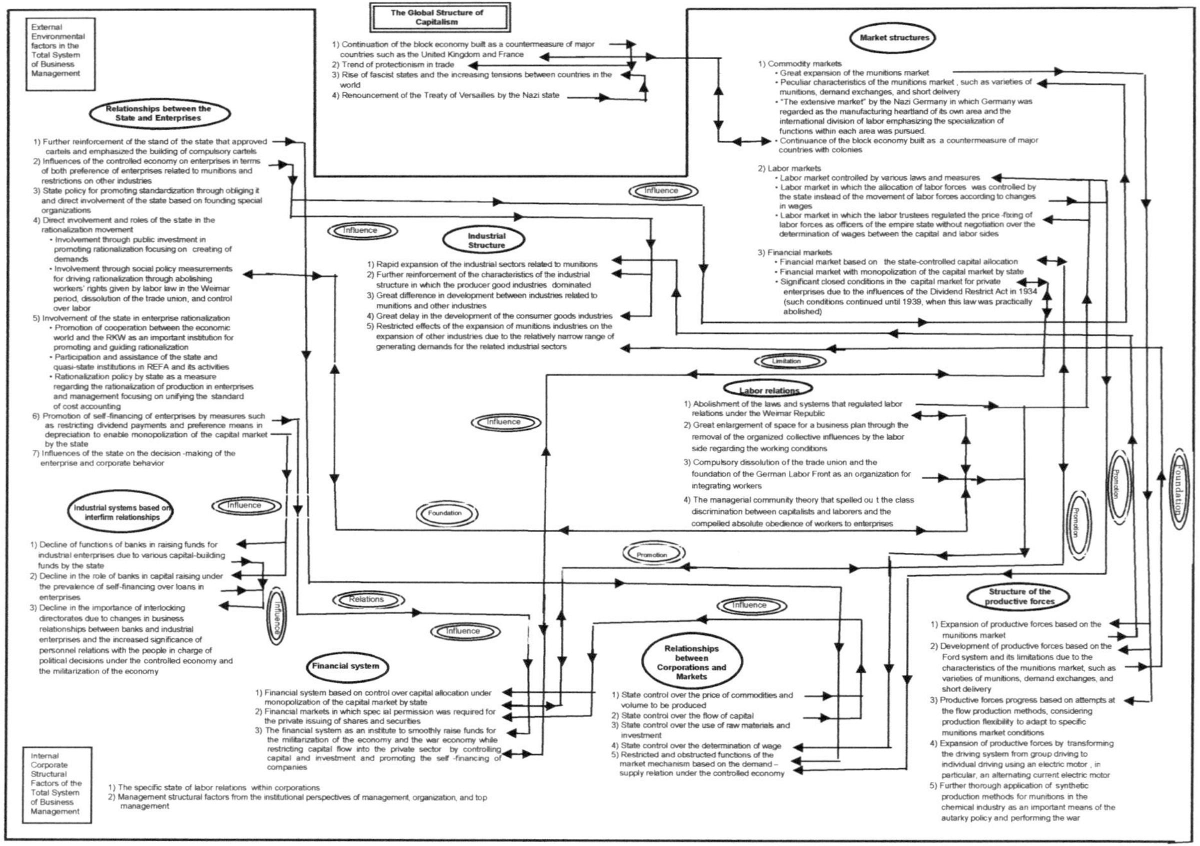

Fig. 3.3 Overview of Germany's total system of business management during National Socialism
Source This figure was compiled by the author, based on discussions in this chapter

II aimed to destroy cartels was enacted on the basis of "prohibition" principles, [*National Archives*, RG59, 862A.054, Developments concerning the German Cartel Law (1956.7.3), pp.1–2; Dyas and Thanheiser 1976, p.132]. Prohibiting cartels was regarded as an American import that did not apply to German economic conditions (Hennecke 2025, S.363). From an industrial perspective, the Restrictive Trade Practices Act weakened the principled prohibition of cartels to the extent that the industrial world was satisfied (Takahashi 1997, pp. 250, 256; Shaev 2022, pp.84–89). Regulatory mechanisms under the Restrictive Trade Practices Act, which dealt with regulatory and anti-monopoly policies influenced business development based on trust, which replaced cartels, and a complementary division of labor in the product fields within large corporate groups (Yamazaki 2024a, 4.2). As Harm G Schröter points out, "even in Germany, where the war had ended both the legal possibility and the unchallenged trust in economic cooperation, the change of paradigm in favor of competition needed considerable time to be implemented" (Schröter 1997, p.201). Furthermore, in the 1930s, the dominant view on international cartels was potentially positive; however, attitudes toward interfirm cooperation drastically changed after World War II and became notably hostile (Fellman and Shanahan 2022a, b, p.10).

Within industrial policy, investment aid policy, as well as currency reform and re-evaluation of company assets, had a significant impact on the financial market by encouraging corporate self-financing and lowering the rate of direct financing through the issuance of securities. The overall industrial structure was also influenced by industrial policy, particularly the heavy and chemical industries. It supported international competitive power in the capital goods market structure, which was the foundation for the industrial structure and heavily weighted toward goods-producing industries. Furthermore, trade policy efforts to form a common market structure, such as that in Western Europe, were underway; however, the government's response to the policy had a significant impact on the structure of commodities markets. The establishment of a common market contributed to the further strengthening and supplementation of the European region's global market connectivity. It also promoted the building of a foreign trade pattern based on German international competitive power, which was biased toward exportation in markets of that region and a "complementary division of labor in industrial and product fields." Economic integration efforts aimed at establishing blocks of a market control system for German enterprises on a Western European scale, against the backdrop of gaps in productive forces and competitiveness gaps with Germany's neighboring countries.

For **labor relations**, the basic characteristics of the new framework for labor relations in postwar Germany can be observed in a dual system (1) the ability to negotiate agreements governing sales conditions for trade unions and the general framework for labor unions and employer associations; (2) works constitutions, which are agreements that specifically govern labor conditions between work councils and management on the basis of collective agreements (Jentsch 1995, p.218). Collective agreements were applied to corporations within a region's particular industry, and as a result, regardless of corporate size, wages tended to be applied horizontally (Allen 2006, pp.81–82). A system of industry-specific collective agreements in each region was an important source of regulatory power for labor unions. Such a system contributed to the reduction of intra-corporate wage disparities in industries, which, together with codetermination at the plant level, strengthened the foundation for employment and wage security, as well as social redistribution in a social market economy. By creating and reinforcing domestic markets, these safety nets coordinated labor markets and expanded commodity markets. The framework for systematic coordination to solve labor management conflicts also contributed to stable and harmonious coordination (Thelen 1991, p.2, p.13).

Furthermore, the codetermination system at the top levels of management secured autonomy in response to capital market pressures on business management caused by worker participation in supervisory boards. This independence was bolstered further by ties between an industrial system based on industry–bank relations. Even investment in vocational education for the company's workforce was encouraged by the systems. Investments in education and training laid the groundwork for diverse quality production that relied on skilled workers, as well as the development of production and marketing strategies in Germany (regarding diversified quality production, see Abelshauser 2003; Streeck 1992; Streeck 1997). As a result, the system promoted German corporate competitiveness and contributed to the building and maintenance of a foreign trade pattern that complemented industrial and product fields in European markets (Yamazaki 2024a, 12.3).

In considering **industrial system based on interfirm relationships** in terms of industry–bank relationships, such a system secured autonomy through coordination among banks and between industries and banks, and the involvement of bank representatives on corporate supervisory boards. The universal banking system, a specific banking sector, is an important component of the German model of capitalism. Expansion of the execution of voting rights using deposit stocks by large banks in the general meetings of industrial enterprises after World War II promoted the personnel ties on the supervisory boards. For example, in German corporations with a total amount of 545 million Deutsche Mark (DM) nominal capital (listed corporations excluding insurance companies), the ratio of deposited stocks of domestic and foreign financial institutions to all stocks was approximately 54% (292 million DM) in 1970 (Arndt 1974, S.16). Considering the proportion of banks' voting rights in AEG, Hoechst, BASF, Siemens, and Bayer as of 1975 was high as 89.29%, 88.62%, 87.15%, 81.02%, and 79.09%, respectively. The figure of August Thyssen was 45.28%. However, the proportion of owner-held stock voting rights held by banks in these corporations in banks was less than 1% (Monopolkommission 1978, S.560). These numerical figures indicate the significance of banks exercising voting rights via the deposited stock system.

Companies can design long-term strategies that are compatible with job security, skill acquisition, and high wages through close relationships between the company and the bank (Amable 2003, pp.12–13). Furthermore, industrial systems based on industry–bank relationships brought about a German-style system of corporate governance. The codedetermination system established by the Codetermination Act of 1976 was based on a structure with an equal number of labor and capital market members on the supervisory board. This type of system weakened the influence of shareholders in capital markets. Moreover, because the system of corporate governance was based on industry–bank coordination, it reinforced autonomy of management against shareholders in collaboration with the codetermination system. This system of industrial concentration hastened building of complementary relationships in product fields on the basis of product quality in the market, which further repressed price competition among enterprises. The system assisted German corporations in avoiding fierce price competition and served as an important foundation for the development of management methods that adopted a management style that focused on competing with quality. In response to global and domestic competition, such reforms aided in the development of large-scale businesses that incorporated cooperative relationships. In this way, industry-bank relationships were at "industrial system" as a German mechanism for developing enterprises, industry, and the economy based on close relationships between industry and banking.

Next, considering **the financial system** which had deep connections with the industrial system based on industry–bank relationships, financial systems had issues related to corporate financing. Mutual ties based on the universal banking system between credit businesses and securities businesses, as well as the role of the house bank among large-scale banks, served as an organizational foundation for the development of the collaborative industrial system based on industry–bank relations. The mutual ties also regulated the financial market structure, where credit and securities businesses were combined; this type of market structure is an important factor that determines the system of corporate governance in Germany.

In addition, one of the most important characteristics of **the structure of productive forces**, an element of German capitalism, was a production system based on vocational education and specialist qualifications, such as those provided under the Meister system. This encouraged the development of experience and skill, as well as investment in vocational education for company employees. Germany had a history of developing production systems based on prewar concepts of flexible production emphasizing quality and development of production systems aimed at achieving improved scale merit through lower production volume and flexibility in response to changes in product demand (von Freyberg 1989; Siegel and von Freyberg 1991; Stahlmann 1993). These built the foundation for the development of diversified quality production that relied on skilled workers. Thus, despite popular perceptions of "Americanization" following World War II, the historical development of productive forces, the system of vocational education and specialized skills, and labor utilization reflected in production all influenced changes in the structure of productive forces.

In the postwar era, **industrial structures** quickly developed in the durable consumer goods industries, as well as in the heavily represented producer goods industries and the heavy and chemical industries, which had international competitive power even before the war. The characteristics of the industrial structures contained (1) formation of German-style production systems, (2) international competitiveness in and skewed exporting toward European markets, and (3) a foreign trade pattern that complemented these industrial and product fields. In terms of the composition of industries with international competitiveness and their characteristics (technological, market, and product characteristics), an obvious nature can be observed in the predominance of sectors where product quality emphasizing functionality based on technological superiority was an important point determining competitive strength in the markets. Germany has built an industrial structure based on such industrial sectors after the war.

Even under the trend seen in the rapid development of consumer goods industries, as pointed out by Wengenroth, despite the universal Americanization of the consumer goods market and the management style, the traditional dominance of the producer goods industry in West Germany was reinforced rather than weakened because of the new competitive advantage pattern among postwar European manufacturers. Of course, a mass consumer society was established after the war; however, certain industrial structure characteristics enabled Germany to keep its own consumer society without developing a consumer goods industry that was strong enough to rival America (Wengenroth 1997, p. 161).

Moreover, looking at **market structures**, they contain commodity, finance, and labor markets. For commodity markets, a country's domestic and export market characteristics, the composition of regions and export market products, trade policy in export destination countries, and competition structures were all deeply concerned with not only price and quality competition and other competitive structures in a market but also company management behavior. Characteristics of German and European markets, which emphasized product quality and functionality, were important in the development of postwar business management and the Americanization of technology and management and were different from those in the US, where standardization was advanced. These market conditions were inextricably linked to corporate product strategy, marketing activities, and labor utilization. These market structures fostered diverse quality production centered on niche market segments and laid the groundwork for a labor division system that supplemented production fields in large corporate groups. Under such market conditions, German competitive strength in European markets, along with the bias toward exporting to these regions, built a pattern of foreign trade with a division of labor in a form complementary to their industrial and production fields. Since before the war, German heavy and chemical industries had a competitive advantage in the European market, and the complementary relationship of industrial and production fields was plain from the rapid development of processing and assembly industries postwar; this type of complementary relationship was stronger in Europe than in other regions. The common market in Europe had great meaning for the capitalistic accumulation of German enterprises. Given European markets that were regulated by a structure of productive forces aforementioned, the mutually complementary relationship among countries in the markets were strong in comparison with other regions. This highlights the importance of Germany's diverse quality production.

Building on the previous analysis, one can see the characteristics of a coordinated market economy in the labor market and its link with labor relations in **enterprise–market relationships** that are related to the state of marketization. In the industrial system, based on the financial system and industry–bank relations, there are characteristics of a coordinated market economy in the financial market. Furthermore, in terms of market structure, it has a relationship with a coordinated market economy in the commodities market, as it avoids price competition by focusing on quality competition through product specialization. The strength of competition is the most fundamental dimension that distinguishes various types of capitalism in product markets. Models of capitalism indicate different characteristics according to the pattern of dominant competition in the product's market (Amable 2003, p.113). In nations characterized as free-market economies such as the US and the UK, regulation of products markets is excessively low (Amable 2003, p.16), competition tend to be intense, and coordination is generally done through price channel. In products markets of nations of continental Europe including Germany, competition is less keen than in the US and the UK (Amable 2003, p.121).

It is worth noting that the market economy, which was coordinated at the highest levels of management through the codetermination system, and the industrial system, which was based on industry–bank relations, were both issues that were closely related to enterprise–market relationships. These issues were facilitated by the development of a German-style system of corporate governance that differed from the market-oriented corporate governance system and emphasized financial markets. To address the "limitations of marketization," measures such as social redistribution functions based on the principles of a social market economy, a framework of industrial relations based on the codetermination system, and an interest coordination system in an industrial system based on the universal banking system and industry–bank relations were implemented. Such characteristics of marketization are deeply integrated with the development of German-style business management emphasizing the significance of enterprise as a "social institution" or "social community."

Figure 3.4 is a graphical overview of the total system of business management in postwar Germany based on our discussions.

(1) The debtor rates in the current calculation of the total number of asset accounts of 19 large banks in Germany were 41% in 1914 (Goldschmidt 1928, S.60).
(2) The annual average amount of issuing industrial securities (stocks and bonds) measured by issue price were 159, 77, 338, 746, 357, and 840 million Mark in the 1883–1890, 1891–1894, 1895–1897, 1898–1900, 1901–1904, and 1905–1913 periods, respectively (Spiethoff 1955, Tafel 3)
(3) Mefo bills were bills issued by munition enterprises and accepted by Mefo (Metallurgidche Forschungsgesellschaft m. g. H.), playing a significant role in raising munition costs (Kawase 1995).

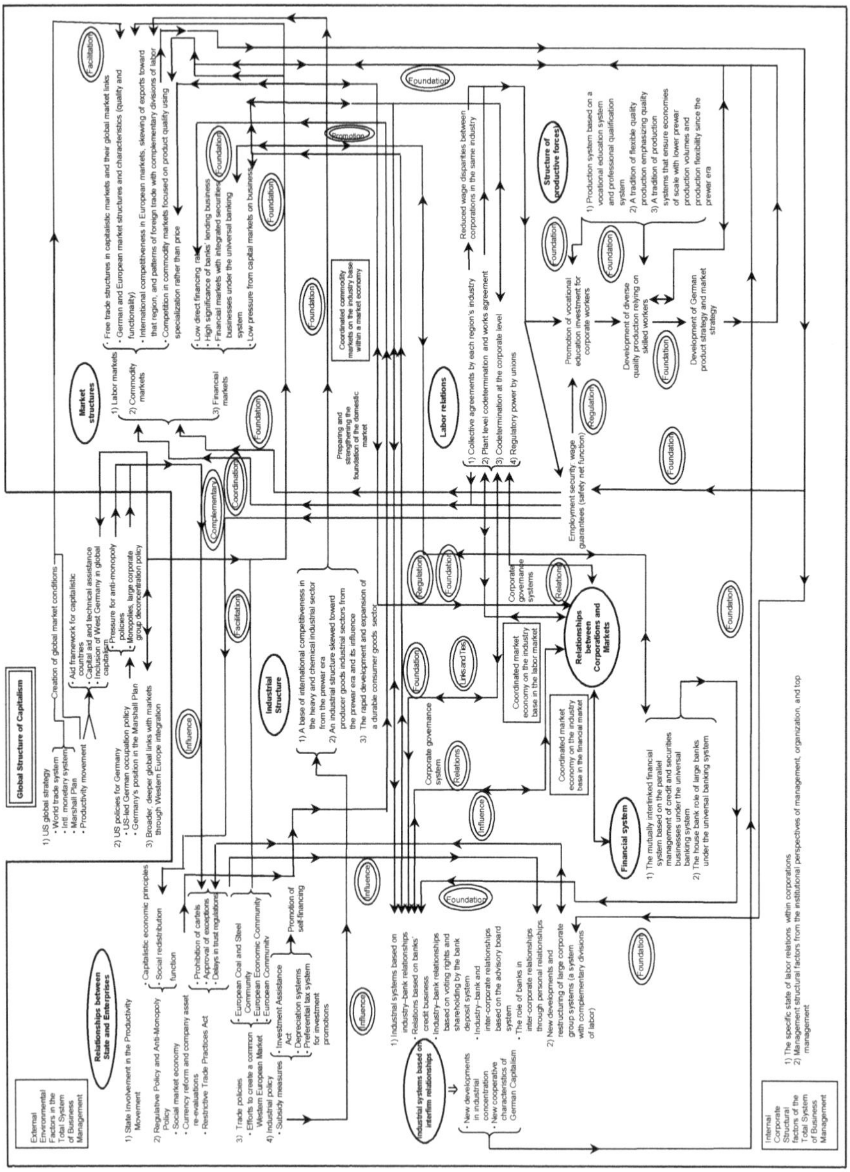

Fig. 3.4 Overview of Germany's total system of business management after World War II
Source This figure was compiled by the author, based on discussions in this chapter

References

Abelshauser W (2003) Kulturkamp. Der deutsche Weg in die neue Wirtschaft und die amerikanische Herausforderung. Kulturverlag Kadmos, Berlin

Abelshauser W, Hesse J-O, Plumpe W (2003) Wirtschaftsordnung und Unternehmen im Nationalsozialismus. Neue Forschungen zur Wirtschaftsgeschichte des Nationalsozilaisumus. In: Abelshauser W, Hesse J-O, Plumpe W (Hrsg) Wirtschaftsordnung, Staat und Unternehmen. Neue Forschungen zur Wirtschaftsgeschichte des Nationalsozilaisumus. Klartext, Essen, S.9–16

Adelmann G (1960) Quellensammlung zur Geschichte der sozailen Betriebsverfassung. Ruhrindustrie unter besonderer Berücksichtigung des Industrie- und Handelskammerbezirks Essen. Peter Hanstein, Verlag G.M.B.H., Bonn

Allen MMC (2006) The Varieties of Capitalism Paradigm. Explaining Germany's Comparative Advantage? Palgrave Macmillan, Basingstoke

Allgemeine Elektricitäts-Gesellschaft (1958) 75 Jahre AEG. Allgemeine Elektricitäts-Gesellschaft, Berlin, Frankfurt am Main

Amable B (2003) The diversity of modern capitalism. Oxford University Press, Oxford

Amamiya A (1994) 1920 nendai Doitsu ni okeru keizai kozo no henka to sono genkai (Change and its limitation of economic structure in Germany during the 1920s). Keizai Kenkyu (Economic Journal of Chiba University) 9(2):263–297

Ambrosius G, Hubbard WH (1986) Sozial- und Wirtschaftsgeschichte Europas im 20. Jahrhundert. C. H. Beck, München

Arndt H (1974) Wirtschaft und Macht. Tatsachen und Theorien. C. H. Beck, München

Bechtold H (1986) Die Kartellierung der deutschen Volkswirtschaft und die sozialdemokratische Theorie-Diskussion vor 1933. Haag + Herchen, Frankfurt am Main

Bergmann J, Jacobi O, Müller-Jentsch W (1975) Gewerkschaften in der Bundesrepublik. Gewerkschaftliche Lohnpolitik zwischen Mitgliederinteresen und ökonomischen Systemzwängen. Europäische Verlag-Anstalt, Frankfurt am Main

Berliner Handels-Gesellschaft (1956) Die Berliner Handels-Gesellschaft in einem Jahrehundert deutscher Wirtschaft 1856–1956. Brüder Hartmann, Berlin

Board of Trade (1904) Statistical abstract for the United Kingdom in each of the last fifteen years from 1889 to 1903. Majesty's. Stationary Office, London

Born KE (1957) Staat und Sozialpolitik seit Bismarcks Sturz. Ein Beitrag zur Geschichte der Innenpolitischen Entwicklung des deutschen Reichs 1890–1914. Franz Steiner Verlag GMBH, Wiesbaden

British Intelligence Objectives Sub-Committee (1946) BMW Passenger Car and Generator Engines. FIAT Final Report No.687, London

Brown WA Jr (1940) The international gold standard reinterpreted, 1914–1934. National Bureay of Economic Research Inc., New York

Chandler A (1990) Scale and scope: the dynamics of industrial capitalis. Harvard University Press, Berkeley, Massachusetts

Dahlem M (2009) Der Professionalisierung des Bankbetriebs. Studien zur Institutionellen Struktur Deutschen Banken im Kaiserreich 1871–1914. Klartext Verlag, Essen

David T, Weserhuis G (2014) Comparing corporate networks in a long-term perspective. In: David T, Weserhuis G (eds) The power of corporate networks. A comparative and historical perspective. Routledge, New York, pp.1–28

Der Deutsche Volkswirt (1937) Gesteuerte Eiseninvestitionen. In: Der Deutsche Volkswirt 11(52):2516–2517

Der Deutsche Volkswirt (1939) Klare Zuständigkeiten in der Rationalisierungarbeit. In: Der Deutsche Volkswirt 14(5):124

Der Vierjahresplan (1941) Der Weg der Rationalisierung. Der In: Vierjahresplan 5(12):657–658

Die Bank (1934) Widerspruchvolle Kartell-Politik? In: Die Bank 27(48):1733–1734

Die Bank (1937) Kartell-Pädagogik. In: Die Bank 30(34):1169–1171

Die Bank (1940) Gewandelte Kartell-Aufgaben. In: Die Bank 33(3):41–42

Duschnitzky Sv (1927) Das Konzern-Problem unter Berücksichtigung der Schwerindustriellen Wirtschaft im Nachkriegs-Deutschland: eine Sozialökonomischen Studie zu den Phänomenen der modernen kapitalistischen Konzentration. Kommissionsverlag der Deutschen Buchhandlung, Kaunas
D.W.I.-Bericht (1961) Die Deutsche Bank—Zentrum des deutschen Finanzkapitals. In: D.W.I. Bericht 12(15):1–23
Dyas GP, Thanheiser TH (1976) The emerging European enterpreise. Strategy and structure in French and German industry. The Macmillan Press, London
Erdmann G (1957) Die Entwicklung der deutschen Sozialgesetzgebung. 2. Erweiterte Auflage, Musterschmidt-Verlag, Göttingen
Fear JR (2005) Organizing control. August Thyssen and the construction of German corporate management. Harvard University Press, Cambridge, Massachusetts, London
Fellman S, Shanahan M (2022) International cartels in the real world: business, politics and diplomacy. In: Fellman S, Shanahan M (Hrsg) A History of Business Cartels. International Politics, National Policies and Anti-Competitive Behavior. Routledge, New York, pp 1–24
Goldschmidt RW (1928) Das deutsche Groβbankkapital in seimer neueren Entwicklung. Emil Ebering, Berlin
Hachtmann R (1989) Industriearbeit im 》Dritten Reich《. Untersuchungen zu den Lohn- und Arbeitsbedingungen in Deutschland 1933–1945. Vandenhoeck & Ruprecht, Göttingen
Hagemann H (1931) Das Verhältnis der deutschen Grossbanken zur Industrie. W. Christian, Berlin
Hardach G (1984) Banking and industry in Germany in the interwar period 1919–1939. In: J Eur Econ Hist 13(2):203–234
Etzold H (1988) Die Entwicklung der Produktivkräfte in der Industrie. In: Institut für Wirtschaftsgeschichte der Akademie der Wissenschaften der DDR, Berthold R et al. (Hrsg) Produktivkräfte in Deutschland von 1917/18 bis 1945. Akadermie Verlag, Berlin, S.36–223
Fellman S, Shanahan M (2022) International cartels in the real world: business, politics and diplomacy. In: Fellman S, Shanahan M (eds) A history of business cartels. international politics, national policies and anticompetitive behavior. Routledge, New York, pp 1–24
Hennecke R (2025) Wettbewerbsregulierung im Wirtschaftswunder. Die Kartellrechtspraxis in Westdeutschland unter den allierten Delartellierungsgesetzen, 1947–1957. De Gruyter, Berlin
Homburg H (1991) Rationalisierung und Industriearbeit: Arbeitsmarkt—Management—Arbeiterschaft im Siemens-Konzern Berlin 1900–1939. Haude & Spener, Berlin
Honma Y (1984) Gendai shihonshugi bunseki no kiso riron (Basic theory for analysis of modern capitalism). Iwanami shoten, Tokyo
Isay R (1955) Die Geschichte der Kartellgesetgebung. W. de Gruyter, Berlin
Iwamura M (2020) Kokka, kigyo, currency. Gurobarizumu no futsugona mirai (State, enterprise and currency: The unwarrantable future of globalism). Shinchosha, Tokyo
Jentsch WM (1995) Doitsu kigyo ni okeru roshikankei (Industrial relations in German enterprise). In: Ohashi S, Oda A, Schanz G (eds) Nihonteki keiei to Doitsuteki keiei (Japanese business managementand and German business management*)*. Chikura shobo, Tokyo, pp 217–234
Kaskel W (1920) Das neue Arbeitsrecht. Systematische Einführung. J. Springer, Berlin
Kato E (1973) Waimaru taisei no keizai kozo (Economic structure of the Weimar system). Tokyo daigaku shuppankai, Tokyo
Kawase Y (1995) Schacht no Mefo tegata (Mefo bill of Schacht). In: Shakai-keizai-shigaku (Socio-economic history) 60(5):655–682
Keiser G, Benning B (1931) Kapitalbildung und Investitionen in der deutschen Volkswirtschaft 1924 bis 1928. In: Institut für Konjunkturforschung, *Vierteljahrheft zur Konjunkturforschung*, Sonderheft 22, Reimar Hobbing, Berlin, 1-210
Kessler G (1907) Deutsche Arbeitgeber=Verbände. In: Schriften des Vereins für Socialpolitik 124:1–386
Kirchhoff HG (1958) Die staatliche Sozialpolitik im Ruhrbergbau 1871–1914. Westdeutscher Verlag, Köln, Opladen

Koch H (1907) Arbeiterausschüsse. Verlag der Zentralstelle des Volksvereins für das kath. Deutschland, M. Gladbach
Koehn O (1942) Normung und Leistungssteigerung. In: Zeitschrift des Vereins Deutscher Ingenieure 86(45/46):665–669
Kudo A, Kipping M, Schröter HG (2004) Americanization. Historical and conceptual issues. In: Kudo A, Kipping M, Schröter HG (eds) German and Japanese business in the boom years. Transforming American management and technology models. Routledge, London, New York, pp 1–29
Kuhlemann W (1908) Die Berufsverein. Gemeinsame Organisation. Dritter Band, Organisation der Arbeitgeber. Verlag von Gustav Fischer, Leipzig
Lampe L (2012) Der Bankbetrieb in Krieg und Inflation. Deutsche Groβbanken in den Jahren 1914 bis 1923. Franz Steiner Verlag, Stuttgart
Lenin WI (1953) Bericht über das Parteiprogramm auf dem VIII. Parteitag der KPR (B). In: Ausgewählte Werke: in zwei Bänden. Bd.II, Diez Verlag, Berlin, S.506–541
Ленин ВИ (1962) Империализм, как высшая стадия капитализма: популярный очерк. In: Полное собрание сочинений. Том 27, ос. изд-во полит. лит-ры, Москва, pp.299–426
Liefmann R (1897) Unternehmensverbände (Konvention, Kartelle). Ihr Wesen und ihre Bedeutung. J.C.B. Mohr, Leipzig
Liefmann R (1923) Kartelle. In: Elster L, Webwer A, Wieser F (Hrsg), Handwörterbuch der Staatswissenschaft, vierte, gänzlich umgearbeitete Auflage., V. Band, G. Fischer, Jena, S.611–630
Liefmann R (1932) Cartels, concerns and trusts. Methuen & Co., London
Lütcke K-P (1978) Dokumentation zur Organisationsgeschichte des deutschen Metallarbeiter-Verbandes. In: Quellensammlung zur Geschichte der deutschen Sozialpolitik 1867 bis 1914, Beihefte II. 2.12, S.1–148
Lurié S (1947) Private investment in a controlled economy. Germany, 1933–1939. Columbia University Press, New York
Maekawa K, Yamazaki T (1995) Doitsu gorika undo no kenkyu (Study of the German Rationalization movement). Moriyama shoten, Tokyo
Marshall A (1970) Industry and trade. A study of institutional technique and business organization; and of their influences on the conditions of various classes and nations. Fourth edition, Augustus M. Kelley, New York
Marx C (2013) Paul Reusch und die Guttehofnungshütte. Leistung eines deutschen Groβunternehmens. Wallstein Verlag, Göttingen
Milward AS (1987) War, economy, and society 1939–1945. Penguin Books, Harmondsworth
Mommertz KH (1981) Bohren, Drehen und Fräsen. Geschichte der Werkzeugmaschinen. Rowohlt, Hamburg
Monopolkommission (1978) Fortschreitende Konzentration bei Groβunternehmen: Hauptgutachte 1976/77 (Haupugutachten der Monopolkommission;2). 1.Auflage. Nomos-Verlagsgesellschaft, Baden-Baden
Mottek H (1964) Wirtschaftsgeschichte Deutschlands. Ein Grndriβ, Bd II, Von der Zeit der Französischen Revolution bis zur Zeit der Bismarckschen Reichsgründung. VEB Deutscher Verlag der Wissenschaften, Berlin
Mottek H, Becker W, Schröter A (1975) Wirtschaftsgeschichte Deutschlannds, Ein Grundriβ, Bd.III, Von der Zeit der Bismarchschen Reichsgründung 1871 bis zur Niederlage des faschistischen deutschen Imperialismus 1945, 2. Aufl., VEB Deutscher Verlag der Wissenschaften, Berlin
Müller H (1918) Geschichte der deutschen Gewerkschaften bis zum 1878. Paul Singer, Berlin
Naphtali F (Hrsg) (1928) Wirtschaftsdemokratie. Ihr Wesen, Weg und Ziel, 3., unveränderte Aufl., Verlagsgesellschaft des Allgemeinen Deutschen Gewerkschaftsbundes GmbH, Berlin
National Industrial Conference Board (1931) Rationalizatin of German Industry. National Industrial Conference Board, Inc., New York
Neumann F (1942) Behemoth: The structure and practice of National Socialism. V. Hollancz, London

Nitta S (1971) Kokka dokusen shihonshugi to gorika (State monopolistic capitalism and rationalization). Gendai hyoronsha, Tokyo
Nomura M (1980) Doitsu roshi kankeisi ron (Labor relations in Germany). Ochanomizu shobo, Tokyo
Ohashi S (1999) Doitsu keizai minshushugironshi (History of economic democracy theory in Germany). Chuo keizaisha, Tokyo
Okamoto T (1993) Taisenkanki shihonshugi no kenkyu (A study of capitalism in the interwar period). Hassakusha, Tokyo
Otsuka T (1987) Roshi kankei ron—Doitsu daini teiseiki ni okeru tairitsuteki roshi kankei no shoso—(Labor relations—Various aspects of the oppositional labor relations in Germany during the period of the Second Reich—). Kansai daigaku shuppanbu, Osaka
Petzina D (1977) Die deutsche Wirtschaft in der Zwischenkriegszeit. Steiner, Wiesbaden
Pieper L (1903) Die Lage der Bergarbeiter im Ruhrrevier. J. G. Cotta'sche Buchhandlung Nachfolger G.m.b.H., Stuttgart, Berlin
Plumpe W (2003) Unternehemen im Nationalsozialismus. Eine Zwischenbilanz. In: Abelshauser W, Hesse J-O, Plumpe W (Hrsg) Wirtschaftsordnung, Staat und Unternehmen. Neue Forschungen zur Wirtschaftsgeschichte des Nationalsozilaisumus. Klartext, Essen, S.243–266
Plumpe W (2018) Unternehmensgeschichte im 19. und 20. Jahrhundert. DeGruyter Oldenbourg, Berlin
Plumpe W (2022) Chemische Industrie. In: Boldorf M (Hrsg) Deutsche Wirtschaft im Ersten Weltkrieg. De Gruyter, Berlin, S.193–225
Pohl H (1978) Die Konzentration in der deutschen Wirtschaft vom ausgehenden 19. Jahrhundert bis 1945. In: Pohl H, Treue W (Hrsg) Die Konzentration in der deutschen Wirtschaft seit dem 19. Jahrhundert. Steiner, Wiesbaden, S.1–44.
Polanyi K (2001) The great transformation. The political and economic origins of our time. Beacon Press, Boston
Prion W (1931) Organization des deutschen Kapitalmarktes und der deutschen Bankwirtschaft. In: Harms B (Hrsg) Kapital und Kapitalismus: Vorlesungen gehalten in der Deutschen Vereinigung für Staatswissenschaftliche Fortbildung. Rear Hobbing, Berlin, S.327–355
Rassow P, Born KE (1959) Akten zur staatlichen Sozialpolitik in Deutschland, 1890–1914. Fritz Steiner Verlag GmbH, Wiesbaden
Reichskuratorium für Wirtschaftlichkeit (1930) Handbuch der Rationalisierung, Zweite, unveränderte Auflage. Spaeth & Linde, Berlin
Reuter UK (1967) Erfahrungen mit staatlicher Kartellpolitik in Deutschland von 1900 bis 1964 unter besonderer Berücksichtung der Zellstoffindustrie. Polygraphischer, Zürich
RKW-Nachrichten (1935) Rohstoff-Umstellung. In: RKW-Nachrichten 9(10):131–132
RKW-Nachrichten (1944) Normung. In: RKW-Nachrichten 18(5):72
Saul K (1974) Staat, Industrie, Arbeiterbewegung im Kaiserreich: zur Innen- und Aussenpolitik des Wilhelminischen Deutschland 1903–1914. Bertelsmann Universitätsverlag, Düsseldorf
Schmeer R (1939) Leistungssteigerung? In: Der Deutsche Volkswirt 13(18):845–848
Shaev (2022) International cartels in the political origins of German competition policy, 1949–1973. In: Fellman S, Shanahan M (eds) A History of Business Cartels. International Politics, National Policies and Anti-Competitive Behavior. Routledge, New York, pp.83–102
Shiomi H, Mizota S, Tanigchi A, Miyazaki S (1986) Amerika・Biggu bijinesu seiritushi (History of birth of big businesses in the United States). Toyo keizai shinposha, Tokyo
Schröter HG (1997) Small European nations: cooperative capitalism in the twentieth century. In: Chandler AD, Amatori F, Hikino T (eds) Big business and the wealth of nations. Cambridge University Press, Cambridge, pp 176–204
Schröter HG (2005) Americanization of the European economy. A compact survey of American economic influence in Europe since the 1880s. Springer, Dordrecht
Siegel T, von Freyberg T (1991) Industrielle Rationalisierung unter dem Nationalsozialisumus. Campus, Frankfurt am Main

Spiethoff A (1955) Die Wirtschaftliche Wechsellagen: Aufschwung, Krise, Stockung. II, Lange statistische Reihen über die Merkmale der wirtschaft-lichen Wechsellagen. J. C. B. Mohr, Tübingen

Spitzley H (1980) Wissenschaftliche Betriebsführung. REFA Methodenlehre und Neuorientierung der Arbeitswissenschaft. Bund-Verlag, Köln,

Spoerer M (1996) Vom Scheingewinnen zum Rüstungsboom. Die Eigenkapitalrentabilität der deutschen Industrieaktiengesellschaften 1925–1941. Franz Steiner, Stuttgart

Statistisches Reichsamt (1902) Statistisches Jahrbuch für das Deutsche Reich 1901. Puttkammer & Mühlbrecht, Berlin

Statistisches Reichsamt (1930) Gewerbliche Betriebszählung. Die Verwendung von Kraftmaschinen und Kraftfahrzeugen im Deutschen Reich und in den Ländern und Landesteilen. Teil I, Einführung in die Methode der Erhebung und Bearbeitung. Die Verwendung von Kraftmaschinen und Kraftfahrzeugen im Deutschen Reich. In: Statistik des Deutschen Reichs, Band 414, Verlag von Reimar Hobbing, Berlin: 1–147

Statistisches Reichsamt (1931) Statistisches Jahrbuch für das Deutsche Reich 1930. Verlag von Reimar Hobing, Berlin

Statistisches Reichsamt (1936) Statistisches Jahrbuch für das Deutsche Reich 1935. Verlag von Reimar Hobing, Berlin

Statistisches Reichsamt (1937) Statistisches Jahrbuch für das Deutsche Reich 1936. Verlag für Sozialpolitik Wirtschaft und Statistik, Berlin

Stolper G, Häuser K, Borchardt K (1964) Deutsche Wirtschaft seit 1870. J. C. B. Mohr, Tübingen

Streeck W (1992) Social institutions and economic performance: studies of industrial relations in advanced capitalist economies. Sage, London

Takahashi I (1997) Doitsu kyoso seigen kinshiho no seiritsu to kozo (Formation and structure of the Restrictive Trade Practices Act in Germany*)*. Sanseido, Tokyo

Teuteberg HJ (1961) Gechichte der industriellen Mitbestimmung in Deutschland. Ursprung und Entwicklung ihrer Vorläufer im Denken und in der Wirklichkeit des 19. Jahrhunders. J. C. B. Mohr, Tübingen

The United States Strategic Bombing Survey (1947a) Adam Opel, Rüsselsheim, *Final reports of the United States Strategic Bombing Survey*, No.81, second edition, Washington

The United States Strategic Bombing Survey (1947b) Volkswagen-Werke, Fallersleben, *Final reports of the United States Strategic Bombing Survey*, No.88, second edition, Washington

Thelen KA (1991) Union of parts. Labor politics in postwar Germany. Cornell University Press, Ithaca

Tohara S (1963) Doitsu kinyu shihon no seiritsu katei (Establishment of Finance capital in Germany). Tokyo daigaku shuppankai, Tokyo

Tokunaga Y (1977) Doitsu shihonsyugi to roshi kankei (German capitalism and labor relations). In: Tozuka H, Tokunaga Y (eds) Gendai rodo mondai (Modern labor problems). Yuhikaku, Tokyo, pp 217–314

Tsukamoto T (1964) Natisu keizai—Seiritsu no rekishi to ronri—(The Nazi economy. History and logic of its birth). Tokyo daigaku shuppankai, Tokyo

Ullmann P (1977) Tarifvertärge und Tarifpolitik in Deutschland bis 1914: Entstehung und Entwicklung, interessenpolitische Bedingungen und Bedeutung des Tarifvertragswesens für die sozialistischen Gewerkschafte. Peter Lang, Frankfurt am Main

Voelcker H (1904) Verhandlungen über den Halbzeug-Verband am 2. Und 3. Dezember 1903 im Reichstagsgebäude zu Berlin. Kontradiktorische Verhandlungen Über Deutsche Kartell 6:367–573

von Freyberg T (1989) Industrielle Rationalisierung in der Weimarer Republik: Untersucht an Beispielen aus dem Maschinenbau und der Elektroindustrie. Campus, Frankfurt am Main

Wagenführ R (1933) Die Industriewirtschaft: Entwicklungstendenzen der deutschen und internationalen Industrieproduktion 1800 bis 1932. In: Institut für Konjunkturforschung, *Vierteljahrheft zur Konjunkturforschung*, Sonderheft 31, Reimar Hobbing, Berlin, 1–69

Weigel W (1939) Elektrische Antrieb von Drehbänken. In: Maschinenbau 18(7/8):167-170

Weis J (2004) Die deutsche Automobilindustrie in der nationalsozialistischen Kriegswirtschaft —Opel, Daimler-Benz und Volkswagen, 1st edn. GRIN Verlag, München

Weiss H (1926) Rationalisierung und Arbeiterklasse:Zur Rationalisierung der deutschen Industrie. Führer-Verlag, Berlin

Wengenroth U (1997) Germany: competition abroad—cooperation at home, 1870–1990. In: Chandler AD, Amatori F, Hikino T (eds) Big business and the wealth of nations. Cambridge University Press, Cambridge, pp 139–175

Windolf P (2002) Corporate networks in Europe and the United States. Oxford University Press, New York

Windolf P (2014) The corporate networks in Germany, 1896–2010. In: David T, Weserhuis F (eds) The power of corporate networks. A comparative and historical perspective, Routledge, New York, pp.66–85

Wirtschaft und Statistik (1927) Erste Reichsgebiete der gewerbliche Betriebszählung vom 16. Juni 1925. In: Wirtschaf und Statistik 7(4):158–173

Wirtschaft und Statistik (1933) Die Investitionen in der deutschen Industrie 1924 bis 1931. In: Wirtschaft und Statistik 13(9):594–597

Witte IM (1930) Ford, fordismus. In: Giese F (Hrsg) Handwörterbuch der Arbeitswissenschaft, Bd. 1, C. Marhard, Halle, Spalte 1856–1865

Wixforth H (1995) Banken und Schwereindustrie in der Weimarer Republik. Böhlau, Köln, Weimar, Wien

Wixforth H (2006) Expansion der Dresdner Bank in Europa. R. Oldenbourg Verlag, München

Wixforth H, Ziegler D (1994) The Niche in the universal banking system: private bankiers within German industry, 1900–1933. In: Fin Hist Rev 1(1):99–119

Yamaguchi H (2006) Doitsu shoken shijyoshi kenkyu—Torihikisho no chiiki tokusei to togo katei—(Study of history of German securities markets—Regional characteristics and integration process of exchanges—). Hokkaido daigaku shuppannkai. Sapporo

Yamazaki T (2001a) Vaimaruki Doitsu gorika undo no tenkai (The development of the Rationalization movement in Germany during the Weimar era). Moriyama shoten, Tokyo

Yamazaki T (2001b) Nachisuki Doitsu gorika undo no tenkai (The development of the Rationalization movement in Germany during the Nazi era). Moriyama shoten, Tokyo

Yamazaki T (2024a) Japanese and German enterprises: Comparison of industrial concentration system and business management. Springer-Nature, Singapore

Yamazaki T (2024b) Relationships between Industry and Bank in Germany: A Historical Analysis of Personnel Connections through Interlocking Directorate and Bank's Advisory Council System. Springer-Nature, Singapore

Yanagisawa O (2006) Shihonshugishi no renzoku to danzetsu (Continuity and discontinuty in the history of capitalism). Nihon hyoronsha, Tokyo

Yanagisawa O (2013) Nachisu Doitsu to shihonshugi: Nihon no moderu he (Nazis Germany and capitalism: Model for Japan). Nihon Keizai hyoronsha, Tokyo

Yoshida K (1976) Doitsu gourika undo ron (German Raionalization movement). Mineruva shobo, Kyoto

Zigitschko A (1970) Ein ökonomisches Rätsel der Vergangenheit (Über den tendenziellen Verlauf der Fondintensitätsentwicklung in den USA seit 1880). In: Gesellschaftswissenschaftliche Beiträge, Jahrgang 1970, Heft 2:162–173

Part II
Business Management in the Second Reich Era

Chapter 4
Enterprise Concentration, Formation of Monopolistic Capitalism, and Business Management

Abstract Part I considered (1) the history of globalism of nations with hegemony and its influences on other countries and (2) the overall system of business management in Germany in each major period as a structural framework for conditions that define the established methods of business management within the characteristics of capitalism. Based on the discussions in Part I, Part II explores business management in Germany during the Second Reich, the period from the shift to monopolistic capitalism to the end of World War I. This chapter considers enterprise concentration, the building of monopolistic capitalism, and changes in business management with such phenomena from the perspective of international comparison with the United States (US) and industrial comparison. It first examines the first movement of enterprise concentration and its background. This chapter then analyzes the processes of concentration and the characteristics of monopoly formation that differ from those in the US. Furthermore, a monopolistic regulation policy is considered concerning trade and industrial policies. Moreover, the significance and limitations of enterprise concentration concerning business management problems will be clarified through a comparison with experiences in the US.

Keywords Cartel · Managerial coordination · Monopolistic capitalism · Monopolistic regulation · Syndicate · Trade policy · Trust

Part I examined the history of globalism of countries with hegemony and its influences on other countries and Germany's total system of business management as the structural framework defining a country's management style by applying the author's original framework. Following the analyses in Part I, Part II considers business management changes in the Second Reich. Part II covers three themes: (1) enterprise concentration and monopoly formation based on it, (2) labor management changes, and (3) the rise of modern business enterprises and changes in organizational structure.

The first movement of enterprise concentration occurred at the turn of the twentieth century in the United States (US) and Germany when both countries reached

T. Yamazaki, *A History of German Business*,
https://doi.org/10.1007/978-981-96-8476-2_4

the monopolistic stage of capitalism. This transformation led to business management changes. Therefore, Chapter 4, as Part I's first chapter, considers enterprise concentration and business management for the period from the shift to monopolistic capitalism to the end of World War I from a comparative perspective with the US. Section 4.1 examines the historical background of the movement toward enterprise concentration. In Sect. 4.2, actual situations of such concentration processes are analyzed to understand the German characteristics of enterprise concentration and the formation of monopolies. Section 4.3 clarifies the significance and limitations of enterprise concentration in relation to business management problems.

4.1 The First Movement of Enterprise Concentration and Its Historical Background

First, the historical background of the movement toward enterprise concentration that began at the late of the nineteenth century is considered. This movement occurred in the US and Germany and monopolies were promptly built. The appearance of this movement was determined by structural changes in capitalism in both nations brought about by the 1873 economic crisis. Crises in 1857 and 1866 were phenomena that occurred in the United Kingdom (UK) that had a high level of productive force and international competitivness and other capitalistic countries received the after-effects of these crises (Ono 1965, p.32). In contrast, economic crises caused by overproduction exceeding demand broke out in 1873 in both Germany and the US. As there were simultaneous crises in both countries during this period, the possibility of expanding exports was restricted. Therefore, conditions were extremely serious for these nations.

Furthermore, crises tended to be chronic phenomenon occurring at approximately 10-year intervals. This means that the level of productive force tended to exceed the scale of markets. An important change in the structure of capitalism can be seen at this point. Under such serious conditions, there were two effective methods to be chosen as countermeasures. The first was to maintain prices through regulations and to avoid competition. Enterprise concentration was an important measure and monopolistic system by some large enterprises built through such concentration. The second was attempts to reduce costs. In this period, reform of labor management systems by strengthening control over labor became an effective measure for reducing production costs.

Under such conditions, in Germany, building cartels or syndicates as higher levels of cartels progressed rather than trusts. However, monopolization and control of prices and markets by cartels or syndicates did not unconditionally become possible by agreement or consolidation but presupposed that the concentration of production had already progressed to a certain degree.

Another important movement of the formation of cartels in Germany aside from the crises after the 1873 excessive production crisis was the shift to a conservative customs system in 1879. The customs rate set in 1879 made it possible to promote concentration without considering foreign competitors and made it easy to reach an agreement regarding combination. Conservative customs made it easy to build cartels by decreasing the number of enterprises that were in competition and accelerated the establishment of such monopolistic organizations. Cartels were built internationally in case there were no conservative customs (Liefmann 1923, S.614; Liefmann 1897, S.66). For example, in the 1880s when efforts to establish pig iron cartels began in Germany, the strict building of the cartel was supported by the movement to set conservative customs (Wagenführ 1931, S.63).

In the domestic market, cartels set prices and allotments to each organization member. In contrast, in the foreign market, the volume that could be sold at the global market price was open for member enterprises and exceeded that in this market. Under such situations, belonging to a cartel was very profitable. As a result, the unified price and volume policy in the domestic market became possible in the middle term. Therefore, the conservative customs policy starting in 1879 was an important premise for the concentration process and cartelization (Bechtold 1986, S.81–82; Wengenroth 1985, S.18).

Without conservative customs setting high prices, cartels were unable to compete against the lower prices of imported products. Thus, the cartelization of Germany's national economy before 1914 was the result of customs policy. For example, customs on iron and steel products enabled domestic suppliers to absorb a part of the custom as producer rent. However, the premise for the custom was the exclusion of domestic competitors by the formation of a cartel. Cartels in the raw material industries promoted the formation of cartels and vertical concentration in the processing industries (Bechtold 1986, S.114). For example, in the pig iron cartel, maintaining high prices became possible by utilizing customs. As a result, customs and differences in freight were utilized in price-setting, despite the fact that production exceeded demand in Germany (Doering 1925, S.325–326). The formation of cartels was promoted by the exclusion of foreign competitors by regulating trade with conservative customs and protecting the domestic market. In addition, in the international market, the enlargement of the market became possible by dumping based on special profits in the domestic market. Thus, restrictive trade usage by cartels was inseparable from the conservative trade system (Yanagisawa 2006, pp.162–163). Cartels needed a protective duty for their existence (Morgenroth 1907, S.8–9). Protective tariffs were a measure to maintain domestic prices higher than those in the world market and load costs on domestic consumers to overcome the free competition of foreign competitors in the world markets (Morgenroth 1907, S.12).

The movement toward enterprise concentration in this period was promoted by the development of production technology and, remarkably, the development of industries based on it, the birth and expansion of new types of industries, and the development and diffusion of the joint-stock company system. The development of new industries (e.g., the electrical and chemical industries) was promoted by new technology such as electrification and chemicalization as well as key industrial sectors (e.g., the mining and iron and steel industries). The scale of required invested capital in these industries was very large. Under this situation, the rapid accumulation of capital became possible by preserving the joint-stock company system, which was useful as a means of concentrating capital (Maekawa 1993, pp.112–113). In addition, concentration and accumulation progressed in the banking sector. The bank functioned as the organizer of industrial enterprise concentration, which strongly promoted enterprise concentration (Jeidels 1905).

Regarding the development of the cartel-building movement in Germany until 1914, Ulrich Wengenroth pointed out some factors that made cartels stable—first, the state's competition policy and the Supreme Court's cartel-friendly jurisdiction. Second, there was a close connection between industry and large banks. Third, a protective tariff enabled the restriction of competition threatened by foreign countries. Fourth, the appearance of the labor movement was strictly organized on the basis of the essential prerequisite for putting through its requirements and position in concentration into large associations (Wengenroth 1985, S.23–24). Regarding the fourth point, cartel problems broadly included the labor market and, in a narrow sense, included only the commodity market (Hermann 1985, S.49).

4.2 Enterprise Concentration and the Formation of Monopolies in Germany Compared with the United States

4.2.1 Enterprise Concentration and the Formation of Monopolies in the United States

This section examines enterprise concentration and formation of monopolies in Germany. From the perspective of international comparison, cases in the United States will be considered.

In the US, the formation of cartels began around the 1870s. The decline in the prices of both industrial and farm products was remarkable in this period. The wholesale price index on all commodities fell by no less than 45.7% from 1869 to 1886. Under these conditions, "to most manufacturers, the only practical response to rising output and falling prices was to form national associations to maintain prices by curtailing production." As a result, by the "1880s these federations had become part of the normal way of doing business in most American industries." Trade associations were created in many industries to control prices and production. They appeared in the mechanical industries, including those producing lumber, woodwares, flooring, and furniture as well as those making shoes, saddlery, and other leather products. Such associations were also built in the reefing and other chemically oriented industries such as those producing petroleum, rubber footwear, explosives, glass, paper, and leather and in industries fabricating metals into products such as bars, wire, rail, nails, sheets, and all types of metal implements and machines as well as in the foundry and furnace industries (Chandler 1977, pp.316-317).

However, many such trade associations were not able to achieve their goals. A. D. Chandler, Jr. pointed out that "the temptation always existed to increase returns by cutting prices through direct rebates, by falsifying reports, or by dialing to record sales." Cases in which manufacturers left a cartel or openly cut prices to obtain more trade after the association succeeded in stabilizing prices could often be observed. Even in such situations, the agreement did not have the binding effect of a legal contract and could not be enforced in courts of law since cartels were illegal (Chandler 1977, p.317).

Therefore, a merger of the constituent forms into a single, legally defined company was required to realize more effective control over the member enterprises in the cartel association (Chandler 1977, p.319). Movement toward the formation of trusts began in the 1880s and became a general phenomenon in the 1890s. Most typical cases can be observed in the birth of the Standard Oil trust in 1882 and US Steel in 1901. The holding company prevailed as a form for concentrating an enterprise instead of a trust due to the Sherman Antitrust Act, which prohibited such concentration measures. This was deeply concerned with the existence of the New Jersey General Company Act, which enabled enterprises headquartered in this state to combine with other companies using a holding company. However, the role that the holding company played in concentration was not different from that of a trust. In the US at that time, merger or consolidation as a strategic option that enterprises could select was historically the first choice of many companies in various industries. Thus, many large enterprises that never existed until then were created with a stroke (Taniguch 2002, pp.6–7).

Regarding trusts or holding companies, the role of such concentration measures is more important for business management. Indeed, these forms of concentration functioned more effectively in restricting and regulating compared with cartels. However, the function of rationalization was more important. Trusts enabled the reduction of excess production capacity and concentration of production on the most advantageous plants in terms of technology and locating conditions among all manufacturing establishments of an enterprise that were included in a merger. Regarding this point, Chandler pointed out that all six of the successful pioneering trusts of the 1880s (Standard Oil trust, Cottonseed Oil trust, Linseed Oil trust, Sugar trust, Whiskey trust, and Lead Processing trust) had been formed to concentrate and rationalize production (Chandler 1977, pp.320–321). In the US, the consolidation or acquisition of enterprises was implemented repeatedly and ineffective plants were closed or reduced and production was concentrated on superior factories in this process (Maekawa 1993, p.164). As a result, a high level of productive forces was built.

Compared with attempts by individual, independent enterprises to reduce excess production capacity and concentrate production on specific plants or manufacturing establishments among maintained manufacturing equipment, such rationalization by consolidated companies such as trusts had a much larger effect. Maintaining and raising prices using monopolization delayed coordination between demand and supply through market mechanisms and was not always effective when the productive force exceeded demand. Overproduction tends to be a chronic phenomenon. The situation in which controlling falling prices could function more effectively was accomplished by consolidating enterprises through the rationalization function. This point is important in examining the functional problems of monopolies such as market control and price regulation.

4.2.2 Enterprise Concentration and the Formation of Monopolies in Germany

4.2.2.1 Enterprise Concentration and Its Characteristics

This subsection considers conditions in Germany. This country's domestic market was relatively small due to the characteristics of the birth and development of capitalism and pressure from other capitalistic nations such as the UK and the US was also strong. Under such conditions, a high rate of conservative customs was set, and dumping exports was often done to expand exports. Control by monopolies became necessary to shift domestic consumer profit losses caused by such dumping. As a result, a monopolistic system was built prematurely and monopolistic organizations such as the cartel were formed for enterprise concentration (Maekawa 1993, pp.163, 179). "Whereas cartels were still the exception and still a transitory phenomenon and were not durable despite of their development after the crisis of 1873," cartels became "one of the foundations of the whole of economic life" at the end of the nineteenth century (Ленин 1962, S.317).

Exports at low prices were promoted by cartels and export dumping in German industries based on price controls in the domestic market through cartels, which secured and increased their economic power in foreign countries [Liefmann 1897, S.167; *Bundesarchiv Berlin*, R1501/107158, Bericht der Zentral-Stelle für Gewerbe und Handel betreffend Erhebungen über Zahl, Bestand und Wirksamkeit der in Württemberg ansässigen Kartelle (11.6.1902), S.6]. As Jefferey R. Fear points out, German industrialists tended to long regard foreign markets as a "safety valve" to keep production volume high (Fear 2005, p.256) and export dumping was considered an essential means of increasing sales in foreign markets. In the acquisition of enterprises, many cases were implemented with the purpose of increasing allotments under such conditions. In concentration by the vertical combination of multiple industries or production processes, there were many cases in which enterprises in the raw materials and semifinished products sectors were acquired to cope with changes in product prices in these sectors by cartels and syndicates. Thus, interests tended to be emphasized on share to be obtained in aspect of distribution (Maekawa 1993, p.165; Tohara 1974, pp.273–276, 305).

However, without simultaneous regulation of production, as well as price, markets could not be controlled by means of sales and prices (Maschke 1969, p.231). Therefore, many cartels and syndicates gave member companies an allotment of production volume for the purpose of regulating output. For instance, the purpose of the Rheine-Westphalia Coal Syndicate (Rheinisch-Westfälisches Kohlen-Syndikat), established in 1893, was "to regulate the output of coal by quotas given to the different members and to prevent price competition through price fixation" (Michels 1928, pp.68–69). However, each member enterprise could abandon production equipment and close ineffective plants on the basis of free decision-making. In addition, decisions regarding allotment volume were often based on criteria such as actual production. In reality, cases in which drastic reduction of excessive production capacity was accomplished and rearrangements that enabled the best productive structures through concentration and production specialization, as seen in rationalization by trusts in the US, were rare. As a result, enterprises in Germany were forced to bear disadvantageous production costs compared with American companies.

In Germany, consolidations such as trusts and mergers occurred, but cartels or syndicates were the main forms for concentrating enterprises. In general, cartels tended to be suitable and effective in sectors in which the production process was relatively simple, such as the coal mining industry. However, in industrial sectors in which the production process was complicated and many kinds of products were manufactured and new products would be developed in a relatively short term, it did not have major significance (Liefmann 1932, p.29; Liefmann 1897, S.61; Maekawa 1993, p.165). Most suitable commodities can be seen in the material sectors fields such as coal, iron, and potash, where cartelization was realized first and most completely (Maschke 1969, *op. cit.*, p.228).

For example, in the mining industry, the equality of products, the commonality of interests and similarity of mining costs determined by the geographical conditions of coal production, and the limited value of products in relation to transportation costs were factors that made agreement between enterprises easy. A memorandum submitted to the Imperial Parliament in 1907 regarding cartel organization pointed out that cartelization movements were most broadly developed in the mining industry [*Bundesarchiv Berlin*, R/3001/7921, Denkschrift über das Kartellwesen, Dritter Teil, Die Kartelle des Kohlenindustrie (21.3.1907), S.1–2]. In the raw material industries, the required volume of consumption was determined by the production volume of products manufactured by using and processing such raw materials. Therefore, the higher the concentration degree covered by the cartels was, the higher the possibility of controlling the price.

In contrast, for example, in the electrical industry, cartels were forced to encounter difficulties due to the variety of products. In addition, the rapid tempo of technological development made formation of cartels impossible for certain products (Wagenführ 1931, S.143). In the mechanical engineering industry, cartelization faced the greatest difficulties. The great variety of products required for the purpose of countering the customer's own specifications made such attempts extremely difficult (Maschke 1969, p.238).

Under such conditions, in Germany, cartels were formed first in industrial sectors that manufactured interchangeable products or mass products such as the coal, iron and steel, and chemical industries. In industries that fabricated specialized products or treated semifinished products, cartels were the weakest and fewest. Cartelization progressed most slowly in cases in which there was little production of mass-produced products and a limited number of large companies (Riesser 1912, S.147).

When examining the number of cartels, in 1905, in the mining and iron and steel industries there were 19 and 62, respectively, but in the electrical industry, there were only two. There were great differences between these industries in the ratio of the production of cartel member enterprises to total production. In 1907, the number of cartels in the mining industry was 74%. Those in coal and crude steel were 82% and 50%, respectively, and greatly exceeded the numerical value of the entire German industry (about 25%). In contrast, in the electrical industry, this number was only 9% (Fischer 1976, S.811; König 1960, S.307, 310–311).

Therefore, in considering conditions in the iron and steel industry, the number of cartels in the steel industry exceeded that in the coal and iron industries, since the steel industry produced many different kinds, grades, and forms of steel (Michels 1928, pp.94–95). However, there were differences in terms of the effects of price regulations among products. "Unlike the coal and pig-iron cartels, which handled relatively homogenous products," the important Steel Works Association (*Stahlwerksverband*) was "a comprehensive, national cartel that encompassed an extensive array of heterogenous steel products" (Fear 2005, p.245). In this association, which was established in 1904, "A" products such as semifinished products, rails, and form irons were under syndicate agreement regulations on all points. In contrast, other rolling mill, "B" products such as bar iron, rolled wire, steel plate, and steel tube steel tubing, which were not considered A products, only the decisions regarding the allotment of supply to each plant were planned. These products were sold not by the cartel organization but by each steel manufacturer or by the cartel to which they belonged such as the rolled wire cartel or steel tube cartel. Such conditions differed greatly from that of the steel cartel in the Oberschlesien region (Böllter 1907, S.77–78; Tohara 1974, p. 309). Despite fewer companies making B-products, cartelizing B-products was harder than A-products due to the greater heterogeneity of B-products compared with the more homogenous A-products. Furthermore, a strong outsider existed (Mannesmann) and "August Thyssen, who insisted on having B-products completely syndicated or not at all" (Fear 2005, p.246). In this way, attempts to eliminate competition through price- and production-allotment cartels and their effects differed between production process departments. The conditions in the sector producing pig irons as the most homogeneous products were more favorable than in other sectors (Fremdling and Krengel 1985, S.33).

In examining the effects of the cartel, the prices of pig iron in Germany exceeded those in the UK from 1900 through the outbreak of the World War I. In contrast, the price of rolled iron in Germany was lower than that in foreign countries, especially in the UK. The main reason for this was because in Germany, strong syndicates did not exist in the finished products industry with any characteristics of equity (Doering 1925, S.321, 323–324, 326–328), whereas strong cartelization of products such as pig iron and semifinished products with characteristics of equity existed before World War I.

In the coal and the iron and steel industries, the existence of mixed enterprises that integrated businesses in both industries greatly influenced the effect of cartels and the controlling power of monopolies. In the production of pig iron, sales were not the main problem, as seen with other large cartels, but self-consumption was the main issue. Mixed enterprises consumed the most pig iron in the company and were able to build high-level competitiveness by selling the remaining pig iron at a lower price. Unequal competitive conditions between mixed enterprises and furnace enterprises that did not integrate other production process and were therefore forced to sell all of their pig iron in markets became an important conflict between the parties (Pinner 1908, S.971–972). The existence of mixed enterprises also caused opposition between coal mining companies and companies integrating ironworks. The behavior of the latter was determined not by its interests in coal but in iron (Silberberg 1910, S.1046–1047).

Mixed enterprises took control over the largest part of production volume from cartels. The more the mixed enterprises prevailed, the less effective the cartels became. Thus, the development of such enterprises as typically German brought big changes in the controlling power of monopolies. Such power was not limited to only individual production departments such as coal, pig iron, or steel but came to reach all heavy industries, including the coal and iron and steel industries, through unified methods. Institutions for the reproduction of capital during the stage of control by mixed enterprises were established (Tohara 1974, pp.310–313).

In the iron and steel industry, competition within the cartel system could not be excluded for several reasons. (1) "since sales or production quotas would be renegotiated in the near future, industrialist attempted to put themselves in the best possible position for the next round of negotiations." (2) "German steel industrialist competed across a broad array of syndicated and non-syndicated goods." (3) "cartels altered the strategic incentives of German steel companies." (4) "because the prices of raw materials and of many intermediate products were guaranteed, profit margins could rise by increasing the difference between the cartel-set price and production costs through greater scale or scope economies, or higher technical efficincy, or both." (5) "since domestic market share was regulated, the export market was one way of dumping excess production." (6) "excess production could be consumed by oneself if downstream parts of the vertical combine processed materials into finished products" (Fear 2005, pp.254–257).

In the iron and steel industry, the appearance of competition was probable by the most effective substitutes for German pig irons, such as the iron and steel scraps and foreign pig irons that both served as substitute materials for German foundries and steel plants (Fremdling and Krengel 1985, S.35). This situation was also an important factor restricting the effects of cartels or syndicates in the iron and steel industry.

In the electrical industry, in contrast to situations in the iron and steel industry, the formation of cartels based on cooperation in the field of techniques including license pool agreements had significance due to factors such as the importance of technology and the rapid tempo of technological progress. In addition, in heavy electrical department products in which order production was fundamentally dominant, setting cartel prices as seen in standardized products was not possible. Especially when the tender system was adopted, tender agreements in which contract prices were manipulated were created (Yoshida 1987, pp.57–62). The formation of cartels had special characteristics in the electrical industry compared with other industrial sectors. In this industry, enterprises attempted to extend their control into fields supplying all or a considerable part of their raw materials by means of methods such as fusion, special participations, and agreements or contracts from the beginning (Brady 1933, p.177). The consolidation of enterprises can be observed in, for instance, the merger of Union or Lahmeyer group by AEG in 1903 or 1910, respectively, and the merger of Schuckert by Siemens & Halske in 1903. In these mergers, rationalization measures such as cutting down overlapping departments, rearranging production departments, and downsizing management departments were performed (Ishiro 1972, pp.115–120).

In the chemical industry, although cartels encountered limitations due to the large number and variety of products in this industry, enterprise concentration began early. Erich Maschke pointed out that "since only homogenous commodities could be cartelized, one at a time, with the object of achieving a uniform market price, a very large number of cartels representing various chemicals—bromide, ferro-cyanide, etc.—were formed" (Maschke 1969, p.230). However, a stronger form of enterprise concentration tended to be adopted in this industry.

Two representative attempts to form a community of interests could be observed starting in the 1900s. One was the "Three Association" among Hoechst, Cassel, and Kalle; the other was the "Three Union" among BASF, Bayer, and Agfa. In addition to these concentrations, enterprises in the pharmaceutical industry formed a community of interests in 1905. Except for these three concentrations, cartel agreements were also created with other enterprises. Various production programs and the specialization of companies in the chemical industry prevented enterprises from intense competition. Situations in which all enterprises were members of many cartels contributed to the restraint and exclusion of competition (Pohl 1978, S.11–12; Kudo 1999, Chapter 1).

The Three Union, which was formed in 1904, was a community of interests of which the core agreement was the "concentration and distribution of interests" that cooperated in issues such as preventing patent trouble; eliminating competition that could occur with the appearance of new dye products; exchanging production methods; unifying sales organizations, especially foreign sales organizations; and keeping up with other members in the increase of capital. Whereas the exchange of shares was not implemented in this agreement, in the Three Association among Hoechst, Cassel, and Kalle, cooperation in purchasing, the exchange of patents and licenses, the common construction of foreign plants, and collaboration in the production and sale of products were decided on the basis of interlocking stock holdings or participation (Kudo 1999, pp.28–29). These two enterprise concentrations enabled a broader range of cooperation and stronger collaboration than cartels.

4.2.2.2 Policies Regarding the Regulation of Monopolies

This section examines enterprise concentration problems in relation to monopoly regulatory policies in Germany. In Germany, cartels were regarded as "a particular form of self-regulation" and "intermediate organization that helped to coordinate individual actions with the greater goals of the community, industry, and the nation" (Fear 2005, p.237). The development of such concentrations in which cartels were dominant was deeply intertwined with typical German monopoly regulatory policies. In contrast to the US, in Germany, state policies prohibiting cartels had not been adopted; rather, cartels were approved from the perspective of industrial and trade policy before World War II. M-L. Djelic pointed out that "German political authorities envisioned industrial development at the national level as a rational and orderly process rather than as an open, unrestricted, and competitive free for-all" (Djelic 2002, p.237). According to Imperial Supreme Court decisions in 1890 and 1897, cartels were not contradictory to the freedom of business prescribed by the Trade Regulation Act of the 1860s. Duties concluded in cartel agreements were regarded as binding (Pohl 1978, S.8; Reuter 1967, S.34; Fear 2005, p.238). The Imperial Court regarded cartels as "measures to prevent economic turmoil" and "agreed upon by voluntary association for purpose of private self-regulation" (Fear 2005, p.238). Such recognition was exactly opposite of the US.

Before World War II, according to the judgment of the Imperial Supreme Court, cartels were regarded as being contrary to Article 138 of the Civil Code establishing acts against good customs only in cases in which it restricted the personal freedom of each person or the public interest protected by the freedom of business. In reality, being based on this regulation, the existence of a cartel did not become a subject of discussion [*Bundesarchiv Berlin*, R43-1/1201, Die Schrift von der Sozialisierungs-Kommission an den Herrn Staatssekretär in der Reichskanzelei (22.2.1923), S.15–16; Leske 1901]. During this period, the Imperial Supreme Court approved cartel agreements as valid and again rejected the view that cartels were contradictory to good customs and therefore invalid (*Bundesarchiv Berlin*, R1501/107163, Denkschrift über das Kartellwesen, Zweite Teil, Vorschriften des inländischen Zivil und Strafrechts unter Berücksichtigung der Rechtsprechung des Reichsgerichts, S.7–9). Originally, a fundamental trend of cartel legislation was directed toward restricting the influence and power of cartels, except for compulsory cartels (Mayer 1959, S.34). However, in Germany, according to contemporary legal opinion, cartel agreements were regarded as not being contrary to the public interest and lawful from the perspective of civil law (Reuter 1967, S.34–35).

In Germany, there was a tendency to regard the cartel as an appropriate means of easing business fluctuations and a passive standpoint against legal regulations. For instance, in questionnaires regarding cartels in 1902 and 1906, the view that the danger of cartels could not justify legal intervention was indicated. It was concluded that the behavior of cartels was sufficiently controlled by competition with outsiders, potential foreign competition, and cartel members who were dissatisfied with cartels (Isay 1955, S.32). The German Court reached a conclusion on the basis of cartel theory of the Historical School that the cartelization of national economy was a necessary step to higher level, more appropriate, and stable production methods (Bechtold 1986, S.114). Before 1914, the Imperial Parliament had discussions regarding solving market control problems that could be implemented as economic policy (Blaich 1973, S.293). Although in such discussions, cartel problems were disputed, the precise of criticism against cartels was not indicated. As a result, insufficient criticism against cartels and monopolies influenced the formation of German characteristics of the cartel-friendly thought (Tano 1991, p.54). The German regal conditions surrounding the industrial combination were "no impediments such as that of the English or American law against restraint of trade had to be encountered or taken into account." Regarding the legal attitude responsible for the specific form of organization, German cartels illustrated it in contrast to the formation of trust (Levy 1935, p.226).

German cartel policy made collective monopolies almost completely free and cartels became dominant (Reuter 1967, S.34, 39). The Cartel Ordinance (the Cartel Law) in 1923 first regulated cartels. This law did not lay down any new legal principles but merely provided a new legal foundation for more intense regulation of the abuses arising from monopolistic combinations [Liefmann 1932, pp.173–174; *Bundesarchiv Berlin*, R/3101/12362, Die Schrift des Reichsrates, Nr.78, Tagung 1922 (29.3.1922), *Bundesarchiv Berlin*, R/3101/12361, Denkschrift betr. Schaffung eines Kartellgesetzes (Oktober 1921), S.2; *Bundesarchiv Berlin*, R43-1/1201, Vortrag des Referenten (30.10.1923); *Bundesarchiv Berlin*, R43-1/1201, Verordnung gegen Mißbrauch wirtschaftlicher Machtstellungen (Oktober 1928)].

The Restrictive Trade Practices Act passed after World War II aimed to destroy cartels on the basis of "prohibition" principles, while the Cartel Ordinance of 1923 was based on "abuse regulations" principles [*National Archives*, RG59, 862A.054, Developments concerning the German Cartel Law (1956.7.3), pp.1–2; Dyas and Thanheiser 1976, p.132]. The Cartel Ordinance depended on the view that the Cartel Court took the duties that were assigned to it. The Court tended not to interfere excessively in the German economy (Liefmann 1932, p.174). Thus, before the end of the World War II, even during the period after the promulgation of the Cartel Ordinance of 1923, economic concentrations emphasizing cartels were maintained under loose regulations against monopolies.

4.2.3 Significance and Limitations of Enterprise Concentration During the Shift to Monopolistic Capitalism

4.2.3.1 Significance and Limitations of Enterprise Concentration Based on Cartels

One significant aspect of enterprise concentration during this period was coping with structural changes in capitalism by creating market control institutions. However, the treatment of such changes by cartels in Germany was forced to face limitations compared to the pursuit of rationalization functions by trusts in the US. For instance, when the Rheine-Westphalia Coal Syndicate was founded in 1893, its production allotment volume was 33,579,309 tons, whereas it increased by 89% to 63,606,440 tons in 1903. In 1908, it was further increased to 77,754,834, making it 2.32 times that of 1893. However, the actual mining volume increased more rapidly than the allotment volume (Mendel 1908, S.1086–1087). A similar trend can be observed in the Steel Plant Association, which promoted an increase in production despite production volume restrictions (Mendel 1908, S.1090). The activities of the enterprise combinations in coal and iron were not able to obstruct the rapid increase and expansion of production and the conditions in which production exceeded demand continued. In this way, overproduction could not be decreased by cartels. Indeed, the enterprise combinations succeeded in maintaining prices at a high level. However, they were powerless against the members' desire to expand production and production restrictions were only a myth (Mendel 1908, S.1093).

In addition, insufficient attempts to pursue rationalization functions due to a delay in the formation of trusts and the limitations of coordinating production capacity and demand using production allotment, cartels obstructed the functioning of the market pricing mechanism by fixing prices at an artificially high level. In cartels combining enterprises of very different sizes, the higher production costs of smaller and weaker firms than those of large-scale plants had to be considered in price fixing for the purpose of guaranteeing a certain profit to even the weakest firms enjoying the protection of the cartel (Maschke 1969, p.247). The cartels in the iron and steel industry "did allow a greater number of vertically integrated firms with smaller scale and market share to remain extant in Germany than in the United States" (Fear 2005, p.258). Thus, prices tended to be set at a higher level. Above all, assembly industries without cartelization suffered damage from domestic competitors that were not members of the syndicate and foreign competitors and by sudden increases in the domestic prices of raw materials and semifinished products (Riesser 1912, S.152).

Maintaining high prices through cartels or syndicates delayed achieving balance between demand and supply through market mechanisms and prevented market recovery. Thus, such monopolistic organizations were forced to face limitations in coordinating productive forces and the market. As a result, the high-cost structures of German enterprises created by long-term imbalances between demand and supply, maintaining excess production capacity, and decreasing operating rates were maintained. Under such conditions, the differences in competitive power between Germany and the US in which the rationalization function of trust was pursued had to become larger. Whereas trusts were an attempt to decrease production costs and increase profits, cartelization was an attempt to improve profitability by raising prices (Silberberg 1910, S.1049). The cartel attempts to bring the price concerning total production cost; however, trust seeks to reduce cost price and expand consumption through lowering price. Trust in the United States enabled enormous strengthening of US production and developed into a risk to German economic life more and more. In contrast, the price was not cheapened by the cartel, reinforcing German industry against foreign competitors as the goal of the cartel policy was achieved only the least of all (Schact 1902, S.7–8). Therefore, cartelization in itself was contradictory. As will be considered in Chapter 7, in the 1920s, when the rationalization movement was implemented through the formation of trusts and pursuit of rationalization, the effects of such concentration measures progressed. However, the number of cartels greatly increased in the 1920s. It increased from 300 in 1900 to 2,500 in 1925 and 3,000 in

1930 (König 1960, S.304). Cartels had been an important means of concentration in the 1920s, as well as trusts.

Furthermore, dumping in the export market based on special profits in the domestic market controlled by cartels or syndicates could be a critical factor restricting the competitiveness of German enterprises. For example, while the price of steel billet per ton was 90 Marks in the German market in 1902, that sold in Rotterdam as an important international trade port was 72 Marks (Voelcker 1904, S.402). The greater part of the export volume of half-finished products manufactured by German iron and steel companies was for the UK, where processing companies that used such semifinished goods sold at dumping prices appeared (Voelcker 1904, S.515–516). This situation increased the competitiveness of UK companies in the international market and became a serious obstacle to the export of products processed in Germany. In this way, a cartel impaired competition among suppliers of the same products and could influence product-processing companies through its price policy (Mathis 1988, S.80). German enterprises in the processing industries were forced to encounter problems of high domestic prices of materials and semifinished products, which, despite export subsidy by cartels of raw materials and semifinished goods to the processing industries, lowered the competitiveness of enterprises in these sectors (Morgenroth 1907, S.50–51, 116), Cartel exports were "a dangerous present" for foreign manufacturers (Morgenroth 1907, S.112). The price policy of cartels, such as in the cheap export in case of high domestic price, could affect disadvantageous on export interests of the national economy (Morgenroth 1907, S.44–45, 116).

4.2.3.2 Significance and Limitations of the Integration of Sales Functions Through Syndicates

Next, in examining enterprise concentration in relation to changes in the internal structure of companies and management behavior, in Germany at the time, syndicates had major significance as a form of enterprise combination. It often played a significant role as a means of forward integration into the sales function. Jürgen Kocka stated that "membership in a tight cartel or syndicate can be regarded as one way for a firm to integrate forward without establishing its own sales organization, since such a cartel sold the products of member firms collectively" (Kocka 1980, p.80). Generally speaking, the movement toward partial integration through participation into suddenly increasing syndicates was especially important during the 1887–1907 period. This trend was particularly prominent in the coal mining, iron and steel, and metal industries (Kocka 1981, S.48–50; Siegrist 1980, S.69–72).

However, when examining the integration of sales in relation to the problem of managerial coordination, the function of coordinating of demand and supply had to face great limitations compared with the method of integration by establishing a company's own sales organization. As A. D. Chandler, Jr. clarified in cases in the US, the function of managerial coordination by integrating production and distribution enabled manufacturing enterprises to coordinate production and market (consumption) by understanding market conditions and achieving throughput and economy of speed through such coordination functions (Chandler 1977). Such managerial coordination was an important enterprise-level measure to cope with the limitations on the coordination of demand and supply through market mechanisms, dubbed the "Invisible hand" by economist Adam Smith (Smith 1993, pp.291–292).

Essentially, the function of coordinating demand and supply through market mechanisms can only bring balance in a certain regional market at a certain time. For an individual enterprise, equilibrium between demand and supply using market principles does not mean that coordinating production and the market by each company can be realized automatically by reflecting situations such as product differentiation and competitiveness. Therefore, an important foundation for realizing more effective reproduction of capital can be created through an enterprise's attempt to cope with "contradictory between production and consumption" determined by characteristics of the capitalistic economy. Structural changes in capitalism began with the 1873 crisis, meaning that the enterprise-level coordination of production and the market became indispensable for the survival of big business.

In examining changes in enterprise concentration during this period from such perspectives, even though the coordination of the production volume and sales of all member companies in a syndicate could be realized to a certain degree, such coordination on the level of an individual enterprise was not always achieved. Vertical integration through the internalization of functions such as sales and purchasing enabled enterprises to achieve the effects of managerial coordination. In contrast to cases in the US where the integration of distribution functions progressed by establishing sales organizations in many large enterprises, the function of coordinating production and the market (consumption) through syndicates in Germany faced significant limitations.

References

Bechtold H (1986) Die Kartellierung der deutschen Volkswirtschaft und die sozialdemokratische Theorie-Diskussion vor 1933. Haag + Herchen, Frankfurt am Main

Blaich F (1973) Kartell—und Monopolpolitil im kaiserlichen Deutschland. Das Problem der Marktmacht im deutschen Reichstag zwischen 1879 und 1914. Droste Verlag, Düsseldorf

Böllter A (1907) Eisenindustrie und Stahlwerksverband. Eine wirtschaftliche Studie zur Kartellfrage. G. Böhme, Leipzig

Brady RA (1933) The Rationalization movement in German industry. A study in the evolution of economic planning. University of California Press, Berkeley, California

Chandler AD Jr (1977) The visible hand: Managerial revolution in American business. Harvard University Press, Cambridge, Massachusetts

Djelic M-L (2002) Does Europe mean Americanization? The case of competition. In: Compet Change 6(3): 233–250

Doering M (1925) Die Entwicklung des deutschen Eisenpreises im internationalen Zustimmung. In: Weltwirtschaftliches Archiv 22 (II): 320–348

Dyas GP, Thanheiser TH (1976) The emerging European enterpreise. Strategy and structure in French and German Industry. The Macmillan Press, London

Fear JR (2005) Organizing control: August Thyssen and the construction of German corporate management. Harvard University Press, Cambridge

Fischer W (1976) Bergbau, Industrie und Handwerk 1914–1970. In: Aubin H, Zorn W (Hrsg) Handbuch der deutschen Wirtschafts- und Sozialgeschichte. Bd 2, Das 19. und 20.Jahrhundert, Klett Cotta, Stuttgart, S.527–562
Fremdling R, Krengel J (1985) Kartelle und ihre Volks-bzw. Einzelwirtschaftliche Bedeutung bis 1914. In: Pohl H (Hrsg) Kartelle und Kartellgesetzgebung in Praxis und Rechtsprechung vom 19. Jahrhunder bis zur Gegenwart. Franz Steiner, Stuttgart, S.29–41
Hermann K (1985) Die Haltung der Nationalökonomie zu den Kartellen. In: Pohl H (Hrsg) Kartelle und Kartellgesetzgebung in Praxis und Rechtsprechung vom 19. Jahrhunder bis zur Gegenwart. Franz Steiner, Stuttgart, S.42–50
Isay R (1955) Die Geschichte der Kartellgesetgebung. W. de Gruyter, Berlin
Ishiro H (1972) Doitsu denki kogyo no dokusen keisei katei (Ge) [Process of monopolization in the German electrical industry (2)]. In: Keizaigaku Kenkyu (Econ Stud) 21(4): 113–156
Jeidels O (1905) Das Verhältnis der deutschen Groβbanken zur Industrie mit besonderer Berücksichtigung der Eisenindustrie. Duncker und Humblot, Leipzig
Kocka J (1980) The reise of the modern industrial enterprise in Germany. In: Chandler AD Jr, Daems H (eds) Managerial hierarchies: comparative perspectives on the rise of the modern industrial enterprise. Harvard University Press, Cambridge, pp 77–116
Kocka J (1981) Groβunternehmen und der Aufstieg der Manager-Kapitalismus im späten 19. und frühen 20. Jahrhundert, Deutschland im internationalen Vergleich. In: Historische Zeitschrift 232: 39–60
König H (1960) Kartelle und Konzentration (unter besonderer Berücksichtung der Preis- und Mengenabsprachen). In: Arndt H (Hrsg) Die Konzentration in der Wirtschaft, Erster Band, Stand der Konzentration, Duncker und Humblot, Berlin, S.303–332
Kudo A (1999) Gendai Doitsu kagaku kigyoushi (Modern business history in the German chemical industry). Mineruva shobo, Kyoto.
Ленин ВИ (1962) Империализм, как высшая стадия капитализма: популярный очерк. In: Полное собрание сочинений. Том 27, ос. изд-во полит. лит-ры, Москва, pp 299–426
Leske F (1901) Vergleichende Darstellung des Bürgerlichen Gesetzbuches für das Deutsche Reich und des Preuβischen Allgemeinen Landrechts. O. Liebmann, Berlin
Levy H (1935) Industrial Germany: a study of its monmopoly organisations and their control by the state. Cambridge University Press, Cambridge
Liefmann R (1897) Unternehmensverbände (Konvention, Kartelle). Ihr Wesen und ihre Bedeutung. J.C.B. Mohr, Leipzig
Liefmann R (1923) Kartelle. In: Elster L, Webwer A, Wieser F (Hrsg) Handwörterbuch der Staatswissenschaft, vierte, gänzlich umgearbeitete Auflage., V. Band, G. Fischer, Jena, S.611–630
Liefmann R (1932) Cartels, concerns and trusts. Methuen & Co., London
Maekawa K (1993) Gendai kigyou kenkyu no kiso (Foundation of study of contemporary enterprise). Moriyama shoten, Tokyo.
Maschke E (1969) Outline of the history of German cartels from 1873 to 1914. In: Crouzet F, Chaloner WH, Stern WM (eds) Essays in European economic history 1879-1914. Edward Arnold, London, pp 226–258
Mathis F (1988) Kartelle, Fusionen und Multinationale Unternehmen in Grossbritanien, Frankreich, Deutschland, den USA und den wichtigsten Staaten der übrigen Welt bis 1914. In: Pohl H (Hrsg) Wettbewerbsbeschränkungen auf internationalen Märkten. Franz Steiner, Stuttgart, S.79–96
Mayer L (1959) Kartelle, Kartellorganisation und Kartelpolitik. Th. Gabler, Wiesbaden
Mendel J (1908) Die produktionsregelnde Tätigkeit der Syndikate. In: Die Bank 1: 1084–1093
Michels RK (1928) Cartels, Combines and Trusts in Post-War Germany. Columbia University Press, New York
Morgenroth W (1907) Die Exportpolitik der Kartelle: Untersuchungen über die handelspolitischen Bedeutung des Kartellwesens. Duncker & Humblot, Leipzig
Ono E (1965) Doitsu shihonshugi ron (German capitalism). Miraisha, Tokyo
Pinner F (1908) Der Zusammenbruch der deutschen Roheisensyndizierung. In: Die Bank 1: 963–973

Pohl H (1978) Die Konzentration in der deutschen Wirtschaft vom ausgehenden 19. Jahrhundert bis 1945. In: Pohl H, Treue W (Hrsg) Die Konzentration in der deutschen Wirtschaft seit dem 19. Jahrhundert. Steiner, Wiesbaden, S.1–44

Reuter UK (1967) Erfahrungen mit staatlicher Kartellpolitik in Deutschland von 1900 bis 1964 unter besonderer Berücksichtung der Zellstoffindustrie. Polygraphischer, Zürich

Riesser J (1912) Die deutsche Groβbanken und ihre Konzentration im Zusammenhang mit der Entwicklung der Gesamtwirtschaft in Deutschland, 4. Aufl., G. Fischer, Jena

Schacht D (1902) Trust oder Kartell? In: Preuβische Jahrbücher 110: 1–18

Siegrist H (1980) Deutscher Groβunternehmen vom späten 19. Jahrhundert bis zur Weimarer Republik. In: Geschichte und Gesellschaft 6(1): 60–102

Silberberg L (1910) Aus der deutschen Kohlenindustrie. Zum Stande der Kartelbewegung. In: Die Bank 3: 1046–1055

Smith A (1993) An inquiry into the nature and causes of the wealth of nations. A selected edition, edited with an introduction and commentary by K. Sutherland, Oxford University Press, Oxford

Taniguch A (2002) Kyodai kigyo no seiki. 20 seiki Amerika shihonshugi no keisei to kigyo godo (A century of huge enterprises. The formation of the US capitalism and corporate behaviors in the Twentieth century). Yuhikaku, Tokyo

Tano T (1991) Dai itiji taisen mae no Doitsu ni okeru karuteru mondai (Cartel problems in Germany before World War I). In: Wayo Jyoshi Daigaku Kiyo (Bull Faculty Human) 31: 43–56

Tohara T (1974) Nishi Doitsu ni okeru sengo kaikaku (Postwar reform in West Germany). In: University of Tokyo Institute of Social Science (ed) Sengo kaikaku: kokusai kankyo (Postwar reform: international environment), vol 2. Tokyo daigaku shuppankai, Tokyo, pp 91–151

Voelcker H (1904) Verhandlungen über den Halbzeug-Verband am 2. Und 3. Dezember 1903 im Reichstagsgebäude zu Berlin. In: Kontradiktorische Verhandlungen über Deutsche Kartell 6: 367–573.

Wagenführ R (1931) Kartelle in Deutschland. Krische, Nürnberg

Wengenroth U (1985) Die Entwicklung der Kartellbewegung bis 1914. In: Pohl H (Hrsg) Kartelle und Kartellgesetzgebung in Praxis und Rechtsprechung vom 19. Jahrhunder bis zur Gegenwart. Franz Steiner, Stuttgart, S.15–27

Yanagisawa O (2006) Shihonshugishi no renzoku to danzetsu (Continuity and discontinuty in the history of capitalism). Nihon hyoronsha, Tokyo

Yoshida M (1987) Amerika oyobi Doitsu denki sangyo ni okeru karuteru keisei to sono kokusaika ni tsuite (Formation of cartels in the American and German electrical industries and their Internationalization). In: Mita Shogaku Kenkyu (Mita Bus Rev) 30(4): 51–75.

Chapter 5
German Enterprises' Attempts at Labor Management System Reforms and Deployment of the Taylor System

Abstract This chapter analyzes efforts to reform the labor management system from a comparative perspective with the United States. First, it considers the background of attempts to change the management system concerning the structural change of German capitalism beginning with the 1873 crisis in the late nineteenth century. Next, this chapter examines the emphasis on labor management reform. It also considers endeavors to separate the planning and execution functions by dividing the former foreman function and deploy the Taylor system in major industrial sectors. Based on these discussions, the significance and limitations of the labor management reform in this period are explored through comparison with phenomena in the US. The limitations in management reform determined by the peculiar conditions of the market, wage standards, and labor relations are clarified.

Keywords Industrial relations · Internal subcontracting system · Labor management · Labor market · Taylor system

A field in which important business management changes appeared during the period from the shift to monopolistic capitalism to the outbreak of World War I can be observed in labor management system reforms. In Germany, enterprises performed not only their own attempts to change the labor management system but also efforts to deploy the Taylor system. In this chapter, the way that German enterprises changed in the process of labor management system reforms is analyzed by comparing it to the United States, in which the Taylor system was the first modern management system created between the end of the nineteenth century and the beginning of the twentieth century.

Section 5.1 examines the historical background of labor management system reform. In Sect. 5.2, the emphasis of these attempts is analyzed. Section 5.3 considers representative cases of management reform. Based on these discussions, limitations of labor management system reforms in this period and their factors are clarified in Sect. 5.4.

T. Yamazaki, *A History of German Business*,
https://doi.org/10.1007/978-981-96-8476-2_5

5.1 Historical Background of Labor Management System Reform

First, the historical background of the labor management system reform that began at the end of the nineteenth century is analyzed. Such change was bought about by the economic crises resulting from the 1873 overproduction crisis. Structural changes in capitalism occurred in Germany as well as in the United States during this period. As was clear in Chapter 4, whereas the crises in 1857 and 1866 were phenomena that occurred in the United Kingdom (UK) with the highest productive force and international competitiveness and influenced other capitalistic nations (Ono 1965, p.32), the 1873 crises were brought about by overproduction in both the United States and Germany simultaneously. The crises in this year were simultaneous crisis and remarkably restricted to expanding exports. Furthermore, crises tend to become chronic phenomena, occurring at about 10-year intervals. As a result, the level of productive force tended to exceed the scale of markets. An important change in the structure of capitalism in this period can be seen at this point. Under such a serious situation, there were two effective countermeasures. One was maintaining prices by limiting and avoiding competition. Enterprise concentration was an important measure and monopolistic systems controlled by large enterprises were established through such concentration processes (see Chapter 4). The other was reducing costs. During this period, labor management system reform by strengthening control over labor became an effective measure to cut production costs.

Under such conditions, in Germany, as well as in the United States, labor management system reform became an important issue. At the time, the technological possibilities of the First Industrial Revolution were already exhausted (Landes 1969, p.237). Possibilities to reduce production costs by replacing machinery and equipment were restricted due to the burden of fixed costs arising from existing production equipment under the lower operating rate brought by the longtime depression. As a result, "the one area that offered large opportunities to cut costs was that of organization and administration" and "the one factor that was compressible was labor" (Landes 1969, p.302). Under such conditions, strengthening management by reforming labor organization became an important problem.

In addition, internal contracting system limitations as a dominant form of labor management were prominent during this period. In this system, each workshop could not be managed in a centralized form and workers were managed only indirectly through internal contracting foremen from the enterprise perspective. For instance, at Loewe, a machine company, the workers complained about cutting the piece wage rate repeatedly implemented by internal contracting foremen, which, in turn, became a factor for the systematic soldiering of workers as a group action to intently restraint work volume. Such resistance caused stagnation and a decrease in labor productivity (Reichelt 1906, S.87–88). Strong expansion of American machine sales in the German market at the end of the nineteenth century made improvements in product quality and cost-cutting the largest problem to be solved by German enterprises (Koda 1982, p.99).

In the electrical industry, breaking up the control power of all-around skilled foremen in workshops that were a foundation of worker resistance tended to be an important management problem to implement production process reform effectively while restraining the systematic soldiering of workers and controlling the autonomous behavior of assembly worker groups (Imakubo 1995, p.376). Under such conditions, the rationalization and modernization of workshop organization began in the 1880s (Möller 2004, S.295) and labor management system reforms were performed consciously at the beginning of the twentieth century.

5.2 Emphasis of Labor Management System Reforms

Next, this section considers the emphasis of labor management system reforms during this period. One is the deployment of the Taylor system. The deployment of this American management system was due to the appearance of large-scale enterprises and plants with the development of German capitalism after 1871 and the necessity of their effective management. Engineers perceived the United States as a competitive threat because of the technological gap between Germany and the US (Ohashi 1984, p.51). It was the German Association of Engineers (*Verein deutscher Ingenieur*) that had a strong interest in implementing the Taylor system in Germany. It played an important role in the introduction and examination of this system's deployment and was an important advocate of Management Science (*Betriebswissenschaft*). Members of this organization regarded the United States as important competitor in world markets. They emphasized the "American threat" in 1903 and had the dominant opinion that opposing the United States should be done with new technological and organizational measures (Trieba and Mentrup 1983, S.79). Thus, attempts to transfer new American methods into German plants began at the beginning of the twentieth century by engineers who believed in the new efficiency improvement measures of F. W. Taylor (Merkle 1980, S.177).

Heidrum Homburg considered the deployment of the Taylor system in this period as occurring in two stages. One can be observed from 1902 to 1908; the other can be seen after 1908. In the first stage, the depression from 1900 to 1902 made it plain that enterprises could not achieve sufficient effects with traditional forms of management organization. Discussions by engineers on American methods of modern plant organization concentrated on comparisons between the piece wage system that was dominant in Germany at the time and modern American wage systems, such as the premium wage system proposed by Halsey and the differential piece rate system developed by Taylor. Taylor's wage system was now well-known. During the second stage, the Taylor system attracted broad attention during the depression from 1907 to 1908, not only its wage system but also other elements. Companies that attempted to introduce individual elements of the Taylor system increased (Homburg 1978, S.174–176).

In addition, trends to separate the planning and execution functions by dividing the former foreman function appeared between the end of the 19th and beginning of the twentieth centuries. Disputes regarding rationalization by the Free Trade Union began in 1908 as discussions on the Taylor system. G. Stollberg pointed out that development from the plant foreman system in the 1870s to the technical management office occurred in some enterprises at the time. In this process, a few attempts to predetermine work time and wages on the basis of time studies, the division of foreman functions, and Taylor-style machine tests were performed. In such attempts, in contrast to the United States, time studies were implemented sporadically, and the functional foreman system and predetermination of wages by technical offices were introduced. Such typical cases can be observed in two machine-producing companies (Berlin Anhalt Maschinery and Borsig) and two electrical companies (AEG and Siemens) (Stollberg 1981, S.31, 36, 41).

Otto Jeidels visited about 60 plants in the iron industry of the Rein-Westfalia region and performed interview research. According to his research results, the person in charge of setting wages in underdeveloped, legacy enterprises was the foreman. In such enterprises, because calculation of accounting and setting of piece wages were not a very large burden, he could still maintain his independence from enterprise management and avoid such management. However, the tendency to divide the foreman's function into two departments with the expansion and intensification of plants appeared. The first was the division into the general foreman, who was well-versed in theoretical calculations and who set piece wages with production engineers, and the lower foreman, who was responsible only for assigning and supervising work. The second was to move decisions of calculatable piece wages to the technical department. This meant reorganizing the office that took charge of setting piece wages (Jeidels 1907, S.1, 4, 106). The arbitrariness of foreman decisions on piece wages and employment (rate cutting) was a large factor in such reform (Jeidels 1907, S.116–117). Regarding the former trend, whereas continuous improvements of contents of piece rate work became a main issue of the general foreman's duties, the lower foreman's duties included the supervision of work rather than the setting of piece wages (Jeidels 1907, S.137).

In this way, attempts to modernize the labor management system were going in two directions. However, in both Germany's original attempts and the deployment of the Taylor system as an American management system, the foundation of calculating the piece wage rate was based not on labor science or Taylorism but on experience (Stollberg 1981, S.35).

During this period, the main industrial sectors in which labor management system reforms were attempted can be seen in the electrical and machine industries. The following points can be stated as the reasons why such attempts were relatively many in these industries. In the industrial sectors in which production equipment among mechanical facilities was the main equipment, there were workers who took charge of various kinds of machines and many types of jobs, which made the problems of management more complicated. In addition, these industries belonged to the most important sector in terms of the number of enterprises and workers and were major sectors of industrial export products. Therefore, in these industries, competition with the UK and the United States was especially intensive and labor management system reform became more necessary than in other industrial sectors (Koda and Ito 1990, pp.160–161).

5.3 Representative Cases of Labor Management System Reform

Based on discussions, in Sect. 5.2, representative cases of enterprises that performed labor management system reforms are explored.

Case of Ludwig Loewe: In this company, Libby was an American engineer employed as chief engineer in 1897. He abolished the piece wage system that was popular in Germany at the time and changed it to the wage system under strict work time decision and management by plant managers. However, production volume decreased by 20% within a year and this reform failed. Georg Schlesinger, who was called the "German Taylor," was sent to Glasgow and studied the premium system under persons such as Rowan (Stollberg 1981, S.37). The reasons for their failure included the opposition of workers and strikes. However, the modern piece wage system fixed by understanding data regarding wages and costs by the company instead of by internal contracting foremen (Koda 1994, p.256). The contracting foreman system was abolished, and technical and calculation offices were completely equipped. Moreover, office work, including deciding wages, was taken away from foremen. The work of skilled workers was also directed with various kinds of cards (Koda and Ito 1990, p.175). Thus, attempts to change the wage system became an important management reform.

Furthermore, systems of every kind of slip were arranged so that enterprises could hold cost accounting, taken charge of by contracting foremen. Non-manual workers who were in charge of accounting were increased and plant accounting departments were adjusted. New bookkeeping systems in plants were adopted and slips such as order slips, production slips, and parts lists moved through each production process and were finally added up in the accounting office (Koda 1994, p.257; Lilienthal 1907, Einleitung, S.3–4, Die Geschäftsbuchführung, S.5–40, Die Betriebsbuchführung, S.40–139).

In addition, a sort of functional foreman system was adopted (Wegeleben 1924, S.145, S.151–152). Loewe performed a time study of machine tool operating work, assisted by the cooperation of Georg Schlesinger. Data obtained were used not only for plant management but also as an index of strengthening management in many machine shops where the machine tools produced by this company were stationed. Therefore, the effects of the time study became very significant (Koda and Ito 1990, p.175).

As a result of such efforts, the old type of all-around mechanical skills changed and semi-skilled workers increased on the one hand, and skill itself became limited and standardization was promoted on the other hand. In accordance, the internal contracting system was broken up and line and staff management organizations were created. Cost accounting functions that internal contracting foremen usually took charge of were taken over by the calculation office and enterprises started better understanding the production process (Koda 1982, pp.116–117).

However, it was in mass production departments, such as weapons producing departments, that such reforms were performed. In contrast to departments of military affairs and mass consumer goods, machine equipment for industrial use as producer goods was not unsuitable for mass production. Therefore, labor management reform still did not progress and faced certain limitations in producing machine tools (Koda 1982, p.118). Thus, standardization did not progress sufficiently, and various products were manufactured, which became an obstacle to Taylorization in studying elements of work (Wegeleben 1924, S.146–147).

Case of Auar: In examining the case of Auer as the manufacturer of the incandescent lamp, F. B. Gilbreth as an assistant to F. W. Taylor worked at this company as the rationalization consultant from late 1914 to the end of 1915 (Pechhold 1974, S.36; Stollberg 1981, S.38). He established the Planning Department with six American engineers and 30 German assistants and performed labor organization reforms in production, inventory, and management. As a result, the duties of non-manual workers who were in charge of the management and allotment of work were decided in detail in the manufacturing department and further prescriptions regarding work were decided. Documents and the classification of tools and materials were arranged on the basis of the Taylor system. In addition, adjusting office desks were fixed on the basis of a motion study developed by Gilbreth. An established form was simplified and the central recording office was organized. Female, a shorthand typist, prepared the 10-finger blind typewriter system (Stollberg 1981, S.38).

In this way, attention to the individual elements of the Taylor system increased, even though individually. However, time studies were not implemented in most of the companies and those that introduced them were rare. The control of labor and strengthening of management based on the direct management of work became possible by standardization through time studies. It was Bosch (Robert Bosch GmbH) that performed the deployment of the Taylor system most positively and attempted to implement it in its entirety.

Case of Robert Bosch: This enterprise already established a tool plant in 1904 with the adoption of American machine tools and the maintenance of tools handled by skilled workers who were absorbed into this plant. The cost management department was organized in 1907 and 1908 and the piecework department was created in 1908 and piece wage rate decisions were moved to this organization. Foremen came to be not charged with piece rate decisions and were responsible for supervising production and its improvement. In 1909, an individual piece wage system was adopted instead of a group piece wage rate system, which had been dominant until then. Individual functions were separated from traditional complicated foreman activities and moved to the central plant management department as a specialized organization (Homburg 1978, S.183; Robert Bosch 1936, S.208, 210; Kenngott 1923, S.114; Krauβ 1924, S.131). The functional foreman system was also introduced, even if only partially (Ito 2002, p.90). Time studies with stopwatches by non-manual workers were implemented. This company faced stagnant sales from 1912 to 1913 and needed to become as effective as possible. Methods of the Taylor system were adopted to achieve this goal (Homburg 1978, S.181). When the inactivity of sales became prominent in 1913, this company attempted to strengthen control of piece work on the basis of minute work analysis and time studies (Ito 1985, p.76).

Starting in 1909, the tempo of work at Bosch was set at such a high level that ordinary workers could not achieve it and it became known as the "Bosch tempo" and had a bad reputation. Bosch attempted to cope with the stagnation of sales in 1912 and 1913 by setting tasks regarded as possible to the highest level and cutting the piece wage rate. As a result of worker oppression by the uncritical introduction of the Taylor system, a strike occurred on May 31, 1913.

Before this strike occurred at Bosch, the right of codetermination regarding setting the piece wage rate was admitted to workers and labor and the involvement of workers in changing the piece wage rate and dismissal was also possible. Work agreements that guaranteed workers such rights had become an obstacle in implementing the Taylor system. Management of this company attempted to abolish these worker rights, reorganize, and strengthen its labor organization and management structure using the Taylor system. The strike was caused by increasing dissatisfaction with management's attempts to take away such rights from workers (Homburg 1978, S.184–189; Kenngott 1923, S.114). The strike began on May 31, 1913, and came to an end with the defeat of the worker and trade union. As a result, this enterprise acquired management autonomy over shop management and became autonomous against labor unions (Homburg 1978, S.192).

Workers and labor unions did not always oppose Taylor's rationalization measures but the introduction of this system at the sacrifice of workers. Central labor disputes were not the Taylor system itself but problems of worker participation in the management of workers and trade unions (Stollberg 1981, S.117). However, at Bosch, the Taylor system did not realize its assertion that it would improve labor productivity and keep social peace. The separation of planning work and executing work had to bring decisive ruptures in the relationship between management and the workers (Homburg 1978, S.193).

Case of Siemens: Another representative case in which labor management modernization was attempted can be observed in Siemens of the electrical industry. Fundamental contents of this company's labor management system reforms can be seen in the shift to direct management system and the centralization of management based on the separation between planning and execution and the formation of the line and staff organization as institutions to realize this purpose. This process is to be understood as the first actual development of direct management of the labor process by company management (Imakubo 1995, pp.335–337; Geck 1931, S.55; Sombart 1927, S.891–894; Riedler 1916, S.141–151).

In reform in the latter half of the 1880s when the transformation from the "foreman economy" to the "engineer economy" began, emphasis was put on adoption of the senior engineer system as a measure to respond to the dysfunction of the foreman economy with the enlargement and differentiation of workshops, particularly, the appearance of the work organization formed by kinds of machines. The senior foreman system was connected with changes in multi-purpose staff departments needed by the differentiation of staff duties and an increase in personnel per duty (progress of cooperation based on the division of labor) with the appearance of such work organizations. However, the senior foreman system did not mean the disappearance of the foreman economy and a shift to the engineer economy would be regarded as an epoch-making change. It was only a preparatory stage of the engineer economy [Imakubo 1995, pp.390–391; *Siemens Archiv Akte*, 68/Li180, Verfügung (31.12.1887)]. In work organizations formed by types of machines, the condition that enabled the final removal of the foreman economy still did not exist (Imakubo 1995, p.417). In addition, in the production process in which mass production and standardization could not come into question, they were very far from realizing the separation between planning and execution in the workshop. The rate of skilled workers measured was high and in each key department such as assembly, the rate of all-around work and elements of handicraft skill based on intellectual ability was large. Skilled workers were still key and their autonomous control to work was maintained (Imakubo 1995, p.408).

The shift to mass production using work organization formed by product type that occurred since the latter half of the 1890s made management organization changes necessary. Siemens & Halske built two kinds of line and staff organizations (engineer economy), composed of the plant engineer system observed in high-voltage electrical plants and the improved senior foreman system seen in low-voltage electrical plants, according to whether high-voltage or low-voltage except for assembly at spot. In the plant engineer system, regulation power of managers was fundamentally broken up through the direct control of production and labor management by managers such as plant engineers, production group chiefs, and the production group section. Office organization at each level was the most advanced plant management organization that changed to the object of management or the executor. This improved foreman system, as well as staff organization, expanded at the same time and became a form of modern management (Imakubo 1995, pp.457–458).

However, the transformation from the foreman to the engineer economy did not mean that all problems concerning plant management and influencing capital accumulation and industrial relations could be solved. Such limitations were due to boundaries of the work organization formed by product type and the engineer economy itself, such as the lack of compulsory work time at the flow production, the mechanization of managerial instruments, and forced mechanization. The ratio of skilled workers to all workers was still high, even at the beginning of the twentieth century (Imakubo 1995, pp.495–496, 498; Imakubo 1990, pp.99–100, 103, 105, 107).

Such limits were essentially determined because management could not directly and scientifically grasp contents of works of skilled workers and thoroughly manage and control their work using task management, of which fundamental content was setting tasks based on time and motion studies (Imakubo 1995, pp.499, 597, 603). For example, in an electric motor plant as a representative production department of Siemens-Schuckert, a time study began at length after moving the plant from Schalrotenberg to Nonnendam in 1912, progressed by the establishment of the rating office (*Siemens Archiv Akte*, 11/Lf494, Bericht über die betriebstechnische Konferenz am 2. Februar 1921, S.4).

Plant management reform in the electrical industry progressed more than in the machine industry, in particular, the machine tool industry. Machines in machine tool producing plants were arranged according to the kind of machine, even in the most advanced cases. This was different from machines being stationed on the basis of the products manufactured in mass production plants, such as electric products, armaments, and sewing machines. In machine tool plants, even for products with the highest demand, production lots could not be as large as that of consumer goods due to the characteristics of producer goods. In addition, in manufacturing machine tools in which roundabout production was prominent, the flexible formation of workshops was needed to avoid management risk. In Germany's machine tool industry, even in large enterprises, specialization in mass production of the same kinds of machines did not progress and methods that mixed mass production with order production were maintained (Koda 1994, pp.174–175). When examining the transportation equipment industry in which the scale of production was still small at the time, for instance, at Opel, scientification of management was not yet identified and the wage and rating offices did not exist until the outbreak of the World War I (Kugler 1985, S.21).

Cases of iron and steel industry: When considering the iron and steel industry compared with the process and assembly industries, the efficiency wage was useful as an important means of management; however, regarding the efficiency of the wage system, scientification and systematization began and could be regarded as "partly scientific." Such systemization and bureaucratization progressed through the making of wage lists and the establishment of wage offices that took charge of payments, control, and preliminary calculation of wages. Kleinschmidt (1993, S.81, 83–84) pointed out that it was impossible to state the scientification of the piece wage system based on the methods of F. W. Taylor or work and time studies in the iron and steel industry before World War I. Business strategy regarding rationalization in the iron and steel industry meant management progress of labor processes as well as securing the continuation and control of production flows. However, such management progress was achieved in the fields of work time and wage policy and cases in which it was realized by appropriate changes in labor organization were rare (Kleinschmidt 1993, S.78). It was in the 1870s that attempts to shift to "the engineer economy" began in the large iron and steel enterprises of the Ruhr region such as Krupp (Otsuka 1987, p.278; Otsuka 1986, pp. 132–136,163–170). In this process, experiments making use of science as much as possible were performed repeatedly and the rationalization of production was pursued. However, systems in which experience at production spots were predominant were slow to be collapsed, even at Krupp (Otuska 1986, pp.132, 134).

5.4 Limitations of Labor Management System Reform and Their Factors

In this way, in Germany, some enterprises attempted not only to change labor management systems in their own way but also deploy the Taylor system as an effective American system. Indeed, companies such as Robert Bosch that attempted to implement many elements of the Taylor system existed. However, cases in which elements of this management system were adopted and implemented individually were usual. Principles of the Taylor system such as the centralization of management, the implementation of piece wages based on tasks, and the standardization of work execution based on time saving principles prevailed in many industries. However, organized work studies in all forms were implemented hesitatingly until the outbreak of the World War I. Time and motion studies (stopwatch method) diffused slowly (Hinrichs 1981, S.53). For instance, they were performed in large enterprises of the machine and electrical industries. Representative cases can be observed at Siemens, AEG, Robert Bosch, Daimler, and Benz (Pechhold 1974, S.35).

It was after World War II, during the period of rationalization (1924–1929) in which the Taylor system prevailed, that direct control of labor force expenditure processes based on time and motion studies by enterprises became possible and management systems that enabled companies to directly manage workers and workshops were established. Attempts to reform labor management or deploy the Taylor system before World War I can be observed only at some big companies in industries such as the electrical and machinery industries. Even looking at enterprises in these industrial sectors, companies that were strongly oriented toward exports were the majority. In Germany at the time, the modernization of the labor management system became an important issue due to situations in which the thorough reduction of costs was needed to strengthen competitiveness in export markets and expand exports. Under such conditions, in the machine industry, transformation from indirect labor management by internal contracting foreman system to a direct management system by enterprises was attempted, technical and management staff departments were arranged, and adoption of the functional foreman system progressed (Borgmann 1981, S.108–111).

In contrast, internal contracting foremen at small and medium enterprises were maintaining a large amount of authority as they did before, despite the partial restriction of their power caused by the establishment of the cost accounting system (Koda 1994, p.178). In the machine tool industry, this held true of large companies in which small lot production of various products was performed as well as small and medium firms. In these enterprises, the judgment of turner based on certain experiences and theory had to be left continued (Koda 1994, pp.280–281). In the electrical industry, as well at small and medium companies, management reforms such as the shift to the engineer economy were not performed as seen at large enterprises such as Siemens & Halske or their plants. Limits in the point of disappearance of workers' regulatory power in workshops and work held true of small and medium companies to a stronger degree (Imakubo 1995, p.500).

In Germany, even during the outbreak of the World War I, the introduction of the Taylor system was delayed by far compared with the United States. There was no organization such as the Taylor Association in the United States and F. W. Taylor's management system was not taught at commercial colleges (Burchardt 1977, S.73).

Building upon these discussions, next, the reason why the Taylor system or labor management system reform was not implemented thoroughly and did not prevail broadly in many enterprises of various industrial sectors is examined.

In Germany, in contrast to the United States, a technical department that should play an important role in management reform was not needed in mass production plants such as steel plants, rolling mill plants, and bicycle or furnace plants; however, in the machine industry where mass production had not yet been observed, there was a requirement of the technical department owing to labor management reforms and the characterization of production processes (Stollberg 1981, S.34).

In addition, the need to achieve work standardization based on time studies was not necessarily as significant as in the United States. The Taylor system is a high-level measure to improve efficiency and mass production techniques based on standardization and specialization principles. Therefore, the implementation of the Taylor system premised mass sales that enabled mass production and was impossible without such market conditions. However, in Germany at the time, in contrast to the United States, the consumer goods market that enabled mass sales had not yet developed (Ohashi 1984, pp.52–53). Therefore, for many enterprises, except for companies strongly oriented toward the expansion of exports and mass production in the electrical and machine industries, the need to broadly and thoroughly introduce elements of the Taylor system was not always large.

Furthermore, in Germany, as a general trend, workers were abundant and skilled workers were also not lacking. As a result, the cost of workers was not as large as in the United States. Therefore, even in relatively large plants, low wage levels tended to obstruct mechanization and adoption of special-purpose machines. Under such conditions, the internal contracting foreman system was still strong and the paternalistic relationships among internal contracting foreman, craftsman, and apprentices were kept up and the formation of new labor organizations based on the division of labor in plants could be seen in only a limited number of companies or plants (Maekawa 1993, p.168).

Finally, in examining the attitude of labor unions to the introduction of the Taylor system, many trade unions and persons concerned with the Social Democratic Party refused this management system as "American bacillus" until the outbreak of World War I (Trieba and Mentrup 1983, S.84). However, trade unions did not necessarily refuse the Taylor system itself wholeheartedly. The Free Trade Union stated that it would not always oppose the Taylor system as long as dangerous aspects and elements of this system from the perspective of workers could be eliminated by worker participation in management and that sacrifices would not be shifted on workers (Ohashi 1984, pp.31–32). However, the Taylor system was regarded as unacceptable for workers and labor unions under the condition in which such control by workers through worker participation in management was not easy to realize.

It was during the rationalization movement after World War II that such limitations in labor management system reform were overcome. The Taylor system was deployed broadly and prevailed in many enterprises of German industries in the form of REFA system, which was a modified Taylor system, in process of the rationalization movement that began in 1924. This research problem will be analyzed in Chapter 8.

References

Borgmann M (1981) Betriebsführung, Arbeitsbedingungen und die sozaiale Fragen. Eine Untersuchung zur Arbeiter- und Unternehmergeschichte in der Berliner Maschinenindustrie zwischen 1870 und 1914 unter besonderer Berücksichtigung der Großbetriebe. Lang, Frankfurt am Main

Burchardt L (1977) Technischer Fortschritt und sozialer Wandel. Das Beispiel der Taylorismus-Rezeption. In: Treue W (Hrsg) Deutsche Technikgeschichte. Vorträge vom 31. Historikertag am 24.September 1976 in Mannheim. Vandenhoeck und Ruprecht, Göttingen, S.52–98.

Geck LH Ad (1931) Die soziale Arbeitsverhältnisse in Wand der Zeit. Eine geschichtliche Einführung in die Betriebssoziologie. Springer, Berlin

Hinrichs P (1981) Um die Seele des Arbeiters. Arbeitspsychologie, Industrie- und Betriebssoziologie in Deutschland 1871–1945. Pahl-Rugenstein, Köln

Homburg H (1978) Anfänge des Taylorsystem in Deutschland vor dem Ersten Weltkrieg. In: Geschichte und Gesellschaft 4(2): 170–194

Imakubo S (1990) 19 seiki matsu Doitsu denki kogyo ni okeru keiei romu seisaku (10) (Management, personnel affairs, and policy in the German electrical industry at the End of the Ninetieth century). In: Saga daigaku Keizai Ronshu (Saga Univ Econ Rev) 22 (5): 71–118

Imakubo S (1995) 19 seiki matsu Doitsu no kojyo (Factories in Germany at the end of the Nineteenth century). Yuhikaku, Tokyo

Ito M (1985) Dai ichiji taisenzen no Doitsu heno Taylor sisutemu no donyu (Introduction of Taylor system into Germany before World War I). In: Keiei Ronshu (Meiji Bus Rev) 32(4): 61–79

Ito M (2002) Doitsu kagakuteki kanri hattatsushi (History of development of scientific management in Germany). Tokyo keizai jyoho shuppansha, Tokyo

Jeidels O (1907) Die Methoden der Arbeiterentlohnung in der rheinisch-westfälischen Eisenindustrie. L. Simion, Berlin

Kenngott E (1923) 25 Jahre treuer Arbeit. In: Der Bosch=Zünderder 5(3): 114

Kleinschmit C (1993) Rationalisierung als Unternehmensstrategie. Die Eisen und Stahlindustrie des Ruhrgebiets zwischen Jahrhundertwende und Weltwirtschaftskrise. Klartext, Essen

Koda R (1982) Loewe sha ni okeru kojyo kanri (The organization and management of Lowe's new factory before World War I). In: Keizai Ronso (Econ Rev) 130(1–2):97–119.

Koda R (1994) Doitsu kosaku kikai kogyo seiritsushi (History of the formation the German machine tool industry). Taga Shuppan, Tokyo

Koda R, Ito M (1990) Doitsu ni okeru kagakuteki kanriho no tenkai (Development of scientific management in Germany). In: Hara T (ed) Kagakuteki kanriho no donyu to tenkai (Deployment and development of scientific management). Showado, Tokyo, pp 159–207

Krauß K (1924) Ein Kurzer Rückblick. In: Der Bosch=Zünder 6(6): 131

Kugler A (1985) Arbeitsorganisation und Produktionstechnologie der Adam Opel Werke (von 1900 bis 1929). Wissenschaftszentrum, Berlin

Landes DS (1969) The unbound prometheus. Technological change and industrial development in Western Europe from 1750 to the present. Cambridge University Press, Cambridge

Lilienthal J (1907) Fabrikorganisation, Fabrikbuchführung und Selbstkostenberechnung der Firma Ludw. Loewe & Co. Actiengesellschaft. J. Springer, Berlin

Maekawa K (1983) Gendai kigyo kenkyu no kiso (Foundation of study of contemporary enterprise). Moriyama shoten, Tokyo
Merkle JA (1980) Management and Ideology. University of California Press, Berkley, Los Angeles, London, The Legacy of the International Scientific Management Movement
Möller A (2004) Kienzle. Ein deutsches Industrieunternehmen im 20. Jahrhundert. Steiner, Stuttgart
Ohashi S (1984) Doitsu ni okeru Taylor sisutemu no donyu katei (II) [Deployment of the Taylor system in Germany (II)]. In: Shogaku Ronshu (Bus Rev Kansai Univ) 29(5): 467–493
Ono E (1965) Doitsu shihonshugi ron (German capitalism). Miraisha, Tokyo
Otsuka T (1986) Ruhr tekkogyo no rodo shijyo to chingin 1865–1880 (Labor market and wages in the iron-and steel industry of Ruhrdistrict 1865-1880). In: Keizai Ronshu (Econ Rev Kansai Univ) 36(1): 119–177
Otsuka T (1987) Roshi kankei shi ron (Industrial relations). In: Kansai daigaku shuppanbu, Suita
Pechhold E (1974) 50 Jahre REFA. Beuth, Berlin, Köln, Frankfurt am Main
Reichelt H (1906) Die Arbeitsverhältnisse in einem Berliner Grossbetrieb des Maschinenindustrie. Leonhard Simion, Berlin
Riedler A (1916) Emil Rathenau und das Werden der Groβwirtschaft. J. Springer, Berlin
Robert Bosch AG (1936) Fünfzig Jahre Bosch 1896–1936. Robert Bosch AG, Stuttgart
Sombart W (1927) Das Wirtschaftsleben in Zeitalter des Hochkapitalismus. 2. Halbband, Duncker & Humblot, München, Leipzig
Stollberg G (1981) Die Rationalisierungsdebatte 1908–1933: Freie Gewerkschaften zwischen Mitwirkung und Gegenwehr. Campus Verlag, Frankfurt am Main
Trieba V, Mentrup U (1983) Entwicklung der Arbeiswissenschaft in Deutschland: Rationalisierungspolitik der deutschen Wirtschaft bis zum Faschismus. Minerva, München
Wegeleben F (1924) Die Rationalisierung im Deutchen Werkzeugmaschinenbau. Dargestellt an der Entwicklung der Ludw. Loewe & Co. A.-G. J. Springer, Berlin

Chapter 6
Rise of the Modern Business Enterprise and the Formation of Managerial Hierarchies

Abstract This chapter explores the rise of modern business enterprises with multi-business units and managerial hierarchy and the structural changes of big business. First, this chapter considers the historical background of the birth of the modern business enterprise in Germany. Next, based on cases in key industrial sectors such as the iron and steel, chemical, electrical engineering, machine, and mining industries, changes in organizational structures and their characteristics are considered concerning the scale expansion of companies and regional dispersion of business units, vertical integration, and diversification. Moreover, this chapter considers the establishment of the central office concerning the functional separation of the directors' duties, the reform of the accounting system, and the establishment of the executive's representative organization and committee organizations. Furthermore, issues concerning the appearance of salaried managers and the rise of managerial enterprises are clarified concerning the type of enterprises in Germany, the retrocession of owner–managers, and the rise of salaried managers from the comparative viewpoint with the United States.

Keywords Divisional structure · Diversification · Functional structure · Managerial enterprise · Managerial hierarchy · Moder business enterprise · Salaried manager · Vertical integration

Regarding business management problems during the Second Reich, two fields—enterprise concentration and labor management system reform—were considered in Chapters 4 and 5, respectively. In addition to these two fields, another important change in business management during this period can be observed in the rise of modern business enterprises that integrated multiple functions such as production, sales, purchasing, managerial hierarchies, and managerial enterprises run by salaried managers.

As Alfred. D. Chandler, Jr. made clear, in the United States (US), modern business enterprises that had multiple business units and managerial hierarchies were created by integrating production and distribution. The managerial hierarchy was an important institution for managing, controlling, and coordinating multiple business

T. Yamazaki, *A History of German Business*,
https://doi.org/10.1007/978-981-96-8476-2_6

units consolidated by vertical integration. "Modern business enterprise took the place of market mechanism in coordinating the activities of the economy and allocating its resources." Thus, "in many sectors of the economy the visible hand of management replaced what Adam Smith referred to as the invisible hand of market forces" (Chandler 1977, p.1).

In this period, structural changes in capitalism in Germany as well as in the US occurred with the 1873 crisis and chronic crises occurring at 10-year intervals thereafter. As a result, the level of productive force tended to exceed the scale of markets, making the internalization of the sales function necessary for understanding market conditions and responding to changes. The internalization of the sales functions as well as the integration of the purchasing function became an effective way to achieve harmonious business process flow and throughput. In this manner, functional vertical integration progressed and organizational structure reform became necessary with such movements. Managerial hierarchies were built as an effective countermeasure.

Therefore, in Chapter 6, the birth of the modern business enterprise with multiple business units and managerial hierarchies run by salaried managers will be explored from the perspective of comparison with the US.

Section 6.1 examines the rise of the modern business enterprise and its factors. In Sect. 6.2, changes in organizational structure are analyzed. Section 6.3 considers the appearance of managerial enterprises run by salaried managers and their roles.

6.1 Rise of the Modern Business Enterprise and Its Historical Background

6.1.1 Rise of the Modern Business Enterprise

First, in examining the factors underlying the rise of the modern business enterprise and changes in management in Germany as well as in the US, the appearance of such enterprises was related to the development of modern industrial capitalism. According to Jürgen Kocka, what made growth possible in the first phase—which began around 1840 and ended with the economic crisis in 1873—was "an integrated market that was enlarged through the expansion of transportation (primarily the railroads) and through the attainment of economic and political unity" (Kocka 1980, p.77). Although this first breakthrough ended with the crisis of 1873, the steady and rapid expansion of the economy began again in the mid-1890s and continued until World War II with short interruptions. Thus, the second phase of industrialization in Germany occurred from 1873 to 1913 (Kocka 1980, p.78). The ratio of the national wealth created in the manufacturing and mining sectors to all national wealth increased from about 33% in 1873 to 45% 1913, and the annual growth rate of these sectors, including handicrafts, was 3.7% during this period (Hoffmann 1965, S.65, 454–455).

In this way, this age was the period of new development of German capitalism and the modern business enterprise was born, and changes in management and organization occurred. Jürgen Kocka pointed out that from the 1870s through World War I, the modern business enterprise emerged in Germany. In this country as well as the US, although developments in technology and the market in the latter half of the nineteenth century were major factors in the structural change of enterprises, five major, interrelated factors lay at the center of the rise of the modern business enterprise: (1) the process of expansion, integration, and diversification, (2) the emergence of cartels and associations, (3) changes in the relationship between industry and banks, (4) the rise of managerial capitalism with its tendency toward the separation of ownership and control and the appearance of salaried entrepreneurs, and (5) the increasing importance of science and systems in production, distribution, and management (Kocka 1980, p.78).

Although the process of expansion, integration, and diversification can be regarded as the most important factor, cartels became "one of the foundations of the whole of economic life" in Germany during the boom at the end of the nineteenth century and during the crisis of 1900–1903 (Ленин 1962, S.317). Syndicates played a significant role as form of enterprise combination. Participation in a tight cartel or syndicate can be regarded as one means for a company integrating forward without founding its own sales organization, because such a cartel sold the products of the member companies collectively (Kocka 1980, p.80). As a form of forward integration, enterprises sometimes used syndicates to market undifferentiated, commodity-like products but tended to rely on their own sales forces to sell more technologically complex products (Feldman 1977, p.30; Chandler 1990, pp.423–424).

In examining the changes in the relationship between industry and banks, the supervisory board was one way for banks to influence corporations directly by holding mandates on this top management organ. Before 1914, bank directors formed the largest single group among the supervisory board members of German corporations and occupied 20% of all mandates. However, in the early twentieth century, the rate of self-financing in large manufacturing enterprises increased. As a result, enterprises tended to be more and more independent of the capital market and banks. In addition, sometimes an inner circle of the supervisory board collaborated closely with boards of directors instead of supervising its activities. In long-term management, the managing board became more influential than the supervisory board and this shift gradually reduced the bank's control over industrial enterprises and raised the power of salaried managers (Kocka 1980, pp.91–92). In managerial enterprises, the achievement of managers could be more significant as a criterion for hiring and promotion than cases in which ownership and control were inseparable. Thus, the "increasing importance of salaried entrepreneurs or managers reinforced the trends toward professionalism and scientific management in industry" (Kocka 1980, p.94).

6.1.2 Expansion of Enterprise Scale

Economic development in Germany after the middle of the nineteenth century can be characterized by the strong expansion of company scale. It required changes in the organizational structure and the development of the division of labor in management (Feldenkirchen 1982, S.304). Increasing enterprise scale promoted the concentration of production. The ratio of the number of workers in companies with over 50 employees to the total number of workers in the manufacturing and handicraft industries rose from 22.8% in 1882 to 42.2% in 1907. The ratio of the number of workers in companies with over 1000 employees to the total number of workers in such sectors increased from 1.9% in 1882 to 3.3% in 1895 and further increased to 4.9% in 1907 (Hoffmann 1965, S.212). In looking at similar figures by industrial sector (see Table 6.1), sectors such as mining, engineering, electrical engineering, chemicals, and textiles led the trend toward concentration. In each field of these industries, more than two-thirds of all employees worked in plants with over 50 employees. In contrast, the least concentrated areas were observed in the manufacturers of clothing, food, and wood and leather products (Kocka 1980, p.79).

Regarding changes in the legal form of the largest 100 companies in the German manufacturing and mining sectors, the number of unincorporated firms decreased from 15 in 1887 to 1 in 1927, whereas the number of joint-stock companies increased from 79 to 88 in same period. Transformations to the joint-stock company form progressed with the expansion of enterprise scale. This trend can be observed particularly in capital-intensive industrial sectors, such as the iron, metal smelting, electrical engineering, and chemical industries. This pattern of development in Germany was different from that in the US in that the producer goods industry was superior to the consumer goods industry (Kocka 1981c, S.45–48).

6.1.3 Trend Toward Vertical Integration

In Germany, cases in which the expansion of enterprises was accompanied by vertical integration and diversification were not rare, as in the case of American enterprises (Kocka 1980, p.79). Therefore, next, in examining the progress of integration, Table 6.2 indicates the integration conditions of the largest 100 manufacturing and mining firms in 1887, 1907, and 1927, the number of firms that integrated both forward and backward increased from 6 in 1887 to 17 in 1907. Regarding membership in cartels or syndicates as a means for a firm to integrate forward without establishing its own sales organization, the number of firms that integrated in both directions increased from 13 to 62 and the number of firms that integrated only forward increased from 12 to 20 in same period. In contrast, the number of companies that integrated only backward significantly decreased from 48 to 6. The number of companies that integrated neither forward nor backward decreased from 27 to 12 in same period. Thus, the trend toward vertical integration can be observed in

Table 6.1 The 100 largest German enterprises in the mining and manufacturing industries based on capital amount

Nominal capital	1887											1907				
	Mining	Stone and clay	Iron and metal	Machine	Electrical	Chemical	Textile	Rubber	Wood	Food	Total	Mining	Stone and clay	Iron and metal	Machine	Electrical
more than 500																
100–499														3		2
80–99.9																
60–79.9												2				
40–59.9												2		6		1
30–39.9			2								3			4		
20–29.9	1		4								5	7		9	3	
15–19.9	1		8	2		2					13	7	1	5	3	
10–14.9	1		5			3					9	5	2	4	7	1
5–9.9	11	1	9	7	1	5	1			1	36					
~4.9	10	2	4	3		2	4	1	1	7	34					
Total	24	3	32	12	2	12	5	1	1	48	100	23	3	31	13	4
Average capital	7.6	5.7	13.9	7.3	17.5	8.7	5.0	4.5	4.9	4.4	9.4	25.3	13.2	36.7	15.1	78.4

(continued)

Table 6.1 (continued)

Nominal capital	1907					1927											
	Chemical	Textile	Paper	Food	Total	Mining	Stone and clay	Iron and metal	Machine	Electrical	Chemical	Textile	Paper	Leather	Rubber	Food	Total
more than 500								1			1						2
100–499					5	2		2		2	2						8
80–99.9						2		2			2						6
60–79.9					2	1		1	1			1					4
40–59.9					9	2		4	4	1	1	1					13
30–39.9					4	1		3	1	1	1	1	2		1	2	13
20–29.9	5	1		1	26		4	3	3	1	4	3		1		2	21
15–19.9	4		2	1	23			4	7		1	2		2		3	19
10–14.9	8	2		2	31	1	1	2	4		1	2	1	1		1	14
5–9.9																	
~4.9																	
Total	17	3	2	4	100	9	5	22	20	5	13	10	3	4	1	8	100
Average capital	16.1	14.2	17.6	14.6	26.8	65.3	22.1	82.5	27.2	99.6	132.6	27.5	26.4	17.7	34.1	22.4	59.2

Source This figure was compiled by the author, based on Siegrist (1980, S.76)

almost the same period as when modern business enterprises rose in the US. The trend toward integration was strongest in the chemical, primary metal, and mining industries. Such enterprises integrated all of the various stages of production from the mining of coal and iron or via the production of pig iron and steel through many stages of metal processing and occasionally even to heavy machinery (Kocka 1980, p.87).

In examining the conditions of vertical integration in the major industrial sectors, in the **iron and metal industries**, regarding the integration of the sales function, the movement of partial integration through membership in syndicates was especially prominent from 1887 to 1907. In contrast, remarkable expansion of the company's own sales organization (establishing of such an organization or strong capital participation in commercial enterprises) was observed.

In the **mining industry (including petroleum extracting and refining)**, when comparing the sales strategies of mining firms in 1887, 1907, and 1927, the manner of independent trade (in 1887), that of partial integration by syndicates (in 1907), and that of the integration of the sales function by establishing the company's own sales organization appeared.

In the **machinery industry**, the integration of sales tended to progress compared to the conditions in the mining and iron and metal industries in 1907 (see **Table** 4.2). Backward integration toward raw materials was not frequently compared with the former period even in 1927, and it was pointed out that such a strategy would never be attractive for precious processing manufacturers (Siegrist 1980, S.69–72).

In the **food and semi-luxury products industries**, a part of large manufacturers pursued a decisive integration policy early (Siegrist 1980, S.75). By 1887, the integration of sales had already become a usual phenomenon, particularly in the electrical, chemical, and distillation industries (Kocka 1981c, S.50). In the distillation industry, the rise of large, integrated enterprises was observed earlier, as in the case of the US. In the 1880s, the sales equipment of big distillation firms came to first be composed of a few of their own stores and, in some cases, refrigerator cars. However, the sales organizations of large distillation firms were giant even compared to them (Siegrist 1980, S.75) and vertical integration progressed strongly during the first 20 years of the twentieth century.

In this way, in Germany, although the trend toward vertical integration occurred from 1887 to 1907, the integration of raw materials rather stagnated for the whole industry (Siegrist 1980, S.79). Jürgen Kocka pointed out that backward integration was often adapted at the late of the 19th century because the relations of industrial technique and defensive market policy were already observed and this held true for the coal industry in particular, and the iron and steel and chemical industries as well. However, the movement toward backward integration was not very active after 1907, except after World War I, until the ceasing of inflation. In contrast, the integration of sales tended to become a usual strategy in enterprises of not only the electrical, chemical, and distillation industries in which it came to be the first common phenomenon but also of all industrial sectors. As a means of integration, increasing membership in syndicates was the main method from 1887 to 1907, and the integration or establishment of a company's own sales organization became the

Table 6.2 Changes in forms of integration in the 100 largest German enterprises in the mining and Manufacturing industries

Industries	1887									1907			
	Number of companies	ab[1)]	abc	abcd	abd	b	bc	bcd	bd	Number of companies	ab	abc	abcd
Mining	24	16	2	0	0	6	0	0	0	23	3	1	2
Stone, clay, and ceramics	3	3	0	0	0	0	0	0	0	3	0	2	0
Iron and metal	32	21	2	0	5	3	0	0	1	31	1	1	7
Machine and transportation equipment	12	1	0	0	0	9	2	0	0	13	0	0	0
Electrical	2	0	1	0	0	0	1	0	0	4	0	0	1
Chemical	12	5	0	0	2	2	3	0	0	17	1	3	0
Textile	5	0	0	0	0	5	0	0	0	3	0	0	0
Paper and printing	–[2)]	–	–	–	–	–	–	–	–	2	1	0	0
Leather, linoleum, and shoe manufacturing	–	–	–	–	–	–	–	–	–	–	–	–	–
Rubber	1	0	0	0	0	0	1	0	0	–	–	–	–
Wood and wood processing	1	0	1	0	0	0	0	0	0	–	–	–	–
Food and favorite food	8	2	0	0	0	2	4	0	0	4	0	0	0
Total	100	48	6	0	7	27	11	0	1	100	6	7	10

Industries	1907					1927								
	abd	b	bc	bcd	bd	Number of companies	ab	abc	abcd	abd	b	bc	bcd	bd
Mining	14	0	0	0	3	9	0	0	7	2	0	0	0	0
Stone, clay, and ceramics	1	0	0	0	0	5	0	2	0	3	0	0	0	0
Iron and metal	20	2	0	0	0	22	1	1	12	2	1	5	0	0
Machine and transportation equipment	2	6	4	1	0	20	0	0	2	1	6	11	0	0
Electrical	0	0	2	1	0	5	0	0	1	0	0	2	2	0
Chemical	8	2	2	0	1	13	0	0	4	5	0	4	0	0
Textile	0	2	1	0	0	10	0	1	0	0	2	5	1	1

(continued)

Table 6.2 (continued)

Industries	1907					1927								
	abd	b	bc	bcd	bd	Number of companies	ab	abc	abcd	abd	b	bc	bcd	bd
Paper and printing	0	0	1	0	0	3	0	2	0	0	0	1	0	0
Leather, linoleum, and shoe manufacturing	–	–	–	–	–	4	0	0	0	0	0	4	0	0
Rubber	–	–	–	–	–	1	0	1	0	0	0	0	0	0
Wood and wood processing	–	–	–	–	–	–	–	–	–	–	–	–	–	–
Food and favorite food	0	0	4	0	0	8	2	0	0	0	0	6	0	0
Total	45	12	14	2	4	100	3	7	26	13	9	38	3	1

Note 1) a = raw materials, b = production, c = sale, d=syndicate
2) No company concerned
Source This figure was compiled by the author, based on Kocka (1980, pp.85–86), Kocka (1981c, S.45–47), and Siegrist (1980, S.90–92).

main measure from 1907 to 1927. Jürgen Kocka stressed that the gradual shift from "market" to "organization" can be clearly traced along the integration of functions that progressed in large enterprises (Kocka 1981c, S.48–50).

6.1.4 *Trend Toward Diversification*

Furthermore, in considering diversification, it remained a much more limited phenomenon in the less capital-intensive industries and the consumer-goods industries in general. Integrating and running a heterogenous concern was considered an extremely difficult problem that required more organizational and managerial skills than were available at the time. Therefore, before World War I, highly diversified combinations were exceptional in the labor-intensive industries other than the raw materials and heavy machinery industries (Kocka 1980, p.88).

In Germany, the tendency toward diversification was seen in a relatively early period. In looking at the largest 100 manufacturing and mining enterprises (see Table 6.3), the number of enterprises that did not diversify decreased from 16 in 1887 to 5 in 1907, whereas the number of enterprises that had more than 10 production fields increased from 9 to 19 in same period. By 1927, this trend further progressed and the number of enterprises with no diversification decreased to only one. The number of enterprises that had over 10 production fields increased to 30. When considering conditions according to the industrial sector, companies with over 10 production fields were of the highest number in the iron and metal, machinery and transportation equipment, and electrical engineering industries. In 1907, the number of such companies was 11 out of the 31 companies in the iron and metal industries. A similar numerical figure in the machinery and transportation equipment industry was 4 out of 13 companies, and in the electrical engineering industry was 4 out of 4 companies. For enterprises, diversification was an attractive strategy for using capital-intensive equipment and existing valuable know-how more effectively. There was a definite tendency toward the production of products outside of the department in the 1920s (Siegrist 1980, S.81–82). This point is in contrast to the number of firms that did not diversify being 23 out of the largest 82 American industrial enterprises and there only being 8 firms with over 10 production fields (see Table 6.3).

In this way, in German big businesses, although integration was slightly ahead of diversification, both progressed at almost the same time. Hans Siegrist pointed out that A. D. Chandler, Jr. regarded the 1920s as the beginning of strong diversification in the US and compared with Germany, great delays in the US became apparent. Differences between the nations were due to the scale of the market (Siegrist 1980, S.82–83). Progressing diversification in big companies can be regarded as the gradual complementation of market principles according to organizational principles of a certain formality. Jürgen Kocka indicated the delay in the development of the social division of labor and the characteristics of the domestic market as the reasons why the tendency toward diversification appeared early in Germany (Kocka 1981c, S.50).

Regarding the delay in developing the social division of labor, German businessmen in important industrial sectors could not depend upon a well-developed industrial and commercial tradition. There were no specialized merchants and shippers who were able to provide raw materials and sell their products in sufficient numbers. Jürgen Kocka pointed out that a low degree of division of labor in the economy as a whole led to a high degree of division of labor within the new enterprises—if they got off the ground at all. This process explains, at least in part, why large-scale, highly integrated, diversified firms existed even in the first phase of German industrialization, during the second third of the nineteenth century and even earlier, especially in the production of raw materials and machinery (Kocka 1980, p.108).

The German domestic market was relatively undeveloped, and its transparency was low. Therefore, entrepreneurs in the first period promoted diversification of products early. If they attempted to make the most of advanced equipment based on European nations' model and decrease risk, such action was needed (Kocka 1981c, S.59). Entrepreneurs aimed for as wide a range of products as possible due to the lack of efficient markets. A form of functional and enterprise diversification was not only the mark of an advanced stage of industrialization but also the result of delayed economic development in the first stage and a gap for which the late industrial countries attempted compensate (Kocka 1975a, S.218; Pohl 1981, S.150, 1982, p.98). This trend of German enterprises toward diversification reflected the characteristics of industrialization related to market conditions. Jeffrey R. Fear points out that "while Americans concentrated on economies of scale and speed, the Germans pioneered in economies of scope and vertical integration" (Fear 2005, p.734).

Table 6.3 Conditions of diversification in the 100 largest German mining and manufacturing Enterprises and the 82 largest American industrial enterprises

Industries	Largest 100 mining and manufacturing enterprises in Germany									
	1887					1907				
	Number of companies	A[1)]	B	C	D	Number of companies	A	B	C	D
Mining	24	7	17	0	0	23	3	17	3	0
stone and clay and ceramics	3	0	2	1	0	3	0	3	0	0
Iron and metal	32	1	11	16	4	31	0	1	19	11
Machine and transportation equipment	12	0	1	7	4	13	0	2	7	4
Electrical	2	0	1	0	1	4	0	0	0	4
Chemical	12	3	8	1	0	17	1	13	3	0
Oil distillation	–[2)]	–	–	–	–	–	–	–	–	–
Textile	5	1	4	0	0	3	1	2	0	0
Paper and printing	–	–	–	–	–	2	0	2	0	0
Leather, linoleum, and shoe manufacturing	–	–	–	–	–	–	–	–	–	–
Rubber	1	0	1	0	0	–	–	–	–	–
Wood and wood processing	1	0	1	0	0	–	–	–	–	–
Food and favorite food	8	4	4	0	0	4	0	4	0	0
Total	100	16	50	25	9	100	5	44	32	19
Industries	Largest 100 mining and manufacturing enterprises in Germany					Largest 82 industrial enterprises in the United States				
	1927					1929				
	Number of Companies	A	B	C	D	Number of companies	A	B	C	D
Mining	9	0	4	2	3	–	–	–	–	–
stone and clay and ceramics	5	0	3	2	0	1	0	0	0	0
Iron and metal	22	0	2	7	13	20	0	8	11	1

(continued)

Table 6.3 (continued)

Industries	Largest 100 mining and manufacturing enterprises in Germany					Largest 82 industrial enterprises in the United States				
	1927					1929				
	Number of Companies	A	B	C	D	Number of companies	A	B	C	D
Machine and transportation equipment	20	0	6	6	8	12	4	4	4	0
Electrical	5	0	2	0	3	3	0	0	0	3
Chemical	13	0	6	4	3	6	2	0	2	2
Oil distillation	–	–	–	–	–	19	16	3	0	0
Textile	10	0	4	6	0	1	0	0	1	0
Paper and printing	3	0	1	2	0	2	0	0	2	0
Leather, linoleum, and shoe manufacturing	4	1	3	0	0	–	–	–	–	–
Rubber	1	0	1	0	0	4	0	2	2	0
Wood and wood processing	–	–	–	–	–	1	0	0	1	0
Food and favorite food	8	0	4	4	0	13	1	6	5	1
Total	100	1	36	33	30	82	23	23	28	8

Note: 1) A = 1, B = 2–4, C = 5–9, D=more than 10 production fields (product fields)
2) No company concerned
Source This figure was compiled by the author, based on Kocka (1980, pp.81–84), Siegrist (1980, S.82, S.90–92), and Porter and Livesay (1969, pp.293–294)

As early producers in relatively undeveloped industrial areas did not face established competitors, they had little to fear when they entered new markets or introduced new product lines. "As a result, patterns of expansion, diversification, and integration developed that seem to have lacked parallels in Britain or even in the US." However, some of the "factors that brought about diversification and integration became less powerful as the economy became more developed, as the overall division of labor became more elaborate, and as markets became more transparent or predictable" (Kocka 1980, pp.108–109).

The progress of the expansion of enterprises, integration, and diversification caused changes in organizational structures. Therefore, the next section considers this point.

6.2 Changes in Organizational Structures and Their Characteristics

6.2.1 The Scale Expansion of Enterprises, Regional Dispersion of Business Units, and Changes in Organizational Structures

The enlargement of enterprise scale after the latter half of the nineteenth century led to regional dispersion of business units in many cases. Companies were generally directed by owners during the industrialization phase. However, management was increasingly taken charge of by people employed for this purpose who were responsible for delegated tasks in the expansion stage. Most factory owners in the early period were practical men who had a commercial or trade background (Pohl 1981, S.154–155; 1982, p.101). When small and medium business units were dominant, it was easy to secure direct contact with employees and understand an outline of the business. As a result, most enterprises did not need independent management to be separated from the enterprise's production and commercial departments. They also did not need a well-designed division of authority and functions, special organization of management, or deliberate securing of the information flow (Kocka 1969a, S.336).

Under such conditions, the management and organization of individual companies generally reflected the owner's personality and were regarded as "the product of his particular style of management" in "the period of founder." However, once a company grew to a certain size, it was no longer effective or possible to use only an owner's personal style of management. Direct contact with employees and obtaining detailed information regarding various production processes became more difficult. Furthermore, enterprise growth often entailed geographical decentralization. Branches were created at some distance from the main plant. As a result, the supervision of these branches became more difficult (Pohl 1981, S.155; 1982, pp.101–102).

For instance, in examining the iron and steel firms in the Ruhrdistrict from 1879 to 1914, a remarkable expansion of enterprises required changes in the organizational structure and management based on the division of labor. For example, in business units of the Phönix or the Union located in a separated region, centralization of all decision-making and the dispersion of production were not appropriate. As necessary and rapid adaptation to economic changes was not possible, it became clear that the organizational structures of both enterprises were insufficient in the next depression. The separation of business unit locations and their scale expansion created problems of coordination, information, and control not seen in large enterprises concentrated in a certain region or in small and medium firms (Feldenkirchen 1982, S.304–305; Stillich 1904, S.93).

The degree of the division of labor and decentralization depended on the number of business units and the scale of business and top managers in individual enterprises. Around 1914, there were definite differences between giant enterprises such as Gelsenkirchener Bergwerks-AG that composed of business units located in separate regions, including Phönix and Deutsch-Luxembourg, and smaller enterprises such as Hoesch, Rheinsiche Stahlwerke, and Bochumer Verein whose business units were not dispersed locationally. For instance, at Phönix, after the adoption of an organizational structure in 1907, the management of each business unit was handled by one person who took charge of technical or commercial affairs (Feldenkirchen 1982, S.314–315).

At all large companies, activities shifted from duties related to production techniques or technical innovation to the total planning of commercial issues and were almost moved to managers and their representatives. The management of technical innovation was taken charge of by various layers of middle management. The introduction of new organizational structures was generally performed in three steps that progressed intermittently: (1) enlargement of duty, (2) increasing the possibility of personnel arrangement by establishing new positions or management levels, and (3) adaptation of organizational structures to changes in the relationship between purpose and means (Feldenkirchen 1982, S.304–305).

The importance of middle management increased with enterprise expansion and the decentralization of decision-making. According to Wilfried Feldenkirchen, in all iron and steel companies researched by him, a new layer of middle management with staff and management positions existed. These staff positions for management made it possible for managers to adjust to the growth of the enterprise and were aimed at decreasing the burden of managers in business units and departments at that time and securing the desirable centralization of decision (Feldenkirchen 1982, S.314).

From 1879 to 1914, these organizational changes in the iron and steel industry of the Ruhr region were determined by the movement of decision-making authorities from an upper level to a lower level. The degree of decision-making decentralization depended on factors such as (1) the scale of the enterprise and horizontal and vertical expansion, (2) the form of company growth preferred by each firm, (3) the composition of shareholders and their influence on management, (4) the financing methods of the company, (5) the location of each business unit, and (6) the degree of the shift in authority from the supervisory board to the board of directors (Feldenkirchen 1982, S.307).

6.2.2 *Progress of Vertical Integration and Changes in Organizational Structure*

Next, this section examines the development of vertical integration and changes in the organizational structure. Different vertical integration strategies can be observed between industrial sectors. Therefore, the conditions in important industries are considered.

6.2.2.1 Development of Vertical Integration in Major Industries

Cases in the Iron and Steel Industry

In the iron and steel industry, at least within a country, as selling was performed through cartels and syndicates, the sales department was generally expanded only slightly in contrast to systems of management and calculation. Nevertheless, daily relationships regarding business between the sales office of syndicates and the enterprise were taken charge of by the sales office. Therefore, the existence of a combination of enterprises increased the necessity for enlarging the middle management layer (Feldenkirchen 1982, S.315).

In addition, among large companies that invested in new technology on a large scale and significantly expanded their production facilities, there were companies that created large marketing organizations. A. D. Chandler, Jr. pointed out that by the end of the nineteenth century, "the German steelmakers, again like the Americans but unlike the British, were beginning to build extensive marketing organizations" (Chandler 1990, p.491). The enterprises of the Thyssen groups had distribution offices and facilities in Berlin, Stettin, Duisburg, Ludwigshafen, Königsberg, and Buenos Aires in Argentina before the outbreak of World War I (Treue 1966, S.157). "Gelsenkirchener Bergwerks-AG, as a giant, integrated mining and steel-producing company, had offices and subsidiaries in a dozen German cities and exclusive agents in as many more, as well as branch offices and agents in nearly all the major European cities and also in China, Egypt, Morocco, Ceylon, South Africa, Brazil, Uruguay, and Chile." Thus, large German firms in the iron and steel industry, as well as its American counterparts, invested more in new technology than their British rivals and created essential and quite similar organizations to run the new production and distribution processes (Chandler 1990, p.491).

Cases in the Machinery Industry

In the machinery industry, large production companies attempted to establish their own marketing organizations. Some German heavy machinery manufacturers provided even more comprehensive marketing services than those of American and German light machinery makers. Regarding international sales forces, A. D. Candler, Jr. pointed out that "they spent more time with industrial customers in designing products to meet their specific needs. They worked out arrangements to extend extensive credit and provide elaborate repair and service guarantees." "The German machinery makers recruited extensive managerial hierarchies to supervise and integrate their processes of production and distribution, hierarchies that were probably even larger than those of the American machinery companies" (Chandler 1990, p.457). At heavy machinery producers, "their sales departments supervised a global marketing network. They usually had their own branches in Europe and relied on exclusive agents elsewhere. Their technical and design departments had subdivisions for the different major product lines" (Chandler 1990, p.462).

Cases in the Electrical Engineering Industry

When examining cases in the electrical industry as well as the chemical industry, large enterprises vigorously attempted to perform forward integration by establishing their own sales organizations. Jürgen Kocka pointed out that "by the mid-1880s, the technical complexity of finished products and services had already led the large electrical engineering and chemicals concerns such as Siemens. AEG, and Bayer, to take over retailing through sale to the final customer" (Kocka 1980, p.88).

Siemens did not have a special sales network in the first period except for the subsidiaries founded in each European country. Even in the case of founding a sales base, this company used external companies, such as commercial firms and agents in each region, instead of integrating the sales function within the company. However, circumstances surrounding this enterprise changed remarkably as "the high-voltage electric revolution" progressed starting in the 1880s. Until then, the passive sales policy was not able to satisfy the new needs of the age. When Siemens transformed toward the growth strategy under Wilhelm von Siemens starting in 1890, the sales policy was reconsidered. The transformation of the sales policy of this company in the 1890s had two pillars: (1) replacing sales agents with technical offices (*Technisches Büro*) as the company's own base and (2) the arrangement of a sales management organization inside the central office corresponding to establishing the sales base. This enterprise decided to establish its own sales base in 1892 due to difficulties of control and understanding the sales network and problems with final responsibility for products under the traditional ways of using agents (Takenaka 1991, pp.38–40; Siemens 1961, S.370).

In examining the condition outside of the country, the foreign sales office of Siemens & Halske was composed exclusively of sales agents until the end of 1889. The first sales office was established in Munich on January 25, 1890, immediately after Wilhelm von Siemens took over management of this company (Mass 1958, S.195). After that, the foundation of the sales office progressed both inside and outside of the country, step by step. The Tokyo office established in 1893 was the first oversees technical office. The total number of technical offices reached 30 in 1903, the number of domestic offices was 22, and that of foreign offices was eight (Takenaka 1991, p.41; Siemens 1961, S.371; Chandler 1990, p.465). In 1914, Siemens had foreign corporate bodies with plants in 10 foreign countries and 168 technical offices, branches, and agents in 49 nations (von Weiher and Goetzler 1981, S.60). Differences did not exist between the organization of the offices in Germany and abroad at the time. Each technical office had "a commercial head alongside the technical managers" and a large staff of trained electrical engineers who were in charge of designing, installing, and servicing customers' electrical equipment (Siemens 1957, p.305; Chandler 1990, p.465). At **AEG**, international sales and service networks were established as well. The number of bureaus in Germany and other European nations was 42 and 37, respectively, and the number of overseas offices reached 38 around 1900 (Hasse 1902, S.35).

The sales offices of these two companies played an important role in the development of the business. A. D. Chandler, Jr. pointed out that "as at the American companies, the sales offices of AEG and Siemens provided their production, design, and research departments with a steady flow of information about customers' needs that propelled the rapid development of new technology. Again, like General Electric with its Electric Bond and Share Company, these German firms created financial institutions that provided customers with the funds necessary to finance their purchases" (Chandler 1990, p.465).

At Siemens, backward integration into raw material departments progressed as well as the forward integration of sales functions. Some factories producing raw materials and semi-finished goods such as rubber, wires, china, and paper were acquired while creating a very elaborate network of sales departments and offices staffed with salaried personnel and centrally controlled by the head office in Berlin (Kocka 1971, p.148).

Cases in the Chemical Industry

The chemical industry belonged to an industrial sector in which large companies pursued vertical integration vigorously. The technical characteristics of this industry promoted such movement from the beginning. Production processes were complex and required many intermediate steps and an enormous number of plants. In addition, competition drove companies to expand not only their production facilities but also their marketing efforts (Feldenkirchen 1987, p.429; Paschke 1925, S.25–26).

A. D. Chandler, Jr. stressed that "from the late 1870s on the leaders invested heavily in marketing and distributing facilities and then in research facilities and personnel to improve product and process" and "the new marketing organizations with their worldwide network of branches and agents were among the largest in the world." "Branch offices included experienced chemists and dyers who, like the trained sales forces of the electrical equipment manufacturers, worked closely with their customers. These offices sent in a steady flow of information about the strengths and weaknesses of the products and suggestions for improvement—information that commercial intermediaries were rarely competent to supply. The staff people in the central sales office in Germany who received these reports worked closely with processing departments and research laboratories, both to improve and to innovate" (Chandler 1990, p.475).

At the time, in the business structure of German chemical enterprises, dye was the main field. Until around 1885, in the industrialized countries of Europe and in the US, sales were performed through local wholesalers that took charge of the role as agent and usually limited their sales to the products of a single color company. In contrast, the dye enterprises in Germany depended largely on export companies to sell their colors to the underdeveloped nations of the world. However, afterward, each major dye firm began to take over the wholesaling of their own products. As contracts with many exporting and marketing companies were expiring, these enterprises decided not to renew them. Instead, they tried to establish their own sales offices in the main commercial centers of the world by sending trained salesmen and traveling consultants (Beer 1959, pp.94–95).

For instance, at **Bayer**, a worldwide marketing organization was created. It was divided into six regional groups: (1) Teutonic (Germany, Austria, Holland, and Scandinavia), (2) Latin (France Italy, Spain, Belgium, and Switzerland), (3) Eastern Europe, (4) Britain, (5) North America, and (6) one for South America, Australia, and the Far East. The Sales Department included a worldwide marketing organization for dyes since the 1880s and, after that, a smaller one for pharmaceuticals, that had entirely different personnel, a third organization for marketing photographic film, and a fourth and even smaller one for selling intermediate products (Chandler 1990, pp.477–478). Thus, at Bayer, in addition to sales and purchasing organizations of inorganic chemical products and organic intermediate products, sales organizations for (1) dye, (2) pharmaceuticals, and (3) photographic products were established and were put in charge of each region and country (*Bayer Archiv*, 010-003-001, Tabellarische Uebersicht über die Organisation des Gesamtgeschäfts der Farbenfabriken vorm. Friedr. Bayer & Co. zu Elberfeld, *Bayer Archiv*, 010-004). A memorandum of this company on organization in 1906 pointed out that the purchasing organization was divided into two sections of chemical products and machine products according to the characteristics of the products sold and sales units of inorganic chemical products produced in this company should be included in these two sections [*Bayer Archiv*, 010-003-001, Denkschrift über die Organisation des Gesamtgeschäfts der Farbenfabriken vorm. Friedr. Bayer & Co. zu Elberfeld (Februar 1906)].

6.2.2.2 Management Functions with the Development of Vertical Integration

The development of vertical integration increased the importance of management. In his study of the US, A. D. Chandler, Jr. pointed out that "the coordination and monitoring of current production and distribution of goods" and "the allocation of resources for future production and distribution" were two basic functions of the modern business enterprise (Chandler 1977, p.450). Regarding middle management, he explained that "the tasks of the managers on the lower level who had charged of the operating units did not differ greatly from those of men who owned and managed a single independent factory or commercial office. But the tasks of the middle managers were entirely new. Middle managers had to pioneer in the ways of modern administrative coordination" (Chandler 1977, p.411).

In Germany, similar conditions can be observed. Integration and diversification in large companies required highly qualified management. The integration of a raw materials base and the foundation of the company's own sales organization required the division of entrepreneurial functions into departments that needed the appropriate specialists in the acquisition of raw materials, further processing, and sales and distribution to run them (Pohl 1981, S.155; Pohl 1982, p. 102).

Under such conditions, in Germany, as well as in the US, centralized functional structures were created in many cases. Jürgen Kocka pointed out that "presumably, vertically integrated, centralized, functionally departmentalized organizations were predominant in Germany, as they were in the United States, at the time" (Kocka 1980, p.98).

However, there were differences between Germany and the US in securing personnel for management. In Germany, as well as the US, considerable progress was achieved by the enterprises in marketing and accounting late in the nineteenth century. As manufacturing firms took over wholesale functions and, to a certain degree, retail functions, the development of new marketing methods became necessary. However, it was not necessarily connected to greater academic training. Progress in this period was achieved not so much by managers with academic business training as by practical men who received a middle-level, commercial-school education at best (Kocka 1980, p.96; Hartmann, 1955, p.18. Regarding commercial education in Germany at the time, see Farrington 1914).

6.2.2.3 Influence of Bureaucracy on Changes in Organizational Structure

In examining the German characteristics of building management organizations, one of them can be observed in the influence of bureaucracy. At the middle and lower levels of management, the growing staff of a company was organized on the basis of "models borrowed from the public bureaucracy." Jürgen Kocka pointed out the following: Written procedures and regulations and systematic job descriptions were emphasized in the technical and marketing offices as well as in the company's central administration. The division of labor was complex and far-reaching; the hierarchy was carefully defined, and lines of authority and procedures for transmitting information were highly formalized. As a result, private bureaucracies sprang up that differed little from those in the government and in state enterprises (Kocka 1980, p.97). A more systematic approach was adopted by top management, and they kept some impersonal, general rules. At the level of middle management, bureaucratic trends became more evident than ever before in the huge white-collar departments and in factory management (Kocka 1981a, p.459).

According to Jürgen Kocka, "as a result of the specific conditions of German industrialization, bureaucratic patterns strongly influenced the development of industrial management." Whereas they were induced mainly from outside in the first stage, "later on, under new technological and commercial conditions, bureaucratization continued, more as a result of changes within the enterprise than as a result from external influences. While being modified and adjusted, existing bureaucratic structures and dispositions could be utilized by German large-scale enterprises in later periods of growth, even though they had to be adjusted to new strategies and operations" (Kocka 1981a, p.461). However, a growth crisis occurred in the 1880s and the disadvantages of bureaucratic organization became more apparent. They can be observed in slow responses, organizational bottlenecks, and excessive formalization (Kocka 1981a, p.459). Bureaucratic structures and techniques had to be fused with other patterns, in particular, with personal, family-based managerial techniques and with market mechanisms and incentives to become functional. "All the limits to bureaucratization in the industrial enterprises resulted from its market dependence and particular achievement orientation, and the fact that private property remained its major source of legitimate power which could successfully refuse to yield to the pressures of bureaucratization" (Kocka 1981a, p.461).

6.2.2.4 Changes in Organizational Structures and the Increase in Non-manual Employees

Managerial organization with the layers of middle and lower management brought an increase in the number of non-manual employees as a new class within the company. As progress of both the division of labor and functional complexity increased the need for coordination, more management personnel had to be arranged (Klatzky 1970, p.429). R. Stockmann pointed out that in manufacturing departments, the rate of commercial personnel can be regarded as a criterion for the scale of the management organization (Stockmann 1987, S.174). With a further increase in duties based on changes in circumstance, the growing necessity for coordination as a result of a more complicated organizational flow promoted the expansion of commercial personnel (Stockmann 1987, S.198). According to Jürgen Kocka, although the semantic distinction between workers and non-manual workers or between workers and private officers was not very common outside individual companies, this condition radically changed by the beginning of World War II. The problems of non-manual personnel were taken up in books, pamphlets, periodicals, and public debates, and the term "non-manual personnel" ("*Angestellte*") was fully established by this time (Kocka, 1981a, p.464).

In 1895, the ratios of the number of commercial personnel to all employees in the electrical and chemical industries were 7.3% and 7.6%, respectively, the highest numerical figure. Similar numerical values increased to 9.8% and 9.9% in 1907 and further to 11.3% and 12.6% in 1925, respectively. Such figures in the iron and steel, machinery, and transportation equipment industries were 3.3% in 1895, 4.3% in 1907, and 7.4% in 1925 [Stockmann 1987, S.270 (Tabelle 5)]. Thus, in the industrial sector, a trend of significant increase in the number of non-manual personnel can be observed.

6.2.3 Progress of Diversification and Changes in Organizational Structure

6.2.3.1 Managerial Problems Brought About by Diversification

Next, in considering changes in organizational structure brought about by diversification, it was after World War I that diversification became evident as a growth strategy in Germany as well as in the US. In enterprises in which diversification was performed, difficult managerial problems appeared under the functional structure. The heads of departments faced difficulties in handling many diverse products. For instance, sales departments were forced to sell different kinds of products. The procurement of raw materials and routing of the production of different goods also became the cause of difficulties. Under such limits of operational management at the level below middle management, top management too often became busy making administrative decisions rather than entrepreneurial, executive decisions (Krooss and Gilbert 1972, p.253). As a result, they tended not to be able to concentrate on top management functions such as allocating corporate or long-term business resources. The appearance of such managerial problems was due to investing capital of industrial enterprises into many different kinds of production departments (Nakata 1983, p.120). Thus, functionally departmentalized organizational structures that had worked so well for a single product line enterprise were not good enough for a multiproduct enterprise.

In addition, as A. D. Chandler, Jr. made clear, "if expansion resulted only in the development of a full line of goods that continued to use much the same type of resources, the recognition of the marketing department so that it had an office for each major type of customer was usually sufficient." However, "where business diversified into wholly new lines for quite different customers with quite different wants, then more reorganization was needed. It became increasingly difficult to coordinate through the existing structure the different functional activities to the needs of several quite different markets" (Chandler 1962, p.393).

In this section, whether German enterprises in major industrial sectors encountered the abovementioned managerial problems under the functional structure with the progress of diversification from the late nineteenth century to World War I is examined. Three industries—the chemical, machinery, and electrical engineering industries—in which the diversification trend appeared more strongly than in other industries are considered.

6.2.3.2 Cases in the Chemical Industry

First, when examining cases in the chemical industry, diversification in this period tended to be limited to expanding from dye as a main product to fields such as pharmaceuticals and intermediate products. These product lines had a certain commonality in terms of production and a decisive difference could not necessarily be seen. For instance, inorganic chemicals, the all-important intermediate products of tar dye, all alizarin-, aniline-, azo-, and sulfur dyes, pharmaceuticals, and photographic products can be pointed out as production fields of Bayer in 1907 (Handbuch der Deutschen Aktien-Gesellschaften 1908, S.1230). These product fields were developed in relation to the dye production process as an important key product of German chemical enterprises at the time. Therefore, in the condition in which products were manufactured, there were not always decisive differences between these product fields.

In addition, as already considered in Sect. 6.2.2.1, at Bayer, its own sales organizations that took charge of marketing were established for pharmaceuticals, photographic film, and intermediate products as well as dye. This means that there was a certain organizational response to deal with multiple product lines by this enterprise. It can be considered that managerial problems with diversification under the functional structure, as seen in the pioneering companies of the 1920s, were still not decisively caused.

6.2.3.3 Cases in the Machinery Industry

The machinery industry belongs to an industrial sector in which the development of diversification using economies of scope had major significance. For example, **Machinenbau-Anstalt Humboldt** began to produce locomotives and railroad cars and other transportation equipment to make use of its underutilized production facilities in 1895 (Beckmann 1916, S.20–23, 136–147; Handbuch der Deutschen-Aktien-Gesellschaften 1912, S.659). It had seven departments in development after 1903. Among them, production departments such as (1) locomotives, (2) machinery, bullets, products supplied for the army, and transmissions, (3) railroad cars and transportation equipment, and (4) finished products such as steel frames, boilers, corrugated plates, and founding were included. In the machinery department, they produced products such as distillatory equipment, cooling machinery, and machines for mining (Chandler 1990, p.457).

At **Borsig,** which was famous for its steam locomotive production, in addition to steam locomotives, stationary steam engines, boilers, and other equipment used in steel mills, pumps, and pipelines were supplied to the oil industry, equipment for chemical factories, turbines, compressors, and cooling machinery for other industries were manufactured in the two decades after 1869 when this company delivered a Siemens-Martin open-hearth work that was the first one constructed in Germany as well as another one created by other company (Rheinmetall=Borsig Aktiengesellschaft 1937, S.34–40; Pierson 1973, S.176, 185–189). However, among the various products, locomotives still remained this company's primary product at this time (Chandler 1990, p.459).

Hannomag was also a steam locomotive maker in the first stage. Afterward, it manufactured products such as steam engines, boilers, pumps, heating equipment, cultivators, iron foundry products, centrifuges (after 1907), and ship engines (Däbritz and Metzeltin 1935, S.96–100, 117–118; Handbuch der Deutschen Aktien-Gesellschaften 1900, S.440; Chandler 1990, p.459). In contrast to Borsig, the ratio of its steam locomotive business to all business decreased to only 19% by 1900 (Chandler 1990, p.459).

In examining other machinery enterprises, similar patterns of diversification can be observed (Chandler 1990, p.460). For instance, **Maschinenfabrik-Augsburg-Nürnberg (MAN)**, a large enterprise with over 15,000 employees, pursued the economies of scope in its three works by producing a variety of machines for the mining, metal, and metal processing industries and for utility businesses by World

War I. Indeed, some heavy machinery companies with the same scale existed in the US and in the United Kingdom. However, firms with the same diversity of product lines as German firms did not exist (Chandler 1990, pp.460, 462).

Regarding the tendency toward diversification by German enterprises, Hans Pohl pointed out that in the mechanical engineering industry in which a relatively high degree of diversification appeared at the start due to the lack of the division of labor in the economy and efficient domestic sales markets, "a trend to greater specialization can be traced as production programs became more stable and companies changed to mass production for wider sales markets" (Pohl 1981, S.150; 1982, p.98). Trends toward diversification in large-scale machinery enterprises was a characteristic German phenomenon under such specific situations. It was after World War I that diversification was made a definite growth strategy in Germany. For instance, after 1924, the manufacturers of heavy industrial machinery quickly again became "the leading producers of machines for European factories, mines, ports, railway terminals, utilities, and commercial centers." The leading companies expanded their number of product lines. A. D. Chandler, Jr. stressed the wide variety of markets served by MAN in the late 1920s (Chandler 1990, p.535).

In this way, the trend toward diversification observed in the chemical and machinery industries from the late nineteenth century through World War I differed from cases in the 1920s in which the capital of industrial enterprises was broadly invested in different production areas. This was related to the formation of organizational structures.

6.2.3.4 Cases in the Electrical Engineering Industry

As was previously mentioned, in Germany at the time, as well as in the US, centralized functionally departmentalized organizations were predominant. However, exceptional cases can be observed. Jürgen Kocka pointed out that "there were many variations and combined structures—well-integrated concerns at the center and loose federations at the periphery." He regarded the decentralized multidivisional structure of the interlocking Siemens' enterprises composed of Siemens & Halske and Siemens-Schuckert Werke as at least one exceptional case (Kocka 1980, p.98).

The electrical engineering industry can be regarded as an industrial sector in which modern business enterprises achieved prominent growth by pursuing economies of scale and scope. A. D. Chandler, Jr. pointed out that "at the same time Siemens and AEG, in unparalleled burst of entrepreneurial energy" (Chandler 1990, p.466). In the Siemens group, by means of a merger in 1903, the Siemens-Schuckert Works that covered the entire heavy-current fields came to be in charge of "the production and distribution of equipment of power, light, and traction and railway systems; small parts and accessories (such as switches, fuses, plugs, sockets); and the high-voltage electric cables used in such systems," and Siemens & Halske took charge of the light-current sectors and continued to produce "low-voltage telegraph and telephone equipment, railway signals, and cables, in addition to electro-chemicals, light bulbs, and measuring instruments." "Both companies were managed from the same central administration building" (Chandler 1990, p.468; Siemens 1957, p.196, Handbuch der Deutschen Aktien-Gesellschaften 1903, S.512; Handbuch der Deutschen Aktien-Gesellschaften 1904, S.1634; Feldenkirchen 1999, pp.50–52). On the other hand, at the beginning of the twentieth century, AEG produced and supplied products such as (1) electric light equipment and electric supply equipment, (2) central electric power plants, (3) electric railroads, (4) electro-chemicals, (5) steam turbines, in particular, large iron-producing plants and mining, and (6) automobiles (Handbuch der Deutschen Aktien-Gesellschaften 1908, S.668–669), and the core area of this company was the heavy-current sectors. In considering the fact that GE and Westinghouse, two American giants in the electrical engineering industry at the time, exclusively produced and sold light and power equipment (See annual reports of General Electric and Westinghouse at the time), Siemens and AEG continued to manufacture more extensive product lines than the Americans (Chandler 1990, p.472). Therefore, the problem to be examined is the organizational structures of German enterprises. In the case of Siemens, although Siemens-Schuckert Werke and Siemens & Halske were managed by the same central office, each company had its own organizational structure.

At **Siemens-Schuckert Werke**, once the reorganization following the merger in 1903 was completed, this enterprise was managed by two giant functional departments—the production department and the sales department. After moving the head office to Nonnendamm in 1913, the administrative structure of this company remained relatively unchanged until the outbreak of World War II. "By a plan that went into effect on August 1, 1913, the organization of the Production Department—renamed the *Zentral-Werksverwaltung* (ZW)—remained much as it had been before, though its specialized staff offices increased in number and in size." In contrast, the sales department, called the *Zentral-Verkaufsverwaltung* (ZV), supervised six major divisions each responsible for a major line of products. In 1913, the major product lines that can be seen are central power stations, electrical machinery for industrial, military and naval equipment including electrical equipment for merchant marines, electric trams and railways, and a small machinery and accessories department (Chandler 1990, pp.469–470; Siemens 1957, XIX). In the field of power current, although each of the Siemens-Schuckert Werke units lacked either the sales or the production department, "they were relatively autonomous units in the corporation's internal price system" (Kocka 1971, p.153).

At **Siemens & Halske**, the management system was influenced by the divisional structure based on the self-supporting accounting system. Plural product fields were organized into three divisions—(1) the electric light and strong electric, (2) the signal for railroads, and (3) the telegraph and telephone—that operated under the self-supporting accounting in organizational reform in 1882 (Tanaka 2023, p.42). A new structure organized according to divisions was created in the 1890s. The electric railway department was separated as the sales department from the Chalrotenburg plant after 1890. By this means, this company's own management system in which each factory and sales department formed a connection mutually as a division with the characteristics of "the profit center" was fundamentally established (Imakubo 1995, pp.52, 58; Takenaka 1991, Chapter 1). Furthermore, the general office was founded and a system that controlled each division was built on the basis of decentralization according to a divisional structure. The goals of this organization were (1) further increasing the efficiency of the internalization of capital competition into individual capital and (2) avoiding or mitigating the evil caused by the anarchical persuasion of individual profit (Imakubo 1995, p.64). As A. D. Chandler, Jr. pointed out, the structure of Siemens & Halske seems to have been more decentralized, even if the production of railway signals and light bulbs was controlled by this company's hierarchy that administrated the Werner plant (Chandler 1990, p.470).

In the organization created in 1890, persons who took charge in full authority independently managed production, sale, revenue, and expenditure according to diversified product fields, and each manager engaged in profit management of factory and division, including plural product fields. Furthermore, ten directors in the head office were in charge of the management and control of divisions as executives who were in high positions (Tanaka 2023, p.52). The head office also attempted uniform management of the whole company. Standard methods of acccounting and cost management that differed in sections were unified. Furthermore, the price that added 7.5% to the manufacturing cost was set as the price for transactions between factories or between divisions within the company (transfer price) and regarded as the standard profit rate. The head office could grasp the conditions of the whole company with numerical figures by a uniform view of sales and profit rates in each product field. At the same time, according to products, factories, divisions, and organizations came to be conscious of their own sales and profit rates in competition with other sections (Tanaka 2023, pp.53–55).

Regarding the characteristics of the organization of Siemens, Jürgen Kocka pointed out that "unlike corporations resulting from mergers (like General Electric), organization-building at Siemens required systematic and planned decentralization, delegation of authority, as well as the creation of counter-balancing tools for control and efficient central decisions." "The product of these deliberate changes was a new organizational pattern which successfully combined systematic orderliness and centralized policy making with flexible decentralization in a highly diversified, multi-divisional firm." At Siemens & Halske, all except one unit had a production department, a technical and planning department, a sales department, an accounting and administrative department, and a central office. "This company was not organized along functional, but along product (or regional) lines." Kock stressed "in essence, though not in a pure form and with some restrictions (especially on the power current side) the Siemens concern had thus developed the specific decentralization pattern of the highly diversified, multi-divisional enterprise 10 to 20 years before du Pont and General Motors first adopted it in the US during the early 1920's" (Kocka 1971, pp.152–154). Thus, "by the outbreak of World War I the Siemens enterprises were operating through a single administrative structure which, with a corporate office of senior executives and with several autonomous product divisions, was the forerunner of the multidivisional structure which Du Pont and General Motors began to fashion in the United States shortly after the war" (Chandler 1990, p.471).

However, in Germany, except for the case of the Siemens, the formation of a divisional structure that integrated the production and sales functions of one product line in each division could not be observed from the late nineteenth century through the Weimar Republic. This meant that the organizational structure of Siemens was an exceptional case (Siegrist 1980, S.87–88; Kocka 1971, pp.154–155). After World War II, in particular, during the latter half of the 1960s, divisional structures prevailed in German enterprises (Siegrist 1980, S.88; regarding the adoption of the divisional structure in Siemens after the 1960s, see Yamazaki 2024, Chapter 11).

Organizations similar to divisional structures were created in the early stage at Siemens because of the three following points. First, the high degree of diversification was an important factor. Siemens was a general maker that produced various products in both the heavy- and light–current fields, including telecommunications, unlike companies in the US. Therefore, coping with management problems caused by diversified product lines was necessary. Second, the tradition of family-ism promoted top managers to display paternalistic leadership in organizational reforms. Third, the bureaucratic tradition functioned effectively in the formation of the organization (Kobayashi et al. 1982, pp.136–137). Among these three factors, the first one is the most important. For example, Jürgen Kocka pointed out that the elaborate pattern of diversification appears to have induced Siemens management to develop a complex organizational device such as an organization similar to a divisional structure very early (Kocka 1971, pp.154–155). Siemens diversified their business to new fields such as incandescent lamps, measuring equipment, electro-chemicals, and telecommunications equipment. In such products, product lines that required their own standards, procedures, and principles to perform fundamental functions such as production, purchasing, and sales were included. Therefore, the centralized departmental organizational structure that was appropriate for a company that dealt with a single product line encountered difficult managerial problems. At Siemens, the early adoption of an organizational structure similar to the decentralized product divisional structure at the end of the nineteenth century was due to this situation.

Based on the preceding discussion, the next section considers how the central office administrated, controlled, and coordinated multiple business units and allocated resources from the perspective of the entire enterprise.

6.2.4 Establishment of the Central Office

6.2.4.1 Establishment of Central Offices in Major Industries

Cases in the Iron and Steel Industry

Functional Separation of the Duties of Directors and Its Significance

First, when looking at the iron and steel industry, in most enterprises, management at the level of the managing board was functionally divided into directors in charge of either technical affairs or commercial affairs (Kocka 1969a, S.343; Kocka 1975b, S.112). This point can be observed in mechanical processing industries as well (Roesky 1878, S.33). Regarding duties, everything to be done other than technical affairs was included in the jurisdiction of commercial affairs. In such management organized on the basis of the division of labor, the importance of the commercial director increased with the passage of time (Feldenkirchen 1982, S.311).

For instance, at **Krupp**, the organizational scheme was planned by Friedrich Krupp in 1872. Accordingly, this company should be fundamentally composed of the technical and commercial departments, and, in addition to these departments, the legal department would be established. The former two functional departments were considered to be administrated by a director who took charge of technical affairs (Lorsbach) and two directors who were responsible for commercial affairs (E. Eichhoch and Wiegand). At **Gutehoffnungshütte**, the work regulation of the board of directors was based on the new corporation law of 1870 [Bongartz 1984a, S.47–48; *Historisches Archiv Krupp*, WA41/2–108. Regarding the prescription of managing board members determined by Krupp in 1872, see *Historisches Archiv Krupp*, WA41/2–105, General-Regulative für die Firma Frid. Krupp. (9.9.1872); *Historisches Archiv Krupp*, WA41/2–105, Geschäftsordnung für die Procura, Geschäfts-Ordnung für das PROCURA der Firma FRIED. KRUPP in Essen a.d. Ruhr.]. The managing board should be composed of two directors for technical affairs and one of each director who was in charge of commercial affairs or legal affairs. However, the position of director responsible for legal affairs was not established in a definite form before 1914. Members of the managing board should discuss on the basis of principle of mutual consent (Bongartz 1984a, S.48; Kocka 1969a, S.343; Roesky 1878, S.35).

However, in the period after the transformation from the 19th to the twentieth century, the importance of an appropriate organizational structure came to be recognized more and more. As a result, duties were divided into the three fields of manufacturing, commercial management, and the entire management. The shift from a system of two directors who had same authority to the hierarchical organizational structure in which a representative director was at the top of the organizational structure formed on the basis of the division of labor principle progressed (Feldenkirchen 1982, S.311–312).

At **Krupp**, in 1879, a foundation was laid to divide the duties of directors into the production department, commercial management, and the entire management. Functionally dividing the duties among four directors became the foundation of labor division, wherein a director who took no certain field of duty was at the top position (Bongartz 1984a, S.47–48). The foundation of the organization was strengthened by representative persons at the lower level who took charge of duties or representatives who were in charge of commercial affairs. On July 1, 1896, members of the board of directors increased to 12 and a system supported by eight persons was created. In October 1989, a system composed of 12 persons was established (Bongartz 1984b, S.81–82). According to an internal document of this company from March 14, 1888, work regulation of the leading managerial organization was decided and prescriptions regarding issues such as constitution, rights, and duties of directors were made. The principle of collegial management based on a board-majority system was fixed [*Historisches Archiv Krupp*, WA41/2–108, Geschäfts-Ordnung für das Direktrium der Firma FRIED. KRUPP in Essen a.d. Ruhr (14.3.1888)].

In this period, as the enterprise grew, a part of the duties that were taken charge of by the supervisory board was entrusted to the board of directors and the duties of the managing board increased. For instance, at Phönix, after the reorganization of management in 1907, in almost all cases, the managing board came to be given the authority of implementing measures to be considered as necessary and expedient in the interest of the company without receiving the recognition of the supervisory board or the general meeting. Although the board of directors had to delegate part of the duties by such an increase in authority, the duties of this organ and staff department included decisions on investment, purchasing and sales, cost accounting, mutual transfer prices between individual business units and principles maintaining the balance sheet, and the coordination of problems of important associations, in addition to long-term goals of the company. After the new organization was adopted, the management of each business unit was performed by each director who took charge of technical affairs or commercial affairs. In this period, in almost all enterprises, the central office had staff positions such as (1) administration and secretary, (2) accounting and receipts and disbursements, (3) purchasing, (4) sales, (5) calculation department, and (6) sending (Feldenkirchen 1982, S.312–315).

Reform of the Accounting System and Strengthening of the Central Office Function

In addition, the functions of the central office were strengthened by the reform of the accounting system and a foundation of organization for such a purpose. For instance, at Krupp, Alfred Krupp attempted to perform thorough reform and improvement of the accounting system as a means for coping with a serious shortage of working capital during the overproduction crisis in 1873. New guidelines regarding the accounting system were created and sections for the management of time and wages, a calculation inspection department, and a special department of calculations were established. Since such means appeared to be very elaborate and appropriate for conditions at the time and future economic changes, at Gutehoffnungshütte, a competitor of Krupp, similar organizational reform became an important problem to be solved (Bongartz 1984b, S.113).

At **Krupp** as a representative case, a "general calculation system" was created on January 1, 1866. It was regarded as a measure that could contribute to three purposes: (1) the management of transactions between individual business units and transactions of materials used, (2) making lists of achievements, and (3) calculations regarding new equipment and business expansion. However, calculations regarding the purchase of materials from outside of the company and wages were handled by the central office. In examining this system from the perspective of "verification of uneconomical business unit and processes of business, rationalization for cost reduction, and foundation of higher competitive ability," the defects in this system were large. Therefore, in 1874, old prescriptions were abolished and reforms in the calculation system were implemented. The characteristics of new regulations can be seen in the accuracy of important details and the concentration of reports on the central office bureau (Bongartz 1984b, S.87–88).

Furthermore, the calculation inspection department was established as a means of strengthening control as an organization for internal management and audits to control all management duties regarding investigating calculations, income and expenditures, increases and decreases in movables and real estate, and loan management. This control not only covered the classical field of the modern controller system, such as revenue and expenditures of all business and management sections, but also aimed at making clear to what degree all business units observed regulations by comparisons of numerical figures on goals and actual results. Directors who managed the calculation inspection department were responsible for making their own annual reports as well as inspecting each report regarding income and outflow of the business units and annual statements of the accounts for the whole company to be made by commercial directors with the assistance of the accounting department chief (Bongartz 1984b, S.92–93).

In this way, in large iron and steel enterprises such as Krupp and Gutehoffnunghütte, strengthening of function of central office was attempted through establishing calculation department and calculation inspection department. Although improvement of the annual statement of accounts progressed only gradually, organizational capability of private officers who were entrusted it first opened opportunities to indicate each part and each work process in relation to costs and to secure universal validity to demand of enterprise for efficiency of production in each business (Bongartz 1984b, S.112).

Section 6.2.3.4 considered that Siemens unified accounting standards regarding cost management and a profit rate that differed in sections, creating an important base for strategic decision-making. A similar case occurred in Thyssen & Co. In the 1880s, managerial accountancy was in its infancy, with few standards outside conventions (Fear 2005, p.161), and improvements in accounting for control were attempted (Fear 2005, Chapter 4). Fear points out "given Siemens' reputation for bureaucracy, Thyssen & Co. had a more coherent system of controls than Siemens & Halske" (Fear 2005, p.186).

Cases in the Chemical Industry

Similar tendencies can be observed in chemical industry. Regarding **Bayer** as one of largest chemical enterprises in Germany at the time, A. D. Chandler, Jr. pointed out that "even more than at Siemens, the physical location of the many processing plants within the works determined the overall administrative structure of the enterprise." "The heart of the Bayer works was Central Administration (Department VII), the building which housed top management and the offices of the sales, purchasing, accounting, patent, and statistical departments, and also the library." Five senior managers who worked in the largest office of "Central Administration" were responsible for the health and continuing growth of this enterprise and had a variety of functional activities. They were members of the directorate ("Directorium"), which was equivalent to the board of directors. Whereas Carl Duisburg and Friedrich Bayer, as a son of the founder of this company, became largely responsible for production, engineering, and research, "the other three concentrated more on purchasing and, much more important, on sales." The administrative structure defined in 1899 remained with few changes until the middle of the 1920s when this enterprise merged with other leading chemical enterprises to form I.G. Farben (Chandler 1990, pp.476–477).

In a memorandum of this company in 1906, at the level of top management, directors were arranged in three departments of purchasing, sales, and engineering. Ordinary business was administrated and performed on the basis of the division of labor among each director. In contrast, decision-making regarding problems of the general business and all business issues with high uncertainty were considered to be handled at the meeting of the managing board on the basis of the board-majority system [*Bayer Archiv*, 010-003-001, Denkschrift über die Organisation des Gesamtgeschäfts der Farbenfabriken vorm. Friedr. Bayer & Co. zu Elberfeld (Februar 1906)].

Cases in the Electrical Engineering Industry

Next, in examining the electrical engineering industry, as already considered in the previous section, at **Siemens**, the decentralization of management and the adoption of a decentralized organizational structure similar to the divisional structure was attempted. An important characteristic of its organizational structure can be seen in "an intricate and highly sophisticated mixture of centralization and decentralization, of administrative mechanism and internal price system, and of boards, committees, and hierarchies" (Kocka 1971, pp.152–154; 1980, p.98). "An elaborate and systematic administration was established which provided for central control, decision-making, and administrative supervision at the top. Top managers were free to concentrate on basic policy, the allocation of capital equipment and personnel, external relations, legal topics, patents, overall organization, and labor management." Two managing board members including most of the unit heads, as well as top officers who were charge of functionally defined activities, met regularly. "Two differentiated general offices existed which participated in the formulation and administration of the companies' overall policies." Effective surveys and controls were enabled by "regular reports, statistics, charts, and a high degree of administrative standardization." An increasing number of central staff departments performed several functions either for one company or for both Siemens & Halske and Siemens-Schuckert Werke together and "specialized systematically on activities necessary for the supervision, coordination, and standardization of the whole." Central staff departments were organizations for functions such as (1) the coordination of construction, research and development, (2) purchasing of raw materials, (3) supervision of the sales field offices, (4) organization of overseas exports, (5) legal, economic, and public relations, and (6) central accounting (Kocka 1971, pp.153–154).

When considering the activities of the board of directors at Siemens, the number of meetings including the financial committee decreased considerably from 168 from 1889 to 1902 (33.6 times per year on average) to 57 from 1908 to 1913 (9.5 times per year an average). The centralized coordination functions that were previously insufficiently performed by the managing board were taken over by representative executers on the board through the executive decisions of Wilhelm von Siemens and his personal contact with individual directors. Thus, the need for the executive board to meet tended to decrease. Although the interval between meetings became longer, the number of items written in minutes decreased as a whole and the number of items of proceedings considered within a month decreased from 83 in 1898 to only seven in 1913/14. Jürgen Kocka pointed out that three trends could be observed from such changes: (1) the managing board became free from confusion of decision-making at the lower levels by delegation of authority, (2) after 1903, the board of directors lost the authority of important decision-making to representatives of the supervisory board, individual directors, the management board's own committees, and new central office departments, and (3) among two primary functions of the place as administrative institution with authority of order and that for exchange of information, the managing board emphasized the latter more and more (Kocka 1969b, S.415–418).

6.2.4.2 Establishment of Executive's Representative Organizations

During this period, strengthening of central office functions was attempted by creating an execution organization representative of top management. There was a trend in which the core of the top management organ moved from the whole supervisory board to representative persons of the organization, such as chairman and leading person of the managing board, in particular chairman. In case this combination was favorable and positive initiative of the latter functioned effectively with support by the former, company growth by forming integrated and diversified large enterprises tended to be possible. In such cases, increasing the influence of directors on business policy was definite compared with that of representative members of the supervisory board from the bank. This can be generally observed in the representative executing organization called "*Direktion*" (Fukuo 1982, p. 71).

For instance, at **Gelsenkirchner Bergwerks-AG**, a system of execution by leading management persons was formed. The general directorate composed of directors of this company and sometimes including persons responsible for each department and directors of group enterprises had characteristics as an enlarged managing board and substantially decided business policy. At such meetings, which were held 13 times in 1908, Ardolf Kirdorf attended as the only member of the supervisory board and the establishment of the executing system by Kirdorf brothers and representatives of leading management can be observed (Fukuo 1982, p.68).

At **Krupp**, under attendance of chief of operating departments, Goose proposed organizing of committee to discuss problems of technical affairs. However, Hagemann considered this plan negatively on May 11, 1874, and insisted that the foundation of such an organization was too complicated. Instead of establishing such an organization, an inner circle, of which the members were Diechmann, R. Eichhoch,

C. Ulenhaut, O. E. Richter, and Lemer, should be created as well as the narrow extent of an executing organ composed of managing directors (Bongartz 1984b, S.75).

6.2.4.3 Establishment of Committees and Their Roles

In large enterprises during this period, various kinds of committee organizations were founded for the purpose of supporting execution of jobs of representative executing organ and persons who took charge of such duties.

At **Siemens**, three kinds of organizations could be seen. The first one was committees as preparatory institutes and consulting organizations with no authority of decision on functional fields that required fundamental special preparation. These were constant committees that took charge of staff function. The managing board already built system in 1899 where all applications from each department regarding new construction, rebuilding, and purchasing of machines for business and machine tools were first estimated in "the Construction committee" and was then suggested to the board of directors. The executive board that was burdened with trifling issues attempted to rationalize its own activities without missing the tendency of decision-making until then.

The second type of committee was organizational and would provisionally suspend its activity after the end of duty. As occasions demanded, the managing board delegated temporary duties concerning inappropriate fields for any competent area or plural competent fields to small groups composed of members of this committee. At Siemens & Halske, a committee to examine attendance problems into the Association of Berlin Metal Manufacturer was established in 1903 and the rationalization committee was created in 1908.

In these two types of committees, other persons, except for members of the board of directors, were often appointed. They influenced the decision-making process through selection, preparation, and recommendation on decisions. In contrast to this, the third type of committee had more or less definite decision-making authority. Immediately after Wilhelm von Siemens took over as chairman of the managing board of Siemens & Halske in 1903, the Finance Committee composed of Berliner, Schpieker, Schpiegel, and Budde as well as von Siemens himself was established with his initiative.

These three kinds of committees aimed at simplification methods of decision-making. They enabled this company to quickly cope with the frequently changing problems without encountering the necessity of changing the allocation of the authority decided by the prescription regarding positions among competent areas and job descriptions. Furthermore, a small scale of elite groups within the managing board that indicated an important entanglement of the two enterprises of Siemens & Halske and Siemens-Schuckert Werke were created by holding other posts on various committees. Thus, this committee system enabled them to subdivide duties effectively among a lot of directors and executing directors (Kocka 1969b, S.436–439). Directors were usually composed of at least two people who were in charge of either sales or production, and a counsel system was adopted for management in case of multiple members. When many directors existed, the chief executive, who was chairman of the managing board and at the top of the board majority system, was elected. In addition, committee systems built departmentally and functionally in the managing board were established to cope with the limits of management based on the board majority system and realize quick decision-making. The purpose of this committee system was to secure uniformity of operation execution to cope with various forms of business brought about by diversification and functional integration and expansion of the scale of business, and personal nature did not play an important role in establishing such committees (Fukuo 1982, pp.62–63; Passow 1922, S.381–383).

At **Krupp**, committees to take charge of a wide range of job areas, such as staff organization, and in which non-manual employees who were in charge of only a certain "role" worked, were established instead of business execution by enlarged executive boards. These committees should assist managing directors (Bongartz 1984b, S.78).

6.3 Appearance of Salaried Managers and the Rise of Managerial Enterprises

6.3.1 Types of Enterprises in Germany and Their Characteristics

Building upon the foregoing analysis, this section considers the emergence of salaried managers and the rise of managerial enterprises. A. D. Chandler, Jr. classified a type of enterprise from the perspective of "how business is administrated and managed" and "who controls management" into three types: (1) "personal enterprises," (2) "entrepreneurial enterprises" "family-controlled enterprises," and (3) "managerial enterprises." Personal enterprises, as the first type, include enterprises "administrated without benefit of an extensive managerial hierarchy." Entrepreneurial enterprises or family-controlled enterprises, as the second type, include those enterprises "where the founders and their heirs recruited managerial hierarchies but continued to be influential stockholders and senior executives in their companies." Managerial enterprises are companies "in which the executives in the administrative hierarchy have no connection with the founders or their families and have little or no equity in the company" (Chandler 1990, p.240).

In entrepreneurial enterprises or family-controlled enterprises, primarily at the level below middle management, the delegation of authority of decision-making to managers who comprise managerial hierarchy was performed. At the level of top management, the founders and their families were still in a dominant position. In contrast, enterprises in which salaried managers are in charge of decision-making in top management are regarded as managerial enterprise (Abe 1994, p.58). However, as a criterion for the rise of such a type of enterprise, situations wherein several skilled individuals are already fixed in a company as a team are important rather than a single individual with sufficient knowledge taking charge of top managerial functions (Abe 1994, p.61). Regarding this point, Hidemasa Morikawa regards the birth of managerial hierarchy composed of layers of managers who have skills and a personnel network among these managers as an essential condition of the shift to a managerial enterprise (Morikawa 1996, p.23).

In examining conditions in Germany at the time from this perspective, it can be stated that as a general trend, the influence of owner–managers in German firms was stronger than its counterparts in the US. The period of the industrial revolution from the period from 1815 until the March 1848 Revolution to the birth of the Second German Empire in 1971 was the golden age of owner enterprises. However, during the Weimar Republic, at the top class of large enterprises, capital ownership and the administration of enterprises were separated to a certain degree and these two functions were divided into capitalists who were not in charge of management on the one hand and managers with no ownership on the other hand. Although owner-entrepreneurs continued to be the majority among all entrepreneurs, their predominance was much more evident than before a few decades ago (Kocka 1983, S.8–9). Jürgen Kocka pointed out that in 1887 and 1907 almost no personal firms were represented among the largest enterprises. Enterprises of the managerial type clearly increased from 1887 to 1907. In mining, firms had often been managerial enterprises since their foundation; they were also strong in chemicals and formed a substantial minority in iron and steel. Even as late as 1907, however, most of the 100 largest corporations were still entrepreneurial, and managerial firms were even rarer among the smaller companies (Kocka 1980, p.93).

Owner enterprises and entrepreneurial enterprises comprised the majority before 1914 and sufficiently developed managerial enterprises maintained only an extremely partial existence (Kocka 1975a, S.222). Hans Pohl pointed out that unlike the development of the management structure in North America, until the outbreak of World War II, "the 'entrepreneur enterprise' whom Chandler sees as a transitional phenomenon was the dominant type of entrepreneur in Germany" (Pohl 1981, S.158; 1982, p.104).

As Chandler made clear, "in both the United States and Germany, the enterprise became managerial and quickly developed effective organizational capabilities." An important difference between the German and the American enterprises can be seen in that "the family often continued to have a powerful, even a decisive, say in management" in Germany (Chandler 1990, pp.500–501). However, in the iron and steel industry, "the managerial teams recruited in the 1880s and 1890s to exploit the economies of throughput were as large as those of the American steelmakers." These salaried managers increasingly took part in top-level decisions (Chandler 1990, p.491).

6.3.2 *Retrocession of Owner–Managers and the Rise of Salaried Managers*

Next, when considering the influence of owners and its role in business management, as Jürgen Kocka pointed out, family structure and resources greatly and positively contributed to the development of capitalism in the early period. Two premises of it existed. One was the underdevelopment of an effective alternative. The other was the economic functionality of a family. During the first two-thirds of the nineteenth century, both the market and state system were unable to solve central business economy problems in the first stage and depending on family appeared to be effective and the only possible measure to solve such problems (Kocka 1979, S.133). Therefore, family resources were used to solve industrial business management problems that could not be settled by other means (Kocka 1979, S.110). However, relationships between families and capitalism in the early stage of industrialization changed and loosened over dozens of years thereafter. In 1914, families were no longer needed to provide a driving force in the development of industrial capitalism as they did in 1850 (Kocka 1979, S.133–135).

One of the most central factors bringing about the retrocession of owner–managers was the expansion of enterprise scale and the dispersion of ownership. However, in companies such as Krupp, Gutehoffnungshütte, and Hoesch, the separation of capital ownership and management did not occur. Although Hoesch was administrated by a member of family and the number of personnel increased with company expansion, it was supported only by some managers at a lower level. Albert Hoesch kept position of president as co-owner president until 1897, and the administrative board was composed of almost exclusively members of the Hoesch family or his intimate persons. At Gutehoffnungshütte, indeed, members of the Haniel family did no longer belong to the board of directors. However, the influence of the supervisory board composed entirely of family members on the managing board was extremely large (Feldenkirchen 1982, S.308–309). In this company, the definite interests of the Haniel family to influence the company through its own representatives by not only supervision but also administration, advice, and support can be observed (Junkers 1970, S.287). However, family members withdrew from daily decision-making more and more with the laps of time. Similar movement can also be observed at Krupp. Alfred Krupp was still very directly involved in the business policy of his enterprise in the 1880s. But after 1903, his direct influence became weak due to changes in the legal form of this company and the situation that his successor was a juvenile. Gustav Krupp attended the supervisory board in 1909 and next year took over chairman of such an organization. Afterward, he still played a decisive role in the development of this firm. However, he no longer directly participated in any decision-making (Feldenkirchen 1982, S.309–310).

In addition, in examining the behavior of salaried managers, the tendency to emphasize long-term planning, preserving, and expanding the company and preferring future profits to short-term opportunities to maximize profits and regard the continuance of the company as his main purpose could be seen. They, generally, made efforts at the stable development of their company and tended to reject sudden, short-term profit if necessary. Thus, a trend of emphasizing re-investment rather than dividend payments can be observed (Kocka 1978, pp.581–582; 1980, pp.93–94).

Patterns of recruitment and careers of salaried entrepreneurs at the level of top management in managerial enterprises differed from that of the owner-entrepreneur. Salaried entrepreneurs tended to have received more secondary and university-level education than owner-entrepreneurs. "One of the most important results of the first rise of salaried entrepreneurs in terms of economic history was that it helped make specialized technical, business, legal, and organizational skills and knowledge available to corporations through their leaders." In addition, "in managerial enterprises, achievement could be more important as a criterion for hiring and promotion than it was when ownership and control were inseparable" (Kocka 1978, pp. 582–583; 1980, p.94).

However, the decline in the meaning of capital ownership as a premise for engaging in top management positions and the tendency for capital ownership to be replaced by general secondary education and secondary professional training progressed only extremely gradually and over the long term (Kocka 1981b, S.112). Prominent difference from the condition in which a high-level professional education at university played a significant role in the education of salaried managers in the US can be seen in this point.

In Germany, like in the US, the trend toward the emergence of salaried managers and the rise of managerial enterprises can be observed in integrated and partial cases of diversified large firms. A. D. Chandler, Jr. pointed out that "far more important to the building of organizational capabilities and the resulting market power of the German enterprises than geographical proximity was the willingness of German entrepreneurs to rely on teams of salaried managers, in contrast to continuing preference of British entrepreneurs" (Chandler 1990, pp.499–500).

As Hans Siegrist pointed out, generally speaking, Chandler's hypothesis concerning the gradual shift from "personal enterprise" through the enterprise of "entrepreneurial" types as the intermediate form to managerial enterprise can be observed in Germany's development. Large companies of the "personnel enterprise" type were probably already in the minority in the late nineteenth century. Although entrepreneurial enterprises formed the majority in 1907, managerial enterprises increased until then. Even though a considerable number of entrepreneurial firms still existed among the largest 100 firms in 1927, the number of managerial firms further increased. However, even in this year, industrial sectors in which managerial enterprises were predominant were limited to the mining, iron-producing, metal-producing, and chemical industries and generally to the largest enterprises. In looking at the general trend, in the US, managerial enterprises became dominant earlier than in Germany. According to Hans Siegrist, a comparison of both countries indicates that between the type of enterprise and choice of a diversification or integration strategy there was no definite relationship, as pointed out by A. D. Chandler, Jr. and H. Deams (Siegrist 1980, S.88). Jürgen Kocka also noted that although good quantitative evidence for comparing the US and Germany was unfortunately lacking, "the major growth of the managerial enterprise probably took place after World War

I in Germany, and even then, many entrepreneurial firms remained among the 100 largest" (Kocka 1980, p.105).

Regarding the reasons for continuing family-controlled enterprises, Akira Kudo stressed that the rise and expansion of such companies, which continues today, occurred during the period of industrial structural transformation caused by "the second industrial revolution" from the late nineteenth century to the beginning of the twentieth century, and that these enterprises established a competitive advantage by displaying vigorous entrepreneurship. However, as part of the dynamism of the growth of German capitalism, these family-controlled firms were forced to transform to a defensive strategy and make their way toward company reorganization and consolidation under industrial rationalization in the 1920s (Kudo 1995, p.152).

In the three chapters of Part II, changes in business management that occurred during the period from the shift to monopolistic capitalism that began in the late nineteenth century through the outbreak of World War I were analyzed. Building upon these discussions, the topics to be considered include business management problems after the war during the Weimar Republic. In Part III, these research issues will be examined.

References

Abe E (1994) Chandler moderu to Morikawa Hidemasa shi no keieisha kigyoron (Managerial enterprise: conceptional difference between A. D. Chandler and Hidemasa Morikawa). In: Keiei shigaku (Jpn Bus Hist Rev) 28(4):55–65

Beckmann Z (1916) Führer durch die Maschinenbau-Anstalt Humboldt: 60 Jahre technischer Entwicklung 1856–1916. Ziegler Beckmann, Köln

Beer JJ (1959) The emergence of the German Dye industry. University of Illinois Press, Urbana

Bongartz VW (1984a) Unternehmensleitung und Kostenkontrolle in der Rheinische Montanindustrie vor 1914, dargestellt am Beispiele der Firmen Krupp und Gutehofnnungshütte (Teil I). In: Zeitschrift für Unternehmensgeschichte 29(I):33–55

Bongartz VW (1984b) Unternehmensleitung und Kostenkontrolle in der Rheinische Montanindustrie vor 1914, dargestellt am Beispiele der Firmen Krupp und Gutehofnnungshütte (Teil II). In: Zeitschrift für Unternehmensgeschichte 29(2):73–113

Chandler AD Jr (1962) Strategy and structur: chapters in the history of the industrial enterpreise. MIT Press, Cambridge, MA

Chandler AD Jr (1977) The visible hand: managerial revolution in American business. Harvard University Press, Cambridge, MA

Chandler AD Jr (1990) Scale and scope: the dynamics of industrial capitalism. Harvard University Press, Cambridge, MA

Däbritz W, Metzeltin E, (1935) Hundert Jahre Hanomag. Geschichte der Hannoverschen Maschinenbau Aktiengesellschaft vormals Georg Egestorff in Hannover 1835 bis 1935. Stahleisen, Düsseldorf

Farrington FE (1914) Commercial education in Germany. Stahleisen, New York

Fear JR (2005) Organizing control. August Thyssen and the construction of German corporate management, Harvard University Press, Cambridge, MA, London

Feldenkirchen W (1982) Die Eisen- und Stahlindustrie des Ruhrgebiets 1879–1914. Wachstum, Finanzierung und Struktur ihrer Großunternehmen. Steiner, Wiesbaden

Feldenkirchen W (1987) Big business in interwar Germany: organizational innovation at Verenigt Stahlwerke, IG Farben, and Siemens. In: Bus Hist Rev 61(3):417–451
Feldenkirchen W (1999) Siemens 1918–1945. Ohio State University, Ohio
Feldman GD (1977) Iron and Steel in the German Inflation 1916–1923. Princeton University Press, Princeton
Fukuo T (1982) Seiki kotaiki Doitsu no kabushiki gaisha "Kansayaku Aufsichtsrat" (*Aufsicftsrat* in German corporations during the turn of the ceentury). In: Keiei shigaku (Jpn Bus Hist Rev) 17(3):53–77
Handbuch der Deutschen Aktien-Gesellschaften (1900) Hannoversche Maschinenbau-Actien-Gesellschaft vormals Georg Egestorff in Linden vor Hannover. In: Handbuch der Deutschen Aktien Gesellschaften 1899–1900, Bd. II, 440–441
Handbuch der Deutschen Aktien-Gesellschaften (1903) Siemens & Halske, Akt.-Ges. in Berlin, SW. Askanischer Platz 3. Fabriken in Berlin, Charlottenburg, Spandau und Wien. In: Handbuch der Deutschen Aktien-Gesellschaften 1902–1903, Bd.II, 512–514
Handbuch der Deutschen Aktien-Gesellschaften (1904) Siemens-Schuckert Werke, Ges. m. beschr. Haftung, Berlin SW., Askanischer Platz 3, mit Zweigniederlassung in Nürnberg. In: Handbuch der Deutschen Aktien-Gesellschaften 1903–1904, Bd.I, 1634–1635
Handbuch der Deutschen Aktien-Gesellschaften (1908) Allgemeine Elektricitäts-Gesellschaft in Berlin, NW. Friedrich Karl-Ofer 2/4. In: Handbuch der Deutschen Aktien-Gesellschaften 1907–1908, Bd.II, 667–672
Handbuch der Deutschen Aktien-Gesellschaften (1912) Maschinenbau-Anstalt Humboldt in Cöln-Kalk. In Handbuch der Deutschen-Aktien-Gesellschaften 1911–1912, Bd.II, 659–660
Hartmann H (1955) Education for business leadership. Organisation for European Economic Co-operation, Paris
Hasse H (1902) Die Allgemeine Elektrizität-Gesellschaft und ihre wirtschaftliche Bedeutung. Karl Winter, Heidelberg
Hoffmann G (1965) Das Wachstum der deutschen Wirtschaft seit der Mitte des 19. Jahrhundert. Springer-Verlag, Berlin
Imakubo S (1995) 19 seiki matsu Doitsu no kojyo (Factories in Germany at the end of the nineteenth century). Yuhikaku, Tokyo
Junkers H (1970) Entwicklung und Wachstum der Stahl- und Walzwerke Oberhausen und Neu-Oberhausen 1880–1890. Beispiel unternehmerischer Entscheidungen in der GHH. Thesis, Ruprecht-Karl-Universität, Heidelberg
Klatzky SR (1970) Relationship of organizational size to complexity and coordination. In In: Adm Sci Q 15(4):428–438
Kobayashi K, Yonekawa S, Hukuo T (1982) Seiyo keieishi wo manabu (Ge) [Learning about Westen business history (2). The age of integrated management]. Yuhikaku, Tokyo
Kocka J (1969a) Industrielles Management: Konzeptionen und Modelle in Deutschland vor 1914. In: Vierteljahrschrift für Sozial- und Wirtschaftsgeschichte 56(3):332–372
Kocka J (1969b) Unternehmensverwaltung und Angestelltenschaft 1847–1914: Zum Verhältinis von Kapitalisumus in Bürokratie in der deutschen Industrialisierung. Klett, Stuttgart
Kocka J (1971) Family and bureaucracy in German industrial management, 1850–1914, siemens in comparativ perspective. In: Bus Hist Rev 45(2):133–156
Kocka J (1975a) Expansion—Integration—Diversifikation. Wachstumsstrategien industrieller Großunternehmen in Deutschland vor 1914. In: Winkel H (Hrsg) Vom Kleingewerbe zur Großindustrie. Quantitätivregionale und Politischrechtliche Aspekt zur Erforschung der Wirtschafts- und Gesellschaftsstruktur in 19. Jahrhundert. Duncker & Humblot, Berlin
Kocka J (1975b) Unternehmer in der deutschen Industrialisierung. Vandenhoeck und Ruprecht, Göttingen
Kocka J (1978) Entrepreneurs and managers in German industrialization. In: The Camb Econ Hist Europe 7(1):492–589
Kocka J (1979) Familie, Unternehmer und Kapitalismus. An Beispielen aus der frühen deutschen Industrialisierung. In: Zeitschrift für Unternehmensgeschichte 24(3):163–186

Kocka J (1980) The rise of the modern industrial enterprise in Germany. In: Chandler AD, Daems H (eds) Managerial hierarchies. Comparative perspectives on the rise of the modern industrial enterprise. Harvard University Press, Cambridge, MA, pp 77–116
Kocka J (1981a) Capitalism and bureaucracy in German Industrialization before 1914. In: Econ Hist Rev 34(3):453–468
Kocka J (1981b) Die Angestellten in der deutschen Geschichte 1850–1980. Vom Privatebeamten zum angestellten Arbeitsnehmer. Vandenhoeck & Ruprecht, Göttingen
Kocka J (1981c) Groβunternehmen und der Aufstieg der Manager-Kapitalismus im späten 19. und frühen 20.Jahrhundert, Deutschland im internationalen Vergleich. In: Histrische Zeitschrift 232:39–60
Kocka J (1983) Legitimationsprobleme und -strategien der Unternehmer und Manager im 19 und frühen 20. Jahrhundert. In Pohl H (Hrsg) Legitimation des Management im Wandel. Steiner, Wiesbaden, S.7–21
Krooss HE, Gilbert CC (1972) American Business History. Prentice-Hall, Engle-wood Cliffs, New Jersey
Kudo A (1995) Doitsu dozoku kigyo no unmei (Destiny of German family business). In: Shakaikagaku Kenkyu (J Soc Sci) 46(4):143–161
Mass R (1958) Die auswärtigen Geschäftsstellen der Siemens-Werke und ihre Vorgeschichte. Ein Erinnerungsblatt an Wilhelm von Siemens. Prestel-Verlag, München
Morikawa M (1996) Topu manejimento no keieishi (Business history of top management). Yuhikaku, Tokyo
Nakata M (1983) Gensdai kigyo kozo to kanri kino (Structure of modern enterprise and management function). Chuo keizaisha, Tokyo
Paschke C (1925) Der Aufbau der deutschen Teerfarbenindustrie und ihre Stellung in der Zollpolitik des Auslandes. Thesis, Hessische Ludwigs Universität zu Gieβen
Passow R (1922) Die Aktiengesellschaft. Eine wirtschaftswissenschaftliche Studie.2., neu bearbeite und erweiterte Aufl., G. Fischer, Jena
Pierson K (1973) Borsig. Ein Name geht um die Welt, Die Geschichte des Haus Borsig und seiner Lokomotiven. Rembrandt Verlag, Berlin
Pohl H (1981) Zur Geschichte von Organization und Leitung deutscher Grossunternehmen seit dem 19. Jahrhundert. In: Zeitschrift für Unternehmensgeschichte 26(2):143–178
Pohl H, Livesay HC (1982) On the history of organization and management in large German enterprise since the ninetieth century. In: German yearbook on business history, Springer, Berlin, New York, 91–122
Porter PG, Livesay HC (1969) Oligopolists in American manufacturing and their products 1909–1963. Appendix for "The structure of American industry in the twentieth century: A historical overview" by A. D. Chadler, Jr. In: Bus Hist Rev 43 (3): 293–294
Rheinmetall=Borsig Aktiengesellschaft (1937) Deutscher Maschinenbau 1837–1937. Im Spiegel des Werkes Borsig. Rheinmetall-Borsig Aktiengesellschaft, Berlin
Roesky E (1878) Die Verwaltung und Leitung von Fabriken speciell von Maschienen-Fabriken unter Berücksichtigung des gegenwärtigen Standes der deutsche Industrie mit besonderer Bezugnahme auf die Eisenbranche. M. Schäfer, Leipzig
Siemens G (1957) History of the House of Siemens, Vol. 1, The Era of Free Enterprise, K. Alber, München
Siemens G (1961) Der Weg der Elektrotechnik. Geschichte des Hauses Siemens. Bd. I, K. Alber, München
Siegrist H (1980) Deutscher Groβunternehmen vom späten 19. Jahrhundert bis zur Weimarer Republik. In: Geschichte und Gesellschaft 6(1):60–102
Stillich O (1904) Eisen- und Stahl-Industrie. Siemenroth, Berlin
Stockmann R (1987) Gesellschaftliche Modernisierung und Betriebsstrukture: Die Entwicklung von Arbeitsstätten in Deutschland 1875–1980. Campus, Frankfurt am Main, New York
Takenaka T (1991) Siemens to Meiji Nihon (Siemens and Japan in the Meiji era). Tokai daigaku shuppankai, Tokyo

Tanaka Y (2023) Siemens. Jiritsuteki jigyobu ni motoduku sekai saisho no sogo denki kigyo (Siemens. The first general electrical company based on independent divisions in the world). In Taniguchi A (ed) Sogo denki kigyo no keieishi (Formation and disbanding of general electrical engineering companies). Yuhikaku, Tokyo, pp 26–68

Treue W (1966) Die Feuer verlöschen nie. August Thyssen-Hütte 1890–1926. Eco Düsseldorf, Wien

von Weiher S, Goetzler H (1981) Weg und Wirken der Siemens-Werke im Fortschritt der Elektrotechnik 1847–1980. F. Steiner Verlag, Wiesbaden

Yamazaki T (2024) Japanese and German enterprises: comparison of industrial concentration system and business management. Springer Nature, Singapore

Ленин ВИ (1962) Империализм, как высшая стадия капитализма: популярный очерк. In: Полное собрание сочинений. Том 27, ос. изд-во полит. лит-ры, Москва, pp 299–426

Part III
Business Management in the Weimar Era

Chapter 7
The Development of Trusts and the Division of Labor in Production

Abstract Based on Part II's examinations regarding the period of the Second Reich, Part III analyzes business management during the Weimar period. Chapter 7 explores enterprise concentration and its special function in business management. It first examines the historical background of the concentration of enterprises in the wave of mergers called "the Second enterprise concentration." Next, it considers the development of trust and the division of labor in production within the merged enterprise using two representative cases in the iron and steel and chemical industries. Based on the cases of Vereinigte Stahlwerke AG and IG Farbenindustrie AG, this chapter analyzes how reducing excessive production capacity and reorganizing the division of labor in the production system was implemented using fusion. These examinations clarify the characteristics and significance of enterprise concentration in this period for the subsequent rationalization process.

Keywords Cartel · Enterprise concentration · IG Farben AG · The second movement of enterprise concentration · Rationalization · Trust · Vereinigte Stahlwerke AG

Part II considered changes in business management during the Second Reich. Following these analyses, Part III analyzed changes in German business management during the Weimar Republic period in terms of the rationalization movement of the 1920s. The research topics to be considered are as follows: (1) enterprise concentration in the form of trusts and their function, (2) the deployment and diffusion of the Taylor system and changes in labor management by introducing the REFA system as an original German system, (3) the deployment of the Ford system, and (4) changes in the organizational structure with rationalization and business diversification.

In the 1920s, the field of rationalization can be seen in three spheres as follows: (1) the rationalization and reorganization of industry using enterprise concentration, (2) rationalization based on developing technology and techniques (technical rationalization), and (3) rationalization based on improving labor organization and management. The latter two spheres were concerned with rationalization at the level of the individual enterprise.

T. Yamazaki, *A History of German Business*,
https://doi.org/10.1007/978-981-96-8476-2_7

Rationalization at the industrial level based on enterprise concentration was implemented on the basis of a fusion form called a "trust." In this process, eliminating or reducing excess production capacity and reorganizing the division of labor in production systems within large enterprises using fusion became important issues. Therefore, Chapter 7 examines the development of the trust as a major form of enterprise concentration in the 1920s and its function, considering the reorganization of the division of labor in production within giant enterprises created as a result of mergers.

Jürgen Bönig considered rationalization processes in the 1920s by dividing them into the three following phases. In the first phase, from 1925 to 1926, capital was more concentrated and accumulated than before 1914, particularly in industrial sectors such as heavy industry, the chemical industry, and the machinery industry. Arrangement processes—closing down of certain business units or factories, dismissals, and production specialization—were implemented following capital concentration. In the second stage, from 1926 to 1927, the rationalization process began at the level of the individual enterprise with the assistance of foreign countries, in particular, the United States (US). Technical rationalization with the investment of capital was also implemented. However, in the third phase, such rationalization had already moved to the background, and the intensification of labor by reorganizing production organization, making wage system changes, and the confronting the pressure of economic crisis appeared in the foreground (Bönig 1980, S.398–399; see also Schmiede and Schudlich, 1981, S.288, regarding the third phase of the rationalization process).

Rationalization and industry reorganization through enterprise concentration occurred during the first phase of the rationalization process in the 1920s. The major characteristics of enterprise concentration in the latter half of the 1920s can be observed in horizontal concentration to achieve the advantages of mass production and mass selling of certain products in contrast to vertical concentration with raw material departments to cope with shortages of goods until the end of inflation after World War I (Kambayashi and Inoue 1976, pp.230–231; Varga 1926, S.432). Typical cases of trusts in the latter half of the 1920s were the foundation of Vereinigte Stahlwerke AG in heavy industry in 1926 and IG Farbenindustrie AG in the chemical industry in 1925.

In Sect. 7.1, the historical background of enterprise concentration and industry rationalization is considered. In Sect. 7.2, the characteristics of rationalization by concentration are examined. Section 7.3 analyzes cases of heavy industry (mining and the iron and steel industry) and the chemical industry. Based on these discussions, in Sect. 7.4, the significance of the rationalization of industry at the enterprise level is clarified.

7.1 Historical Background and Tasks of Enterprise Concentration

A concentration wave called "the second movement of concentration of enterprise" occurred in Germany and the US during the 1920s. In this section, the historical background of such concentration processes is considered in heavy industry and the chemical industry as representative industrial sectors of such change.

The damages that Germany suffered due to its defeat in World War I were tremendously large. Above all, the loss of production capacity and demolition of the division of labor in industrial regions such as the Rheine-Westfalen district due to the alienation of territories caused heavy industry composed of the mining and iron and steel industries, very serious damage. Indeed, in several years after World War I, not only combining old equipment but also producing new production equipment was achieved. However, there were many facilities produced on the basis of outdated technologies. As a result, at the beginning of the inflationary period, a lot of incorrectly combined production equipment existed in Germany. Proper and truly modern production facilities were strikingly lacking (Rauecker 1926, S.35). In addition, many speculative foundations and company acquisitions aiming at the inflation effect were performed. Among the production equipment accumulated in this process were several equipment with no technologically organic relationship to the entire production process.

Thus, when the rationalization movement began in 1924, large enterprises in German heavy industry had excessive production equipment, bad equipment, and unprofitable plants. Therefore, it became important for these companies to eliminate excess production capacity and perform rationalization of the industry as a whole by consolidating them into trusts using enterprise concentration. The number of cartels increased significantly in the 1920s (in Germany, they increased from 1,000 in 1920 to 3000 in 1930; König 1960, S.304). However, it became clear that cartels were not appropriate for restricting production capacity and reorganizing production. The "Steel Trust" project, as seen in the foundation of Vereinigte Stahlwerke, meant a new form of coordinating industry that was superior to already established cartels (Reckendrees 2000, S.567). Vereinigte Stahlwerke was an attempt "to break out of the logic of German cartel-concern capitalism" and "to reorder the competitive dynamics of the whole steel industry" (Fear 2005, p.523). A document kept in the ThyssenKrupp Corporate Archives regarding its foundation also emphasized that the company aimed to achieve the economic rationalization of a part of the Rhein-Westfalen mining and iron industries (*thyssenkrupp Corporate Archives*, VST/3844, Vereinigte Stahlwerke, Aktiengesellschaft, Düsseldorf). The Founding of Vereinigte Stahlwerke was "an attempt by German steel industrialists to create American-style mass production economies, rationalize the industry, and deliver productivity and profitability from their investments" (Fear 2005, p.523) and one of its goal was "to help the steel industry match production with demand" (Fear 2005, p.549). Two strategic goals of this company were "to reduce industry capacity and to rationalize itself in the interest of profitability" (Fear 2005, p.553).

Next, the situation surrounding the German chemical industry changed remarkably with the World War I. The rapid development of chemical production in many nations that were Germany's best customers before 1914 but were cut off from their sources of supply during the war led to the relative decline of Germany's chemical industry (National Industrial Conference Board 1931, p.119). Whereas the US chemical industry increased its ratio of production to the world production from 34% before the outbreak of World War I to 47% by 1923, and the German chemical industry decreased its ratio from 24% to 17% over the same period (International Economic Conference 1927, p.21). Thus, the difference between the countries became larger. The shares of the US and France in all global chemical exports increased from 10% in 1913 to 16% in 1925 and from 9.7% to 13.3%, respectively. In contrast, Germany decreased from 28.4% to 23% over the same period (International Economic Conference 1927, p.41).

Whereas in the US, Great Britain, and France dye production increased, in Germany it decreased tremendously. This was a very serious blow to the German chemical industry in which dye was one of its dominant products. For instance, Germany's share in world aniline dye production significantly decreased from 82% in 1913 to 46% in 1924 (International Economic Conference 1927, p.28). As a result, operating rates of German enterprises decreased remarkably. For example, according to an internal Hoechst document, the operating rate of this company's dye manufacturing plants (except for indigo dye) was only about 18% in 1924 (*Hoechst Archiv*, IG214, Besprechung technischer Fragen. Zusammenlegung der Fabrikationen, S.1).

Under such serious conditions, the reduction of excess production capacity in the dye field and the rapid expansion of new production areas became important tasks for the German chemical industry. In the dye field, (1) moving dye production to the most productive plants, (2) reducing excess inventory, and (3) decreasing the tremendous number of dyes produced became central problems (Tammen 1978, S.29; Lindner 2005, S.32; Thiel 2020, S.254). Moving the emphasis of production to excellent plants of the highest technological level and the production concentration of certain products into these plants by abandoning old, low efficiency equipment, eliminating excess equipment, and closing down unprofitable, low productivity plants became important goals of realizing effective production at the level of individual enterprises. Thus, the most important purpose of concentration into IG Farben was the exclusion of mutual competition in the field of sales and dissolution and coexistence of plants with low operating rates and individual factories with low profitability (Tammen 1978, S.21).

In the chemical industry, the thorough rationalization of the dye department as a core business field and business structure reorganization through diversification were regarded as important purposes of enterprise concentration. The transformation from a chemical company in which the dye department was central to a general chemical company, including business fields in which high profitability and growth could be expected, was deeply concerned with the rationalization of dye department. The World War I promoted efforts for further use of the synthesis production methods, especially in high-pressure synthesis, to substitute substances (Plumpe 2022, S.221–223); however, such endeavors were further driven in the 1920s when the rationalization movement was developed. At IG Farben, the thorough rationalization of older fields such as the dye department, expansion of investments in nitrogen, and research and development in new fields such as synthetic ammonia, synthetic methanol, artificial oil, synthetic rubber, light metal, artificial and staple fiber, and synthetic resin were pursued on the basis of consolidation leader Carl Bosch's "generalization plan" in 1925. In his plan, improvement of dye department profitability was considered to provide financial support for research and development in these new departments. The consolidation of enterprises was regarded as an indispensable premise for the implementation of the thorough rationalization of the dye department (Kudo 1999, pp.84–85; Kudo 1978, pp.55–56).

Thus, in heavy industry and the chemical industry, the reduction of excessive production capacity was strongly propelled by enterprise concentration. R. A. Brady pointed out that the earlier phase of the rationalization movement in the 1920s was largely concerned with "problems of retreatment which involved elimination of the worst features of the industrial and organizational heritage from the war, revolution, and inflation periods" (Brady 1933, p.xii). Attempts to concentrate and specialize production in a certain plant according to product type by discarding excessive and inefficient equipment and closing down unprofitable plants were regarded as important ways of improving productivity, cutting production costs, and increasing profit by means of rationalization. As important feature of such processes was "grouping of individual businesses in large combinations and the elimination of inefficient producers in order to balance supply and demand," "rationalization" was understood by many people only in this sense (Urwick 1929, p.14). Such rationalization was generally called "negative rationalization." It was a process in which technologically unfavorable plants or business units were reduced or abandoned to concentrate production on certain technologically advantageous plants or business units and achieve specialization in certain types of production (regarding the conception of "negative rationalization," see Bauer 1931, S.195–196; Enquete Ausschuβ 1930a, S.22–23).

This period saw a wave of enterprise concentration. In addition to the challenging economic and business circumstances in German industry and the severe problems of excessive production capacity, aid from the state regarding tax created an important foundation for promoting consolidation. For example, as typically seen in the merger leading to the founding of Vereinigte Stahlwerke AG in 1926, various measures of tax reduction made this amalgamation easier, and the delay in the enactment of the tax reduction law became a factor determining the time needed for concentration (Kleinschmidt 1993, S.198–199; Krohn 1974, S.203–204). Furthermore, as seen in the case of a merger that created a steel trust (Vereinigte Stahlwerke AG), consolidation had great significance for acquiring urgently needed foreign loans (Kleinschmidt 1993, S.200), as did the development of rationalization (Reckendrees 1996, S.166).

7.2 Characteristics of the Rationalization of Industry by Enterprise Concentration

Next, this section considers the features of the rationalization of industry using enterprise concentration, in particular, trusts. One important origin of the wave of concentration in this period was the "agreement" regarding specialization. Before this time, specialization was achieved by separating a part of manufacturing that had previously belonged to a department as an independent business. This process was generally the result of relatively long market development (for instance, the case of Bücher regarding the specialization of craftsmen of nails, horseshoes, and arms being separated from the handwork of smiths). It was based on the free decisions of individual economic players and not the result of agreements between individual economies (Schiffer 1928, S.30). However, in the 1920s, specialization was implemented by mutual allotment of production based on the specialties of individual companies in certain products. Unlike the previous period, this specialization pursued "a division of labor based on contract" (Schiffer 1928, S.30; Schuster 1923, S.433). In this way, concentration and production specialization according to products were driven by enterprise concentration in this period, which resulted in building of an organization based on labor division such that each enterprise or plant specializes in the development of specific products by making the best use of their expertise.

An important feature of enterprise concentration during this period can be seen in the consolidation of firms that integrated different production processes. This had major significance for attempts to concentrate and specialize production according to product. Horizontal concentration, such as cartelization and enterprise trusts, which produced the same products and company consolidation, which integrated plural production processes, were dominant in Germany during this period. E. Varga highlighted that in 1926, it was important that the fusion of vertically integrated enterprises became dominant, and in individual business units of enterprise created by fusion, the trust-based specialization of fusion was pursued on the basis of locational and production technological advantages (Varga 1926, S.432). In case of vertically integrated enterprises in the iron and steel industry, as well as the allotment of production capacity of each kind of product in the rolling mill department, the allotment of production capacity in the manufacturing process of pig iron and steel was determined by concentrating and specializing production in the rolling mill process, as a final production process in this industry, according to the kind of product (Maekawa and Yamazaki 1995, p.39). Therefore, more thorough implementation of production concentration and specialization became possible compared with enterprise consolidation, which did not integrate different production processes mutually concerned with regrouping production organizations within firms created by trusts. David E. McNabb (2016, p.84) points out that prominent features of German big business in the Weimar period can be observed in "a multiplicity of ties and webs" through cartels and a high level of vertical integration (McNabb 2016, p.84). Moreover, the development of trust increased the significance of such integration.

Another characteristic of trusts in the iron and steel and chemical industries can be observed not in the simple consolidation of two capitals, but in the concentration of more capitals or the same kind of production department into one large capital (Kambayashi and Inoue 1976, p.231). Therefore, large trusts born by fusion occupied overwhelming weight in the industrial sector to which they belonged in terms of both the degree of production concentration and market share. As a result, they were able to realize the "division of labor based on contract," which was not possible before. In the 1920s, "negative rationalization" meant the rationalization of an entire industry that exceeded the level of individual enterprises. Trusts in Germany in the 1920s significantly exceeded the function of trusts in the US during the shift to monopolistic capitalism (see Chapter 4).

7.3 Production Concentration and Specialization Based on Product Type in Major Industries

Building on the foregoing discussions, the concentration and specialization of production according to product type in heavy industry and the chemical industry are examined next. This section considers the cases of Vereinigte Stahlwerke and IG Farben.

7.3.1 Production Concentration and Specialization Based on Product Type at Vereinigte Stahlwerke

As the German Steel Trust, Vereinigte Stahlwerke AG was formed out of four large groups of mining combines and the production processes of the iron and steel industry: (1) the Rhein-Elbe-Union, (2) the Thyssen Group, (3) The Phönix Group, and (4) Rheinstahl (Vereinigte Stahlwerke A.G. 1926, S.10; National Industrial Conference Board 1931, pp.82–83; Lasch 1930, S.92). The purpose of this company was to integrate their mining, iron plants, steel and rolling mills, and business units with the aim of rationalizing mining and the iron manufacturing industry [*thyssenkrup Corporate Archives*, A596/2, Gründungsvertrag der Vereingte Stahlwerke Aktiengesellschaft (14.1.1926), S.3]. Each enterprise and plant integrated into Vereinigte Stahlwerke was included in the overall plan of trusts from the perspective of "a division of labor based on contract." Elisabeth Schalldach highlighted that technical rationalization and other rationalization measures within the company required planned organization of all production processes to effectively accomplish the task of manufacturing and processing of iron and metal; this rationalization further led to the foundation of Vereinigte Stahlwerke and the crude steel community of interests in continental Europe

(Schalldach 1930, S.125). Vereinigte Stahlwerke's plants were "technically obsolete, and badly located with respect to raw materials, markets, or other plants with which they were closely related in the technique of production, were either completely reorganized or closed down permanently" [(1)]. R. A. Brady stressed "with this policy went the plan for concentrating the manufacture of particular products in a few specially equipped and favorably located plants" (Brady 1933, p.110).

In the iron department, pig iron production specialization was performed among the combines with steel producing and rolling mill equipment as well as blast furnace and simple blast furnace enterprises. Concentrations were implemented so that the simple blast furnace and casting companies of Schalkel Verein, Friedrich Wilhelm Eisenhütte, Meiderich Eisenhütte, Vulkan Eisenhütte, and Concordia Eisenhütte could produce as much of one or two kinds of special pig iron as possible, and, in the blast furnace equipment of the combines, only Thomas pig iron was manufactured (Stahl und Eisen 1927, S.474–475; Wolff 1930, S.109).

In regrouping the iron and steel and processing departments, three principles were regarded as standard: (1) integrating neighboring companies previously administrated separately due to differences in the enterprises to which they belonged, (2) specializing the production of each enterprise as much as possible and enabling the highest efficiency both quantitatively and qualitatively in each special department, and (3) making plants along the River Rheine in the eastern-most region favorable for exports, concentrating on export production and letting other plants take charge of production for the domestic market (Shimada 1940, p.19). First, the business units of Phönix (Ruhrort) and Rheinstahl (Meiderich) that were located in neighboring regions were fused into one industrial plant on the basis of the first principle. Business units of Dortmund and Hörder Verein were concentrated under united management in a similar way and various kinds of production were unified (Vereinigte Stahlwerke A.G. 1927, S.12, Wolff 1930, S.109).

As a result of such concentration and unification of business units among groups of major combines that integrated mining and iron and steel production, four groups of combines were administrated as a unified unit: (1) Dortmund-Hörder Verein, (2) the Rheine group composed of plants of Rheinstahl and Phönix, (3) the Hamborn group that had August Thyssen Hütte, and (4) the Bochmer Verein (Enquete Ausschuβ 1930a, S.32, S.130).

Production concentration and specialization based on product type among these groups was driven so that the effective division of labor in production among many rolling mill products might be achieved while avoiding duplication and maintaining the continuity of each production process as much as possible.

In **the Rheine group**, orders for export, specifically, bar iron and form iron, were allotted to the Ruhrort-Meiderich iron plants because of their favorable location on the Rheine River. In the production of semi-finished products, this group was also in charge of the supply of sheet bar and the production of semi-finished steel tube of various thin plate plants of Vereinigte Stahlwerke.

In the **Hamborn group**, August Thyssen Hütte, with its favorable plant locations, mainly took charge of production for export, and a large proportion of structural steel production was allotted to this business unit as well. This group also became engaged in the mass production of semi-finished products intended for export such as bar iron, form iron, and structural shapes.

In contrast to the two former groups, **the Dortmund-Hörder Verein** was primarily in charge of production of products for the domestic market because it had no advantage in transportation costs. The supply of semi-finished products and form iron was taken charge of by the Hörde group. On the other hand, the Dortmund Union produced mostly rail, structural steel, universal iron, and bar iron for the domestic market. The Dortmund group also specialized in a variety of workshop products including tools, bridges, and constructional engineering.

The Bochmer Group took charge of the production of products for the domestic market as it also did not have a locational advantage, like the Dortmund-Hörder Verein group. This group did not produce any mass products such as bar iron, form iron, or steel plates. The production equipment of this group was arranged primarily for the production of high-grade steel. The Bochmer Verein that absorbed Westfälische Stahlwerke specialized in quality production such as high-grade steel, railway rolling stock, cast steel bells, springs, rivets, bolts, and nuts. The production of tubes, rolled wire, and wire products was placed under one central administration. The reason why this group specialized in high-grade products was because these were high value-added products and they were able to absorb high transportation costs (Vereinigte Stahlwerke A.G. 1927, S.12; Ufermann 1927, S.175; Enquete Ausschuβ 1930a, S.32–33; Stahl und Eisen 1927, S.475; National Industrial Conference Board 1931, p.85; Shimada 1940, pp.19–20).

In this way, Vereinigte Stahlwerke was able to make better use of the larger potential of rationalization than other company groups as competitors. Whereas technological modernization and rationalization based on it in the second phase of the rationalization movement did not contribute to any further increase in productivity, the regrouping of production did decisively contribute to the improvement of productivity (Reckendrees 2000, S.434). One result of "the steel trust project," as seen in the foundation of Vereinigte Stahlwerke AG, was the reorganization of production programs based on economies of scale within enterprises borne by trusts created through fusion (Reckendrees 2000, S.590).

7.3.2 Production Concentration and Specialization Based on Product Type at IG Farben

Next, regarding the chemical industry, the case of IG Farben is considered. Measures to rationalize production began after the merger in 1925 as a means of (1) adapting production capacity to address the minimization of sale opportunities in many fields caused by the World War I, (2) integrating production equipment to create the same products in many plants, and (3) improving and cost-cutting of products (*Hoechst Archiv*, IG194, Über Struktur und wirtschaftliche Verflechtung der westdeutschen Werks der I.G. Farbenindustrie Aktiengesellschaft, S.6). After the consolidation in 1925, the "division of labor based on contract" was first completely implemented by specializing in certain products on the basis of each plant's own specialty from the unified perspective (Schiffer 1928, S.86). Consolidation enabled IG Farben to implement planning and create continuity for the first time (I.G. Farbenindustrie A.G. 1938, S.145). In this enterprise, to reorganize production organization, the principle of two-fold production, wherein the same product was produced in two former companies or plants, was adopted. It emphasized competition within the company and effective management (*Bayer Archiv*, 004/B-14-3-6, Einführung neuer Farbstoffe ab 1925, S.4; Gross 1950, S.8; Kudo 1999, p.130). However, as rationalization progressed, superfluous production of the same product was gradually abandoned (*Bayer Archiv*, 004/B-14-3-6, Einführung neuer Farbstoffe ab 1925, S.4, 5; Reichelt 1956, S.35). The principle of ideal competition within IG Farben was given up in the process of implementing the integration of production capacity in 1930. As a result, one product came to be produced in only one place (Meer 1953, S.35; Stolle 1980, S.103–104) and this enterprise pursued thorough simplification (*Bayer Archiv*, 004/B-14-3-6, Einführung neuer Farbstoffe ab 1925, S.5).

Concentrating and specializing production based on product type was strongly driven by the regional arrangement of production determined by each company location that was part of the merger. At IG Farben, which was created by the fusion of eight enterprises, a wide range of locational separation of production spots with various production plans required a mixture of centralization and regional autonomy (Etzold 1988, S.103). As a result, four regional operating groups called "*Betriebesgemeinschaft*" ("the Operating Community") were established—(1) the Upper Rheine, (2) the Middle Rheine, (3) the Lower Rheine, and (4) the Middle Germany (Brady 1933, p.237; Tammen 1978, S.21–22; Chandler 1990, p.568; Plumpe 1991, p.225)—on the basis the "decentralized centralism" principle.

Therefore, how production concentration and specialization based on product type was accomplished is considered according to the location of production capacity. Among various product fields, departments that needed to eliminate excessive production capacity and concentrate and specialize production according to product type were the largest and this change was accomplished most thoroughly in the dye field. Whereas tar dyes were produced in more than eight plants until then, most products were manufactured in only one plant and only a few mass products were manufactured in two places. Indanthrene dye was produced only in Ludwigshafen and the production of wool and silk dyes and vat dyes was concentrated in Hoechst's plants. Production of dyestuff ceased in Elberfeld plant as the smaller of Bayer's two plants, at the Weiler-ter Meer works in Uerdingen, at the Kalle plant in Biebrich, and at Griesheim works (Enquete Ausschuβ 1930b, S.36, 113; Brady 1933, p.237; Chandler 1990, p.569).

As a result of implementing such thorough production concentration and specialization based on product type, all dyes came to be produced in only one place, although a few exceptional cases existed. Carl Bosch pointed out that at IG Farben, most products were manufactured in only one place and a few mass products were produced in two places when each plant's production capacity was insufficient (*Hoechst Archiv*, IG 194, Über Struktur und wirtschaftliche Verflechtung der westdeutschen Werks der I.G. Farbenindustrie Aktiengesellschaft, S.7; Enquete Ausschuβ 1928, S.437). Plans to concentrate and specialize production on a product basis brought desirable results (Enquete Ausschuβ 1930b, S.113). As a result of this reorganization, BASF and Bayer's Leverkusenplant increased dyestuff production by 6.2% and 27.4%, respectively. In contrast, Hoechst decreased dye production by 2.5% (Bäumler 1963, p.103). According to an internal IG Farben document on April 13, 1927, whereas Hoechst abandoned some production departments of brands such as triphenylmethane dye, alizarin dye, and alkylated dye, it increased production of other dyes to a certain degree. As a result, plants of rest dyes and primary processing products indicated rational operating [*Hoechst Archiv*, IG200, Bericht an den Aufsichtsrat. Betriebsgemeinschaft Mittelrhein 1926 (13.4.1927), S.1–2].

The reorganization and regrouping of the dye department occurred in each primary factory that belonged to each Operating Community. For instance, in Hoechst's plants producing dyes and intermediate chemicals, the integration of each production department was performed in 1926 for the purpose of fostering more effective activities. Rationalization was implemented at the end of this year as a whole. Considerable simplification of production began to be achieved. The reduction of dye plants at the Biebrich factory was almost completely implemented in the fiscal year 1927 and almost all of them were then moved to Hoechst [*Hoechst Archiv*, IG200, Bericht an den Aufsichtsrat. Betriebsgemeinschaft Mittelrhein 1926 (13.4.1927), S.1, 4].

Furthermore, the sorts of dyes produced tremendously decreased through the rationalization process. According to an internal document from 1925 in the Hoechst archives, a new list about dye products included no less than 32,000 types. The technical committee, the top institution of technical affairs (see Chapter 10), considered the number of dye types to be too high and made a vigorous effort and ultimately agreed to reduce the types of dye produced (*Hoechst Archiv*, IG214. Besprechung technischer Fragen. Zusammenlegung der Fabrikationen, S.2). An internal document of the Middle Rheine Operating Community from September 22, 1927, also pointed out endeavors to reduce production costs by decreasing the product types produced and accurate cost management were further prompted at the time in the rationalization process of Hoechst's plant [*Hoechst Archiv*, IG200, Betriebsgemeinschaft Mittelrhein erstes Halbjahr 27 (22.9.1927), S.1–2; Meer 1953, S.36; Chandler 1990, p.571].

A similar principle as that governing the dye department production—that certain products or product groups should be produced in only one place on the basis of the most appropriate production conditions—was adopted in other product fields as well (*Hoechst Archiv*, IG194, Über Struktur und wirtschaftliche Verflechtung der westdeutschen Werks der I.G. Farbenindustrie Aktiengesellschaft, S.8). As a result, plant specialization similar to the dye department could be observed in other product departments such as pharmaceuticals, artificial silk, and fertilizer.

BASF, the headquarters of the Upper Rheine Operating Community, continued to produce intermediate chemicals, dyes, and organic chemicals closely related to dyes. However, its primary activity moved synthetic ammonia and nitrogen fertilizer to the Oppau plant and the Leuna plant located in neighboring Ludwigshafen.

Hoechst, as the headquarters of the Middle Rheine Operating Community, was the primary manufacturer of pharmaceuticals as before, as well as Leverlusen. Hoechst also took over production of vat dyes and all chemical products such as polyvinyl acetate, which was produced with the material acetylene.

At **Bayer,** as the headquarters of the Lower Rheine Operating Community, the Leverkusen plant as the core of this organization focused on the production of dye. Many other plants had to move their emphasis to products other than dye.

The Bitterfeld factory in **Griesheim,** the headquarters of the Middle Germany Operating Community, concentrated its production on light metal, in particular, magnesium. It also focused on the production of aluminum through a joint venture.

Agfa concentrated on business related to photography. It changed the production of photographic film and took over the management, production, and sale of photographic products such as printing paper manufactured in Leverkusen and cameras produced in Munich.

Furthermore, whereas the Uerdingen plant became the supplier of intermediate chemicals of a large size, the Kalle plant began to produce cellophane as a new product. Köln-Rotweil produced all three types of rayon (Chandler 1990, p.571; Haber 1971, pp.285–287; Hauser 1956, S.85, 89).

In this way, in fields other than dyes, the regrouping of production organization was implemented on the basis of concentrating and specializing production according to product type. L. F. Haber pointed out "the reorganization of the 1920s gave the main works a characteristics product mix and allowed them to enlarge their product range within the broad lines assigned to them." The chief feature of such reorganization can be seen in the "tendency towards product specialization (except for heavy inorganic chemicals) in the main works" (Haber 1971, pp.286–287).

However, there were considerable differences in the conditions of the concentration movement and the integration capacity between industries and between individual enterprises due to technical reasons or in terms of capital and purchasing equipment and other economic reasons (Enquete Ausschuβ 1930b, S.36). For instance, according to an internal document from October 1929 in the Hoechst archives, even after the first integration of the entire field of dye over three years, overcoming the still-existing duplication of many products was regarded as the most important goal to achieve (*Hoechst Archiv*, IG214, Niederschrift der Sitzung des TEA am Diensstag, den 1. Oktober 1929 vormittags $9\frac{1}{2}$ Uhr in Ludwigshafen a. Rhein, S.4).

Along with the elimination of duplicate production facilities in plants, the relocation and reallocation of plants and productive schedules and the concentration and specialization of production in many fields, the reorganization and combination of laboratories was pursued as well. Research in various fields had been concentrated in "a few well-equipped and thoroughly modernized laboratories attached to the larger specialized works in Ludwigsafen, Leverküsen, Höchst, etc." Smaller laboratories were ruthlessly scrapped in whole or in part whenever unnecessary duplication was discovered. Laboratories that were not closed down were either concentrating on some relatively narrow and highly specialized field of research, or, more likely, were kept primarily for control purposes (Brady 1933, p.238).

For instance, the Central Laboratory of the Upper Rheine Operating Community, which was headquartered at BASF, pursued the development of synthetic intermediate chemicals such as resins, styrene, and ethylene. The laboratory in neighboring Oppau concentrated on high-pressure synthesis. The Central Laboratory of the Lower Rheine Operating Community, whose headquarters was Bayer, naturally focused on dyes. In the lower Rheine region, the specialized Color Laboratory, the Moth Laboratory, and the Rubber Laboratory existed. Although research in Hoechst focused on pharmaceuticals, the Central Laboratory for the Middle Rheine continued to concentrate on vat dyes. Other laboratories took charge of research on acetylene (Chandler 1990, p.571).

Thus, at IG Farben and Vereinigte Stahlwerke, production concentration and specialization based on product type was implemented according to primary plants and regions and the system of the division of labor in new large enterprises created by trusts was established. Figure 7.1 indicates the locations of various IG Farben factories and mines.

When looking at problems of production concentration and specialization based on type of product in comparison with heavy industry, in the chemical industry, unlike heavy industry, the need to eliminate or reduce excessive production capacity was not due to the low technological level of production facilities of German chemical enterprises, but was determined by excessive changes in the relationship between demand and supply caused by World War II and the increase of production and competitiveness among foreign enterprises after the war. A. D. Chandler, Jr. pointed out that "the companies coming into the merger had been able to maintain their facilities and the skills of their personnel at close to the state-of-the-art level. The German still led the way in most industrial chemicals. Rationalization, therefore, was marked less by the massive closing down of old works, the reshaping of other works, and the building of new ones than occurred in iron and steel. More often it took the form of changing the product mix and concentrating products in plants best suited for their manufacture" (Chandler 1990, p.569).

In contrast, Vereinigte Stahlwerke AG was only a compromise and a "half consolidation" of enterprises with the same product programs in the heavy industry. This situation occurred because some leading companies, such as Krupp, Mannesmann, Hoesch, and Gutehoffnung, did not participate in the merger, and as a result, powerful outsiders continued to exist. These outsider enterprises selected their independence (Kleinschmidt 1993, S. 202–208). Planned operations cutbacks, plant closures, and

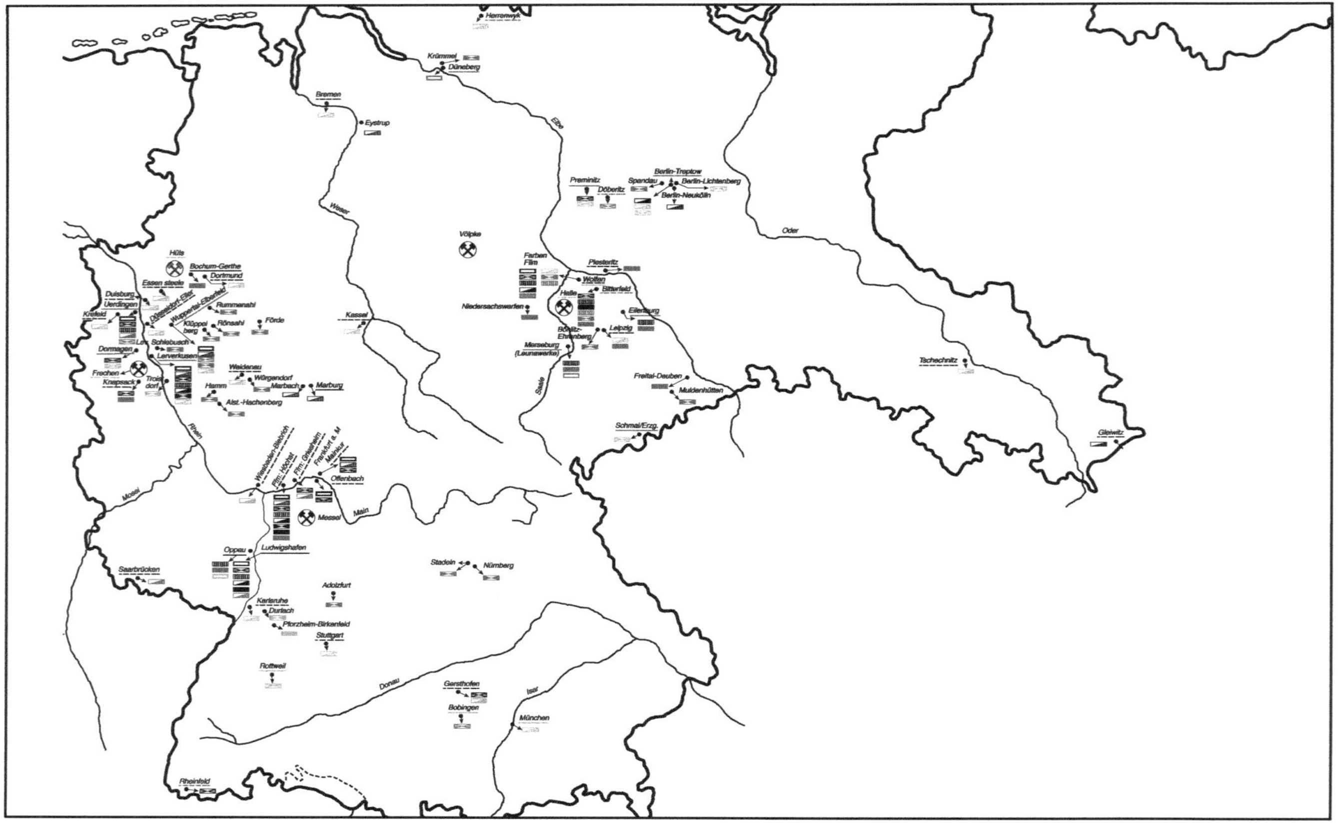

Fig. 7.1 Location of plants of IG Farbenindustrie AG and those combined by communities of interest or letting and hiring agreements (September 1930)
Source Hoechst Archiv, IG 194, Organisation, Betriebsgemeinschaften

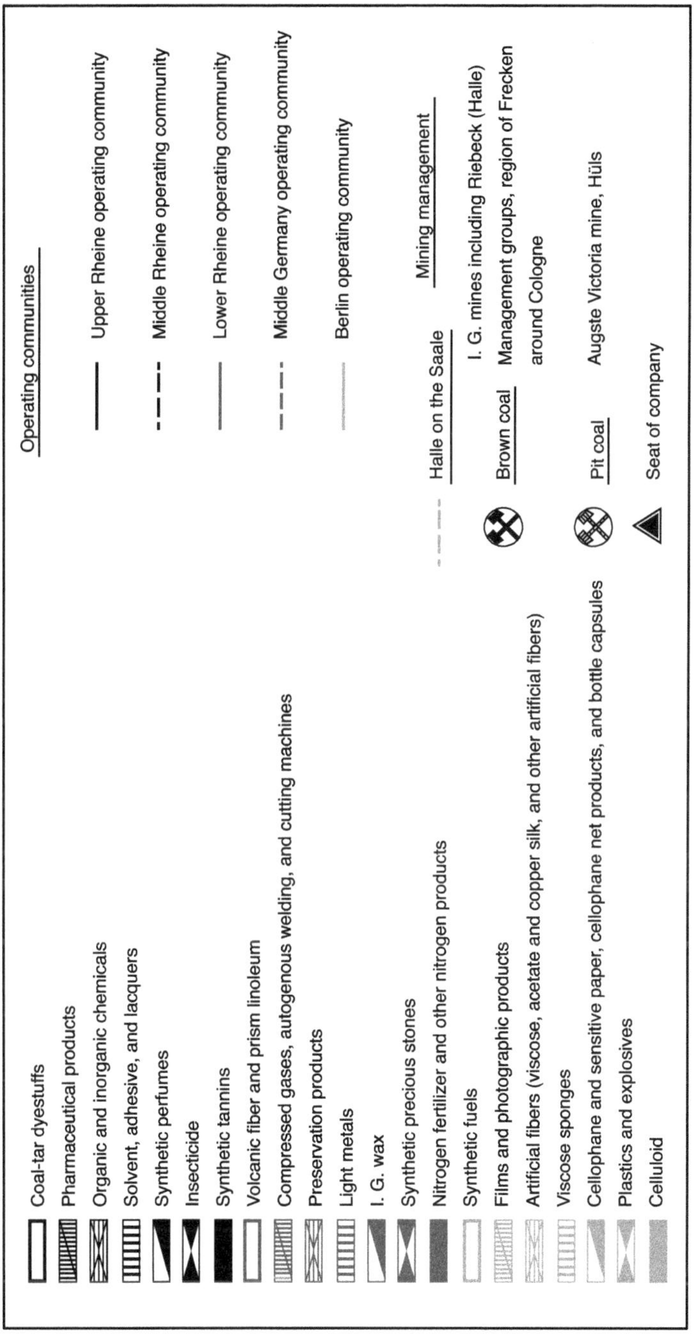

Fig. 7.1 (continued)

coordination of production programs (particularly similar product groups of mass producers concentrated on a relatively small extent measured by the sum of manufacturers) (Kleinschmidt 1993, S. 207) drew attention to the effects of concentration and specialization of production based on the product division of labor in production using trust.

Furthermore, the method for creating trust influenced the subsequent development of equipment investment in Vereinigte Stahlwerke AG and IG Farbenindustrie. In IG Farben, the total amount of capital participation securities and other securities at the foundation of the company (December 31, 1925) was significantly large (242,536,340 RM) (IG Farbenindustrie AG 1926) due to the merger covering the entire German chemical industry. Their ratio to all assets was 20% and nearly equivalent to that of fixed equipment (26.9%) at the company's establishment. Similar numerical figures at the end of the financial year 1927 (December 31, 1927) were 296,143 RM and 16.3%, respectively (IG Farbenindustrie AG 1928). Therefore, the increase in securities afterward was not significantly large. In contrast, Krupp was expected to be the biggest object of the Vereinigte Stahlwerke AG merger; however, it did not participate in the trust, and the combination of the promoting enterprise was not completely fused. Due to such situations, Vereinigte Stahlwerke AG attempted to expand and strengthen the trust, resulting in considerable capital participation (Maekawa 1970, p.55). The total amount of securities of capital participation and other securities on April 1, 1926, was 92,906,446 RM, and the ratio of them to all assets was only 6.6%. In contrast, the ratio of fixed equipment to all assets was 77.1% and significant (Vereinigte Stahlwerke AG 1927, S.16–17; Handbuch der Deutschen Aktien-Gesellschaften 1926, S.4162). The total capital participation securities and other securities at the end of the financial year 1927 (September 30, 1927) increased to 295,159,000 RM and their ratio to all assets rose to 14.2%, respectively (Vereinigte Stahlwerke AG 1928, S.16–17). This became an important factor restricting the development of equity investment afterward (see Yamazaki 2001, Chapter 2, 3, and 4). Therefore, when investment in the heavy and chemical industries is examined, comparing the roles and conditions of equipment investment between these industries, particularly in this context, is important.

7.4 Significance of the Rationalization of Industry Using Trusts

Building upon these discussions, Sect. 7.4 attempts to clarify the significance of the rationalization of industry by enterprise concentration in the form of trusts for enterprise-level rationalization in the second and the third phases of the rationalization process.

The second stage of the rationalization process in the 1920s was when enterprise-level rationalization was pursued at full scale on the basis of foreign credits, in particular, from the US. In this stage, rationalization was implemented primarily in the fields of technology, technique, and management represented by changes in labor organization. An important premise of the effective rationalization of individual companies is that production fields that enterprises control are broad and have conditions enabling the development of mass production. However, at the beginning of the relatively stable period of capitalism when the rationalization movement began, it was necessary to consolidate firms in the same types of industrial sector using trusts as a means of horizontal enterprise concentration, as well as eliminate unnecessary excessive equipment and concentrate and specialize production on the basis of product type by moving production to superior plants and business units with technological and locational advantages and thus achieve industry-level rationalization and the reorganization of the industry (Maekawa and Yamazaki 1995, pp.51–52).

In rationalization during this period, the emphasis was placed on two aspects—(1) the efficiency of production and (2) market stability (National Industrial Conference Board 1931, p.33). As A. P. Young pointed out, the "rationalization process started as an attempt to ration output within the limits of the existing market demands, simultaneously to reduce production costs in face of the handicap inherently arising from the low load conditions obtaining in the carious factories" (Young 1929, p.12).

Rationalization during this period played an important role as a countermeasure on the side of not only production but also sales. Enterprise concentration implemented at the beginning of the rationalization movement was driven to overcome the imbalance between production and sales as well as cost reduction. Hilde Weiss pointed out that production equipment had to be decreased in all kinds of ways to overcome the contradiction between production foundations enlarged before and the existing possibility of sales (Weiss 1926, S.8).

In this way, the rationalization of industry in the first phase of the rationalization process was an attempt to create a more effective foundation of production and sales by enabling large enterprises formed by trusts to eliminate excessive production capacity and achieve the division of labor in production based on product type within a company. This created favorable conditions for rationalization at the level of individual enterprises and was regarded as phenomenon with, so to speak, "preparatory characteristics" for subsequent industry-level rationalization.

Therefore, the next important research topics to be analyzed are how business at the level of individual enterprises and their significance. In the following three chapters (Chapter 8, 9, and 10) these problems will be considered.

(1) In Vereinigte Stahlwerke AG, there were many cases of closing and discarding plant and production equipment from 1926 to 1933. Decreases occurred in the number of blast furnace plants (23 to 9), open-hearth furnace plants (20 to 8), bar iron and form iron plants (17 to 10), strip steel rolling plants (7 to 3), and wire plants (7 to 2). Similar decreases occurred in sheet bar plants (13 to 6), steel tube plants (8 to 3), press and forging plants (8 to 4), cast steel plants (10 to 4), wire processing plants (9 to 4), and wheel plants (6 to 1) [*thyssenkrup Corporate Archives*, VST/1588, Der Umbau der Vereinigte Stahlwerke (2.11.1933), Anlage 2].

References

Bäumler E (1963) Ein Jahrhundert Chemie. Econ Verlag, Düsseldorf

Bauer O (1931) Rationalisierung und Fehlrationalisierung. Wiener Volksbuchhandlung, Wien

Bönig J (1980) Technik und Rationalisierung in Deutschland zur Zeit der Weimarer Republik. In: Trotzsch U, Wohlauf G (Hrsg) Technikgeschichte. Historiche Beiträge und neuere Ansätze. Schulkamp, Frankfurt am Main, S.390–419

Brady RA (1933) The rationalization movement in German industry. a study in the evolution of economic planning. University of California Press, Berkeley, California

Chandler AD Jr (1990) Scale and scope: the dynamics of industrial capitalism. Harvard University Press, Berkeley, Massachusetts

Enquete Ausschuβ (1928) Wandlungen in den wirtschaftlichen Organization. (I)-3, E. S. Mittler & Sohn, Berlin

Enquete Ausschuβ (1930a) Die deutsche eisenerzeugende Industrie. (III)-2, E. S. Mittler & Sohn, Berlin

Enquete Ausschuβ (1930b) Die deutsche chemische Industrie. (III)-3, E. S. Mittler & Sohn, Berlin

Etzold H (1988) Die Entwicklung der Produktivkräfte in der Industrie. In: Institut für Wirtschaftsgeschichte der Akademie der Wissenschaften der DDR, Berthold R et al. (Hrsg) (1988) Produktivkräfte in Deutschland von 1917/18 bis 1945. Akadermie Verlag, Berlin, S.36–223

Fear JR (2005) Organizing control. August Thyssen and the construction of German corporate management. Harvard University Press, Cambridge, Massachusetts, London

Gross H (1950) Material zur Aufteilung der I.G. Farbenindustrie Aktiengesellschaft. Kiel Institut für Weltwirtschaft, Kiel

Haber LF (1971) The chemical industry, 1900–1930. International growth and technological change. Oxford University Press, Oxford

Hauser H (1956) Geschichte des Werks Uerdingen der Farbenfabriken Bayer Aktiengesellschaft. Werk Uerdingen der Farbenfabriken Bayer, Krefeld

Handbuch der Deutschen Aktien-Gesellschaften (1926) Vereinigte Stahlwerke Aktiengesellschaft, Düsseldorf. In: Handbuch der Deutschen Aktien-Gesellschaften 1926, Bd.III, 4158–4163

IG Farbenindustrie AG. (1926) Bericht des Vorstandes und des Aufsichtsrates über das Geschäftsjahr 1925. IG. Farbenindustrie AG., Frankfurt am Main

IG Farbenindustrie AG. (1928) Bericht des Vorstandes und des Aufsichtsrates über das Geschäftsjahr 1927. IG. Farbenindustrie AG., Frankfurt am Main

IG Farbenindustrie AG. (1938) Zur Erinnerung an die 75 Wiederkehr des Gründungstages der Farbwerk vorm: Meiste Lucius & Brunning. IG. Farbenindustrie AG., München

International Economic Conference (1927) The chemical industry. League of Nations, Geneva

Kambayashi T, Inoue K (1976) Kogyo no keizai riron (The economic theory of industry). Zoho ban, Mineruva shobo, Kyoto

Kleinschmidt C (1993) Rationalisierung als Unternehmensstrategie. Die Eisen- und Stahlindustrie der Ruhrgebiets zwischen Jahrhundertwende und Weltwirtschaftskrise. Klartext, Essen

König H (1960) Kartelle und Konzentration (unter besonderer Berücksichtung der Preis- und Mengenabsprachen). In: Arndt H (Hrsg) Die Konzentration in der Wirtschaft, Erster Band, Stand der Konzentration, Duncker und Humblot, Berlin, S.303–332

Krohn CD (1974) Stabilisierung und ökonomische Interessen. Finanzpolitik des Deutschen Reichs 1923–1927. Bertelsmann Universitätsverlag, Düsseldorf

Kudo, A (1978) IG Faruben no seiritsu to tenkai (1) (Founding and development of IG Farben). In: Shakai Kagaku Kenkyu (J Soc Sci) 29(5):1–62

Kudo A (1999) Gendai kagaku kigyoushi (Modern business history in the German chemical industry). Mineruva shobo, Kyoto

Lasch K (1930) Entwicklungstendenzen für die Zusammenschuβformen in der deutschen Groβindustrie seit 1914. Industrie-Verlag und Dr, Düsseldorf

Lindner SH (2005) Hoechst. Ein I.G. Farben Werk im Dritten Reich. 2. Auflage, C. H. Beck, München

Maekawa K (1970) Doitsu dokusen kigyo no hatten katei (Development of monopolistic enterprise in Germany). Mineruva shobo, Kyoto
Maekawa K, Yamazaki T (1995) Doitsu gorika undo no kenkyu (Study of the German rationalization movement). Moriyama shoten, Tokyo
McNabb DE (2016) Converging trends and the future of the global market (A comparative history of commerce and industry, vol II). Palgrave Macmillan, Basingstoke
ter Meer F (1953) Die IG Farbenindustrie Aktiengesellschaft: Ihre Entstehung, Entwicklung und Bedeutung. Econ Verlag, Düsseldorf
National Industrial Conference Board (1931) Rationalization of German industry. National Industrial Conference Board, Inc., New York
Plumpe G (1991) The Political framwork of structural modernization: The I.G. Farbenindustrie A.G., 1904–1945. In: Lee WR (ed) German industry and German industrialization: Essays in German economics and business history in the nineteenth and twentieth centuries. Routledge, London, New York, pp 220–264
Plumpe W (2022) Chemische Industrie. In: Boldorf M (Hrsg) Deutsche Wirtschaft im Ersten Weltkrieg. De Gruyter, Berlin, S.193–225
Rauecker B (1926) Rationalisierung und Soziakpolitik. Sieben Stäbe-Verlag, Berlin
Reckendrees A (1996) Die Vereinigte Stahlwerke A.G. 1926–1933 und „das glänzende Beispiel Amerika". In: Zeitschrift für Unternehmensgeschichte 41(2):159–186
Reckendrees A (2000) Das ≪Stahltrust≫-Projekt. Die Gründung der Vereinigte Sthalwerke A.G. und ihre Unternehmensentwicklung 1926–1933/34. C. H. Beck, München
Reichelt WO (1956) Das Erbe der IG-Farben. Econ Verlag, Düsseldorf
Schalldach E (1930) Rationalisierungsmaβnahmen der Nachinflationszeit im Urteil der deutschen freien Gewerkschaften. G. Fischer, Jena
Schiffer C (1928) Die ökonomische und sozialpolitische Bedeutung der industriellen Rationalisierunsbestrebung. G. Braun, Karlsruhe
Schmiede R, Schudlich E (1981) Die Entwicklung der Leistungsentlohnung in Deutschland: Eine historische Untersuchung zum Verhältniss von Lohn und kapitalistischen Produkutionsbedingungen. 4. Aufl., Campus Verlag, Frankfurt am Main, New York
Schuster E (1923) Typisierung als Wirtschaftsorganisation. In: Weltwirtschaftliches Arch 19(3):429–438
Shimada C (1940) Doitsu Godo Seiko no kako oyobi genzai (3) [The past and present of Vereinigte Stahlwerke AG in Germany (3)]. In: Tekko Renmei Chosa Geppo (Mon Res Rep Jpn Iron Steel Fed) 24: 18–26
Stahl und Eisen (1927) Vereinigte Stahlwerke, Aktiengesellschaft, Düsseldorf. In: Stahl und Eisen 47(11):474–477
Stolle U (1980) Arbeiterpolitik im Betrieb: Frauen und Männer, Reformisten und Radikale, Fach- und Massenarbeiter bei Bayer, BASF, Bosch und in Solingen (1900–1933). Campus Verlag, Frankfurt am Main, New York
Tammen H (1978) Die I.G. Farbenindustrie Aktiengesellschaft [1925–1933]: Ein Chemiekonzern in der Weimarer Republik. H. Tammen, Berlin
Thiel C (2020) Entscheidungen und Anpassungspraktiken. Die BASF zwischen 1865 und 1965. Campus, Frankfurt am Main
Ufermann P (1927) Der Stahltrust. Verlagsgesellschafts des Allgemeinen Deutschen Gewerkschaftsbundes
Urwick LF (1929) The meaning of rationalization. Nisbet, London
Varga E (1926) Die marxistische Sinn der Rationalisierung. In: Die Internationale 9(14):431–439
Vereinigte Stahlwerke AG. (1927) Bericht über das 1. Geschäftsjahr vom 14. Januar bis 30. September 1926 für die ordentliche General-Versammlung am 28. März 1927, Vereinigte Stahlwerke A.G., Düsseldorf
Vereinigte Stahlwerke AG. (1928) Bericht über das 2. Geschäftsjahr vom 1. Oktober 1926 bis 30. September 1927 für die ordentliche General-Versammlung am 28. März 1928, Vereinigte Stahlwerke A.G., Düsseldorf

Weiss H (1926) Rationalisierung und Arbeiterklasse:Zur Rationalisierung der deutschen Industrie. Führer-Verlag, Berlin
Wolff E (1930) Die Unternehmungs-Organisation in der deutschen Eisen-Industrie. C Heymann, Berlin
Yamazaki T (2001) Vaimaruki Doitsu gorika undo no tenkai (The development of the rationalization movement in Germany during the Weimar era). Moriyama shoten, Tokyo
Young AP (1929) Rationalization of industry. New York

Chapter 8
Deployment of the Taylor System and the REFA System

Abstract This chapter examines the deployment of the Taylor and the REFA (*Reichsausschß für Arbeitszeitermittlung*) systems as "German Taylor systems" in relation to changes in historical conditions. First, it considers the deployment of the Taylor system during and after World War I until 1924. In addition, the introduction of the Taylor and REFA systems during the relatively stable period of the 1920s is discussed. The social and economic backgrounds of the Taylor system diffusion, modification of the Taylor system into the REFA system, and the roles of rationalization science in implementing the REFA system are explored. Furthermore, the management functions of the REFA system and its influence on workers are examined and compared with those of the Taylor system. Based on these discussions, the introduction of the REFA system in major industrial sectors, such as the iron and steel, electrical engineering, machinery, mining, and chemical industries, is considered, and the overall conditions are elucidated. Through these discussions, changes in labor management will be clarified.

Keywords Economic democracy · Labor science · Management science · Rationalization · Rationalization science · REFA system · Taylor system

Important business management changes in Germany during the Weimar Republic can be seen in the deployment and diffusion of the Taylor system and improvement in the labor management system through the introduction of the REFA system as an original German system, the deployment of the Ford system, and organizational structure reform with business rationalization and diversification. Attempts to deploy the Taylor system can already be observed from the beginning of the twentieth century to World War I; however, it was not adopted sufficiently by German enterprises and did not prevail during this period.

In the 1920s, the German industry lagged behind the United States (US) in respect of rational organization. J. Ermansky stressed that even in countries with a high technological level such as Germany, losses arising from irrational production organization were undoubtedly larger than in the US, and rational organization in Germany

T. Yamazaki, *A History of German Business*,
https://doi.org/10.1007/978-981-96-8476-2_8

was not equal to the US (Ermanski 1928, S.216). Under these circumstances, rationalization in the field of labor organization and management reform became an important problem in Germany. American management methods represented by the Taylor and Ford systems drew attention and their deployment was attempted to strengthen Germany's international competitiveness. The Taylor system was modified according to the German situation and as a result of these revisions, the REFA system was created as a "German" Taylor system.

This chapter considers the deployment of the Taylor system and clarifies business management changes in the field of labor organization and management after World War I. In Sect. 8.1, attempts to deploy the Taylor system during the war and the postwar period through 1924 are examined. In Sect. 8.2, the transformation of the Taylor system into the REFA system and characteristics of this revised German system are explored. Based on these discussions, in Sect. 8.3, how the REFA system was introduced and labor management and organization changed are analyzed.

8.1 Deployment of the Taylor System During and After World War I

8.1.1 Deployment of the Taylor System During World War I

As considered in Chapter 5, attempts at reforming the labor management system and deploying the Taylor system in Germany from the end of the nineteenth century to World War I did not progress sufficiently, and as such, developments lagged behind the US. However, as well as in the United States where the demands of World War I again brought scientific management to the forefront (Hunt 1922, p.xi), conditions surrounding the deployment and implementation of the Taylor system changed considerably in the period during and after World War I.

Organized endeavors to achieve the mass production of munitions became an urgent problem with the outbreak of war and the shift to a war economy and labor organization reform using the Taylor system came to have major significance. The use of rational production methods, work forms making it possible to save time, raw materials, and energy, and organizational measures to promote the increase of output gave rise to unexpected possibilities under the almost unabsorbable, massive demand for munitions during wartime (Pechhold 1974, S.40). Munitions were mass produced on a scale almost equivalent to the US in German munitions industries (Spitzley 1980, S.62).

Changes in industrial relationships with the outbreak of the war also had great significance. The Social Democratic Party adopted a cooperative policy with the war and the Free Trade Union under this party decided to abandon the strike entirely (Nomura 1980, p.182). This policy had major significance in promoting increasing munitions production and the Taylor system was regarded as an important means of coping with the national task of achieving the enlargement of munitions production for war. Therefore, the introduction of the Taylor system became an important problem transcending the level of the individual enterprise.

8.1.2 Deployment of the Taylor System After World War I Until 1924

At the beginning of the period after the war, the significance of introducing the Taylor system was further increased to address the need for rebuilding the economy. Such a national task was emphasized due to a tremendous decline in domestic production, a remarkable decrease in exports, and enormous reparation payment requests by victorious nations. Problems concerning the introduction of the Taylor system were considered under this national economic perspective.

Under this environment, in terms of capital, economic concessions offered to the worker class to avoid the success of the 1918 German Revolution imposed large shackles on the subsequent resurrection and development of enterprises. Therefore, introducing the Taylor system had greater meaning as an effective means of increasing Germany's productive forces.

In examining the attitude of labor unions, changes in the political framework brought about due to the Social Democratic Party's participation in the Weimar government increased the importance of introducing the Taylor system in relation to its "socialization plan." For many labor union functionaries, socialization was regarded as a problem of expanding production. However, as there were no effective means under the contemporary German situation except for improving productivity, increasing production was synonymous with addressing the problem of improving productivity (Ohashi 1999, p.89). Among the Free Trade Union functionaries, persons who entered the Weimar government ministry appeared and considered reconstruction and developmental problems under such conditions. Introducing the Taylor system to address the problem of socialization and increasing production came to have a more positive meaning (Ohashi 1984, p.36).

The situation greatly changed during the inflationary period. In Germany, the monetary incentive wage was traditionally dominant until the beginning of the 1920s and individual piece rates were decided through negotiations between workers and foremen. However, inflation motivated the adoption of the time incentive wage combined with a stronger introduction of the time study (Trieba and Mentrup 1983, S.99). The pressure of economic anxiety on workers weakened their resistance and promoted their acceptance of time incentive wages that promised them a more stable income (Schmiede and Schudlich 1981, S.264–265). The consideration of time as "measure of value of work output" rather than monetary value increased due to a remarkable decline in the value of money as a result of inflation. Thus, adoption of the time incentive wage rather than the monetary incentive wage became a necessary and important problem (Henzel 1927, S.509; Reichskuratorium für Wirtschaftlichkeit

1930, S.259; Kobayashi 1979, p.123). This promoted the study of labor processes conducted by "the Committee of Time Study" (*Ausschuß für Zeitstudien*) founded within the Economic Production Committee (*Ausschuß für wirtschatliche Fertigung*) (Homburg 1991, S.291–294).

However, during this period, attempts to implement the Taylor system by German enterprises were not organizational and were only partial. In 1919, the Taylor system was discussed, and the possibility of its use was examined again; however, few plants implemented this system in its strictest form due to the considerable time spent on implementing time study, the necessity to build the special work office and increase staff, and the intense distrust of workers. Furthermore, the characteristics of the German market, such as the narrow domestic market, were important in determining the insufficient deployment of Taylor's management. Instead, it was a matter of high-grade products, not a larger volume of objects of the same kind (Hartmann 1921, S.445–446). Around 1922, time studies were implemented only sporadically due to their high cost and worker opposition, and the use of instruction cards was limited (Söllheim 1922, S.148, 168, 175–181). This situation did not change until the relatively stable period of capitalism during which the introduction of the Taylor system in the form of the REFA system progressed (Homburg 1991, S.297).

8.2 The Taylor System and REFA System During the Relatively Stable Period of the 1920s

8.2.1 Social and Economic Background of Taylor System Diffusion

During the relatively stable period from 1924 to 1929, conditions changed tremendously. Rationalization was regarded as an extremely important measure that indicated that this means of economic reconstruction was driven as a "national movement," so to speak, with the strong state involvement and trade union cooperation. Under these conditions, the introduction of the Taylor system as well as the Ford system became an important issue. How did the factors that had previously restricted the deployment of the Taylor system change?

The domestic market became narrower due to hyperinflation, causing the expansion of exports to become an urgent task for achieving the resurrection and development of enterprises and the reconstruction of the national economy. In the inflationary period, it was possible for German companies to increase exports to a certain degree by means of the dumping effect caused by the decline in the currency exchange rate. However, such competitiveness in exports disappeared with the end of inflation and the stabilization of the German Mark. As a result, thorough cost-cutting became an indispensable task for all industrial sectors.

Factors such as eight-hour labor time, wage system improvement, and labor union approval of agreed-upon wages brought about the tendency that wages were hard to fall. Such a situation did not change fundamentally, despite the amendments implemented around the stabilization of the German Mark (Kato 1973, p.363). This was a factor in the important tasks of increasing wages and cutting labor costs.

The possibility of shifting to socialism in industrial relations disappeared with the defeat of revolutionary influences, which promoted the cooperation of labor and capital. The Economic Democratic Theory of the Free Trade Union appeared as an ideology to drive rationalization instead of socialization. It was closely connected with the assertion that improving the economic position of workers would be realized by cooperating in economic development measures, including rationalization. Collaboration in economic development or rationalization occurred under the name of socialization during the revolutionary period after World War I. In contrast to this, such cooperation was promoted under the name of "democratization" or "economic democratization" during the relative stable period between 1924 and 1929. This perspective was based on productivity. Among trade union leaders, a high level of productivity was indispensable for realizing a high-level standard of living, as seen in the US at the time, and rationalization was regarded as the most effective means to achieving their goals (Ohashi 1999, p.107). The Taylor system was considered one of the most important rationalization measures under these circumstances.

The condition of the financial market also increased the necessity to deploy the Taylor system. A shortage of capital manifested as constant credit shortages (Amamiya 1994, p.295), causing the development of rationalization with its capital expenditures to be forced within a certain limit due to the capital shortage and the burden of capital costs [(1)]. Therefore, the Taylorsystem was particularly significant as a rationalization measure that did not require special capital expenditures.

8.2.2 *Modification of the Taylor System and REFA System*

Thus, the introduction of the Taylorsystem began at the outset of the twentieth century as one of the most important issues after 1924 regarding the reconstruction of the national economy. However, the Taylor system was transformed into the REFA system on account of worker influence and opposition. REFA (*Reichsausschß für Arbeitszeitermittlung*) played a significant role in this modification. It was established in 1924 and named by the General Association of German Metal Manufacturers (*Gesamtverband Deutscher Metallindustrieller*) and the German Association of Engineers (*Verein deutscher Ingenieure*) (Pechhold 1974, S.56). The REFA system developed by REFA was a rationalization measure created under the special German situation after World War I and could be considered the "German" Taylor system or the revised Taylor system.

The purpose of REFA as an institute can be seen in the following four points. The first is to prompt education on work time calculators and organize training courses that were useful for such purposes. The second is to integrate local institutions that were beneficial to the first purpose. The third is to prepare the needed teaching aids as uniformly as possible to consistently and systematically implement training of work time calculators. The fourth is to promote further development of scientific and practical study in every manner in the field of work measurement (Reichskuratorium für Wirtschaftlichkeit 1930, S.36–37). In considering tasks of the REFA more specifically, it aimed (1) to replace the monetary incentive wage system that was traditionally dominant in Germany with the time incentive wage system newly adopted by the REFA system, (2) implement work-study based on time study, and (3) provide the possibility to remove continuous conflicts over setting standard output from the plant by "securing of objectivity" of time measurement. The second point indicated that manufacturing technical and work organizational changes were implemented from a work-study to achieve work effectiveness and increase labor intensity (Spitzley 1980, S.101). Regarding the third point, Eduard Michel (1924, S.195) stressed that the REFA's negotiation table could reach an agreement on fundamental economic issues better than when mutual consent was possible in dissipating workshop or plant conflicts (Michel 1924, S.195).

The commonalities between the Taylor system and the REFA system lie in the following four points. First, we deal with labor intensity as a measurement of the performance parameter. In both systems, work performance was not measured by the manufactured physical product; instead, a criterion of labor intensity was found by the difference between the actual output and the standard output, which was regarded as the basis of the wage payment. Second, the wage policy and performance policy should be separated. Third, the power of the trade union and workers should be restricted when determining workload. Fourth, time studies should be uniform—labor became comparable and calculable by a unified time study form (Trieba and Mentrup 1983, S.104–105).

Two differences between the Taylor system and the REFA system can be observed. One is changes in the task standard of the work volume to be accomplished. Whereas the task standard in the Taylor system was to achieve "maximum output" based on the fastest time of a first-class worker, the basis of tasks in the REFA system was to achieve "normal output" based on the average time of a mean worker. The other was the modification of the wage system. Whereas the relationship between wages and output changed progressively in the Taylor system, this relationship changed proportionally in the REFA system (Trieba and Mentrup 1983, S.106; Schmiede and Schudlich 1981, S.271–276).

In addition to the influence of workers, the following situation was concerned with changes in task standards. In the Taylor system, the significance of standardization was not admitted without unifying the task base at the highest level. In contrast, since such standardization did not progress in Germany, the arrangement of miscellaneous processes, consequently unifying them at a certain standard, had important significance. Therefore, taking up not only individual workers and problems on the spot as seen in the Taylor system but standardization from a social perspective, including the entire enterprise and industry, became important. If standardization was attempted in, the rather average, normal conditions had to be a basis (Kobayashi 1979, pp.123–124).

In the REFA system's wage system, the relationship between wages and output was modified. German workers avoided compulsory tasks as observed in the differential piece wage system of the Taylor system. This point should have had great significance for workers.

Nevertheless, the definition was repeatedly changed in the history of REFA theory. In the real experiences of enterprises, the actual difference between the Taylor and REFA systems in tasks was not as large as generally considered (Schmiede and Schudlich 1981, S.268, 271–274). This means that the difference between the two systems was only a relative problem. The Taylor system could be accepted by workers in the form of the REFA system by modifying the task standard from "maximum output" to "normal output." Using the concept of "normal output" was only a tactical concession on the side of capital to drive rationalization for German entrepreneurs (Trieba and Mentrup 1983, S.107).

In this way, the Taylor system with revisions prevailed as the German REFA system. Time studies that were not implemented until then diffused broadly throughout enterprises and the separation of planning and execution using task-setting progressed. As a result, the leadership in decisions regarding the speed of work moved from workers to companies and direct control over work by enterprises became possible (Inamura 1985, p.194). Volker Trieba and Ulrich Mentrup pointed out that concerning time and motion studies and saving time, German capital was able to achieve higher-level unification and standardization with the REFA system than with the Taylor system (Trieba and Mentrup 1983, S.103–104). For German firms that attempted to promote rationalization, the diffusion of the REFA system signified the most progress in introducing the Taylorsystem that had been achieved since World War I. The deployment of the Ford system also made it more important to implement the Taylor system. One of reasons why scientific management represented by the Taylor system became an important topic for discussion in the 1920s was the special impact of Fordism (Guillén 1994, p.103).

The revision of the Taylor system and the resultant introduction of the REFA system were significant for deploying the Ford system. To organize the flow production method as an important element of the Ford system, we apply the study results of Frederic W. Taylor regarding interdependent quantitative relations among work time, work volume, and manufactured product. Such a scientific building of labor organization is based on the "principle of rational arrangement of social labors" through the standardization of each partial labor (Nakata 1983, p.104). This approach provides an important basis for building the flow production organization, focusing on the significance of time study in setting the work takt. The Taylor system time study provides the rational criterion for the determination of the peace rate and was also used as the standard of setting procedure planning; it was also used as the base for organizing the production line in the Ford system (Shiomi 1978, p.237; Barnes 1937, p.v). In this way, Taylor's work and time studies (and therefore the REFA system as well) found further development in the work structure of belt conveyors and flow production characterized as "Fordism" (Schmiede and Schudlich 1981, S.284).

A significant difference can be observed in Germany when comparing conditions in the US. During the 1920s, a management system was adopted in the US, expanding to the field of scientific management in a broad sense that included the study results of H L. Gantt and the Gilbreths over the Taylor system (Drury 1922, pp.105, 139; Barnes 1937, pp.v, 16; Witte 1930a, Spalte 2085; Witte 1930b, Spalte 2262–64). After Frank Bunker Gilbreth decided to raise himself as a "consulting engineer" in 1912 (Kijne 1996, p.69), he abandoned the contracting business and focused on introducing scientific management into factories (Drury 1922, p.121). Gilbreth undertook his important work in the German industry (Drury 1922, p.171); however, in Germany, the separation between planning and execution could be realized, and the deployment of the Taylor system and its principle was an indispensable task in the 1920s. Although the Gantt chart prevailed in countries other than the US in the mid-1930s (Clark 1935, pp.ix and Chapter IX), such movement tended to be in a fair way to diffusion in the 1920s. Therefore, the development of labor management did not occur at such a stage, vastly differing from situations in the US [(2)].

8.2.3 The REFA System and Rationalization Sciences

During this period, the rationalization sciences such as management science (*Betriebswissenschaft*) and labor science (*Arbeitswissenschaft*) played a major role (Trieba and Mentrup 1983, S.99; Bauer 1931, S.165). Trieba and Mentrup pointed out that the period between 1917 and 1924 had decisive significance for the systematization, concentration, and unification of the German rationalization sciences (Trieba and Mentrup 1983, S.99).

Management science played a large role in introducing the Taylorsystem at the beginning of the twentieth century. In contrast, although labor science already performed active studies before World War I, it played a significant role in the transformation of the Taylor system into the REFA system and in the introduction of the REFA system to German enterprises. This especially concerned the study of the problem of fatigue at setting tasks. Studies during this period achieved a certain result. For instance, according to Bruno Rauecker, whereas the Taylor school attempted to cope with exhaustion problems using only business statistics and rest without considering fatigue experiments, the German post-Taylor school placed the largest value on the study of fatigue in enterprises based on psycho-technology. German labor science, psycho-engineering, or management science had to first mitigate distrust in "the scientific management," at least. Such efforts could only be successful when these sciences focus on the sociopolitical secondary object of their research over the labor technical object (Rauecker 1925, S.688–689).

However, during this period, new sciences such as labor science and psychotechnology were too new to establish study results as popular or universally valid and were still only in the first stage of scientific development (Schiffer 1928, S.26). Nevertheless, labor unions had a friendly perspective of studies in the field of psychotechnology and tended to overestimate the utilization and effect of these studies' results (Eliasberg 1926, S.84, 86).

During this period, as seen in all labor sciences since Josepha Ioteiko, labor science always prescribed its objects of study as superhistorical categories such as "general labor," "human labor," "human structure of labor," and "the workforce." Therefore, it was not able to understand labor under capitalistic labor processes in spite of being oriented toward science exceeding simple natural science (Utsusmi 1954, pp.195–196). As a result, labor science became the common ground and the neutral field on which managers and workers connected and might cooperatively struggle over fundamental tasks for the national economy such as the rationalization of labor formations (Schalldach 1930, S.44; Lipmann 1925, S.478).

In Germany, labor science institutes felt obligated to consider the interests of entrepreneurs during the Weimar Republic; however, they also maintained contact with the labor movement, which provided additional value as a factor in integrating workers. The ambivalent reaction of the German General Labor Union (Allgemeiner Deutsche Gewerkschaftsbund) and the Social Democratic Party to bourgeois labor science reflected such a function. Even when labor unions accepted individual research results of labor science in their sociopolitical activities, trade unions tended to combine their demands and goals with the acceptance of reform to correct capitalism's defects (Hinrichs and Peter 1976, S.83–84).

8.2.4 Management Functions of the REFA System and Its Influences on Workers

Next, the management functions of the REFA system realized the concentration of the planning function in the management on the company side and the separation between planning and execution. In the Taylor system, "the discovery of a science of work meant a transfer of skill from the worker to management and with it some transfer of power" (Haber 1964, pp.24–25). "Taylor's methods placed greater power in the hands of the employers, for they gave him knowledge of, and control over, the factors of production than he had ever had before" (Nadworny 1955, p.53). As the American did, "countless German workers opposed Taylorism as they saw it as giving management more control over the workplace and work routine, as de-skilling, and as a possible cause of unemployment" (Hughes 2004, p.286).

In the REFA system, knowledge regarding the labor process was also transferred to management, and all expertise was transferred to the planning function. In particular, calculating standard time and determining the peace rate based on it became a "black box" for workers. H. Spitzley (1980, S.140–142) stressed that disciplined implementation and socialization of subordination under the company's control were a premise and result of the management organization succeeding from "scientific management" to the REFA system. The systematic separation of planning and work execution was a premise and consequence of the REFA system and meant the centralization of all knowledge and planning capabilities on managers (Spitzley 1980, S.140–142).

Entrepreneurs and labor scientists stressed a scientific method to find the "righteous" wage used with the REFA system, and reference to "scientific characteristic" could evaluate the allowed time standard found out with the REFA methods as "just" and "fair." Trade unions regarded this system's "scientific character" as merit in the determination of piecework, which served employers as excluding piecework as materials for negotiation and concretely denying the codetermination of employee representatives. However, this point was a part of the minimum premise of labor unions for the acceptance of the piece wage (Schmiede and Schudlich 1981, S.265–266).

The possibility of an accurate and objective calculation of peace work time using the REFA system was why trade unions accepted such German methods; however, whether the decision to achieve objective and fair standard work volume and exclude the arbitrariness of former forepersons was able to be made is doubtful. The standard work volume was never naturally scientifically accurately measured and was not uniform even in the long term. Instead, "thinking regarding standard" was generally in the head of individual time study staff, who tended to depend on their feelings and social influences (Spitzley 1980, S.109–110). Under the separation between planning and execution, staff personnel (such as planners, work time calculators, and engineers) played significant roles in the rationalization movement, making all people achieve the maximum in the shortest time unit and inspiring workers to become time-conscious, forcing them into a new work rhythm (Borscheid 1996, S.134).

One of the defects of the REFA system for workers was that they were continually faced with the risk of lowering wages and piece rates. In the REFA system, workers were generally unable to control the conversion of the piece rate or know the criterion on which such changes were based (Richter 1926, S.638). In this system, when workers achieved a piece wage at a certain level, many cases arose where the piece rate was lowered via changes in the standard of calculation, analysis of motion, and measurement of the shortest time of elements of motions explained as "re-examination" (Schalldach 1930, S.46–47). Such reductions in piece rate were enabled because knowledge regarding setting the piece rate was entirely unknown to workers, and the wage decision could be performed at the capitalist's discretion. In this way, one of the most considerable risks of the REFA system for workers was the possibility of lowering piece rates. For example, of the 717 departments in the German industry that adopted a wage system based on the REFA system, the decline in the piece rate and increase in the working output was achieved in 492 departments, equivalent to 68.6% (Deutscher Metallarbeiter-Verband 1932, S.192–194). In the automobile industry, an increase of 70% in working output was realized by lowering the piece wage by 50% (Trieba and Mentrup 1983, S.103).

The task standard in the REFA system was changed to "normal output" based on the average time of a mean worker instead of "maximum output" based on the fastest time of a first-class worker in the Taylor system. However, it was not always easy for workers to accurately grasp the basis of the tasks and their decision process. Furthermore, in the Taylor system, the differential piece wage system played a significant role in complementing the management function based on the task system. In comparison, in the REFA system, German workers succeeded in hindering the adoption of such a wage system. However, when workers achieved their tasks and gained certain wages, the piece rate was lowered for "re-examination"; therefore, the influences of the REFA system on workers were not significantly different from those in the Taylor system, and the differences in both were relative.

Indeed, the Works Council Law allowed the working class to influence management, but the influential power of the Works council could hardly be founded in the period of the Weimar Republic. Works councils could neither require the introduction of a new work organization nor conversely constrain its adoption by the company side (Kaskel 1920, S.205). As Michael Stahlmann (1994, S.231) stresses, in the automobile industry, the Works Council Act enacted in 1920 hardly allowed labor representatives to influence management (Stahlmann 1994, S.231). In reality, the monopolization of employers regarding the job design and management of the work organization did not change (Spitzley 1980, S.67). Under such conditions, the setting of the standard work volume was forced to be performed in an autocratic manner according to the capitalist's will; therefore, labor unions could not hamper the imputation of sacrifice to workers as intended.

Regarding the attitude of labor unions to the Taylor and REFA systems, attempts were made during the 1920s to provide workers with a share of results realized by rationalization through the REFA system by laborer influencing management instead of fundamentally refusing the Taylor system (Spitzley 1980, S.67). Participation in management through the works council was regarded as a potent measure for trade unions. The idea of emphasizing the development of productive forces, as seen in the Economic Democratic Theory of the Free Trade Union (Ohashi 1999, p.107), was representative. In the US, as typically seen in the American Federation of Labor (AF of L), a line of cooperation between management and labor in the labor union movement took root, and the involvement of trade unions in management was approved and promoted. Trade unions played a significant role in labor relations, as seen in the introduction of the Taylor system (Nadworny 1955, Chapter 8 and Chapter 9, especially pp.122, 131–132, 143). As Nadwony pointed out, "the developers and proponents of the scientific management program not only encouraged the trade unionists to participate in their organization and technical meetings, but also proposed that the installation of their management methods in business firms take place under conditions of union participation." Labor unions chose "taking advantage of a rather unusual opportunity to prepare themselves to cope with important industrial developments" (Nadworny 1955, p.151). Indeed, in this aspect, conditions in Germany were somewhat similar to those in the US. However, in Germany, labor unions' attempts to influence management and regulative power were minimal, and relationships between management and labor did not reach the level in the US during the 1920s. Although the Works Council Act was enacted in 1920, the involvement and participation of labor unions and labor-capital cooperation in Germany differed from the US. In 1930, despite such conditions, from the official standpoint, no fundamental view of trade unions or an opinion regarding individual methods led back to the Taylor system could not be found (Schalldach 1930, S.37).

8.3 Introduction of the REFA System and Changes in Labor Management

This section considers the implementation of the REFA system and labor organization changes and management in German enterprises.

8.3.1 Overall Conditions of the REFA System's Introduction

The REFA system was implemented in many industries, including primary industrial sectors such as the metal, machinery, electrical engineering, iron and steel, mining, and chemical. According to research by the Metalworker Union (*Deutscher Metallarbeiter Verband*) from 1927, of 1,102 departments obtaining answers from the metal industry in a broad sense, 717 (65.1%) of them used the REFA wage system. The ratios of the piece wage system, premium wage system, Bedaux system, and other systems to all wage systems were 23.7% (261 departments), 9.3% (103 departments), 1.3% (14 departments), and 0.6%, respectively (Deutscher Metallarbeiter-Verband 1932, S.192). Thus, use of wage payment methods, standard time, and its calculation based on the REFA system progressed. The REFA system was introduced as an original German method and replaced the Taylor system in many industries.

In examining the REFA system, the problem of time studies was central. This institution organized educational courses for time study personnel and promoted the implementation and diffusion of time studies through such courses. According to the first edition of "*the REFA book*" published in 1928, 115 educational courses for piece wage calculators were implemented in 45 cities from 1924 to 1928 and over 5,000 personnel responsible for calculation called "work time calculators" ("*Arbeitzeitberechner*") were trained by September 1929 (Stitz 1930, S.182; Verband für Arbeitsstudien 1952, S.32). After REFA was founded in 1924, the number of these training courses increased dramatically (see Fig. 8.1) and the number of places holding them reached about 20. The number of participants in these educational courses was approximately 1,800 in 1924, more than four times the number in 1923.

8.3.2 Introduction of the REFA System and Changes in Labor Management in Major Industries

Next, the conditions of introduction of the REFA system and labor organization changes and management with it in some major industrial sectors are examined.

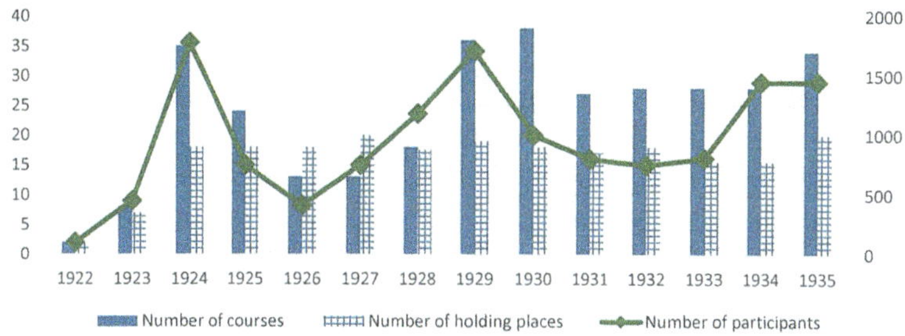

Fig. 8.1 Number of REFA's courses, places of holding courses, and participants
Note Numerical figures in 1922 and 1923 are those of the Committee for Economic Manufacturing (Ausschuss für wirtschaftliche Fertigung); numerical figures in 1924 include those of this committee
Source This figure was compiled by the author, based on Pechhold (1974), S.67

8.3.2.1 Introduction of the REFA System and Labor Management Changes in the Electrical Engineering Industry

When considering the electrical engineering industry, attempts to transform management from the older, empirical methods to systematic, scientifically based, and analytical methods had already begun at Siemens in 1913/14. However, it was only after World War I that "these methods were systematically adapted and realized on a company-wide level" (Homburg 1983, pp.148–149). At the beginning of the twentieth century, the factors determining and influencing performance in assembly were not sufficiently clear and wage decisions imposed greater difficulty than in mechanical works. Therefore, conducting a time study was an indispensable method for making detailed wage decisions in the assembly department. On the one hand, as all of the factors determining and affecting the efficiency of machines had already been investigated in detail, the processing time of machine parts and equipment was accurately calculated and decided (Lange 1922, S.249, 251). However, in calculating the processing time of machine parts and equipment, personnel taking charge of time exposure filming could not depend on accurate sources, such as the calculable performance of machine tools (Homburg 1991, S.509). Therefore, the modernization of labor management based on labor process studies became a very important task.

At **Siemens-Schuckert Werke**, the technical and organizational formation of production was taken charge of by production engineers and foremen. However, the rationalization of production became a central activity of the Central Plant Department in the 1920s and rationalization policy became strict for the first time by combining the initiatives of individual plants and management and Central Plant Department control (von Freyberg 1989, S.182). At Siemens, the piece rating office was in charge of work time decisions using time studies, although in many cases, work offices were created in major plants such as the electric motor plant from 1920 to 1921 (*Siemens Archiv Akte*, 11/Lf494, Bericht über die betriebstechnische Konfernz am 2. Februar 1921, S.2–6). During the second production engineering meeting on November 3, 1921, among the seven points of a broad program, themes on the function and role of the work office were first set up (*Siemens Archiv Akte*, 64/Lc511, Niederschrift der 2. betriebstechnische Konfernz am 3. November 1921). Although the duty of the work office was to introduce scientific management using time studies of machine tools and tool standardization, this organization played a dominant role in the thorough reorganization of production processes. The electric motor plant at Siemens-Schuckert Werke was a pacemaker of introducing the work office (von Freyberg 1989, S.191). Until 1924 when the rationalization movement began, rationalization activities in factories such as the electric motor plant promoted the implementation of time studies and standardization. The work office became the decisive, central institution in plants in reorganizing production processes on the basis of production flow principles that started during the 1924–1925 period (von Freyberg 1989, S.193). Standard work decisions based on the REFA system progressed through such activities during the relatively stable period of 1924–1929.

At the Werner F plant at **Siemens & Halske**, the piece rating office made an effort to understand work time using time studies (Bönig 1993, S.310). A large part of frequently repeated work and operations was based on standard time. As a result, most wage decisions were made by the piece rating office [*Siemens Archiv Akte*, 15/Lc816, Jaresbericht 1926/27. Wernerwerk F, S.2 (in: Jahresbericht WWF 26/27)]. According to a plant report in the fiscal year 1926/27, the large-scale transformations of the organization began in the latter half of the fiscal year 1924/25 and most of them were implemented in the fiscal years 1925/26, 1926/27, and 1926/27. This held true for calculation and costs as well as inventory in particular [*Siemens Archiv Akte*, 15/Lc816, Jaresbericht 1926/27 (5.11.1927), S.1 (in: Jahresbericht WWF 26/27)]. According to a report by the Werner F plant in the fiscal year 1927/28, the increasing importance of understanding production costs strongly burdened preliminary calculations [*Siemens Archiv Akte*, 15/Lc816, Bericht der K.I.F. über das Geschäftsjahr 1927/28 (Oktober 1928), S.2–3 (in: Jahresbericht WWF 27/28)]. The number of works analyzed by time studies increased from 23 in 1927 to 155 in the autumn of 1928. In the fiscal year 1929/30, approximately 100% of works was analyzed by time studies. In the fiscal year 1927/28, of the preliminary calculations of all new production, 60% of them had already been implemented by the piece rating office. However, a standard time [*Siemens Archiv Akte*, 15/Lc816, Jahresbericht der Fabrikleitung F 1927/1928, S.8–9 (in: Jahresbericht WWF 27/28)] regarding one-third of the work at the First Werner F plant had still not been decided upon even by 1930 (Bönig 1993, S.310). Standard times set up by the piece rating office were only half of assembly works and parts production until 1930/31. Piece rate decisions were almost completely moved to the piece rating office for the first time in 1928/29 (Schmidt 1993, S.138–139). The number of card files regarding the piece rate increased from 60,000 to 75,000 during this fiscal year [*Siemens Archiv Akte*, 15/Lc816, Jahresbericht 1928/29 der Kfm. Leitung F (30.10.1929) (in: Jahresberichte WWF 1928/29)]. Thus, at the Werner F plant, piece wage rate decisions were no longer performed by foremen during this period. However, all decisions except for partial works came to be implemented by the piece rating office. Almost all preliminary calculation workshops and most assembly workplaces systematically and sufficiently calculated standard times on the basis of data for work time per unit and preliminary calculations [*Siemens Archiv*

Akte, 15/Lc816, Jahresbericht der Fabrikleitung F 1928/1929, S.7 (in: Jahresberichte WWF 1928/29)]. Piece wage rate decisions were made on the basis of REFA system methods by plant engineers (Bönig 1993, S.309–310). According to research by the German Metalworker Union, of 98 departments in the electrical engineering industry that received reports regarding the wage system, the REFA wage payment system was adopted by 74.5% of them (73 departments) (Deutscher Metallarbeiter-Verband 1932, S.195).

8.3.2.2 Introduction of the REFA System and Labor Management Changes in the Machinery Industry

As considered in Chapter 5, the machinery industry was the industrial sector in which attempts to deploy the Taylor system and reform labor management systems had already been partially implemented in large enterprises before World War I. However, in this industry comprised of many small and medium firms, the analysis of production processes by time and work studies was conducted by only a few large companies, even in 1923 (von Freyberg 1989, S.130). Preliminary calculations were regarded as the only problem concerning wage payment and in the most enterprises, their level at that time was insufficient from the perspective of modern calculation goals (Hegner 1924, S.701).

The implementation of time studies progressed primarily in large-scale companies that manufactured in series or implemented mass production at a certain scale. Time studies had especially major significance in developing the production flow. All work and time studies progressed with the production flow principle. Once such production was implemented, in the operation and process planning stages, the need to perform new time study works became unnecessary (von Freyberg 1989, S.137).

In Germany, many time and work studies were implemented on the basis of the REFA system as a modified Taylor system. According to research by the German Metalworker Union in 1927, the REFA wage payment system was adopted by 80.7% (197 departments) of 244 machinery industry departments that received reports regarding the wage system. Similarly, in the agricultural machine and office machine industries, 95.6% (22 departments) of 23 departments and 87.9% (29 departments) of 33 departments, respectively, adopted the REFA wage system (Deutscher Metallarbeiter-Verband 1932, S.195). In addition, in the automobile industry, output increased by 70% after cutting the piece wage rate by 50% (Trieba and Mentrup 1983, S.103).

8.3.2.3 Introduction of the REFA System and Labor Management Changes in the Mining Industry

The mining industry's differences from the process and assembly industries such as the electrical engineering and machinery industries are examined next. The REFA system was broadly implemented and used not only in the metal industry but also in many other manufacturing departments after the foundation of REFA in 1924 (Preger and Reindl 1940, S.684). The thinking of F. W. Taylor played an important role in the mining industry. Progress in mechanization during this period was related to organizational changes on a larger scale (Schalldach 1930, S.102). For instance, the work form of miners changed from isolated individual work to group work under task and time control. This indicated the application of Taylor's thinking (Vahrenkamp 1981, S.243). One such case can be observed in business units using the shaker conveyor (Schalldach 1930, S.102–103; Hinrichs and Peter 1976, S.30). The introduction of the shaker conveyor as transportation equipment in a pit brought not only the mechanization of coal transportation but also strict organization of transporting work and enabled the smooth implementation of the three-shift work system and compelled all miners to task work (Etzold 1988, S.113; Ota 1979, pp.47–48). The introduction of task management systems such as the Taylor system can be observed in brown coal mining in middle Germany and in the transformation to more rational working methods in the mid-1920s. The intensification of work using the Taylor system as well as new machinery equipment played a significant role in such transformation (Friedlich 1926, S.168).

Mechanization was accompanied by labor organization changes in miners and assistant personnel, changes in the wage system, and the strengthening of management in the mining industry. These measures complemented the technological changes introduced by mechanization. For example, in the coal mining industry, since work performance still depended on the contribution of human effort, managers attempted to complement technological change by means of labor organization and management (Bönig 1993, S.401; Enquette Ausschuβ 1928, S.151–152). As a result of the further strengthening of management based on tasks calculated by stopwatch measurements, individual workers were no longer as free as before and became unable to freely coordinate their own work time (Schalldach 1930, S.103). Thus, such organizational changes enabled enterprises to further intensify labor and played a big role in improving labor productivity by combining it with mechanization (Schalldach 1930, S.101). However, in the mining industry, scientific management was still only partially introduced even during the latter half of the 1920s (Schalldach 1930, S.109).

8.3.2.4 Introduction of the REFA System and Labor Management Changes in the Iron and Steel Industry

As the piece wage rate stabilized in the iron and steel industry, calculating work time was not as important as in the mechanical industrial sectors due to the characteristics of their production processes; time studies of work were not observed before World War I (Schmiede and Schudlich 1981, S.254; Kleinschmidt 1993, S.84; Jeidels 1907, S.121–122). However, after postwar inflation, the arrangement of labor forces in iron-producing plants became the object of systematic work and time analyses. The wave of rationalization that started in 1924 led to dependence on the knowledge and methods of work and time studies (Schmiede and Schudlich 1981, S.259–260).

In the iron and steel industry, the concentration and integration of steel production reached a new level with the further development of the "integrated economy" ("*Verbundwirtschaft*"). Setting the time needed for production volume and manufacturing was premised on the accurate coordination of individual production progress. The pace of individual production could be maintained smoothly in operations based on accurate time. Therefore, calculation and preliminary calculation of each part of the production process came to have a major significance (Schmiede and Schudlich 1981, S.282–283).

It was the REFA system that played an important role in organizing production. According to research by the German Metalworker Union in 1927, REFA's wage payment system was adopted in 44.3% (113 departments) of 255 departments in the iron and steel and metal producing industries that received wage system reports (Deutscher Metallarbeiter-Verband 1932, S.195). Time studies based on REFA methods were useful as the basis of new classifications of the piece wage and premium wage (Tillmann 1926, S.1152, 1154; Polak 1929, S.871). The foundation of calculating working time and wages was changed by scientific work and time studies. This meant that the disappearing function of the foreman progressed at the same time in this field. More accurate fundamental materials for measuring work time and wages made changes in the calculating formular of the piece wage and adaptation to rapid changes in the business cycle easy (Kleinschmidt 1993, S.282–283; Lutz 1975, S.125–127).

However, there were differences between production processes due to the characteristics of each process. Work studies in the steel-producing process concentrated on improving production and transportation equipment. Since the ratio of wages to the entire cost of the steel plant was relatively low, utilizing production facilities as effectively as possible became important rather than cutting wage costs. Therefore, as observed at Dortmund Union, the primary viewpoint was directed at avoiding the interruption of work and waiting time and such time losses became clear through time studies. In contrast, work and time studies played a big role in the rolling mill plant on account of a situation wherein the cooperation of workers had more significance than in the blast furnace and steel plants. Time studies provided information regarding the possibility of making the rolling method more suitable by comparing plants with the same operating conditions. Time studies were also useful for decisions and setting the new piece wage rate. After the latter half of the 1920s, time studies were a means of implementing managerial social policy that became important for coping with conditions in which a wage increase and legal shortening of working time were processed (Kleinschmidt 1993, S.277–281; Cromberg 1930, S.732, 736–738).

Rationalization measures in the field of labor organization in the iron and steel industry did not play as a large role as in the process and assembly industries due to the characteristics of its production processes. Generally speaking, under changes in the wage system and the influence of the US, the introduction of labor management measures based on the REFA system was attempted only partially compared with the process and assembly industries such as the electrical engineering and machinery industries.

8.3.2.5 Introduction of the REFA System and Labor Management Changes in the Chemical Industry

Finally, rationalization based on enterprise concentration and technological rationalization were central measures of the time in the chemical industry as well as heavy industry. Technological innovation contributed significantly to increasing the economic efficiency of the production process of the chemical industry, which was characterized by process engineering. This is generally indicated in the higher degree of integration of individual production equipment and better time coordination of individual production stages (Schmiede and Schudlich 1981, S.252). However, rationalization measures in labor organization played a larger role as a means of supplementing the effectiveness of technological rationalization during this period of rationalization in the 1920s.

The chemical industry was a capital-intensive rather than a wage-intensive industry and the entire wage cost, including labor for repair and expansion, comprised only 10% to 25% of all costs, on average, at the time. At **IG Farben**, wages only comprised 20%–25% of all costs. As a result, profitability did not depend on the wage level to the same degree in the chemical industry as in other labor-intensive industries (Zollitsch 1990, S.72; Tammen 1978, S.194). The dependence of production on special chemical reactions and automatically operating apparatuses eliminated the adoption of the incentive wage and piece wage systems. Therefore, 80% of workers were paid time wages with or without a general production premium wage. The necessity of deciding wages on the basis of time and work studies was low compared with the introduction of the piece wage. However, in processing shops, auxiliary branches, and departments such as maintenance, packaging, and loading, the incentive wage or piece wage was primarily used and only approximately one-third of workers worked for pure time wages without a premium wage. Preliminary decisions on wages based on time and work studies played a big role in this point (Tammen 1978, S.74).

In the chemical industry, the broad introduction of the piece wage faced very intensive opposition from workers at the beginning of the 1920s (*BASF Archiv*, Ohne Signatur, Der Mensch in der BASF. 1865–1939, S.158). Rationalization measures in the latter half of the 1920s brought changes in management organization that enabled the piece wage to be raised to a quasi-scientific level. The calculation of the piece rate was no longer entrusted to foremen but came to be the charge of the company's own engineer and section (Zollitsch 1990, S.76).

The calculation office was established at Badische Anilin- und Soda-Fabrik AG (**BASF**) to measure the fair wage as accurately as possible after World War I. There were two primary activities of the section that took charge of preliminary calculations including (1) the introduction of the piece wage and (2) creating data for the production bonus wage. This company adopted the premium wage again in 1920, calculated the standard time and the time actually required on the basis of experience, work studies, and lists, and implemented piece rate work, which became an important duty. As a result, the piece rating offices, whose duty was training preliminary calculation staff as quickly as possible, were created in the machine technical department at Ludwigshafen, the nitrogen department, and the construction and technical departments at Oppau. They took charge of calculating the standard time, making data of time regarding continually repeated works, and introducing the piece wage into workshops. Such attempts brought about amazing effects. Adoption of the piece wage was not limited to handicraft workers and auxiliary branch personnel as before and was expanded to all producing business units. However, staff who were well-trained in such work were still lacking. The education of personnel taking charge of preliminary calculations became an important problem. The number of such personnel increased from only a few in 1920 to 230 in 1928. They measured standard time and the output of individual work and production processes. Such changes in management reform required the thorough reorganization of the sections charged with preliminary calculations. The Central Preliminary Calculation Department was organized from the aforementioned three coexisting piece wage offices (*BASF Archiv*, Ohne Signatur, Der Mensch in der BASF. 1865–1939, S.156–160, 162, 165).

However, workers' estimation of calculating working time using a stopwatch and calculator was not very good. When work performance exceeded the standard numerical value, the piece rating office was able to easily modify the standard time to the working time achieved in the execution of work. Therefore, the strategy wherein workers performed work intentionally slowly as a countermeasure in the calculation of time often succeeded, although only for the short term. In calculating wages on the basis of time studies, the introduction of the REFA system as the German Taylor system progressed. This system was one reason why workers agreed with the new piece wage method. Since it measured not the highest output but normal output, the piece wage could not move below a certain level very frequently because of the "normal output" principle (Zollitsch 1990, S.76). Thus, the "piece wage based on rough estimates" used until then in Ludwighhafen at BASF was replaced by the REFA system's time incentive wage by 1932 at the latest (Schmiede and Schudlich 1981, S.258).

The importance of these reforms based on preliminary calculations is that the evaluation of work performance was attempted by considering more perspectives as well as time, recording not only the time but also the burden and progress of work. With such methods, the worth of work could be calculated by considering not only the flow of time but also many other aspects such as experience, mental and physical burden, skillfulness of workers, and pleasure. At this company, a different side could be observed from American methods such as "Taylorism" that prevailed after World War I (*BASF Archiv*, Ohne Signatur, Der Mensch in der BASF. 1865–1939, S.160–161).

At **Bayer**, preliminary calculations were taken charge of by foremen until the beginning of the 1920s and time studies were not well-performed (*Bayer Archiv*, 1/6-6-25, Arbeitsbüro, S.4-5a). Although the activity of the piece rating office in Leverkusen was limited to advice (*Bayer Archiv*, 1/6-6-25, Arbeitsbüro, S.5b), time to be summed up in the piece wage list was increasingly calculated by work and time studies starting in 1928. Such measurements were implemented in accordance with the REFA system. Thereafter, the Bedaux system exerted a positive influence on time study methods and their use to a certain degree (*Bayer Archiv*, 1/6-6-25, Arbeitsbüro,

S.11). At the end of the 1920s, the time recorder was introduced as an instrument for recording work execution time and preliminary calculations in workshops (*Bayer Archiv*, 1/6-6-25, Arbeitsbüro, S.23). The piece rating office had 16 times inspectors in 1927, which increased to 25 the next year. The training of inspectors and calculators (*Bayer Archiv*, 1/6-6-25, Arbeitsbüro, S.11)started in 1927 (*Bayer Archiv*, 1/6-6-25, Arbeitsbüro, S.17) and 81 persons were trained by 1930 (*Bayer Archiv*, 1/6-6-25, Arbeitsbüro, Anlage 2). At the Dormagenplant, piece rating office activity began in 1924 when this plant started expanding. The continual increase in the scale of the required calculations precipitated the establishment of this organization (*Bayer Archiv*, 1/6-6-25, Arbeitsbüro, S.27). The premise for a systematic piece wage system and a premium wage system in the transportation department was created by appropriate time and work studies conducted after 1929 (*Bayer Archiv*, 1/6-6-25, Arbeitsbüro, S.31).

Labor management reform progressed in the chemical industry in the 1920s. It became possible to constantly maintain the quality of production and products by improving equipment, planning management, introducing machines that determined the rhythm of work and production flow, and maintaining the terms of production at a unified level. This contributed to stabilizing workers' income in the form of the piece wage and their stronger agreement. One important characteristic of management reform in the 1920s can be seen in this point. Thus, the premise of implementing the piece wage was that the calculation of this wage became possible on a technical and organizational level (Zollitsch 1990, S.77).

As American management and production systems, the Taylor and Ford systems caused important changes in business management during the Weimar period. Rationalization measures greatly contributed to improving productivity, developing mass production, and economic development in the US. Under these conditions, German enterprises increasingly needed to deploy the Ford system to cope with competition with foreign companies including US enterprises. Therefore, building upon this chapter's analysis, important research topics that should be considered include the deployment of the Ford system and the problems with using it to shift to mass production. In the next chapter, this research issue will be examined.

(1) For instance, the average discount rates of American central bank in 1925 and 1929 were 3.421% and 5.163%, respectively. In contrast, similar numerical figures in Germany were 9.153% and 7.107%, respectively. Whereas the average discount rates of private banks in the United States in 1925 and 1929 were 3.315% and 5.099%, respectively, similar numerical values in Germany were 7.62% and 6.87%, respectively. Ledermann (1933), S.63.

(2) Urwick and Brech (1951, p.142) pointed out in 1951 that in Great Britain, the development of motion study has been even more neglected than scientific management itself. They stressed that in the past years, motion study became more accepted as the basic principles upon which the science of management had been developed; however, adequate attention was not paid to that particular feature connected to the analysis of movements and their surroundings. Urwick and Brech (1951), p.142.

References

Amamiya A (1994) 1920 nendai Doitsu ni okeru keizai kozo no henka to sono genkai (Change and its limitations on Germany's economic structure during the 1920s). In: Keizai Kenkyu (Econ J Chiba Univ) 9(2):263–297

Barnes RM (1937) Motion and time study. Jon Wiley & Sons Inc., New York

Bauer O (1931) Rationalisierung und Fehlrationalisierung. Wiener Volksbuchhandlung, Wien

Bönig J (1993) Die Einführung von Fließbandarbeit in Deutschland bis 1933. Zur Geschichte einer Sozialinnovation. Teil I, Lit, Münster, Hamburg

Borscheid P (1996) Die Tempomacher. Die Rationalisierungsbewegung und die Beschleunigung des Lebens in den Weimarer Jahren. In: Zeitschrift für Unternehmensgeschichte 41(2):125–138

Clark W (1935) The Gantt chart. A Working Tool of Management. SIR Isaac Pitman & Sons Ltd., London

Cromberg O (1930) Die Betriebsführung im Siemens-Martin-Werk mit Hilfe von Zeitgedingen. In: Archiv für das Hüttenwesen 3(12):731–744

Metallarbeiter-Verband D (1932) Die Rationalisierung in der Metallindustrie. Zusammengestellt und bearbeitet nach Erhebungen des Vorstandes der Deutschen Metallarbeiter-Verband. Verlagsgesellschaft des Deutschen Metallarbeiter-Verbandes, Berlin

Drury HB (1922) Scientific management. A history and criticism, 2nd edn. Columbia University, New York

Eliasberg W (1926) Richtungen und Entwicklungstendenzen in der Arbeitswissenschaft (I). In: Archiv für Sozialwissenschaft und Sozialpolitik (56):66–101

Enquette Ausschuß (1928) Die Arbeitsverhältnisse im Steinkohlenbergbau in der Jahren 1912 bis 1926. (IV)-2, E. S. Mittler & Sohn, Berlin

Ermanski J (1928) Theorie und Praxis der Rationalisierung. Verlag für Literatur und Politik, Berlin

Etzold H (1988) Die Entwicklung der Produktivkräfte in der Industrie. In: Institut für Wirtschaftsgeschichte der Akademie der Wissenschaften der DDR. Berthold R et al. (Hrsg) Produktivkräfte in Deutschland von 1917/18 bis 1945. Akadermie Verlag, Berlin, S. 36–223

Friedlich A (1926) Die „Rationalisierung" der deutschen Wirtschaft: Zu den Denkschriften der Industrie und der Freien Gewerkschaften. In: Die Internationale 9(6):165–171

Guillén NF (1994) Models of management. Works, authority, and organization in a comparative perspective. The University of Chicago Press, Chicago, London

Haber S (1964) Efficiency and uplift. Scientific management in the progressive era 1890~1920. The University of California Press, Chicago, London

Hartmann K (1921) Das Taylor-System in der Parxis. Nach den Jahresberichten der preußischen Regierungs- und Gewerbefräte für 1920. In: Technik und Wirtschaft 14(7):447–449

Hegner K (1924) Das Problem der Vorkalkulation. In: Maschinenbau 6(19):701–702

Henzel Fr (1927) Zeitbeobachtung und Zeitrechnung im Fabrikbetrieb. In: Zeitschrift für Betriebswirtschaft 4(7):507–508

Hinrichs P, Peter L (1976) Industrielle Friede? Arbeitswissenschaft und Rationalisierung in der Weimarer Republik. Pahl-Rugenstein, Köln

Homburg H (1983) Scientific management and personel policy in the modern German enterprise 1918-1939: The Case of Siemens. In: Gospel, HF., Littler, CR (eds) Managerial strategies and industrial relations. A historical and comparative study. Heinemann Educational Books, London, pp 137–156

Homburg H (1991) Rationalisierung und Industriearbeti: Arbeitsmarkt—Management—Arbeiterschaft im Siemens-Konzern Berlin 1900–1939. Haude & Spener, Berlin

Hughes TP (2004) American genesis. a century of invention and technological enthusiasm 1870–1970, 2nd edn. The University of Chicago Press, Chicago

Hunt EE (1922) Introduction. In: Hunt EE (ed) Scientific management since Taylor. A collection of authoritative papers. McGraw-Hill, New York, pp xi–xv

Inamura T (1985) Keiei kanrironshi no konpon mondai (Fundamental problems in the history of management theory). Mineruva shobo, Kyoto

Jeidels O (1907) Die Methoden der Arbeiterentlöhnung in der rheinisch-westfälischen Eisenindustrie. Leonhard Simion, Berlin
Kaskel W (1920) Das neue Arbeitsrecht. Systematische Einführung J. Springer, Berlin
Kato E (1973) Waimaru taisei no keizai kozo (Economic structure of the Weimar system). Toko daigaku shuppankai, Tokyo
Kijne HJ (1996) Time and motion study: Beyond the Taylor-Gilbreth controversy. In: Spender JC, Kijne H (eds) Scientific management. Frederick Winslow Taylor's gift to the world. Kluwer Academic Publishers, Boston, pp 63–92
Kleinschmidt C (1993) Rationalisierung als Unternehmensstrategie. Die Eisen- und Stahlindustrie der Ruhrgebiets zwischen Jahrhundertwende und Weltwirtschaftskrise. Klartext, Essen
Kobayashi Y (1979) Keiei romu ron (Labor problem in business management). Chikura shobo, Tokyo
Lange L (1922) Grundsätze für zweckmäβige Montage mit einigen Beispielen. In: Maschinenbau/ Betrieb 4(17):249–251
Ledermann F (1933) Fehlrationalisierung—der Irrweg der deutschen Automobilindustrie seit der Stabilisierung der Mark. C. E. Poeschel, Stuttgart
O Lipmann (1925) Zur Methodik der Arbeitswissenschaft. In: Die Arbeit 2(8):476–478
Lutz B (1975) Krise des Lohnanreizes. Ein empirisch-historischer Beitrag zum Wandel der Formen betrieblicher Herrschaft am Beispiel der deutschen Stahlindustrie. Europäische Verlagsanstalt, Frankfurt am Main, Köln
Michel E (1924) Arbeitsvorbereitung: Als Mittel zur Verbilling der Produktion über das Beschleuningen der Materialbewegung durch flusslaufähnliche Übersichten und Erhöhen der Arbeitsleistung mit Hilfe des "freien Zeitauftrages," 2. verbesserte Auflage, VDI-Verlag, Berlin
Nadworny MJ (1955) Scientific management and the unions 1900–1932. A historical analysis. Harvard University Press, Cambridge, Massachusetts
Nakata M (1983) Gendai kigyo kozo to kanri kino (Contemporary enterprise and management functions). Minerva shobo, Kyoto
Nomura M (1980) Doitsu roshi kankeihi ron (German labor relations). Ochanomizy shobo, Tokyo
Ohashi S (1984) Doitsu ni okeru Taylor sisutemu no donyu katei (II) [Deployment process of the Taylor system in Germany (II)]. In: Shogaku Ronshu (Bus Rev Kansai Univ) 29(5):467–493
Ohashi S (1999) Doitsu keizai minshushugironshi (History of economic democracy theory in Germany). Chuo keizaisha, Tokyo
Ota K (1979) 1920 nendai Doitsu tankogyo ni okeru gijyutsu hatten (On the change of the construction of laborers in the German coal-mining industry in 1920's). In: Kaihatsu Ronshu (J Dev Policy Stud) (26–27):49–59
Pechhold E (1974) 50 Jahre REFA. Beuth, Berlin, Köln, Frankfurt am Main
Polak V (1929) Zeitstudie und Arbeitszeitermittlung. In: Archiv für das Hüttenwesen 2(12):871–875
Preger E, Reindl R (Hrsg) (1940) Klingelnberg Technisches Hilfsbuch. J. Springer, Berlin, Heidelberg
Rauecker B (1925) Die Bedeutung der Rationalisierung. In: Die Arbeit 2(11):683–690
Reichskuratorium für Wirtschaftlichkeit (1930) Handbuch der Rationalisierung, Zweite, unveränderte Auflage. Industrieverlag Spaeth & Linde, Berlin
Richter O (1926) Die Refa-Kalkuration. In: Betriebsräte-Zeitschrit für Funktionäre der Metallindustrie 7(20):636–640
Schiffer C (1928) Die ökonomische und sozialpolitische Bedeutung der industriellen Rationailsierungsbestrebung. G. Braun, Karlsruhe
Schalldach E (1930) Rationalisierungsmaβnahmen der Nachinflationszeit im Urteil der deutschen freien Gewerkschaften. G. Fischer, Jena
Schmidt D (1993) Weder Ford noch Taylor. Zu Rhetorik und Praxis der Rationalisierung in den Zwanziger Jahren am Beispiel dreier Siemens Werke. Universität Bremen, Bremen
Schmiede R, Schudlich E (1981) Die Entwicklung der Leistungsentlohnung in Deutschland: Eine historische Untersuchung zum Verhältniss von Lohn und Leistung unter kapitalistischen Prodokutionsbedingungen, 4. Auflage. Campus Verlag, Frankfurt am Main, New York

Shiomi H (1978) Gendai tairyo seisan taiseiron (The modern mass production system). Moriyama shoten, Tokyo
Söllheim F (1922) Taylor=System für Deutschland: Grenzen seiner Einführung in deutschen Betriebe. R. Oldenbourg, Berlin
Spitzley H (1980) Wissenschaftliche Betriebsführung. REFA Methodenlehre und Neuorientierung der Arbeitswissenschaft. Bund-Verlag, Köln
Stahlmann M (1994) Von der Werkstatt zur Lean-Production. Arbeitsmanagement und Arbeitsbeziehungen im sozialen Wandel. In: Zeitschrift für Unternehmensgeschichte 39(3):219–243
Stitz A (1930) Das Refa-System. In: Betriebsräte-Zeitschrift für die Funktionäre der Metallindustrie 11(6):180–184
Tammen H (1978) Die I.G. Farbenindustrie Aktiengesellschaft [1925–1933]: Ein Chemiekonzern in der Weimarer Republik. Tammen, Berlin
Tillmann H (1926) Aufbau der Stücklohne auf Grund von Zeitstudien in der Gieβerei. In: Stahl und Eisen 46(34):1149–1154
Trieba V, Mentrup U (1983) Entwicklung der Arbeiswissenschaft in Deutschland: Rationalisierungspolitik der deutschen Wirtschaft bis zum Faschismus. Minerva, München
Urwick L, Brech EFL (1951) The making of scientific management, vol 1. Sir Issac Pitman & Sons Ltd., London
Utusmi Y (1954) Rodo kagaku jyosetsu (Introduction to labor science). Horitsu bunkasha, Kyoto
Vahrenkamp R (1981) Die "goldnen Zwanziger"—wirklich die groβ Zeit der Rationalisierung? In: REFA-Nachrichten 34(5):243–246
Verband für Arbeitsstudien (1952) Das REFA Buch. Bd.1, Arbeitsgestaltung, Hanser, Müchen
von Freyberg T (1989) Industrielle Rationalisierung in der Weimarer Republik: Untersucht an Beispielen aus dem Maschinenbau und der Elektroindustrie. Campus, Frankfurt am Main, New York
Witte IM (1930) Gantt, Henry L. In: Giese F (Hrsg) Handwörterbuch der Arbeitswissenschaft, Bd. 1, C. Marhard, Halle, Spalte 2084–2086
Witte IM (1930) Gilbreth, Frsank B. In: Giese F (Hrsg) Handwörterbuch der Arbeitswissenschaft, Bd. 1, C. Marhard, Halle, Spalte 2262–2266
Zollitsch W (1990) Arbeiter zwischen Weltkwirtschaftskrise und Nationalsozialismus. Ein Beitrag zur Sozialgeschichte der Jahre 1928 bis 1936. Vandenhoeck & Ruprecht, Göttingen

Chapter 9
Deployment of the Ford System and Its Characteristics

Abstract This chapter examines the deployment of the Ford system in German-specific conditions, such as the commodity and labor markets, considering the implementation of production standardization and the flow production system. First, this chapter considers the discussion on and attitudes toward the Ford system in Germany at the time. It then examines the progress of the standardization of production under the standardization movement in Germany during the 1920s in relation to specific historical circumstances, clarifying the significance and limitations of such efforts. Furthermore, this chapter analyzes the introduction of the flow production system and the German-style mass production system in relation to market conditions represented by the narrow and changing domestic commodity market and difficulty in the export market. Cases in the processing and assembly industries, such as the electrical engineering, automobile, and machine industries, are discussed from the comparative viewpoint of these industrial sectors. Based on these examinations, the characteristics and limitations in the deployment of the American mass production system represented by the Ford system are clarified in two points. The first point regards implementing mass production, and the second is how the deployment of the Ford system in the automobile industry influenced the national economy by creating demands in related industries.

Keywords Economy of scale · Flexibility · Flow production · Ford system · Mass production · Production management · Standardization of production

The deployment of American management methods and production methods such as the Taylor and Ford systems to perform rationalization of labor organization during the Weimar Republic became an indispensable problem. The Ford system was a key measure for realizing cost reduction and mass production. In the United States (US) in the 1920s, mass production based on the Ford system spread throughout the process and assembly industries such as the automobile, electrical, and machine industries and the economic effects of mass production were expanded broadly throughout the national economy. Therefore, German enterprises had to deploy the Ford system and

T. Yamazaki, *A History of German Business*,
https://doi.org/10.1007/978-981-96-8476-2_9

attempt to achieve mass production to overcome competition with companies from foreign countries, in particular, the US.

By nature, mass production is premised on the existence of a mass market that enables it. However, rationalization during this period was pursued under strict conditions represented by a narrow domestic market and difficulties in export markets. Therefore, in this chapter, how the deployment of the Ford system progressed is examined using case studies of representative enterprises in the process and assembly industries such as the electrical engineering, automobile, and machine industries. This chapter elucidates the actual conditions of the implementation of the Ford system, characteristics of German-style deployment, and the economic effects of mass production caused by the implementation of this production system.

First, Sect. 9.1 considers the discussion on and attitudes toward the Ford system in Germany at the time. Next, in Sect. 9.2, the standardization of production as a pillar of the rationalization measures developed by Henry Ford is considered. In Sect. 9.3, deployment of the flow production system is analyzed. In these two sections, cases in the electrical engineering, automobile, and machine industries are considered. Building on these discussions, in Sect. 9.4, the influence and economic effects of attempts to shift toward mass production will be clarified.

9.1 From the Taylor System to the Ford System

This Section considers the discussion on and evaluation of the Ford system in Germany at the time. In the 1920s, "Fordism invaded Europe as a progressive idea," and it was "future-oriented, flexible, and melioristic" (Rodgers 1998, p.375). During the latter half of the 1920s, unlike the preceding period, discussions on the Taylor system in Germany were replaced with the Ford system for the following two points. The first is that the Ford system was regarded as an alternative to the new economic policy (maintaining a capitalistic system with slight changes). The second is that the Ford system's methods were considered more compatible with the management climate in Germany (Trieba and Mentrup 1983, S.107).

Regarding the appearance of the Ford system as an alternative economic policy, Henry Ford's low-price and high-wage policy, particularly the cooperative policies between the capital and labor sides, was considered different from the capitalistic principle and more similar to the socialistic one. It was not considered "red socialism" but "white socialism" (Gottl-Ottlienfeld 1926, S.39–40). Labor union leaders and revisionist socialists regarded Fordism as "a peaceful transition to white socialism" (Hughes 2004, p.290). The mission members of the German General Labor Union [Allgemeiner Deutsche Gewerkschaftsbund (ADGB)] who visited factories in Ford Motor in 1925 considered that this company achieved a harmonized combination of "the Organized capitalism," namely the technological progress and increase of mass purchasing power (Hinrichs and Peter 1976, S.79). From a national economic perspective, the most prominent attention was focused on the Ford system, which was characterized as a new phase and a new era of capitalism (Witte 1924, S.63).

As regards the significance of understanding that methods of Ford can be more compatible with the managerial climate in Germany, they were combined with the idea of a works community and were considered to have the possibility to bring the further diffusion of such an idea (Trieba and Mentrup 1983, S.107). Gottl-Ottlienfeld (1926, I., especially S.3) pointed out that Ford's idea exceeded Taylor's idea and made efforts to lead to industrial peace. Irene M. Witte (1930, Spalte 1859–1860) also insisted that the Ford Company realized the highest wage and the cooperation of employees by removing class opposition and promoting cooperation with workers. In this way, managers, labor scientists, and a part of the trade union movement understood that the Ford system could overcome the negative influences of the Taylor system (Trieba and Mentrup 1983, S.108). In the 1920s, as Thomas P. Hughes points out, "Ford supplanted Taylor as the American messiah who could show the way to mass production and social harmony" (Hughes 2004, p.286).

In addition to these discussions, the Ford system was taken up as a countermeasure to problems regarding labor organization in German enterprises. In 1925, although the Taylor system was regarded as the most progress for management organization among specialists, with the appearance of Ford's idea, whether management organization was appropriate until then became an important issue. Furthermore, in discussions regarding the increase of work output between employer associations and labor unions, the necessity to first use all possibilities by improving working machines and labor organizations to achieve productivity improvement was stressed. Such discussion helped promote a positive evaluation of the Ford system (Woldt 1925, S.187–188).

In this period, Jakob Walcher, one of the leading members of the German Communist Party (Kommunistische Partei Deutschlands), wrote in his book "*Ford order Marx*" (Walcher 1925) that severe criticism of the Ford system also occurred; however, theoretically, valid critical evaluations regarding the Ford system were scarce. Even criticism on the side of Marxism that described Ford as the most sophisticated exploiter and violent adversary against the labor movement who excluded workers' influence through his partnership model could not successfully appeal for pushing class conflict (Hinrichs 1981, S.199).

As seen in the Economic Democratic Theory of the Free Trade Union as an ideology to drive rationalization, Ford's rationalization model played a significant role as a measure of production rationalization and further strengthened the cooperative relationships between capital and labor. Due to the idea emphasizing the increase of productive forces, this trade union regarded the Ford system as a meaningful measure of realizing the high-life-level society already observable in the US (Ohashi 1999, pp.105, 107).

Based on these discussions, the optimistic attitude of labor unions toward the Ford system decreased compared with the period at the beginning (Schalldach 1930, S.55); however, unlike with the deployment of the Taylor system, their attitude remained relatively positive.

The Ford system has two aspects: (1) a labor management system and (2) a production system. The significance of the mass production system of this American management method was concerned with a relatively affirmative evaluation due to its significant economic effects, such as the decline of costs and product prices and the promotion of consumer society. "White socialism" was based on the effectiveness and possibility of developing a society that mass production could create. In comparison, the aspect of the labor management system of the Ford system tended to be negatively evaluated due to the significant increase in labor intensity and monotone in the flow production system. Therefore, it is important to distinguish these two aspects when evaluating the Ford system.

9.2 Standardization Movement and the Standardization of Production

9.2.1 Standardization Movement and Its Characteristics

When examining the standardization of production in the 1920s, standardization became an important issue as an influential means of efficiency improvement and an important basis for the introduction of the flow production method. The implementation of rationalization measures in the field of technology encountered limitations due to a lack of capital and the burdensome of capital costs it required. Therefore, standardization had great significance as one rationalization method that did not entail capital expenditure. Carl Schiffer classified production rationalization into three types as follows: (1) the rationalization of products according to sort, form, and volume (= standardization), (2) the rationalization of production equipment (= technical rationalization), and (3) the rationalization of labor (= labor policy rationalization) (Schiffer 1928, S.11). Hans Siegrist highlighted that in the 1920s, a movement toward strong standardization and reductions in type contributed to the rationalization of the national economy (Siegrist 1981, S.164).

It was during World War I that reduction of type and standardization were systematically driven as a movement for the first time. The standardization agencies that took charge of establishing norms for munitions production were founded throughout the country during wartime (Bauer 1931, S.131). The German Standards Committee of Industry (*Normenausschuß der deutschen Industrie*) that was in charge of creating and enacting norms was formed in 1917 (Reichskuratorium für Wirtschaftlichkeit 1930, S.14). However, it was during the relatively stable period of the 1920s (1924–1929) that reduction of type and standardization were aggressively pursued. Standardization was pursued as the "Standardization movement," which developed as a line in the chain of the rationalization movement. The German Standards Committee (*Deutscher Normenausschuß*, "DNA"), founded in 1926, played a significant role. The number of norms (standards) set by such committees increased from 6 in 1918 to 748 in 1924 and further to 3,336 in 1930 (DNA 1957, S.71; Brady 1933, p.428).

Thus, in Germany, the reduction of type and standardization movement were more systematically driven than in other countries. Robert Alexander Brady highlighted that the German experience differed from other countries and this movement was more systematically organized in Germany than elsewhere (Brady 1933, p.183). During the interwar period, the rationale of standardization prevailed not only in many industries but also it permeated down to the level of small and medium firms (Reichskuratorium für Wirtschaftlichkeit 1930, S.127–165; Takahashi 1993, p.38).

The enterprise concentration that took place at the beginning of the rationalization movement built the foundation for standardization activities of this period. In Germany, unlike the US, consumer individualism was dominant. This situation became an obstacle to standardization. It prevented the unification of demand even during the emergent period of World War I and in the first years after the war, which hindered production and sales standardization of necessities of life such as food and clothing (Rauecker 1925, S.744). The restriction of competition and influence of consumer individualism made it easy for German enterprises to specialize in the production of a few types of products through enterprise concentration (Bauer 1931, S.136–137).

9.2.2 *Standardization of Production in Major Industries*

Next, this section considers the progress of production standardization in major industrial sectors. The electrical engineering, automobile, and machinery industries in the processing and assembly sectors, in which the deployment of the Ford system became an important task, are considered.

9.2.2.1 Standardization of Production in the Electrical Engineering Industry

In considering the electrical engineering industry in Germany, association organizations such as the Central Association of the German Electrical Industry (Zentralverband der Deutschen Elektrischen Industrie) had great significance in pursuing standardization, and their influence was strengthened. Two monopolistic giants, Siemens and AEG, played a leading part in this association (2022, S.246). A high degree of concentration by Siemens and AEG facilitated the progress of standardization. R. A. Brady stressed that the concentration of output in the hands of a few large producers had promoted "the process of standardization and introduction of standards into practice" (Brady 1933, p.183). In the German electrical industry, the degree of dependence on exports was relatively high and systematic efforts at standardization as an important basis of mass production became an emergent problem to overcome foreign enterprises.

Considering cases of production standardization at representative large companies, at Siemens & Halske, reducing the number of types had been thoroughly implemented for the past few years using a suitable new design, according to an annual report from fiscal year 1924/25 (Siemens & Halske Aktiengesellschaft 1925). In fiscal year 1925/26, continuing endeavors over several years to cut production costs by type reduction, the use of the most modern production methods, the adaptation of design to them, and the further development of the organization succeeded when the same kinds of commodities came into question (Siemens & Halske Aktiengesellschaft 1926).

At AEG, production volume could be remarkably increased. Prices were reduced by the reduction of type and introduction of the flow production method in machine plants (Allgemeine Elektricitäts-Gesellschaft 1925, S.8). In fiscal year 1926–1927, unproductive costs were saved, and liquid capital was decreased via technical improvements in production equipment, reduction of type, design improvements, and the formation of organizations (Allgemeine Elektricitäts-Gesellschaft 1927, S.9). An annual AEG report in fiscal year 1927/28 stressed that this company paid the greatest attention to this point (Allgemeine Elektricitäts-Gesellschaft 1928, S.9).

These activities progressed relatively easily with consumer goods products such as the vacuum cleaner. However, for products in which the tempo of innovation was fast and product innovation was rapidly implemented as well as for producer goods, the situation differed. For example, at the Werner F plant of Siemens & Halske, reductions in the types of switches and conductors were performed and the number of electric bell types was decreased by 50% in fiscal year 1926/27 [*Siemens Archiv Akte*, 15/Lc816, Kurz Bericht der Abteilung für Telegraphie, Fernsprechwesen und Grubensignalanlagen über das Geschäftsjahr 1926/27, S.5 (in: Jahresbericht WWF 26/27)]. In relays produced at the Werner F plant, 8 types with 68 variations were decreased to 4 types with 21 variations. The number of types of relay caps and baseplates for relays and control switches decreased from 15 to 8 and from 19 to 8, respectively. However, for parts and many instruments, each product was divided into many variants. For instance, no less than 1,280 different types of the direct current type of signal apparatus with approximately 200 parts existed even after the reduction of type. For the frequency meter, there were 675 variants under three voltages (Schmidt 1993, S.121–122). In fiscal year 1927/28, various types of waterproof intercommunication apparatuses for mining and ships were replaced with one cheap, unified type and efforts to reduce type continued to be implemented [*Siemens Archiv Akte*, 15/Lc816, Jahresbericht des C.B.F. 1927/1928 (22.10.1928), S.5 (in: Jahresbericht WWF27/28)].

However, efforts to reduce the number of specifications and types were hindered by new product structures. Such cases could be observed in new small pre-selector and flat-type relays (Schmidt 1993, S.123). Above all, in instruments for multiple connection telephones and dial phones, important type-reducing activities came to an end in about 1926 to 1927. However, types with a new structure were created at the same time. In the telephone manufacturing department, endeavors to create a unified type of dial phone or telephone apparatus for the switchboard were newly performed. Reforms that brought many more types occurred concurrently [*Siemens Archiv Akte*, 15/Lc816, Jahresbericht 1926/27. Wernerwerk F, S.3 (in: Jahresbericht WWF 26/27); *Siemens Archiv Akte*, 15/Lc816, Jahresbericht des C.B.F. (4.11.1927), S.1 (in: Jahresbericht WWF 26/27); Schmidt 1993, S.124]. According to a report from the Werner F plant at Siemens & Halske in fiscal year 1927/28, this plant succeeded in again unifying the types of primary instruments such as the rotary system and relay at the end of this fiscal year. As a result, in fiscal year 1928/29, the volume enabling complete line production came to be reconsidered by the creation of new types [*Siemens Archiv Akte*, 15/Lc816, Jahresbericht der Fabrikleitung F 1927/1928, S.7 (in: Jahresbericht WWF 27/28)].

Nevertheless, the appearance of types with new structures became a factor aggressively influencing this effect. When engineers taking charge of standardization ended their activities concerning certain norms, the effects of standardization were often ruined by the next new development. The design department, which played an important role in attempts to reduce type, repeatedly encountered dilemmas between realizing reforms and endeavoring to further drive standardization (Schmidt 1993, S.94–95,121), which became a large obstacle to standardization.

In large electrical engineering industry enterprises, standardization was implemented and led by the core institutions of the company such as the central norms department. For instance, the central norms department at Siemens was not only involved in the activities of the German Norm Committee and other special norm committees but also pursued the development of international norms and cooperated with the establishment of individual norms [*Siemens Archiv Akte*, 15/Lc815, Jahresbericht der Abteilung C.B.Z. über das Geschäftsjahr 1930/31 (November 1931), S.3 (in: Jahresbericht WWZ 30/31)].

9.2.2.2 Standardization of Production in the Automobile Industry

The automobile and electrical engineering industries were the industrial sectors in which the standardization of production was most aggressively pursued. Until World War I, the plan of parts standardization did not progress as the machine industry avoided the costs brought about by such measures, and companies feared being pushed away from the world market with remarkable foreign sales (Filk 2001b, S.127). After the war, in the production of small and popular cars, the shift to mass production by deploying American production systems was vigorously performed and production standardization was implemented as an important foundation. However, standardization never progressed uniformly, and all the various stages of development could be observed (Hänecke 1927, S.157).

In examining the reduction of product types, Bruno Rauecker pointed out that in 1926, despite the tremendous global sales volume of only one type of cheap automobile by the Ford Motor Company, the German automobile industry could not reduce type in a similar fashion until then. Considering the production costs of about 80 types of cars displayed at the Berlin automobile exhibition in December 1925, the ratio of wages and salaries to all costs increased from 20 to 25% on average; a large part was material costs that were still 40% to 50% more expensive than those in the US (Rauecker 1926, S.14–15). This situation occurred because many types of automobiles were manufactured in Germany, and the reduction of product types and parts standardization had not progressed sufficiently. Richard Woldt pointed out that special automobiles were still produced according to demand in 1925 (Woldt 1925, S.191).

When the rationalization movement was implemented in the latter half of the 1920s, the shift to small and popular cars progressed and the reduction of product type was aggressively pursued. However, various types of products required large expenditures for production equipment and repair parts stock, enabling production in only relatively small series on the one hand and preventing the effective use of cost-cutting measures on the other. In this situation, the consolidation of automobile enterprises was an important foundation for the reduction of various types. It was pointed out that only the Auto Union created by merger in 1932 and some large corporate groups were able to implement the reduction of type (Blaich 1973, S.20); however, the reduction of the type of passenger car from 14 to 11 in the Auto Union was insufficient considering that the relatively small sales volume of the product program of 11 was regarded as substantial. Specialization was also attempted; however, the effects of such efforts were restricted because the possibility of specialization within the company depended on the standardization level and product type reduction (Maurer 1936, S.159–163).

A sharp reduction in product types was implemented by consolidating Daimler and Benz in 1926 (Nishimuta 1987, p.40; Nishimuta 1999, pp.33, 37). In the board of directors meeting on March 29, 1926, it was pointed out that truck standardization had to be implemented as rapidly as possible and that competition in foreign markets and achieving higher sales were possible by producing a unified type (*Mercedes-Benz Clasic Archiv*, Kissel Protokolle, I/1, Protokoll der Sitzung des Gesamtvorstandes am 29. März 1926 in Stuttgart, S.2–4). For example, an internal document dated November 27, 1927, stressed that implementing rational production in large lots was needed to develop an advantageous price policy and attempts to produce and supply as many automobiles as possible by the end of the year were necessary [*Mercedes-Benz Classic Archiv*, Kissel Technische Protokolle, 1.22., Protokoll Nr.175 über die Direktions-Besprechung am 14. & 15. November 27 in Gaggenau (15.11.1927), S.1, 3]. The reduction of product type was an important premise. However, there were cases in which planned production volumes could not be achieved due to defects and changes in design [*Mercedes-Benz Classic Archiv*, Kissel Technische Protokolle, 1.22, Protokoll No.173 über die Direktionsbesprechung am 24.25 und 26.Oktober 1927 in Gaggenau (28.10.1927), S.2; *Mercedes-Benz Classic Archiv*, Kissel Technische Protokolle, 1.22, Protokoll No.176 über die Direktionsbesprechung am 23.November 1927 in Gaggenau (24.10.1927), S.1; *Mercedes-Benz Classic Archiv*, Kissel Technische Protokolle, 1.22, Protokoll Nr.175 über die Direktions-Besprechung am 14. & 15.November 27 in Gaggenau (15.11.1927), S.1]. The progress and effects of efforts to reduce product types were related to design problems. Even in July 1928, the fundamental premise at Daimler-Benz for rational production by the reduction of type was to lighten the burden of the work methods caused by producing too many types and further drive the standardization and unification of structures by implementing measures such as unifying the chassis types produced [*Mercedes-Benz Classic Archiv*, Kissel Technische Protokolle, 1.23, Protokoll No.191 über die Direktionsbesprechung am 25. Juli 1928 in Gaggenau (26.7.1928), S.1–2].

As a result of enterprise and industry concentration, including the elimination of weaker units, the number of automobile factories in Germany was reduced from 86 to 17 and the number of types produced decreased from 146 to 40 between 1924 and 1929 (Brady 1933, p.147). However, in 1929, of the 34 primary types of passenger cars produced by a total of 17 manufacturers, the number of types of cars of 1,000 cubic centimeters (cc) to 1,500 cc and less than 1,000 cc were 1 and 3, respectively; the number of types of cars over 3,000 cc, of 2,000 to 3,000 cc, and of 1,500 cc to 2,000 cc were 18, 7, and 5, respectively (Schmidt 1933, Anlage 1). Thus, except for small and large cars, differences in the progress of the reduction of type can be observed. Even in 1929, over 50% of the total passenger car production in Germany was still in the mid-range category between upper class and luxury cars (Stahlmann 1993, S.79).

When considering parts standardization, B. Rauecker pointed out that in 1926, although only the standardization of parts was effective in decreasing the ratio of raw materials costs to all German automobile production costs, it was not implemented in spite of many discussions (Rauecker 1926, S.15). It was after 1926 when the German Norm Committee was founded that efforts to standardize parts further progressed. For instance, at Opel, standardizing parts and sizes in factories decreased production costs. The need to set up machines according to new fittings disappeared because of the unified sizes of screws, key ways, and toothed wheels (Kugler 1985, S.31). At Daimler-Benz, the importance of common body use between 2-L and 2.6-L cars was emphasized in a discussion on October 4, 1928 (*Mercedes-Benz Classic Archiv*, Kissel Protokolle, I/23, Protokoll der Besprechung am 4. Oktober 1928, S.2). There were cases in which the standardization of parts, in particular, core unit parts, was performed considering the relationship of the supply between plants within a company. For example, at Daimler-Benz, the products program at the Sindelfingen plant was coordinated according to a chassis program at the Untertürkheim plant. In 1928, the stock of approximately 200 bodies for the 2-L car could be accurately coordinated with the chassis program by reducing product types (*Mercedes-Benz Classic Archiv*, Kissel Protokolle, I/4, Protokoll No.16 der Gesamtvorstandssitzung vom 28. Juni 1928 in Untertürkheim, S.7–8). The premise for cutting body manufacturing costs was unifying the body to a standard type. This unification was an important premise underlying the strong development of flow production (*Mercedes-Benz Classic Archiv*, Kissel Protokolle, I/4, Protokoll der Vorstandssitzung vom 24. Oktober 1928, in Mannheim, S.14).

Plant and equipment specialization also progressed. At the managerial board meeting of Daimler-Benz held on June 10, 1926, it was decided that toothed wheels would be produced at the Mannheimplant, whereas the Untertürkheim plant would focus on automatic machine parts and runners. Regarding the gray cast iron plant and aluminum plant, which were separated in three places until then, gray cast iron should be produced only in Mannheim and aluminum casting should be manufactured in Untertürkheim. Furthermore, whether or not all body production should be moved to Sindelfingen was discussed (*Mercedes-Benz Classic Archiv*, Kissel Protokolle, I/1, Protokoll über die Sitzung des Gesamtvorstandes am 10. Juni 1926 in Untertürkheim, S.1–2) and, as a result, body production specialization was implemented.

Such production specialization was implemented in not only parts production but also automobile manufacturing. With the sharp reduction in the types of automobiles produced by consolidating Daimler and Benz, a production line of one kind of car was fundamentally arranged in one plant (Nishimuta 1987, p.40; 1999, pp.33, 37). For example, the transfer of 5-ton truck production from Marienfelde to Gaggenau was implemented. Savings of over 2 million Reichsmark (RM) and the expectation of achieving optimal operating rate of approximately 100% by increasing production in the Gaggenau plant were the primary reasons (*Mercedes-Benz Classic Archiv*, Kissel Protokolle, I/2, Protokoll der Sitzung des Verwaltungsausschuβ vom 18.10.1926 in Berlin, S.2). The division of labor by enterprise concentration and production specialization between plants created an important foundation for the subsequent rationalization of production technology and labor organization (Thirme 2004, S.189–190, 296).

However, Fred Ledermann pointed out that concerning the actual conditions of production standardization in 1933, the effect of parts standardization was still very small, the reduction of product type was insufficient, and the specialization of production was late. Such delays in specialization were due to the insufficient progress of parts standardization and the destination of the German market in which other products needed to compensate for the decline in the sale of certain products (Ledermann 1933, S.68–71).

9.2.2.3 Standardization of Production in the Machinery Industry

In the machinery industry, even at the end of 1925, numberless, excessive types that did not contribute to productivity and increased production costs still existed (Rauecker 1926, S.16–17). Under such conditions, it was the development of manufacturing in series and flow production on the one hand, and high-precision requirements on the other hand, that made the problem of standards decisively important (Brady 1933, p.148). However, in Germany at the time, there were some factors that made standardization difficult.

First, many small and medium firms existed in the machinery industry. According to statistics in 1925, the average number of workers in a company with over 25 employees was only 184.2. A similar numerical figure in 1930 decreased to 142.8. Among large enterprises to which the Association of German Machine Manufacturers (*Verein Deutscher Maschinenbau-Anstalten*) belonged, the average number of workers per enterprise in 1930 was only 252.1 (Brady 1933, p.143). Indeed, large manufacturers actively pursued standardization, but many companies, in particular, those operating on a small scale, could not effectively use and establish special standards (Brady 1933, p.150).

Second, many manufacturers in the machinery industry did not sufficiently understand the merits of standardization or have an interest in standardization activity. The primary reason for opposition to early attempts at machine standardization in the first stage was that standards would prevent technical development (Brady 1933, p.149).

Systematic standardization activities and their effects were not sufficiently recognized even in the period of rationalization in the 1920s. One speaker at a meeting in Saarbrücken on May 22, 1930, stressed that many manufacturers did not know at all about the existence of DIN standards as the German industrial norm or were indifferent to all organized work standards. Many people perceived all proposed or established norms with doubt and distrust. DIN standards often came into conflict with carefully worked out and systematically applied work standards (Brady 1933, p.153).

Third, delays in concentration caused standardization limitations. The number of combinations in the German mechanical industry in 1927, 1928, and the first quarter of 1929 were 50, 65, and 65, respectively. Of these, the number of combinations implemented in mechanical engineering proper (i.e., locomotives, boilers, railway carriages, and machine tools) was 42. In nature, the advantage of horizontal combinations lay in the "reduction of unit manufacturing and selling costs, primarily by way of increased factory specialization and the economies of continuous standardized production" (Brady 1933, pp.143–144, 147). Delays in concentration also became a factor determining the limits of plant and equipment specialization. The standardization of parts was an important foundation of the specialization of plants and production locations (Mori 1965, p.138; Hänecke 1927, S.157). Delays and limitations in the reduction of product types and parts standardization determined by the existence of many small and medium plants and manufacturing locations and the low level of concentration in the machinery industry restricted production specialization between plants or production locations.

Next, how production standardization progressed is examined using cases in some product sectors of the machinery industry.

In the **machine tool industry**, the reduction of innumerable types and models was vigorously attempted. Efforts were driven to create a standard type enabling effective production at appropriate costs everywhere (Deutscher Metallarbeiter-Verband 1932, S.88).

In the **agricultural machine industry**, the difficulties to overcome included making suitable enterprises specialize in certain kinds of machines and reducing product types. For instance, in threshing machine and compressor production, the number of types decreased from 200 to 30. Therefore, the first task was to thoroughly reconsider the design of individual parts and equipment. Groups of machine parts were standardized according to the soil conditions of agricultural land at home and abroad, temperature and weather conditions to adapt product types to all situations, and purchaser demands by various product constitutions. Thus, large-scale production was realized with a daily manufacturing capacity of 25 tractors, 35 threshing machines, and 50 straw compressing machines (Duvigneau 1932, S.49).

In the **sewing machine industry**, the introduction of flow production was an important motive underlying standardization. The concentration of representative enterprises was implemented to drive common work in the standardization of appurtenances such as wrenches, replacement presser feet, and oilers, and, for instance, individual parts such as screws and bolts (Duvigneau 1932, S.49).

In the **railway car building industry**, standardization efforts were propagated. R. A. Brady pointed out that although this industry lay on the fringe of the machine-producing field and should be classified as an "engineering industry," it illustrated "the problems common to the entire machine field" fairly well. The Association of German Railway Car Builders (*Deutsche Waggonbau Vereinigung*) attempted to reduce the number of car types produced in various plants in cooperation with the National Railways (*Reichsbahn*). Each plant specialized in one or a narrowly limited number of types through the efforts of the association. Such means were prepared and used for the standardization of single and component parts. Brady stressed the "utilization of standard parts and car types practically eliminated the former designing and drafting departments" and the necessary supervisory and highly skilled working classes tended to be reduced by the use of simple but precise gauges and other control instruments (Brady 1933, pp.156–158). As a result of such endeavors, in the 1920s, only 11 unified types of freight cars and four basic types of passenger cars for the trunk line existed. In the repair plant, the effects of standardization were large. The stock of repair parts decreased from 14,000 to 4,000 types. By parts standardization, the average time required for the basic repair of a type of locomotive decreased from 11 to 4 days and the abolishment of 19 locations and 48 plant departments became possible. In parts standardization, standardizing fittings played a big role in making finishing work unnecessary by the simple fitting of repair parts (Iltgen 1929; pp. CXXV-1–2; Klein 1929, pp. CXXVI-1–2). A similar shortening of the time required for parts standardization could also be observed in railway car maintenance (DNA 1957, S.62–63).

9.2.3 Limitations on the Standardization of Production and Their Factors

In Germany, standardization was more systematically pursued by the involvement of institutions such as the German Norm Committee than in other countries under the rationalization movement in the 1920s. However, such endeavors in Germany encountered larger obstacles than they did in the US.

First, consumer individualism inveterately dominated. This custom made it difficult to subordinate consumers' demands to the purpose of rationalization called "standardization." Second, cases in which the amount that product prices declined equaled the cut in production costs enabled by standardization were rare in Germany. Therefore, consumers could not enjoy the effects of such rationalization measures. Reductions in price as observed at the Ford Motor Company were never implemented.

In Germany, thinking of entrepreneurs' service to society did not prevail and there was no preparation for them to pay workers a higher wage (Trieba and Mentrup 1983, S.111). Hilde Weiss pointed out in 1926 that whereas there was a slight decrease in prices due to rationalization, if Mr. Opel had given up part of his own profits, the lack of sales in the automobile industry would have made lowering the price impossible despite the transformation that had already begun at the Opel plant (Weiss 1926, S.19). Indeed, strict market conditions in Germany at the time made price reduction difficult. However, the situation in which there were very few consumer benefits for standardization made it difficult to sufficiently recognize the benefits of mass-producing standardized products. This became an important factor restricting the progress of standardization.

9.3 Deployment of the Flow Production System and Its Characteristics

Building on these discussions, this section considers the introduction of flow production as a core mass production system represented by the Ford system.

In Germany, the conveyor as mechanical transportation equipment was adopted by Opel in 1923 for the first time and also by AEG the next year. Its introduction then progressed, particularly in the electrical engineering and metal processing industries (Trieba and Mentrup 1983, S.108). However, in Germany at the time, the flow work method and conveyor work method were not always differentiated (Stollberg 1981, S.49–51; Stahlmann 1993, S.71). Clarifying which flow production method was implemented became important. Belt conveyors were arranged primarily in pre-assembly, final assembly, and packaging and their degree of diffusion differed significantly between individual industrial sectors (Etzold 1988, S.61–61). Therefore, it is necessary to concretely examine the conditions of the representative industries and primary production processes. In particular, it is important to regard the electrical engineering and machinery industries by analyzing each constituent primary product sector.

9.3.1 Conditions of the Deployment of the Flow Production System in German Industry

First, in this subsection, the overall conditions for adopting the flow production system are considered. According to research by the German Metalworker Union in 1930, introducing rates of flow work were 19.3%, 14.6%, 18.6%, 13.3%, 10.5%, and 9.6% in the transportation equipment, the electrical engineering, watch and clock-making, optical, machinery, and precious machine industries, respectively (Vorstand des Deutschen Metallarbeiter-Verband 1930, S.89–90). The introductory rates of flow work in all these industries were higher compared with similar numerical figures in all industrial sectors. Gerhard Duvigneau pointed out that in 1932, at most, only 2% to 3% of all German enterprises researched performing production using flow work (Duvigneau 1932, S.68). In 1930, approximately 80,000 workplaces with flow work and conveyor work were established in the entire industry. This number was equivalent to only 1% of employed people in plants with more than 50 people and was less than 0.5% of all workers in business enterprises (Bönig 1993b, S.699). The introductory rates of conveyor work were 16.6%, 15.5%, 7.0%, 5.6%, 7.9%, and 6.2% in the transportation equipment, the electrical engineering, watch and clock-making, optical, machinery, and precious machine industries, respectively (Vorstand des Deutschen Metallarbeiter-Verband 1930, S.90–91), whereas in the transportation equipment and electrical engineering industries, the differences in the introductory rates of flow work and conveyor work were very small, the introductory rates of conveyor work were much lower than those of flow work in other industries.

According to research by the German Metalworker Union in 1931, in the electrical engineering industry, of the 181 departments researched, 57 (31.5%) and 53 (29.3%) introduced flow work and conveyor work, respectively. In the automobile and bicycle industries, out of the 94 departments researched, 30 (31.9%) and 20 (21.3%) implemented flow work and conveyor work, respectively. Therefore, the introductory rates of either the flow work or conveyor work method in the electrical engineering and automobile and bicycle industries were 60.8% and 53.2%, respectively, and both figures were high. In contrast, in the machinery industry, of the 475 departments researched, 77 (16.2%) and 11 (2.3%) introduced flow work and conveyor work, respectively. Therefore, the introductory rate of either the flow work or conveyor work method was only 18.5% (Deutscher Metallarbeiter-Verband 1932, S.86,117, 138).

Next, the situation in which the flow production system was introduced in major industries is considered. Cases in the electrical engineering, automobile, and machinery industries are considered.

9.3.2 Deployment of the Flow Production System in Major Industries

9.3.2.1 Deployment of the Flow Production System in the Electrical Engineering Industry

In the electrical engineering industry, transformation to the flow production method was first implemented in the production of meters, home appliance instruments, and radios and was then gradually expanded to other mass products, in particular, material for equipment installation and the manufacturing of small electric motors and measuring instruments (Keiser and Benning 1931, S.57). The introduction of the flow production system progressed primarily in the manufacturing of standardized products in which mass sales were possible. According to a report of the Werner F plant of Siemens & Halske in fiscal year 1927/28, flow production was organized in various fields such as producing parts, radios, loading coils, condensers, fuses, and photomatons and work process of coil winding and painting [*Siemens Archiv Akte*, 15/

Lc816, Jahresbericht der Fabrikleitung F 1927/1928, S.7–8 (in: Jahresbericht WWF 27/28].

However, there were also sectors in which the introduction of the flow production method was not possible. The production and repair of heavy electric motors was always implemented on the basis of individual orders and therefore the form of manufacturing was individual production. This form of processing was adopted because of the technical consideration that the transportation of heavy, partly finished goods was more difficult than that of machine tools (Duvigneau 1932, S.57).

Therefore, the situations of the individual product sectors are examined next.

Introduction of the Flow Production System to Major Product Sectors

Cases in the Electric Motor Sectors

Cases of Electric Motor Production

The electric motor sector was one of the product fields in which the introduction of the flow production system was attempted most aggressively. R. A. Brady stressed that within the individual plants, flow production had been introduced in "nearly all manufacturing operations of a repetitive, automatic or semiautomatic, and standardized character," and the case of the Elmo Works at Siemens-Schuckertwerke was typical (Brady 1933, p.176). An annual report of this plant in fiscal year 1926/27 pointed out that the transformation to flow production in various workshops combined with rationalization was promoted considerably [*Siemens Archiv Akte*, 15/Lg562, Jahresbericht des Elektromotoren Werkes 1926/27, S.2 (in: Chronik 1926/27); *Siemens Archiv Akte*, 15/Lg562, Direktionsbericht der Zentral-Werksverwaltung 1926/27, S.10 (in: Chronik 1926/27)]. A similar report in fiscal year 1928/29 stated that further expansion was being considered [*Siemens Archiv Akte*, 15/Lg562, Jahresbericht des Elektromotoren Werkes 1928/29, S.24 (in: Chronik 1928/29)].

In this factory, the introduction of this production method was implemented in not only the assembly plant but also in the casting and forging and parts production plants.

Therefore, the situation of the flow production of the electric motor is considered first.

In the **casting and forging process**, the Pasewalk casting iron works were included in Elmo Works and cast metal production was inserted into the flow production plan. The transformation to flow production was implemented on this basis. However, this movement was at the beginning (von Freyberg 1989, S.218–219). In casting iron work, the transformation to flow production was implemented in January 1927 and conveyor belts formed production lines for processes such as casting and cooling [*Siemens Archiv Akte*, 15/Lg562, Jahresbericht des Elektromotoren Werkes 1926/27, S.16 (in: Chronik 1926/27)].

In the **mechanical processing process**, a special production series was created for various parts. Machine tools were arranged according to the order in which they were used for processing. A series of flow production methods were created for the mechanical processing of electric motor cases and bearing pedestals of various sizes and forms (Vrang 1927, S.424; Bönig 1993a, S.262). However, unlike assembly work, in the transportation of partly finished goods from one mechanical processing location to the next, simple auxiliary devices such as sliding rails, chutes, and tin pates stands were enough. In reorganizing the mechanical work, belt conveyors that set predetermined work cycles beforehand were impossible (Köttgen 1928a, S.3–4, 7–8; Vrang 1927, S.413–414; Homburg 1991, S.514). The introduction of flow production brought a "compulsory work tempo" to only a relatively small group of workers (Homburg 1991, S.514).

In the **assembly process**, primary manual work that could not be replaced by machines appeared. Work methods caused situations in which assembly work could not be sufficiently managed by the work office, its plant engineers, and staff for the time exposure photography. The transformation to conveyor work was a decisive measure to overcome this issue (Homburg 1991, S.508–511; Köttgen 1928c, S.1127). Two solutions could be considered. One was a shift from serial production to line production principles. The other was to set work cycles (time) to intermittent, rhythmic conveyor advances. However, the production volume of an individual series was not always enough to assemble electric motors using belt conveyors. Furthermore, a determined series was sometimes changed in the very short-term and even among partial works, different work tempos were created with such a change. Therefore, not the "production of one type" as observed at the Ford Motor Company but "changeable flow production" (*die wechselnde Fliessarbeit*) came into question (Homburg 1991, S.511; Köttgen 1928b, S.105–107). Indeed, partial work at the conveyor no longer required workers with broad, special abilities as were required in serial production assembly. However, their knowledge and abilities were still needed and when viewed as a whole, even in cases in which such supplements were performed, replacement was achieved in only a few partial workshops (Homburg 1991, S.508–512).

Such production methods were an attempt to organize flow production to flexibly change large volumes and diverse types (von Freyberg 1989, S.158). It was the flow production system in which production in small series and in larger series was performed with the same workers at the same conveyor (von Freyberg 1989, S.158; Köttgen 1928a, S.12). With this method, the demand determined for a certain year or half-year was divided into individual production lots or series. Lots or series of a product and other products were not produced in turns and, except for individual parts, for instance, a volume equivalent to the demand for one year or a half-year of each product should be individually manufactured continuously and after the production of such volume was completed, other products would be produced in the same way (Schulz-Mehrin 1927, S.817).

One of the other main products manufactured at the Elmo Works of Siemens-Schuckertwerke was the vacuum cleaner. Its manufacturing indicated the most advanced case of flow production development using the conveyor. According to a report of Central Plant Management in fiscal year 1924/25, all work in the production of the vacuum cleaner, from the casting to the packaging, was performed in one place on the basis of flow production principles [*Siemens Archiv Akte*, 15/Lg562.,

Direktionsbericht der Zentral-Werksverwaltung 1924/25, S.2 (in: Chronik 1924/25]. It was pointed out that vacuum cleaner manufacturing was a case in which 100% of the work was implemented by the flow production method (Duvigneau 1932, S.69). At AEG, the vacuum cleaner was the first home appliance product manufactured using modern belt conveyor production (Strunk 2000, S.46).

Cases of Vacuum Cleaner Production

The conditions of vacuum cleaner flow production are explored next. The type of vacuum cleaner produced at the Elmo Works of Siemens-Schuckertwerke was reduced to only one type called "the Protos" (Dransfeld 1929, p.923). In both the mechanical processing and assembly processes, the flow production system was introduced for the effects of its manufacturing. At the Elmo Works of Siemens Schuert Werke, complete transformation to belt conveyor work was implemented for the desk types, ceiling hanging type fans, and other products in fiscal year 1926/27 [*Siemens Archiv Akte*, 15/Lg562, Jahresbericht des Elektromotoren Werkes 1926/27, S.2 (in: Chronik 1926/27), *Siemens Archiv Akte*,15/Lg562, Direktionsbericht der Zentral-Werksverwaltung 1926/27, S.10 (in: Chronik 1926/27)].

Figure 9.1 indicates the overall layout of the Elmo Works' vacuum cleaner plant. In the **mechanical processing process**, the various parts of the cleaner were produced in the different departments of the factory in which work of similar character was performed. In this production process, equipment such as grinders, turret lathes, and varnish benches existed. In the machine shop, chutes and belt conveyors were used to carry the parts from the lathes to the drill presses. Chutes carried parts from the lathes to a belt conveyor running lengthwise through the department. This conveyor carried them to the women operating the drill presses. In this department, the parts were passed by hand from operator to operator between successive processes. No work stock was allowed to accumulate between processes. Whereas the conveyor was used to carry work objects from machine to machine, mechanical transportation equipment was not used to carry objects from worker to worker.

All finished parts were collected in the stockroom from which they were delivered to the assembly belt. Finished parts passed from operator to operator and then to the assembly department. The assembly plant had a maximum capacity of 1,000 cleaners per each 8-h day. When operating at full capacity, the stockroom for parts supplying the assembly line had space for only a few hours' requirements of the assembly department. Material handling equipment conveyed these parts to the assembly room.

In the **assembly process**, many small tools were installed in the assembly room. These tools were used to machine the aluminum parts and assembly work was facilitated using this combination. In the assembly room, assembly lines were arranged on both sides of the conveyor. On the left-hand side of Fig. 9.1, the electric motors were assembled. After inspection and testing, they were returned to the middle section of the conveyor and then back on the belt to the stockroom. From the stockroom they were sent along the right-hand side of the conveyor, as indicated in Fig. 9.1, together with other parts. Assembly operations were performed on this conveyor. Vacuum cleaner casings were taken from the enameling shop to the assembly room on special racks. These racks were carried by electric carts. A total of 120 casings was

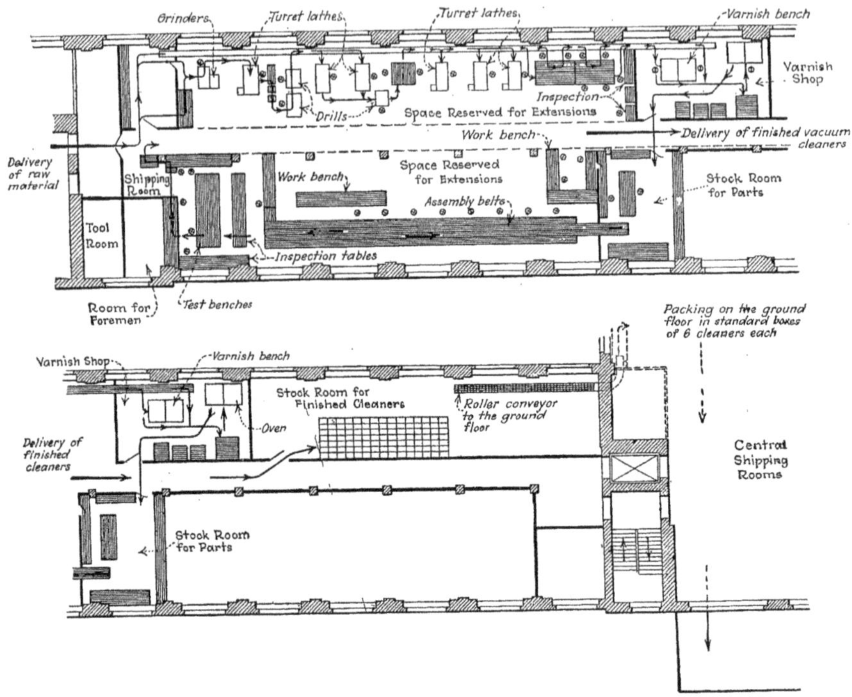

Fig. 9.1 Layout of the Department for the Assembly of the Vacuum Cleaners in Siemens-Schuckertwerke

carried in one load (Dransfeld 1929, pp.923–925) Parts were attached to the body on the conveyor and the vacuum cleaners were assembled. In this way, conveyors were installed in both the subassembly and final assembly processes.

After the cleaners were tested, they were packed in cardboard cases and delivered to a stockroom for finished products by another conveyor of the overhead type. This conveyor consisted of a series of trolleys equipped with anti-friction bearings and driven by chain. Packed vacuum cleaners were hung on hooks and delivered by the conveyor (a chain and trolley conveyor) to a chute and slid by gravity to the main stockroom. Three different handling systems were adopted to remove the containers from the stockroom as follows: (1) a "paternoster" to transport them to the main stockroom, (2) a chute to carry them to the shipping room in which the cleaners were packed in shipping boxes containing six each, and (3) a conveyor to load the packed cleaners directly onto railroad cars or ships (Dransfeld 1929, p.923).

According to the annual report of Elmo Works in the fiscal year 1928–1929, the change in the packaging in this plant progressed with the transformation to flow production. The packaging works were included in the production of the box and wooden frame and the flow production system [(*Siemens Archiv Akte*, 15/Lg562, Jahresbericht des Elektromotoren Werkes 1928/29, S.5 (in: Chronik 1928/29)]. The plant's fiscal year 1929–1930 report pointed out that the packaging of products such as the desk-type and the ceiling hanging type fans was also inserted in the flow production. The standardization of packaging adjusting to such production method was implemented [*Siemens Archiv Akte*, 15/Lg562, Jahresbericht des Elektromotoren Werkes 1929/30, S.4 (in: Chronik 1929/30), *Siemens Archiv Akte*, 15/Lg562, Direktionsbericht der "Zentral-Werksverwaltung" 1929/30, S.5 (in: Chronik 1929/30)].

In this way, the manufacturing of vacuum cleaners represented the most advanced case of implementing the flow production system. However, in the transportation between departments combining each production line, a universal type of mechanical transportation was used that carried partly finished goods of a certain volume within time intervals. Therefore, different departments were mutually independent and the coordination and integration of time between different production processes became an important managerial task (Shiomi 1978, p.286). A systematic process for the management of mutual production lines was needed (Shiomi 1978, p.282) and transportation between departments based on production planning was performed by electric trucks (Vrang 1927, S.425; Gelbsattel 1926, S.633; Bönig 1993a, S.261; von Freyberg 1989, S.185). Decisions regarding the transportation plan had great significance for the control of the flow of conveyance and coordination and the integration of production processes.

Differences Between Electric Motor and Vacuum Cleaner Flow Production

As may be clear from these discussions, the implementation of the flow production method differed for the primary products produced at the Elmo Works. Heidrum Homburg pointed out that although the flow production method developed by Henry Ford was used to a much broader extent than standardized mass production in a changed form, the Elmo Works at Siemens-Schuckertwerke unexpectedly became a two-fold experiment. Whereas vacuum cleaner manufacturing appeared to be the most suitable field of activity in which to pursue the American model, electric motor production was indicated as the most fitting activity for building the German variant of flow production (Homburg 1991, S.449).

One of the essential factors of this difference can be observed in the differences in the standardization degree determined by the market characteristics and conditions of both products. Various installation conditions of motor and possibilities of electric motor use, varied customer demands for generating electric power, and the character, size of motor, and structure of the motor's mechanical parts required an extraordinarily broad width of electric motor supply (Kölb 1953, S.528; Kinkel and Feill 1963, S.62–64, 66–67; Scharll 1963, S.176–177; Homburg 1991, S.441; *Siemens Archiv Akte*, 64/Lc511, 12. Betriebstechnische Konferenz 1928. Nürnberger Werk, S.1). The standardization of the main products of the Elmo Works encountered limitations because the demand for electric motors for various uses was determined by the special characteristics of electricity, the volume of generating power, and structure (Homburg 1991, S.444). Unlike the mass production of "Protos" as a single type of vacuum cleaner, in the production of the partial small electric motor, many variations of the model prevented thorough integration and compulsory progressing transportation as observed in the flow production of the vacuum cleaner (Bönig 1993a, S.261).

Cases in the Meter Sector

The meter sector was another field in which flow production was first introduced to the electrical engineering industry. The first conveyor at AEG was installed in this sector (Stollberg 1981, S.148; Strunk 2000, S.49) and all precise work was performed in the form of flow production. In the 1920s, mass low-voltage measurement instruments and more expensive ones with fewer orders could be produced on the conveyor at the same time and in various combinations (Duvigneau 1932, S.55). An annual AEG report from fiscal year 1925/26 pointed out that the transformation to flow production in the meter plant could be regarded as complete (Allgemeine Elektricitäts-Gesellschaft 1926, S.14). This plant was already understood as a "model of completely implemented flow production" (Ledermann 1928, S.480). With the meter, the possibility of work allotment and more effective management of each working process under the belt conveyor were decisive merits for the introduction of flow production due to the existence of manual work that was not replaced by machine work (Ferrari 1928, S.760). The moving stand was arranged, and relatively light machines were installed according to the purpose of the workflow; thus, the rational flow of work was created (Mirus 1929, S.43–44).

In the **mechanical processing process**, automatic machines were widely used in the manufacturing of parts and stamped base plates, hoods, and central plates made of iron and aluminum. The moving stand carried these parts (Mirus 1929, S.47–48; Bönig 1993a, 270). Roller conveyors and belt conveyors were used to transport parts and carry them to machines such as punching machines, boring machines, milling machines, and riveting machines; 1,000 to 1,400 parts were carried to the small punching shop per hour (Mirus 1929, S.45–49).

In the **assembly process**, moving stands were used. In 1929, there were 50 moving stands with a total of 1,500 m and a width of 30 or 60 cm, and they controlled the flow of production. However, in a large part of the cases, female workers did not perform assembly work on the conveyor directly but implemented their work beside the conveyor at a fixed desk. The piece wage was adopted for all production work due to such work forms securing the flexibility required to change the meter type (Mirus 1929, S.41, 44, 51, 55–56; Ferrari 1928, S.761; Bönig 1993a, S.271–272). Moving stands were also used in electrical inspection and packaging. The work rhythm created by the tempo of moving stands contributed to the acceleration of production (Ferrari 1928, S.764).

Cases in the Radio Manufacturing Sector

At the AEG plant, the mechanical processing and assembly processes of the radio producing sector were arranged continuously (see Fig. 9.2).

In the **mechanical processing process**, various parts provided to the assembly process passed through many work processes. Such tasks could be solved only if

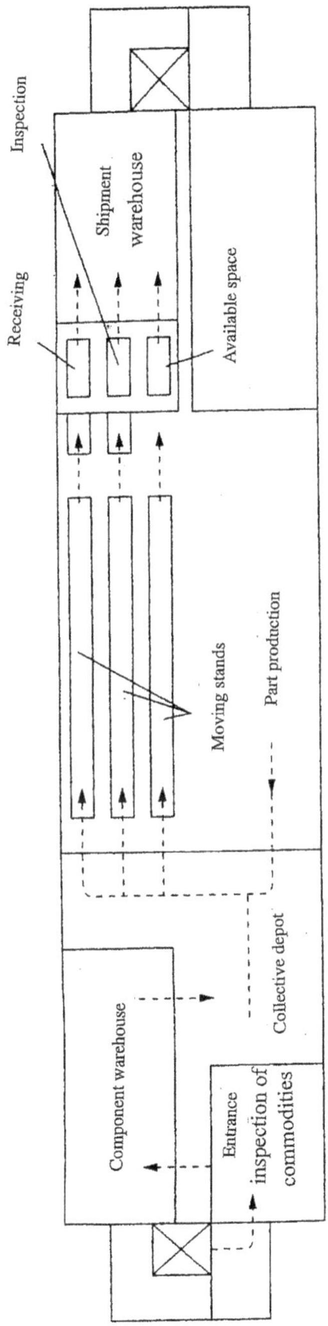

Fig. 9.2 Layout of AEG's Radio Manufacturing Plant

accurate general surveys concerning the arrangement of each machine existed. Large planning boards combined with card boxes to be accurately managed played a key role in providing information regarding the work condition of each part and enabled such general surveys (Moellendorff 1929a, S.576; Bönig 1993a, S.321–328). The production of radio parts was performed at primary integrated workshops such as the punching shop, lacquer painting shop, electric plating shop, and winding shop. Some parts that passed more work processes were always included in each flow cycle. Thus, the production of base plates was implemented in one flow cycle including machines and works such as the press, drawings, punching works, and welding machines for angle brackets (see Fig. 9.3). All parts produced by such production methods were carried to the central storehouse after being checked for the stability of size, function, and volume. All materials were conveyed from there to the flow production line for assembly in the production plan rhythm with 100 pieces per trip (Moellendorf 1929a, S.578–579).

In the **assembly process**, the production plan was made according to the predetermined production volume per day. This plan for flow production included all of the indications concerning equipment such as standard tools, special equipment, and transportation equipment needed under the moving stand (Moellendorff 1929a, S.576).

In the production of radio sets, production method development considering flexible adaptation to market changes was attempted due to market characteristics' dependence on seasonal and fashion changes (Bönig 1993a, S.325). The reorganization of production was implemented to quickly enable the transformation of different parts and products. Ulrich von Moellendorff pointed out that in 1929 in AEG's radio manufacturing, changeable flow production was implemented as a much more elastic and flexible system in which continuous mass production of the same type of product was out of the question. Moving stands, roll gangs, and chutes were used in radio production and tasks such as drawing, punching, and welding were performed in one flow. There were often parts where many tasks were performed for a very long time. Regarding these parts, organizing the original work field was effective. However, as the continuous use of this field could not be expected, work fields had to be created so that the same work field could be used for the production of other parts with similar work processes without setting up machines requiring time and cost. In addition, flexibility in flow production was needed in two directions as follows: (1) making production volume rapidly adapt to economic conditions within a certain time and (2) paying attention to the possibility of various modifications of the same instrument with slight losses caused by transformation to the same flow production line (Moellendorff 1929b, S.395–398). Before the introduction of flow production, fitting work was performed by skilled workers on a fixed working stand without strict binding of time by measures such as work preparation and materials, reconsideration of workshop and equipment, and the preliminary inspection of raw materials. Such work methods changed to simple assembly work for which time was accurately determined (Bönig 1993a, S.326).

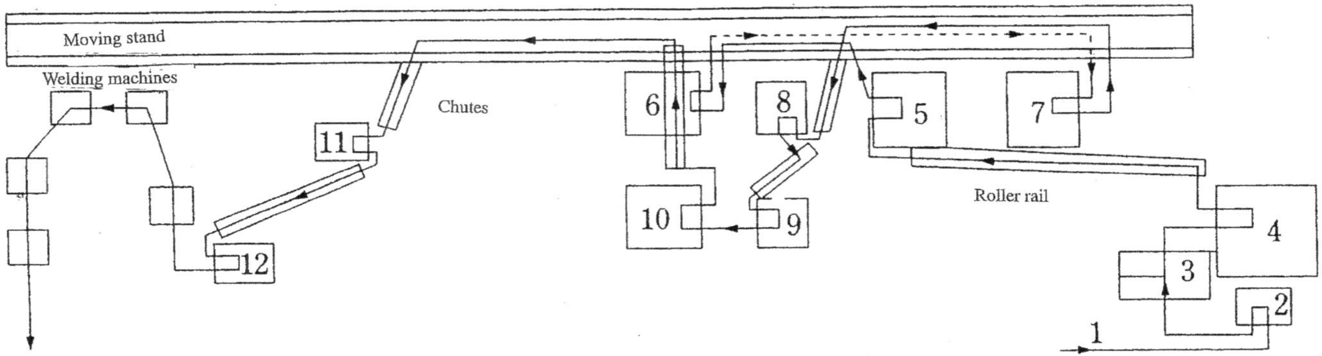

1 Cutting of stripes and heads
2 Cutting of corners
3 Greasing
4 Drawing of base plates
5 Cutting of edge
6 Finishing the drawing
7 Punching of the bottom
8 Punching of one short side
9 Punching of one long side
10 Completing the punching of the bottom
11 Punching of the other short side
12 Punching of the other long side

Fig. 9.3 Flow production of the base plates in AEG's Radio Manufacturing Plant

Cases in the Equipment-Installing Products Sector

Gehard Duvigneau pointed out that although the continuous mass production of small products such as plug sockets, switches, and sockets by the equipment-installing product sector was possible from the perspective of consumption volume, inevitably advancing flow production could not be introduced as even the largest series was manufactured very rapidly. Orders changed constantly under the existence of many types and variations of over 20,000 small parts for household equipment and were influenced by likes and fashion, which led to continual changes in products. Therefore, peculiar special equipment was not used and equipment for flow production that could be assembled quickly such as work stands with chutes, short moving stands, or stands made for partly finished goods that slid from one worker to the next were used (Duvigneau 1932, S.56).

In the production of these products, work stages were divided into very broad ranges. The flow work process with avoidable compulsory progress could not achieve benefits worth mentioning. Nevertheless, in the equipment-installing product plant at Siemens-Schuckertwerke, flow production was introduced because the volume of parts being manufactured could be reduced sharply using flow production (Vrang 1927, S.417). This attempt was implemented for the first time at the end of 1924 (Bönig 1993a, S.292). An annual report about the small product plant in fiscal year 1924/25 pointed out that the introduction of flow production for the production of switches, plug sockets, fuses, and bell transformers greatly contributed to shortening the appointed delivery time [*Siemens Archiv Akte*, 15/Lg562, Jahresbericht des kl. W. I und II für 1924/25, S.3 (in: Chronik 1924/25)].

In examining **fuse production** at Siemens-Schuchertwerke, the work course indicated in Fig. 9.4 was adopted. A box for receiving each of 100 cartridges existed, inclining backward and made a pair at each workshop. This incline made it easy to grasp, take out, and look over. Personnel at some work stands performed work on the same product in parallel. This work stand was tied to one side by a belt conveyor advancing it to the place of inspection. The belt conveyor remained in the final workshop at all times. Female workers arranged their filled out saucers and put them on the conveyor for the purpose of transportation. By a simple, well-devised signal system, an inspection stand taking charge of tests had to pay attention to arrivals. Saucers for various products were used and all dishes were equipped with the same long metal bar. This metal bar crashed contact installed on the conveyor immediately before the inspection stand and blocked it up. The signal turned on at this stand and it became necessary to remove the dish from the conveyor (Vrang 1927, S.419–420).

Flow production without a conveyor was the main form of the flow production system for fuse manufacturing at Siemens. Conveyors were used for the transportation of assembled products to be placed in this section [*Siemens Archiv Akte*, 15/Lg562, Jahresbericht des kl. W.I und II für 1926/27, S.4 (in: Chronik 1926/27); *Siemens Archiv Akte*, 15/Lg562, Jahresbericht des kl. W.I und II für 1928/29, S.4 (in: Chronik 1928/29); *Siemens Archiv Akte*, 15/Lg562, Jahresbericht des kl. W.I und II für 1929/30, S.2 (in: Chronik 1929/30); *Siemens Archiv Akte*, 15/Lg562, Direktionsbericht der Zentral-Werksverwaltung 1928/29, S.5 (in: Chronik 1928/29)]. In

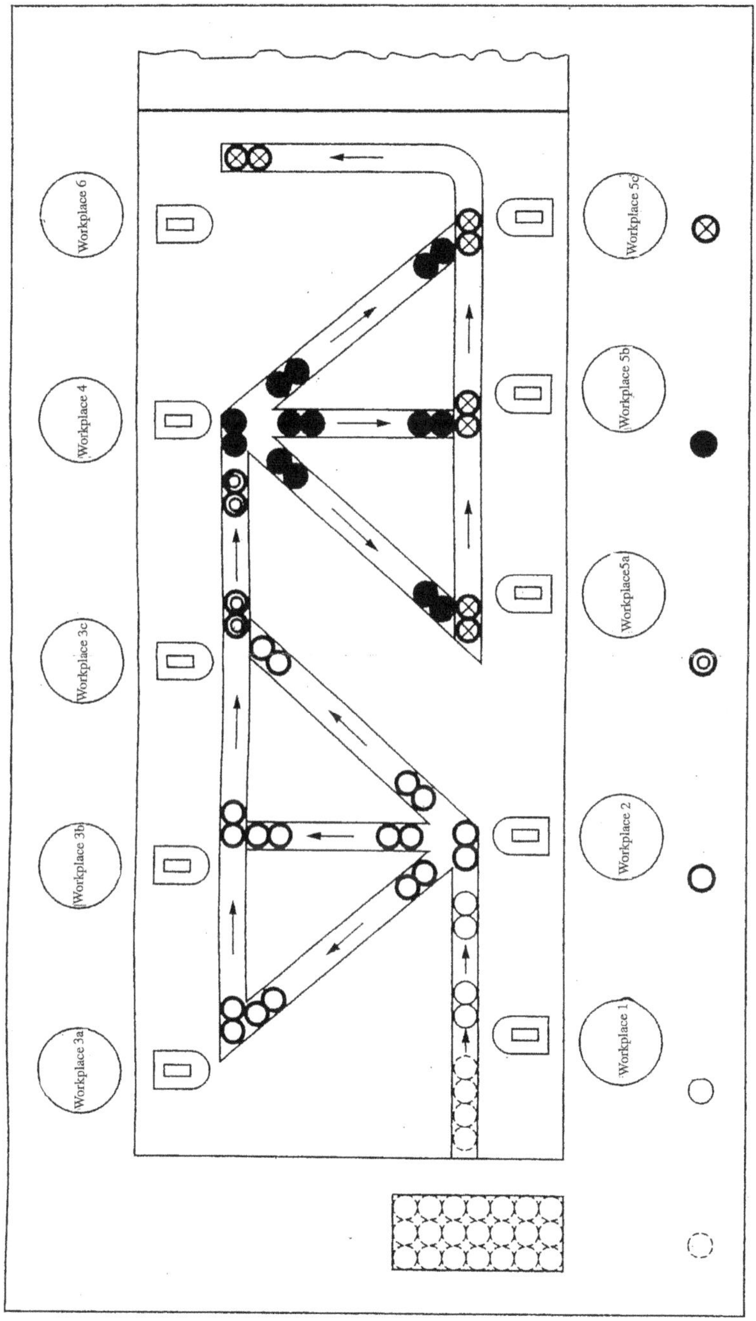

Fig. 9.4 Flow of transporting semifinished products from workplace to workplace in the equipment installing product plant of Siemens-Schuckertwerke

contrast, at AEG, flow production of fuses using conveyors could be observed (Die Rote Fahne 1926).

In switch manufacturing, each special form of flow production had to be selected according to different lots and types due to the existence of many types. Therefore, flow production did not progress as it did in fuse manufacturing (Bönig 1993a, S.295). Standardization of parts by reconsidering design had major significance for the development of mass production using the flow production method (Dominik 1929, S.7–8). For example, in the switch plant at Siemens, instruments and parts were produced on the work stand. However, they needed one or two times, according to circumstances, three or four times per day, the transformation of production due to small production volumes and short tacts (*Siemens Archiv Akte*, 64/Lc511, Niederschrift über die betriebstechnische Konferenz am 16.u. 17. Oktober 1928 im Kinosaal des Verwaltungsgebäudes Berlin-Siemensstadt, S.62). In switch production, although the introduction of conveyors was implemented since the fault rate rose under such compulsory work, work processes with unavoidable advances was not realized as seen in the electric motor plant (Gelbsattel 1926, S.633). In this way, there were differences between products and enterprises in the equipment-installing products sector.

The flow production system using the conveyor was also implemented in the AEG; however, its prominent characteristic can be seen in adopting piecework using such a production method. The Ford Company adopted the time wage system due to the achievement of driving workers to abide by the set tact time through the mechanism of the flow production system. In contrast, management could compel workers to work faster in dual ways by combining conveyor work with peace work. Furthermore, the piece wage was applied to workers at the group unit, which pressured them to keep tact time more strongly through promoting solidarity among them. The highest speed of the most skilled and fastest workers was measured with a stopwatch, and the tempo of the belt conveyor was set on the basis of such time. Furthermore, the moving speed of the conveyor gradually increased, and the intensity of labor significantly increased under the group piece wage system (Die Rote Fahne 1926). In this way, the task standard that was once "normal output" based on the average time of a mean worker in the REFA system instead of "maximum output" based on the fastest time of a first-class worker in the Taylor system was altered to the maximum and fastest output.

Cases in the Electric Heating Instrument Sector

In manufacturing electric heating instruments, for instance, at Siemens-Schuchertwerke, the assembly of flatirons and water heaters was performed using flow production in 1924 and by the end of 1925, respectively (Bönig 1993a, S.245).

At Siemens Elektrowärme GmbH, the belt conveyor and flow production groups were arranged so that even smaller series for various products could be manufactured under the most favorable conditions. This held true for the punching shop and new assembly hall in particular [*Siemens Archiv Akte*, 15/Lg562, Bericht zum Geschäftsjahr 1929/30, S.13 (in: Chronik 1929/30), *Siemens Archiv Akte*, 15/Lg562,

Direktions-Bericht der "Zentral-Werksverwaltung" 1929/30, S.5 (in: Chronik 1929/30)].

When examining flatiron production, in the **mechanical processing process**, workers pushed the bottom part from the metal plate with a 250-ton press and carried them to the grinder by chute, roller conveyor, and belt conveyor. They were then carried to the profile cutter, to grind, polish, and bore two fastening holes and push bolts. The milling machine and grinder worked continuously, and a conveyor transported the parts. Small accessories such as protection apparatuses, installation instruments, and hoods were carried to machines for processing by simple conveyors and chutes (Wolf 1929, S.252–252; Bönig 1993a, S.247). However, such transportation equipment was used primarily to carry work objects and it was in the assembly process that they played a great role as a means of establishing continual and compulsory of work.

The **assembly process** was completely transformed to flow production with the use of the belt conveyor. O-form assembly stands were combined and pulled by chain with a carrying car on which each of five flatirons was installed. This carrying car could be moved forward and continued to a stop until the chain was pulled again. Work on partly finished goods was performed in this time. Tools and parts that were easy to use were arranged so that workers could look over them, which made work easy. For example, in the workshop for attaching angles of contact to hood, it was possible to easily take the hood out of the inclined box. Parts to be screwed fell to female workers who took them out of the container placed in front of this workshop. After finishing assembly, electric inspection was automatically performed. After this inspection, completed flatirons were put into cardboard boxes on the conveyor and carried to an apron conveyor that carried them to the warehouse and packaging plant. Cars with no loads returned to the first workshop (Vrang 1927, S.428–429). Assembly conveyors installed for flatiron production carried pallets in which five flatirons were placed. "The well-devised better flow production" already combined 12 female workers at the end of 1925 (Bönig 1993a, S.248). Such flow production was the "standstill work type of flow production" and the method called the "conveyor type of tact system."

Thus, in electric heating instrument manufacturing, the introduction of the flow production system was relatively aggressively pursued. However, flow production could not be developed as observed in American automobile plants and electrical enterprises due to production volume restrictions determined by market conditions. Although the work tempo was determined beforehand by the final assembly conveyor, workers could influence the speed of the conveyor belt to a certain degree (Wolf 1929, S.254–255).

Cases in the Telephone Manufacturing Sector

Considering the telephone manufacturing sector, in the Werner plant at Siemens & Halske, wonderful results could be achieved in telephone and dial phone manufacturing through the introduction of flow production (Vrang 1927, S.430). The production of communication instruments such as the telephone was implemented in the Werner F plant, which was the biggest factory in this company with the most employees and the most equipment (Bönig 1993a, S.302–304). Jürgen Bönig highlighted that when automatic production equipment could not replace human work, flow production line and belt conveyor became a means of accelerating it (Bönig 1993a, S.308).

At the Werner F plant, the first attempt to introduce flow production was made at the end of 1924, and in telephone manufacturing, this production method was implemented in March 1927. In dial phone production, a lot of special equipment was used for flow production (Bönig 1993a, S.315; Schmidt 1993, S.128). In this plant, an increase in production exceeding that of labor time was achieved by expanding line production, installing new automatic machines in almost every department, strictly organizing the transportation system, and improving the overall work method in fiscal year 1926/27. Thorough cost reduction was realized in tool manufacturing by introducing flow production and arranging special machines [*Siemens Archiv Akte*, 15/Lc816, Jahresbericht 1926/27. Wernerwerk F, S.1 (in: Jahresbericht WWF 26/27)]. In this fiscal year, setup time and machine loss time were shortened in parts manufacturing by systematic work preparation, conveyor transportation, and flow production expansion. Flow production was further expanded into assembly, and by increasing line production, an approximate 10% reduction in the time of all assembly workshops and a decline in the piece wage were realized by using special work-saving machines [*Siemens Archiv Akte*, 15/Lc816, Jahresbericht der Fabrikleitung F 1926/27, S.2–5 (in: Jahresbericht WWF 26/27)].

In 1927/28, the order of production progress, the flow of products, and flow production planning from the raw materials to the finished product came into question. In 1928/29 at the punching shop, regular transportation based on plans using electric trucks was implemented, increasing output by 50%.

In small products, flow production was profitable for the first time in cases of volume of over 500. However, at the Werner F plant, small orders less than 50 increased after 1927 and in the world crisis afterward, the ratio of such small orders to all orders increased to over half. As a result, the time for preparation and setting up made mass assembly unprofitable. Under this situation, changes in the manufacturing method were made between flow production without motor compelling and conveyor work. In addition, “changeable flow production,” which made it possible to exchange tools and equipment easily and rapidly when the model to be produced was changed, was attempted as a countermeasure (Bönig 1993a, S.316).

Cases in the Incandescent Lamp Manufacturing Sector

Finally, the incandescent lamp manufacturing sector is considered. Incandescent lamp production experienced its own development until the end of the 1920s due to much of the work being manual. The introduction of flow production progressed in relation to mechanization. Osram and other German manufacturers not only attempted to replace manual work with mechanical work but also combined assembly mechanization with the flow production line.

In lamp bulb production, AEG made some attempts at mechanization at the beginning of the 1920s. However, at Osram, lamps were produced by manual or blowing work until the introduction of American machines protected by patents. Although flow production was limited to detaching bottles, inserting them into a cooling furnace, and manual work by rake and scoop, the belt conveyor made such manual work unnecessary at the end of the 1920s (Bönig 1993a, S.277–278; Hanfland 1929, S.855–858; AFAB 1928, S.477; Zschacke 1931).

In incandescent lamp assembly, during the 1920s, work mechanization was attempted without combining semiautomatic and automatic machines with one system or the flow production process at the beginning (Bönig 1993a, S.282). Osram tested the introduction of new machines and flow production at a moment of stagnant sales in the summer of 1924 (Osram GmbH 1924; Bönig 1993a, S.284). It combined the partial work processes of individual workshops with flow organization. Machines for embedding molybdenum anchor wire, automatic exhaust and pouring, and applying adhesive agent were arranged. Manual processes such as mounting work were performed in the production flow near the chain conveyor. As the arrangement of partial automated machines and transportation equipment set the work rhythm, in 1926, production could be regarded as flow production (Bönig 1993a, S.284).

Looking at incandescent lamp production at the end of 1925 on the basis of Fig. 9.5, a combination of machines under flow production can be observed. First, cut tubes, galas bars, and leading-in wires were carried to machines to produce the stem (a) in which two female workers were arranged. Finished stems were automatically moved to the anchor wire embedding machine, which embedded molybdenum anchor wire into the galas bar, (b) "stem with anker" passed near five female workers on the chain conveyor, (c) and as "mounts" arrived at the machine that sealed the glass envelop. (d) It was sealed with a glass bulb by one female worker and then set on the pump as a "lamp sealed with glass." (e) Exhaust and pouring gas were automatically performed. Automatic evacuating equipment (f) dropped an "evacuated lamp" on the troughing conveyor. (g) Evacuated lamps reached the basing machine and machine for flashing that attached the base. Female workers received bases that were applied with an adhesive agent from the machine. (h) In the "basing and flashing processed lamp," conducting wire was put on to the sockets and (i) brand marks and seals were pasted and packed. (j) "Packaged lamps" were finally moved to a storehouse or shipped (Mäckbach and Kienzle 1926, S.194–195).

Regarding the development of flow production, Jürgen Bönig stressed that incandescent lamp flow production manufacturing played an important role in the framing of the mechanization strategy. As far as completely automated equipment could not be freely used, organizing flow production had to put all processes under a unified rhythm (Bönig 1993a, S.287).

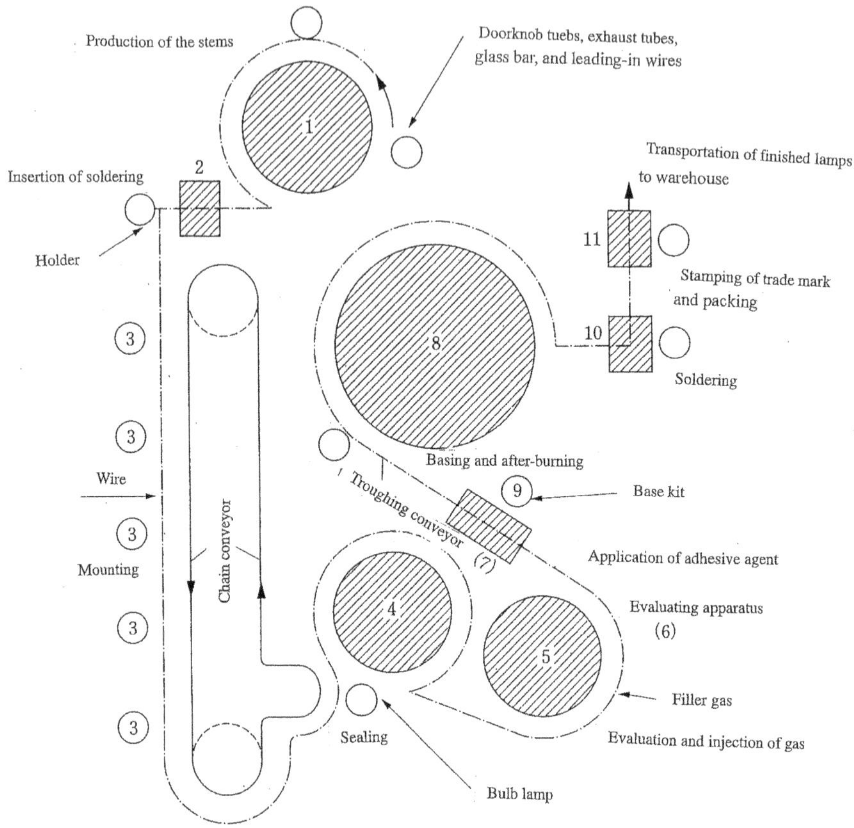

Fig. 9.5 Flow production of incandescent lamps in Osram (end of 1925)

Characteristics of the Introduction of the Flow Production System to the Electrical Engineering Industry

Even in the electrical engineering industry as a typical industrial sector in which the introduction of the flow production method progressed broadly, cases in which transformation to this production system were performed in all casting and forging processes, mechanical processing, and assembly, and a high-level transportation system between processes was introduced, were limited to the electric motor plant, vacuum cleaner manufacturing in particular. In many product sectors in which flow production was implemented, cases in which the conveyor as mechanical transportation equipment was installed were not many in the mechanical processing process, and even in the assembly process, there were not many cases of flow production adoption with conveyors. Even in product sectors and production processes in which the new production system using the conveyor was introduced, they did not all mean "the conveyor system" in which each task was performed with moving forms according to conveyor movement. Actually, there are many cases in which flow production systems termed as "conveyor type of tact system" and "the changeable flow production" were introduced. Heidrum Homburg pointed out that "the conveyor belt was extended to some metalmaking departments and finally to the casting departments in 1927–28. The introduction of the conveyor belt to a few production units was, however, the most salient of the changes, which included the future subdivision of work and the general changeover from the driving belt to the separate drive" (Homburg 1983, pp.149–150).

9.3.2.2 Introduction of the Flow Production System to the Automobile Industry

Overall Conditions of the Introduction of the Flow Production System to the Automobile Industry

Shifts from production by machine type to production by product type were observed in some automobile industry enterprises in the 1910s (Lang 1919, S.4–5; Filk 2001b, S.225–226). In the latter half of the 1920s, transformation to flow production was pursued in many large enterprises under delays in technology and labor organization compared with the US. It was pointed out that in 1927–1928, representative automobile plants that did not implement production based on the flow production principle almost did not exist. However, in reality, such attempts were prominent only in some companies producing small and popular cars. Even though it was often thought that flow production with the completely inevitable advancement of work as observed at the Ford Motor Company at the time was a general case, the allotment of predetermined time meant that this could not be observed everywhere. As G. Duvigneau pointed out, in many cases, a sort of "elastic flow production" could be seen (Duvigneau 1932, S.51–51).

Michael Stahlmann pointed out that a model of rationalization emphasizing labor process flexibility and product variation interchangeability prevailed during Daimler-Benz's second modernization phase from the middle of the 1920s to the outbreak of World War II and can be characterized as a "flexible production concept with an emphasis on quality" (Stahlmann 1993, S.175–177, 243–244; Feldenkirchen 2003, S.149). This company succeeded in producing all six-cylinder and eight-cylinder engine models using flow production. Nevertheless, product variants continued to be maintained to a certain degree and the level of the production structure greatly differed from that of the Ford Motor Company (Stahlmann 1993, S.176). At Daimler-Benz, takt time, as had been observed in the American automobile industry for the preceding 15 to 20 years, was not achieved until the late 1930s (Stahlmann 1993, S.179). Daimler-Benz attempted to develop the more typical German flow production and began flow production in 1926 for the first time, introducing the first belt conveyor in 1928; however, this company did not reach the level of production technology of Adam Opel until 1934 (Kugler 1987, S.337).

Among the enterprises that produced small and popular cars, as a representative case of conveyor system development characterized by the Ford system, in contrast to generally known impressions, automobile production at Opel was not performed using the continuous belt conveyor in the 1920s. There were many individual belts and their tempos were coordinated by foremen (Radkau 2008, S.278). The length of the final conveyor of this company was only 45 m and the work tact was approximately 30 min in 1924 (Braun 1991, S.198; Kugler 1987, S.337). The workshops of the semifinished product department were connected by belt conveyors until 1926, and the length of conveyors of this firm's whole automobile factory reached 2,000 m in 1929 (Bönig 1993a, S.445; Dresler and Lambert 1988, S.67). However, the system combining work flow and work conveyors was only dominant until 1929 (Braun 1991, S.198; Kugler 1987, S.337). Only 19% of the employees worked directly under conveyors in 1928 (Kugler 1987, S.337; Bönig 1993a, S.445).

The introduction of the flow production system to various production processes differed greatly. Therefore, the implementation of this production method in major production processes is considered next.

The casting and forging processes: At Daimler-Benz, casting plants were traditionally organized according to product type. This was due to the variety of engines produced. Casting works were mechanized in 1929. Sand reclamation was automated, and underground transportation equipment carried the molded sand to a large mixer. It was then moved to the ground by elevator and carried to a tank arranged on a founder workshop again by a conveyor (Stahlmann 1993, S.161–162). Rudolf Hoffmann (1930, S.41) pointed out that in 1930, in Daimler-Benz's bronze casting shop, mass production was implemented, and flow production was performed with belt conveyors installed in a large hall (Hoffmann 1930, S.41).

The body manufacturing process: According to an internal Daimler-Benz document from September 29, 1927, at the Untertürkheim plant, the body manufacturing plant's transformation to flow production was completely implemented (*Mercedes-Benz Classic Archiv*, Kissel Protokolle, I/3, Protokoll Nr.7 der Sitzung des Arbeitsausschusses vom 29.9.27. in Mannheim, S.4). The moving assembly line for body production was arranged in the Sindelfingen plant in 1925–1926 (Laux 1992, p.92). The implementation of flow production using conveyors in this plant was chosen in October 1929 (*Mercedes-Benz Classic Archiv*, Kissel Protokolle, I/5, Protokoll über die Direktionssitzung vom 2. und 3. Oktober 1929 in Untertürkheim, S.13). Two body assembly conveyors installed in this plant had a production capacity of 600 to 700 car bodies in the usual labor time. The possibility of letting various types of flow individually in a line and at various tempos was created by the body assembly conveyor (*Mecedes-Benz Classic Archiv*, Kissel Protokolle, I/5, Anlage zum Protokoll über die Arbeitsausschußsitzung vom 22. Oktober 1929. Betrifft Umstellungsprojekt Sindelfingen, S.1–2). To organize production using two mutually independent conveyors, flexibility was required (Thieme 2004, S.199). The body production cost of the 2-L type of limousine could be reduced to RM 210 by introducing a belt conveyor with a RM 600,000 investment from October 1919 to May 1930 [*Mercedes-Benz Classic Archiv*, Kissel Protokolle, I/5, Vorstandsbericht über die Gesamtlage des Konzerns (26.6.1930), S.4; *Mercedes-Benz Classic Archiv*, Kissel

Protokolle, I/5, Protokoll über die Direktionssitzung vom 2. und 3. Oktober 1929 in Untertürkheim betreffend Personenwagen und allgemeine Verwaltungsfragen, S.13]. However, a maximum production capacity of 1,000 to 1,100 bodies in 1928 could not be exploited as production using conveyors became profitable only with passenger cars. Due to the manufacturing of a large series, it was introduced only in the body production of passenger cars (Stahlmann 1993, S.161). Since type reduction was performed thoroughly for passenger cars, flow production using conveyors was dominant in the production process. In contrast, truck bodies had to be individually adjusted to the things transported and the carrying volume of consumers. The conditions making production using conveyors economical were secured due to the necessity of designing them according to such demand (Hoffmann 1930, S.88). At Opel, flow production was introduced in body manufacturing after 1926. After body parts passed the body painting process, they were assembled using conveyors (Kugler 1985, S.49–50).

The painting process: In the painting process, although manual work was dominant until then, for instance, at Adler, a high-temperature immersion method using conveyors was introduced. The individual processing of mudguards, coated metal plates, and wheels depending on manual work that took time were driven away by it. Degreasing, painting, and drying were implemented by flow production. Painting came to be performed in the unified, continuous flow and its time was shortened to approximately three to four hours (Jurthe 1931, S.601–602). At Opel, the introduction of the American painting method using conveyors was implemented after 1928 (Kugler 1985, S.50).

The chassis producing process: At Opel, individual parts produced in this department were assembled to finished part units on the subassembly conveyor and carried to the chassis assembly conveyor and then assembled to finished chassis (Kugler 1985, S.46). In the chassis department at the Untertürkheim plant at Daimler-Benz, transformation to flow production was implemented at a rate of 80% of all work in September 1927 (*Mercedes-Benz Classic Archiv*, Kissel Protokolle, I/3, Protokoll Nr.7 der Sitzung des Arbeitsausschusses vom 29.9.27. in Untertürkheim, S.4). A final moving assembly line for chassis was installed this year (Laux 1992, p.92).

The mechanical processing process: In the mechanical processing process in which the production of each kind of part was performed, there were many cases in which flow production using transportation equipment other than the belt conveyor was introduced. In cases in which sufficient production volume could be secured, implementing mechanical processing in the form of flow production often promised much larger benefits. However, even in such cases, neither mechanical transportation nor expensive special equipment was decisively needed and implementing flow production was possible with relatively simple means (Hänecke 1927, S.160). For instance, at the boring line using the drilling machines at Opel, workers carried partly finished goods from one machine tool to the next one by roller conveyor (Bönig 1993a, S.447).

In this way, the introduction of the belt conveyor as mechanical transportation equipment was still beginning in mechanical processing. Even at the Ford Motor Company, belt conveyors in the mechanical processing department were adopted for the transportation of articles in which mechanical processing work was finished to the assembly process at the beginning of introducing a new production system. Such transport equipment did not play a role as a means of combining machines (Shiomi 1978, pp.227–228; Arnold 1914, pp.347–349). At Opel, introducing conveyors did not progress in mechanical processing (Weiss 1926, S.19). It was in the assembly process that the establishment of the moving type of flow work organization called the "conveyor system" had epoch-making significance.

The assembly process: Opel reduced car types produced from five to one at the end of 1923 to achieve the volume needed for flow production and released a small unified standard automobile in the spring of 1924 (Kugler 1985, S.30; Kroth 1928, S.103, 106; Bönig 1993a, S.443). The first conveyor was introduced in the final assembly process and flow production was implemented (Sehrr-Thoss 1979, S.86; Löwisch 2011, S.195). Although assembly using belt conveyors started in the transmission manufacturing department in 1926 (Kugler 1987, S.337), the introduction of such equipment in engine assembly occurred one year before in 1925. The assembly of engines was done on the belt conveyor with a special clamping device by which parts were turned in all directions and fixed. In rear axle assembly, conveyor belts secured the regular advancement of transportation and work processes everywhere (Schlesinger 1926, S.611–612). The final assembly of individual parts into finished chassis was performed at the lowest floor of the plant where engines were installed and parts such as radiators, bodies, switchboards, and wheels were attached, and one finished car left the assembly line every 4.5 min. According to Karl Schmidt, in 1926, the Opel plant was still not at a high level and there were cases in which workers interrupted the working process of individual, partly finished goods even though only for a short time, and they still influenced the progress of conveyors to a certain degree (Schmidt 1927, S.45–46). Productivity, work dividing degree, and conveyor tact speed could not be achieved as observed in the US. The rate of skilled workers was still high. According to German Metalworker Union research, an average of 56.8% of workers were skilled workers in the German automobile industry whereas a similar figure for Opel was 66%. The average rate of unskilled workers in the German automobile industry was 11.7%, whereas a similar figure for Opel was only 5% (Vorstand des Deutschen Metallarbeiter-Verband 1930, S.8–9, 13–14).

In this way, even at Opel, a typical case of Ford system deployment, the breaking up of skilled work as observed in the US did not occur despite of the transformation to the flow production system (Stahlmann 1994, S.228). At Opel, there were many inspectors. The limitations on the introduction of flow production can be understood from this point. Whereas the ratio of inspectors to workers was 1:15 at the Ford Motor Company's Highland Park Plant, a similar figure for Opel in 1929 was approximately 7:1 (Kugler 1985, S.58). Thus, in the assembly process, only a part of production was first transformed to conveyor work in the 1920s, and flow production differed from the work form compelled by conveyors existed in many places (Hänecke 1927, S.159; Schultz 1927).

In Germany, flow production was generally used only in individual business units and was never observed throughout an entire enterprise until 1933 (Hachtmann 1989, S.68). Even at Opel, where the introduction of the Ford system was pursued as an eminent breakthrough, manufacturing using the flow production method did not reach the level of the Ford Motor Company even in 1929 (Kugler 1987, S.336–337). In 1935, the system regarded as 100% flow production composed of machine lines, complete automatic belt conveyors, and final assembly conveyors was realized at the Brandenburg Truck Plant at Opel; by this time, this company had reached a high level of development of the Ford system (Seherr-Thoss 1979, S.295) (see Chap. 12).

Joachim Radkau highlighted that even at Opel in the 1920s, the production of interchangeable parts was not introduced and skilled workers were indispensable in fitting them. Since the ratio of wages to total production costs was only one-tenth in automobile production, there was not a great incentive to save skilled workers in assembly. In the automobile industry, there were causes for strengthening the necessity for production in small lots determined by the German market. Production of such a small series was regarded as an incomplete variant of the Fordism appropriate for poorer countries in which the automobile was still a privilege for higher class (Radkau 2008, S.278–279).

Hans Joachim Brown stressed that a large part of German automobile manufacturers performed rational behavior in rationalization endeavors only partially implemented and the "the changeable flow production" concept played a decisive role in such efforts (Braun 1991, S.183). There were many cases in which the belt conveyor itself was used in various forms. According to Rüdiger Hachtmann, many intermediate forms existed between the two poles of flow production—with and without the conveyor. The flow production system organized until 1933 can generally be regarded as a primitive form rather than the "complete" form (Hachtmann 1989, S.69–70). Paul Berkenkopf pointed out that particularly with passenger cars, production methods that enabled the application of American technical results (especially various methods of flow production) in Germany to an extent suitable for the possibility of much smaller sales had to be developed (Berkenkopf 1933, S.48). As H. J. Brown pointed out, many studies concerning rationalization were published in the 1920s, but they should not be identified with the extent of transformation to flow production or conversion work and rationalization actually being implemented. The authors of these publications pursued publicity and tended to exaggerate the benefits and actual real-world implementation of rationalization. He stressed that the results of "real production" by enterprises indicated by these publications would create a distorted image (Braun 1991, S.194–195).

Limitations on the Introduction of the Flow Production System and Their Factors

The introduction of the flow production method did not progress as well as it did in the US, even in the automobile industry. The following points can be considered major factors determining such limitations.

The production of passenger cars increased from 38,988 in 1925 to 91,936 in 1929 (Statistisches Reichsamt 1929, S.123; Statistisches Reichsamt 1932, S.129); however, they were overwhelmingly fewer than similar figures in the US (3,186,000 and 4,587,000, respectively) (The Bureau of Foreign and Domestic Commerce 1930, p.806). Automobile production lots in Germany were forced to be smaller due to strict and unfavorable market conditions and a small number of manufactured automobiles. In Germany, cases in which 50–100 cars of the same kind were produced per day using the belt conveyor were regarded as profitable (Ledermann 1933, S.26). When estimating automobile production from an international perspective, in world markets, only enterprises manufacturing at least 50 cars per day could be competitive. However, in Germany, only Opel, with the highest production capacity of approximately 100 cars per day, reached this level (Weiss 1926, S.23; Löwisch 2011, S.195). In the US, the daily production volume on average was about 255 in 1929 whereas in Germany, a similar figure was approximately 2.7—with the exception of Opel (Adelt 1930, S.72). The Ford Motor Co. needed the day labor of approximately nine people to produce one finished car. In contrast, similar numerical figures for well-organized German plants and those manufacturing luxurious cars with highly qualified workers were about 80–90 persons and about 350 people, respectively. These figures were significant compared with the numerical value of modern British plants (approximately 35–44) (Stahlmann 1993, S.68–69).

Regarding the prevalence of automobiles, while the numbers of populations per motor vehicle in the US, the United Kingdom, and France in 1927 were 5.3, 43, and 44, respectively, a similar numerical value in Germany was 196 (National Automobile Chamber of Commerce 1927, p.44). In addition to conditions in which the German automobile market was incomparably smaller than the US market, the sale of American automobiles with a large price advantage in the German market increased remarkably in the 1920s. The ratio of American passenger car sales to total sales in the German market increased from only 2.6% in 1921 to 12% in 1924 and further to 38.5% in 1929 (the average until September). Similar numerical figures concerning trucks increased from 0.9% to 5.1% and further to 33.4% in the same years (Vorstand des Deutschen Metallarbeiter-Verband 1930, S.51). In a 1928 meeting of Daimler-Benz's managing board, the difficulties caused by competition with American enterprises were emphasized. This meeting pointed out that Daimler-Benz's product prices were at as high as before and the main reason for the difficulties surrounding the German automobile industry was low import customs (*Mercedes-Benz Classic Archiv*, Kissel Protokolle, I/4, Protokoll der Vorstandssitzung vom 2. Oktober 1928 in Untertürkheim, Blatt 3; *Mercedes-Benz Classic Archiv*, Kissel Protokolle,I/4, Protokoll No.16 der Gesamtvorstandssitzung vom 28.Juni 1928 in Untertürkheim, S.3).

Under this condition, specialization in the smallest car enabled companies to avoid competition with American companies or the high-class automobile market segment in which differences in production technique were not great and the German wage level made use of advantageous handiwork techniques that were profitable for German passenger car manufacturers (Flik 2001a, S.83–84; *Mercedes-Benz Classic Archiv*, Kissel Protokolle, I/4, Protokoll der Vorstandssitzung vom 24. Oktober 1928 in Mannheim, S.19). In the emphasis on the high-class car segment, product differentiation on the point of quality had major significance. For example, at Daimler-Benz, even the prices of smaller and cheaper 2-L and 2.6-L cars were absolutely high and securing competitive power using models emphasizing quality was regarded as an important task (*Mercedes-Benz Classic Archiv*, Kissel Protokolle, I/4, Protokoll der Vorstandssitzung vom 24. Oktober 1928 in Mannheim, S.1–2). However, in both cases, production volumes and lots per type had to be small under strict market conditions.

Customers' preference for motorcycles and the high diffusion rate of motorcycles also became important factors in determining the limitation of the mass production of automobiles. Technically excellent and highly efficient motorcycles drove property and maintenance costs better than small automobile types (Blaich 1973, S.31).

As a result of such severe situations, attempts to shift to mass production by deploying the Ford system caused the expansion of excess production capacity. "Productivity tripled between 1925 and 1929. However, plants were heavily underutilized" (Link 2020, S.141). It was pointed out that large automobile enterprises expanded their production capacity by 2–3 times between 1927 and 1928 (Feldmann 1999, S.7) and that a sharp increase in production capacity was created in a relatively short term. However, the operating rates of German companies were forced to decline tremendously under the market conditions caused by the expansion of American automobile imports and assembly progress by rival foreign enterprises in Germany. The operating rates of Opel, BMW, Adler, and Brenabor in 1928 were 60.72%, 60%, 30.14%, and 9.04%, respectively. A similar average figure for these four enterprises was only 36.27% (Ledermann 1933, S.82). The utilization rate of workers measured by hours worked in the German automobile industry decreased from 44.8% in 1928 to 38.8% in 1929 and further to 28.8% in 1930; these numerical figures were lower than those in the whole industry (64.5%, 63.3%, and 49%, respectively) (Ludwig 1932, S.123).

The rationalization of the German automobile industry with a large investment in production capacity was known as "failed rationalization," as is clear from these low operating rates. In such cases, the flow production system became the "too expensive production method" (Nishimuta 1999, p.95; Flik 2001b, S.237–238). Fritz Blaich pointed out that transformation to the belt conveyor was not only unprofitable but also the source of large financial losses (Blaich 1973, S.29; Flik 2001a, S.84; Pierer 2011, S.195–196, 201–202). Therefore, as Michael Stahlmann insisted that the introduction of Henry Ford's production system in Germany was not advisable (Stahlmann 1993, S.71). Newly created equipment could never be effectively used and attempts to transfer American production methods into Germany were regarded as general failures (*Der deutsche Volkswirt* 1933, S.X, S.XII).

One of the largest factors determining this limitation was market conditions. According to F. Blaich, such "mis-rationalization" appeared as a deep, difficult distance to be overcome between technical and organizational rationalization and the "rationalization" of infrastructure, which the state had almost neglected, on the one hand, and the "rationalization" of tax legislation and the legal order on the other (Blaich 1973, S.33).

In Germany at the time, there were some factors restricting demand for automobiles such as the completion of the freight railroad network and passenger transportation, state transportation policy emphasizing railways, insufficient road construction, and the heavy tax burden of automobile ownership and use due to state tax policy and customs (Nishimuta 1999, Chap.5). Such restrictive conditions were significantly changed by the National Socialist motorization policy (see Chap. 12).

9.3.2.3 Introduction of the Flow Production System to the Machinery Industry

Overall Conditions of the Introduction of the Flow Production system to the Machinery Industry

Next, in examining the machinery industry, the shift from individual production to series production progressed in individual partial fields and the introduction of flow production was implemented in some departments suited to this production method. This trend can be observed in the production of motors, machine tools, high-speed pressing machines, typewriters, and other smaller machines primarily for consumers such as sewing machines, gas ranges, and cooking appliances (Keiser and Benning 1931, S.58). In the entire machinery industry, except for partial product sectors, almost all of the introduction of the flow production system was organized without the conveyor. As already considered in Sect. 9.3.1, the diffusion rate of conveyor work in the machine industry was much lower than in the electrical engineering or automobile industries. In the machinery industry, particularly, the machine tool industry, the possibility of mass production was low and there were still intermediate forms of production methods, and the flow production system existed in many places due to market limitations.

The first way to establish flow production was production by product type. The shift from production by type of machine to production by type of product could be observed in enterprises in which mass production by flow production could not be developed due to market restrictions. T. v. Freyberg pointed out that production by type of product was the highest and broadest form to reach flow production for many medium firms in the machinery industry, particularly, the machine tool industry. The introduction of the pure flow production system could not be considered for small series (von Freyberg 1989, S.156–157).

The second method for introducing flow production was the way in which production for both smaller and larger series was performed with the same workers and at the same conveyor. Special emphasis on development activity to make flow production more flexible according to large changes in volume and various types by technical and organizational measures lay in this point. This form of flow production was a compromise between time economy and market economy. It was often only possible to organize flow production despite small volume and higher costs were allowed to secure greater elasticity (von Freyberg 1989, S.158; Köttgen 1928a, S.12). The shift from production of one product to another made the transformation of working machines and equipment on a large-scale necessary, which required costs (Schulz-Mehrin 1927, S.814). Schulz-Mehrin pointed out that when continuous flow production of the same object was out of the question, "changeable flow production" was chosen instead of manufacturing in series (Schulz-Mehrin 1927, S.817). As already considered in this chapter, this production method was attempted in the electrical engineering and automobile industries.

The third method for forming flow production in the German machinery industry was "mixed production" in which series production was performed in mechanical processing and flow production was implemented in the assembly process. Whereas assembly by the flow production method could be realized relatively easily due to the high rate of manual work, mechanical production with various machine tools and different processing processes generally caused major difficulties. Time had to be equalized between processing machines and the full operation of machines was a premise in flow production with a relatively large volume of the same product. The development of machine tools (higher processing speed and therefore shorter tact time) made this problem acute. As such difficulties could be very large due to the small volume and large differences in the efficiency of machine equipment, there were many cases in which series production was maintained in mechanical production and the flow production principle was realized only in assembly (von Freyberg 1989, S.161).

Next, the introduction of the flow production method to some product sectors in the machinery industry is examined.

Introduction of the Flow Production System to the Agricultural Machine Industry

According to research by the German Metalworker Union in 1931, in the agricultural machine industry, of the 41 departments researched, 15 (36.6%), 3 (7.3%), and 11 (26.8%) introduced flow work, conveyor work, and manufacturing in series, respectively (Deutscher Metallarbeiter-Verband 1932, S.99). The most important problem in transforming to flow production was markets restrictions. Forecasting a certain sales volume was difficult due to intense changes in the sales and characteristics of agricultural machines as a seasonal product and therefore production plans based on the smallest volume had to be made (Duvigneau 1932, S.50; Deutscher Metallarbeiter-Verband 1932, S.99).

Many enterprises implemented the transformation to the flow production of agricultural machines in 1925 and 1926 under such difficulties. Deutsche Industrie-Werke AG in Spandau implemented assembly by flow production as broadly as possible in four products—grass cutters, reapers, automatic harvesting and bundling machines, and threshing machines (Maschinenbau 1926, S.727). According to a report in the magazine "*Werkstattstechnik,*" in June 1926, tractor assembly was performed using the same method as automobiles and there were cases in which a working method using assembly rails was adopted and the processing of shaft journals was performed in flow production using conveyors that carried partly finished goods between a series of machines (Werkstattstechnik 1926, S.358). In 1926, Heinrich Lanz AG began the first flow production of tractors in Germany using an assembly conveyor that was 175 m in length (Herrmann 1985, S.93). Whereas transmissions and tractor casings manufactured by Hannomag and automatic harvesting and bundling machines were assembled using the flow production method, at Friedrich Krupp AG the threshing machine was manufactured in series. R. Sack AG in Leipzig casted hubs of toothed plow wheels and developed flow production or manufacturing in series for the assembly of potato diggers and dumping device production by 1931 (Bönig 1993a, S.542; Bünge 1928, S.VII-VIII; *Jahresberichte der Gewerbeaufsichtsbeamten und Berghörden für das Jahr 1927* 1928c, S.247). At Hannomag, the driving apparatus of agricultural machines was assembled with the flow production method using a moving assembly rail (Müller 1927, S.512).

However, even in the latter half of the 1920s, only a small number of plants introduced flow work or conveyor work in a few parts of smaller agricultural machines due to obstacles such as changes in the price of agricultural products, market scale, capital equipment, and the agricultural business structure. In 1926, only the largest plants could realize flow production with the flexibility of existing machines and equipment (long tact time and low level of inevitable advancement of work within a predetermined time) under the lowest possible capital expenditure (Bönig 1993a, S.551).

In this way, there were efforts to organize flow production more elastically in the agricultural machine industry as well as the machine tool industry due to strict market conditions. In threshing machine production at Heinrich Lanz AG, the variety of products made it impossible to completely shift to flow production in metal parts manufacturing as well. An essential difference between Germany and the US lay in the necessity of elastic adjustments. In the equipment for all flow production lines for threshing machine parts and element groups, the primary task was to arrange the work process and auxiliary equipment so that the elements of the small threshing machine and a small volume of larger threshing machines could be processed, carried, and assembled effectively. Although in manufacturing the straw bundling machine, in particular, assembly by pure flow production was implemented for the threshing machines and straw bundling machines at Heinz Lanz Company; the flow production method using belt conveyors was not possible as observed in tractor production due to its scale in the 1920s (Hofer 1929, S.70, 72, 74–75, 77).

Manufacturing a very small threshing machine and a small number of large threshing machines using the flow production lines was desired because of the sales structure. As a result, compelling efficiency by special wage forms and work instruction cards was needed due to the uncertainty of assembly work time. In the production of tractors at Heinrich Lanz AG, the assembly conveyor for the Burdog HRII type as a small tractor was installed in 1926. However, the necessity for high flexibility, the low capital cost, and the expected rapid change in products excluded a continuous flow production line or conveyor work because of the intensely changing seasonal business in which the sales volume during the summer was many times greater than that in the winter (Bönig 1993a, S.547–548; Müller 1927, S.510).

Introduction of the Flow Production System to the Sewing Machine Industry

The sewing machine industry was one of the machinery industries in which the reduction of type and standardization of parts and the introduction of flow production progressed relatively smoothly. The concept of flow production was thoroughly implemented, primarily in small parts casting shops, wood processing shops, assembly, and packaging. In contrast, when examining intermediate processing workshops for lathe work of individual parts and small parts, boring work, and milling, the conditions were not different from general situation previously observed. G. Duvigneau pointed out that in sewing machine production, the flow production system with the unavoidable progress of work within a determined time was introduced as well as a working form without the compulsion of production and tact determining the time for each work. In the process of flow production, there were many kinds of transportation equipment. There was equipment such as the trolley conveyor in the casting plant, apron conveyors made of iron in the scaling shop, short chutes for carrying objects from machine to machine in the processing of main parts, transportation from worker hand to worker hand in the production of stands, overheads, and belt conveyors in assembly lines, and manual trollies in packaging. Individual special machines for processing primary parts were also included in flow production processing (Duvigneau 1932, S.53). In sewing machine manufacturing, the production of parts and painting was often performed using flow work and assembly and packaging were implemented using conveyor work (*Jahresberichte der Gewerbeaufsichtsbeamten und Berghörden für das Jahr 1927* 1928b, S.XLV-XLVI; *Jahresberichte der Gewerbeaufsichtsbeamten und Berghörden für das Jahr 1927* 1928c, S.246; *Jahresberichte der Gewerbeaufsichtsbeamten und Berghörden für das Jahr 1927* 1928a, S.39–40, S.399).

A report of the German Metalworker Union pointed out cases of conveyor introduction in the assembly of shuttles and the adoption of the flow production of throat plates and wire (Deutscher Metallarbeiter-Verband 1932, S.105). For instance, Nähmaschinenfabrik G. M. Pfaff A.G. began flow production in a series of workshops instead of production by machine type for the first time between 1924 and 1927 (Lüth 1936, S.20–21).

At this company, although two kinds of conveyors were used, they contributed only to each product group and the transportation of parts. Assemblers stood at two machines and moved between belt conveyors that could be put forward intermittently. A "moving vise," which could fix an object in an optional place, and a simple belt conveyor were installed. These two types of conveyors moved fitfully with the tact, enabling flexible coordination. Therefore, skilled workers did not perform fitting work directly on the conveyor but could do it at a stilling machine. Nähmaschinenfabrik Karlsruhe vorm. Haid & Neu introduced flow production using trolleys and chutes in 1925 and 1926. The unification of machine operating times was attempted to equalize work tact. Cutting speed was increased to avoid the accumulation of materials and processing machines were combined by chutes. Electric trucks were used for transportation from casting plants to the storehouse and overhead chain conveyors were used for transportation within the assembly plant. In 1927, Dürkoppwerke AG, which had highest rate of sewing machine production for business use, followed the case of Nähmaschinenfabrik Karlsruhe vorm. Haid & Neu (Bönig 1993a, S.349, 351, 353–354).

In Mundlos AG, 700 women workers produced 13% of the sewing machines by flow work (Duvigneau 1932, S.69). In Nähmaschinenfabrik Karlsruhe vorm. Haid & Neu, a 40%–60% increase in production volume was achieved compared with previous methods as a result of the entire reorganization of the plant. The time needed to produce one product was shortened from 90 days in 1925 to 16 days in 1926 and the number of workers who took charge of direct production decreased from 648 to 383. The number of transportation workers also decreased from 87 to only 6 (Oesterreocher 1927, S.39, 51).

However, the introduction of the flow production system in the manufacturing of sewing machines for business use greatly differed from the production of sewing machines for family use. For example, at H. Koch & Co. AG, and later, at Kochs Adlernähmaschinen Werke A.-G., there were restrictions on the flow production of sewing machines for business even in 1935. Since special machines and sewing machines for business use could not be sold in large numbers, production lots of their parts were small. Flow production was organized only in the assembly process under such conditions. Motivating workers in this plant to achieve higher efficiency was accomplished not by flow production but by implementing the individual piece wage system supplemented by premium wages, which were introduced after World War I (Bönig 1993a, S.358).

Introduction of the Flow Production System to the Office Machine Industry

In the office machine industry, almost every enterprise was forced to maintain business units at a high level (Deutscher Metallarbeiter-Verband 1932, S.101–102). However, many plants were too small to introduce flow production even in 1925. Of 172 plants, only eight business units employed over 500 employees. In many cases, these enterprises produced other precision machines such as bicycles, autocycles, and machine tools as well as typewriters and calculating machines (Bönig 1993a, S.359) and there were many mixed businesses.

In the office machine sector, cases relatively similar to sewing machine production could be observed. However, the flow production was not implemented as observed in the production of sewing machines. Implementing all production in plants using flow production with the inevitable advancement of work within a determined time frame was impossible. Plants using essential flow production first became dominant in the assembly of groups of parts and this production method was later implemented sufficiently in final assembly. Especially interesting auxiliary equipment was the rolling table installed on the table, which made it possible to turn partly finished goods in all directions and change direction on the plane. The supply of parts to assembly was performed by a small overhead chain conveyor (Duvigneau 1932, S.54).

At Wandler-Werke, A.-G., the flow work of office machines began late compared with bicycle and automobile production. This company introduced the flow production system using the moving stand for the first series of "Small Continental" small typewriters. However, it was limited only to assembly. At Mercedes Büromaschinen-Werke AG's Tella Plant, flow production came into question in all production and assembly processes in 1929. However, even in such cases, a relatively large amount of activity had to be left to trained, skilled workers. With the typewriter, special fitting work prevented the implementation of flow production unlike in subassembly, stand assembly, and final assembly. In manufacturing precision machines, such limitations in organizing flow production continued to be an influence until at least 1936 (Bönig 1993a, S.361–364).

Introduction of the Flow Production System to the Railway Car Building Industry

Finally, cases in the railway car building industry are examined. According to research by the German Metalworker Union in 1931, of the 76 departments researched, 28 (36.8%), 4 (5.3%), and 16 (21%) introduced flow work, conveyor work, and manufacturing in series, respectively (Deutscher Metallarbeiter-Verband 1932, S.123). Flow production meant a continuous moving belt and conveyor system was not suitable for this industry and was not regarded as recommendable due to the character of the work (Brady 1933, p.158). The size of the objects produced and the low production hindered continuous flow production (Bönig 1993a, S.554).

In this industry, flow production was organized by the "conveyor type of tact system" method. In the assembly process, conveyors moved parts to the next operating place and "came to a stop for a definite interval of time sufficiently long to permit (the necessary operations, and once more moved on)." Trucks, the framework, the floor, and other heavy parts were mounted as the car moved through the shop. Most of the work had been subdivided to the point at which a high degree of precision and finishing could be performed by unskilled workers without any more training than the ability to read and follow simple instructions concerning the highly routinized tasks to be performed.

As a result of such reorganization, the time needed to produce freight cars was shortened from 24 days by unit production to 15 and 1/2 days by introducing plant and personnel systematization and then further to 8 and 1/2 days by adding flow production methods (Brady 1933, p.158). At the National Railways (*Reichsbahn*) repair plant, the time needed to attach freight car brakes was shortened from 154 to 46 h by introducing flow production. In engine manufacturing, the necessary work time decreased from 1,500 min to 550 min and the time savings in assembly, painting, and packaging reached approximately 70% (Rocker 1927, S.33). In attaching breaks to railroad cars at the Grünewald plant of the National Railways, the work tact of flow production advancing intermittently took 45 min in 1928. The essential series of flow production was composed of nine workshops. At each series of flow production, 2 to 12 workers performed tasks and 47 persons worked as a whole (Lauke 1928, S.66).

Even after the introduction of flow production, the effort to shorten work tact using measures such as work process improvement and the further division of labor was achieved. In freight car production, work tact was about three hours at the beginning whereas it was initially shortened to 1.5 h in short-term development and finally to 20 min as the shortest work tact achieved to that point (Reichskuratorium für Wirtschaftlichkeit 1930, S.1102).

However, in the railway car building industry, transformation to mass production by introducing the flow production system encountered certain limits due to market conditions such as large changes in demand. For example, "anticipation of impending increases in certain types of the fall and winter traffic was the occasion in 1927 for the placing of an order on short notice which kept the fright-car plants busy overtime, while leaving the passenger car part of the industry completely idle." In addition, the introduction of the 2-class system in 1928 resulted in a sudden need for large members (8,000) of the cushion and their types of passenger coaches, and overburdened this portion of the industry, while leaving the freight car section idle. Thus, the effect of such policies largely offset the cost advantages arising from reorganization, which became a factor discouraging further endeavors along these lines" (Brady 1933, pp.159–160).

In this way, the introduction of the flow production system was attempted only in a limited number of sectors in the machinery industry under strict market conditions. Such market conditions can be seen particularly in the narrowness and intensity of changes in the domestic market. Cases in which systems that aimed at securing a certain level of flexibility to deal with demand fluctuations between products and obtaining some benefits of mass production, even with decreased production output under the market constraints, were more than in the electrical engineering and automobile industries.

The introduction of the flow production method was implemented later in the machinery industry than in the electrical engineering or automobile industry, which influenced the actual conditions of production reorganization and the effect of such efforts. Whereas mass production in the electrical engineering industry using the flow production system already prevailed in many sectors before 1927, the machinery industry first started on broader transformation to this production system during the last years of the rationalization movement in the 1920s. Therefore, as T. v. Freyberg pointed out, the actual difference between the industries would be greater than the results of the aforementioned research by the German Metalworker Union to certain degree (von Freyberg 1989, S.34–35). This point holds true for comparison with the automobile industry as well. In the machinery industry, the introduction of the flow production system could not achieve enough short-term effects and encountered great limitations under the pressures of the world economic crisis that began in 1929.

9.3.3 German Development of the Flow Production System and Its Limitations

As is clear from the preceding discussions, attempts to deploy the Ford system progressed in the processing and assembly industries. Originally, the introduction of this American production method premised the existence of specific products enabling mass production and market stability. However, as T. Siegel and Thomas von Freiberg pointed out paying particular attention to the machine tool industry, special German conditions represented by the existence of excess production capacity and a narrow and intensely changing market did not enable the acceptance of the modern American production system (Siegel and von Freyberg 1991, S.267). Even though there were differences between industrial sectors, generally, such market conditions aggressively influenced the introduction of the Ford system in the 1920s. In addition to the restricted sales potential determined by market circumstances, the lower concentration degree was also an important factor that brought limitations in the managerial rationalization movement, including introducing the flow production system in Germany (Hachtmann 1996, S.219). It restricted the production volume even in large enterprises.

The introduction of the flow production system could be observed only in certain large enterprises in the processing and assembly industries or in their most advanced plants, specific production processes, and product sectors, in particular departments in which standardization progressed and had a suitable character for mass production. Moreover, the introduction of the flow production system aimed at obtaining some of the benefits of mass production, even with decreased production output, and securing a certain level of flexibility for dealing with demand fluctuations between products, was attempted in many enterprises and plants instead of a method without production elasticity such as the Ford system. Regarding this point, T. v. Freyberg highlighted that restrictive German market conditions forced the secession from the ideals of the flow production method, highly integrated and mechanically combined, such as observed with the Ford system. Temporal economic integration of production processes was realized in the machinery and electrical engineering industries only to the degree to which the flexibility needed for production would not be sacrificed (Siegel and von Freyberg 1991, S.390). This point holds good for the automobile industry as well. Carl Köttgen stressed in 1928 that in the German industry, in contrast to the US, specialty in development could be observed in the pursuit of methods enabling an advantage of flow production even under smaller production volumes (Köttgen 1928a, S.12). Such methods observed in Germany at the time aimed at increasing the operating rate and realizing the economies of scale of mass production by securing lots on the basis of the production of multiple products in the same manufacturing line and flexibility for dealing with demand fluctuations between products by forming production on the basis of "universalization" instead of "specialization."

In this way, the shift to the flow production system was implemented according to Germany-specific conditions. In reality, in many cases, there were some variants of these methods. The Ford system itself was only, as it were, "an ideal type" that was regarded as a goal in Germany at the time. Such attempts were determined by market limitations during the stage of the first shift to mass production. As can be observed in the Ford Motor Company during the latter half of the 1920s to the beginning of the 1930s, the situation greatly differed from that in the US, where methods called "flexible mass production" were aimed at "greater flexibility in assembly rather than cost advantages through a single-purpose approach" and using a machine tool system that "could accommodate changes in design of the Ford automobile without totally tearing out machinery used to produce the old model" (Hounshell 1984).

Regarding conditions in the electrical industry, Heidrum Homburg highlighted that technical and organizational reforms were not implemented in all fields simultaneously and not only financial conditions but also the premises in terms of science, technique, and design, in part, personnel premise was insufficient. All changes were connected to many years of preparatory activities and their "ripeness" under production conditions was only gradually realized after several months or years of the first actual attempt. In this way, the experimental character of rationalization efforts in the 1920s was a prominent feature (Homburg 1991, S.525–526). Tilla Siegel stressed if the evident symbol of "technical rationalization," that is, the belt conveyor, and the scientific selection of the workforce were first introduced by the work office to Siemens plants relatively late compared with organizations broadly based on Taylor's principle and production management, it was due to a lack of not intention but possibility (Siegel and von Freyberg 1991, S.311).

Such restrictive market conditions greatly changed with the militarization of the economy and the war economy during the Nazi era. Under this new situation, the introduction of the Ford system and the shift to mass production were more aggressively driven (see Chap. 12).

9.4 Limitations on the Deployment of the Ford System and Their Influence on the National Economy

Building upon the foregoing examinations, finally, the influence of limitations on the deployment of the Ford system, particularly in the automobile industry, and on the development of Germany's national economy is considered.

Generally, the economic effect of mass production in the durable consumer goods industries such as the automobile industry on many related industrial sectors and the overall national economy was very large. Considering the characteristics of each industry from the perspective of production flow and process, in the processing and assembly industries such as the automobile, electrical, and machinery industries, many types of materials were at the starting point of production and were processed and assembled and finally a single product was completed (Sakamoto 1978, pp.48–49). In this type of industry, mass production at large enterprises of the last process (for instance, final assembly manufacturers in the automobile industry) can create a great economic effect on many industrial sectors at the preceding process in the production flow by creating demand. In addition, decisive elements and the national economic effectiveness of mass production were much bigger in consumer goods departments than in producer goods departments and historically, mass production in the consumer goods industries provided the initial foundation for the shift to the mass production of producer goods (Mottek et al. 1975, S.31). Therefore, among the processing and assembly industries, it was not producer goods such as machine tools but consumer goods such as automobiles that could create a much larger economic effect of mass production. Furthermore, the wider the range related to other industries, the larger the economic effect of mass production in certain industries caused by creating demand in the related industrial sectors. At this point, the effects of mass production in the automobile industry were larger than those in the electrical engineering industry. Thus, generally, mass production in the automobile industry played a decisive role in the establishment of the mass production economic system upon which the market foundation enabling mass production could be built through such relationships between industries.

It was in the US that such economic development was first realized. In the US, the reorganization of industries progressed around World War I and the railway and coal mining industries declined. Instead of these departments, the automobile, oil, and electric power industries became key industries. Whereas the development of American industry was based on relationship between "railway, iron and steel, and coal mining" before World War I, it changed to a system based on the relationship between the "automobile, iron and steel, and oil and electric power" in the 1920s (Shiomi et al. 1986, p.139). In contrast, the delay of mass production in Germany's automobile industry not only became a restrictive factor for mass production in the machinery industry but also made machine production costs higher, which came to be limiting factors for rationalization in the electrical engineering and the automobile industries themselves. Such negative influences can be observed in the chemical industry as well. One important characteristic of the industrial composition of German capitalism in the Weimar era was that while the development of the heavy and chemical industries progressed, the growth of new industries such as the automobile industry was weak. The delay in the development of new product fields while expanding old product sectors using negative rationalization at IG Farben as the largest core of capital in the German chemical industry can be regarded as an expression of the influence of such industrial structural characteristics (Kudo 1976, p.182).

In this way, during the Weimar Republic, the influence of the mass production delay in the automobile industry, which should take leadership of the development of mass production in many industrial sectors under the very strict market conditions at home and abroad, was tremendously large. In Germany, a system in which driving capital accumulation based on mass production systems such as the Ford system itself created enough of a market base that it enabled mass production could not be built as it was in the US. Limitations on the rationalization movement in this period were indicated at this point.

Attempts to overcome these mass production delays and the economic development system upon which they were based were aggressively driven by state involvement in the economy and under tremendous changes in market conditions during the Nazi era from 1933 to 1945. In this period, rationalization in the field of labor organization using the REFA system was driven by the involvement of state institutions in REFA and under a lack of workers. Therefore, the research topics to be further analyzed are changes in the business management of German enterprises during the Nazi era. This will be considered in Part III.

References

Adelt R (1930) Die Krise in der deutschen Personenautomobil-Industrie. Thesis (doctoral), Ludwig-Maximilians-Universität zu München, München

AFAB (1928) Grundlagen und Richtlinien Gewerkschaflicher Rationalisierungspolitik. Bund der Industrieangestellten Österreichs, Wien

Allgemeine Elektricitäts-Gesellschaft (1925) Geschäftsbericht über das Geschäftsjahr vom 1. Oktober 1924 bis 30.September 1925. Allgemeine Elektricitäts-Gesellschaft, Berlin

Allegemeine Elektricitäts-Gesellschaft (1926) Geschäftsbericht über das Geschäftsjahr vom 1. Oktober 1925 bis 30.September 1926. Allgemeine Elektricitäts-Gesellschaft, Berlin

Allgemeine Elektricitäts-Gesellschaft (1927) Geschäftsbericht über das Geschäftsjahr vom 1. Oktober 1926 bis 30.September 1927. Allgemeine Elektricitäts-Gesellschaft, Berlin

Allgemeine Elektricitäts-Gesellschaft (1928) Geschäftsbericht über das Geschäftsjahr vom 1. Oktober 1927 bis 30.September 1928. Allgemeine Elektricitäts-Gesellschaft, Berlin

Arnold HL (1914) Ford Methods and the Ford Shops, (IX). In: Eng Mag 48(3):338–366.

Bauer O (1931) Rationalisierung und Fehlrationalisierung. Wiener Volksbuchhandlung, Wien

Berkenkopf P (1933) Die deutsche Automobilindustrie in der Krise. In: Wirtschaftsdienst 18(2):46–50

Blaich F (1973) Die „Fehlrationalisierung“ in der Deutschen Automobilindustrie 1924 bis 1929. In: Tradition 18:18–34

Bönig J (1993a) Die Einführung von Fließbandarbeit in Deutschland bis 1933. Zur Geschichte einer Sozialinnovation, Teil I. Lit, Münster, Hamburg

Bönig J (1993b) Die Einführung von Fließbandarbeit in Deutschland bis 1933. Zur Geschichte einer Sozialinnovation, Teil II. Lit, Münster, Hamburg

Brady RA (1933) The rationalization movement in German industry: a study in the evolution of economic planning. University of California Press, Berkeley, California

Braun HJ (1991) Automobilindustrie in der USA und Deutschland in den 20er Jahren—ein Vergleich. In: Pohl H (Hrsg) Traditionspfleg in der Automobilindustrie. F. Steiner, Stuttgart, S.183–200

Bünge P (1928) Das Fließband im Landmaschinenbau. In: Das Industrieblatt 33(49):VIII–VIV

Der deutsche Volkswirt (1933) Automobilbau 1913–1933. In: Der deutsche Volkswirt 7(19): I–XIX

Deutscher Metallarbeiter-Verband (1932) Die Rationalisierung in der Metallindustrie. Zusammengestellt und bearbeitet nach Erhebungen des Vorstandes der Deutschen Metallarbeiter-Verband. Verlagsgesellschaft des Deutschen Metallarbeiter-Verbandes, Berlin

Die Rote Fahne (1926) Die Arbeit „fließt“. In: Die Rote Fahne 9(90):18.4.1926.

DNA (1957) Die deutsche Normung, 1917–1957. Oskar Zach, Berlin

Dominik H (1929) Das Schaltwerk-Fabrikhochbau und Hallenbau—der Siemens=Schuckertwerke A.=G. S. Hirzel, Berlin

Dransfeld H (1929) Vacum Cleaner Manufacture in the Siemens-Schuckert Works. In: Am Machinist 71(23):923–926

Dresler A, Lambert N (1988) Die Arbeit. In: Schirmbeck P (Hrsg) 》Morgen kommst Du nach Amerika 《.Erinnerungen an die Arbeit bei Opel 1917–1987. J. H. W. Dietz, Berlin, Bonn, S.168–192
Duvigneau G (1932) Untersuchungen zur Verbreitung der Fließarbeit in der deutschen Industrie. Eine wirtschaftlich-technische Studie. Dissertation, Technische Hochschule Breslau
Etzold H (1988) Die Entwicklung der Produktivkräfte in der Industrie. In: Institut für Wirtschaftsgeschichte der Akademie der Wissenschaften der DDR, Berthold R et al. (Hrsg) (1988) Produktivkräfte in Deutschland von 1917/18 bis 1945. Akadermie Verlag, Berlin, S.36–223
Feldenkirchen W (2003) „Vom Guten das Beste". Von Daimler und Benz zur DaimlerChrysler AG. Band 1, Die ersten 100 Jahre (1883–1983), 1. Aufl., Herbig, München
Feldmann GD (1999) Die Deutsche Bank und die Automobilindustrie. In: Zeitschrift für Unternehmensgeschichte 44(1):2–14
Ferrari F (1928) Fließfertigung im Elektritzitätszählerbau. In: Maschinenbau 7(16):760–765
Flik R (2001a) Automobilindustrie und Motorisierung in Deutschland bis 1939. In: Boch R (Hrsg) Geschichte und Zukunft der deutschen Automobilindustrie. Tagung in Rahmen der "Chemnitzer Begegnungen" 2000. F. Steiner, Stuttagart, S.49–84
Flik R (2001b) Von Ford lernen? Automobilbau und Motorisierung in Deutschland bis 1933. Böhlau, Köln, Weimar, Wien
Gelbsattel H (1926) Die "Fließarbeit" in der elektrotechnischen Industrie. In: Z Betriebswirt 3:631–633
Gottl-Ottlienfeld F v (1926) Fordismus. Über Industrie und technische Vernunft. 3. Aufl., Verlag von Gustav Fischer, Jena
Hachtmann R (1989) Industriearbeit im 》Dritten Reich《. Untersuchungen zu den Lohn- und Arbeitsbedingungen in Deutschland 1933–1945. Vandenhoeck & Ruprecht, Göttingen
Hachtmann R (1996) Industriarbeiterschaft und Rationalisierung 1900 bis 1945. Bemerkungen zum Forschungsstand. In: Jahrbuch für Wirtschaftsgeschichte 37(1):211–258
Hänecke H (1927) Fließarbeit im deutschen Maschinenbau. In: Maschinenbau 6(4):157–162
Hanfland C (1929) Der neuzeitliche Maschinenbau. Ein Handbuch zum Studium und zum Nachschlagen. Bd. 2, Verlag der Literaturwerke "Minerva" R.M. Lippold, Leipzig
Herrmann K (1985) Ackergiganten. Technik, Geschichte und Geschichten. Westermann, Braunschweig
Hinrichs P (1981) Um Seele des Arbeiter. Arbeitspsychologie, Industrie- und Betriebssoziologie in Deutchland 1871–1945. Pahl-Rugenstein, Köln
Hinrichs P, Peter L (1976) Industrieller Friede? Arbeitswissenschaft, Rationalisierung und Arbeiterbewegung in der Weimarer Republik. Pahl-Rugenstein, Köln
Hofer M (1929) Der Landmaschinenbau Heinrich Lanz A.G., Mannheim. Organisation Verlagsgesellschaft M. B. H., Berlin
Hoffmann R (1930) Daimler=Benz Aktiengesellschaft Stutgart=Untertürkheim. Organisation Verlagsgesellschaft, Berlin
Homburg H (1983) Scientific management and personel policy in the modern German enterprise 1918–1939. In: Gospel HF, Littler CR (eds) Managerial strategies and industrial relations. Heinemann Educational Books, London, pp 137–156
Homburg H (1991) Rationalisierung und Industriearbeit: Arbeitsmarkt—Management —Arbeiterschaft im Siemens-Konzern Berlin 1900–1939. Haude & Spener, Berlin
Hounshell DA (1984) From the American system to mass production, 1800–1932. The Johns Hopkins University Press, Baltimore
Hughes TP (2004) American genesis. A century of invention and technological enthusiasm 1870–1970. 2nd edition. The University of Chicago Press, Chicago
Iltgen G (1929) Die Anwendung der Normung bei den Lokomotiven der Deutschen Reichsbahn. In: International Management Congress (ed) L'organisation scientique du travail. IVe Congres International. Comité national de l'organisation française, Paris, pp. CXXV-1-CXXV-4
Jahresberichte der Gewerbeaufsichtsbeamten und Berghörden für das Jahr 1927 (1928a) Jahresberichte der Gewerbeaufsichtsbeamten und Berghörden für das Jahr 1927, Bd. I, Preußen, Reichsamt des Innern, Berlin, S.1–703

Jahresberichte der Gewerbeaufsichtsbeamten und Berghörden für das Jahr 1927 (1928b) Jahresberichte der Gewerbeaufsichtsbeamten und Berghörden für das Jahr 1927, Bd. II, Berlin, Reichsamt des Innern, Berlin, Bayern (2), 2. V-LXXIII, S.1–270

Jahresberichte der Gewerbeaufsichtsbeamten und Berghörden für das Jahr 1927 (1928c) Jahresberichte der Gewerbeaufsichtsbeamten und Berghörden für das Jahr 1927, Bd. II, Berlin, Reichsamt des Innern, Berlin, Sachsen (3), 3. S.1–349

Jurthe E (1931) Die Rationalisierung der Lackierverfahren des Automobilbaues der Adlerwerke. In: Automobiltechnische Zeitschrift 34(27):601–604

Keiser G, Benning B (1931) Kapitalbildung und Investitionen in der deutschen Volkswirtschaft 1924 bis 1928. In: Institut für Konjunkturforschung, *Vierteljahrheft zur Konjunkturforschung*, Sonderheft 22. Reimar Hobbing, Berlin, S.1–210

Kinkel H, Feill W (1963) Klein- und Kleinstmaschinen. In: Schweder B (Hrsg.), Forschen und Schaffen. Der Anteil der AEG an die Entwicklung der Deutschen Technik, Allgemeine Elektricitäts-Gesellschaft, Berlin, S.300–308

Klein F (1929) Die Anwendung der Normung bei den Wagen der Deutschen Reichsbahn. In: International Management Congress (ed) L'organisation scientique du travail. IVe Congres International. Comité national de l'organisation française, Paris, pp. CXXXVI-CXXVI-4

Kölb W (1953) Das Elektromotorenwerk in Neustadt/Saale. In: Siemens-Schuckertwerke (Hrsg) Die Entwicklung der Starkstromtechnik. Berlin, Erlangen, S.527–535

Köttgen C (1928a) Die allgemeinen Grundlagen der Fließarbeit. In: Zentralblatt für Gewerbehygiene und Unfallverhüttung, Beiheft 12, "Fließarbeit," 1–17

Köttgen C (1928b) Das fließende Band. In: Industrie- und Handelskammer zu Berlin (Hrsg) Die Bedeutung der Rationalsierung für das deutschen Wirtschaftsleben. Stilke, Berlin, S.77–125

Köttgen C (1928c), Grundsätzliches über Fließarbeit. In: Maschinenbau 7(23):1126–1127

Kroth KA (1928) Das Werk Opel. Inseldruckerei, Berlin

Kudo A (1976) Sotaiteki anteiki no Doitsu kagaku kogyo (German chemical, 1925-1929). In: Shakaigaku Kenkyu (J Soc Sci) 28(1):144–203

Kugler A (1985) Arbeitsorganisation und Produktionstechnologie der Adam Opel Werke (von 1900 bis 1929). Wissenschaftszentrum, Berlin

Kugler A (1987) Von der Werkstatt zum Fließband. Etappen der frühen Automobilproduktion in Deutschland. In: Geschichte und Gesellschaft 13(1):304–339

Lang R (1919) Gruppenfabrikation. In: Daimler Werkzeitung 1(1):4–5

Lauke HL (1928) Die Vornahme der Leistungsabstimmung bei Einführung fließender Fertigung. In: Betriebs-Technik (5):65–67

Laux JM (1992) The European Automobil Industry. Twayne Publishers, New York

Ledermann S (1928) Fließarbeit in der Zählerfabrik der AEG. In: Werkstattstechnik 22(17):448–482

Ledermann F (1933) Fehlrationalisierung—der Irrweg der deutschen Automobilindustrie seit der Stabilisierung der Mark, Fehlrationalisierung C. E. Poeschel, Stutgart

Link SJ (2020) Forging Global Fordism. Nazi Germany, Soviet Russia and the Contest over the Industrial Order. Princeton University Press, Princeton, New Jersey

Löwisch R (2011) Auto-Mobilität. Wie der Mensch das Laufen verlernte 500,000 v. Chr. bis heute. Monsenstein & Vannerdat, Münster

Ludwig H (1932) Die Arbeitlosigkeit in der deutschen Automobilindustrie. In: Schriften des Vereins für Sozialpolitik 185(2):121–154

Lüth E (1936) G.M. Pfaff A.-G., Kaiserlautern. J. J. Arnd, Leipzig

Lutz M (2022) Elektroindustrie. In: Boldorf M (Hrsg) Deutsche Wirtschaft im Ersten Weltkrieg. De Gruyter, Berlin, S.227–249

Mäckbach F, Kienzle O (1926) Fliessarbeit. Beitrage zu Ihrer Einführung. VDI-Verlag, Berlin

Maschinenbau (1926) Fließarbeit. In: Maschinenbau 8(15):727

Maurer H (1936) Das Zusammenschlußproblem in der deutschen Automobilindustire mit Berücksichtigung der Auto-Union AG. Buchdrückerei Meier & Cie, Schauffhausen

Mirus RR (1929) Allgemeine Elektricität-Gesellschaft. Die Organisation der AEG-Zählerfabrik. Organisation Verlagsgesellschaft, Berlin

Moellendorff Uv (1929a) Fließende Fertigung von Rundfunkgeräten. In: AEG-Mitteilungen 23(9):576–581

Moellendorff Uv (1929b) Wechselnde Fließarbeit. In: Der Werksleiter 3(16):395–398

Mori S (1965) Keiei kanri soron (The general theory of management), 2nd new edition. Chikura shobo, Tokyo

Mottek H, Becker W, Schröter A (1975) Wirtschaftsgeschichte Deutschlannds, Ein Grundriß, Bd.III, Von der Zeit der Bismarchschen Reichsgrndung 1871 bis zur Niederlage des faschistischen deutschen Imperialismus 1945, 2. Aufl., VEB Deutscher Verlag der Wissenschaften, Berlin

Müller W (1927) Allgemeine Grundlagen und Arbeitsvorbereitung im Landmaschinenbau. In: Maschinenbau 6(10):509–512

National Automobile Chamber of Commerce (1927) Facts and figures of the automobile industry. National Automobile Chamber of Commerce, New York

Nishimuta Y (1987) Daimler=Benz A.G. no seiritsu (The establoshment of Daimler-Benz A.G.). In: Shakaikagaku Kenkyu (J Soc Sci) 38(6):1–40

Nishimuta Y (1999) Nachizumu to Doitsu jidosha kogyo (Nazism and German automobile industry). Yuhikaku, Tokyo

Oesterreocher K (1927) Einige Rationalisierungsmaßnahmen und ihre Ergebniss. In: Reichskuratorium für Wirtschaftlichkeit (Hrsg) Die Vorträge der RKW-Tagung vom 15. März 1927. Reichskuratorium für Wirtschaftlichkeit, Berlin, S.535–547

Ohashi S (1999) Doitsu keizai minshushugironshi (History of economic democracy theory in Germany). Chuo keizaisha, Tokyo

Osram GmbH (1924) Geschäftsbericht 1924. Osram GmbH, München

Pierer C (2011) Die Bayerischen Motoren Werke bis 1933. Ein Unternehmensgründung in Krieg. Inflation und Weltwirtschaftskrise. Oldenbourg, München

Radkau J (2008) Technik in Deutschland vom 18. jahrhundert bis zur Heute. Campus, Frankfurt am Main

Rauecker B (1925) Wege und Möglichkeiten der Rationalisierung. In: Die Arbeit 2(12):743–751

Rauecker B (1926) Rationalisierung und Sozialpolitik. Sieben Stäbe-Verlag, Berlin

Reichskuratorium für Wirtschaftlichkeit (1930) Handbuch der Rationalisierung. Zweite, unveränderte Auflage. Spaeth & Linde, Berlin

Rocker R (1927) Die Rationalisierung der Wirtschaft und die Arbeiterklasse. Verlag "Der Syndikalist" F. Kater, Berlin

Rodgers DT (1998) Atlantic Croosings. Social Politics in a Pregressive Age. Harvard University Press, Cambridge, Massachusetts

Sakamoto K (1978) Gendai kyodai kigyo to dokusen (Modern huge enterprise and monopoly). Aoki shoten, Tokyo

Schalldach E (1930) Rationalisierungsmaßnahmen der Nachinflationszeit im Urteil der deutschen freien Gewerkschaften. G. Fischer, Jena

Scharll R (1963) Der elektrischer Antrieb von Werkzeugmaschinen. In: Schweder B (Hrsg) Forschen und Schaffen. Der Anteil der AEG an die Entwicklung der Deutschen Technik. Allgemeine Elektricitäts-Gesellschaft, Berlin, S.176–180

Schiffer C (1928) Die ökonomische und sozialpolitische Bedeutung der industriellen Rationalisierungsbestrebung. G. Braun, Karlsruhe

Schlesinger G (1926) Arbeitsstätten des deutschen Automobilbaues. In: Werkstattstechnik 20(20):608–635

Schmidt K (1927) Die deutsche Automobil-Industrie und ihre Leistungsfähigkeit auf dem Weltmarkt. Thesis, Hessische Ludwigs Universität zu Gießen, Gießen

Schmidt B (1933) Wege zur Verbesserung der Produktions- und Wettbewerbslage der deutschen Personenkraftwagen-Industrie. Diss. Technische Hochschule Darmstadt, Darmstadt

Schmidt D (1993) Weder Ford noch Taylor. Zu Rhetorik und Praxis der Rationalisierung in den Zwanziger Jahren am Beispiel dreier Siemens Werke. Universität Bremen, Bremen

Schultz F (1927) Rationalisierung in der Motoren-industrie. In: Reichskuratorium für Wirtschaftlichkeit (Hrsg) Die Vorträge der RKW-Tagung vom 15. März 1927. Reichskuratorium für Wirtschaftlichkeit, Berlin, S.10–16

Schulz-Mehrin (1927) Kosten bei Einzel-, Reihen- und Fließfertigung. In: Maschinenbau 6(16):813–818

Seherr-Thoss HCGv (1979) Die deutsche Automobilindutrie. Eine Dokumenten vom 1886 bis 1979, 2., korrigierte und erweiterte Auflage, Deutsche Verlags-Anstalt, Stuttgart

Shiomi H (1978) Gendai tairyo seisan taiseiron (Modern mass production system). Moriyama shoten, Tokyo

Shiomi H, Mizota S, Tanigchi A, Miyazaki S (1986) Amerika biggu bijinesu seiritushi (History of big business in the United States). Toyo keizai shinposha, Tokyo

Siegel T, von Freyberg T (1991) Industrielle Rationalisierung unter dem Nationalsozialismus. Campus, Frankfurt am Main, New York

Siegrist H (1981) Vom Familienbetrieb zum Managerunternehmen. Vandenhoeck & Ruprecht, Göttingen

Siemens & Halske Aktiengesellschaft (1925) Dreigster Geschäftsbericht vom 1. Oktober 1924 bis 30. September 1925. Siemens & Halske Aktiengesellschaft, Berlin

Siemens & Halske Aktiengesellschaft (1926) Einunddreigster Geschäftsbericht vom 1. Oktober 1925 bis 30. September 1926. Siemens & Halske Aktiengesellschaft, Berlin

Stahlmann M (1993) Die Erste Revolution in der Autoindustrie. Management und Arbeitspolitik von 1900–1940. Campus Frankfurt am Main, New York

Stahlmann M (1994) Von der Werkstatt zur Lean-Production. Arbeitsmanagement und Arbeitsbeziehungen im sozialen Wandel. In: Zeitschrift für Unternehmensgeschichte 39(3):219–243

Statistisches Reichssamt (1929) Statistisches Jahrbuch für das Deutsche Reich 1928. Verlag von Reimar Hobbing, Berlin

Statistisches Reichssamt (1932) Statistisches Jahrbuch für das Deutsche Reich 1931. Verlag von Reimar Hobbing, Berlin

Stollberg G (1981) Die Rationalisierungsdebatte 1908–1933: Freie Gewerkschaften zwischen Mitwirkung und Gegenweh. Campus Verlag, Frankfurt am Main, New York

Strunk P (2000) Die AEG. Aufstieg und Niedergang einer Industrielegende, 2. Auflage, Nicolai, Berlin

Takahashi H (1993) Doitsu kikai kogyo gorika katei (Process of rationalization in the German machine industry). In: Takeoka Y, Takahashi H, Nakaoka T (eds) Sin gijyutsu no donyu (The introduction of new technology). Dobunkan, Tokyo, pp.25–48

The Bureau of Foreign and Domestic Commerce (1930) Statistical Abstract of the United States 1930. G.P.O, Washington, D.C.

Thieme C (2004) Daimler-Benz zwischen Anpassungskrise, Verdrängungswettbewerb und Rüstungs-Konjunktur 1919–1936, 1. Aufl., Vaihingen/Enz: IPa, Stuttgart

Trieba V, Mentrup U (1983) Entwicklung der Arbeitswissnschaft in Deutschland: Rationalisierungspolitik der deutschen Wirtschaft bis zum Faschismus. Minerva, München

von Freyberg T (1989) Industrielle Rationalisierung in der Weimarer Republik: Untersucht an Beispielen aus dem Maschinenbau und der Elektroindustrie. Campus, Frankfurt am Main, New York

Vorstand des Deutschen Metallarbeiter-Verband (Hrsg) (1930) Die Frauenarbeit in der Metallindustrie. Verlagsgesellschaft des Deutschen Metallarbeiter-Verbandes, Stuttgart

Vrang WL (1927) Fließarbeit in der Siemens-Werken. In: Siemens-Jahrbuch: 409–432

Walcher J (1925) Ford order Marx. Die praktische Lösung der sozialen Frage. Neuer Deutscher Verlag, Berlin

Weiss H (1926) Rationalisierung und Arbeiterklasse: Zur Rationalisierung der deutschen Industrie. Führer-Verlag, Berlin

Werkstattstechnik (1926) Massenfertigung in einer Traktorenfabrik. In: Werkstattstechnik 20(11):358–364

Witte IM (1924) Taylor, Gilbreth, Ford. Gegenwartsfragen der amerikanischen und europäischen Arbeitswissenschaft. R. Oldenbourg, München, Berlin
Witte IM (1930) Ford, Fordismus. In: Giese F (Hrsg) Handwörterbuch der Arbeitswissenschaft, Bd. 1, C. Marhard, Halle, Spalte 1856–1865
Woldt R (1925) Die Heutige Krise in der deutschen Betriebsorganisation. In: Gewerkschafts-Archiv 3(4):186–192.
Wolf J (1929) Fließarbeit in der Herstelleung elektrisch beheitzer Bügeleisen. In: Der Werksleiter 3(10):251–256
Zschacke FA (1931) Selbsttätige Förder und Eintragvorrichtungen für Kühl= und Brennöfen. In: Der Werksleiter 5(15/16):317–322

Chapter 10
Changes in Organizational Structure: The Case of IG Farben

Abstract This chapter analyzes organizational reform in a large German company, IG Farben. In the 1920s, not only were rationalization efforts implemented, but organizational structure reform was also pursued. Enterprise concentration in the form of trust and consistent rationalization, production concentration and specialization based on product type, and the regrouping of production organizations and diversification have made organizational structure a critical problem. This chapter examines two stages in the organizational reform of IG Farben from a comparative viewpoint, with Du Pont as the leading chemical company in the United States. How organizational reform in this German company was implemented and why such attempts encountered limitations (in contrast to Du Pont's success) are clarified.

Keywords Central office · Committee organizatio Decentralized centralization · Diversification · Divisional structure · Enterprise concentration · IG Farben · Rationalization

Business management in Germany experienced significant changes in the process of implementing rationalization measures during the 1920s. In addition to these changes, organizational structure reforms associated with enterprise concentration in the form of trusts, rationalization development, and business diversification and the way rational organizational structures managed, controlled, and coordinated activities in large enterprises created by consolidation became important problems. Moreover, in enterprises that adopted a diversification strategy, difficult managerial issues inevitably arose under functional structures as diversification progressed. IG Farben pursued diversification and was forced to pursue organizational reforms to resolve such managerial problems. In the United States (US), organizational reforms such as those related to divisional structures were performed. This can typically be observed at Du Pont. Therefore, organizational structure reforms are essential to consider from the perspective of comparison with US experiences.

This chapter clarifies changes in organizational structure with business rationalization and diversification in Germany. The case of IG Farben is compared with the case of Du Pont, a pioneering company that adopted a divisional structure in

T. Yamazaki, *A History of German Business*,
https://doi.org/10.1007/978-981-96-8476-2_10

the 1920s. First, Sect. 10.1 considers organizational reforms at IG Farben and their factors. Following this, Sects. 10.2 and 10.3 address organizational reforms in the first and second stages. Based on these discussions, Sect. 10.4 clarifies the significance and limitations of the organizational reforms at IG Farben.

10.1 Organizational Reforms at IG Farben and Their Factors

When examining the development of organizations and decision-making systems at IG Farben during the interwar period, three stages were observed, including (1) organizational reform based on the "decentralized centralism" principle (compromise of the organizational plans of founders Carl Duisberg and Carl Bosch), (2) from the end of the 1920s to the beginning of the 1930s, organizational change to cope with global economic crises and organizational defects during the first stage (creation of a divisional organizational structure), and (3) polycentrism as a result of rapid expansion in the 1930s (Plumpe 1990, S.154, 163; regarding the plans of the organization of IG Farben and their discussions between Carl Duisberg and Carl Bosch, see Fischer 1979). This chapter examines organizational changes during the first and second stages.

As considered in Chap. 7, enterprise concentration in 1925 led to the foundation of IG Farben and the subsequent rationalization and transformation of strategy were aimed primarily at the thorough implementation of concentration and specialization based on product type in legacy departments represented by the dye field and reorganization of the business structure by diversification. Organizational reforms in this company were implemented as countermeasures to manage problems caused by these two changes. Helmut Tammnen highlighted that the rationalization of the legacy production field and expansion of new production areas were related to strengthening superimposed organizational fields (Tammnen 1978, S.29).

10.2 Organizational Reform in the First Stage and Its Characteristics

10.2.1 Production Concentration and Specialization Based on Product Type and Regrouping of Production Organizations

Organizational reform in the first stage was performed as a countermeasure to managerial problems caused by the concentration and specialization of production based on product type. Such concentration and specialization meant dividing markets according to products from the perspective of "division of labor based on contracts" and allotting production on the basis of such principles. Each plant that continued to exist without ceasing its operations was dispersed according to product or region, and groups of plants that produced specific products or related products were formed in primary regions. Therefore, the central task for each plant, scattered in regions, was to formulate its own manufacturing plan for each region and analyze the most favorable production conditions. The improvement of initiatives on the level of these operating departments by management decentralization through a broad delegation of authority regarding autonomous management activities became an effective means for making plans according to products and executing production on that basis.

As Robert Alexander Brady stated that although Vereinigte Stahlwerke was organized vertically, the main principle guiding decentralized management was horizontal integration. Such integration made it easy "to avoid duplication of facilities and to prevent undue expansion along any particular line within any individual plant" as well as offered "a basis for securing maximum flexibility and individual initiative in the management of the separate plants" (Brady 1933, p.121).

The progress of horizontal integration promoted management decentralization. Realizing effective production under the most advantageous conditions by coordinating production schedules and promoting initiatives of different plants located in various places was regarded as the central responsibility of management. Thus, the separation of production locations with various production plans in different regions required a mix of centralization and regional autonomy. As a result, "centralized, vertically formed according to product management" and "regional, horizontal management of individual production locations" were promoted (Etzold 1988, S.103).

Four (later, five) regionally divided groups called "*Betriebsgemeinschaft*" ("the Operating Community") were formed on the basis of Duisberg's principle "decentralized centralization" to realize such a management system. Although central management held the final authority in all policy matters, all routine factory problems were relayed to one of the four subsidiary managerial groups. Each group enjoyed complete autonomy within the rules established by the central office (Brady 1933, p.237; Tammnen 1978, S.21–22; Plumpe 1991, p.225). Whereas financial matters, patents, raw material purchases, and commercial intelligence were to be dealt with centrally, each individual plant was responsible for its own technical direction, labor, and (initially) sales (Waller 1928, S.18). The decision-making concerning production, research and development (R&D), and many other functions remained in the hands of the work groups (Abelshauser et al. 2004, p.220; Stokes 2007, S.233).

Thus, a system of management based on "decentralized centralization" was established by the creation of operating communities in each region wherein enterprises that were part of the 1925 fusion were located (Enquete Ausschuβ 1928, S.443; Hayes 1987, p.20; Tammnen 1978, S.21–22). Founding these groups was aimed at achieving savings in various fields, such as avoiding unneeded duplication, facilitating improvements in technological aspects, administration, and holding and managing inventory [*BASF Archiv*, I.G. C0/2, Eidesstattliche Erklarung von Ernst Struss über die Betriebs gemeinschaften und die Sparten, S.3 (Document No. NI-9487 of the Nuremberg Trials)].

The following regional operating groups were established corresponding to the concentration and specialization of production based on product type: (1) the Upper Rhine, (2) the Middle Rhine, (3) the Lower Rhine, and (4) Middle Germany.

(1) **The Upper Rhine Operating Community** (with a headquarters in Ludwigshafen where many BASF plants were located).

Intermediate chemicals, dye, and organic chemicals closely related to dye were produced in the beginning. However, its primary activity moved to synthetic ammonia and nitrogen fertilizer. In addition, synthetic tannin, solvent, and paints were produced.

(2) **The Middle Rhine Operating Community** (with a headquarters in Frankfurt am Main where many Hoechst plants were located)

The primary products of this group included pharmaceuticals, vat dyes, and all chemical products made with acetylene. Furthermore, solvents, adhesive agents, paints, synthetic tannin, nitrogen fertilizer, other nitrogen products, insecticides, and cellophane were handled.

(3) **The Lower Rhine Operating Community** (with a headquarters in Leverkusen where many Bayer and Weiler-ter Meer plants were located).

This group produced primarily dyes. In addition, insecticides, intermediate chemicals, antiseptics, pharmaceuticals, solvents, adhesive agents, paints, and film and photographic products were produced.

(4) **The Middle Germany Operating Community** (composed of two subgroups of Wolfen-Bitterfeld and Frankfurt am Main where Griesheim Elektron, Köln-Rotweil, and Agfa plants were located).

In the Wolfen-Bitterfeld subgroup, light metal, magnesium in particular, was produced in Bitterfeld. In Wolfen, photographic film, printing paper, and artificial silk were produced. In addition, organic chemicals, solvent, adhesive agents, paints, nitrogen fertilizer, and other nitrogen products were manufactured. In the Frankfurt am Main subgroup, compressed gas, autogenous welding machines, gas cutting machines, organic chemicals, and inorganic chemicals were produced [*Hoechst Archiv*, IG200, Betriebsgemeinschaft "Mittelrhein" neu (8.3.1927), S.1; *Hoechst Archiv*, IG200, Betriebsgemeinschaft Mittelrhein, S.1, *Hoechst Archiv*, IG194, Über Struktur und wirtschaftliche Verflechtung der westdeutschen Werke der I.G. Farbenindustrie Aktiengesellschaft, S.3–4; *Hoechst Archiv*, IG194, Ausführliche Geschichte des Technischen Ausschusses, S.11–14; *Hoechst Archiv*, IG194, Eichwerk Heinz Aufzeichnungen über Gründung und, Entwicklung, Organisation und Mitglieder von TEA-Hauptgruppe-2-Kommissionen der I.G. Farbenindustrie A.G., Bd.I (Frankfurt 1943), S.11–13; *Hoechst Archiv*, IG194, Gründung und Entwicklung der I.G. (Oktober 1936); Plumpe 1990, S.142; Tammnen 1978, S.21; Feldenkirchen

1987, pp.436–437; Haber 1971, pp.339–340; Chandler 1990, pp.569–571; Schneckenburger 1988, S.33–34]. According to an internal document of Bayer, the purpose of establishing the Lower Rhine Operating Community was to integrate the production locations of IG Farben downstream of the Rhine River to achieve rational production in primary production locations and production managed from a unified viewpoint. [*Bayer Archiv*, 004/C-19, Richtlinien für eine Fusion der I.G. und für die Bildung einer Betriebsgemeinshaft der Farbenfabriken vorm. Friedr. Bayer & Co. (Leverkusen) mit den Chemischen Fabriken vorm. Weiler-ter Meer (Uerdingen), S.2].

IG Farben decided to separate Maingau plants from the Middle German Operating Community and integrate them into the Middle Rhine Operating Community on November 22, 1929. Furthermore, plants producing photographs, artificial silk, and plastics were separated from the Middle Rhine Operating Community and included in the newly founded Berlin Operating Community. Agfa became the headquarters of this group [*Hoechst Archiv*, IG194, Eichwerk Heinz Aufzeichnungen über Gründung, Entwicklung, Organisation und Mitglieder von TEA-Hauptgruppe-2-Kommissionen der I.G. Farbenindustrie A.G., Bd.I (Frankfurt 1943), S.12–13; *Hoechst Archiv*, IG200, Auszug aus der Niederschrift über die Sitzung des Arbeits-Ausschusses vom 22.11.29, S.1–2; *Hoechst Archiv*, IG194, Ausführliche Geschichte des Technischen Ausschusses, S.12; *Hoechst Archiv*, IG200, Brief an Pistor (18.9.1929); Tammnen 1978, S.21–22].

The management system based on the "decentralized centralization" principle promoted competition within the company. The promotion of ideal competition among these operating communities was Duisberg's concept of decentralization (Chandler 1990, p.568). Increasing the active initiatives of each plant was pursued by such internal competition under central office control. Carl Bosch pointed out that cutting production costs and maintaining ideal competition among the manufacturing locations was important for the success of mergers and therefore the autonomously managed four Operating Communities developed ideal competition under the supervision of the Working Committee of the managing board (Enquete Ausschuβ 1930, S.113). The purpose of founding these operating groups was to secure uniformity above all in the plant management of the same field regarding managerial perspectives and problems such as social policy and the energy supply (*Hoechst Archiv*, IG194, Über Struktur und wirtschaftliche Verflechtung der westdeutschen Werks der I.G. Farbenindustrie Aktiengesellschaft, S.5).

In examining the function and operation of the operating community, an internal document of the Middle Rhine Operating Community on March 8, 1927, pointed out in a meeting of this group that only more important issues such as organization problems, personnel affairs, credit requests for larger amounts, and relations with other operating and sales communities should be discussed from a unified standpoint. This conference was held before about eight days of the Technical Committee meetings as the highest organization concerned with technological affairs and managers from each plant participated. When there was a difference of opinion in this discussion and a difficult situation could not be broken through, the authority for the final decision was given to the head or its deputy of operating community [*Hoechst Archiv*, IG200, Betriebsgemeinschaft "Mittelrhein" neu (8.3.1927), S.1].

A similar internal document on October 16, 1929, pointed out that the managers of the three plants in Hoechst, Mainkur, and Griesheim gathered at meetings regularly held in approximately one-week intervals and in addition to the abovementioned affairs, the calculation of costs and projects under planning to be submitted to the Technical Committee were discussed and decided in collaboration (*Hoechst Archiv*, IG200, Geschäftsordnung und Aufgabenkreis der Betriebsgemeinschaft Mittelrhein, S.1). In the operation and management systems within the operating community, managers were arranged to combine competent functional fields such as science, production, inventory, shipment and packaging, accounting and calculation, patents, laboratory, technical affairs, education, and wages and salaries within each plant [*Hoechst Archiv*, IG200, Betriebsgemeinschaft MITTELRHEIN. Sachbearbeiter (Vertrauensleute)].

10.2.2 Centralization of the Sales Department and Sales Management Problems

Centralization of the sales department was attempted to make the best use of very abundant experience of marketing of merged enterprises. Five sales groups were organized according to product: (1) dye, (2) chemicals, (3) pharmaceuticals, (4) photo graphy and artificial silk, and (5) nitrogen. This sales group was called the "Sales Community." The headquarters were located in Frankfurt am Main, Leverkusen, and Berlin and actual sales were made by these regional groups [*Hoechst Archiv*, IG194, Über Struktur und wirtschaftliche Verflechtung der westdeutschen Werks der I.G. Farbenindustrie Aktiengesellschaft, S.11–12; *Hoechst Archiv*, IG194, Gründung und Entwicklung der I.G. (Oktober 1936); *Hoechst Archiv*, IG235, Verkaufs gemeinschaft Farben und Farbereihilfsprodukte. Geschäftsordnung des Farben-Ausschusses, S.1–2; *Hoechst Archiv*, IG235, Ländereinteilung der Verkaufsgruppen für Farben und Färbereihilfsprodukte; Feldenkirchen 1987, p.438; Meer 1952, S.786–787; Tammnen 1978, S.22–23; Brady 1933, pp.238–239; Chandler 1990, p.572]. Each sales group had its own accounting, statistics, and legal departments. For example, the legal department dealt with contracts concerning sales, cartels, agreements, and legal problems of the applied technology department (Meer 1952, S.787; *BASF Archiv*, I.G.C0/2, Organisation der Verkaufsgemeinschaft Pharmazeutika ≫Bayer≪, Dental ≫Bayer≪, Pflanzenschutz ≫Bayer≪, Sera- u. Vet.-Med. Produkte ≫Behringswerke≪, Leverkusen a. Rh.).

The establishment of the sales community meant the centralization of the sales department implemented on the basis of principle that the plant did not manage its own sales organization (*Hoechst Archiv*, IG194, Über Struktur und wirtschaftliche Verflechtung der westdeutschen Werks der I.G. Farbenindustrie Aktiengesellschaft,

S.9, 11). In the selection of products allotted to each sales community, the principle of integrating products with the same chemical characteristics and in the same fields of use was regarded as standard. In addition, in forming fields of activity of each sales community, special advice regarding the use of individual consumer products to coping with same stratum of consumers only by one section as much as possible was emphasized (*Hoechst Archiv*, IG194, Über Struktur und wirtschaftliche Verflechtung der westdeutschen Werks der I.G. Farbenindustrie Aktiengesellschaft, S.12–13). In each sales community organized on the basis of product type, committee organizations in charge of advice were founded. For instance, the dye committee concerning with the dye sales community was composed of members taking charge of commercial affairs of the Working Committee responsible for the management of the dye business and assumed responsibility for the supervision of all sales of dyes and dyeing auxiliary agents. It was in charge of not only providing advice regarding problems such as sales business organization, decisions on the constitution of products, sorts of dyes, changes in price, and publicity but also all agreements and contracts, agents, and personnel affairs concerning the dye business (*Hoechst Archiv*, IG235, Verkaufsgemeinschaft Farben und Farbereihilfsprodukte. Geschäftsordnung des Farben-Ausschusses, S.2–3). There were cases in which subcommittees such as the small sales committee were convened to examine desirable products. For instance, in September 1928, each one was called from Frankfurt am Main, Hoechst, Leverkusen, and Ludwigshafen and a list of desirable products was made. This subcommittee created a list of desirable products as new products by considering the products and the country that was the sales target (*Hoechst Archiv*, IG234, Auszug aus dem Protokoll über die 15. Sitzung der käufmannischen Kommission vom 12. September 1928 in Höchst am Main; *Hoechst Archiv*, IG234, Auszug aus dem Protokoll über die 16. Sitzung der käufmannischen Kommission vom 24. Oktober 1928 in Frankfurt am Main; *Hoechst Archiv*, IG235, Wunschliste für Neue Produkte. Beschluss zu Punkt 3 der Tagesordnung der Sitzung der Käufmannischen Kommission vom 12. September 1928).

The concentration of sales and marketing control in the hands of the sales community as specialized sales organizations made it possible "to simplify greatly the whole commercial end of the chemical industry, and greatly to reduce marketing cost" (Brady 1933, p.239).

10.2.3 Establishment of Committees and Their Significance

Furthermore, each kind of committee was founded at IG Farben. According to Fritz ter Meer, a member of the board of directors, organization of this company was a very elaborate structure of technical, commercial, and administrative committees that worked together or on their own without a hitch and that dealt correctly with countless problems of the concern or presented them for a final decision by the managing board (Meer 1953, S.47). Gottfried Plumpe pointed out that the prominent characteristics of organization of this enterprise lay in the committee systems that created the necessary flexibility within before making decisions (Plumpe 1990, S.163). The Working Committee (*Arbeitsausschβ*), the Technical Committee (*Technicher Ausschuβ*), and the Commercial Committee (*Kaufmännischer Ausschuβ*) were important such committees.

10.2.3.1 Working Committee

At the time of foundation of IG Farben, the executive board consisted of no less than 83 members, so this organization was obviously quite unwieldy. Therefore, the Executive Committee (and later, the Working Committee), composed of fewer members, was established (Meer 1953, S.51; Haber 1971, p.339; I.G. Farbenindustrie Aktiengesellschaft 1925). This committee made and implemented important decisions. It was established for the purpose of increasing the managing board's efficiency and supervising day-to-day operations (Feldenkirchen 1987, p.434). According to Carl Bosch's reference in 1928, the Working Committee had 26 members of which was he chair. It had initiative. Members of the managing board other than those who were department managers were no longer called to meetings concerning the whole company. Although they legally had the same obligation as members of this committee, the Working Committee took charge of business administration (Enquete Ausschuβ 1928, S.439).

The functions of the Working Committee were as follows: (1) decision-making on capital expenditures including participation in other companies, (2) closing down and reshaping the plant and other reorganizational matters, (3) agreements, cartels, and syndicates, (4) all labor affairs, (5) recruiting and promoting all managers with salaries over 10,000 Reichsmarks (RM), and (6) all financial affairs including dividend payments. Carl Bosch feared that the weakness of IG Farben's existing form of governance would not be overcome without concentrated executive control by representatives executing the organization of the managing board (Chandler 1990, pp.567–568).

According to Working Committee regulations, meetings of this organization should be held at least 14 days per year. Meetings should be held in Frankfurt am Main where the company's central office was located or at one of the operating or sales community bases in turns. In addition, the division of labor was introduced by committee members. Furthermore, managers of the operating and sales communities or subgroups thereof as well as all members of the managing board in their respective fields should be called at a meeting held in the location where they worked on a certain day at least once per week. Special committees composed of managers of the same types of departments, plants, and offices were organized according to the need for uniformity and the consistency of the execution of duties in all business units at various places. Members of these organizations were appointed by the Working Committee (*Hoechst Archiv*, IG194, Geschäftsordnung für die Mitglieder des Vorstandes der I.G. Farbenindustrie Aktiengesellschaft, S.3, 5–6). The decision-making and principles of the Working Committee became the policy of IG Farben (Plumpe 1990, S.145, 149–150, 152) until the establishment of the Central Committee on February 25, 1931 [*Hoechst Archiv*, IG 194, Eichwerk Heinz Aufzeichnungen über Grüdung, Entwicklung, Organisation und Mitglieder von TEA-Hauptgruppe-2-Kommissionen der I.G. Farbenindustrie A.G., Bd.I (Frankfurt 1943), S.17].

10.2.3.2 Technical and Commercial Committees

Whereas company-level decision-making as well as management duties were performed by the Working Committee, the division of labor was allotted to subordinate organizations. The Technical Committee, which was in charge of investment, maintenance, and fundamental technical affairs, and the Commercial Committee, which made fundamental decisions concerning purchases and sales and the management of other affairs, were founded. These two committees aided the activities of the Working Committee (Etzold 1988, S.103; Plumpe 1991, pp.225–227). Thus, very elaborate committee organizations that dealt with the many businesses of the IG Farben group professionally or took charge of preparing for final decision-making of the managing board were built (Meer 1953, S.47).

The Technical Committee was the highest organization concerning technical affairs. In addition to the examination and recognition of credits for all expansion and replacement investments, the rational use of production locations, the reduction of production items and decisions about effective composition considering inventory and similar problems, and investigations on the integration of production locations were its primary duties in the first year [*Hoechst Archiv*, IG194, Ausführliche Geschichte des Technischen Ausschusses, S.6–7; *Hoechst Archiv*, IG214, Besprechung technischer Fragen. Zusammenlegung der Fabrikationen, S.1–2; *Hoechst Archiv*, IG214, Tagesordnung für die Sitzung des Tea am Dienstag, den 1. Oktober, vormitags 9 $\frac{1}{2}$ Uhr in Ludwigshafen (1.10.1929), S.1; *Hoechst Archiv*, IG214, Niederschrift der Sitzung des TEA am Dienstag, den 1. Oktober 1929 vormittags 9 $\frac{1}{2}$ Uhr in Ludwigshafen a. Rhein, S.3; Tammnen 1978, S.24]. There were cases in which the problems of integrating production locations and reducing product types were entrusted to subcommittees within the Technical Committee and discussed by investigating this committee's suggestions (*Hoechst Archiv*, IG214, Niederschrift über die Sitzung des Tea am Donnerstag, dcn 28. Oktober 1926, Vormittags 9 $\frac{1}{2}$ Uhr in Frankfurt a. M., Feuerbachstrasse 50, S.2, 5; *Hoechst Archiv*, IG214. Gemeinschaftliche Sitzung des TEA mit dem Farbenausschuss und der Koloristischen Kommission am Freitag den 4. Februar 1927 vorm. 9 $\frac{1}{2}$ Uhr in Frankfurt a. M., Feuerbachstr.50, S.1–2).

The Technical Committee had 12 members at the time of its foundation (*Hoechst Archiv*, IG194, Ausführliche Geschichte des Technischen Ausschusses, S.8) and was composed of directors in charge of technical affairs, senior engineers of the primary operating group (the Operating Community), and a few heads of small-scale plants. The following issues can be identified as functions of this committee: (1) providing the statistical date of changes in production, costs, and positions of employees, (2) investigation of credit proposals for new equipment from plants and decisions on circulation to all members of the executive board, (3) discussions regarding conventions, fundamental license agreements, and patent affairs. Specialist lectures and reports on new scientific and technological results from IG Farben and discussions concerning production and depreciation were also duties of this committee. The decisions of this organization required admission [*Hoechst Archiv*, IG194, Anlage zu den 126 Job sheet for executives of the former I.G. Farbenindustrie A.G. Arbeitsteilung und Verantwortung der IG-Vorstandsmitglieder und Direktoren(14.4.1946); *Hoechst Archiv*, IG214, Niederschrift über die Sitzung des Tea am Donnerstag, den 28. Oktober 1926, Vormittags 9 1/2 Uhr in Frankfurt a. M., Feuerbachstrasse 50, S.1; *Hoechst Archiv*, IG214, Niederschrift über die Sitzung des Tea am Donnerstag, den 10. März 1927, vormittags 9 1/2 Uhr in Frankfurt a. M., Feuerbachstr. 50; *Hoechst Archiv*, IG214, Niederschrift der Sitzung des TEA am Dienstagg, den 1. Oktober 1929 vormittags 9 $\frac{1}{2}$ Uhr in Ludwigshafen a. Rhein, S.1, F. ter. Meer, Die I.G., S.783].

Many subcommittees that gave advice concerning problems related to activities concerned specifically with production, the business economy, and science existed in the Technical Committee. Representative organizations included dye, dye applying, intermediate chemicals, and patent subcommittees. After October 1926 when the first large-scale integration in the dye field occurred, 11 subcommittees were integrated into four primary subcommittees [*Hoechst Archiv*, IG194, Ausführliche Geschichte des Technischen Ausschusses, S.9–11, Anlage zu den 126 Job sheet for executives of the former I.G. Farbenindustrie A.G. Arbeits teilung und Verantwortung der IG-Vorstandsmitglieder und Direktoren (14.4.1946); *Hoechst Archiv*, IG 194].

Company managers could better understand accurate outlines of production and costs in various factories according to the activities of the Technical Committee. The R & D policies of the IG Farben group were coordinated by this committee. This committee was the central source of information for the board of directors and was operated with the support of staff departments (Plumpe 1990, S.146).

The Commercial Committee, composed of directors who was in charge of commercial problems and managers of important departments, was the highest institution concerned with fundamental and important commercial matters for all sales group issues such as price policy, convention, personnel matters, problems of foreign sales companies and agents, and publicity [*Hoechst Archiv*, IG194, Anlage zu den 126 Job Sheet for executives of the former I.G. Farbenindustrie A.G. Arbeitsteilung und Verantwortung der IG-Vorstandsmitglieder und Direktoren (14.4.1946); Meer 1952, S.787; Meer 1953, S.46]. Although the sale of each product itself was managed by the sales community, the commercial committee was in charge of the unified activities of sales at home and abroad and securing uniformity in price and sales policies. The Commercial Committee played a major role in the IG's considerable movement toward centralization of function within the first few years after the merger (Abelshauser et al. 2004, p.219; Stokes 2007, S.233). This committee was responsible for the board of directors (*Hoechst Archiv*, IG194, Über Struktur und wirtschaftliche Verflechtung der westdeutschen Werks der I.G. Farbenindustrie Aktiengesellschaft, S.13). It was also the coordinating committee for commercial problems in which all or many sales communities and other departments concerning commercial affairs had a general interest [*Hoechst Archiv*, IG194, Die Funktion des Kaufmännischen Ausschusses (KA)].

The commercial committee supervised the activities of sales communities and was responsible for controlling the sale of products such as dyestuffs and chemicals. The plants made product invoices at cost for sales communities as the marketing combines (*Hoechst Archiv*, IG194, Über Struktur und wirtschaftliche Verflechtung der westdeutschen Werks der I.G. Farbenindustrie Aktiengesellschaft, S.11). "The proceeds from the sales, after deducting expenses, were credited to the concern's central financial administration." However, Ludwig Frits Haber pointed out that "under such conditions it must have been difficult to monitor costs efficiently" (Haber 1971, p.34). The commercial committee provided information regarding market trends and the international position of IG Farben until 1928 (Feldenkirchen 1987, p.436; Tammnen 1978, S.24).

Necessary close contacts between technical and commercial operation were created by special committees in which the directors in charge of technical or commercial matters were called with persons in charge. The Dye Committee, the Chemicals Committee, and the Central Pharmaceuticals Meeting existed as such committees [*Hoechst Archiv*, IG194, Anlage zu den 126 Job Sheet for executives of the former I.G. Farbenindustrie A.G. Arbeitsteilung und Verantwortung der IG-Vorstandsmitgliederund Direktoren (14.4.1946); *BASF Archiv*, I.G. C0/2, Organisation der I.G.; Meer 1952, S.787]. Whereas the technical and commercial committees aided the Working Committee, these special committees functioned as specialist staff.

10.2.4 Establishment of the Central Department

Furthermore, a series of central departments to deal with problems of the entire enterprise was created as staff organization. The central finance, national economy, economic policy, central purchasing, and press departments were established in Berlin. The central accounting, central tax, central insurance, and public relations departments were founded in Frankfurt am Main. The central contract and traffic departments were located in Ludwigshafen. The economic policy department was established in 1932 (Meer 1952, S.787; Plumpe 1990, S.153). As time passed, the central finance department was forced to face new requirements in addition to the fields of duty handled by various financial sections until then. The integration of the national economic department and the economic policy department in Berlin was implemented considering negotiation with the competent authorities and organizations concerning the economy. Similar needs can also be observed in relation to foreign government offices and quasi-national institutions [*Hoechst Archiv*, IG194, Entstehung und Aufgabengebiet der I.G. Berlin NW.7 (20.8.1937), S.1–3; *BASF Archiv*, I.G. C0/3, Entstehung und Aufgabengebiet der I.G. Berlin NW.7 (20.8.1937), S.1–3; Meer 1953, S.47]. These departments functioned primarily as controlling staff.

There were many cases in which a central department was divided into one or more sections. For instance, the central financial department was divided into six sections including the financial secretary, management of currency, accounting, credit, and promotion of exports. The national economy department had five sections as follows: (1) the entire economy, (2) observation of foreign countries, (3) market research, (4) enterprise and finance documents, and (5) the Frankfurt am Main branch (*BASF Archiv*, I.G. C0/3, Organisationsplan der I.G. Belin NW7, *Hoechst Archiv*, IG194, Organisationsplan der I.G. Belin NW7).

10.2.5 Characteristics of Organizational Reform in the First Stage

Building on these discussions, this section clarifies the characteristics of organizational reform in the first stage. According to an IG Farben annual report in the fiscal year 1925, with the merger, simplification and more effective use of business units were pursued by the rational integration of the sales and production departments (I.G. Farbenindustrie Aktiengesellsachaft 1926, S.2). Alfred D. Chandler, Jr. pointed out that "the new structure was essentially a compromise in which all agreed that the goal of the merger should be to bind together more effectively the existing administrative offices and committees" (Chandler 1990, p.569).

Within each of IG Farben's major and minor managerial groups, the division of authority and responsibility had been functional. Each producing, distributing, or special staff unit was able to specialize in a narrow range of functions while it was simultaneously closely combined with the larger company. This enterprise was able to secure a high degree of individual and group responsibility and established a managerial system that was responsive and flexible in the face of either major or minor changes by the systematic application of these organizational principles (Brady 1933, p.237; Thiel 2020, S.262).

Regarding organizational structures at the time, R. A. Brady pointed out that "functional organization of plant, division of the duties of all workers, salaried employees, and executives, and methods of fixing responsibility and assessing success and blame" had been carried into all or nearly all phases of the productive and commercial activities of various enterprises. He emphasized that the larger application of these principles was best exemplified by Vereinigte Stahlwerke and IG Farben in Germany while also being observed at the American Telephone and Telegraph Company (AT&T) and General Motors (GM) in the US (Brady 1933, p.46). The organization of IG Farben was modeled after the system laid down in the organization of GM and AT&T and the managerial pattern of Vereinigte Stahlwerke was borrowed from IG Farben (Brady 1933, p.121).

The goal of management organization in the first stage lay in increasing positive initiative through the decentralization of management and further specialization. In the case of Vereinigte Stahlwerke, the creation of a system of administration based on the "decentralized centralization" principle was pursued with such a purpose.

10.3 Organizational Reform in the Second Stage and Its Characteristics

10.3.1 Reorganization of Business Structures and the Foundation of Divisions

10.3.1.1 Reorganization of Business Structures and Management Problems

Next, this section examines organizational reform in the second stage. One of its most important characteristics can be observed in its attempt to handle the managerial problems arising from business diversification. In individual industrial departments, different types of organizational structures were formed (Kieser and Kubicek 1983, S.249; Schmalenbach 1959, S.9). As is typically observed in divisional structures, the degree of organizational change depended heavily on the types of products manufactured and their increase (Wolf 2000, S.320, 322; Stockmann 1987, S.87). In departments that had very diverse product lines, duties such as calculation, production planning, and holding of inventory increased and there was a need for a higher level of coordination and control due to differences in their product lines (Stockmann 1987, S.199).

As discussed in Chap. 6, when companies with functional structures implemented diversification, difficult managerial problems arose. The heads of departments confronted difficulties in dealing with many diverse products. For example, sales departments were forced to sell different types of products. The procurement of raw materials and routing of the production of different goods also became the cause of difficulties. Under such limited middle- and lower-level operational management, top management was often too busy making administrative rather than entrepreneurial or executive decisions (Krooss and Gilbert 1972, p.253; Chandler 1962). As a result, top managers were not able to concentrate on top management functions such as allocating business resources from the perspective of long-term administration and the entire enterprise. Thus, the functionally departmentalized organizational structure that had worked so well for a single-product enterprise was inappropriate for a multi-product enterprise.

Although diversification was implemented at IG Farben after the merger, attempts to reform the organizational structure during the first stage were limited to measures to coping with managerial problems arising from the consolidation of the enterprise and production concentration and specialization based on product type. However, one of the most important managerial problems with diversification appeared to be investment decision difficulties. In this company, departments and plants that intended to invest submitted a detailed credit application document in which the reason and expected results were communicated to the operating community. This application was sent to suitable, special committees. However, the operating communities and large plants as institutions that made investment applications tended to diversify broadly and sometimes had activities that competed with other plants as the center of decentralized decision-making. Therefore, it was not easy to uniformly manage investments in all fields from research to new equipment and further to unified repair from the technical aspect. Decisive defects in the organizational structure of this enterprise lay in his point (Plumpe 1990, S.146–147).

10.3.1.2 Foundation of Divisions

In this way, IG Farben's organizational principle was the decentralization of both technical and commercial management based on regional and practical perspectives, the integration of responsibilities, and securing a unified business policy by the board of directors or its committees concerned (*Hoechst Archiv*, IG194, Über Struktur und wirtschaftliche Verflechtung der westdeutschen Werks der I.G. Farbenindustrie Aktiengesellschaft, S.2). However, the limits of the management organization formed in the first stage of reform became prominent. In 1929, current income became less than expenditures and the enormous cost of R&D became a big problem. Under such conditions, the firm's activities were integrated into three large divisions (Sparten). Carl Bosch decided to entrust management of investment in these three divisions to three especially capable, suitable, younger managers. The foundation of divisions aimed at reducing R&D investment and expenditures under the pressure of the world economic crisis (Plumpe 1990, S.148, Plumpe 1991, pp.228, 235). Directors took charge of one of these divisions to administrate, above all, problems with production planning, investment, and new construction plans.

Immediately before the world crisis (August 1929), three divisions were organized to create an appropriate foundation to recognize future credit and observe the limits of freely usable funds and achieve higher production and research economy and better individual plant cooperation (Tammnen 1978, S.23). Technologically or chemically related products were consolidated in each division.

Division I (Sparte I) (headed by Karl Krauch): Products such as nitrogen, methanol, synthetic fuels, synthetic oil, lubricants, metal carbonyl, nickel, pit coal, and lignite were treated.

Division II (Sparte II) (headed by Fritz ter Meer): Products such as heavy chemicals, organic intermediates, dyestuffs, pigments, magnesium, pharmaceuticals, pesticides, dissolvents, softening agents, plastics, synthetic rubber, detergents, synthetic tans, compressed gas, autogenous welding tools, and gas cutting tools were handled.

Division III (Sparte III) (headed by Fritz Gajewski): Products such as photo articles, cellulose, artificial silk, synthetic fibers, celluloid, vulcanized fiber, and plastics processing were handled (*Hoechst Archiv*, IG194, Die Aufteilung der I.G. in 3 Sparten; *Hoechst Archiv*, IG194, Über Struktur und wirtschaftliche Verflechtung der westdeutschen Werks der I.G. Farbenindustrie Aktiengesellschaft, S.3;

Hoechst Archiv, IG194, Gründung und Entwicklung der I.G. (Oktober 1936); *Hoechst Archiv*, IG214, Aufstellung der in der Sitzung des Technischen Ausschusses am 21.November 1929 in Leverkusen zur Beratung vorliegenden Kreditforderungen; *BASF Archiv*, I.G.C0/2, Organisation der I.G.; *BASF Archiv*, I.G.C0/2, Sparten, Betriebsgemeinschaften und Werke der I.G. bei Kriegsende; Tammnen 1978, S.23–24, Plumpe 1990, S.147–149; Meer 1952, S.783; Feldenkirchen 1987, p.437; Chandler 1990; Haber 1971, p.339).

The chairmen of these divisions were responsible to the managing board for R&D programs, all problems relating to salaried staff, and technical matters of their own divisions. Technical affairs within each department were handled by the standing committee composed of specialists and these committees were involved in process improvement, applied techniques for original products of each department, technical questions related to chemical apparatuses, and packaging and storage problems (Haber 1971, p.339). Investigation of credit applications submitted by the division was first performed by the Technical Committee and sent to upper-level institutions such as the Working Committee (*Hoechst Archiv*, IG214, Aufstellung der in der Sitzung des Technischen Ausschusses am 21. November 1929 in Leverkusen zur Beratung vorliegenden Kreditforderungen; *Hoechst Archiv*, IG214, Niederschrift der Sitzung des TEA am Mittwoch, den 23 Juli 1930, vormittags 9 $\frac{1}{2}$ Uhr in Frankfurt a. M., Feuerbachstrasse 50, S.4). These divisions were suitable for management of the company's technical aspects (Plumpe 1990, S.148). Dividing all fields of activity into three divisions was implemented to cope with the need for new controls emphasizing fund allotment problems. General managers supervised the expenditure budgets of their own plants (Tammnen 1978, S.24). However, "the chairmen of the Division did not have responsibility for the profit and loss account of their product groups, in this important respect they differed from Du Pont's General Managers" (Haber 1971, p.339).

10.3.2 Establishment of the Central Committee and Its Significance

Another important point of organizational reform in the second stage was the establishment of the Central Committee (*Zenralausschuß*) as the top decision-making institution composed of fewer members than the Working Committee. At the end of the 1920s, there was a need to coordinate production and distribution more closely and further centralize control at the level of top management to complete the rationalization of production and regain world markets (Chandler 1990, p.573). Under such conditions, Carl Bosch, as the chairman of the board of directors, pointed out that the Working Committee, comprised of over 25 members, did not function sufficiently as the responsible top management organization due to its scale. The Working Committee's lack of decision-making ability and its slow and bureaucratic behavior were pointed out. In the first stage of organizational reform, "attempts at forming central organizations were tentative and did not yet represent a coherent strategy for integrating the former components into a new firm" (Abelshauser et al. 2004, p.220).

Establishing a central institution composed of the chairman of the managing board and four or five formal directors was proposed for the purpose of coping with this condition. Thus, a new managing board committee was formed in 1931 (Plumpe 1990, S.149–150, 152; Tammnen 1978, S.27; Meer 1952, S.789; Feldenkirchen 1987, p.434; Chandler 1990, p.575). The most important duties of this committee were decisions regarding fundamental principles of business policy and the selection of managers. In contrast, the Working Committee continued to be in charge of daily duties including a large part of investment decisions [*Hoechst Archiv*, IG194, Anlage zu den 126 Job Sheet for executives of the former I.G. Farbenindustrie A.G. Arbeitsteilung und Verantwortung der IG-Vorstandsmitglieder und Direktoren (14.4.1946); Plumpe 1990, S.152]. The orders of the Central Committee were binding on all divisions, operating communities, sales communities, and any other kind of committee (Tammnen 1978, S.28). The purpose of establishing the Central Committee was to make members of this organization devote themselves to essential top management functions such as allocating business resources from the long-term perspective of the entire enterprise by separating their tasks from day-to-day operational duties and achieving the division of labor in general management functions between the Central Committee and the Working Committee.

Thus, members of the Central Committee were regarded as the leaders of the managing board. This committee took complete responsibility for IG Farben policy. It was in charge of company administration until 1937 when organizational reform in the third stage was implemented. Gottfried Plumpe pointed out that members of this committee were entrepreneurs, meaning that they were in charge of the enterprise's strategic decision-making (Plumpe 1990, S.150); however, the influence of the Central Committee decreased. Moreover, the administration of divisions and product departments became central to critical decision-making within IG Farben following the shift of Carl Bosch from the managing board to the supervisory board (Reuber 2012, S.51).

When examining the composition of this organization's members from 1930 to 1945, the rate of chemists was high. Of the 14 members during this period, nine were chemists and chemists were positioned at the top of three divisions and operating communities (Plumpe 1990, S.152). L. F. Haber pointed out that "the looked-for qualifications were chemical knowledge, an understanding of industrial economies, and the ability to take charge of plant operations" (Haber 1971, p.342). These points were considered in personnel disposition within the Central Committee. Figure 10.1 illustrates an overall view of IG Farben's organizational structure.

Fig. 10.1 Organizational structure of IG Farbenindustrie AG (September 1931) *Source Bayer Archiv*, 13/2, Kommision der I.G., S.72

10.4 Limitations of Organizational Reform at IG Farben

Did IG Farben's organizational structure, created by reform in the second stage, build a system that enabled effective decision-making and the rational allocation of business resources? First, an evaluation by A. D. Chandler, Jr. pointed out the following:

The staffs of the committees and the functional staff officers were large, specialized, and well trained. The information the senior managers received at their many meetings was probably as accurate and detailed as the foundation produced at that time by staff offices in any industrial enterprise in the world. Yet, given the number of meetings that the senior executives had to attend in different places, they had little time to absorb and evaluate the massive data they received for long-term strategic planning. Instead, they continued to use the data more for short-term decisions concerning the day-to-day production and distribution activities in which they were so intimately involved. Unlike Du Pont, they had no corporate or general office where general executives, largely free from operating duties, concentrated on monitoring performance; on allocating resources on the basis of that monitoring and of their own understanding of economic, technical, market, and political considerations; and then on defining and implementing long-term strategies (Chandler 1990, p.579).

Based on the preceding examinations in this chapter, the significance and limitations of IG Farben's organizational reform in the second stage and its factors are clarified next.

First, at IG Farben, only three divisions were departmentalized according to product type despite the company featuring a broader range of product lines than Du Pont. Even though technologically and chemically related products were consolidated, in reality, multiple product lines in which fundamental functions such as production, sales, and purchasing differed greatly were forced to be handled by one division. Under this situation, managerial problems that functionally departmentalized structures often encountered in the diversification of products could not be solved sufficiently. In contrast, at Du Pont, in spite of having fewer product lines than IG Farben, five product divisions were established as follows: (1) explosive, (2) dyestuff, (3) pyralin, (4) paint and chemicals, and (5) artificial leather and film (see for instance, Chandler 1962). Each division was founded according to the product field in which fundamental functions such as production, sales, and purchasing differed greatly and as a result, created desirable conditions for top executives to allocate business resources effectively from the perspective of long-term administration and the entire company. In contrast, in IG Farben, "a clear separation of operational and corporate management, and the position of the general manager responsible for the development, production, and marketing of one product line" as "the crucial elements of the multidivisional structure" were not adopted (Dornseifer 1995, pp.222–223) despite the foundation of three divisions and the Central Committee.

Second, a self-supporting accounting system was not adopted in the division of IG Farben and a profit center system of the division was not built. The responsibility of each division for profit and control of the division based on measuring and evaluating business results using measures such as the return on investment was not introduced. This included important factors that made it difficult for the head office to evaluate the business results of each division and manage and control business units such as the operational department and allocate business resources effectively from the standpoint of the whole enterprise. L. F. Haber pointed out that in addition to funds and markets, managerial ability and the careful measurement of each division's performance, assigning responsibility for the department's profit and loss account to each general manager, seemed to have been Du Pont's recipe for success (Haber 1971, p.342). As is clear from this reference, whether each division took responsibility for not only its sales volume and costs but also for the profit of its own business, each division functioned as a profit center closely concerned with the effects of introducing and using the divisional structure. The organizational structure of IG Farben had to face large limitations in contrast to the success of Du Pont regarding this point.

Third, at IG Farben, an organization that should function as general staff, supporting and advising top management, Central Committee members in particular, taking charge of allocating resources from the viewpoint of the long-term and the entire company was not established; this was also an important factor determining the limitations of organizational reform. Indeed, the technical and commercial committees as institutes to aid the Working Committee responsible for function of general management existed. However, as the Working Committee mainly took charge of day-to-day business, they primarily performed preparatory activities and provided advice concerning business and operations and did not assist the Central Committee through functions as general staff. In addition, the central departments organized in three regions as staff organizations to handle problems of the entire enterprise functioned primarily as controlling staff. Thus, the leaders of top management represented by members of the Central Committee had to attend many meetings to gain various information due to the disestablishment of an organization that should function as general staff. Under such conditions, it seems to have been difficult for them to secure enough time to absorb and evaluate the massive amount of data to formulate a long-term strategy.

Furthermore, the committee organization system also had some defects. Bernd Dornseifer points out, "even though the establishment of committees resembled the formation of product divisions in many respects, that mode of organization had two major flaws." The first was the division of responsibility between various committee members or even different committees, while the second was the lack of commercial marketing expertise in these committees (Dornseifer 1995, p.225).

In this way, in IG Farben's organizational structure, executive functionaries in the head office such as Central Committee members could not sufficiently devote themselves to strategic decision-making and allocating business resources from the perspective of long-term company growth and the whole enterprise due to the following three factors: (1) lack of a system in which each division dealt with only one product line and fundamental functions such as production, sales, and purchasing did not differ, (2) lack of profit center system based on the self-supporting accounting of the divisions, and (3) disestablishment of organizations that should function as general staff. Such limitations meant insufficiency of organizational reform to cope with managerial problems caused by business diversification. In reality, in contrast to the success of Du Pont, limits on attempts to reform IG Farben's organizational structure influenced decisions and the effects of their investments during the period of the world economic crisis and national socialism (Yamazaki 1997, Chap. 9). Success or failure of organizational reform became an important factor greatly affecting the subsequent growth of both enterprises.

References

Abelshauser W, von Hippel W, Johnson JA, Stokes RD (2004) German industry and global enterprise. BASF: the history of a company. Cambridge University Press, Cambridge

Brady RA (1933) The rationalization movement in German industry. A study in the evolution of economic planning. University of California Press, Berkeley, California

Chandler AD Jr (1962) Strategy and structure: chapters in the history of the industrial enterpreise. MIT Press, Cambridge, Massachusetts

Chandler AD Jr (1990) Scale and scope: the dynamics of industrial capitalism. Harvard University Press, Cambridge, Massachusetts

Dornseifer B (1995) Strategy, technological capability, and innovation: German enterprises in comparative perspective. In: Caron F, Erker P, Fischer W (eds) Innovations in the European economy between the wars. Walter de Gruyter, Berlin, pp 197–226

Enquete Ausschuβ (1928) Wandlungen in den wirtschaftlichen Organization. (I)-3, E. S. Mittler & Sohn, Berlin

Enquete Ausschuβ (1930) Die deutsche Chemische Industrie. (III)-3, E. S. Mittler & Sohn, Berlin

Etzold H (1988) Die Entwicklung der Produktivkräfte in der Industrie. In: Institut für Wirtschaftsgeschichte der Akademie der Wissenschaften der DDR, Berthold R et al. (Hrsg) Produktivkräfte in Deutschland von 1917/18 bis 1945. Akadermie Verlag, Berlin, S.36–223

Feldenkirchen W (1987) Big business in interwar Germany: organizational innovation at Verenigt Stahlwerke, IG Farben, and Siemens. In: Bus Hist Rev 61(3):417–451

Fischer W (1979) Dezentralisation oder Zentralisation—kollegiale oder autoritäre Führung? Die Auseinandersetzung um die Leitungsstruktur bei der Entstehung des I.G. Farben-Konzerns. In: Horn N, Kocka J (Hrsg) Recht und Entwicklung der Groβunternehemen in 19. und 20. Jahrhundert. Wirtschafts-, sozial- und rechtshistorische Untersuchungen zur Industrialisierung in Deutschland, Frakreich, England und den USA. Vandenhoeck und Ruprecht, Göttingen, S.476–488

Haber LF (1971) The Chemical Industry, 1900–1930. International growth and technological change. Oxford University Press, Oxford

Hayes P (1987) Industry and Ideologie. IG Farben in the Nazi Era. Cambridge University Press, Cambridge, Massachusetts

I.G. Farbenindustrie Aktiengesellschaft (1926) Bericht des Vorstandes und Aufsichtsrates über das Geschäftsjahr 1925. I.G. Farbenindustrie Aktiengesellschaft, Frankfurt am Main

Kieser A, Kubicek H (1983) Organisation. 2.neubearbeitete und erweiterte Auflage, de Gruyter, Berlin, New York

Krooss HE, Gilbert C (1972) American business history. Prentice-Hall, Englewood Cliffs, New Jersey

Meer F ter (1952) Die I.G.: Ihre Entstehung, ihre Entwickung und Bedeutung. In: Chemische Industrie 4(10):777–806.

Meer F ter (1953) Die IG Farbenindustrie Aktiengesellschaft: Ihre Entstehung, Entwicklung und Bedeutung. Econ Verlag, Düsseldorf

Plumpe G (1990) Die I.G. Farbeinindustrie A G: Wirtschaft, Tecknik, Politik 1904–1945. Duncker & Humblot, Berlin

Plumpe G (1991) The political framwork of structural modernization. In: Lee WR (ed) German industry and German industrialization: essays in German economics and business history in the nineteeth and twentieth centuries. Routledge, London, New York, pp 220–264

Reuber C (2012) Der lange Wege an die Spitze. Karrieren von Führungskräften deutscher Groβunternehmen im 20. Jahrhundert. Campus, Frankfurt am Main

Schmalenbach E (1959) Über Dienststellengliederung im Groβbetriebe. Westdeutscher Verlag, Köln, Opladen

Schneckenburger A (1988) Die Geschichte des I.G. Farbenkonzern. Bedeutung und Rolle eines Grossunternehmen. Pahl-Rugenstein, Köln

Stockmann R (1987) Gesellschaftiche Modernisierung und Betriebsstruktur. Die Entwicklung von Arbeitsstätten in Deutschland 1875–1980. Campus, Frankfurt am Main, New York

Stokes RG (2007) Von der I.G. Farbenindustrie AG bis zur Neugründung der BASF (1925–1952). In: Abelshauser W (Hesg) Die BASF. Eine Unternehmensgeschichte. 3.Auflage, C. H. Beck, München, S.221–358, 670–688

Tammnen H (1978) Die I.G. Farbenindustrie Aktiengesellschaft [1925–1933]: Ein Chemiekonzern in der Weimarer Republik. H. Tammnen, Berlin

Thiel C (2020) Entscheidungen und Anpassungspraktiken. Die BASF zwischen 1865 und 1965. Campus, Frankfurt am Main

Waller P (1928) Probleme der deutschen chemischen Industrie. H. Meyer, Halberstadt

Wolf J (2000) Strategie und Struktur 1955–1995. Ein Kapitel der Geschichte deutscher nationaler und internationaler Unternehmen. Gabler, Wiesbaden

Yamazaki T (1997) Doitsu kigyo kanrishi kenkyu (History of management in German enterprises). Moriyama shoten, Tokyo

Part IV
Business Management in the Nazi Era

Chapter 11
Implementation of the REFA System and Changes in Labor Management

Abstract Based on discussions regarding changes in business management during the Weimar Republic in Part III, Part IV analyses business management in the Nazi period. Two research topics, the REFA system implementation and the Ford system deployment, are examined. This chapter considers the deployment of the REFA system by the strong involvement of the Nazi state. First, it explores the expansion of REFA activity and examines the progress of implementing and diffusion of the REFA system in major industrial sectors emphasized by the state for expanding munition production as well as the general conditions. The differences in the implementation of the REFA system between industries are discussed, and changes in labor management are clarified. Based on these examinations, the characteristics and significance of the diffusion of the REFA system supported by the Nazi policy are elucidated.

Keywords Labor management · Labor science · Munition production · Rationalization · Rationalization science · REFA system · Work study

In Part IV, the business management changes in the Nazi era from 1933 to the end of World War II are considered relative to the economic system under National Socialism, changes in market conditions brought about by the militarization of economy and the shift to the war economy, and the state-led rationalization movement. Rationalization was a movement promoted by the strong involvement of the fascist state starting in the latter half of the 1930s. It was developed primarily in the fields of production technology and labor organization. The rationalization of labor organizations caused significant business management changes. Although the Taylor system diffused the REFA system as a typical German system in the 1920s, the implementation of the REFA system was more strongly driven under REFA's expansion of activities from time studies to work studies and the involvement of the Nazi state in REFA. In addition, under the striking expansion of munitions-related markets, many industrial sectors were given the possibility of implementing the Ford system and pursuing mass production. Thus, the shift to mass production through Ford system implementation progressed on the basis of new market conditions based on munitions.

T. Yamazaki, *A History of German Business*,
https://doi.org/10.1007/978-981-96-8476-2_11

The REFA system's "scientific" work and time studies brought modernization and diversification of wage forms and became an important rationalization measure and labor management system. The fields of use for these studies were expanded by further increasing the importance of production and time economies under the planning framework of the entire Nazi state economy (Hachtmann 1989, S.175). In this period, REFA system developed as an effective means of work study and for the rationalization of work preparation, work management, and work design (Schmiede and Schudlich 1981, S.304). Thus, the diffusion of the REFA system was an important factor for business management transformation.

Chapter 11 considers the expansion of the REFA system and changes in labor management from the perspective of comparison with the Weimar period. Section 11.1 examines the activities and characteristics of the REFA system. Section 11.2 analyzes the general conditions of implementing the REFA system. Section 11.3 considers various cases in major industrial sectors such as the electrical engineering, automobile, machinery, iron and steel, and chemical industries.

11.1 Activities of the REFA and Their Characteristics

11.1.1 Involvement of the State in REFA and Its Significance

An important characteristic of REFA activity can be observed in the strong state involvement in this organization. The importance of REFA activity increased, and the fields of its activity were expanded through the involvement of state institutions in promoting rationalization and initiatives. Attempts to realize rational methods of human work as one of the emphases of the National Committee for Production Increase and committees thereunder were implemented depending on REFA activities. Thus, the field of REFA activity was expanded (Hachtmann 1989, S.74).

Cooperation with other institutions concerned with problems in the labor science field, in particular, state and quasi-state institutions, determined another characteristic of REFA activity. The Agency of Professional Training and Corporate Leadership (*Amt für Betriebsführung und Berufserziehung*) within the German Labor Front (*Deutsche Arbeitfront*), which was created from the German Technical Labor Education Institute (*Dinta*) in 1935, is such an institution (Hachtmann 1989, S.180). Cooperation between REFA and the German Technical Labor Education Institute that began before 1933 became official according to an October 1935 agreement (Hachtmann 1989, 181; *thyssenkrupp Corporate Archives* (below *tkA*), VST/590, Richtlinien für organisatorische Fragen innerhalb der Refa-Ausschüsse, S.2: Pechhold 1974, S.83). The goal of this collaboration was to provide enterprises with knowledge regarding the business economy required for achieving best results (Maschinenbau 1934, S.602). Later, REFA educational courses were jointly implemented by REFA and the Agency of Professional Training and Corporate Leadership. Whereas the former was responsible for providing lecturers and teaching materials, the latter took charge of publicity and inviting participants. As a relatively large personnel organization to which the Agency of Professional Training and Corporate Leadership contributed significantly, it represented the most significant expansion of REFA activity since 1935 [*tkA*, VST/590, Arbeitsrichtlienien für die Einrichtung und Durchführung von Refa-Kursen (4.10.1935), S.1; *tkA*, VST/590, Richtlinien für organisatorische Fragen innerhalb der Refa-Ausschüsse, S.3; *tkA*, VST/590, Vereinbarung zwischen Amt für Arbeitsführung und Berufserziehung und Refa; Hachtmann 1989, S.181; Kothe 1936, S.65; Winkel 1938, S.505].

Those who did not have the knowledge required about time measurement and calculation activities took REFA educational courses. A two-member committee for the smooth execution of work was established by the Agency of Professional Training and Corporate Leadership and REFA. It became an active part prior to the implementation of work to exclude unfavorable conditions in the first stage [*tkA*, VST/590, Arbeitsrichtlienien für die Einrichtung und Dürchführung von Refa-Kursen (4.10.1935), S.2]. As long as the demand for individual enterprises did not become problematic, support for rationalization by the Agency of Professional Training and Corporate Leadership was usually implemented with the mediation of the state industrial group. REFA was able to sufficiently maintain its organizational autonomy and contents even under this influence (Pechhold 1974, S.82; Hachtmann 1989, S.181). However, regarding the formation of the REFA organization, regional committees were expanded on the basis of requests for this national institute, which was comprised of broad regional organizations. Thus, the influence of the state on REFA was not insignificant (*tkA*, VST/590, Richtlinien für organisatorische Fragen innerhalb der Refa-Ausschüsse, S.2; *tkA*, VST/590, Verzeichnis der Refa-Gau-und Refa-Ortsausschüsse im Reich).

In this way, the REFA system prevailed in a broad range of industries in a relatively short time. Rüdiger Hachtmann highlighted that the rapid expansion of the REFA system could not have been realized without the support of quasi-state institutions, such as the German Labor Front (Hachtmann 1989, S.303). It was particularly important to Germany's industrial economy that labor rationalization was not only approved but also promoted strongly or implemented immediately by state institutions and managers (Pentzlin 1938, S.40). National Socialists promoted various modernization and rationalization movements, as without modern industry, the state could not win the war. They knew the effect of stable rules using such processes. It became clear from the promise of Taylorism that measures such as the active acceptance of F. W. Taylor's time and motion studies and the expansion of REFA activity post-1934 would decisively contribute to "scientific" solutions, mitigation of social conflicts within enterprises, and realization of a socially harmonious "community within a company" ("*Betriebsgemeinschaft*") (Hachtmann 1989, S.303). Studies and concepts in labor science, labor psychology, and industrial sociology fields created a broader sensation behind the progress of the "Americanization" of industrial production and rapid changes in social relationships within companies (Hachtmann 1989, S.81).

The independence of REFA and the German Technical Labor Education Institute, which appealed to "neutrality," was no longer completely lost under the Nazi's acquisition of administrative power and the German Labor Front's enforcement of labor control. Educational REFA courses were implemented at its own expense and did not receive support from the German Labor Front (*tkA*, VST/590, Richtlinien für organisatorische Fragen innerhalb der Refa-Ausschüsse, S.3). However, problems such as the pursuit of the most suitable worker efficiency performed by managers and labor scientists after the introduction of scientific management were not emphasized. Instead, underlying the increase in community consciousness and the loyalty of workers to the state were stressed and the foundation for a shift to a general mobilization of workers for wartime was built (Koda and Ito 1990, p.201). Institutions such as REFA were forced to become part of complex state and party organizations so that they could continue (Pechhold 1974, S.82–83).

The Nazi regime attempted to apply scientific management consistent with its ideology and to combine scientific management with its idea of "community" and "leadership." The German Labor Front played a significant role in the ideological campaign to raise productivity and stressed the task of maximum productivity for the German people (Guillén 1994, pp.122, 126). It used the experience and organizational capabilities of the German Technical Labor Education Institute (*Dinta*) to develop such ideological propaganda (Guillén 1994, p.123). Thus, achieving essential goals of REFA such as securing "neutrality" and "objectivity" became very difficult due to the involvement of quasi-state institutions, such as the German Labor Front.

11.1.2 Expansion of REFA Activity

Next, this section considers REFA activity and its emphasis. In the Nazi era, as seen in the change of REFA's name to the "National Committee for Work Study" ("*Reichsausschuß für Arbeitsstudien*") in March 1936, the emphasis of this institution's activity shifted from time studies to broad work studies (Hachtmann 1989, S.180; Maschinenbau 1936, S.215; Winkel 1938, S.505; Spitzley 1980). The time study was the main field of REFA. However, in the mid-1930s, understanding not only how quickly work could be performed using the predetermined work method but also how the work was performed, whether certain work could be better designed, and how such designs could theoretically be most suitably implemented became important issues (Pentzlin 1935, S.228).

Thus, in 1936, REFA activity reached all work studies such as setting standard time, job design, job evaluation, and work guidance (Schlaich 1974, S.190). A. Winkel pointed out that the development of job design was strongly promoted and further driven by the influence of the German Labor Front on REFA activity. As a result, the demand for the most expedient job design became a fundamental principle of the most superior rank (Winkel 1938, S.505). After 1933, during the implementation of work and time studies by enterprises, psychological results were used and diffused for the first time. In this process, a guide concerning the "mental and physical conditions of human labor in enterprise" that plainly yet minutely collected labor productivity problems from the viewpoint of the "human perspective" according to the newest level of knowledge had especially important meaning (Böhrs 1942, S.70). In this way, as in the 1920s, the scientific study of labor played a great role in rationalization sciences.

During World War II, the significance and role of the work study further increased to expand munitions production and address the issue of lack of skilled workers. Among all measures useful for mobilizing the still-existing preparatory production capacity for the war economy, the use of the results of working technique and work studies could play an important role (Pentzlin 1942, S.59). Securing skilled workers for particularly important purposes and replacing them with semiskilled workers had to be taken into consideration. Therefore, independent departments that took charge of work studies exclusively and sufficiently promoted organizing and expanding them were needed for plants with modern equipment (Weigel 1942, S.46). G. Peiseler highlighted that in 1943, the comparison of business units to achieve the best output premised appropriate time and work studies (Peiseler 1943, S.26–27).

REFA activity rapidly expanded with the munitions boom and lack of workers. Efforts to increase the intensity of labor were strengthened due to the lack of workers in all parts of German industry. They rapidly increased the number of, and participants in, educational REFA courses after 1936 (Hachtmann 1989, S.176). Whereas the number of REFA training courses was less than 100 in 1935, it increased to approximately 230 in 1939 when World War II began. The number of participants increased from about 2000 to approximately 6000 during the same period (Pechhold 1974, S.86–87).

The demands of the war economy further accelerated such developments. The number of participants in REFA courses reached a peak in 1943 with nearly 12,000. "The wage catalog concerning iron and steel and metal work" ("*Lohnkatalog Eisen und Metall*") that came to have a binding force on all metal enterprises after 1942 also brought a repeated, strong rush of REFA activity in the same year (Hachtmann 1989, S.176). This change was related to the introduction of job evaluations. Work studies necessary for job evaluations made it possible to accurately analyze and estimate individual activities and work forces (Schmiede and Schudlich 1981, S.305). Making complex plans punctually beforehand without any loss of time, calculating in advance, and using the remaining room to increase output for the war economy on the basis of accurate time measurements would have been impossible without tables and standard values created by REFA (Wirtschaftsdienst 1942, S.460).

An internal document dated October 20, 1942, from the thyssenKrupp Corporate Archives pointed out that realizing requests for an increase in armament production depended decisively on the success of REFA activity. The three most significant activities included (1) creating work studies for the best work improvement designs, (2) conducting studies to decide accurate time, and (3) grading work based on its value. The measurement of time and job evaluation also had significance. The regrouping of wages throughout the entire industry was indispensable—fair wages were a basis for employee satisfaction, and the foundation of increasing production was built upon such wages. Many countermeasures to these wage problems were taken charge of by REFA as trained staff. The need arose to implement intensive education to train REFA representatives to be well versed in such problems in REFA's regional committee organization, and such activities were performed in cooperation with the German Labor Front. Thus, the role of REFA in education and providing materials further increased [*tkA*, VST/590, Leistungssteigerung in der Rüstungsindustrie (20.10.1942), S.1–3)].

However, observing production-related economic principles and implementing time economy measures became much more difficult and became impossible under constant changes in the war economy. This can be observed in the decrease in REFA activity (Schmiede and Schudlich 1981, S.312). The number of REFA training courses and participants therein decreased after 1943. The number of participants decreased to approximately 1600 in 1945 and fell below this level in 1935 (Pechhold 1974, S.87). Indeed, the best solutions that enabled the progress of individual works in the workshop and office departments using work and time studies were pursued and such studies continued to play a role (Die Deutsche Volkswirtschaft 1943, S.470). However, the defects observed in, for instance, the procurement of raw materials, the replacement of production equipment, sensitivity to disturbances, and bureaucratic economic organization could not be compensated by increases in human performance, so the use of the work study progressed toward failure as the burden caused by the war increased (Pechhold 1974, S.89). REFA activity stopped for the first time with the end of the Nazi rule (Hachtmann 1989, S.176).

In this period, the intensity of labor was significantly increased by using work and time studies and the labor force was saved. Insistence on "scientificness" and "objectivity" of the REFA system was thought to create an opportunity to secure an "industrial piece" within the "works community" by implementing wage payments suitable to worker performance (Hachtmann 1989, S.178–179). Since decisions to create piece wage payment stability under the same conditions could not be made until the mid-1930s, the scientific measurement of work and time studies did not address conflicts over piece wage payments (Schwenger 1935, S.159). Although the endeavor to achieve industrial peace using the REFA system had significance, complications over the piece wage system nonetheless occurred. The restraint of output could become a struggle over the piece work wage system that was adopted by workers. Indeed, the REFA system prevailing, especially in the introduction of the belt conveyor (which controlled the work tempo by a mechanical flow), was an attempt to gain more accurate knowledge about workers' operative capabilities and performance possibilities and set narrow limits on workers' own "piece wage policy" by eliminating workers' ability to repress output. Trouble over the use of the stopwatch and calculator occurred frequently in parallel with the diffusion of the REFA system (Hachtmann 1989, S.201–203).

11.2 General Conditions of the Implementation of the REFA System

REFA system prevailed primarily in the metal industries in a broad sense, similar to the period in which REFA was founded in 1924. In the metal processing industry, the fundamental modernization of labor organizations promoted by REFA and the Agency of Professional Training and Corporate Leadership in many metal processing industry enterprises contributed to the transformation of productivity trends, which decreased until the 1932–1934/35 period. Productivity as measured by work time increased by 34.4% between 1934 and the first quarter of 1939 (Hachtmann 1989, S.228).

In REFA educational courses, in addition to the fundamental course in which work study principles and methods were taught irrespective of the department in 26 two-hour lectures, special training courses for using the REFA system in fixed fields were comprised of 12 lectures totaling 24 h. From 1939 to 1945, 47 three-week courses were organized in the Augstusburg School of the German Labor Front. Of them, 26 were for the metal industry and there were many other courses. The number of courses for the metal, clothing, sawing, paper manufacturing, and casting industries was 26, seven, three, three, and two, respectively. A course was established for the glass, ceramic, shipbuilding, mining, rubber, and printing industries (Pechhold 1974, S.88). Thus, educational REFA courses prevailed in several industrial sectors, which included the metal industry and its related industries, among others. During the World War II period, stronger expansion of the REFA system and the introduction of "the wage catalog concerning iron and steel and metal work" after 1942 promoted the intensification of labor, particularly in metal processing industries that were important for munitions (Hachtmann 1989, S.230–231; Schmiede and Schudlich 1981, S.306). Implementing work studies was never limited to the mechanical industrial sectors or large enterprises but REFA activities could also be observed in the metallurgy industry, forging factories, timber processing industry, clothing industry, and the shoe manufacturing industry (Der Vierjahresplan 1939a, S.881).

However, despite the existence of departments in which the diffusion of the REFA system further progressed, there were still industrial sectors in which systematic work and time studies encountered many difficulties. The shipbuilding industry was a representative case. Efforts to introduce the REFA system in shipbuilding plants were strongly supported, and until the beginning of 1941, this system was adopted in almost every plant except for a few smaller shipbuilding factories. Managers of many companies knew the REFA system well. However, in the shipbuilding industry, there was still distance from the complete understanding of this system. As the accurate calculation of piece work wages required a long period of time, relatively roughly estimated, predetermined time generally had to be used. In addition, urgent tasks often had to take precedence due to constant changes in the plans of the navy; as predetermined work processes were disturbed by these changes, thorough production scheduling was almost impossible. Furthermore, during wartime, the necessary personnel for the piece rating office was lacking. The accurate measurement of the piece wage rate was difficult for these reasons. Therefore, there were a few shipbuilding factories in which activities based on the REFA system were sufficiently performed (Hachtmann 1989, S.179–180). For instance, in the German Shipbuilding Corporation, work and time studies depending on methods of REFA and piece wage based on them were adopted immediately after the acquisition of administrative power by the Nazis.

However, most of other enterprises in the shipbuilding industry began to standardize works for shipbuilding at last in 1938/39 for the first time. In a few smaller shipbuilding yards that did not use the REFA system until 1941, enterprises in which repair work made REFA system adoption impossible appeared (Hachtmann 1989, S.367). The chemical industry also belonged to the industrial sector in which the introduction of the REFA system was not heavily pursued. At least in part of this industry, efforts to increase the intensity of labor using the special wage system and time studies were performed (Schmiede and Schudlich 1981, S.304).

In this way, the rush of the economic situation that began in the mid-1930s did not immediately increase work and time studies in all industrial sectors. Control of economic policy by the Nazi state was concentrated on industries that had significance for armaments. Such conditions caused arrears in work and time studies in industrial sectors that were not emphasized by the state, in particular, the consumer goods industries (Schmiede and Schudlich 1981, S.295).

11.3 Implementation of the REFA System and Changes in Labor Management in Major Industries

Building upon the foregoing analysis, next, this section considers how the REFA system was implemented and how it changed labor management in major industrial sectors.

11.3.1 Implementation of the REFA System and Changes in Labor Management in the Electrical Engineering Industry

In the electrical engineering industry, the study of work time was an important activity responsible for work preparation and the use of REFA principles generally indicated the best form of work time measurement during the period of national socialism (Frenz 1935, S.299). Gustav Leifer pointed out that in 1939 in electrical engineering plants, REFA thinking was adopted more often in recent years (Leifer 1939, S.667–668). According to an internal AEG document dated June 1940, the measurement of work time at this company based on REFA system principles was performed on vacuum tube production. In the Berlinvacuum tube plant, work and time studies were regarded as a means of creating fundamental materials for the improvement of plants, fair wages, and rough calculations based on REFA principles. The work planning office brought together the fundamental concepts of this institution, considering that the same kinds of materials would be used in all sections and future comparisons would become possible and that the appropriate utilization of the unified concept could be achieved using fundamental REFA concepts [*Historisches Archiv der Deutschen Technikmuseums*, GS6385, Arbeitszeitermittlung nach den Grundsätzen des Reichsausschuβ für Arbeitsstudien (Refa) bei der Herstellung in der Röhrenfabrikation (7.6.1940), S.1]. In June 1940, the principles concerning the observation of time and the use of the time exposure filming method (*Zeitaufnahme*) were explained (*Historisches Archiv des Deutschen Technikmuseums*, GS6385, Richtlinien über Zeitbeobachtung und Auswertung von Zeitaufnahme). In January 1941, the problem of time loss in the measurement of work time based on the REFA system was taken up and decisions regarding generally applicable time were planned [*Historisches Archiv des Deustchen Technikmuseums*, GS6385, Verlustzeiten bei der Arbeitszeitermittlung nach Refa (17.1.1941), S.1]. In this period, the introduction of job evaluations also progressed. At AEG, the recognition of work process evaluation had already spread throughout the various units responsible for costs. Keeping close contact with the job evaluation field was recommended to apply such evaluations to other sections [*Historisches Archiv des Deutschen Technikmuseums*, GS6385, Bericht über eine Besprechung über Arbeitsbewertung und Zeitaufnahme am 14.1.41(15.1.1941), S.1].

Regarding the conditions of the primary product departments, when examining the **electric motor sector** in the Elmo Works at Siemens-Schuckert Werke, the time exposure filming was implemented continuously for effective production in 1934 in boring and screw cutting [*Siemens Archiv Akte*, Ls101, Technischer Bericht der Elektromotoren-Werk, Metallgieβerei und Eisengieβerei Pasewalk des 3. Vierteljahr (Monate April-Juni) 1934 (2.7.1934), S.2 (in: Technische Vierteljahrsberichte 3., Monate April-Juni 1934)]. Saving approximately 40% of the time in producing rotor cores of slip rings became possible using time studies [*Siemens Archiv Akte*, Ls101, Technischer Bericht der Elektromotoren-Werk, Metallgieβerei und Eisengieβerei Pasewalk des 2. Vierteljahr (Monate Juli-September) 1934 (18.4.1934), S.2 (in: Technische Vierteljahresberichte 2., Monate Januar/März 1934)]. As a result of a time exposure filming, 20 new memos for preliminary calculations were made for the purpose of subsequent management [*Siemens Archiv Akte*, Ls101, Technicher Bericht der Elektromotoren-Werk, Metallgieβerei und Eisengieβerei Pasewalk des 4. Vierteljahr (Monate Juli-September) 1934 (13.10.1934), S.2 (in: Technische Vierteljahresberichte 4., Monate Juli-September 1934)].

Thus, the implementation of work studies that progressed during the Weimar Republic was further expanded. In 1935, an extension of time and motion study implementation was reported and saving time over 20% was expected (Siegel and von Freiberg 1991, S.356). The term system was newly established and the planning office prepared to expand production of products such as the electric refrigerator and electric motor in the fiscal year 1937/38 (Siegel and von Freiberg 1991, S.359). According to a magazine called "*The Four-Year Plan*" (*Der Vierjahrplan*), in June

1939 in the field of electric motors, the ratio of skilled workers to semiskilled workers in parts production and assembly changed from 7:3 in the previous period to 5:95 and from 8:2 to 1:9, respectively (Der Vierjahresplan 1939b, S.735), and the ratio of semiskilled workers increased.

When considering the **equipment-installing products sector** at Siemens-Schuckert Werke, time and motion studies were implemented and time savings of 15–20% were achieved using the time exposure filming method (Siegel and von Freiberg 1991, S.356). In this enterprise's switch plant in the fiscal year 1935/36, replacing old machine tools on a larger scale became necessary and hard metal was used instead of high-speed steel. In using hard metal in machines and partly finished goods especially appropriate to such tool use, time study made it clear that the time needed to process casting iron, steel, and casting steel could be shortened to one-third, one-fifth, and one-eighth, respectively, of the time required for high-speed steel [*Siemens Archiv Akte*, 15/Lg562, Jahresbericht des Schaltwerks für das Geschäftsjahr 1935/36 (31.12.1936), S.3–4 (in: Chronik 1935/36. Bericht der ZW und der Werke, S.97–98].

In the **telephone manufacturing sector** of the Werner F plant of Siemens & Halske, the systematic education of workers and decision on piece wage payments based on a scientific method were important elements of a personnel policy that aimed at putting the right workers in the right places, which, in turn, led to enhanced long-term performance (Siegel and von Freyberg 1991, S.34).

In the **radio manufacturing sector**, various tools and equipment were required due to the many forms of production (Moellendorff 1935, S.81). This further increased the significance of work preparation. In January 1941, the introduction of the punch card system using the Hollerith code as a tool of work preparation and management in the Berlin vacuum tube plant at AEG was discussed and works that were taken charge of by eight workers in the plant accounting office until then were implemented by machines with the introduction of the Hollerith card [*Historisches Archiv des Deutschen Technikmuseums*, GS6385, Besprechung über Einführung des Hollerith-Lochkartenverfahrens in der Röhrenfertigung des RöwB (14.1.1941), S.1].

11.3.2 Implementation of the REFA System and Changes in Labor Management in the Automobile Industry

In the automobile industry, wage calculation and the field of design problems made the role of work preparation more important (Dyckhoff 1942, S.296; Eichwald 1935, S.310–311). Werner von Schütz pointed out that in 1942, the most efficient management was pursued by the organizational formation of the plant, rationalization over the last 10 years, and the most economic labor force management during wartime and work preparation. Work preparation prevailed in a very broad range under the situation in which demand significantly exceeded supply by many times (Schütz 1942, S.580). In all German automobile firms, work preparation organized the labor process at the end of the 1930s. It performed the processing of work order decisions and parts and unit production as well as machine settlement, tools, and equipment for this work. However, unlike large American automobile enterprises, foremen and skilled workers were in charge of the task of achieving the most well-suited conditions. Unlike the Ford Corporation, at which it was only possible for workers to execute their work according to predetermined time due to very detailed work planning, at Opel, as a typical case of the deployment of American production methods, even though it was within the determined framework, there was room for the autonomous organization of work execution (Stahlmann 1994, S.228).

During this period at both Daimler-Benz and Opel, the work management planning function was moved from lower management to newly created middle management. This can be observed in the decisions and piece wage calculations and control of work output. The foundation of modern work management was already created and new work management with further functional specialization was continually constructed for the managerial differentiation of operations before World War II (Stahlmann 1994, S.234).

In addition, when examining the changes in wage system management at Daimler-Benz, depending on a new method of "analytic job evaluation" whose value was already demonstrated in the US, eight new labor groups were chosen instead of five wage classes in accordance with the introduction of special machine tools with individual drive systems and modern equipment after 1936 and changes in the training system implemented during this period (*Mercedes-Benz Classic Archiv*, Kissel Protokolle, I/15, Protokoll der Vorstandssitzung in UT am 23./24. März 1942, S.17–19; Schriften der Hamburger Stiftung für Sozialgeschichte des 20. Jahrhunderts 1987, S.158). Regarding this point, Bernard P. Bellon pointed out that under rapid expansion and rationalization in the late 1930s, Daimler-Benz implemented the first wage system reform by creating categories based on worker skill and ability (i.e., skilled, semiskilled, and unskilled workers) that had been maintained since the nineteenth century (Bellon 1990, pp.224–225). As more authorities were moved to the time study and work preparation offices according to the enterprise's efforts to make the wage system more objective and use more elaborate job evaluation methods, such endeavors encountered the opposition of foremen and department managers in some cases (Stahlmann 1992). At this company, the REFA system was introduced to measure standard time. According to the minutes of a managing board meeting on March 23/24, 1942, at the Genshagen plant, the measurement of time was consistently performed on the basis of the REFA system. When the largest part of work time was determined by machines, the use of this system was possible. However, in cases of handicrafts such as assembly and body assembly, implementing the REFA system was difficult (*Mercedes-Benz Classic Archiv*, Kissel Protokolle, I/15, Protokoll der Vorstandssitzung in UT.am 23./24. März 1942, S.18–19).

11.3.3 Implementation of the REFA System and Changes in Labor Management in the Machinery Industry

The machinery industry was also an industrial sector in which the work study method such as the REFA system had significance. In the machine tool industry, technical and organizational changes were driven by the preparation for work and operation scheduling, training the managerial ability and flexibility potential of skilled workers, and further development of the systematic management of costs and time after 1933 (Siegel and von Freyberg 1991, S.258). In this industrial sector, the themes of work preparation, work management, and job design gained a special driving force in the labor force arrangement due to an increasing lack of labor. Movements toward the thorough division of work, the complete transformation of the old standard wage group, and methods to establish more just wages were connected to new complex demands for work preparation (Siegel and von Freyberg 1991, S.265; Haase 1937, S.59). For example, in MAN (Maschinenfabrik-Augsburg-Nürnberg), expansion of the operation scheduling office was implemented in 1942, and arranging three young engineers who were in charge of increasing output at production spots in such an office was effective [*MAN Archiv*, 2.3, Nr.27, Leistungssteigerung; 23. Betriebskommission—Punkt 19 (14.4.1942) (Betriebskommissionssitzung am 15. u. 16. Mai 1942 in Düsseldorf), S.1]; such methods became more important in the 1930s.

One effect of time and work studies that played an important role in the work preparation was decreasing workers' work burden. Improvement in the disposition of workers at forging locations was pursued. Work studies brought time and labor savings of forging and ancillary workers by enabling a better arrangement of workers. Great results were achieved by accurate work studies in term observations as well. In a company producing machine tools, the ratio of workers that kept the time limit to all workers was only 27%. In contrast, in other enterprises that decided the term systematically on the basis of a work study, similar figures reached 65% (Kothe 1936, S.65–66).

Work and time studies enabled enterprises to draw effective conclusions concerning the organization of the whole plant, for instance, work preparation, allocation of work, term, holding inventory, planning work, work accuracy, and lacking equipment and apparatuses (Mayer 1939, S.509).

11.3.4 Implementation of the REFA System and Changes in Labor Management in the Iron and Steel Industry

In the iron and steel industry, belonging to a different type of industrial sector from the processing and assembly industries such as the electrical engineering, automobile, and machinery industries, the measurement of time could be performed on the basis of the REFA system using a combination of time studies, rough estimates, calculations, and comparisons with value based on experience (Rossie 1939, S.1067). In iron works, the time study served its most efficient use for production equipment and shortening production time and as a means to indicate ways to manage operation scheduling and term management (Springorum 1936, S.1046). In a hot rolling mill plant, the new piece wage (i.e., the time incentive wage) was adopted to each group in the finishing plant on the basis of detailed time and work studies using the REFA system (Hoppe 1937, S.306–307; Veit 1932, S.544–545). In the cold rolling mill plant, an individual piece work rate was introduced on the basis of minute work and time studies. The results of a time study concerning manual and machine work were recorded in one part of a table and the table of the second sheet, respectively, and the predetermined time as standard time was measured on their basis (Weichselmann 1940, S.170). In the casting plant, the use of time studies progressed. The time needed for completion of one product had to be divided into the time for individual manipulation to generate complete data for the standard value of preliminary calculations and output and in such attempts, the principles of the REFA system had decisive significance (Schütte 1940, S.1108).

Motion studies were also introduced. For instance, at August Thyssen-Hütte, the time exposure photography by film was implemented and performance was calculated. As a result, the highest production volume per 24-h period and the average throughput of the blast furnace was recorded at approximately 1000 tons and 815 tons, respectively. These numerical figures were regarded as binding and became the basis of the production plan (Skroch 1935, S.547–548; Monden 1934, S.539–546; Stahl und Eisen 1934, S.986–988). During the national socialism period, management using the Gantt Chart was also observed (Schmidt 1937, S.156–162).

In the iron and steel industry, changes in labor management were enforced on the basis of work studies, including time and motion studies, although the situation differed greatly in other enterprises. Herbert Rossie pointed out in 1939 that the tools available for measurement in reality were still lacking at the time and therefore the fields in which accurate time study methods were used were limited. Particularly, in small and medium enterprises, a very large part of decisions regarding predetermined time as standard time depended on rough calculations (Rossie 1939, S.1067). For example, at Krupp, according to an internal document dated April 21, 1937, cases arose in various plants where the piece work rate was being implemented, and the company implemented efforts to keep the piece wage rate at a low level and the intentional restraint of labor by workers was attempted as a countermeasure to rate-cutting. Such rate-cutting caused protests and requests for improvement by workers (*Historisches Archiv Krupp*, WA41/6-207, Niederschrift über die Sitzung des Vertrauensrats der Gußstahlfabrik am 21. April 1937, vormittags 10 Uhr, im Hauptverwaltungsgebäude, S.1–2).

11.3.5 Implementation of the REFA System and Changes in Labor Management in the Chemical Industry

In the chemical industry, time and work studies played a big role in piece wage rate decisions. The piece wage system at IG Farben was completed up to the smallest part. For instance, in Leverkusen, there were approximately 30,000 piece wage rates and hundreds of prescriptions for a premium wage system concerning individual plants and products (Zollitsch 1990, S.80). At Bayer's Dormagen plant, the piece wage rate system with premium wages was adopted for all production locations on the basis of work and time studies with one exceptional case after 1935 (Schmiede and Schudlich 1981, S.28). Implementation of time and work studies became more significant in introducing sophisticated systems for the piece wage. As previously mentioned in Sect. 8.3, although the chemical industry was not an industrial sector in which the introduction of methods such as the REFA system was strongly driven, endeavors to increase labor intensity by using a special wage system and time studies were pursued, at least in part of this industry (Schmiede and Schudlich 1981, S.304–305).

For example, at **BASF,** as a constituent part of IG Farben, the primary fields of preliminary calculation were divided into two large groups: (1) implementing piece work and (2) making data for the production premium system. The production premium plan was appropriately based not on individual performance but on the performance of all plant employees during a certain term, usually one month. Such changes needed to be thoroughly reformed by the preliminary calculation department. Therefore, the Central Preliminary Calculation Department was established instead of three piece rating offices. The number of personnel in this department increased from 67 in 1932 at its lowest level to 222 in 1940 [*BASF Archiv*, Vogtländer-Tetzner V, Werksgeschichte Heft IX, Chronik der BASF 1865–1940, VII. Periode (1933–1940), S.1343–1344]. The number of persons who were in charge of preliminary calculations increased from only 18 in 1933 to 142 in 1940 [*BASF Archiv*, Vogtländer-Tetzner V, Werksgeschichte Heft IX, Chronik der BASF 1865–1940, VII. Periode (1933–1940), S.1539].

At **Bayer**, a subdivision of IG Farben, the work office (*Arbeitsbüro*) was founded as the section in charge of preliminary calculations and time and work studies. The piecework committee (*Akkordkommission*) established in August 1920 was its beginning. The piece rating office was created as a supervisory institution to provide advice to business units (*Bayer Archiv*, 1/6-6-25, Arbeitsbüro, S.1). In the latter half of the 1920s, the preliminary calculation function, which was exclusively taken charge of by foremen until the beginning of the 1920s (*Bayer Archiv*, 1/6-6-25, Arbeitsbüro, S.4–5), came to be performed with time studies by the piece rating office. Preliminary calculations were implemented on the basis of the REFA system. In the Nazi era, such efforts further progressed. The piece rating office was put in charge of not only measuring incentive time (*Akkordzeit*) but also job design, wage payment methods, and problems concerning the wage level at the end of the 1930s. With this expansion in the extent of the job, the piece rating office was changed to the work office in January 1940 (*Bayer Archiv*, 1/6-6-25, Arbeitsbüro, S.11–12).

However, in Leverkusen, the two-hold form, in which the calculation function was taken charge of by a time inspector and foreman, was adopted in the 1930s. This meant that shifting the calculating function to the work office or the piece rating office was still in a transitional stage. Even after this transformation, preliminary calculations were implemented primarily by employees at locations as before. Endeavors to move all duties concerning preliminary calculations to the work office were driven more intensely after 1942. However, it was in 1946, after World War II, that preliminary calculations came to be under the purview of an independent calculator. This transformation brought a significant increase in the staff of the work office. The number of such personnel was 75 in 1946 (*Bayer Archiv*, 1/6-6-25, Arbeitsbüro, S.14–15), which increased to about three times the number (28) in 1933 (*Bayer Archiv*, 1/6-6-25, Arbeitsbüro, Anlage 4). In the education of persons in charge of setting the piece wage rate, the number of such trained personnel reached 32 in 1928 and was highest in the late 1920s. However, there were similar figures in 1934 and 1938 of 92 and 80, respectively. The number of persons trained during the period from 1933 to 1945 reached 501 (*Bayer Archiv*,1/6-6-25, Arbeitsbüro, Anlage 2). Uniformly applying data concerning the piece wage and premium wage to all locations and business units determined a shift in responsibility for the calculating function from the foreman to the work office as a neutral institution (*Bayer Archiv*, 1/6-6-25, Arbeitsbüro, S.38).

In the iron and steel and chemical industries, work studies were implemented to make wage decisions. However, in the field of labor organization and management, the role that rationalization played was not as great as in the processing and assembly industries such as the electrical engineering, automobile, and machinery industries due to characteristics of production processes of the iron and steel and chemical industries.

In Germany, except for the brief regarding the necessity to use science to reduce waste, the ideology of scientific management itself was neither wholeheartedly adopted nor widely accepted. However, the implementation of the techniques of scientific management was extensive in the interwar period (Guillén 1994, pp.267–269, 283) and this trend can be prominently observed in the Nazi era.

During the period of national socialism, realizing mass production became a much more important goal under the militarization of economy and the shift to a war economy. Tremendous expansion of the munitions markets demanded and promoted mass production in the munitions industries and related industrial sectors. The deployment of the Ford system became one of the most important tasks for realizing such goals. Therefore, the next research topic to be considered is how the Ford system was deployed and how the shift toward mass production progressed and the results of such movements. The next chapter will examine this research problem.

References

Bellon BP (1990) Mercedes in peace and war. Cambridge University Press, New York
Böhrs H (1942) Leitfaden für das Arbeitsstudium. In: Technik und Wirtschaft 35(4):70–71

Der Deutsche Volkswirt (1939) Klare Zuständigkeiten in der Rationalisierungsarbeit. In: Der Deutsche Volkswirt 14(5):124
Der Vierjahresplan (1939a) Arbeitsstudien fördern die Leistung. In: Der Vierjahresplan 3(14): 880–881
Der Vierjahresplan (1939b) Innerbetriebliche Leistungssteigerung. In: Der Vierjahresplan 3(11):734–735
Die Deutsche Volkswirtschaft (1943) Rationalisierung nach Erzeugnissen. In: Die Deutsche Volkswirtschaft 12(15):470–471
Dyckhoff O (1942) Grundlagen für eine Groβproduktion und deren maschinelle Ausrüstung im Kraftfahrzeugbau. In: Automobiltechnische Zeitschrift 45(11):293–300
Eichwald E (1935) Arbeitsvorbereitung im Konstruktionsbüro von Kraftwagenfabriken. In: Automobiltechnische Zeitschrift 38(12):310–313
Frenz G (1935) Aus der Praxis der Arbeitsvorbereitung. In: Maschinenbau 14(11/12):229–300
Guillén NF (1994) Models of management. Works, authority, and organization in a comparative perspective. The University of Chicago Press, Chicago, London
Haase K (1937) Aufgaben des deutschen Werkzeugmaschinenbau. In: Werkstatt und Betrieb 70(5/6):57–59
Hachtmann R (1989) Industriearbeit im 》Dritten Reich《. Untersuchungen zu den Lohn- und Arbeitsbedingungen in Deutschland 1933–1945. Vandenhoeck & Ruprecht, Göttingen
Hoppe C (1937) Zeitakkorde in Zurichtereien, besonderers in Walzwerken für mittlere und schwere Form- und Profilstähle. In: Archiv für das Eisenhüttenwesen 11(6):303–306
Koda R, Ito M (1990) Doitsu ni okeru kagakuteki kanriho no tenkai (Development of scientific management in Germany). In: Hara T (ed) Kagakuteki kanriho no donyu to tenkai (Deployment and development of scientific mangement). Showado, Tokyo, pp 159–207
Kothe E (1936) Bestgestaltung der Arbeit durch Arbeitsstudien. In: Maschinenbau 15(3/4):63–66
Leifer G (1939) Der Einfluβ des planmäβigen Arbeitseinsatzes auf die Leistung der Betriebe. In: Der Vierjahresplan 3(10):666–670
Maschinenbau (1934) Schulungsarbeit des Refa. In: Maschinenbau 13(21/22):602
Maschinenbau (1936) Refa=Reichsausschuβ für Arbeitsstudien. In: Maschinenbau 15(7/8):215
Mayer F (1939) Arbeits- und Zeitstudien in der Schlosserei und im Zusammenbau. In: Maschinenbau 18(19/20):507–509
Moellendorff UV (1935) Werkzeuge und Vorrichtungen im Rundfunkgerätebau. In: Maschinenbau 14(3/4):81–83
Monden H (1934) Leistungsüberwachung im Walzwerken in Anlehnung an das Gantt-Verfahren. In: Archiv für das Eisenhüttenwesen 7(9):539–546
Pechhold E (1974) 50 Jahre REFA. Beuth, Berlin, Köln, Frankfurt am Main
Peiseler G (1943) Rationalisierung der Zeit- und Arbeitsstudien. In: Technik und Wirtschaft 36(2):25–28
Pentzlin K (1935) Die Zweckstudie. Beitrag zum Neuaufbau der Arbeitswissenschaft. In: Technik und Wirtschaft 28(8):225–232
Pentzlin K (1938) Grundsätzliches zur deutschen Arbeitsrationalisierung (Kritik des Bedaux-System). In: Technik und Wirtschaft 31(2):33–40
Pentzlin K (1942) Arbeitsforschung und Betriebspraxis. In: Technik und Wirtschaft 35(4):57–61
Rossie H (1939) Zur Frage der Schätzung von Arbeitsvorgabezeiten bei Akkordarbeit. In: Stahl und Eisen 59(38):1967–2069
Schlaich K (1974) Stand und Weiterentwichklung der REFA-Lehre. In: REFA-Nachrichten 27(3):190–192
Schmidt G (1937) Zeitstudien in Schmiedebetrieben und ihre betriebswirtschaftliche Verwaltung. In Archiv für das Eisenhüttenwesen 11(3):157–162
Schmiede R, Schudlich E (1981) Die Entwicklung der Leistungsentlohnung in Deutschland: Eine historische Untersuchung zum Verhältniss von Lohn und Leistung unter kapitalistischen Prodokutionsbedingungen, 4. Auflage. Campus Verlag, Frankfurt am Main, New York

Schriften der Hamburger Stiftung für Sozialgeschichte des 20. Jahrhunderts (Hrsg) (1987) Das Daimler-Benz Buch. Ein Rüstungskonzern im >Tausendjährigen Reich<. Delphi Politik, Nördlingen

Schütte W (1940) Betriebswirtschaftliche Maβnahmen zur Leistungssteigerung in der Eisenhüttenindustrie, 2 Teil. In: Stahl und Eisen 60(49):1107–1113

Schütz Wv (1942) Betriebsführung und Betriebswissenschaft. In: Automobiltechnische Zeitschrift 45 (21):580–582

Schwenger R (1935) Das soziale Frage im Betrieb. In: Jahrbuch für Nationalökonomie und Statistik 142:49–163

Siegel T, von Freyberg T (1991) Industrielle Rationalisierung unter dem Nationalsozialismus. Campus, Frankfurt am Main, New York

Skroch K (1935) Leistungsüberwachung in Feinblechwalzwerken. In: Stahl und Eisen 55(20):544–549

Spitzley H (1980) Wissenschaftliche Betriebsführung, REFA Methodenlehre und Neuorientierung der Arbeitswissenschaft. Bund-Verlag, Köln

Springorum F (1936) Die technische Entwicklung der deutschen Eisen- und Stahlerzeugung während der letzten fünfzehen Jahre. In: Stahl und Eisen 56(38):1042–1063

Stahl und Eisen (1934) Leistungsüberwachung in Siemens-Martin Werken mit Hilfe des Gantt-Verfahrens. In: Stahl und Eisen 54(38):986–988

Stahlmann M (1992) Management, Modernisierung- und Arbeitspolitik beider Daimler-Benz AG und ihren Vorläuferunternehmen von der Jahrhundertwende bis zum Zweiten Weltkrieg. In: Zeitschrift für Unternehmensgeschichte 37(3):147–180

Stahlmann M (1994) Von der Wekstatt zur Lean-Production. In: Zeitschrift für Unternehmensgeschichte 39(3):219–243

Veit K (1932) Betriebswirtschaftliche Untersuchung in einer Zurichterei. In: Stahl und Eisen 52(22):544–545

Weichselmann F (1940) Betriebswirtschaftliche Maβnahmen zur Leistungssteigerung in der Eisenhütten- industrie. In: Stahl und Eisen 60(9):169–173

Weigel W (1942) Neuzeitliche Arbeitsuntersuchung im Zusammenbau. In: Werkstattstechnik und Werkswleiter 36(3/):46–49

Winkel A (1938) Die Auswirkung der Refa-Arbeit im Unternehmen. In: Maschinenbau 17(19/20):505–506

Wirtschaftsdienst (1942) Refa-Vorstufe der Rationalisierung. In: Wirtschaftsdienst 27(26):460

Zollitsch W (1990) Arbeiter zwischen Weltwirtschaftskrise und Nationalsozialismus. Ein Beitrag zur Sozialgeschichte der Jahre, (1928) Bis 1936. Vandenhoeck & Ruprecht, Göttingen

Chapter 12
Expansion of the Munitions Market and Deployment of the Ford System

Abstract This chapter considers the deployment of the Ford system in the German-specific conditions represented by the munition markets in the Nazi era. This chapter analyzes the implementation of standardization of production with the force of government and the flow of production systems based on the expanding munition markets. The chapter first discusses the progress of the standardization of production under the strong involvement of the state. It then examines the introduction of the flow production system and efforts to develop a German-specific style of mass production concerning the characteristics of the munition market. Cases in the electrical engineering, automobile, and machinery industries are explored from the comparative perspective of these industrial sectors. Based on these discussions, the characteristics and limitations in the deployment of the American mass production system represented by the Ford system are clarified in two points: implementing mass production and how the Ford system, based on munition markets, influenced the national economy by creating demands in related industries.

Keywords Economy of scale · Flexibility · Flow production · Ford system · Mass production · Munition market · Production management · Standardization of production

During the period of National Socialism, munitions demand was tremendously expanded with the militarization of economy caused by the Second Four-Year Plan, which began in 1936, and the shift to a war economy starting in 1939. Under such extensive changes in market conditions, many industries experienced remarkable development and the shift to mass production progressed. During this period, systematic attempts at standardization were pursued under the strong involvement of the state. These favorable situations gave enterprises in many industries the possibility of further introducing the Ford system and the realization of mass production. Therefore, it is important to clarify how production standardization was a significant foundation for realizing mass production and how the deployment of the flow production system progressed.

T. Yamazaki, *A History of German Business*,
https://doi.org/10.1007/978-981-96-8476-2_12

The chapter examines the implementation of the Ford system and the progress of mass production based on the tremendous expansion of the munitions market. It explains the significance and limitations of Ford system deployment and attempts to realize an economic system based on mass production relative to the special character of the munitions market as opposed to private demand by comparing it to the development after World War II when the consumer goods markets, in particular, the durable consumer goods markets, expanded tremendously. In this chapter, the problem of realizing of mass production by implementing the Ford system is examined considering the characteristics of the munitions market.

In Sect. 12.1, production standardization as an important pillar of the Ford system is considered. In Sect. 12.2, the deployment of the flow production system is analyzed. In these two sections, cases in the electrical engineering, automobile, and machine industries are examined in relation to the expansion of the munitions market and the character of this market. Based on these discussions, in Sect. 12.3, the significance and limitations of the munitions market in the development of mass production are clarified.

12.1 Standardization of Production and Its Characteristics

12.1.1 Standardization in the Nazi Era and the Role of the State

Considering production standardization, the economic policy of the Fascism regarded standardization and reduction of type as new goals. This was indicated in the benefits of standardization for production enabling the savings and efficient use of raw materials (Etzold 1988, S.91; RKW-Nachrichten 1935, S.131). Norms and unified delivery conditions became an indispensable pacemaker for the appropriate management of raw materials (RKW-Nachrichten 1938, S.54). The necessity and importance of standardization came to be broadly recognized from this perspective. The total number of norm lists increased remarkably from approximately 3,000 in 1929 to over 6,000 in 1936. It increased further to over 6,400 at the beginning of 1939 and reached its peak of 8,200 in 1942 until the end of World War II (DNA 1957, S.71; Zeitschrift des Vereins Deutscher Ingenieure 1939, S.787). In 1936, the number of norm lists related to shipbuilding, railway, machine manufacturing and material inspection was 1,250, 650, and 630, respectively. Similar figures related to electrical engineering, construction, mining, tools and machine tools, and automobile manufacturing were 450, 410, 400, 250, and 170, respectively (RKW-Nachrichten 1936, S.136). The number of norm lists concerning the processing and assembly industries were relatively high. Although the number of norm lists increased to about 7,700, items of each related department tended to be the same as in 1936 (Freitag 1942, S.178–179).

The progress of standardization in this period was due to the involvement of the state in promoting technical rationalization in this field under the militarization of economy (Hachtmann 1989, S.71). Whereas the observation of norms was obligatory in supplies for the Armed Forces, the National Railways (*Reichsbahn*), and the National Post (*Reichspost*), participation in the creation of norms was generally unrestricted and regarded only as a recommendation except for government and public authorities. However, this situation changed with the Second Four-Year Plan in 1936. Applying standardization became a primary obligation by order of the minister of the economy. In addition, compulsory adoption was implemented after the foundation of the "National Committee for Production Increase" in February of 1939. Under such conditions, standardization activity became a central task decided in the urgent plan of the Ministry for the Economy in May 1939. Orders for changing the number of types and product kinds were promulgated on the basis of the orders of the administrator of the Four-Year Plan on September 8, 1939. It gave the minister of the economy the authority to declare that norms were obligatory. Appropriate direction by the industrial group concerning standardization, the reduction of type, and cost-cutting was provided on September 28, 1939 (Koehn 1942, S.666; Etzold 1988, S.91–92; Der Vierjahresplan 1941, S.658).

The outbreak of World War II made standardization efforts more urgent and systematic. The significance of standardization and the reduction of type for the war economy lay in (1) making production easy, (2) securing the exchangeability of parts of the same equipment, and (3) ensuring the exchangeability of parts of various equipment. In particular, the third point contributed to the transformation of important industries for the war (Schnitt 1936, S.219). The orders of the minister for the economy and the administrators of each department and other orders for reductions in the number of types made reduction of type a duty of the war economy. Thus, unlike the Weimar era when attempts to reduce product types were able to achieve only small effects (Etzold 1988, S.92), such endeavors became a primary, central problem during the Nazi era (Olk 1941, S.539–541). In the machine tool industry, the reduction of type was promoted by order on May 28, 1941, which introduced the obligation of reporting the starting and stopping of machine tool manufacturing (RKW-Nachrichten 1939, S.176). In other departments and the metal processing industries, the number of types was thoroughly reduced (Hachtmann 1989, S.77). In the fiscal year 1942/1943, the simplification of production based on specialization and the reduction of type in the mining industry were required by the command of Adolf Hitler himself (Buskühl 1942, S.218).

In 1942, of 1,700 norms, approximately 1,500 were compulsory (Koehen 1942, S.666). However, the "Committee for Standardization and Reduction of Type," the chairman of which was the head of the German Norm Committee, was organized by order of the minister of armaments on June 24, 1944, to improve the efficiency of standardization activities to enable an increase in wartime production. The authority to declare that norms were obligatory was given to chairman of this new committee. He was responsible for "duties of strict integration and promotion of standardization and the reduction of type" and for implementation of measures by the minister of armaments. His duty was to begin the appropriate measures for introducing norms (RKW-Nachrichten 1944, S.72).

Whereas cartel policy was pursued as a measure to cope with the high market risk of specialization in the Weimar era, state forces replaced such means in the Nazi era. During the Weimar Republic, specialization in the form of being limited to a few types of similar machines was associated with high market risk. Since many machine tool manufacturers feared such risks, improving the premise for specialization (standardization, reduction of type, and industrial concentration) became an important task of cartel policy in this period (Siegel and von Freyberg 1991, S.203–205). In contrast, during the national socialism period, such rationalization measures were enforced by the state. The promotion of interfirm rationalization through monopolistic capital organizations was emphasized to increase organizational efficiency for the wartime economy by centralizing state monopolistic regulations. Standardization and strengthening the division of labor in production and assembly processes were pursued by such rationalization (Mottek et al. 1975, S.339).

12.1.2 Standardization of Production in Major Industries

This section examines the progress of production standardization in the major industrial sectors, including the electrical engineering, automobile, and machinery industries belonging to the processing and assembly industries in which Ford system deployment became an important task.

12.1.2.1 Standardization of Production in the Electrical Engineering Industry

Many norms became compulsory in the electrical engineering industry on the basis of orders by the head of this industry's economic group. The thorough reduction of type in the field of radio vacuum tubes was directed by the Administrator of Communication Technology. Thus, standardization was driven by the force of the state (Wagner 1942, S.533). The Main Committee for the Electrical Equipment Industry (*Hauptausschss Elektrotechnik*) was founded in the spring of 1943 as a committee in the Alfred Speer Ministry to achieve greater increases in the production of the electrical equipment supplied to the Armed Forces. It directed the allotment of metal, standardization of products, and the simplification of processes and drove the standardization of production and eliminated certain non-essential products (The United States Strategic Bombing Survey 1947c, pp.2–3, 20).

Cartel organization also played a big role in driving standardization. In this period, there were various cartels formed to regulate prices, allocate to territories outside of Germany, implement production standardization, and exchange general technical information (The United States Strategic Bombing Survey 1947c, p.13).

The number of German industrial norms related to the electrical industry increased from about 50 in 1925 to over 200 in 1930. However, it was in the 1930s that further increases progressed. The number of such norms increased to over approximately 500 after the first few years of the 1940s (Wagner 1942, S.531). Important characteristics of production in the electrical industry could be seen in the striking variety of products and fields of use (Braun 1935, S.11). Production standardization in major product sectors is considered next.

Electric Motor Sector: As a result of the variety of products primarily related to generating power, the number of revolutions, protection methods, operating times, and sizes, many products were created in the field of electric motors. In 1940, there were only 3.7 types of open three-phase motors operated in the iron producing plant that integrated other production processes. It was necessary to limit electric motor production to one or two suppliers to reach a satisfactory level to a certain degree. However, such attempts were not implemented in all cases and never indicated a solution to the problem (Schiz 1940, S.275–276, 278). Around the end of World War II, efforts to adopt separate drive methods for various working machines triggered very high demand for the three-phase short circuit motor primarily and reducing the types of electric motor as broadly as possible became necessary (Götz 1944, S.207). However, even right before the end of the war, the reduction of type of the electric motor did not progress sufficiently. The magazine "*Der Vierjahresplan*" in February 1944 pointed out that even in this year, the reduction of type of the electric motor should be continued in many fields (Der Vierjahresplan 1944, S.45). In parts standardization, norms for shaft ends, belt pulleys, and fixed flanges of the electric motor were created with DIN VDE2,942 as one of the norms of the German Standards Committee. DIN747 was followed for the shaft height (Schiz 1940, S.277).

Communications Equipment Sector: In telephone manufacturing, the total weight of telephones produced at Siemens, the weight of metal parts, and the number of parts were reduced by 16%, 56%, and 13%, respectively, and the wages required for production were cut by 38% through the simplification of structure and the standardization of parts (Siemens-Mitteilungen 1939, S.106; Leifer 1939, S.666). In the fiscal year 1937/38, the number of individual parts of the newest telephone was significantly decreased from 116 to 58 (Der Deutsche Volkswirt 1939a, S.924). H. Wagner highlighted that in 1942, the standardization of communications equipment parts such as condensers and resistors had been receiving a special driving force and varied equipment types were assembled with relatively few elements without any new or special design on the basis of "the unit system." This method of standardization often led to the reduction of product type (Wagner 1942, S.530).

In radio production, all enterprises abandoned specific products with a special structure on the basis of special group demand and, as a result, the number of types decreased from over 200 to fewer than 170 (Der Deutsche Volkswirt 1937a, S.2197). In the rationalization plan for the radio manufacturing industry, which members of state institutions created at the end of the 1930s to achieve mass production of radio sets for the Armed Forces, the number of equipment types should have been reduced from 266 to 138 in 1940/1941. Previously existing requests were achieved with the standardization of individual parts and the reduction of type (Der Deutsche Volkswirt 1939d, S.2238; Der Deutsche Volkswirt 1940, S.616).

Equipment-Installing Products Sector: According to *Der Vierjahresplan* magazine in February 1944, the time needed for production was abbreviated by over 80%

and the consumption of raw materials and costs was reduced by approximately 30% and 40%, respectively, by the unification of contact springs for plug sockets (Der Vierjahresplan 1944, S.45). A report in 1944 pointed out that all manufacturers of plugs for communications equipment were obligated to implement the new design of the triple-pohl plug featuring a 5.77-mm (mm) diameter on the basis of DIN41,700 (Biniek 1944, S.131–132).

Incandescent Lamp Manufacturing Sector: With the outbreak of World War II, rationalization measures previously started in the field of incandescent lamps had to be expanded to make production adjustments to the constantly increasing demands of specific munitions industries. One of the most important means for doing so was standardization (Abshagen and Koetz 1943, S.79). Surprisingly good effects were achieved by the cooperation of manufacturers integrated in the "Electric Lamp Community," particularly after the foundation of the circle organization in the middle of 1942. As a result, in May 1944, the number of types was reduced to approximately 330 instead of no less than 27,000 types before World War I. Similar attempts can be also observed in special large and small lamps. The Electric Technical Special Committee and the Electric Lamp Technical Special Committee played a major role in the incandescent lamp manufacturing department and contributed decisively to such wonderful results (Freiberger 1944, S.124; Abshagen and Koetz 1943, S.79–80).

Other Product Sectors: Whereas 100 types were previously produced in the **loudspeaker sector**, only 14 types were produced in 1940 (Der Vierjahresplan 1940a, S.13). According to an April 1943 report, not only was a series of prescriptions and norms issued by the Association of Electric Engineers, but alterations were also made in overhead wire manufacturing to enable the use of interchangeable raw materials in the **electric wire sector**. This association was involved in rationalization measures in the field of overhead wire and isolator parts as well as the reduction of type (Jacottet and Lieber 1943, S.196). The number of types of high-voltage isolators in the **isolator sector** was reduced from 120 to 19 by the first half of 1943 (Speer 1943, S.242). During this period, appropriate Deutsches Institut für Normung (DIN) norm lists were made, along with attempts to adjust to the situation (Jacottet and Lieber 1943, S.197). According to a report by Rudolf Winkler in 1944, the thorough standardization of lead accumulators for transportation equipment was implemented in the **storage battery sector** on the basis of DIN72,311 immediately before new unified norms were created in October 1943. However, whereas there were favorable conditions regarding the norms related to fixed-type shortage batteries, the situation in other fields of the lead accumulator differed. Thus, there were differences between products in the progress of standardization (Winckler 1944, S.315). In the **generator sector**, the number of types of generators with engines decreased from 415 to 51 in 1944. The types of **electric soldering irons**, **electric measurement appliances**, and large **cooking appliances** were reduced from 105 to 66, from 260 to 8, and from 150 to 9, respectively (Der Vierjahresplan 1944, S.45).

In this way, standardization and reduction of type activities in the electrical engineering industry were driven by the compulsion of the state. Standardization progressed more effectively during wartime and engendered many beneficial results. Wilfried Felsenkirchen pointed out that the greatest effects of rationalization at

Siemens during World War II were related to reorganizing the range of types on rational principles (Feldenkirchen 1995, S.199). British research on the electric motor and power transformer plants of five enterprises in the German electrical industry stressed that the degree of standardization was high and that such measures were applied to product components and other manufacturing data and encouraged "production along the most efficient and economic lines" (British Intelligence Objectives Sub-Committee 1946b, p.3). The United States (US) Strategic Bombing Survey pointed out that "production continued to increase until November 1944 due to extensive reductions in types of products and simplification of production processes" despite the striking loss of plant facilities to bombing (The United States Strategic Bombing Survey 1947c, p.39).

12.1.2.2 Standardization of Production in the Automobile Industry

Unlike the US, the degree of capital concentration in the German automobile industry was low, so extremely small production lots of any kind of product tended to be developed for a narrow domestic market (Oshima 1991a, p.10). In 1937, the number of types of passenger cars, trucks, motorcycles, tractors, and three-wheel vehicles was 52, 113, 150, 105, and 20, respectively (Schell 1939a, S.1011; Schell 1939b, S.363; Automobiltechnische Zeitschrift 1939, S.239–241, Oshima 1991a, p.10). There were no less than 15 to 16 classes of effective loads of trucks. Countless types of truck trailers existed due to fact that a considerable portion of those produced was manufactured by handicraft (Der Vierjahresplan 1939, S.531; Schell 1939a, S.1011–1012, Automobiltechnische Zeitschrift 1939, S.241). In 1939, the number of types, including variations, totaled 1,367 (The United States Strategic Bombing Survey 1947d, p.11). However, in reality, there were two to three variations on one main type in addition to no less than 440 primary types of automobiles. As a result, approximately 1,200 types existed overall (Schell 1939a, S.1011).

One of the primary factors determining the high cost of raw materials for the German automobile was the delay in parts standardization. According to a 1934 report, the cost of raw materials in Germany was 49% higher than in the US. The difference between the two countries in the cost of steel, copper, pressed parts, and rubber was 25%, 30%, 60%, and 40%, respectively, and costs in the German automobile industry were higher than their American counterparts. The costs of parts such as gray casting iron, screws, rivets, and bolts in Germany were 2.25 times higher than in the US (Schwenninger 1934, S.316). A 1939 report pointed out that there were no less than 5,381 types of 123 kinds of parts; therefore, on average, approximately 44 types existed for each part (Der Deutsche Volkswirt 1939c, S.2039; Schell 1939a, XS.1012). The high cost of repair parts was also due to the existence of many automobile types (Der Deutsche Voklswirt 1937b, S.1054). The standardization of primary unit parts became an important task under these conditions. In a discussion at Daimler-Benz on September 20, 1938, the decision on whether the rear axle of the L66 type could be used for the production of future economic cars was important [*Mercedes-Benz Classic Archiv*, Kissel Technische Protokolle, 1.30, Protokoll Nr.316 über die Aussprache am 20. September 1938 in Gaggenau (21.9.1938), S.6].

In the automobile industry, involvement and compulsion by the state became a special form to overcome this situation. Automobile enterprises maintained their autonomy on decisions regarding product type until 1938 (Pohl and Habeth 1986, S.65). At Daimler-Benz, the selection of type was performed autonomously and in a board of directors meeting on November 12, 1937, the company's type program was significantly adjusted [*Mercedes-Benz Classic Archiv*, Kissel Protokolle, I/10, Protokoll der Vorstandssitzung vom 12. November 1937 in U.T. (3.12.1937), S.3, *Mercedes-Benz Classic Archiv*, Kissel, Werk Gaggenau, 6.9, Rundschreiben Nr.1629 betreffend Übersicht über das Gaggenauer Nutzwagenprogramm im Jahre 1937 (11.2.1937), S.1]. Another internal Daimler-Benz document dated November 29, 1937, pointed out that their type program was very definitive and simple [*Mercedes-Benz Classic Archiv*, Kissel Technische Protokolle,1.29, Der Brief von Dr. W. Kissel an Herrn Direktor Carl Werner betreffend Typenbegrenzung (29.11.1937), S.1].

Drastic reductions in type were attempted in Germany in preparation for war (Oshima 1991a, p.10). From the perspective of the entire automobile industry, increasing munitions production standardization had not made very much progress at the time. Therefore, a system was created to drive standardization more intensely by state involvement and enforcement. Adolf von Schell, the colonel of the Supreme Order of the Army was appointed Chief Representative for Motor Vehicles in November 1938. After an order regarding the reduction of type in the automobile industry was issued on March 2, 1939, he set a goal to decrease the number of automobile types from 335 to 81 by December 31, 1939 (Hachtmann 1989, S.72–73; Der Vierjahresplan 1940a, S.13; Meyer 2009, S.436).

Schell's plan set the goal of reducing the number of **passenger car** types from 52 to 30. Five primary types of cars with engines smaller than 1.2 L should be produced by four enterprises and six main types of cars with an engine size between 1.2 and 2 L should be manufactured by six enterprises. Eleven primary types of cars with 2- to 3-L engines should be produced by 10 companies and three main types of cars with 3- to 4-L engines should be manufactured by three enterprises. In passenger cars with an engine size greater than 4 L, five primary types should be produced by three enterprises. The emphasis of the reduction of type was placed specifically on cars with an engine size greater than 1.3 L.

The goal was to reduce the number of **truck** types from 113 to 19. Of the 15–16 effective load classes, only 1.5-ton, 3-ton, 4.5-ton, and 6.5-ton trucks should be produced. In trucks with a 1-ton nominal maximum load, only one type of 1-ton truck should be produced by one company and five primary types of 1.5-ton trucks should be produced by five companies. Six main types of 3-ton trucks should be manufactured by seven firms and four main types of 4.5-ton trucks should be manufactured by eight firms. Three primary types of 6.5-ton trucks should be produced by six enterprises. For small trucks, only each one type of three-wheel vehicle and four-wheel trucks with a 650-kg (kg) nominal effective load and a 500-cubic centimeter (cc) engine should be produced by five enterprises; the goal was reducing the number of types from 20 to 2. Therefore, the overall number of types, including small trucks, should be decreased to 21. Similar goals were set for motorcycles, trailers, and tractors. Regarding the former, the reduction from 150 to 30 types became the goal (Der Vierjahresplan 1939, S.530–531; Automobiltechnische Zeitschrift 1939, S.239–241; Hass 1939, S.953; Gentsch 1939, S.1207–1208; Kirchberg 1969, S.135–136; Seherr-Thoss 1979, S.352–353).

As a result of this reduction of type plan, no less than 1,200 types, including car variations, were reduced to 200 and the number of parts-types was decreased from 5,381 to 739 in September 1939. Looking at standardization of main parts shows decreases in the types of generators for lighting (164 to 27), starters (113 to 10), switchboard boxes (114 to 2), ignition plugs (35 to 5), electric bulbs (269 to 26), winkers (38 to 2), fuel cocks (435 to 4), tachometers (215 to 7), tail lamps (50 to 1), and central lubricators (32 to 4). Motorcycle parts also decreased, including the types of horns (25 to 1), starters (212 to 19), saddles (22 to 3), and rear saddles (60 to 1) (Schell 1939a, S.1012). The appointment of A. v. Schell as Chief Representative for Motor Vehicles and his plan for the reduction of types were pursued on the basis of Hermann Gerling's intention to standardize various automobiles and restrict product type from the military perspective (Busch 1966, S.31; Oshima 1991b, p.143). However, standardization did not progress as first planned (Braun 1995, S.65), so Schell attempted to implement further reduction of type and make a new wartime plan simultaneously (Oshima 1991b, p.143).

In his plan, the reduction goal for passenger car types was five (Kirchberg 1969, S.139). However, despite such endeavors, the restriction of types could not be achieved as planned (Oshima 1991b, p.145). There were many kinds of cars for military use compared to the US (Oshima 1993, p.69; Kirchberg 1969; The United States Strategic Bombing Survey 1947d, p.11). Under this situation, 50,000 trucks and trailers—equivalent to the volume produced in six months—were lost due to the battle in Stalingrad (Eichholtz 1985, S.338), which greatly changed the situation. The Central Automobile Committee was organized and decided that production should concentrate on fewer types (Schriften der Hamburger Stiftung für Sozialgeschichte des 20. Jahrhunderts 1987, S.285).

In 1944, it was decided that two types of motorcycles—one with a 125 cubic centimeter (cc) engine and another with a 350 cc engine—should be produced by the Auto Union. Volkswagen was regarded as the only car (jeep) manufacturer. In addition, only one type of 0.65-ton tricycle truck, two types of 1.5-ton trucks, three types of 3-ton trucks, two types of 4.5-ton trucks, and one type of 8-ton truck should be produced by specific enterprises. Regarding special types for military use, it was decided that special types of cars and six types of half-tracks—1 ton, 3 tons, 5 tons, 8 tons, 12 tons, and 18 tons—should be manufactured (The United States Strategic Bombing Survey 1947d, pp.19–20).

After the outbreak of World War II, in contrast to truck production, passenger car production for civil demand was limited to a small extent. Reducing types to a minimum for the German market was thought to be effective from the national economic perspective (Der Deutsche Volkswirt 1939e, S.259); however, at Daimler-Benz, the type program of the Chief Representative for Motor Vehicles essentially influenced the type reduction of trucks. In passenger car production, the production of existing types was fundamentally approved (Der Deutsche Volkswirt 1939b, S.1544). In reality, decisions regarding types were discussed and modified through negotiations with enterprises during the period until a decision by Schell's program [*Mercedes-Benz Classic Archiv*, Kissel Technische Protokolle, 1.30, Protokoll der Sitzung über die Typenbegrenzung bei den LKW. In Untertürkheim am 13.Dezember 1938 (19.12.1938), S.1, 3; *Mercedes-Benz Classic Archiv*, Kissel Technische Protokolle, 1.30, Protokoll der Sitzung in U.T. am 10.1.39 betreffend Fabrikationsprogramm der Werke Gaggenau und Mannheim auf Grund der Typenbegrenzungsaktion (24.1.1939), S.1–4; *Mercedes-Benz Classic Archiv*, Kissel Technische Protokolle, 1.30, Protokoll der Sitzung in U.T. am 23.1.39 betreffend Typenbegrenzung der LKW für das Werk Gaggenau (27.1.1939), S.2, 5; *Mercedes-Benz Classic Archiv*, Kissel Technische Protokolle, 1.30, Protokoll der Sitzung in U.T. am 20.3.39 betreffend Lkw.-Programm Gaggenau (28.3.1939); *Mercedes-Benz Classic Archiv*, Kissel Protokolle, I/15, Protokoll der Vorstandssitzung in UT. am 23./ 24.März 1942 (7.4.1942), S.1]. In March 1939, coordination was attempted in a certain direction. Whereas at Opel, only one type of 3-ton truck would be produced, at Daimler-Benz three types—1.5 ton, 3 ton, and 4.5 ton—would be allotted as primary objects [*Mercedes-Benz Classic Archiv*, Kissel Technische Protokolle, 1.30, Protkoll der Sitzung in U.T. am 9.3.39 betreffend Konstruktion der Lkw.-Typen des Schell-Programmes (14.3.1939), S.1–2]. Thus, the standardization situation differed between enterprises.

Production specialization was attempted within individual companies as well. The minutes of a meeting of Daimler-Benz on March 1, 1938, pointed out that specialization within individual companies had become an important task around the time when A. v. Schell was appointed Chief Representative for Motor Vehicles in November 1938 (*Mercedes-Benz Classic Archiv*, Kissel Protokolle, I/11, Protokoll über die am Dienstag, dem 1. März 1938, nachmittags 4 Uhr, im Sitszungszimmer 10 der Deutschen Bank, Berlin W.8., Mauerstrasse 39, abgehaltene Präsidialsitzung der Daimler-Benz Aktiengesselschaft, Stuttgart-Untertürkheim, S.5). In truck production at this enterprise, the Gaggenau plant produced 2-, 3-, 3.75-, 6-, and 10-ton trucks at the start of the war. As a result of the Schell program that aimed at standardizing the production of the various truck manufacturing factories into a single model, in 1941, it was decided that the Untertürkheim, Mannheim, and Gaggenau plants should produce only 1.5-ton, 3-ton, and 4.5-ton trucks, respectively. As the production orders for older models finished, this program was gradually put in effect (The United States Strategic Bombing Survey 1947b, EXHIBIT D).

12.1.2.3 Standardization of Production in the Machinery Industry

As observed in the machine tool industry, production allotments in the machinery industry were implemented by concentrating the production of specific products at the enterprises with the best possibility for rational production under the militarization of economy. It built a foundation for advancing standardization. In the machine tool industry, the rational arrangement of production capacity could be secured by production coordination. Machines such as radial drilling machines, gear processing machines, and automatic machines were appointed as representative machine tools for which specialization was implemented (Lange 1939, S.1134). Special committees and working committees were organized to implement the reduction of type more rapidly and intensely in all primary special machine tool fields (Free 1943, S.3). The experiences of production planning and control in the machine tool field were used for the entire machine industry and a thorough reduction of type was achieved (Siegel and von Freyberg 1991, S.211–212).

However, despite needing close cooperation between the electrical and machinery industries, such collaboration was not sufficiently established. Kurt Hegner pointed out that the standardization that electric motor manufacturers had to perform was not still achieved in 1937, which caused major difficulties for machine tool plants in design and production techniques (Hegner 1937, S.170).

In January 1940, "*Der Vierjahresplan*" magazine highlighted that the machine tool industry had been the pacemaker for standardization for a long time period and represented a good case study in the reduction of type and specialization (Der Vierjahresplan 1940a, S.13). In 1939, Hein Kiekebusch stressed that this industry actively pursued this purpose by using the unit system, the general use of unified parts and part groups needed for the production of special-purpose machines, the broad use of universal product groups, and purchasing standardized parts outside of the company. Standardization in machine tool manufacturing for machining metals prevailed due to its production and purchasing advantages. However, standardization activities in machines for the forming process progressed partially (Kiekebusch 1939, S.569).

World War II led to an increase in production volume and a reduction in the number of types of machines (Dolezalek 1944, S.29). The aforementioned order on May 28, 1941, that introduced the reporting obligation concerning the starting and stopping of machine tool manufacturing became an important moment in the reduction of type (Olk 1941, S.539–541). In the entire machinery industry, machine types were reduced from 3,637 to 1,011 by 1942. Machine tool types decreased from 1,321 to 526. The reduction of type rate of the lathe, automatic lathe (single axle type), milling machine, planning machine, tool room lathe, wheel hobbing machine, and gear shaping machine was 53%, 70%, 71%, 67%, 84%, 42%, and 22%, respectively. There were similar figures for cutting machine tools and machines for the forming process of 61% and 60%, respectively. Considering machines other than machine tools, the reduction of type rates of sorting machines, agricultural machines and flour grinders, and construction machines was 89%, 81%, and 71%, respectively (Gesell 1942, S.426–427).

At **MAN** (**Maschinenfabrik-Augsburg-Nürnberg**), a representative enterprise in the machinery industry, the drafts of 90 norms were being made or completed as of April 11, 1938. The standardization of equipment and instruments for transportation such as electric trucks, freight cars with cranes, fork-lift trucks, and trailers progressed. Casting and forging equipment were also important areas of standardization [*MAN Archiv*, 2.3, Nr.19, Niederschrift über die zweite Sitzung der

Unterkommission für Betriebsnormen am 11. April 1938 in Nürnberg (Betriesbs-kommissionssitzung am 24./25.5.38), S.2–3, S.7]. The number of norms increased from 138 on September 30 [*MAN Archiv*, 2.3, Nr.24, Niederschrift über die 4. Sitzung der Kommission für Betriebsgeräte am 30. September 1940 in Gustavsburg (Betriebskommissionssitzung am 18./19.Oktober 1940 in Nürnberg), S.2] to 172 on September 12, 1941. The ratios of norm lists related to office machines, transportation equipment for plants, equipment for storehouses, transportation equipment, equipment for workshops, installing instruments, and casting equipment were 3%, 2.5%, 25%, 27.5%, 25%, 13%, and 4%, respectively, for a total 172 norm lists [*MAN Archiv*, 2.3, Nr.26, Niederschrift über die 5. Sitzung der Kommission für Betriebsgeräte am 12. September 1941 in Nürnberg (Betriebskommissionssitzung am 24.u 25.11.1941 in Hamburg), S.3–4]. The number of norm lists increased to 183 on June 30, 1942. At MAN, a total of 22,800 instruments for workshops had been produced on the basis of norms until that point [*MAN Archiv*, 2.3, Nr.28, Niederschrift über die 6. Sitzung der Kommission für Betriebsgeräte am 3.Juli 1942 in Augsburg (Betriebskommissionssitzung am 6. u 7.Nov.1942 in Augsburg), S.5–6]. However, the number of norm lists almost did not increase thereafter. The number of such lists was 183 in 1943 and 185 on January 24, 1944 [*MAN Archiv*, 2.3, Nr.31, Niederschrift über die 8. Sitzung der Kommission für Betriebsgeräte am 24.Januar 1944 in Nürnberg (Betriebskommissionssitzung am 2. u 3.6.44 in Gustavsburg), S.3].

The introduction of plant-developed standards (*Werknorm*) also had major significance. In a meeting of the management committee occurring on December 15–16, 1939, it was decided to mutually coordinate plant-developed standards as much as possible to limit tool varieties in the MAN group. Interchanges concerning the standardization of tools already started made it possible for three MAN plants to take a bird's-eye view of the activities implemented until then to compare them to conditions in other plants. It was decided to use DIN as much as possible on the basis of such standardization [*MAN Archiv*, 2.3, Nr.23, Niederschrift über die Tagung am 15. und 16.12.39 in Werk Gustavsburg (Betriebskommissionssitzung am 5./6.4.40), S.1–2].

At MAN, attempts to reduce product type were continued until the late period. C. Hechner pointed out that in February 1942, he took over the task of attempting all measures that would contribute to rational production in relation to the reduction of type concerning ship engines (*MAN Archiv*, 1.3.3.5, Akt 17, Typenbeschränkung von Marine-Verbrennungsmotoren, S.3). The meeting of the management committee in February 1943 pointed out that special attention would have to be paid to simplification of type and reducing existing instruments in the future [*MAN Archiv*, 2.3, Nr.29, Niederschrift über die 9. Sitzung der Kommission für Betriebsgeräteam 9.Februar 1943 in Gustavsburg (Betriebskommissionssitzung am 9. u 10.April1943 in Nürnberg), S.4].

12.1.3 Limitations of Standardization of Production and Their Factors

In this way, standardization and the reduction of product types were strongly and systematically driven with compulsion by the state in the processing and assembly industries and industrial sectors related to munitions under the task of realizing the mass production of munitions. However, it was pointed out that standardization not only encountered limitations regarding capitalistic competition but also restricted technical advances. Such phenomena could be observed particularly during the years of war production. Strict reduction of type prevented the possibility of new design and restricted the arrangement of special-purpose machines. The Association of German Engineers indicated a situation in which plans for the reduction of type during peacetime had to be considered and those types, once abolished, could easily be adopted again later by such consideration. This recognition clarified that the reduction of product type was not always suitable for mass production (Etzold 1988, S.93–94). Reduction of type was never "almost completed" until the end of 1942 (Ludwig 1974, S.421) and reducing type continued by state initiative afterward as well (Hachtmann 1989, S.77; Wussow 1943).

The reorganization of the production process, changes in the equipment required, and transformation to standardized parts on the user side constantly encountered cost and managerial difficulties in the **electrical engineering industry**. The introduction of standards sometimes encountered difficulties. Whereas costs rose in a short time, the profits obtained from standardization only became clear after the passage of a long time (Wagner 1942, S.534). K. Borbeck stressed in January 1945 that the contribution of standards to rationalization in Germany was not as great as considered and making norms compulsory and maintaining these conditions had to be satisfied to greatly enlarge their effect (Bobek 1945, S.4).

Although attempts to achieve the common use of parts between motor vehicles for military and civilian use on the basis of interchangeability in truck production were made in the **automobile industry**, such attempts did not always succeed due to the dispersion of production (Kirchberg 1969, S.125–126). Whereas in passenger cars there was a vague germination of standardization and reduction of type at the time, in trucks, state intervention was first performed very late. As a result, during wartime, a transitional phenomenon of standardization occurred in which the types chosen in the introductory stage were added to existing standards. It was pointed out that standardization and reduction of type endeavors in the automobile industry began with a 5- to 10-year delay afterward (Schütz 1942, S.580). Kurt Pentzlin stressed in 1943 that the constant change in few existing types was implemented under wartime production; there was a trend to prevent the reduction of type (Pentzlin 1943, S.53).

In parts standardization, efforts to standardize and unify appurtenances could facilitate many changes in engines and automobiles [*Mercedes-Benz Classic Archiv*, Kissel Technische Protokolle, 1.30, Stand der Typen am 1. August 1939 (7.8.1939), S.1]. This could become a factor restricting standardization. The minutes of a managing board meeting of Daimler-Benz on December 5, 1939, pointed out that activities to unify bus bodies were brought to a standstill and unification could not be implemented as planned at the beginning due to structural reasons [*Mercedes-Benz Classic Archiv*, Kissel Protokolle, I/12, Protokoll der Vorstandssitzung in U.T. am 5.12.1939 (13.12.1939), S.3]. The unification of industry-producing appurtenances was restricted by the demand for non-unified repair parts for automobiles still in use and realizing decisive synergy was difficult due to a lack of coordination between industrial sectors. With the effectuation of the wartime plan in 1943, automobile types were essentially produced on the basis of existing standards and since changes in these types should no longer be performed, standardization endeavors reached their peak in 1942 (Pesch 1988, S.160). In reality, even in the automobile industry in West Germany at the end of the 1950s, parts interchangeability was secured by the skilled grinder (Hammer 1959, S.20), and it was in the 1960s that the German automobile industry first reached the same level of mechanization as the Ford Motor Company (Radkau 2008, S.295; Kern and Schumann 1984, S.40).

Even once systematic goals such as the Schell program were established, cases in which enterprises were forced to cope with excessive requests of this plan, worker problems, and difficulty in procuring machine equipment were not few [*Mercedes-Benz Classic Archiv*, Kissel Protokolle, I/13, Protokoll der Vorstandssitzung in Untertürkheim am 2.4.1940 (9.4.1940), S.11; *Mercedes-Benz Classic Archiv*, Kissel Protokolle, I/14, Protokoll der Vorstandssitzung am 21.1.41 in Untertürkheim und 22.1.41 in Sindelfingen (28.1.1941), S.4; *Mercedes-Benz Classic Archiv*, Kissel Protokolle, I/14, Protokoll der Vorstandssitzung in Untertürkheim am 25./26.3.1941 (28.3.1941), S.11; *Mercedes-Benz Classic Archiv*, Kissel Protokolle, I/14, Protokoll der Vorstandssitzung in Untertürkheim am 28. Mai 1941 (29.5.1941), S.8]. The fact that production might be influenced by how decisions concerning the types allotted to each company would be made afterward [*Mercedes-Benz Classic Archiv*, Kissel Protokolle, I/15, Protokoll der Vorstandssitzung in UT. am 3. Juni 1942 (17.6.1942), S.5] could have been a factor restricting organizational standardization efforts.

In pursuit of scale merit by concentration and production specialization of specific types into as few manufacturers as possible, the limitations were prominent. Although the number of truck producers decreased from 22 to 12 between 1940 and 1945, the number itself was as many before. For trailers, the number of producers increased from 6 to 11 by 1943. Although the number of manufacturers decreased to eight again by 1945, it was greater than this in 1940 (Pesch 1988, S.212). Considering the situation, including the reduction of the number of producers in charge of specific types of passenger car production, the reduction in type still did not achieve sufficient effect until the end of 1942 (Pesch 1988, S.141). The goal of rationalization for motorcycles that aimed at reducing producers to one per class type was first achieved in 1944 (Pesch 1988, S.133, 208).

Before World War II, about two-thirds of approximately 6,000 companies in the **machinery industry** were very small enterprises employing 100 workers at most. The aspects of de-concentration in the machine-building industry were primarily seen not only in their dispersion throughout the whole of Germany but also in the lack of specialization by individual enterprises (The United States Strategic Bombing Survey 1947e, pp.20–21; The United States Strategic Bombing Survey 1947f, p.7). In the machine tool industry, the rate of enterprises that produced four or more categories of machines decreased slightly from 24.6% in 1938 to 21.9% in 1944. A report by the US Strategic Bombing Survey pointed out that "the degree of specialization which took place during the war years was very slight, while the number of types of machines produced in each category remained large" (The United States Strategic Bombing Survey 1947f, Exhibit 11–15). According to research that investigated 81 machine tool manufacturers, grinding machines were being produced by 33 enterprises in 1938 and 27 enterprises in 1944. The decrease in the number of enterprises manufacturing this sort of machine was not very large. This research clarified that "before the war, more than 20 firms were producing drill presses, horizontal boring mills, and milling machines" and such cases were still observed at the end of the war (The United States Strategic Bombing Survey 1947e, p.26).

In producer goods departments such as machine tool producers, product characteristics became a factor limiting standardization. Since one of the largest automobile industry customers was the Armed Forces and special customer demands were restricted by their interference, cooperating with customers in this industry to promote the reduction of type was relatively easy. In contrast, in the machine tool industry, thorough standardization was difficult because standard machines had to adapt to the structure and volume of parts to be produced (Boehringer 1939, S,1069). Under this condition, even provisional goals had still not been achieved in the machinery industry at the beginning of 1943 (Jensen and Raupp 1943, S.138).

Building on previous investigations of production standardization, how the introduction of the flow production system progressed and how mass production was developed under the expanded market created by the militarization of economy and the shift to a war economy, considering not only the quantity but also the quality of the munitions market, will be investigated in the next section.

12.2 Development of the Flow Production System and Its Characteristics

12.2.1 Expansion of the Munitions Market and the Development of the Flow Production System

By nature, mass production presupposes the existence of a mass market that enables it. However, rationalization in the 1920s was forced to be pursued under very strict economic conditions represented by the existence of excessive production capacity, a narrow and intensely changing domestic market, and difficulties in export markets. The introduction of the flow production system could only be observed in certain large enterprises of the processing and assembly industries or their most advanced plants, specific production processes, and product sectors, in particular, sectors that were suitable for mass production in which standardization had progressed. Moreover, introducing a system that aimed at obtaining some of the benefits of mass production, even with decreased production output, and securing a certain level of flexibility to deal with demand fluctuations between products were attempted in many enterprises and plants instead of inelastic production methods such as the Ford system.

However, the expansion of flow production system use came to a momentary end with the world economic crisis. A complete conveyor system in which the production functions of human labor and machine equipment were combined, the tempo of work was thoroughly determined by a belt conveyor, and partially automatic and completely automatic machines were observed only in exceptional cases until 1935–1936 (Hachtmann 1989, S.69).

In the Nazi era, the introduction of the flow production method was more strongly driven under the tremendous expansion of the munitions market. Tilla Siegel pointed out that whereas the rationalization process was started on the right lines and rationalization thinking developed into the definite guidelines of business policy in the 1920s, it was not rationalization itself but the peculiar conditions in which it was implemented that became a theme in the 1930s. During the world economic crisis, it became more important "to save" than "to rationalize." When the market was extended afterward and production capacity in the electrical industry was completely used again in 1936, sales conditions almost equal to that of standardized mass production based on the Ford system in the US were created (Siegel and von Freyberg 1991, S.317).

Thus, after the latter half of the 1930s, the rationalization plan already developed and being realized in the 1920s was pursued more intensely on all levels—organizational rationalization, technical production rationalization, design rationalization, and personnel management (Siegel and von Freyberg 1991, S.317) —and rationalization endeavors lost their experimental character at this stage. In the 1930s, thorough attempts to implement the American model of highly mechanized and standardized mass production were made instead of compromising with the temporary equipment absolutely needed under the conditions in the 1920s. In this process, not only flow production but also "Fordization" and thorough work and automation mechanization became a central new goal of rationalization considering the motivation of a serious lack of sufficient labor (Homburg 1991, S.527). At Daimler-Benz, the expansion of the production foundation and the increasing lack of skilled workers with full employment precipitated the shift to capital-intensive production methods in 1936. The mass production method using the flow production system played an important role in this task (Thieme 2004, S.272).

The striking expansion of the introduction of the flow production system during the national socialism period was enabled by market conditions under the militarization of economy. In the munitions economy from 1934 to 1939, state demand became a decisive market for capitalistic industrial production (Mottek et al. 1975, S.141). In addition, the mass production of arms and the creation of the European Extensive Market called "*die Großraumwirtschaft*" under Nazi control expanded the market for mass products considerably. As long as conditions for the expansion of mass production based on the American model were created by such an enlarged market, war—particularly the dispatch of troops to the Western region and the invasion of the Soviet Union by the German Armed Forces afterward—indicated an important turning point for the rationalization movement, especially flow production (Hachtmann 1989, S.77).

In the Nazi era, the introduction of the flow production method was strongly driven further under such conditions. Rüdiger Hachtmann pointed out that flow production was expanded on a scale not previously observed from 1936 to 1944. This method was increasingly used even in departments in which flow production was almost never used prior to the Nazis ascent to power. Although belt conveyors were not observed in very small enterprises until 1933, they were eagerly introduced during the Nazi era. The flow production system was completed and partially or completely automatic machines under the conveyor were installed much more effectively in the metal processing industry, in particular. Above all, in the consumer goods industries, methods such as flow production that were not very developed, even afterward, were used, and the flow production method without a conveyor was also implemented in a few cases (Hachtmann 1989, S.80–81).

Introducing the flow production system in major industries is considered next, including a discussion of cases in the electrical engineering, automobile, and machinery industries.

12.2.2 Development of the Flow Production System in Major Industries

12.2.2.1 Development of the Flow Production System in the Electrical Engineering Industry

Recovery after the world economic crisis progressed relatively rapidly and the introduction of the flow production method began early in the electrical engineering industry. A serious situation during the economic crisis had already been overcome at Siemens in the fiscal year 1933/1934. Reorganization to flow production progressed and a qualitative new wave of rationalization could be observed in production fields such as electric motor plants and home appliance sectors after 1933. However, it was in the latter half of the 1930s that belt conveyors prevailed as a means of "conveyor system" as the moving type of the flow production (Zollitsch 1990, S.22). The tremendous expansion of munitions markets with the Second Four-Year Plan started in 1936 greatly changed the conditions of mass production development using the flow production system.

The situations of individual product sectors are considered next.

Development of the Flow Production System in Major Product Sectors

Cases in the Electric Motor Sector

The electric motor sector was one of the product fields in which the introduction of the flow production system was attempted most intensely in the 1920s (see Chapter 9). At the Elmo Works of Siemens-Schuckert Werke, the business management principle whereby the production of major products and munitions was combined could be realized during the national socialism period. This factory supplied production equipment for munitions industries as well as electric motors and tools and developed small electric motors used for aircraft apparatuses. Intense competition in the home appliance market forced this factory to pay special attention to the economic efficiency of production. As a result, the Elmo Works moved part of its production early and avoided the high wage level in Berlin in the 1930s (Siegel and von Freyberg 1991, S.344–345).

Thus, the second plant was constructed on the Saar River. Belt conveyors moving rhythmically, special-purpose automatic machines, and transportation equipment were developed to achieve vacuum cleaner production at lower cost in the fiscal year 1937/1938. In the construction plan for the second hall started in the first quarter of 1938, a new production line for electric refrigerators was implemented from the perspective of the most modern American production method with a view to effectively automating production of special equipment to work alongside the smallest, most skilled workers (Siegel and von Freyberg 1991, S.348).

In 1935/1936, electric refrigerator assembly was transformed to flow production and packaging using the conveyor was introduced to the smallest electric motor (Siegel and von Freyberg 1991, S.357). The production volume of casings for the electric motor was increased by rearranging the flow production line. Increased demand could not be met with one existing belt conveyor, so two new conveyors were installed for electric motor assembly. Whereas one of these conveyors was used to assemble lightweight electric motors with aluminum casings, the other conveyor was used to assemble all electric motors except for the standard model. Five conveyors were installed to produce the smallest electric motor, ventilating equipment, and electrical tools [*Siemens Archiv Akte*, 15/Lg562, Elektromotorenwerk. Jahresbericht 1935/36 (Chronik) (30.12.1936), S.9 (in: Chronik 1935/1936. Bericht der ZW und der Werke, S.128)]. As the effective production of various types of vacuum cleaners became very difficult due to the frequent transformation of belt conveyors, the design was reconsidered with the aim of attaching the same apparatus to multiple types of vacuum cleaners (Siegel and von Freyberg 1991, S.357).

In the winding shop, tasks influencing the total cost of the electric motor came to be performed by dividing production into stages using a belt conveyor. The time needed to wind wire was abbreviated and the training period of female winding workers shortened from three months to four weeks, thereby decreasing the cost of training for one worker from 220 Reichsmark (RM) to 75 Reichsmark (RM). In 1937/1938, production time was reduced by 16% despite an increase in production. Considering that the ratio of working time for winding to total production time in the first plant was greater than one-fourth, this goal had major significance (Siegel and von Freyberg 1991, S.358).

However, rationalization in the second plant was significantly influenced by further attempts to emphasize munitions production. Indeed, the production of products for civilian demand was aggressively restricted and the prohibition of the production of such goods brought production of the vacuum cleaner using the belt conveyor to almost a complete stop. At the time, an early end of the war was taken into consideration in the electrical industry as well. The accomplishment of completing the building and starting electric refrigerator production was decided to prepare for exports after the war. However, the prohibition of home appliance production was stricter and pursued on a larger scale in 1940/1941. As a result, electric refrigerator production began immediately in the second plant with only a few volumes; however, it was forced to be ceased along with the production of vacuum cleaners, electric floor polishing machines, and ventilating equipment. Instead, the production of aircraft motors was moved from the Berlin plant to the second plant. Parts production for incendiaries also began. Since the production of home appliances was based on small electric motor manufacturing, Siemens-Schuckert Werke could continue the business policy in which apparatuses were adjusted to piece time production and the base of electric equipment production in this company was maintained (Siegel and von Freyberg 1991, S.349). The minutes from the supervisory board's meeting on February 27, 1941, pointed out that the domestic home appliance business was halted. Instead, products with importance for military affairs appeared, and 99% of all domestic businesses became essential for the war (*Bundesarchiv Berlin*, R8119F, Deutsche Bank, P3360, Protokoll über die Aufsichtsratssitzung am 27 Februar 1941, S.2).

Cases in the Meter Sector

There were many standard types according to meter operating conditions in the meter manufacturing sector. There were production volumes of many types that not only made the formation of flow production proper but also decisively necessary. Except for a few heavy machines, light machines came into question and could be included in the flow production process without much difficulty.

In AEG's meter plant, a total of 50 moving stands with a total length of 1,500-m was installed. The average interval between workshops was 1 m to secure freedom for employees to move and place boxes for transportation. Therefore, a large part of many partly finished goods moved between two workshops. Waiting in the transportation of partly finished goods was reduced and the flow elasticity to a certain degree was realized by it. As observed in the large punching shop, in moving stands on which individual tasks had to be done by machines, special equipment to carry partly finished goods directly to the machine was used. Partly finished goods were conveyed to the next machine by rail with points along the direction of the flow and further carried to the machine by roller conveyor. After tasks were completed, partly finished goods were put on another roller conveyor and again carried in the direction of the flow. Hubert Helfort indicated the following points as the advantages of such flow production methods including (1) the possibility of replacing workers due to very easy tasks based on the thorough division of labor, (2) a high level of comfort and ease of work compared with previous working methods, (3) the possibility for female workers to concentrate on parts processing through the automatic transportation of materials and partly finished goods, and (4) the improvement of product quality by concentrating on certain work.

At **AEG,** as a representative model of contemporary modern production, the workflow in the **mechanical processing process** began at the small punching shop. This shop produced 70% of all meter parts. In the punching shop, base plates and hoods were manufactured on a long moving stand and the machines needed for production were arranged to the right and left of the moving stand. Afterward, parts such as hock buckles and clasp lock washers were fixed by electric spot welding or riveting. In the press of another group, frames were processed on a belt conveyor and completed by a riveting or welding machine. There was a core punching shop at another place on the first floor. Two core disks were cut by high-speed automatic punching machine in one process of going there and back. Many moving stands carried individual plates that were conveyed from the punching machine to manual work.

All parts produced on the first floor were carried by elevator to the fourth floor for **painting**. After degreasing, the base plate and hood were conveyed to three moving stands for painting. Hood tasks were performed on the moving stand. Immersion equipment was installed on the immediate side of the moving stand conveyor. As the base plate had to be painted on both sides, this equipment was designed especially for painting it. The base plate was hung on the chain conveyor with blow-shaped metal fittings made of wire and soaked in the paint tank in the process of transportation. Afterward, the base plate left the tank and was put on the moving stand conveyor with blow-shaped metal fittings. The moving stand carried all painted parts a 20-m length across the drying furnace. After an hour, the parts appeared on their side of the furnace for further processing. Aside from this painting by the furnace, many parts were painted with air-drying paint. Such painting had merits due to the short time required for it to dry.

Precision parts manufacturing was performed in a location adjoining the painting shop. Register stands were produced by an automatic metal covering machine on the basis of the precision method. The brass lining and axle were manufactured by many small machines and worm and toothed wheels were produced by a special automatic milling machine.

Register assembly was performed using a moving stand after manufacturing the parts of this apparatus. Parts such as drums, axles, and toothed wheels were assembled with the appropriate fitting apparatus. Registers were carried to the storehouse after inspection at the testing location.

In the **winding process**, series coil winding was performed by a small crank mechanism and voltage coils were produced by a special-purpose machine operating at 3,000 revolutions per minute. This machine performed round winding many times completely automatically and stopped automatically in abnormal cases. After coil completion and flange fixation, these coils reached the driving system assembly with the current coil and driving system was assembled on the conveyor. At another moving stand, the armature was produced in processes beginning from raw materials procurement to development of finished parts.

The final component of the meter was the braking magnet. The moving electric plating equipment in which thousands of copper magnets were carried through many washing baths and gilding baths by a seamless chain was particularly worthy of notice. A chain conveyor carried gilded magnets to the moving stand. They were magnetized and measured accurately with special instruments.

All parts in which assembly works were completed were conveyed at once to the intermediate storehouse. This warehouse not only gathered and classified many parts and arranged them according to their necessity in assembly but also coordinated the time needed for the production of the various parts. This achieved the stable flow of materials to final assembly.

Thus, the last stage of production, **final assembly,** was performed according to the type of electric current needed under many moving stands. Parts such as base plates, hoods, and connecting terminals were first conveyed to each moving stand. Other parts such as registers, driving systems, magnets, and screws were directly placed in the workshops where they were needed to perform tasks. As soon as parts based on customer orders were attached to the meter, cards that contained all of the special instructions were pasted on the base plate that workers could use to check if each part was appropriate for the customer order.

After final assembly was finished, inspection was implemented. The hood was temporarily placed on the end of the moving stand. A finished meter was stored on the moving shelf table and carried to inspection where meters were tested individually. The flow production system was organized in which partly finished goods did not move but the inspector moved from stand to stand. After inspection, meters were conveyed to the connection and a final high-tension test of deflective strength was performed. Finally, the meter left inspection and was taken to the storehouse for packaging, which was also performed on the moving stand (Herfort 1937, S.205–208).

Cases in the Radio Manufacturing Sector

The flow production system had already been introduced to the radio producing sector in the 1920s. Ulrich von Moellendorf pointed out that whereas simple radio sets were previously assembled in only one flow of work and therefore by one moving stand, the production method thoroughly dissolved and was divided into assembly groups that replaced the former method in 1933 (Moellendorff 1933a, S.172). According to him, genuine mass production of radio instruments encouraged the use of the moving stand as a means of combining individual workshops in 1933 (Moellendorff 1933b, S.484).

The production of variable condensers used for all types of radio sets was gathered on one moving stand. Individual rotors and stators were assembled with a well-designed apparatus. The assembly of coils with fixed condensers, condensers, and other individual parts was implemented in the assembly group next to variable condenser production. The assembly of radio set chassis was composed of only attaching components on to the base plate by machine and accurate connections. The completed chassis was attached to the case on the next desk. After verification of the reception capacity and inspection of the assembled loudspeakers, it progressed to final inspection where sound effects were tested. Afterward, the belt conveyor received the radio set from various assembly and inspection stands and carried it to the warehouse for sending via packaging. U. v. Moellendorf stressed that such production organization enabled the timely production of very complex radio sets in large numbers in 1933/1934 (Moellendorff 1933a, S.173–175). In producing the most complicated radio sets with production volumes of thousands per day using the belt conveyor, inspection based on laboratory principles was no longer sufficient and the inspection process and methods were changed. The modern inspection station included five stages as follows: "inspection of individual parts—group inspection—inspection of chassis—inspection of loudspeaker—final inspection of instrument." Inspection tasks were performed on the belt conveyor in the form of flow work (Geuter and Frey 1934, S.248).

In the Nazi era, the introduction of the flow production system was more eagerly pursued due to the necessity of the mass production of radios with the expansion of the munitions market. According to a report by U. v. Moellendorf in 1940, flow production as an effective mass production method particularly needed appropriate transportation equipment for its implementation. It was the moving stand that prevailed most broadly in precision machine production. Whereas the apron conveyor was useful for the transportation of partly finished goods in the direction of the production flow, processing was performed on both sides of the fixed shelf board or on a small flank desk. Partly finished goods were taken out of the conveyor in each workshop and returned to the conveyor after the work processes were completed.

Moving stands that could be used according to production plan changes and were inevitably needed each manufacturing year as various possible stands became necessary for special purposes of producing specific types of instruments in very large numbers and many different types in small numbers in production planning. The moving stand depicted in Figure 12.1 is one such case. In cases of large-scale production, tasks were arranged in the direction of progress on the one hand and in the opposite direction of advancement on the other hand. In cases of manufacturing in small numbers, two types were produced by the same conveyor. In cases in which the first working processes were similar, tasks were performed at the first conveyor together and afterward production was separated into two tracks. The structure of the moving stand enabled a variety of production methods to be implemented.

However, there were cases in which the procurement of new equipment for more effective production was not always possible, and the use of older existing moving stands was implemented by the slight reconstruction or elaborate rearrangement of workshops. Radio set stands were first put on a light car for the attaching stand. Next, an empty case prepared for attachment was put on the belt conveyor of the moving stand. The case was then moved onward to the middle of the assembly line where it was taken down by a female worker for assembly. A car loaded with radio set stands

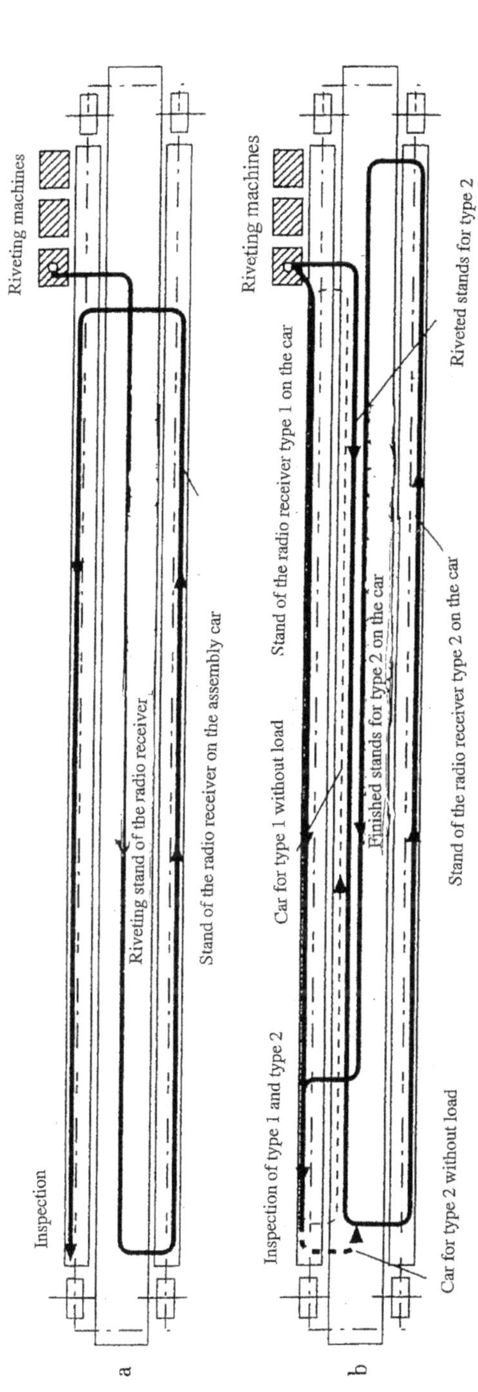

Fig. 12.1 Possibilities of using the moving stand in radio assembly *Note* (1) Both sides were in a flow, (2) Each side was for the special product type
Source Moellendorf (1940, S.131)

advanced to the end of the conveyor and was put on the rail installed at the side of the shelf board. This car proceeded to the attachment place on the rail through working processes and then went forward to the first place on the conveyor again with the assembled instrument. After the radio set was finished, it was put on the conveyor and taken to the management location and conveyed to inspection. An empty car was used again to receive the next stand (Moellendorff 1940, S.131).

In this way, production methods enabling the flexible implementation of product changes were attempted in radio assembly. A US Strategic Bombing Survey report pointed out that planning within the electrical industry was "a short-term affair, with frequent changes occurring, especially in communications equipment" (The United States Strategic Bombing Survey 1947c, p.3). Organizing flow production using the moving stand according to production planning changes was an effective countermeasure to such problems and took flexibility for market changes into consideration.

Cases in the Equipment-Installing Products Sector

Next, considering the condition of the equipment-installing product sector, the average amount of all orders in the equipment-installing product plant of Siemens-Schuckertwerke reached no less than RM 140 in 1936/1937 and the stratums of customers were broadly dispersed. A wide range of product lines at this plant meant that they needed to meet various market demands. Plants in this sector moved parts of production early and avoided the high level of wages in Berlin. In the 1930s, the second plant was expanded for standardized mass production, whereas in the first plant in Berlin, new workshops were organized for the production of instruments for aircraft and the division of labor between the plants was implemented (Siegel and von Freyberg 1991, S.345–346).

In 1939/1940, the "development of new production system and broad rationalization" were slogans of equipment-installing product plants. Production of the selenium rectifier was transformed from experimental production into mass production. In the assembly of the central rectifier for the National Post (*Reichspost*), transformation to line production was implemented. Rationalization of boring and screw cutting was also implemented and assembly in the second plant was further rationalized (Siegel and von Freyberg 1991, S.364–365). In the gilding department, a 50% increase in output was achieved by using the new circular conveyor (Siegel and von Freyberg 1991, S.357). Thus, in this department, the emphasis of rationalization was placed on the second plant, which implemented standardized mass production and the reform of labor organization in this plant using the flow production system was strongly driven.

In switch manufacturing, assembly was performed in the flow production process (conveyor work) regularly advanced by transportation equipment. In work processes performed without predetermined tact, there was the possibility of arranging many machines for assembly with conveyors and shortening work tact by many times by their appropriate operation. The introduction of flow production in such cases became a means of greatly increasing productivity as well as installing machines for assembly (Kaatz 1938, S.517). The production of complex double switches was performed on the semiautomatic assembly stand (Zollitsch 1990, S.22).

Cases in the Electric Heating Instrument Sector

When examining the manufacturing of electric heating instrument, at Siemens-Elektrowärme GmbH, rationalization measures were begun in 1934/1935 with a view to further approaching mass production modeled after the Ford system and gradually implemented after 1935/1936. Anticipation that the market for this company's products would further increase and encounter intensive price competition was the most important reason. In addition, the general lack of skilled workers and raw materials was also deeply connected to the reasons for rationalization. Furthermore, rationalization was promoted on the one hand and prevented on the other hand by specific problems such as the prohibition of core products under the militarization of the economy and the transformation to munitions production. This enterprise's product lines were reduced after 1928/1929 and the factory gradually changed from a plant for small electric instruments to producing ranges and storage batteries. The rationalization of range production was determined under the pressure of price decreases due to strict market conditions. However, in the middle of the 1930s, the time when this firm's products could be sold in spite of the high price was thought to have had passed. Thus, electrical enterprises were forced to put electric ranges on the market at the price of gas ranges and reduce their price by approximately 25%. Devices to improve work methods were attempted in the assembly of ranges already transformed to conveyor work under this situation and transformation was performed in the assembly of other instruments as well (Siegel and von Freyberg 1991, S.326).

At Siemens-Elektrowärme GmbH, in 1934, the shift to flow production using the conveyor was driven with the increase of sales of EKPH type and EKNK type [*Siemens Archiv Akte*, Ls101, Technicher Bericht des Siemens-Elektrowärme G.m.b. H. Werks des 3. Vierteljahr (Monate April-Juni) 1934 (6.6.1934), S.2 (in: Technische Vierteljahresberichte 3., Monate April-Juni 1934)]. All workshops up to packaging were reorganized to improve the flow of production. In range assembly, one large assembly conveyor was installed instead of three small belt conveyors flowing side by side. All models—and yet, constantly only one type—were assembled in greater numbers on this new conveyor. Cost reduction of 13% was achieved and 25% of skilled workers and approximately 13% of semiskilled workers became unnecessary due to these improvements in the range assembly work methods. The rate of female work increased to 63% with this transformation (Siegel and von Freyberg 1991, S.325–326).

Thus, as Fleckenstein's report in 1942 pointed out, the production of electric ranges had become genuine mass production (Fleckenstein 1942, S.285). Whereas the progress of rationalization at Siemens-Elektrowärme GmbH arose from specific sales market conditions until 1935/1936, it was determined by changes in market conditions with the militarization of economy afterward. This company recorded a decrease in sales in the fiscal year 1940/1941. Sales declined by 8% after the prohibition of this enterprise's core products. Since the Armed Forces cancelled short-term orders, the sale of munitions decreased by 31%. In the fiscal year 1941/ 1942, production instability caused by changes in the Armed Forces plan became one factor causing the loss in income and expenditure of this plant (Siegel and von Freyberg 1991, 328–330, 352).

The demand for electric ranges was tied to seasonal changes and required that the arrangement of the flow production line could enable re-composition. In addition, the different demands of each country had to be taken into consideration due to the high rate of exports. Changeable work allotments became necessary under this situation. It was pointed out that such elastic flow production indicated better results and efficiency than rigid flow production with mechanically determined flow tact under the conveyor (Fleckenstein 1942, S.286).

As is clear from the preceding discussion, in the development of the flow production system in the electrical engineering industry, flexible adaptation to extensive changes in the munitions market was needed. Therefore, emphasis had to be placed on securing flexibility rather than the American model of mass production to manufacture the same types of products in massive numbers. The specific characteristics of the munitions market determined the manner of implementing flow production. Diffusion of the Ford system in the German electrical industry progressed in the 1950s and the 1960s as a result of the boom in consumer goods production after World War II. After the war, conveyor work prevailed, particularly in the final assembly of product lines such as radios, televisions, vacuum cleaners, electric washing machines, dishwashers, and ranges (Wittke 1996, S.153).

12.2.2.2 Development of the Flow Production System in the Automobile Industry

In this section, the development of the flow production system in the automobile industry is considered. In this industry, the decision to supply small and popular cars was made due to the poverty of a broad stratum of purchasers during the world economic crisis (Köhler 1966, S.139). Introducing American production methods became less easy as the production and sales situation became more serious. However, conditions (Schütze 1931, S.245) greatly changed under the policy to promote motorization and the militarization of economy. German automobile manufacturers benefited from the regime's favorable policies. "A host of measures—tax incentives, allowing roadside parking, simplifying drivers' licensing, lowering insurance and registration fees, and so on—eased maintenance costs" (Link 2020, S.142). The introduction of the flow production system was more aggressively driven under such circumstances.

American Mass Production and the Introduction of the Flow Production System

First, Opel is examined as a typical case of pursuing the American mass production model. Walter Wahl pointed out that after General Motors in the US took over administration of Opel, all production began to be expanded on the basis of the American model (Wahl 1938, S.98). The most typical case can be observed in the Brandenburg truck plant. Opel decided to move all truck production from Rüsselsheim to Brandenburg on April 1, 1935, and the most modern automobile factory was created in only 190 business days. This company employed the most modern production methods anywhere and thoroughly used all possibilities of the flow work system [*Historisches Archiv des Deutschen Technikmjuseums,* I. 2.032 0007, Auszug aus der Begrssungsrede des Betriebsführung der Adam Opel AG., Dr. R. A. Fleischer, anlässlich der Eröffnung des Opel-Lastwagenwerkes Brandenburug. (6.1.1936), S.1; Adam Opel Aktiengesellschaft 1936, S.3, 17; Automobiltechnische Zeitschrift 1936, S.39–40].

In this truck factory, a very close system that was regarded as 100% flow production composed of 13 machine lines, 27 completely automatic belt conveyors, and a final assembly conveyor was realized after November 1935 (Adam Opel Aktiengesellschaft 1936, S.15, 20, 32; Seherr-Thoss 1979, S.295; Bönig 1993, S.445; Neliba 2000, S.63).

The automobile parts needed for final assembly were produced on the basis of predetermined accurate time under individual belt conveyors and the necessity of placement and installation planning of machines were determined by these parts (Stodieck 1936, S.137; Neliba 2000, S.63). Figure 12.2 depicts the layout of the Brandenburg plant. Unlike former automobile plants, all production—from raw materials to finished vehicles—was performed in one building. This factory employed 800 male workers at the time, 15% of whom were foremen and skilled workers. The production capacity of the plant for each 24-h period consisting of 8-h three shifts staffed by approximately 2,500 workers was 150 cars (Automobiltechnische Zeitschrift 1936, S.39–40; Seherr-Thoss 1979, S.295; Adam Opel Aktiengesellschaft 1936, S.10, 17). The shop floor of the Brandenburg plant "was spacious and light-filled and featured powerful, machines, precise coordination, and partial automation." "Fully laid out according to flow principles, the brand-new plant accomplished the entire fabrication from raw materials to finished truck under one roof" (Link 2020, S.160; Adam Opel Aktiengesellschaft 1936, S.5–6).

The conditions surrounding the introduction of the flow production system to major production processes are considered next.

In **the mechanical processing process**, machine equipment was composed of about 1,200 machine tools with individual drive systems and 13 machine lines. The processing of individual part units, front and rear axles, crank shafts and cam shafts, and cylinder blocks and the manufacturing of transmissions and chassis were organized according to machine lines. Mechanical transportation equipment such as roller conveyors and completely automatic conveyor belts were used exclusively for carrying parts to be processed (Adam Opel Aktiengesellschaft 1936, S.12–13,

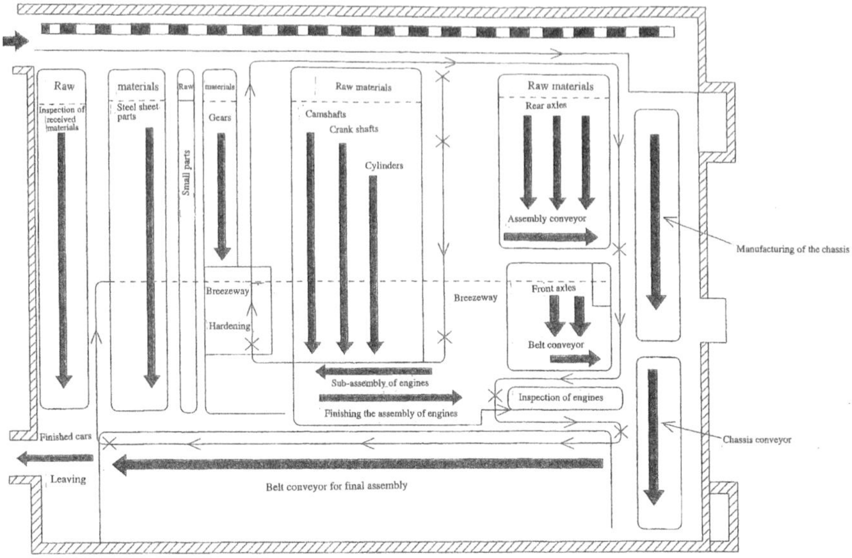

Fig. 12.2 Layout and progress of production in the big hall of Opel's Brandenburg Truck Plant *Source* Automobiltechnische Zeitschrift (1936, S.39) and Hund (1937, S.356–357)

16–17, 20, 24; Automobiltechnische Zeitschrift 1936, S.40; Neliba 2000, S.63). The transportation of heavy partly finished goods from one working machine to the next was performed by roller conveyor (Automobiltechnische Zeitschrift 1937, S.179). Specific parts were produced on the conveyor belt (Hundt 1937b, S.355).

In **the assembly process**, the assembly of engines as a subassembly process was implemented on the turntable put on the conveyor belt. The finished engine was carried from the assembly conveyor to inspection. In final assembly, all mechanical processing lines producing individual parts and part units were connected by the main final assembly line (Automobiltechnische Zeitschrift 1936, S.41–42). Groups of arriving parts progressed to final assembly on an approximately 110-m-long conveyor without an intermediate warehouse. A storehouse for raw materials existed between the two ends of this conveyor (Stodieck 1936, S.137). In final assembly, axles and springs were first attached to the chassis on the conveyor and the engine, steering gear, fuel tank, radiator, step, and mudguard were attached afterward. Final assembly of the rear axle was performed using the belt conveyor. After the differential gear was attached to the rear axle case, the brake drums and hubs were attached; the rear axle was painted with a spray painting machine as the final work process. After finishing these tasks, a crane carried the driving cab. In the meantime, the conveyor advanced to the place where electrical instruments, bonnets, and wheels were attached to the truck. The inspection and testing of already finished cars were undertaken 30 m from the end (Automobiltechnische Zeitschrift 1936, S.41–42; Hundt 1937b, S.355, Adam Opel Aktiengesellschaft 1936, S.22, .31). This organizational integration of production processes in the factory was realized to the broadest extent. Twenty-seven belt conveyors forming tact were flowed into the final assembly conveyor (Stahlmann 1993, S.88; Seherr-Thoss 1979, S.295; Adam Opel Aktiengesellschaft 1936, S17, 31; Automobiltechnische Zeitschrift 1936, S.40) and its total length reached five kilometers (km) (Adam Opel Aktiengesellschaft 1936, S.17; Automobiltechnische Zeitschrift 1936, S.40; Neliba 2000, S.63).

When considering other production processes, in the **hardening process**, quenching works were included in the progress of flow production (Automobiltechnische Zeitschrift 1936, S.40–41; Stodieck 1936, S.137; Seherr-Thoss 1979, S.295) and were performed by production methods using a belt conveyor. The introduction of flow production was first realized in this production process. In the **electrical gilding process**, production was implemented by flow work using a belt conveyor (Adam Opel Aktiengesellschaft 1936, S.17, 25; Automobiltechnische Zeitschrift 1936, S.40–41). In the **body manufacturing process**, even large body parts were assembled using the conveyor (Feldenkirchen 2003, S.149).

Flow work and conveyor work were performed in the primary processes of automobile production in the Brandenburg plant as the newest factory. In transportation between production departments, carrying the finished parts, appurtenances, and smaller parts needed for assembly and attachment was performed by transportation equipment such as the overhead chain conveyor and roller conveyor (Automobiltechnische Zeitschrift 1937, S.179). A truck produced at the Brandenburg plant known as "Opel Britz" was the foundation of the army from 1939 until the end of World War II. Without this truck, the supply of equipment for the army would have been paralyzed. A large part of the delay in the rationalization of the truck industry could be overcome by this truck (Schriften der Hamburger Stiftung für Sozialgeschichte des 20. Jahrhunderts 1987, S.285). The production capacity of this plant was the highest level of production in Germany at the time. The Rüsselsheim plant was also "the most completely integrated automobile plant in Europe with a very large forge, a press shop with 365 presses, a tool and die shop including among its equipment six large Keller machines, and close to 10,000 modern high-grade machine tools" (The United States Strategic Bombing Survey 1947a, p.5; Neliba 2000, S134). This plant had 96 conveyors with a total length of approximately 12 km in 1937 (Stahlmann 1993, S.88).

As is clear from these discussions, Opel represented a typical case of the introduction of the American production system. The essential constituents of modern mass production—manufacturing tasks relatively fragmented using the tact cycle and assembly conveyors, a simple standardized production structure, the pioneering of special-purpose machines and the first automatic transportation conveyor, partial organizational differentiation on hierarchical and functional levels, the horizontal and vertical division of labor, specialized staff for production techniques, planning, and quality control—prevailed in this enterprise until the outbreak of World War II (Stahlmann 1994, S.227).

"The Flexible Production Concept with an Emphasis on Quality" and Its Significance

In addition to these attempts to implement the flow production system based on the American model of mass production in the period of national socialism, there were enterprises that pursued their own attempts to adapt to German-specific conditions. Most typical cases can be observed at Daimler-Benz. "The flexible production concept with an emphasis on quality" that this company continued to pursue after their merger in 1926 enabled them to thoroughly adapt to changes in demand due to the economic crisis and provided them with an opportunity to shift to mass production gradually during the upswing phase (Feldenkirchen 2003, S.149). The need to adjust flow production to the characteristics of its products arose due to the various work plans and traditional restrictions of this firm. The difficult task of achieving a significant increase in the production volume of all models started in 1933 had to be solved in the workshops of their Untertürkheim plant (Hundt 1937a, S.250).

As pointed out in a meeting of top management on February 27, 1936, the simplification of type and the shift to flow production were their primary goals (*Mercedes-Benz Classic Archiv*, Kissel Protokolle, I/9, Protokoll über die Präsidialsitzung der Daimler-Benz A.G. am Donnerstag, dem 27. Februar 1936 im Eichensaal der Deutschen Bank und Discont-Gesellschaft, Berlin W8, S.4). Therefore, the design was investigated and adjusted to manufacture three types—1.3 L, 1.9 L, and 2.6 L—with the same tools and equipment using flow production (*Mercedes-Benz Classic Archiv*, Kissel Protokolle, I/9, Protokoll über die Präsidialsitzung der Daimler-Benz Aktiengesellschaft in Berlin am 27.2.36 11 Uhr vormittags, S.8). In truck assembly at the Mannheim plant, two types were assembled in one line parallel to the existing chassis line [*Mercedes-Benz Classic Archiv*, Kissel Technische Protokolle, 1.29, Protokoll der Sitzung in Bruchsal am 30.12.36 betr. Lastwagen-Fabrikation im Werk Mannheim (5.1.1937), S.3]. Although at Daimler-Benz the reorganization of flow production using the conveyor was implemented in the 1930s, after the transformation of passenger car manufacturing (Mercedes 170) to flow production using conveyors during the first half of the 1930s, in 1938, truck production modernization reached its peak until the outbreak of World War II with the start of mass production at the Mannheim plant (Stahlmann 1992, S.167). Bernard P. Bellon pointed out that "by the mid- and late 1930s, moving belts and assembly lines were central features of the factories in Untertürkheim, Mannheim, and Sindelfingen, and almost certainly the others as well" (Bellon 1990, p.224).

In this way, large-scale technical and labor organizational reforms were implemented. However, in spite of such reorganization continuing until the end of the 1930s (Stahlmann 1993, S.175), a rationalization model emphasizing securing the labor process flexibility and the interchangeability of the product variations to be manufactured was pursued during the second phase of modernization from the middle of the 1920s until the outbreak of the war (Stahlmann 1993, S.243–244).

In the passenger car sector, the emphasis of the German market shifted heavily to segments of the popular car market. Daimler-Benz adopted a strategy to specialize in middle- and high-class cars. As a result, production at this company was composed of two categories: (1) mass production to a certain degree of middle-class cars with an annual volume of thousands to a maximum of approximately 18,000 and (2) individual production of high-grade and luxurious cars based on almost complete handicraft with an annual volume of hundreds, tens, or just a few (Nishimuta 1999, p.168). Recognition that the production of many small, cheap cars in which competitors had a competitive advantage was not expedient under the intense competition at the time, despite understanding the importance of the small car, was the background of this strategy (*Mercedes-Benz Classic Archiv*, Kissel Protokolle, I/8, Protokoll der Vorstandssitzung der Daimler-Benz Aktiengesellschaft in Stuttgart-Untertürkheim am 29. August 1934, S.2–3). It was not possible for German plants to secure large lots as in the US, and in the passenger car sector, the acquisition of munitions demand did not have meaning as it did in the truck sector. Under this situation, Daimler-Benz could compete with such competitors only if it marketed cars of a much higher quality than its American competitors. Indeed, efforts to reduce the variety of products were made in the passenger car sector as well, but it almost never reached the production structure of the Ford Motor Company (Stahlmann 1993, S.176).

In truck production, lots enabling mass production to a certain degree were first realized in the Nazi era when the possibility of such production was increased by the expansion of the munitions market. In truck production at Daimler-Benz, modernization progressed slowly due to the existence of many types in the 1920s. A decisive mass production breakthrough was realized with the transformation to flow production using conveyors at the Mannheim plant (Stahlmann 1993, S.176–177; Stahlmann 1992, S.167). At the Gaggenau plant, the reduction of type was further advanced as a result of the loss of many trucks and trailers in the battle of Stalingrad. Rationalization was implemented in the main plant producing 4.5-ton trucks using rapid tempo and belt conveyor assembly between May and June of 1944 (Schriften der Hamburger Stiftung für Sozialgeschichte des 20. Jahrhunderts 1987, S.285–286).

However, a higher rate of skilled workers than in the American automobile industry was maintained to control the disorder of the production process, despite the installation of the most modern production equipment and labor organization reform (Stahlmann 1992, S.167). A flexible production structure with manufacturing in small series and a high rate of skilled workers was created. Such German-specific methods, referred to as "flexible production with an emphasis on quality," were maintained until the end of the 1930s (Stahlmann 1992, S.175, 178). Daimler-Benz could satisfy the expanding demand for munitions under the Nazi state in a relatively short term with this elastic production structure depending on the potential of skilled workers. Personnel arrangements and the flexibility to change products and elasticity of equipment setups enabled them to cope with the Armed Forces' demand for various munitions rapidly and smoothly (Stahlmann 1993, S.186, 245–247). The Gaggenau truck manufacturing plant realized full operation by orders of the Armed Forces and the state. Daimler-Benz dominated business for government offices in the 1920s and 1930s because of their flexible production structure (Stahlmann 1993, S.177; Feldenkirchen 2003, S.149).

According to the minutes of a supervisory board meeting of this enterprise on April 9, 1937, the ratio of business for government offices to all businesses was 40% (*Mercedes-Benz Classic Archiv*, Kissel Protokolle, I/10, Protokoll über die am Freitag, den 9. April 1937, in Stuttgart-Untertürkheim im Sitzungssaal der Gesellschaft abgehaltene Aufsichtsratssitzung der Daimler-Benz A.G., S.5). In this firm, transportation equipment production was transformed almost entirely to "business for government office" in 1939 (Stahlmann 1993, S.247). Michael Stahlmann pointed out that labor organization reform and technical modernization began in truck production at the Mannheim plant in 1939 and subsequently became the model of the rationalization measures implemented in munitions production (Stahlmann 1992, S.174).

"The flexible production concept with an emphasis on quality" pursued a mixed form of "effects of quantity and quality." Such effects could not be realized with a simple "low trust organization" taking the Taylor system as a model. The introduction of a systematic method of job evaluation and wage payment element based on skill was characteristic. This flexible production concept with a high rate of skilled workers had the advantage that many different small lots were produced and production changes between individual plants were possible in concentrating on the domestic market. This contributed not only to the more effective use of their production capacity but also to their adaptation to the changing demand structure. High rate of skilled workers enabled Daimler-Benz to rapidly build a production system for aircraft engines and ships. Such adaptative flexibility secured the competitiveness of Daimler-Benz (Stahlmann 1992, S.177–179).

In this way, Daimler-Benz became the forerunner of special-purpose machines, assembly conveyors, and automatic transportation conveyors at the end of the 1930s. However, there was no short tact time and performance control was achieved by applying specific group piece wages to production workers in many plants. This measure could replace bureaucratic forms of efficiency control based on the REFA system (Stahlmann 1994, S.227). In spite of such attempts and results, managerial social organizational rationalization and modernization in this company were implemented later and more moderately than the American automobile industry and did not progress as smoothly as management intended, even in the 1930s. Belt conveyors were increasingly and systematically integrated after the middle of the 1930s. However, as long as conveyors were individually arranged in each specific production area and inspection place and buffer stock existed between conveyors, the workers still influenced the working tempo (Stahlmann 1993, S.186–187).

At Daimler-Benz, the production of cars not for the civil market but for the Armed Forces for military use, in particular, cross-country and utility vehicles, became dominant and manufacturing passenger cars no longer played an important role in automobile manufacturing after the outbreak of World War II. In contrast, the production departments of munitions such as engines for aircraft and tanks were expanded remarkably [*Mercedes-Benz Classic Archiv*, Kissel, Werk Untertürkheim, 6.1, Der Brief an die Rüstungsinspektion im Wehrkreis V z. Hd, des Herrn Oberstleutnant Klett (9.12.1939); *Mercedes-Benz Classic Archiv*, Kissel Protokolle, I/12, Protokoll der Vorstandssitzung in U.T. am 12.10.39 (20.10.1939), S.7; *Mercedes-Benz Classic Archiv*, Kissel Protokolle, I/14, Protokoll der Vorstandssitzung am 21.1.41 in Untertürkheim und 22.1.41 in Sindelfingen (28.1. 1941), S.2; *Mercedes-Benz Classic*

Archiv, Kissel Protokolle, I/14, Protokoll der Vorstandssitzung in Untertürkheim am 28. Mai 1941 (29.5.1941), S.7; Stahlmann 1993, S.245]. According to the minutes of a managing board meeting of Daimler-Benz on October 23, 1941, programs for automobile production at the Untertürkheim, Mannheim, and Sindelfingen factories were no longer of importance and the automobile production program was still significant only in the Gaggenau plant [*Mercedes-Benz Classic Archiv*, Kissel Protokolle, I/14, Protokoll der Vorstandssitzung in Ut. am 23. Oktober 1941 (23.10.1941), S.4]. In production related to munitions such as engines for aircraft and tanks, conveyors with hoists in the assembly process and electric carts were installed and the first flow production line of "the tact system" that manufactured in large lots was created (Schriften der Hamburger Stiftung für Sozialgeschichte des 20. Jahrhunderts 1987, S.230–231). This system became a "fundamental mode of advance of production process." For example, at the Berlin-Genshagen plant newly constructed for the production of aircraft engines, the tact was 48 min in 1941 (Nishimuta 1999, p.253).

Skilled workers and flexible personnel arrangements enabled the rapid establishment of foundation for production of engines for aircraft and ship (*Mercedes-Benz Classic Archiv*, Kissel, Werk Untertürkheim, 6.1, Der Brief an den Herrn Reichsstatthalter Gauleiter Wilhelm Murr vom 2. Dezember 1939 über die Entwicklung der Gefolgschaftsstärke der Werke Untertürkheim, S.3). The way of thinking about personnel disposition was changed and skilled workers who did not go to the front were primarily arranged for the production of aircraft engines, ships, and tanks. In contrast, in automobile production, female unskilled workers and captives as workers taking charge of forced labor increasingly went to work (Stahlmann 1994, S.229). As a result, the ratio of skilled workers to all workers in charge of automobile production were only from 7 to 14% in individual departments. For example, even the largest machine department in an automobile plant had only 232 skilled turners out of 1,713 male workers, a ratio of 13.5% (Stahlmann 1993, S.247). In this way, in the proper automobile manufacturing department, it was no longer possible to use skilled workers sufficiently. At both Opel and Daimler-Benz, the arrangement of workers in charge of forced labor became an obstacle to rationalization (Stahlmann 1994, 229).

Regarding conditions until the outbreak of World War II, Hans Joachim Braun pointed out that until the 1940s, in the automobile industry (which was the most pivotal), the types of production organizations were definitively regulated by the markets it supplied. It has been noted that in this meaning, Americanism would only spread on a selective basis (Braun 1995, S.67–68). Indeed, three times the number of passenger cars were produced during this term, increasing from 92,160 in 1933 to 274,849 in 1938, and the number of buses, estate cars, and trucks produced increased 4.8 times during this period (6,470 in 1938) (Länderrat des Amerikanischen Besatzungsgebiets 1949, S.301). However, the ratio of car production in the US to global production was still 78% in 1936 (Ruelberg 1938, S.969). In this situation, the lot produced in the German automobile industry was not entirely equal to that of its counterpart in the US, despite all of the modernization endeavors undertaken since the start of the war (Stahlmann 1994, S.228). The evident advantage that the American automobile industry held before World War II was due to their higher level of standardization, mechanization, and economies of scale than their counterparts in Europe (Laux 1992, p.112). In Germany, passenger car production was greatly decreased during the war and munitions manufacturing was tremendously expanded. The possibility of overcoming the delay in the primary field of automobile production had to be further narrowed under these conditions.

12.2.2.3 Development of the Flow Production System in the Machinery Industry

In the machinery industry, various methods to balance the possibility of rationalization and the need to secure flexibility were attempted under the restrictive market conditions of the 1920s. Such strict conditions greatly changed with the militarization of economy of the Nazi state. In the machine tool industry, demand significantly increased after 1936 and Germany's production capacity was first fully utilized after World War I. The supply of raw materials became heavily dependent on the Armed Forces as the institution in charge of allotment. The lack of a labor force, in particular, skilled workers, became serious (Siegel and von Freyberg 1991, S.274).

These three factors pressured the machine tool industry to use automatic machines, standardize them, divide tasks, reform the organization to accelerate the shift to industrial mass production based on the Ford system, and ultimately rationalize this industry (Siegel and von Freyberg 1991, S.275). However, since it was not possible to use semiskilled workers for special-purpose machine production, in contrast to universal machine tools, special-purpose machines were generally not produced using flow production (Wommerlsdorf 1943, S.223–224). In the machinery industry, the flow work system was more forcefully introduced or further developed during the World War II period (Hachtmann 1989, S.79). The war brought significant changes in the composition of employees. The increase in the production of specific important products for the war made it necessary to use a labor force with no experience for such work and foreigners under the exodus of skilled workers to the military. The flow production line with conveyors driven by mechanical power provided a breakthrough measure in this situation (Dolezalek 1944, S.29).

However, the adaptation of the machinery industry as the primary user of machine tools for munitions production created large-scale and yet intensely changing demand. Certain characteristics of munitions demand—frequent changes of armament plans, the variety of munitions, the short time of technological innovation, and the short-term appointed delivery day—made it difficult to consolidate orders of the same types of products for mass production. In addition, the traditional adaptation of enterprises to flexibility was strengthened by the expectation of an early end to the war and the continuous orientation of machine tool manufacturers toward the future (global) market. Adjusting the capacity of these companies' production processes to changing requests became very important for manufacturers and machine tool users. In the 1920s, a production organization modeled after Ford's rigid workflow became unattractive for many machine manufacturers. Therefore, even in the Nazi era, the machine tool industry continued to adopt a cautious strategy and an elastic approach to flow production in spite of favorable order conditions (Siegel and von Freyberg 1991, S.268–269).

Enterprises regarded securing elasticity (flexibility) as the most important goal because of market conditions. Particularly in representative machine tool companies, flexible forms of mixed flow production were further expanded and enterprise's traditional orientation toward the goal of elasticity to epochal reform and changes in demand were maintained during the period of national socialism as well, which prevented the thorough failure of rationalization policy (Siegel and von Freyberg 1991, S.275–276). The US Strategic Bombing Survey pointed out that the German machinery industry was more flexible than the American industry due to its reliance on pre-mass production methods (The United States Strategic Bombing Survey 1947e, p.27).

Therefore, considering the general machine tool production situation, large-scale automobile manufacturing production in series and even mass production came into question. In contrast to this, the number of parts manufactured in machine tool production at the time was generally 10, 20, or approximately 40 at most, and in Germany, it was rare for machines to be manufactured in a single series with over 40 pieces in 1939 (Fehse 1939, S.142). K. Pentzlin highlighted in 1943 that like products such as aircraft, tanks, locomotives, and cannons, machine tools were previously produced exclusively in the form of individual production and assembled on the basis of method of the job-site production, whereas machine tools were often already manufactured on the basis of tact (Pentzlin 1943, S.52). Herbert Kalveram stressed that in 1944 in Germany, as well as in other countries, machine tools were not manufactured in volume, so enabling the implementation of genuine flow production as observed in the automobile industry, even considering the entire demand for machine tools for an enlarged economic sphere in Europe, was not possible. Flow production was limited to specific work groups, namely assembly and parts manufacturing produced in large numbers (Kalveram 1944, S.45).

In this way, it was in the assembly process that machine tool flow production was implemented most widely and there were not very many cases in which it was introduced in the mechanical processing process.

Next, the introduction of the flow production system is considered on the basis of real-world cases. Wilhelm Fehse pointed out that in 1939 at **Pittler Werkzeugmachinenfabrik AG**, the production of machines in greater numbers was already being done for scores of years and they had produced series of 10 or 20 pieces for a long time. As many Pittzler turret lathes were produced, the introduction of flow production was already considered in 1926. The total number produced per month was approximately 50 in 1939. Machines of each size were not continuously produced every month; a new series was created first after the finished machine was removed from the conveyor and prepared for sale. The number of possible sales greatly differed between the various types of machine tools. Whereas there were machines in which flow production was considered quietly economical, for other machines for which only 10 pieces were needed in approximately two or three months, the conditions for implementing flow production were still not at all mature. The introduction of the flow production method for such products was implemented in three primary groups—rotary slides, spindle headstocks, and beds. For fast headstocks and beds, tractors pulled by a chain were used for flow production. In the flow production of rotary slides, a simple car moved by manual or mechanical power was used. In each manufacturing group, subassembly groups that assembled individual machine parts in subgroups were arranged near the conveyor. Parts processed in advance reached the conveyor and were assembled in each place. Inspection locations were arranged at the conveyor. For instance, bed assembly was performed at 12 assembly points and two inspection places. Slide head assembly was done at 12 assembly points and six inspection places. For rotary slide assembly, there were no less than 20 assembly points with appropriate inspection places. In the mechanical processing shop, the continuous production of parts with various turret lathe sizes became possible and term planning became very simple using this production method. As a result, term observation stability increased and time savings of at least 25% to 30% was achieved in assembly. The introduction of flow work in turret lathe assembly greatly influenced other assembly workshops of machines manufactured in smaller numbers. In these workshops, tasks came to be performed on the basis of the same system as the turret lathe assembly workshops from the perspective of term decisions (Fehse 1939, S.142–144).

At **Loewe**, product types were limited to lathes, milling machines, and boring machines. K. Hegner highlighted that in 1939, the assembly of individual groups of parts, in particular, driving apparatuses, was performed using a sort of flow production at the time. First, 20-piece cases of a driving apparatus were put on an assembly table or fixed with a simple tool according to need. Small groups of parts accurately combined beforehand or newly attached parts were put in front of each case and the attachment of parts and their groups into the driving apparatus cases started in the same order that was accurately decided in advance. Such production and assembly methods were introduced to not only the same types of driving apparatuses but also various types of driving apparatuses such as feed shaft lathes, engine lathes, multi-cut lathe aprons, feed boxes, and turret heads were also produced and assembled on the basis of the same principle (Hegner 1939, S.126–128).

However, there were also enterprises in which the introduction of flow production encountered difficulties and was almost not implemented. At **Gebr. Boehringer-Werkzeugmaschine**, introducing flow work assembly in lathe and turret lathe manufacturing was impossible due to the various lengths of the beds and the many special apparatuses (i.e., water cooling apparatus, taper cutting apparatus or copying attachment, and compressed air chuck) required. In parts manufacturing, common parts of the driving apparatus such as the toothed wheel, shaft, main shaft, and bearings were produced in the part of plant in which manufacturing in series was dominant. In contrast, only parts that were not commonly used were manufactured in the individual parts processing shop or assembly shops for special types of parts (Martin 1939, S.125–126).

The German capital goods industry had not adopted mass production methods due to its individualistic and highly competitive nature. The competitiveness of the German capital goods industry in the export market consisted of "an ability and an intention to satisfy the customers' exact requirements and also to offer a large variety of products." The US Strategic Bombing Survey pointed out that "it was regarded as more important to offer a wide range of products than to supply them more cheaply" and the German capital goods industry avoided specialization, which might have made it possible to maintain the advantage of mass production methods. In wartime, similar conditions could be observed. "When the war began, efforts were made to induce manufacturers to avail themselves of the advantages of specialization and mass production methods." However, such endeavors did not have positive results. The US Strategic Bombing Survey stressed that these measures achieved very little in terms of increasing the productivity of the German capital goods industry and "the diminishing ratio of skilled workers in the industry's total labor force tended to lower the productivity of labor." It pointed out that even considering this factor, "the effects of rationalization could not have been very great" (The United States Strategic Bombing Survey 1947e, p.26). Labor productivity per worker and per hour in the German machine tool industry decreased by 10% in 1942, 18% in 1943, and 24% in 1944, respectively, compared with the level of labor productivity in 1939 (The United States Strategic Bombing Survey 1947e, p.89). In the US, an amazing increase in the production capacity of the machine tool industry was primarily achieved by converting general machinery plants to machine tool manufacturers. One-third of the machinery factories in the US implemented this conversion over the course of the war (The United States Strategic Bombing Survey 1947e, p.27).

The influence of unused, excessive production capacity was significant as well. Indeed, the operating rates in the German machinery industry increased from 32% in April 1933 (Maschinenbau 1933, S.314) to 78.1% in April 1936 (Maschinenbau 1936, S.462) and to over 100% in December 1937 (Maschinenbau 1938, S.199) under the expansion of domestic demand. However, as the US Strategic Bombing Survey pointed out, "not only was there a sufficiency of machine tools in German industry as a whole, but there was actually unused excess capacity in the machine tool industry itself" throughout the course of the war (The United States Strategic Bombing Survey 1947f, pp.3, 5). When examining the allocation of machine tools to the main user groups, all munition industries consumed 74.3% and 83.0% of all machine tools used in Germany in the fourth quarter of 1942 and the second quarter of 1944, respectively (The United States Strategic Bombing Survey 1947e, p.19). The existence of unused excessive production capacity was caused by the lack of urgent demand for machine tools rather than the lack of labor or materials (The United States Strategic Bombing Survey 1947e, p.20). In this way, the full-scale development of mass production could not be realized in the producer goods industries such as the machine tool industry despite the tremendous expansion of the munitions market caused by the militarization of the economy and the war economy.

12.3 Development of Mass Production and the Limitations of the Munitions Market

Building upon the proceeding examinations, the significance and limitations of efforts to develop mass production on the basis of the munitions market are explored next.

Munitions market expansion in the Nazi era made it possible to develop mass production by introducing the Ford system. However, a problem was the quality of the munitions market. Indeed, the munitions market was tremendous, as large as the market scale itself. But the kinds of munitions in demand changed frequently with modifications or fundamental changes in the plans for the munition preparation. Varieties of munitions, the rapidity of technological innovation, and short delivery times were important characteristics of this market. In particular, short-term appointed delivery days made it difficult to gather orders of the same types of products for mass production (Siegel and von Freyberg 1991, S.268, Weis 2004, S.21, 25). Therefore, German enterprises were forced to implement flow production methods taking production flexibility into consideration to adapt to specific munitions market conditions.

Companies that promised a short-term appointed delivery day and were low cost were selected for ordering munitions. Generally, enterprises that had thoroughly rationalized their production could more easily acquire state orders compared with those with legacy production equipment (Hachtmann 1989, S.73; Der Vierjahresplan 1940b, S.103–104). For instance, at Opel, smooth production advances and effective flow production development using belt conveyors were premises for acquiring increasing munitions orders related to aircraft (Weis 2004, S.13).

However, in Germany at the time, frequent changes in the type to be produced and the transformation of production goals prevented the introduction and expansion of flow production (Hachtmann 1989, S.80; Welter 1954, S.29–31; Janssen 1968, S.179). Therefore, even during the period of national socialism, securing production flexibility became an important task in implementing the flow production system to adapt to such market conditions and pursuing methods to elastically cope with changes in demand. Regarding this point, a great difference from the US—where mass production was developed and prevailed on the basis of expanding of the consumer goods market such as automobiles—can be observed.

In addition, mass production based on the enlargement of the munitions market under the militarization of economy encountered great limitations in the development of the national economy. This expansion of the munitions market would definitely end within a relatively certain short period. Moreover, the economic effect created by the mass production of munitions through providing for the demand in related industries tended to be limited to a relatively narrow range of industries. Although a remarkable part of automobile production that was converted to producing munitions and manufacturing products such as aircraft parts, engines for aircraft and ships, and tanks occupied a high rate (The United States Strategic Bombing Survey 1947a, p.1; The United States Strategic Bombing Survey 1947g, p.4; British Intelligence Objectives Sub-Committee 1946a, p.1), the range of industrial sectors that were related to production of these products by providing materials and parts was much narrower than those in the case of automobiles. As a result, unlike the mass production of consumer goods—in particular, durable consumer goods such as automobiles—cases in which the economic effect of the mass production of munitions could generate a demand for many other industrial sectors of the entire national economy were rare.

Considering the automobile industry, of which mass production should greatly contribute to the development of other industries by creating demand, even in the Nazi era, motorization for business use played a big role, whereas diffusion of automobiles for personal use was still only in the first stage (Oshima 1991b, p.126). Passenger cars did not become a mass consumer good unlike the period after World War II. In addition, the emphasis of demand and production was placed on products related directly to munitions such as engines for aircraft, ships, and tanks. The procurement of parts was also greatly influenced by priority of munitions in grading production emergencies [*Mercedes-Benz Classic Archiv*, Kissel Protokolle, I/14, Protokoll der Vorstandssitzung in Untertürkheim am 28. Mai 1941 (29.5.1941), S.7], which became an important factor restricting the mass production of automobiles. Whereas the automobile industry was a leading department both technically and economically in the US, in Europe, particularly in Germany, the leading role of this industrial sector was essentially limited to the technical field before the end of World War II (Kuczynski 1988, S.31).

Whereas the German automobile industry was never a key industry for scores of years after its birth until the 1930s (Kugler 1987, S.307), it first developed into an economically important department and a growing sector in the 1930s (Kugler 1987, S.339; Stahlmann 1993, S.60; Tessner 1994, S.183). There is also reference to the fact that German capitalism began to transform its structure from traditional connections between industries based on "coal–iron–railroad" relationships into a system of mass production in industrial sectors, of which the core was the automobile industry, with the development of this industry in the latter half of the 1930s (Nishimuta 1999, p.141).

However, in spite of active attempts to achieve such development, mass production could only progress by depending heavily on the munitions market due to the great delay in motorization for personal use. German-specific characteristics and the limitations of rationalization and economic development indicated that development based on civilian demand as observed in the US could not be realized.

In this way, the development of mass production based on the munitions market not only restricted the implementation of the American mass production method represented by the Ford system but also prevented transformation into an economic structure in which the expansion of mass production's effects could reach many related industrial sectors. After World War II, the full-scale expansion of the consumer goods market—in particular, the durable consumer goods market—progressed into a modern, economic system as observed in the US and enabled mass production to be established in Germany.

References

Abshagen F, Koetz G (1943) Das Fertigungsprogramm der Glühlampentechnik. Ein Beitrag zur Rationalisierung in der Kriegswirtschaft. In: Das Licht 13(6/7):79–82

Adam Opel Aktiengeselslchaft (1936) Das Neue Werk. Zur offizielle Eröffnung der Lastwagenfabrik der Adam Opel A.G. in Brandenburug. Adam Opel Aktiengeselslchaft, Brandenburg

Automobiltechnische Zeitschrift (1936) Das neue Opel-Lastwagenwerk. In: Automobiltechnische Zeitschrift 39(2):39–44

Automobiltechnische Zeitschrift (1937) Die Tagung der Automobil- und Flugtechnischen Gesellschaft am 25. Februar 1937 anläβlichder 33. ordentlichen Mitgliederversammlung. In: Automobiltechnische Zeitschrift 40(7):179–181

Automobiltechnische Zeitschrift (1939) Die deutsche Motorisierung vor und nach der Typenbe reinigung. In: Automobiltechnische Zeitschrift 42(9):239–249

Bellon BP (1990) Mercedes in Peace and War. Cambridge University Press, New York

Biniek G (1944) Normung der Stöpel für die Nachrichtentechnik. In: Elektrotechnische Zeitschrift 65(13/14):131–132

Bobek K (1945) Rationalisierung und Normen. In: Elektrotechnische Zeitschrift 66(1/2):2–4

Boehringer R (1939) Spezialisierung, Normung und Typung im deutschen Werkzeugmaschinenbau. In: Der Vierjahresplan 3(18):1067–1069

Bönig J (1993) Die Einführung von Flieβbandarbeit in Deutschland bis 1933. Zur Geschichte einer Sozialinnovation. Teil I, Lit, Münster, Hamburg

Braun H-J (1995) Automobilfertigung in Deutschland von den Anfängen bis zu den vierziger Jahren. In: Niemann H, Hermann A. (Hrsg) Eine Entwicklung der Motorisierung im Deutschen Reich und den Nachfolgestaaten. Stuttgarter Tage zur Automobil- und Unternehmensgeschichte. Franz Steienr, Stuttgart, pp 58–68

Braun W (1935) Die Elektroindustrie in der deutschen Wirtschaft. In: Der Deutsche Volkswirt 10(4):11–15 (Sonderbeilage: Die Wirtschaft im neuen Deutschland, 11 Folge: Elektroindustrie)

British Intelligence Objectives Sub-Committee (1946a) BMW Passenger Car and Generator Engines. FIAT Final Report No.687, London

British Intelligence Objectives Sub-Committee (1946b) German Heavy Electrical Industry. Motors and Power Transformers. B.I.O.S. Final Report No.600, London

Busch KW (1966) Strukturwandlungen der Westdeutschen Automobilindustrie. Ein Beitrag zur Erfassung und Deutung einer industriellen Entwicklungsphase im Übergang vom produktionsorientierten zum marktorientierten Wachstum. Duncker & Humblot, Berlin

Buskühl E (1942) Der Ruhrbergbau in der Leistungsprobe. In: Der Vierjahresplan 6(5):218–221

Der Deutsche Volkswirt (1937a) Die Funkgeräte: billiger, besser, weniger. In: Der Deutsche Volkswirt 11(45):2196–2197

Der Deutsche Volkswirt (1937b) Billigere Einzalteile für Kraftfahrzeug. In: Der Deutsche Volkswirt 12(22):1054

Der Deutsche Volkswirt (1939a) Siemens-Gruppe: Siemens & Halske A.-G., Siemens-Schuckertwerke A.-G. In: Der Deutsche Volkswirt 13(19):923–926

Der Deutsche Volkswirt (1939b) Daimler-Benz A.-G., Berlin-Stuttgart. In: Der Deutsche Volkswirt 13(31):1542–1544

Der Deutsche Volkswirt (1939c) Genormte Automobilteile. In: Der Deutsche Volkswirt 13(41):2038–2039

Der Deutsche Volkswirt (1939d) Konsolidierte Rundfunkwirtschaft. In: Der Deutsche Volkswirt 13(45):2237–2239

Der Deutsche Volkswirt (1939e) Die Umstellung des privaten Kraftwagenbedarfs. In: Der Deutsche Volkswirt 14(10):259

Der Deutsche Volkswirt (1940) Rundfunkindustrie in der Umstellung. In: Der Deutsche Volkswirt 14(20):616

Der Vierjahresplan (1939) Die Typenbegrenzung in der Kraftfahrzeugindustrie. In: Der Vierjahresplan 3(7):530–531

Der Vierjahresplan (1940a) Fortschreitende Normung und Typisierung. In: Der Vierjahresplan 4(1):12–13
Der Vierjahresplan (1940b) Die Betriebsgrößen in Kriegswirtschaftlicher Beurteilung. In: Der Vierjahresplan 4(3):103–104
Der Vierjahresplan (1941) Der Weg der Rationalisierung. In: Der Vierjahresplan 5(12):657–658
Der Vierjahresplan (1944) Elektroindustrie—eine Stütze unseres Rüstungspotentials. In: Der Vierjahresplan 8(2):44–45
DNA (1957) Die deutsche Normung 1917–1957. Oskar Zach, Berlin
Dolezalek KM (1944) Fließfertigung auf Maschinenstraßen. In: Technik und Wirtschaft 37(3):29–34
Eichholtz D (1985) Geschichte der deutschen Kriegswirtschaft 1939–1945. Bd.II: 1941–1943, Akademie-Verlag, Berlin
Etzold H (1988) Die Entwicklung der Produktivkräfte in der Industrie. In: Institut für Wirtschaftsgeschichte der Akademie der Wissenschaften der DDR, Berthold R et al. (Hrsg) (1988) Produktivkräfte in Deutschland von 1917/18 bis 1945. Akadermie Verlag, Berlin, S.36–223
Fehse W (1939) Fließzusammenbau der Pittler-Revolverdrehbänke. In: Werkstattstechnik und Werksleiter 33(5):142–144
Feldenkirchen W (1995) Siemens 1918–1945. Piper, München
Feldenkirchen W (2003) „Vom Guten das Beste", Band 1, Die ersten 100 Jahre (1883–1983), 1. Aufl., Herbig, München
Fleckenstein (1942) Fließzusammenbau von elektrisch beheizten Küchenherden. In: Werkstattstechnik und Werksleiter 36(13/14):285–286
Free J (1943) Maschinen, Organisation und Kriegspotential. Ein kurzer Rückblick auf 50 Jahre Entwicklung und ein Ausblick. In: Maschinenbau 22(1):1–4
Freiberger H (1944) Die Glühlampe in der Kriegswirtschaft. In: Der Vierjahresplan 8(5):124–125.
Freitag G (1942) 25 Jahre Normung. In: Technik und Wirtschaft 35(11):177–179
Gentsch E (1939) Die Typenbegrenzung in der Kraftfahrzeugindustrie. In: Der Deutsche Volkswirt 13(25):1206–1208
Gesell H (1942) Typenabrüstung in der Maschinenindustrie (II). In: Der Vierjahresplan 6(9):426–428
Geuter P, Fery H (1934) Prüfung von Rundfunkempfängern am laufenden Band. In: Elektrotechnische Zeitschrift 55(10):248–250
Götz F (1944) Cernavin, B., Berechnung von Typenreihen im Drehstrom-Motorenbau. In: Elektrotechnische Zeitschrift 65(21/22):207–212
Hachtmann R (1989) Industriearbeit im 》Dritten Reich《. Untersuchungen zu den Lohn- und Arbeitsbedingungen in Deutschland 1933–1945. Vandenhoeck & Ruprecht, Göttingen
Hammer M (1959) Vergleichende Morphologie der Arbeit in der europäischen Autoindustrie: Die Entwicklung zur Automation. Kyklos-Verlag, Tübingen
Hass R (1939) Rationalisierung des deutschen Kraftfahrwesen. In: Der Deutsche Vokswirt 13(20):952–953
Hegner K (1937) Normung im Werkzeugmaschinenbau. In: Maschinenbau 20 (5/6): 169–172
Hegner K (1939) Der Getriebebau in den Loewe-Fabriken. In: Werkstattstechnik und Werksleiter 33(5):126–129
Herfort H (1937) Herstellung von Elektrizitätszählern im Fließprozeß. In: Feinmechanik und Präzision 45(14):205–208
Homburg H (1991) Rationalisierung und Industriearbeit: Arbeitsmarkt—Management—Arbeiterschaft im Siemens-Konzern Berlin 1900–1939. Haude & Spener, Berlin
Hundt E (1937a) Besuch bei Daimler-Benz, In: Motorschau 1(3):248–257
Hundt E (1937b) Besuch bei OPEL in Brandenburg. In: Motorschau 1(4):354–359
Jacottet P, Lieber N (1943) Die Mitarbeit des VDE auf dem Gebiete der Austauschwerkstoffe und der Typenbeschränkung im Freileitungsbau. In: Elektrotechnische Zeitschrift 64(13/14):196–198
Janssen G (1968) Das Ministerium Speer. Deutschlands im Krieg. Ullstein, Frankfurt am Main, Berlin

Jensen W, Raupp A (1943) Die VDF-Fertigung bei Heidenreich & Harbeck. In: Hauptausschuss Maschinen beim Reichsminister für Bewaffung und Munition (Hrsg) Fliessende Fertigung in deutschen Maschinenfabriken. W. Girardet, Essen, S.136–152
Kaatz K (1938) Leistungssteigerung durch Anwendung von Zusammenbaumaschinen. In: Maschinenbau 17(19/20):517–522
Kalveram H (1944) Der Gruppenakkord in der Industrie. Frankfurt am Main, Univ, Diss
Kern H, Schumann M (1984) Das Ende der Arbeitsteilung? Rationalisierung in der industriellen Produktion: Bestandaufnahme, Trendbestimmung. C. H. Beck, München
Kiekebusch H (1939) Zur Normung im Werkzeugmaschinenbau. Aufgaben beiden Maschinen spanloser Formung. In: Maschinenbau 18(23/24):569–570
Kirchberg P (1969) Typisierung in der deutschen Kraftfahrzeugindustrie und der Generalbevollmächtigte für das Kraftfahrwesen. Ein Beitrag zur Problematik staatsmonopolistischer Kriegsvorbereitung. In: Jahrbuch für Wirtschaftsgeschichte, 1969, Teil II, 117–142
Koehn O (1942) Normung und Leistungssteigerung. In: Zeitschrift des Vereins Deutscher Ingenieure 86(45/46):665–669
Köhler V (1966) Deutsche Personenwagen-Fabrikate zwischen 1886 und 1965. In: Tradition 11(3):127–151
Kuczynski T (1988) Allgemeine Bidingungen und Tendenzen der Entwicklung. In: Institut für Wirtschaftsgeschichte der Akademie der Wissenschaften der DDR, Berthold R et al. (Hrsg) (1988) Produktivkräfte in Deutschland von 1917/18 bis 1945. Akadermie Verlag, Berlin, S.8–35
Kugler A (1987) Von der Werkststt zum Fließband. Etappen der frühen Automobilproduktion in Deutschland. In: Geschichte und Gesellschaft 13(1):304–339
Länderrat des Amerikanischen Besatzungsgebiets (1949) Statistisches Handbuch von Deutschen Reich 1928–1944. Ehrenwirth, München
Lange L (1939) Werkzeugmaschinen als Grundlage der Produktionssteigerung. In: Der Vierjahresplan 3(19):1113–1134
Laux JM (1992) The European automobil industry. Twayne Publishers, New York
Leifer G (1939) Der Einfluß des planmäßigen Arbeitseinsatzes auf die Leistung der Betriebe. In: Der Vierjahresplan 3(10):667–670
Link SJ (2020) Forging global fordism. Nazi Germany, Soviet Russia and the contest over the industrial order. Princton University Press, Princton, New Jersy
Ludwig K-H (1974) Technik und Ingenieure im Dritten Reich. Droste, Düsseldorf
Martin J (1939) Vom Rohwerkstoff zur fertigen Boehringer-Werkzeugmaschine. In: Werkstattstechnik und Werksleiter 33(5):122–126.
Maschinenbau (1933) Wirtschafts-Kurzbericht. In: Maschinenbau 12(13/14):313–315
Maschinenbau (1936) Die Wirtschaft im Zahlen. In: Maschinenbau 15(15/16):462
Maschinenbau (1938) Der Aufstieg der deutschen Industriewirtschaft. In: Maschinenbau 17(7/8):198–199
Meyer T (2009) Die Daimler-Benz AG 1945 bis 1955. Der Wiederaufbau und die strategische Ausrichtung des Fahrrzeugsgeschäfts, 1. Aufl., Daimler AG, Stuttgart
Moellendorff Uv (1933a) Fertigung der AEG-Rundfunk-Empfänger. In: AEG-Mitteilungen 29 (5): 172–175
Moellendorff Uv (1933b) Fertigungsaufgaben im Rundfunkgerätebau. In: Werkstattstechnik 27(4):481–484
Moellendorff Uv (1940) Leistungssteigerung im Zusammenbau. In: Werkstattstechnik und Werksleiter 34(8):129–132
Mottek H, Becker W, Schröter A (1975) Wirtschaftsgeschichte Deutschlands, Ein Grundriß, Bd. III, Von der Zeit der Bismarchschen Reichsgrndung 1871 bis zur Niederlage des faschistischen deutschen Imperialismus 1945, 2. Aufl., VEB Deutscher Verlag der Wissenschaften, Berlin
Neliba G (2000) Die Opel-Werke im Konzern von General-Motors (1929-1948) in Rüsselsheim und Brandenburg. Produktion für Aufrüstung und Krieg ab 1935 unter nationalsozialistischen Herrschaft, 1. Aufl., Brandes und Apsel, Frankfurt am Main

Nishimuta Y (1999) Nachizumu to Doitsu jidosha kogyo (Nazism and German automobile industry). Yuhikaku, Tokyo

Olk F (1941) Kriegsaufgaben der deutschen Werkzeugmaschinenindustrie. Zur Anordnung über die Meldepflicht von Werkzeugmaschinen. In: Zeitschrift des Vereins Deutscher Ingenieure 85(24):539–541

Oshima T (1991a) Ryo taisenkanki no Doitsu jidosha kogyo (1) [German automobile industry in the interwar period (1)]. In: Aich Daigaku Keizai Ronshu [Staff papers on economy (Aich University Journal of Economics)] 126:1–58

Oshima T (1991b) Ryo taisenkanki no Doitsu jidosha kogyo (2) [German automobile industry in the interwar period (2)]. In: Aich Daigaku Keizai Ronshu [Staff papers on economy (Aich University Journal of Economics)] 27:73–147

Oshima T (1993) Dai niji sekai taisenchu no Doitsu jidosha kogyo (1) [German automobile industry during World War II (1)]. Aich Daigaku Keizai Ronshu (Aich University Journal of Economics)132:23–91

Pentzlin K (1943) Überwindung der Massenproduktion. In: Technik und Wirtschaft 36(4):49–56

Pesch M (1988) Struktur und Funktionsweise der Kriegswirtschaft in Deutschland ab 1942—unter besonderer Berücksichtigung des organisatorischen und produktionswirtschaftlichen Wandels in der Fahrzeugindustrie—. Müller Botermann Verlag, Köln

Pohl H, Habeth S (1986) Brüninghaus, B., Die Daimler-Benz AG in den Jahren 1933 bis 1945. Steiner, Stuttgart

Radkau J (2008) Technik in Deutschland vom 18. Jahrhundert bis zur Heute. Campus, Frankfurt am Main

RKW-Nachrichten (1935) Rohstoff-Umstellung. In: RKW-Nachrichten 9(10):131–132

RKW-Nachrichten (1936) Die Bedeutung der Normung für die Industrie. In: RKW-Nachrichten 10(9):135–137

RKW-Nachrichten (1938) Leitsätz der Rationalisierung. In: RKW-Nachrichten 12(3):54

RKW-Nachrichten (1939) Beschränkung der Typen und Sortenzahl von Erzeugnissen. In: RKW-Nachrichten 13 (9): 175–176

RKW-Nachrichten (1944) Normung. In: RKW-Nachrichten 18(5):72

Ruelberg H (1938) Die deutsche Kraftfahrzeug-Industrie im Aufschwung. In: Der Deutsche Volkswirt 12(21):967–970.

Schell Av (1939a) Nationalsozialistische Wirtschaftsformen und Kraftfahrzeugindustrie. In: Der Vierjahresplan 3(17):1010–1012

Schell Av (1939b) Neue Wege der deutschen Motorisierung. In: Der Vierjahresplan 3(4):362–264

Schiz R (1940) Spezialisierung, Typung und Normung im Elektromotorenbau. In: Elektrotechnische Zeitschrift 61(11):275–278

Schnitt J (1936) Das Poteital der kriegwichtigen Industrie. In: Der Deutsche Volkswirt 11(5):217–220

Schriften der Hamburger Stiftung für Sozialgeschichte des 20. Jahrhunderts (Hrsg) (1987) Das Daimler-Benz Buch. Ein Rüstungskonzern im >Tausendjährigen Reich<. Delphi Politik, Nördlingen

Schütz Wv (1942) Betriebsführung und Betriebswissenschaft. In: Automobiltechnische Zeitschrift 45(21):580–582

Schütze W (1931) Achsschenkelfertigung in Fließarbeit. In: Maschinenbau 10(7):245–248

Schwenninger O (1934) Fertigungsfragen im Kraftwagenbau. In: Maschinenbau 13(11/12):316

Seherr-Thoss HCG v (1979) Die deutsche Automobilindutrie. Eine Dokumenten vom 1886 bis 1979, 2., korrigierte und erweiterte Auflage, Deutsche Verlags-Anstalt, Stuttgart

Siegel T, von Freyberg T (1991) Industrielle Rationalisierung unter dem Nationalsozialismus. Campus, Frankfurt am Main, New York

Siemens-Mitteilungen (1939) Der Einfluß des planmäßigen Arbeitseinsatzes auf die Leistung der Betrieb. In: Siemens-Mitteilungen (207): 106–110

Speer A (1943) Selbstverantwortung in der Rüstungsindustrie. In: Der Vierjahresplan 7(7):242–246

Stahlmann M (1992) Management, Modernisierung- und Arbeitspolitik bei der Daimler-Benz AG und ihren Vorläuferunternehmen von der Jahrhundertwende bis zum Zweiten Weltkrieg. Zeitschrift Für Unternehmensgeschichte 37:147–180

Stahlmann M (1993) Die Erste Revolution in der Autoindustrie. Management und Arbeitspolitik von 1900–1940. Campus, Frankfurt am Main, New York

Stahlmann M (1994) Von der Wekstatt zur Lean-Production. Arbeitsmanagement und Arbeitsbeziehungen im sozialen Wandel. In: In: Zeitschrift für Unternehmensgeschichte 39(3):219–243

Stodieck K (1936) Entwurf und Bau mechanischer Werkstätten. In: Maschinenbau 15(5/6):136–138

Tessner M (1994) Die deutsche Automobilindustrie im Strukturwandel von 1919 bis 1938. Botermann & Botermann, Köln

The United States Strategic Bombing Survey (1947a) Adam Opel, Rüsselsheim, Final reports of the United States Strategic Bombing Survey, No.81, second edition, Washington

The United States Strategic Bombing Survey (1947b) Daimler-Benz Gaggenau Works, Final reports of the United States Strategic Bombing Survey, No.82, second edition, Washington

The United States Strategic Bombing Survey (1947c) German Electrical Equipment Industry Report, Final reports of the United States Strategic Bombing Survey, No.48, second edition, Washington

The United States Strategic Bombing Survey (1947d) German Motor Vehicles Industry Report, Final reports of the United States Strategic Bombing Survey, No.77, second edition, Washington

The United States Strategic Bombing Survey (1947e) Machine Tool and Machinery, Final reports of the United States Strategic Bombing Survey, No.54, second edition, Washington

The United States Strategic Bombing Survey (1947f) Machine Tool Industry in Germany, Final reports of the United States Strategic Bombing Survey, No.55, second edition, Washington

The United States Strategic Bombing Survey (1947g) Volkswagen-Werke, Fallersleben, Final reports of the United States Strategic Bombing Survey, No.88, second edition, Washington

Thieme C (2004) Daimler-Benz zwischen Anpassungskrise, Verdrängungswettbewerb und Rüstungskonjunktur 1919–1936, 1. Aufl., Vaihingen/Enz: IPa, Stuttgart

Wagner H (1942) Normung und Elektrotechnik. In: Elektrotechnische Zeitschrift 63(45/46):529–535

Wahl W (1938) Zwischenbetrieblicher Vergleich in der deutschen Automobilindustrie. Konrad Triltsch, Würzburg

Weis J (2004) Die deutsche Automobilindustrie in der nationalsozialistischen Kriegswirtschaft —Opel, Daimler-Benz und Volkswagen, 1. Aufl., GRIN Verlag, München

Welter E (1954) Falsch und Richtung planen. Eine kritische Studie über die deutsche Wirtschaftslenkung im Zweiten Weltkrieg. Quelle & Meyer, Heidelberg

Winckler R (1944) Die Normung von elektrischen Sammlern (Akkumulatoren). In: Elektrotechnische Zeitschrift 65(27/40):315–316

Wittke V (1996) Wie entstand industrielle Massenproduktion? Diskontinuierliche Entwicklung der deutschen Elektroindustrie von den Anfängen der „großen Industrie" bis zur Entfaltung des Fordismus (1881–1975). Edition Sigma, Berlin

Wommerlsdorf F (1943) Einfluß der Serien- und Massenfertigung auf den Bau von Normal- und Spezialmaschinen. In: Hauptausschuss Maschinen beim Reichsminister für Bewaffung und Munition (Hrsg) Fliessende Fertigung in deutschen Maschinenfabriken. W. Girardet, Essen, S.210–224

Wussow J (1943) Die Schreibmaschine im Krieg. In: Der Vierjahresplan 7(3):110–112

Zeitschrift des Vereins Deutscher Ingenieure (1939) Leistungssteigerung überall. In: Zeitschrift des Vereins Deutscher Ingenieure 83(26):787–791

Zollitsch W (1990) Arbeiter zwischen Weltwirtschaftskrise und Nationalsozialismus. Ein Beitrag zur Sozialgeschichte der Jahre 1928 bis 1936. Vandenhoeck & Ruprecht, Göttingen

Part V
Germany's Globalism, German Capitalism, and Corporate Expansion

Chapter 13
Germany's Globalism and Regionalism: A Historical View

Abstract Based on the discussions in the foregoing chapters, Part V considers the history of Germany's globalism and regionalism and the development of German capitalism and enterprises. Globalism means the principle, norm, and ism of setting the institutional framework and rules for acquiring global hegemony in building the world order. This chapter examines Germany's globalism and regionalism, which are deeply related to the development of German capitalism and enterprises from the late nineteenth century to the present, from a historical viewpoint. Regarding the period until the end of World War II, this chapter considers the three periods of the Second Reich, the Weimar Republic, and National Socialism. Next, the period of the Cold War after World War II is considered. Furthermore, this chapter explores the period after the 1990s to the present, when globalization and regionalization have progressed at full scale. Through these analyses, this chapter clarifies the characteristics and significance of Germany's global strategy in the international circumstances in each period.

Keywords European integration · European Union · Europeanization · German capitalism · Globalism · Globalization · Pax Americana · Regionalism

As discussed in Chapter 1, when looking at the internationality and nationality of capital, it is important to clarify the unique characteristics of capitalism of the concerned country, the generality of capitalistic accumulation, and the power of life of capital by considering the historical conditions and the processes of birth and development of capitalism in each nation (Taguchi 2018, pp.139, 146). The process of how each country's capitalism has maintained and developed its life power in the process of globalization focuses on globalism as the principle and doctrine for competition over acquiring the global hegemony in establishing the dominant order to create the more advantageous foundations for corporate behavior and economic development.

Globalization is a process in which global interdependence in both aspects of markets and productive forces intensifies. In contrast, globalism means the principle, norm, and ism of setting an institutional framework and rules for acquiring global

T. Yamazaki, *A History of German Business*,
https://doi.org/10.1007/978-981-96-8476-2_13

hegemony in building the world order. The latter not only contributes to the development of the concerned country but also can be restrictive conditions for activities to pursue its national interest because a country with hegemony forces other countries to follow the rules set by its own country. Meanwhile, regionalism has characteristics as a countermeasure to "globalism," such as creating the framework, institutions, and rules to control world markets to the maximum degree. Dichotomizing regionalism and globalism highlights these two key aspects of global reality (Pettman 1999, p.181). Regionalization is an attempt to emphasize a certain region in terms of markets and productive forces and form a more advantageous framework for trade in such an integrated region. In contrast, regionalism is an ideology as a behavioral principle and norm that enables building more favorable capital accumulation conditions than nations in other areas by differentiating trade conditions. Regional integration is traditionally regarded as "a harmonization of trade policies" (Hettne 1999, p.xii).

Globalism aims to build hegemony to create more advantage foundations for capital accumulation in one's own country, but it has been an issue with characteristics peculiar to each period. Based on discussions in the previous chapters and discussions regarding the history of globalism in Chapter 2, this chapter attempts to grasp the changes in Germany's globalism and regionalism from the late nineteenth century to the present. We examine five periods: (1) the Second Reich, (2) the Weimar Republic, (3) National Socialism, (4) the Cold War after World War II, and (5) the 1990s to the present. How was Germany incorporated into the globalism of a country with hegemony in each period, and how has Germany coped with such movements by pursuing its globalism and regionalism under such international circumstances? How are the trends seen in Germany concerning capitalistic accumulation development and corporate expansion? This chapter's examination is deeply connected to the problem of how relations between German globalism and regionalism and the development of German capitalism and corporate expansion or business management are to be understood.

First, regarding the period until the end of World War II, Sects. 13.1, 13.2, and 13.3 consider each period of the Second Reich, the Weimar Republic, and National Socialism, respectively. Section 13.4 examines the period of the Cold War after World War II. Building upon these examinations, Sect. 13.5 analyzes the period after the 1990s to the present, when globalization and regionalization have progressed at full scale. Through these analyses, this chapter clarifies the characteristics and significance of Germany's global strategy in the international circumstances in each period.

13.1 Germany's Globalism and Regionalism in the Second Reich Era

In the age from the late nineteenth century to the end of World War I, even though its economic predominance declined due to the rapid increase of industrial productive forces in the United States (US) and Germany, the United Kingdom (UK) maintained its hegemony due to its importance in trade and the international financial market. The remarkable expansion of exports based on high productive forces, a capital accumulation structure complemented by colonies, and the core position in international finance based on the gold standard system was the foundation for the globalism of the UK. The UK's hegemony was grounded on the fact that such a currency system at the time functioned under the international financial system in which only London was a central clearing position (Brown 1940, pp.x–xi), a central market for international transactions in goods, services, and securities, and insurance, and a core remittance channel. The strength of the London market as a financial center was primarily supported by large dealing amounts of commodities and services (Brown 1940, pp.535–536). Thus, attempts to establish hegemony in each nation were deeply concerned with forming its economic sphere by acquiring and maintaining colonies under the UK's hegemony. In this period, the fundamental problem of globalization seen in "estrangement between market and governance" was solved by imperialistic colonial policy partially with force and arms (Rodrik 2011, pp.26, 32–34; Shibayama 2014, p.325). As long as the imperialistic international balance among the world powers was maintained, the disposition mode of excessive capital through the central measure of capital export under the colonial policy could function as the world mechanism in which internal problems were solved externally (Okamoto 1993, p.245). During the period until World War I, in Germany, excessive capital was disposed of through external advances rather than through keeping and concealing unused equipment (Kato 1973, p.206).

In Germany, the rapid expansion of productive forces centered on the heavy and chemical industries progressed after 1871 when the Second Reich was born; however, restrictive conditions, as seen in the narrow domestic market and holding of few colonies, limited capital accumulation structure. To break these restrictions, Germany pursued globalism, aiming to establish a hegemony that enabled it to set the rules. Germany's challenge to redivide colonies under the global capitalistic system, as seen in capitalism on a country base and the colonial economic sphere pursued by the UK and France, led to World War I. This war indicates failure in the abovementioned disposal system of excessive capital (Okamoto 1993, p.245). In this sense, the pursuit of hegemony to build a more favorable foundation for the reproduction of German capitalism had the characteristics of "offensive globalism" and "defensive globalism" as an important countermeasure to the limitation of capitalistic reproduction. The changes in business management analyzed in Part II was an important basis for such challenges and means.

Germany first achieved the shift to monopolistic capitalism, as did the US, and the high level of concentration progressed not only in industries but also in the banking industry compared with the UK. Germany became a typical nation in monopolistic capitalism. State policy permitting cartels, a protective trade policy that functioned as an important foundation for the effectiveness of cartels, and establishing close relationships by combining and knitting industries and banks were important characteristics of prewar German capitalism. Regarding conditions at the time, Lenin pointed out in 1919 that Germany was inferior to the US regarding technique and production; however, it was a model of advanced capitalistic countries that was superior to the US in terms of the high level of organization of monopolistic capitalism and finance capitalism (Lenin 1953, S.511; regarding the relationships between industry and bank based on personnel connections, see Yamazaki, 2024b). Such direction in Germany at the time was an important basis for developing enterprises and the economy by expanding exports and pursuing Germany's globalism as a countermeasure against countries with hegemony and restrictive conditions for behaviors to build hegemony. However, while monopolistic systems with higher concentration were established, adopting management methods to improve productivity was not always widespread or smooth. This situation is true for deploying the Taylor system as an influential American management method. Unlike the US, the scientific building of labor organization based on the "principle of rational arrangement of social labors" (Ленин 1948, p.136) through standardization of each partial labor encountered limitations, which restricted the expansion of productive forces. Thus, changes in business management did not sufficiently contribute to achieving such goals.

13.2 Germany's Globalism and Regionalism in the Weimar Era

However, Germany's globalism as an imperialistic challenge resulted in its collapse with the defeat in World War I. As a result, significant restrictions on resuscitation and development were imposed on Germany by the Treaty of Versailles and the birth of the Weimar Republic. During this period, the US acquired hegemony and pursued globalism most strongly.

The reparation problem was at the core of stabilizing Europe after World War I. The US created a way to solve this problem. Without stabilizing the currency, the "Reichsmark," it was impossible to settle the financial chaos in Germany. The US capital export aimed at reinforcing the influence of this country on the European markets, and, in particular, capital aid to Germany had an important goal of exporting commodities; however, severe unsolved conditions in the reparation problem became an obstacle to US capital exports (Edwards 1924, p.35; Kato 1973, p.134). The Dawes Plan in 1924 was based on the recognition that the reparation problem was, in essence, primarily an economic problem and not a political one (Schmidt 1934, S.24). This plan had some economic and political goals, such as the temporary solution of the reparation problem, countermeasures to the threat brought by the birth of a socialistic country, collection of war credits to the UK and France through capital assistance for Germany and payment of reparations by this country, and high interest in Germany due to a lack of capital. The inflow of the initial 800 million Reichsmarks was important because it entailed postponing the payment of reparations in the first year and strengthened foreign reliance (Schmidt 1934, S.31).

In this way, the US played a great role in both aspects of the provisionary solution of the reparation problem and capital export, and American involvement contributed to creating a foundation for solving serious problems in Europe. Germany's orientation toward globalism aimed at acquiring hegemony was forced to retreat considerably. Instead, the rationalization movement began in 1924 and became the national task of rebuilding exhausted enterprises, industries, and the economy. It was an important countermeasure for defense during the crisis of German capitalism; however, credits provided by the US were the lifeline for the rationalization movement in the period of relative stability. The rebuilding of Germany greatly depended on the US capital exports. For example, 86.7% (12,390,315,000 USD) of the total amount of loans publicly collected in the US States from 1924 to 1930 (14,305,250,000 USD) was issued in Germany (Kuczynski 1933, S.16).

However, Germany was compelled to return to the gold standard system as an indispensable prerequisite for receiving funds from the US (Kato 1973, pp.140–141). In the competition between the US and the UK over whether the USD or the British pound (GBP) acquired the position of core currency, making Germany implement conversion into gold immediately or not became a focus (Link 1970, Zweiter Teil, II; Kato 1973, pp.142–143). The US pursuit of globalism, intended to achieve hegemony in building the world order, can be seen at this point. The United States aimed to make the USD the core currency in exchange for the GBP through the return of Germany to the gold standard system (Link 1970, S.233–236). The rebuilding of such a system as a primary means for integrating the world economy (Polanyi 2001, p.211) progressed, an important trend commonly observed in major capitalistic countries. With such a movement, the position of the US as a nation with the most substantial financial and economic powers was reinforced (Link 1970, S.239).

For Germany, the collapse of its currency meant that relationships with the economy outside the country were cut off (Polanyi 2001, p.238), and in the period of relative stability, Germany was forced to follow American globalism. In the Dawes Plan by the US as an assistance measure for Germany after World War I, debts were created with political grounds such as reparation, and loans were provided due, in part, to political reasons (Polanyi 2001, p.240). The Dawes Plan was a movement to establish hegemony through the temporary solution of the reparation problem and achieving reform of the currency system in Germany, and on its whole, was the premise and an important component of America's ground design (Link 1970, S.240).

The German state was subject to burdened reparation, and domestic conditions changed depending on the partial charge of payment of reparations by the state as a combined body of government and economic world. Thus, the solidarity of a nation was united with the gold standard system due to the supreme duty of maintaining the value of currency against foreign currencies (Polanyi 2001, p.224). However, Germany's return to the gold standard system became a restrictive condition for the rationalization movement that should enable the revival and development of German capitalism, corporate expansion, and economic policy during the great crisis that began in 1929.

In this way, during the Weimar Republic, Germany was forced to pursue globalism to rebuild its economy while coping with the US strategy and rules set by this hegemony state that replaced the UK after World War I. Under such heteronomous and restrictive institutional frameworks, Germany aimed to rebirth and develop monopolistic enterprises by deploying technology and management methods such as the Taylor and Ford systems from the US; however, unlike the US, establishing a mass production system could not be realized at the time. The delay of mass production in the automobile industry significantly restricted the progress of mass production in various related industries due to the limitation in creating demand for these industrial sectors.

The relationship between the industrial sectors fundamentally determined the development and characteristics of the rationalization movement in the 1920s (Maekawa and Yamazaki 1995, p.240). Restrictions on the economic effects in terms of inter-industry relations and the stringent market circumstances, an important limitation for the rationalization movement in Germany during this period, did not enable the expansion process, where the capital accumulation based on the rationalization simultaneously created demand: the market for the more advantageous development could not be realized.

After 1929, the production capacity accumulated in the rationalization movement during the period of relative stability was forced to be greatly excessive under further restrictive market circumstances. Thus, while Germany's defensive globalism collapsed, options for economic policy were limited, and the Brunning cabinet was forced to adopt the deflation policy due to restrictions brought by the gold standard system on issuing currency despite a significantly severe depression (Kato 1973, pp.417–420). In the great depression, building the block economy progressed as a countermeasure of major countries like the UK and France. It limited countries as partners in which free trade was admitted to the extent of core nations (Iwamura 2020, p.103) and promoted more serious economic conditions due to further blockade of markets. Significant limitations represented by the lack of cooperative relations based on global connections of the capitalistic economy in the markets and capital reproduction structure under the system of capitalism at the level of one nation and colonies promoted further serious conditions of economic crisis and excluded Germany from the international circulation of commodities and capital.

13.3 Germany's Globalism and Regionalism in the Nazi Era

Following the failure of the rationalization movement by the world crisis and the period of severe economic situations, Germany shifted to the fascist system of National Socialism. Under this system, the restrictive framework imposed by the Versailles treaty was denounced entirely. In the Nazi era, Germany pursued the building of hegemony, enabling the expansion of the economic sphere that targeted Europe as a core while aiming at realizing world hegemony. Nazi Germany caused World War II (in which Europe was the arena of war) while enlarging munitions and strengthening the Eastern orientation based on the concept of "the extensive market" ("*Großraumwirtschaft*"). The orientation in policy toward the extensive market and autarky and building Germany's own economic block came to the surface (Yanagisawa 2006, p.29).

In this plan, based on the concept of the international division of labor modified into the specialization of function within each area, Germany was regarded as "the manufacturing heartland of its own area, together with the bordering industrial areas of North-east France, Belgium, and Bohemia," "the peripheral regions would supply raw materials and foodstuffs to this developed industrial core." This vision was pursued through a series of bilateral trade agreements signed with underdeveloped South-eastern European countries after 1933 (Milward 1987, pp.9–10). In this plan, the national economies of individual peoples played roles as reservoir of raw materials and labor forces for the German economy and subcontractors. The occupation and economic use of various European countries and areas were for performing war and the most important element for National Socialism that intended to establish the fundamentally new order for the European economy and society (Ambrosius and Hubbard 1986, S.261–262).

In "the extensive market" plan and the related new order, all occupied nations and subordinate countries were integrated into the German system of war economy in very various ways. Through this approach, Germany aimed to use the production capabilities of European national economies for the German war economy in the short term to reduce the economic burdens that could not cover war efforts alone. Some national economies maintained relative independence and were integrated into the war economic system using "voluntary compulsion"; however, in other countries, the Germans relentlessly plundered, snatched, and destroyed. The German Empire forced occupied countries or subordinate nations to participate in trade and settlement in a one-sided way that advantaged Germany after 1940. Important commodities for production in the German war economy were exported from these countries without considering the needs of their national economies. The exchange rate was also treated in favor of the Reichsmark. Nations integrated into "the extensive market" were forced to conclude the bilateral commercial agreement (Ambrosius and Hubbard 1986, S.262).

The "extensive market" plan aimed to realize the more advantageous reproduction of capital under Germany's rules instead of the rules and frameworks set by the US and the victorious nations after World War I. Thus, unlike the "protective" globalism before World War I and in the Weimar era, the "offensive globalism" was pursued despite emphasizing hegemony mainly in Europe. Such attempts can also be regarded as "globalism based on regionalism." It was the development of the rationalization movement and the creation of systems of the controlled economy under the Nazi state that had significance as measures of building hegemony in the imperialistic globalism of German capitalism.

In this way, supported by state institutions, business management was developed as an important measurement of pursuing globalism. Representative examples of such a movement can be observed in the pursuit of standardization led and forced by the state, building compulsory cartels, and the progress of mass production based on the great expansion of munitions markets. Germany's globalism was promoted on a full scale after full employment was achieved by the first four-year plan that began in 1933. Globalism based on the militarization of the economy and the war economy was no longer for coping with and overcoming the limitations of the reproduction structure of German capitalism in the period before World War I. Thus, the characteristics of Germany's globalism changed, and such changes determined the development of business management.

As the previous discussions established, two World Wars were Germany's challenges to establish more stable and favorable foundations for reproducing its capitalism. For each country, it is essential to maintain and develop its life power in globalization by changing limitations to restrictions. Clarifying the German-specific development of business management and its significance and limitations is deeply concerned with these problems. After the breakdown of its globalism until the end of World War II, Germany did not pursue the apparent globalism under the Cold War system and the US hegemony in the capitalistic block. Instead, Germany has emphasized regionalization based on Western Europe. Conversely, in the prewar period, the lack of frameworks of regional economic integration, such as today's European Union (EU), was an important factor determining limitations in Germany while trends toward further focusing trade on the European region as a core of markets.

13.4 Germany's Globalism and Regionalism During the Cold War After World War II

This subsection considers German globalism and regionalism during the Cold War after World War II through comparison with the prewar era. Germany's federal government considered the social market economy in the framework of a postwar economic order as critical for economic policy, particularly to further expand and solidify the domestic market economy and competition (Erhard 1954, S 150). In contrast to the Nazi-controlled economy before the war, postwar, the state played a more regulatory role in economic policy. This economic policy was based on a philosophy emphasizing market mechanisms by limiting government to an auxiliary role and the strict separation of politics and the economy (Noda 1998, pp.196–197). The social nature of government policy was evident in creating a framework for an economic order that guaranteed the equitable distribution of the product and benefits of economic activity (Bundesministrium für Wirtschaft 1959, S 18). The social market economy was based on the combined principle of "freedom in markets" and "social equilibrium" (Müller-Armack 1956, S 390; Müller-Armack 1966, S.243). The new postwar framework for labor relations was based on the codetermination system and the function of safety nets in employment and wage security, which supported conditions for correcting social inequities within a social market economy (Yamazaki 2013, 4.4).

West Germany built a new postwar economic system and economic order as a unique direction of the market economy; it could enjoy the benefits of US-led capitalistic world economic systems, such as the General Agreement on Tariffs and Trade and the International Monetary Fund. Moreover, America's global strategy had stepped toward a major trading country with the Marshall Plan and the productivity movement. One of the initiatives of the Marshall Plan was realizing the integration of and free trade in Western European countries (Stolper et al. 1964, S 272), aiming to build a multinational order for global trade and payments (Buchheim 1993, p.78). The Organization for European Economic Cooperation (OEEC) was built with the goal and regulatory intent to gradually remove trade barriers, such as the allotment system in global trade, and similar discriminatory barriers; the OEEC coordinated various policies to promote international cooperation in Europe and reinforce the capitalist system (Schröter 2005b, S 366, 369; Postan 1967, p.98). While the US worked to create conditions for economic restructuring in European countries under the Marshall Plan, it compelled these countries' governments to open their markets to free trade and international competition (Schröter 2005a, p.8; Kudo et al. 2004, p.8). By laying the foundation for economic rebuilding based on the influx of USD to many participating countries, capital aid under the Marshall Plan served as an important condition for creating the international monetary system after the war, which recognized the USD as the world's key currency. In the 1950s, there was an enormous chasm between Western Europe and the US regarding possible production and demand; thus, another objective of the Marshall Plan was to take advantage of the unsatisfied demands for US production in Western Europe (I.P.W.-Berichte 1978, S 4).

The Marshall Plan was also a core element in rebuilding Germany's economy, its return to the Western European economy, and the complete removal of policies that allowed the weakening of Germany by occupation authorities (Furuuchi 2007, pp.65–66). Aid from the Marshall Plan was kept to a minimum on account of the principles of "independence" and "mutual assistance" for European countries; thus, the promotion of German rebuilding was required to pick up the slack (Manabe 1989, pp.174–175, 177–178, 188, 226). West Germany was supposed to be at the core of the US stabilization efforts for Western Europe. Due to the division of Germany into East and West, opposition to the socialist camp, and being a defeated nation in World War II, Western Germany gained special consideration in the Marshall Plan. Because of West Germany's position at the axis of the capitalistic bloc countries and the relative strength of Germany's industrial productive forces, Germany became a necessary element in reorganizing the US-led system of capitalism.

The Marshall Plan proposed trade policy rules to ease Germany's return to the international scene, revive global markets mid-term, and develop international economic cooperation vehicles like the OEEC (Abelshauser 2004, S 151, S 153). One initial goal was to reduce resistance from each country toward Germany's economic rebuilding by associating it with the rebuilding of Europe's overall economy rather than focusing on the critical role of Germany and how much European countries were needed to restructure the European economy (Suzuki 1977, pp.426–427). Thus, the Marshall Plan was designed to integrate the overall German economy and that of the Ruhr region with the economic system of the West through large-scale financial aid (Schlieper 1986, S 162; Borchardt 1978, S 71–72). From this perspective, West Germany occupied a central position. Extensive congressional research on the European Recovery Program repeatedly emphasized that the Ruhr was the economic heart of Europe. Moreover, Germany was the pillar of the entire restructuring system (Kitamura 1973, p.33), highlighted by Germany's high industrial production and its basis that made it possible. The American-led reintegration of West Germany into the world economy (Berghahn 2024, p.160) was a crucial issue for this country and the United States.

In this way, based on the US government's understanding that the revival and expansion of German industries were necessary for the rebuilding of economic conditions in Europe (Barjot 2002, p.49; Crouzet 2002, p.435), Germany occupied a central role in technical assistance under the Marshall Plan and the productivity movement. The US also regarded West Germany as one of the most important countries in the productivity movement. The international expansion of the productivity movement led by the US due to the creation of the European Productivity Agency was an inevitable result of the fusion of the two primary goals of US policy postwar: improving productivity and promoting European integration (Boel 2002, p.88). In the first few years of the 1950s, among the countries under the Marshall Plan, West Germany was the heart of capitalistic rationalization (Thalmann 1956, S 91) and an important country within Europe for the expansion of the productivity movement (*National Archives*, RG469, Assistant Administration for Production, Productivity & Technical Assistance Division, Records relating to US Advisory Group on European Productivity, 1952–1953, The Concept and Status of the Productivity Program). In this way, America's globalism built a more advantageous foundation for Germany by incorporating it into the regional market and economic relations.

When comparing aid by the US after World War I and after World War II, in the Dawes Plan post-World War I case, the US aid policy was limited to the defeated nation of Germany and focused on capital assistance through private funding. US capital assistance was economically and politically motivated in three ways: (1) keeping Germany in the realm of capitalism; (2) receiving the highest possible interest payments from the strikingly capital-poor Germany (Maekawa 1970, pp.11–14); and (3) reclaiming US war loans from both England and France (Yoshida 1976, pp.26–27). In contrast, post-World War II, aid was primarily from public funding rather than private funding due to the impetus of the Marshall Plan itself (Kudo 1996, p.250).

As part of this technical assistance, the US shared technology with European countries for broadly defined productivity improvements intended to increase the effects of capital aid (Oba 1975, pp.49–50; Takagi 1962, pp.7–8). These points strongly reflected US globalism during the Cold War after World War II.

History after World War II was how independent states with their sovereignty were subordinated through free trade and capital exports (Watanabe 2003, pp.211–212). The triumph of globalism in the US trade policy after the war has been a product of a pattern of global orientation in domestic politics based on the position of the US as a superstate in world trade (Kirshner 2014, pp.24, 167). Under such conditions, Germany has developed a prioritizing regionalization focusing on a specific district, namely Europe, as a core market for this country rather than pursuing its globalism. This was reflected in the history in which Germany pursued European integration, which resulted in today's EU. Being supported by the postwar international economic system prioritizing the interests of advanced countries, not developing countries (Yeates 2001, p.169; Takemura 2020, p.41; Mizuoka 2006, chapter 2; Stiglitz 2002, p.215), and the regionalization in Europe and due to the importance and effectiveness of European markets as an important foundation for capital accumulation, Germany did not need to pursue globalism in each aspect of "defense" and "offense." There was also no room to pursue its globalism like that before World War II under the strong influence of globalism of the US as a hegemony nation.

The breakdown of the Bretton Woods system in the former half of the 1970s brought about a significant change in US hegemony in the capitalistic block. This phenomenon indicates that this hegemonic nation no longer had the power to control the world's financial and currency policies (Harvey 1989, p.164). Under such situations, the US not only pursued but also led the liberalization and globalization of finance and stepped toward acquiring hegemony in international finance since the 1980s, which built the foundation for the prevailing neoliberal American globalism after the 1990s.

13.5 Germany's Globalism and Regionalism After the 1990s to the Present

After the 1990s, the fundamental structure of globalism included three layers. (1) The first layer, neoliberalism, opened up the economy in each country to the global capital and mobilized people for globalization based on a doctrine emphasizing market mechanism in the aspect of ideology. (2) The second layer included multinational enterprises as actors of economic globalization and multinational banks and speculative financial capital that mediate international finance. (3) In layer three, international politics consisted of America's hegemony and government in each country under which it has been created (Mizuoka 2006, pp.86–87). Globalization is a physical process closely related to capital accumulation and includes an ideology such as the belief in free markets based on neoliberalism and the effective role of competition (Mittelmann 2001, p.7; Steger 2009, Preface to the second edition, pp.1–2, 112; Steger 2002, pp.13, 40). The concept related to globalism can be defined as a dominant ideology and subjectivity (subjectivism) concerned with the different historically dominant thoughts regarding global expansion (James 2006, p.22). Today, globalism is led by American attempts to reduce globalization to a single economic dimension and rebuild society as a global market society, and neoliberal globalism is based on sole thinking in this sense (Beck 1997, S.196; Beck 2000, p.118).

By nature, an effective market economy combines (1) the state and the market and (2) laissez-faire and intervention. Their combinations depend on selection by each country, international position, and historical past (Rodrik 2011, p.22). The coordination role of the national state in the twentieth century was based on the instability of laissez-faire and an understanding regarding the needed intervention corresponding to such instability. In contrast, new regulators, such as international economic institutions, intended to enable free operations based on laissez-faire (Kuttner 2000, pp.150–151). The capitalistic market economy is increasingly strengthening the American standard under globalism (Motoyama 2001, p.2).

Even under such significant change, Germany maintains the fundamental principle and system of a "coordinated market economy" (Hall and Soskice 2001), based on and supported by such economic principles and determined by the path dependency after World War II in which manufacturing sectors have built international competitiveness. At the same time, Germany has pursued its own form of globalism, where these industrial sectors are at the core. This approach contrasts with US globalism, which is led by the financial sectors and information and communication technologies (ICT) sectors. The US has pursued establishing a more advantageous foundation for capital accumulation in these departments because the ICT sector, in which the platform is an important base for competitive power, and the financial sector are the core of departments with international competitiveness. In contrast, even in trends in which ICT can standardize all elements of products and fundamentally change the architecture, pursuing a different path from that in the US in building strategy that takes into account "the Fourth Industrial Revolution" has become vital for Germany.

This perspective is deeply concerned with the direction of Germany's regionalization and regionalism. Regionalism based on Europe as an enlarged economic sphere by the Eastern expansion in the EU can be considered a significant axis countermeasure to US globalism. Germany's dependence on this area in both markets and the formation of productive forces has been reinforced within the EU zone, and the interaction within this region has been deepened. This situation signifies regionalization as "Europeanization" as (1) regionalization in which the enlarged EU is a foundation for markets and productive forces and (2) building and deepening a systematic framework, including setting rules for more favorable trade terms in this region that enables advantageous capital accumulation. Germany's regionalism is based on such regionalization and is an important driving force of Europeanization.

In the processing and assembly industries, such as the automobile industry (one of the leading industries with international competitiveness in Germany), geographical proximity and the possibility of building an international division of labor between products and between production processes through spatial separation and reorganization are the bases for incorporating each EU country into elements of productive forces. The moment of such regionalization for German and European enterprises dramatically differs from that of the regionalization of Japanese enterprises (Yamazaki 2024a, 15.4). Under such conditions, Germany has strengthened its reproduction (accumulation) structure while pursuing the most appropriate division of labor with nations in the enlarged Europe and reinforcing the "EU-based capitalism" characteristic based on this region.

German regionalization is based on ideology and behavioral norms to secure more favorable accumulation conditions by differentiating trade terms against enterprises outside the region. Regionalization has progressed due to such regionalism, and Germany has been in the leading position in this movement and has enjoyed the merits of regionalization. The degree of progression of Germany's regionalization focusing on the expanded EU is very high, and the regionalism of this country is stronger than that of other nations. In this way, Germany has pursued globalism with an important axis emphasizing regionalization as a countermeasure to US-led globalization and globalism.

In considering the "globalization" phenomenon in terms of trade, the behaviors of the enterprise as an agent of economic activities do not come within the range. Enterprise development into multinational firms and the internationalization of production progressed after World War II; however, such phenomena were limited in the Cold War compared to the period after the 1990s. It is the phenomenon of the full scale of incorporating countries in the socialist block in terms of both markets and productive forces that marks a new epoch. Regionalization in the aforementioned twofold meanings (namely Europeanization) manifests Germany's globalism and is an important direction in this period.

This chapter clarifies Germany's globalism and regionalism in each period and their significance. Based on these discussions, the next chapter considers the characteristics of German capitalism and corporate expansion until the end of World War II from a comparative viewpoint with the period after the war.

References

Abelshauser W (2004) Deutsche Wirtschaftsgeschichte seit 1945. C. H. Beck, München

Ambrosius G, Hubbard WH (1986) Sozial- und Wirtschaftsgeschichte Europas im 20. Jahrhundert. C. H. Beck, München

Barjot D (2002) Introduction. In: Barjot D (ed) Catching up with America. Productivity Missions and the diffusion of American economic and technological influence after the Second World War. Pressede Lunivesite de Paris-Sor-

Beck U (1997) Was ist Globalisierung? Antworten auf Globalisierung. Schurkamp Verlag, Frankfurt am Main

Beck U (2000) What is globalization? Polity Press, Cambridge

Berghahn VR (2024) The insider-outsider of early 20th century German industry. Güntrt Henle and the Klöckner Steel Conglomerate, 1899–1955. Bloomsbury Academic, London
Boel B (2002) The European productivity agency and American policy toward Western Europe after World War II. In: Barjot D (ed) Catching up with America. Productivity Missions and the diffusion of American economic and technological influence after the Second World War. Presse de Lunivesite de Paris-Sorbonne, Paris, pp 87–97
Borchardt K (1978) Grundriβ der deutschen Wirtschaftsgeschichte. Vanden-hoeck & Ruprecht, Göttingen
Brown WA Jr (1940) The international gold standard reinterpreted, 1914–1934. National Bureau of Economic Research Inc., New York
Buchheim C (1993) Marshall plan and currency reform. In: Diefendorf JM, Frohon A, Rupieper H-J (eds) American policy and the reconstruction of West Germany, 1945–1951. Cambridge University Press, Cambridge, New York, pp 69–83
Bundesministrium für Wirtschaft (1959) Der Sprung in die Marktwirtschaft— Entwicklung zum Wohlstand. In: Das Presse- und Informationsamt der Bundesregierung (Hrsg) Deutschland im Wiederaufbau 1949–1959 und Tätigkeitsbericht der Bundesregierung für das Jahr 1959. Kommissionsverlag, Bonn, S 18–25
Crouzet F (2002) Conclusions. In: Barjot D (ed) Catching up with America. Productivity missions and the diffusion of American economic and technological influence after the Second World War. Presse de Lunivesite de Paris-Sor-bonne, Paris, pp 427-438
Edwards GE (1924) American policy with reference to foreign investments. Am Econ Rev 14(1, Supplement):26–35
Erhard L (1954) Das Bundesministerium für Wirtschaft. In: Das Presse- und Informationsamt der Bundesregierung (Hrsg) Deutschland im Wiederaufbau. Tätigkeitsbericht der Bundesregierung für das Jahr 1954. Kommissionsverlag, Bonn, S 147-176
Furuuchi H (2007) Gendai Doitsu keizai no rekishi (A history of the modern German Eeonomy). Tokyo daigaku shuppankai, Tokyo
Hall PA, Soskice D (eds) (2001) Varieties of capitalism: the institutional foundations of comparative advantage. Oxford University Press, Oxford
Harvey D (1989) The condition of postmodernity. Basil Blackwell, Oxford
Hettne B (1999) The new regionalism: a prologue. In: Hettne B, Inotani A, Sunkel O (eds) Globalism and the new regionalism. Macmillan Press, Basingstoke, Hampshire, pp. xv–xxix
I.P.W.-Berichte (1978) Wissenschaftlich-technischer Fortschritt und Entwicklungstendenzen des gegenwärtigen Kapitalismus. In: I.P.W.-Berichte 7 (10):1–8
Iwamura M (2020) Kokka, kigyo, currency. Gurobarizumu no futsugona mirai (State, enterprise and currency: the unwarrantable future of globalism). Shinchosha, Tokyo
James P (2006) Globalism, nationalism, tribalism. bringing theory Beck in. Sage, London
Kato E (1973) Waimaru taisei no keizai kozo (Economic structure of the Weimar system). Tokyo daigaku shuppankai, Tokyo
Kirshner O (2014) American politics and the triumph of globalism. Routledge, New York
Kitamura J (1973) Sengo Doitsu no seiji to keizai (German policy and economy after WW II). Horitsu bunkasha,Kyoto
Kuczynski R (1933) Wall Street und die Deutschen Anleihen. Bankierprofite und Publikumsverluste. H. Buske, Leipzig
Kudo A (1996) Keizai seicho to chiiki togo (Economic growth and regional integration). In: Hara T, Kudo A (eds) Gendai Yoroppa keizaishi (Modern European economic history). Yuhikaku, Tokyo, pp. 247–279
Kudo A, Kipping M, Schröteret HG (2004) Americanization. Historical and conceptual issues. In: Kudo A, Kipping M, Schröteret HG (eds) German and Japanese business in the boom years. Transforming American management and technology models. Routledge, London, New York, pp. 1–29
Kuttner R (2000) The role of governments in the global economy. In: Hutton W, Giddens A (eds) Global capitalism. The New Press, New York, pp 147–163

Ленин ВИ (1948) СИСТЕМА ТЭЙЛОР АПОРАБОЩЕНИЕ—ЧЕЛОВЕКА МАШИНОЙ. In: Полное собрание сочинений. Том 20, ос. изд-во полит. лит-ры, Москва, pp 134–136
Lenin WI (1953) Bericht über das Parteiprogramm auf dem VII.Parteitag der KPR (B). In: Ausgewählte Werke: in zwei Bänden, Bd.II, Dietz Verlag, Berlin, S.506–541
Link W (1970) Die amerikanische Stabilisierungspolitik in Deutschland, 1921–32. Droste, Düsseldorf
Maekawa K (1970) Doitsu dokusen kigyo no hatten katei (Development of German monopolistic enterprises). Mineruva shobo, Kyoto
Maekawa K, Yamazaki T (1995) Doitsu gorika undo no kenkyu (Study of the German Rationalization movement). Moriyama shoten, Tokyo
Manabe S (1989) Amerika no Doitsu senryo seisaku (America's occupation policy for Germany). Horitsu bunkasha, Kyoto
Milward AS (1987) War, economy, and society 1939–1945. Penguin Books, Harmondsworth
Mittelmann JH (2001) Globalization. Captors and captives. In: Mittelmann JH, Othman N (eds) Capturing globalization. Routledge, London, pp 1–16
Mizuoka F (2006) Grobarizumu (Globalism). Hassakusha, Tokyo
Motoyama Y (2001) Sengo 55 nen (The postwar 55 Years). In: Motoyama Y (ed) Gurobarizumu no shogeki (Shocks of globalism). Toyo Keizai shinposha, Tokyo, pp. 1–8
Müller-Armack A (1956) Soziale Marktwirtschaft. In: Beckerath E v, Brinkmann C, Gutenberg E et al. (Hrsg) Handwörterbuch der Sozailawissenschaften, Bd.9. Gustav Fischer, J. C. B. Mohr, Vandenhoeck & Ruprecht, Göttingen, S 390–392
Müller-Armack A (1966) Wirtschaftsordnung und Wirtschaftspolitik. Studien und Konzepte zur sozialen Marktwirtschaft und zur europäischen Integration. Rombach, Frfeiburg
Noda S (1998) Doitsu sengo seijikeizai chitsujo no keisei (Formation of political economic oder in Germany after WW II). Yuhikaku, Tokyo
Oba K (1975) Seisansei undo (Productivity movement). In: Nihon Seisansei Honbu (ed) Seisansei jiten (Productivity dictionary). Nihon Seisansei Honbu, Tokyo
Okamoto T (1993) Taisenkanki shihonshugi no kenkyu (A study of capitalism in the interwar period). Hassakusha, Tokyo
Pettman R (1999) Globalism and regionalism: the costs of dichotomy. In: Hettne B, Inotani A, Sunkel O (eds) Globalism and the new regionalism. Macmillan Press, Basingstoke, Hampshire, pp 181–202
Polanyi K (2001) The great transformation. The political and economic origins of our time. Beacon Press, Boston
Postan MM (1967) An economic history of Western Europe 1945–1964. Methuen & Co., London
Rodrik D (2011) The globalization paradox. Why global markets, states, and democracy can't coexist. W. W. Norton, New York
Schlieper A (1986) 150 Jahre Ruhrgebiet. Ein Kapitel deutscher Wirtschaftsgeschichte. Schwann, Düsseldorf
Schmidt CT (1934) German Business Cycles 1924~1933. National Bureau of Economic Research, New York
Schröter HG (2005a) Americanization of the European economy. A compact survey of American economic influence in Europe since the 1880s. Springer, Dordrecht
Schröter HG (2005b) Deutschlands Reintegration in die europäischen Wirtschaft. In: North M (Hrsg) Deutsche Wirtschaftsgeschichte. Ein Jahrtausend im Überblick, 2., völlig überarbeitete und aktualisiert Auflage, C. H. Beck, München, S 362–388
Shibayama K (2014) Yakusha atogaki (Postscript by translator). In: Rodrik D (translated by Shibayama K, Okawa Y) Grobarizeshon paradokusu (Globalization paradox). Hakusuisha, Tokyo, pp. 324–329
Steger MB (2002) Globalism. The new market ideology. Rowman & Littlefield Publishers, Lanham
Steger MB (2009) Globalization. A very short introduction. 2nd edition. Oxford University Press, Oxford
Stiglitz JE (2002) Globalization and its discontents. W. W. Norton & Company, Inc.

Stolper G, Häuser K, Borchardt K (1964) Deutsche Wirtschaft seit 1870. J. C. B. Mohr, Tübingen
Suzuki N (1977) Sengo Amerika no taigai enjyo (Foreigen assistance by the USA after WW II). In: Shoken kenkyu (J Financ Secur Mark) 54: 375–427
Taguchi N (2018) Book review: Kigyo keiei no nichi doku hikaku (Comparison of business management in Japan and Germany, Book review). Hikaku Keiie Kenkyu (Journal of the Association for Comparative Studies of Management) 42:139–147
Takagi K (1962) Nishi Yoroppa ni okeru seisansei undo (The Productivity movement in Western Europe). Nihon Seisansei Honbu, Tokyo
Takemura M (2020) Kinyu grobarizumu no keizaigaku—Kakusa shakai no keisei to sekai kinyu kiki no boppatsu (Economics of financial globalization—Formation of unequal society and the outbreak of financial crisis). Kamogawa shuppan, Kyoto
Thalmann H (1956) Durch Rationalisierung ohne Kapital zur verstärkten Ausbeutung der Arbeiterklasse in Westdeutschland. In: Behrens F (Hrsg.), Aktuelle Fragen der Ökonomie und Politik des wiederstandenen deutschen Imperialismus: Festschrift zum zehnjährigen Bestehen des Verlags die Wirtschaft. Verlag der Wirtschaft, Berlin, S 87–114
Watanabe M (2003) Yakusha atogaki (Postscript by translators). In: Ellwood W (translated by Watanabe M, Aneha A, Gurobarizeshon towa nanika (What is globalization?) Kobushi shobo, Tokyo, pp. 207–219
Yamazaki T (2013) German business management: a Japanese perspective on regional development factors. Springer, Tokyo
Yamazaki T (2024a) Japanese and German enterprises: comparison of industrial concentration system and business management. Springer Nature, Singapore
Yamazaki T (2024b) Relationships between industry and bank in Germany: a historical analysis of personnel connections through interlocking directorate and bank's advisory council system. Springer Nature, Singapore
Yanagisawa O (2006) Shihonshugishi no renzoku to danzetsu: Seioteki hatten to Doitsu (Continuity and discontinuity in the history of capitalism: West European development and Germany). Nihon Keizai hyoronsha, Tokyo
Yeates N (2001) Globalization and social policy. Sage, London
Yoshida K (1976) Doitsu gorika undou ron (The rationalization movement in Germany). Mineruva shobo, Kyoto

Chapter 14
German Capitalism and Corporate Expansion Until the End of World War II

Abstract Based on Germany's globalism and regionalism discussed in Chapter 13, this chapter considers German capitalism and corporate expansion concerning special historical conditions in each period, which differed from the postwar period, regional conditions in Europe, and relationships between German and American capital. From the comparative perspective with the period after World War II, the reason why German capitalism and enterprises were forced to face limitations in their development and the full-scale deployment of American management methods ("Americanization") was impossible until the end of World War II but became possible after the war is examined. First, this chapter considers the development of German capitalism and corporate expansion concerning historical conditions before the end of World War II and regional circumstances in Europe. Next, it compares market structures before and after World War II and among the three major countries: Germany, the United Kingdom, and France. Furthermore, the relationships between the German and American capital during the interwar period are discussed. Following these examinations, issues regarding Fordism as a capitalistic accumulation system are analyzed and compared with the period after World War II.

Keywords Americanization · Business management · Fordism · German capitalism · Global capitalism · Market structure · Mass production

After World War II, Germany implemented "Europeanization" in two ways. The first is the development of business management and the accumulation structure (reproduction structure) of German capitalism, which was based mainly on the European region and building complementary relationships in its markets. The second way was apparent in the strong attempts to drive European integration as a foundation for more advantageous development of business management and capital accumulation. This dual approach indicates the significance of regional conditions for Germany's development based on Europe and differing from Japan, as indicated in Chapter 1. However, in the period before the end of the war, Germany was unable to realize development based on the European region. This chapter analyzes the development of German capitalism and enterprises until the end of World War II, giving attention

T. Yamazaki, *A History of German Business*,
https://doi.org/10.1007/978-981-96-8476-2_14

to special conditions that significantly differed from the postwar period, the significance of regional conditions in Europe, and the relationships between German and American capital. This chapter also clarifies why German capital and enterprises faced limitations in developing and deploying American management methods.

First, Sect. 14.1 examines German capitalism and corporate expansion until the end of World War II from a comparative perspective with the period after the war. Section 14.2 compares market structures before and after World War II and among three major capitalistic nations in Europe: Germany, the United Kingdom, and France. Focusing on the specific historical conditions in Germany, Sect. 14.3 considers the relationships between German and American capital in the 1920s; at this time, the lack of capital in Germany became prominent, and the involvement and roles of American capital intensified. Moreover, in Sect. 14.4, issues of the development of Fordism as an important capitalistic accumulation system are examined through comparison with the period after World War II.

14.1 Development of German Capitalism and Enterprises Until the End of World War II

This section considers the development of German capitalism and corporate expansion before the end of World War II concerning the historical conditions of world capitalism and in the context of regional circumstances in Europe. The unique character of German capitalism in this period appeared in the market as a disproportion between the productive force and the market, which had become the largest bottleneck for business management and productivity. Limitations in the reproduction structure (accumulation structure) of German capitalism were determined by blockaded restrictions on export markets under closed conditions, such as the economic sphere of colonies, closed trade relationships, European countries' conservative trade policies, and movement toward the formation of economic blocks after the 1929 global economic crisis. Such limitations were also due to the weakness of the international cooperative system, represented by poor collaboration among nations in the market and trade policies as countermeasures.

In the 1920s, when international cooperation among major capitalistic countries was attempted led by the United States (US), each country could achieve only slight international cooperation and could not prevent the spread of protectionism that hindered world trade due to the preference of economic policy oriented toward each country's national interests (Ambrosius and Hubbard 1986, S.242–243). The League of Nations could not build a liberal and open system of international economy due to member countries' politics, and they refused to renounce monopolistic trading rights with colonies (Suzuki 2017, pp.63–64), leading to further blocking markets. It was not the liberal integration of the world economy emphasizing the balance of the external economy; the stabilization policy within the individual national economy in each country had come to the front. Numerous problems that could only be settled when international cooperation was secured were not solved (Ambrosius and Hubbard 1986, S.249). Thus, worldwide market linkages and capital based on international cooperation in economic affairs—as observed after World War II—were not created, restricting the development of German enterprises and capitalism.

Germany's domestic market was narrow due to the emergence and subsequent development of German capitalism. After World War I, Germany lost all its colonies, and the domestic market became much narrower due to hyperinflation. The importance of the export market remarkably grew in this situation. However, development based on the international market was limited by the aforementioned restrictive conditions. Indeed, after World War I, international economic relationships strengthened from the perspective of anti-Soviet policy. However, the development of the rationalization movement in the 1920s was an important factor that determined the trends and results of German capitalism's development, which encountered severe limitations under the blockaded restriction of export markets due to the world economic crisis and the withdrawal of capital the US lent to Germany. These strict circumstances restricted the improvement of productivity. German innovative industries such as machinery, electrical engineering, and chemistry pursued technological developments akin to those in the US after World War I; however, they could not operate at full potential. The labor productivity gap between both countries by 1936 was mainly due to "the inefficiency with which the newly introduced techniques were used" (Timmer et al. 2016, pp.874,878, 898). Furthermore, policies based on the concept of "the extensive market" ("*Großraumwirtschaft*") in the period of National Socialism and developments supported by this policy could not enable sufficient development in Europe.

Before World War II, it was not possible for markets in Europe to compensate for the restrictions of the narrow German domestic market under the weakness and limitations of the cooperative system among the capitalistic countries despite the high ratio of exports to Europe to all German exports. Under this situation, Germany was not able to make the best use of the export market, in particular, the European market, as a core for developing its productive force and reproduction structure (accumulation structure) sufficiently. This was related to the lack of global connections of the capitalistic economy represented by a deficiency of worldwide market links. Limits of development based on the European region were due to conditions in which patterns of economic development supported by consumer goods market expansion, as observed after World War II, could not be realized in major European countries.

Germany already developed its economy on the basis of expansion of the heavy and chemical industries; international competitiveness in these industrial sectors was strengthened before World War II. However, until the end of World War II, the European market, where quality in terms of product functionality was emphasized, an important factor of competitiveness, as witnessed after the war, did not develop because of the insufficient economic expansion of countries in this region. After World War II, German enterprises had built management systems more appropriate for the European market with characteristics such as emphasizing product functionality by modifying American management methods while deploying and adapting technology and management methods from the US (Yamazaki 2013a, 2013b). The development of "diversified quality production" (Streeck 1997; Abelshauser 2003), relying on skilled workers, market structures, and characteristics focusing on quality and functionality, reflected this. German product quality focuses on functionality and durability and the German production system differentiates on the basis of quality, not price. German corporations have developed on the foundation of a German strategy that builds competitiveness through quality differentiation. Germany sought market positioning by pursuing competitiveness in Europe's relatively high share of exports that were compatible with the characteristics of high-quality European goods. By contrast, before the end of World War II, German enterprises could not establish a foundation of international competitive power on a foundation of product differentiation in spite of their original attempts, which was an important factor determining limitations.

The full-scale deployment of American management methods ("Americanization") was impossible until the end of World War II but became possible after the war. Delay and limitation of the Americanization of business management and the different ways of developing from the US until the war were determined not by the lack of intention of top executives and managers but by a lack of conditions due to great changes in market conditions. The German-specific development of business management and corporate behaviors adapted to the unique conditions surrounding enterprises. Market conditions significantly changed after World War II. First, the domestic market was expanded by realizing equality of rights between both sides of capital and labor. This phenomenon was apparent in Germany and other major European capitalistic countries, which contributed to expanding export markets. Second, the US established international systems for free trade. Furthermore, as considered in Chapters 2 and 13, many countries that received aid from the US under the Marshall Plan were forced to open their markets to free trade. Third, in Western Europe, the common market was formed by European integration attempts and expanded later. Such changes in market conditions significantly contributed to the rise of American management methods and corporate expansion in Germany after World War II.

14.2 Comparison of Market Structures Before and After World War II and Among Those in Germany, the United Kingdom, and France

This section examines market structures as an important factor in determining the limitations of German corporate expansion and the development of business management, comparing market structure in Germany with that in the United Kingdom and France. Although market conditions in the European region were fundamentally the same, the British and French colonial markets had great significance. The ratios of Germany's exports to colonies to the total exports in 1900 and 1913 were only 0.3% and 0.37%, respectively. The ratios of Germany's exports to countries in Europe to the total amount of exports in 1900, 1913, 1928, 1933, and 1938 were 76.9%, 76%,

70.6%, 78%, and 75.9%, respectively (Statistisches Reichsamt 1902; S.139; Statistisches Reischsamt 1915, S.253–254; Statistisches Reichsamt 1931; S.236–239; Statistisches Reichssamt 1935; S.228–229; Statistisches Reichsamt 1943, S.322–323). The ratios of France's exports to European countries to the total exports in the same years were 73.7%, 68.8%, 64%, 52.7%, and 55.5%, respectively (Statistique Générale de la France 1902, p.266; 1917, pp.250–251; 1931, pp.197–198; 1935, pp.195–196; 1941, pp.163–164). Therefore, Germany's numerical values tended to exceed those of France. In contrast, similar figures for the United Kingdom (excluding bullion and specie) in the same years were 39.2%, 33.5%, 27.4%, 33.1%, and 30.7%, respectively (Board of Trade 1904, pp.120–123; 1917, pp.84–87; 1940, pp.378–381) and the dependence rate on European markets was lower than Germany and France.

Such differences highlighted the significance of colonial markets. The ratios of UK's export to colonies and dominions to the total amount of exports in 1900, 1913, 1928, 1933, and 1938 were 32.4%, 37.2%, 45.3%, 44.4%, and 49.9%, respectively(1) (Board of Trade 1904, pp.120–123; 1917, pp.84–87; 1940, pp.378–381), indicating that the capital's reproduction structure heavily depended on these countries. Similar numerical figures regarding France were 11.6%, 13%, 17.3%, 32.4%, and 27.4%, respectively (Statistique Générale de la France 1902, p.266; 1917, pp.250–251; 1931, pp.197–198; 1935, pp.195–196; 1941, pp.163–164). The numerical value in 1933 greatly increased due to the formation of the economic block; however, the dependence rate of the colonial markets of France was lower than that of the United Kingdom, which was deeply connected to France's high weight of European markets in exports. The economic sphere of the United Kingdom, including colonies and dominions, was an important premise for supporting and maintaining capital reproduction without a cooperative system in trade before World War II. Under these restrictive circumstances, Germany's pursuit of globalism (examined in Chapter 13) was deeply concerned with the difficulties of the reproduction structure based on colonial markets in the export of products and the import of materials and natural resources. In the period of National Socialism, the attempt to create the economic sphere of larger areas in Europe was an alternative to such a colonial policy.

After World War II, the differences in the quality of the productive force and the economic power between the US and European countries fell significantly during economic growth between the 1950s and the beginning of the 1970s. The leveling of the structures of the productive force advanced, and the special conditions enabling this recovery were observable in both productivity and the market.

The domestic market's foundation was vastly improved by equalizing labor and capital and by the worldwide linkage of the markets created by establishing the free trade system, the international monetary system, and the common market in Western Europe. The domestic market's improved foundation in some major European countries contributed to the development of German enterprises based on European markets as one of their core export markets. Thus, significant differences in market conditions occurred between the end of World War II and the postwar period, indicating a "discontinuity" between the two periods before and after World War II.

14.3 Relationships Between German Capital and US Capital

14.3.1 Shortage of Capital and Introducing Foreign Capital in the 1920s

This section considers the relationships between German capital and American capital. In the inflation period after World War I, Germany could greatly ease twofold restrictions on capital accumulation by dumping due to the decline in the value of the "Mark" and the restraint of the increase in real wages caused by the Treaty of Versailles and labor relations based on equality between capital and labor under the Weimar state (Kato 1973, p.341)—however, this condition dissolved when the currency stabilized. The general shortage of capital during the relatively stable period in the 1920s became a restrictive factor for private equipment investment and the development of business management, restricting the pursuit of rationalization from the aspect of funds.

The influence of inflation on capital formation was highly significant, and severe inflation brought about a lack of middle class, contributing to capital formation, rentier layer, and bureaucratic layer with property (Prion 1931, S.349), which is a factor determining great restriction in the domestic capital building. Unprecedented inflation brought about the complete disappearance of rentiers, growth of upstart enterprises, and concentration of huge and excessive vertically combined enterprises that began to be dissolved immediately after the stabilization of the currency. Furthermore, the complete collapse of the "Mark" resulted in taking general working capital away from Germany (Harris 1935, pp.2–3).

In Germany at the time, an imbalance between capital demand and capital formation forced the German economy to use foreign capital constantly; however, using foreign capital was only possible when the rate of interest and return of debt could be paid through surplus from exports. Furthermore, unlike the interest rate in the money market, the interest rate in the capital market only changed slightly, even in a recession (Prion 1931, S.350–351). This attribute was a factor restricting the development of rationalization based on capital procurement in the capital market.

In the capital market, the rate of fixed interest-bearing securities increased; however, this was not due to an increase in the rate of industrial loans. The demand for long-term funds from public bodies was brought about by a new function of the state: to tranquilize revolution power and energy, greatly restricting the issuing of private bonds in the market for fixed interest-bearing securities. As a result, most private enterprises were forced to depend on the unstable stock market in the issue of securities. The capital market in this period remarkably depended on foreign capital (Kato 1973, pp.238–239). Social policy was to be developed to counter unemployment by implementing rationalization in the 1920s, and public investment was enlarged. The expansion of public finance by social policy became a factor that oppressed the finances of private enterprises in mobilizing capital from the US

(Okamoto 1993, p.222). For example, the ratio of foreign capital to the total amount of issued stocks (market price), domestic bonds (par value), and foreign bonds (par value) in Germany and foreign countries from 1926 to 1928 was 25.3% (Institut für Konjunktureforschung 1933, S.158). The ratio of foreign bonds to the total amount of shares, domestic bonds, and foreign bonds issued by private and public companies in the same period was 29%, exceeding that of domestic bonds (20.5%) (Statistisches Reichsamt 1936, S.380).

In this way, foreign capital's role in the relatively stable period was significant. While recovery from the stabilization crisis in August and winter of 1924 corresponded to an extensive following of foreign capital, difficulties in the middle of 1925 (such as the liquidation crisis that became increasingly clear) were concerned with a remarkable decrease in the inflow of foreign capital (Schmidt 1934, pp.35–36). Introducing foreign capital at the time faced three problems: (1) the heavy disproportionate emphasis on short-term funds within used foreign capital, (2) a disproportionate emphasis on the US in the inflow of foreign capital, and (3) a high rate of issuing of bonds by entities and institutions with public characteristics, which acted as a direct factor determining instability in the German economy (Kato 1973, pp.176–181). Moreover, a report of the Reparation Commission showed that the ratio of loans of private enterprises to the total amount of loans for Germany from 1925 to 1929 was 39.3% (Reparation Commission 1930, p.214).

Regarding the contents of foreign capital, the ratio of long-term foreign capital to introduced foreign capital from 1924 to 1928 was only 49.3% (The Economist 1932, p.10). Moreover, the ratio of foreign capital to short-term funds in this period was 37.7%; however, the ratio of foreign capital to long-term funds was only 18.2% (Lüke 1958, S.216). Regarding the disproportionate emphasis on the United States in the inflow of foreign capital, the ratio of long-term bonds from the US from 1924 to June 30, 1931, was 52.2%; a similar figure regarding private following was higher and reached 63.2% (Harris 1935, p.95). Moreover, the ratio of private loans to the total amount of long-term loans in the same period was only 37.6% (The Economist 1932, p.16). Furthermore, the capital export of the US to Germany was deeply concerned with the reparations problem and the issue of repayment of the war debts. Through this linkage, US capital directly and indirectly supported capital imported from other countries. Thus, capital export by the US was a prop of international finance in the relatively stable period, which made the world economy at the time unstable (Kato 1973, p.179). In this way, issuing bonds by entities and organizations with public characteristics restricted private equipment investment in terms of funds (Harris 1935, p.95). Moreover, there was a difference in capital raising methods between large companies that could freely use foreign capital and many other companies without such possibility. The latter restriction regarding funds for the development of rationalization was significant.

14.3.2 Involvement of American Capital in German Capital

Considering the involvement of American capital in German capital, the inflow of capital from the US was a critical issue for Germany after World War I. Even before the Dawes Plan in 1924, as an important moment of accepting funds from the US, a bank received one hundred letters from German enterprises within two weeks that demanded loans in the New York market, and the average amount of required loans was approximately five million USD (Dunn 1926, p.146). The prospects for European development depended on capital accumulation in countries like Germany, which was forced to seek the US market for loans, as well as conditions of political and financial stabilization (Dunn 1926, p.185).

As seen in the case of Vereinigte Stahlwerke AG, the development of rationalization was a prerequisite condition for acquiring American loans (Reckendrees 1996, S.166), and American pressure on German enterprises was tremendous. The introduction of funds from foreign countries was an important moment in forming large trusts in the relatively stable 1920s. When the mobilization of funds that heavy and chemical industries in Germany implemented before World War I (in cooperation with credit banks that engaged in current account and securities businesses) was no longer possible, bonds in foreign markets were issued without relying on German credit banks (Okamoto 1993, p.254). Managers who implemented rationalization at that time could not rely on big German banks because these financial institutions lacked the financial resources needed for the modernization and rationalization of large enterprises (Chandler 1990, p.590). "*The Annalist*" journal on November 26, 1924 pointed out that the rehabilitation of Europe demanded significant capital investment; however, such investment could not be found outside of the US. Foreign banks were organized to deal with capital investment apart from their discount and deposit business (The Annalist 1924, p.445). This situation was true for Germany.

Regarding the involvement and role of US capital in capital raising in German companies, of 135 public and private bonds issued on the USD from October 14, 1924, to July 30, 1930, the rate of bonds issued in the US was 86.6%. Many US companies were consortium leaders. Of these 135 bonds, Dillion Read & Co. was the consortium leader in 20, and representative enterprises occupied many of these. For example, two concerned August Thyssen Hütte, three for Vereinigte Stahlwerke AG, three for companies belonging to the Siemens group, one was regarding Deutsche Bank, and two concerned Rudolph Karstadt (Kuczynski 1933, S.10–16). It quickly became evident that without American financial support, Vereinigte Stahlwerke AG could not come into existence (Fear 2005, p.530).

Capital exports from the US to Germany contributed to the recovery of international financial connections between major capitalistic countries through German reparation payments, the related repayment of war debts of the United Kingdom and France to the US, and the return of each country to the gold standard system (Okamoto 1993, p.291). The Dawes Plan created the stage in which US investment banks and capital started full-scale activities to rebuild and stabilize the German and European economies (Abo 1984, p.88). It was the issue of Dawes bonds equivalent to 110 million USD in which Morgan was the underwriter that had epoch-making significance for the movement to issue foreign securities (Abo 1984, pp.141, 154).

According to one study, of the 370 German loans issued after August 1924, 70 were issued chiefly in the US, and their ratio to the total issuing amount reached two-thirds, a very high rate. Such a difference occurred mainly because large loans were only possible in markets such as New York (Kuczynski 1928, pp.174–175). In all cases, the terms in which US loans were permitted for Germany were never easy. Total costs, including issue, interest (and premium), and annexed costs, reached 9.5% on an annual average of the amount gained by borrowers (Kuczynski 1928, pp.174–185). The significant capital cost burden had to be a tremendous restrictive factor for developing rationalization and business management. Furthermore, the high rate of short-term funds became a factor that restricted the progress of rationalization.

Nonetheless, accepted foreign capital could not build a development structure that enabled the increase in exports through the productive use of accepted foreign capital, productivity improvement, and payment of principal and interest (Abo 1984, pp.162–163). Indeed, foreign securities investment by the US in the 1920s helped stabilize the world economy after World War I and played an indispensable role in stabilizing the domestic economy in Germany; however, it could not guarantee full-scale recovery and development. US capital investment resulted in an intermediating collapse in attempts at recovery and development by creating an accumulation process of debts as "excessive lending" (Abo 1984, pp.2–3, 169). For instance, Vereinigte Stahlwerke AG, a huge trust in Germany, was significantly overcapitalized and was burdened with a heavy debt from its inception (Fear 2005, p.551).

Furthermore, the high interest rate as the premise for which Germany accepted foreign funds from the US due to the shortage of capital was a restrictive factor. Indeed, the highly favorable conditions in the money market in 1924, the first year of the Dawes Plan, enabled borrowing at an unusually low interest rate (Feis 1925, p.672). However, interest rates for Germany were high through the relatively stable period, which was a factor restricting rationalization and reforms in business management.

In the relatively stable period after the unprecedented inflation, Germany was incorporated in the framework led by the US to rebuild the world economy in the capitalistic block and rapidly realize the productive forces corresponding to new international competitive circumstances and new wage levels. The rationalization enabling this transition became indispensable under the US attempts in which a return to the gold standard system was fundamental. The essential driving force of rationalization was given by foreign capital. Foreign currency mitigated the radical financial stringency and restriction on rationalization in terms of funds due to the remarkable capital shortage; however, rationalization was forcibly pursued depending on the use of unstable foreign capital. A decrease in the inflow of foreign capital and a pullback of foreign funds suddenly stopped the development of rationalization (Kato 1973, pp.207–209). During this period, business management changes and development were pursued under such restrictive conditions.

14.4 Fordism as the Accumulation System in Germany Before and After World War II

This section examines issues regarding Fordism as a capitalistic accumulation system on the basis of the preceding discussions. The establishment of mass production based on the Ford system created and developed by Ford Motor Co. in the US symbolizes the capitalistic accumulation mode in the twentieth century. A capitalistic accumulation system based on mass production called "Fordism" prevailed globally and became an important model of capitalistic development.

Therefore, comparing the periods before and after World War II concerning the accumulation mode called "Fordism," the largest bottleneck until the end of World War II was the restricted German domestic and export market conditions. Excluding such market conditions, David Harvey points out two significant impediments to the spread of Fordism in countries other than the US during the interwar period. He explains "the state of class relations throughout the capitalist world was hardly conductive to the easy acceptance of a production system that rested so heavily upon the socialization of the worker to long hours of purely routinized labour, demanding little in the way of traditional craft skills, and conceding almost negligible control to the worker over the design, pace, and scheduling of the production process." In the capitalist world, except in the United States, "labour organization and craft traditions were simply too strong, and immigration too weak, to permit Fordism or Taylorism any easy purchase on production, even though the general principles of scientific management were widely accepted and applied." The European automobile industry experienced "a major revolution in class relations—a revolution that began in the 1930s but which came to fruition only in the 1950s—to accommodate the spread of Fordism to Europe." Harvey also points out "the modes and mechanism of state intervention" as the second major barrier to be overcome. He insists "the problem of the proper configuration and development of state powers was resolved only after 1945" and "this brought Fordism to maturity as a fully-fledged and distinctive regime of accumulation." Thus, the foundation for a long postwar boom was formed and was broadly maintained until 1973 (Harvey 1989, pp.127–129).

In Germany during the Weimar period, paternalistic labor relations, an important pillar of Fordism, did not function effectively. Even Ford Motor Company AG, a subsidiary of Ford Motor in Germany, could not exclude trade unions or the high wages seen in the US under the law system in the Weimar Republic (Abo 1984, p.229). Harvey stressed that Fordism depended on the nation-state taking a very special role within the overall system of social regulation (Harvey 1989, p.135).

Meanwhile, the restrictive market condition determined the limitation in building the accumulation mode based on Fordism in Germany until the end of World War II. Such restriction was connected with the delay in mass production in the automobile industry and the limitation of expanding demand in various industrial sectors. Generally, the economic effect of mass production in the durable consumer goods industries, such as the automobile industry, on many related industrial sectors and the overall national economy was substantial. Regarding the characteristics of each industry from the viewpoint of production flow and process, many materials were at the starting point of production in the processing and assembly industries, such as the automobile, electrical, and machinery industries. They were processed and assembled, and finally, a single product was completed (Sakamoto 1978, pp.48–49). Mass production at large final process enterprises (for instance, final assembly manufacturers in the automobile industry) could have a tremendous economic effect by creating demand in many industrial sectors at the preceding process in the production flow. Furthermore, decisive elements and the national economic effectiveness of mass production were much more significant in consumer goods departments than producer goods departments. Historically, mass production in the consumer goods industries provided the initial foundation for the shift to the mass production of producer goods (Mottek et al. 1975, S.31). Therefore, among the processing and assembly industries, consumer goods like automobiles (not producer goods like machine tools) could create a much larger economic effect of mass production. Furthermore, the broader the range related to other industries, the larger the economic effect of mass production in specific industries caused by creating demand in the related industrial sectors. At this point, the effects of mass production in the automobile industry greatly exceeded those in the electrical engineering industry. Thus, mass production in the automobile industry played a decisive role in establishing the economic system upon which the market foundation enabling mass production could be built through such industry relationships. However, in Germany, during the Weimar Republic and the Third Reich, the automobile industry could lead to neither expansion of production in related industries nor enlargement of consumption based on the effects of the growing mass production.

Regarding the diffusion of Fordism after World War II, David Harvey emphasized that “it was primarily through spatial and temporal displacement that the Fordist regime of accumulation resolved the overaccumulation problem during the long postwar boom.” “New geographical centres of accumulation—the US South and West, Western Europe and Japan, and then a range of newly-industrializing countries—were created” (Harvey 1989, p.185). In the discussion based on the regulation theory, Fordism is grasped as a chain of significant transformations in the labor process that is deeply connected with changes in the conditions of the wage worker class. Such changes form a social consumption norm, and the economic class struggle is institutionalized in the form of collective bargaining. Fordism is the principle of combining the process of production and the mode of consumption, which constitutes mass production as the specific element of the universalization of wage labor (Aglietta 1976, p.96). Based on the long-run decline in the social cost, the new mode of integrating capital relations of production made a significant upsurge in accumulation after World War II possible (Aglietta 1976, p.324).

Postwar Germany’s deployment of mass production systems such as the Ford system centered on typical volume production industries like the automotive and electrical industries. Overall, changes in production during the 1950s were not simply a “rebuilding” of the prewar state, as they also became more flexible and dynamic. It has been stated before that rationalization along the lines of Taylor Ford using an American-style mass production model was integrated with the management climate of the 1950s and modified on the basis of collective experience (Radkau 1993, S 139). On this point, A. Ambrosius identifies two important factors in the failure of the Taylor-Ford model of rationalization in quickly spreading in 1950s West Germany: consumer goods production at the time was merely of supplementary significance and German managers had a traditionally skeptical attitude toward American-style Fordism. This not only has to do with the issue of the wide-scale management units necessary to roll out this type of rationalization model, but is also related to the "Made in Germany" brand, combined with flexible labor- and knowledge-intensive production methods instead of globally standardized mass production (Ambrosius 1993, S 117–118).

Deployment of the Ford system and establishment of the Fordism as an important capital accumulation mode greatly progressed after the 1960s (Yamazaki 2024, Chapter 9). Unlike the period until the end of World War II, it was the automobile industry that played significant roles and greatly contributed to diffusion of such accumulation system. This industry became pace maker in diffusion of Fordism through demand creating effect by mass production of cars in other related many industries, high absorption power of employment, and role as the standard of wage level (Wellhöner 1996, Kapitel 3).

For example, Volkswagen played great roles. One secret of Volkswagen's success was its selective approach to the American model. While Volkswagen followed the US expansion, it used specialized know-how such as highly mechanized proprietary transfer machines for body assembly and could thus relax their very strict alignment with US development (Kleinschmidt 2004, pp 82, 88–89). One way that Volkswagen pursued as a German approach to production technology innovation was to replace the US style of automation called "Detroit automation," which impeded flexible production methods, with one adapted to German circumstances. As a follower, Volkswagen was able to learn from others' mistakes and avoid the difficulties that first-moves had experienced in the automation process. In this manner, a new type of typical German Fordism was born, enabling Volkswagen to survive the decline of the 1970s through this application of American methods to German circumstances. The essence of this method could be seen in the diverse, high-quality production that dominated the country in concert with German-style labor relations that were critical to codetermination. This system of harmonious labor relations based on labor resource cooperation in distributing shop floor power between labor and management is said to reflect the essential elements of a classic paradigm of highly skilled labor that values technical precision (Abelshauser 2004, S 376–377; 2005, pp.100–102).

However, conditions significantly changed in the 1970s. David Harvey points out "the crisis of Fordism can to some degree be interpreted, therefore, as a running out of those options to handle the overaccumulation problem" (Harvey 1989, p.185). The emphasis of the US economy changed from the former Fordism system of mass production and consumption to post-Fordism, enabling higher specialization, greater flexibility, and faster turnover (Mittelmann 2001, p.2). In the US, typical Fordist wage bargaining erosion was coupled with a long-term productivity slowdown (Boyer and Durand 1993, p.23). Under the crisis of Fordism, transformation to post-Fordism became important issue (Regarding discussions on post-Fordism, see, for example,

Kato and Steven 1993; Beynon and Nichpls 2006a, 2006b; Amin 1994; Bonefeld and Holloway 1991; Alonso and Lucio 2006; Jessop 1988, 2001; Koch 2006; Giorgi 2006; Thursfield 2000; Wigfield 2001; Brown and Lauder 1992). Flexible accumulation, as opposed to the rigidities of Fordism, relied on flexibility in terms of labor processes, labor markets, products, and consumption patterns (Harvey 1989, p. 147).

Moreover, issues arose regarding flexibility attempted in Germany during the interwar period and was pursued after the 1970s. The Ford system is a mass production method based on the principle of specialization and has contributed significantly to the realization of economies of scale. However, before World War II, restrictive market conditions made it difficult to achieve scale merits based on specialized production lines and workers. Therefore, German enterprises attempted to gain some of the benefits of mass production even with a decreased production output under market constraints and to secure a certain level of flexibility for dealing with demand fluctuations between products (see Chapters 9 and 12). In contrast, from the 1970s to the end of the 1980s, a multi-product business strategy aimed to create new demand under the structural change of capitalism seen in the shift to low economic growth. This approach created a new problem regarding flexibility and resulted in a reform of the production system.

In cases where various products must be manufactured in multiple production lines (organized on the basis of the principle of specialization), securing production flexibility to meet the changing demands of the market is impossible, and such a rigid production method cannot adapt to the changes in the market. Therefore, it was necessary to establish mass markets for specific types of products and ensure the market's stability. Realizing economies of scale is challenging if such conditions cannot be secured; thus, reforms were necessary to allow the production process to cope with decreases in the average production lot per type of product. Moreover, the change in demand for products with diverse types (intended to create new markets) led to the need to reform the production system after the 1970s. In this regard, the increase in the types of products manufactured made it difficult to increase the demand and expand each product in the market. As a result, the average production lot per product type significantly decreased.

Under such situations, in the American mass production system, securing an operating rate that enabled companies to realize economies of scale became extremely difficult. For example, the American mass production method created numerous products, which was difficult given the problems regarding equipment investments and the amortization of fixed costs. Moreover, such efforts were not cost effective and inflexible in the face of changing demands. As a result, mass-producing various products while satisfying demand fluctuations between different types of products became an important issue for top management (Yamazaki 2024, 13.1).

In the interwar period and after the 1970s, the logic enabling the resolution of the management task was transforming the principle of production formation from "specialization" to "universalization." In all production lines, equipment, and labor force, "generalization" was required. The principle of formation of production based on "universalization" is the foundation for securing production flexibility and enables the realization of "economy of scale" and scale by "economy of scope." Given economies of scope, the ability to adjust between supply and demand can be increased. Considering this issue concerning the "historical cognizance" as an attempt at theorization by considering historical contexts ("contextualized theorizing") (Üsdinken and Kipping 2020, pp. 72–275, 282, 288) (see Chapter 1), specific historical conditions determined the flexibility problems seen in the German enterprises during the interwar period. However, the principle of production formation is based on "universalization" as the mechanism in which production flexibility can be achieved for other periods and be generally theorized.

Workers could take charge of multifunctions in the labor force and had the skills needed for such work. In the flexible production structure seen in Germany during the 1920s and the 1930s, the high rate of skilled workers to all workers had great significance for securing flexibility in production. The "dual system" of occupational education was created in the second half of the nineteenth century and played a significant role (Dornseifer 1995, p.207). After World War II, the vocational education system, an important established system that has greatly contributed to bringing up skilled workers, has played a significant role in developing quality production (Yamazaki 2024, Chapter 9, Chapter 13).

(1) The ratios of the UK's exports to the old colonies and dominions to the total exports in 1960, 1970, and 1980 (1980 includes Hong Kong and Tanzania) were 40.3%, 25.3%, and 13.6%, respectively. These ratios tended to decline after the independence of colonial countries (Central Statistical Office 1961, pp.211, 216; 1972a, b, pp.257–258; 1982, pp.318–319).

References

Abelshauser W (2003) Kulturkampf. Der deutsche Weg in die neue Wirtschaft und die amerikanische Herausforderung. Kulturverlag Kadmos, Berlin

Abelshauser W (2004) Deutsche Wirtschaftsgeschichte seit 1945. C. H. Beck, München

Abelshauser W (2005) The dynamics of German industry. Berghahn Books, New York, Oxford

Abo T (1984) Senkanki Amerika no taigai toshi (American foreign investments during the interwar period). Tokyo daigaku shuppankai, Tokyo

Aglietta M (1976) Régulation et crises du Capitalisme: L'expérience des Etats-Unis. Calmann Lévy, Paris

Alonso LE, Lucio MM (eds) (2006) Employment relations in a changing society. Assessing the post-Fordist paradigm. Palgrave Macmillan, Basingstoke

Ambrosius G (1993) Wirtschaftlicher Strukturwandel und Technikentwicklung: Die westdeutsche Gesellschaft der 50er Jahre. In: Schildt A, Sywottek A (eds.) Modernisierung im Wiederaufbau. Die westdeutsche Gesellschaft der 50er Jahre. Dietz, Bonn, S.107–128

Ambrosius G, Hubbard WH (1986) Sozial- und Wirtschaftsgeschichte Europas im 20. Jahrhundert. C. H. Beck, München

Amin A (ed) (1994) Post-Fordism. A reader. Blackwell, Oxford, Cambridge

Beyon H, Nichols T (eds) (2006a) Patterns of work in the post-Fordist era. Fordism and post-Fordism. Edward Elgar, Cheltenham

Beyon H, Nichols T (eds) (2006b) The Fordism of Ford and modern management. Fordism and post-Fordism. Edward Elgar, Cheltenham

Board of Trade (1904) Statistical Abstract for the United Kingdom in each of the last fifteen years from 1889 to 1903. Her Majesty's. Stationary Office, London
Board of Trade (1917) Statistical abstract for the United Kingdom in each of the last fifteen years from 1901 to 1915. Her Majesty's. Stationary Office, London
Board of Trade (1940) Statistical Abstract for the United Kingdom in each of the last fifteen years 1924 to 1938. Her Majesty's. Stationary Office, London
Bonefeld W, Holloway J (eds) (1991) Post-Fordism and social form. A Marxist debate on the post-Fordist state. Macmillan Academic and Professional, Basingstoke
Boyer R, Durand J-p (1993) After Fordism. Macmillan Press, Basingstoke
Brown P and Lauder H (eds) (1992) Education for economic survival. From Fordism to post-Fordism? Routledge, London, New York
Central Statistical Office (1961) Annual abstract of statistics, No. 98, 1961. Her Majesty's Stationery Office, London
Central Statistical Office (1972) Annual Abstract of Statistics 1972. No.109, Her Majesty's Stationery Office, London
Central Statistical Office (1972) Annual Abstract of Statistics. 1982 Edition, No.118, Her Majesty's Stationery Office, London
Chandler AD Jr (1990) Scale and Scope: The Dynamics of industrial capitalism. Harvard University Press, Cambridge, Massachusetts
Dornseifer B (1995) Strategy, technological capability, and innovation: German enterprises in comparative perspective. In: Caron F, Erker P, Fischer W (eds) Innovations in the European economy between the wars. Walter de Gruyter, Berlin, pp 197–226
Dunn RW (1926) American foreign investment. Heubsch and the Viking Press, New York, B. W
Fear JR (2005) Organizing control. August Thyssen and the construction of German corporate management. Harvard University Press, Cambridge, MA, London
Feis H (1925) The export of American capital. In: Foreign Aff 3:668–688
Giorgi AD (2006) Re-thinking the political economy of punishment. Perspectives on post-Fordism and penal politics. Ashgate, Aldershot
Hämmerling F (1960) Die Mechanisierung von Montagen in der Elektroindustrie. In: Brandt L, Gardellini R, King A et al. (Hrsg) Industrielle Rationalisierung 1960. Verkehrs- und Wirtschafts-Verlag, Dortmund, S 127–129
Harris CRS (1935) Germany's foreign indebtedness. Oxford University Press, London
Harvey D (1989) The condition of postmodernity. Basil Blackwell, Oxford
Institut für Konjunktureforschung (1933) Konjunkturestatistisches Handbuch. Reimar Hobbing, Berlin
Jessop B (ed) (1988) Conservative regimes and the transition to Post-Fordism. The Cases of Britain and West Germany. Department of Government, University of Essex, Colchester
Jessop B (ed) (2001) Regulationist perspectives on Fordism and Post-Fordism. Edward Elgar, Cheltenham
Kato E (1973) Waimaru taisei no keizai kozo (Economic structure of the Weimar system). Tokyo daigaku shuppankai, Tokyo
Kato T, Steven R (eds) (1993) Is Japanese management post-Fordism? An international debate. Mado-sha, Tokyo
Kleinschmidt C (2004) Driving the West German consumer society: The introduction of US style production and marketing at Volkswagen, 1945–70. In: Kudo A, Kipping M, Schröter HG (eds) German and Japanese business in the boom year. Transforming American management and technology models. Routledge, London, New York, pp 75–92
Koch M (2006) Roads to post-Fordism. Labour markets and social structures in Europe. Ashgate, Aldershot
Kuczynski R (1928) American loans to Germany. In: Cassel G et al. (eds) Foreign investments. University of Chicago Press, Chicago, pp 167–191
Kuczynski R (1933) Wall Street und die Deutschen Anleihen. Bankierprofite und Publikumsverluste. H. Buske, Leipzig

Lüke RE (1958) Von der Stabilisierung zur Krise. Polygraphischer Verlag, Zürich
Mittelmann JH (2001) Globalization. Captors and Captives. In: Mittelmann JH, Othman N (eds) Capturing globalization. Routledge, London, pp 1–16
Mottek H, Becker W, Schröter A (1975) Wirtschaftsgeschichte Deutschlannds, Ein Grundriβ, Bd.III, Von der Zeit der Bismarchschen Reichsgrndung 1871 bis zur Niederlage des faschistischen deutschen Imperialismus 1945, 2. Aufl., VEB Deutscher Verlag der Wissenschaften, Berlin
Okamoto T (1993) Taisenkanki shihonshugi no kenkyu (A study of capitalism in the interwar period). Hassakusha, Tokyo
Prion W (1931) Organization des deutschen Kapitalmarktes und der deutschen Bankwirtschaft. In: Harms B (Hrsg) Kapital und Kapitalismus: Vorlesungen gehalten in der Deutschen Vereinigung für Staatswissenschaftliche Fortbildung. Rear Hobbing, Berlin, S 327–355
Radkau R (1993) "Wirtschaftswunder" ohne technologische Innovation? Technische Modernität in den 50er Jahren. In: Schildt A, Sywottek A (Hrsg) Modernisierung im Wiederaufbau. Die westdeutsche Gesellschaft der 50er Jahre. Dietz, Bonn, S.129-154
Reckendrees A (1996) Die Vereinigte Stahlwerke A. G. 1926-1933 und „das glänzende Amerika." In: Zeitschrift für Unternehmensgeschichte 41 (2): 159-186
Reparation Commission (1930) The final report of the agent-general for reparation payments (May 21, 1930) H. M. Stationery Office, London
Sakamoto K (1978) Gendai kyodai kigyo to dokusen (Modern huge enterprise and monopoly). Aoki shoten, Tokyo
Schmidt CT (1934) German business cycles 1924–1933. National Bureau of Economic Research, New York
Statistique Générale de la France (1902) Annuaire Statistique 1901. Imprimerie Nationale, Paris
Statistique Générale de la France (1917) Annuaire Statistique 1914 et 1915. Imprimerie Nationale, Paris
Statistique Générale de la France (1931) Annuaire Statistique 1930. Imprimerie Nationale, Paris
Statistique Générale de la France (1935) Annuaire Statistique 1934. Imprimerie Nationale, Paris
Statistique Générale de la France (1941) Annuaire Statistique 1939. Imprimerie Nationale, Paris
Statistisches Reichssamt (1902) Statistisches Jahrbuch für das Deutsche Reich 1901. Puttkammer & Mühlbrecht, Berlin
Statistisches Reichsamt (1915) Statistisches Jahrbuch für das Deutsche Reich 1914. Puttkammer & Mühlbrecht, Berlin
Statistisches Reichssamt (1931) Statistisches Jahrbuch für das Deutsche Reich 1930. Verlag von Reimar Hobbing, Berlin
Statistisches Reichsamt (1935) Statistisches Jahrbuch für das Deutsche Reich 1934. Verlag von Reimar Hobbing, Berlin
Statistisches Reichsamt (1937) Statistisches Jahrbuch für das Deutsche Reich 1936. Verlag für Sozialpolitik, Wirtschaft und Statistik, Berlin
Statistisches Reichsamt (1943) Statistisches Jahrbuch für das Deutsche Reich 1941–42. Verlag für Sozialpolitik, Wirtschaft und Statistik, Berlin
Streeck W (1997) German capitalis: Do it exist? Can It survive? In: Crouch C, Streeck W (eds) Political economy of modern capitalism: Mapping convergence and diversity. Sage, London, pp 33–54
Suzuki M (2017) Gurobaru gabanansuron kogi (Lectures on global governance). Tokyo daigaku shuppankai, Tokyo
The Annalist (1924) America's growing investment abroad. In: Annal 24 (616) (3.11.1924): 445
The Economist (1932) Reparations and war debts. (Supplement). In: Econ 4614 (January 23,1932):1–16
Thursfield D (2000) Post-Fordism and Skill. Theories and Perceptions. Ashgate, Aldershot
Timmer MP, Veenstra J, Woltjer PJ (2016) The Yankees of Europe? A New View on Technology and Productivity in German Manufacturing in the Early Twentieth Century. In: J Econ Hist 76(3):878–908

Üsdinken B, Kipping M (2020) History in management and organization studies: From margin to mainstream. Routledge, New York

Wellhöner V (1996) „Wirtschaftswunder"—Weltmarkt—Westdeutscher Fordismus. Der Fall Volkswagen. Westfälisches Dampfboot, Münster

Wigfield A (2001) Post-Fordism, Gender and Work. Ashgate, Adlershot

Yamazaki T (2013a) Gendai no Doitsu kigyo: Sono grobaru chiikika to keiei tokusitsu (Contemporary German enterprises: Their global-regionalization and characteristics of business management). Moriyama shoten, Tokyo

Yamazaki T (2013b) German business management: a Japanese Perspective on regional development factors. Springer, Tokyo

Yamazaki T (2024) Japanese and German enterprises: Comparison of industrial concentration system and business management. Springer Nature, Singapore

Chapter 15
Conclusion: German Business Management and German Enterprise as a "Social Community"

Abstract Based on the discussions in the preceding chapters, this chapter explains the characteristics and significance of business management changes until the end of World War II. It also explores continuity in business management before and after World War II, the pursuit of economic rationality in Germany, and the origins of the nature of German enterprise as a "Social community." First, the characteristics and significance of business management changes in the periods of the Second Reich, the Weimar Republic, and National Socialism are considered. Next, this chapter examines which "continuity" can be observed in business management before and after World War II, how the progress of business management development until the war's end was, and how it influenced and contributed to business management in the postwar period. Finally, this chapter clarifies the origins of enterprise as "a social community" by examining the pursuit of economic rationality in Germany from a comparative perspective with the United States.

Keywords Americanization · Business management · Corporate structure · Economic rationality · Enterprise concentration · Ford system · Labor management system · Mass production · Organizational structure · Taylor system

In exploring the internationality and nationality of capital, it is essential to clarify the unique characteristics of capitalism of the concerned country, the generality of capitalistic accumulation, and the power of the life of capital by considering the historical conditions and the processes of the inception and development of capitalism in each nation. Considering how German capital had maintained its life by exhibiting nationality and changing limitations to restrictions is an essential viewpoint in the analysis of capitalism (Taguchi 2018, pp.139, 146). One of the primary issues of this book lies in elucidating such research issues by examining changes in enterprise business management as a central behavioral agent.

This book analyzed the history of business management in Germany from the Second Reich to the end of World War II from a comparative perspective with the United States (US), between industries, and between enterprises. Changes in business management during three periods—(1) the Second Reich, (2) the Weimar Republic,

T. Yamazaki, *A History of German Business*,
https://doi.org/10.1007/978-981-96-8476-2_15

and (3) the rise of National Socialism—were deliberated concerning the historical conditions of world capitalism, German capitalism during each period, the character of major industries, and the influence of American management methods. This book broadly examined various significant fields of business management, such as enterprise concentration, enterprise structure, management systems, production systems, organizational structure, and business strategy, without limitation to a specific field. Through the aforementioned analysis, this book attempts to elucidate the overall structure of business management in Germany before the end of World War II and the interrelationships between management systems in each field.

This chapter builds on the preceding examinations to clarify this book's implications by analyzing German-specific characteristics and the significance of business management development. First, Sect. 15.1 describes the characteristics and significance of changes in business management in Germany during three periods until the end of World War II: the Second Reich, the Weimar Republic, and National Socialism. This section examines four main fields: (1) enterprise concentration and its corresponding system of industrial concentration, (2) labor management system and the deployment of the Taylor system, (3) deployment of the Ford system and the transformation toward mass production, and (4) changes in the structure of the enterprise and organizational structure. Next, Sect. 15.2 analyzes "continuity" in business management between the period until the end of World War II and the postwar period and its significance. The significance and limitations of business management are clarified by examining how changes appeared until the end of World War II and understanding the points to be evaluated concerning postwar development. Furthermore, Sect. 15.3 investigates the origins of the nature of enterprise as "a social community" by examining the pursuit of economic rationality in Germany from a comparative perspective with that in the US.

15.1 Changes in Business Management in Germany Until the End of World War II: Their Characteristics and Significance

Based on the discussions in the preceding chapters, Sect. 15.1 describes the characteristics and significance of business management changes in Germany before World War II's end by summarizing the research results in this book. In this way, the German style of business management is clarified.

15.1.1 Enterprise Concentration

First, concerning enterprise concentration, the first great wave of corporate consolidation, known as the First Enterprise Concentration Movement, took place in the

US and Germany during monopoly formation from the late nineteenth century to the beginning of the twentieth century. The socioeconomic background can be seen in the change in the structure of capitalism due to the tendency of productive forces over the scale of markets, such as in chronic crises occurring at approximately 10-year intervals. Furthermore, factors such as the diffusion of the joint-stock company system, which was helpful as a means of concentrating massive capital, and the role of banks as the organizer of industrial enterprise concentration that strongly promoted enterprise concentration, and the development of production technology and the growth of industries based on it, in which the scale of required invested capital was very large, had also promoted the progress of enterprise concentration.

Despite the nearly similar economic backgrounds of such phenomena between the US and Germany, the nature of their concentration greatly differed. Germany's characteristics can be seen in the precocious formation of cartels and syndicates and the development of corporate concentration in which cartels were dominant. This situation was strongly determined by the particularities of the country's capitalist development. The large gaps between the rapid development of industrial productive forces, the absorptive capacity of the domestic market, and the consequent change in the conditions of accumulation were the structural basis for the early formation of German monopolies. The response to the limitations imposed by the narrow domestic market made dumping to promote exports inevitable, and maintaining the declining prices in the domestic market became the lifeline of capital accumulation. Export dumping of raw materials and semifinished products became a factor that decreased the competitiveness of the German processing industry, dealing with foreign firms that imported these materials to produce finished goods.

The formation of monopolies in Germany was also closely related to the country's characteristic monopoly regulation. In the period before the end of World War II, Germany did not adopt a firm state policy regarding monopoly control via cartels, which was in sharp contrast to the US. Instead, from the industrial and trade policies perspective, the German state adopted policies that approved cartels, functioning effectively under a system of protective tariffs. International cartels did develop, but by ensuring the competitiveness of domestic products against lower-priced imports through protective tariff policies, cartels were made easier to establish, and the conditions for them to function effectively were created.

In the raw materials sector, such as the coal and pig iron product sectors (where the products were uniform and the variety was limited), the cartel functioned relatively effectively because the required consumption was determined by the production volume of the products manufactured using or processing the raw materials. In contrast, cartels did not necessarily function effectively in the electrical machinery, chemical, and machinery industries. In these industries, the production process was complex, technological development was rapid, and various products were produced and sold. In the electrical machinery industry, trust was rather important. Furthermore, the formation of cartels based on cooperation in techniques, including license pool agreements, had significance due to factors like the importance of technology and the rapid tempo of technological progress. In the chemical industry, interest communities developed due to limitations caused by the considerable number and variety of products. Cartelization in the mechanical engineering industry faced difficulties due to the variety of products required to counter the customer's specifications. In this way, there were significant differences between industries in the ratio of the production of cartel member enterprises to total production. Furthermore, remarkable differences in the formation of cartels and syndicates and the effects of price regulations by cartels or syndicates can be observed among products in the same industry, such as the iron and steel industry.

Because cartels were the dominant form, the establishment of a system based on the rationalization function of the trust, which was compatible with oligopolistic competition seen in the US at the time, the development of rationalization through concentration and specialization of production in specific plants was delayed. The effect of limiting and restraining production through production quota cartels faced limits, and such a method of production adjustment was a major constraint to the development of rationalization by the trust. These were also among the important factors that led to the disparity in competitiveness between American and German firms. Furthermore, the target level of price maintenance that the cartel pursued had to be higher than when production cost reductions were pursued through the rationalization function of the trust, which could be a factor limiting the effectiveness of the price cartel.

Compared with trusts in the US, the primary limitations of cartels or syndicates can be seen in the following points. First, the production process was complicated in industrial sectors; many products were manufactured, and new products would be developed. In this environment, cartels or syndicates tended to continue only for a relatively short period, and their effects were insufficient. Second, the effectiveness of the cartels tended to be less due to the existence of mixed enterprises through the self-consumption problem in such types of enterprises. Third, there were many cases in which the production allotment volume was increased despite production volume restrictions, which became an important factor in maintaining excessive production capacity. In many cases, enterprises were acquired to increase allotments in cartels and syndicates and strengthen such limitations. Fourth, there were cases in which a higher price was forcibly set in cartels combining enterprises of very different sizes, including smaller and weaker firms with higher production costs than those of large-scale plants due to the necessity to guarantee profit to even the weakest firms. Fifth, the high-cost structures of German enterprises were created by long-term imbalances between demand and supply and the decreasing of operating rates due to maintaining excess production capacity. Moreover, the decline of operating rates became an important factor determining the disparity in competitiveness between American and German enterprises, as well as the influences of the delay in the development of trusts and the lack of the possibility of using rationalization functions based on such concentration forms.

The concentration of enterprises in the form of syndicates with joint sales organizations made it possible to integrate forward without creating their own sales organizations. When such sales integration is viewed concerning the problem of managerial coordination, the function of the syndicate in coordinating supply and demand had to have significant limitations due to no company's own sales organization enabling to directly gain market information compared with that of integration through the creation of its own sales department. Adjusting supply and demand through the market mechanism can only bring about an equilibrium of a particular product's total supply and demand in a given regional market at a single moment. Moreover, reflecting differences in product specifications, characteristics, and competitiveness among firms, the equilibrium between supply and demand through the market mechanism does not automatically guarantee the adjustment between their production and the market at the individual firm level. Therefore, independent coordination of production and the market by individual firms and overall coordination of the business process based on internalizing the sales function within the company were indispensable. Meanwhile, the coordination of production and markets by syndicates does not achieve the coordination of production and markets for each company, even though the syndicates can, to some extent, coordinate the production and sales volumes and determine and adjust prices for all companies that are members of such an organization. The limitation of the syndicate's coordination function can be seen in this point.

In the 1920s, the limitations of enterprise concentration in the period of monopoly formation were largely overcome by the development of new corporate concentration. During this period, a second wave of massive concentration and mergers (the Second Enterprise Concentration Movement) occurred in the US and Germany. It developed as a concentration of companies aiming at industrial reorganization under the severe excess capital after World War I. The most important characteristic in the US was "vertical integration," which combined related heterogeneous production processes and different kinds of business areas (Nakata 1983, pp.80–81, 100, 119). In contrast, Germany's most important management issue was consolidating excess production capacity through corporate concentration and reorganizing production organizations and industrial reorganization using enterprise concentration. This approach was promoted more drastically and is deeply related to the concentration of German companies that developed in the form of trusts during this period.

Regarding the background of enterprise concentration, the significant disparity between production capacity and demand was due to the much narrower domestic market due to hyperinflation and the disappearance of competitiveness of German enterprises in exports caused by the decline in the currency exchange rate with the end of inflation and the stabilization of the German Mark. Such situations were deeply concerned with the inevitable necessity to drastically reduce excess production capacity. Furthermore, the aid of the state in terms of tax also promoted consolidation. As seen in the case of the merger that created Vereinigte Stahlwerke AG, the development of trust had great significance in acquiring urgently needed foreign loans.

During the 1920s, factories of the company established by the trust were selected for closure or disposal. Among the remaining factories that had not been closed, reorganization of production was promoted in the form of concentration and specialization of production by product kind in the most suitable factories in terms of location conditions and technological level. This situation further evolved the rationalization function of trusts during monopoly formation in the US. It was an advanced form of rationalization with the same function as the concentration of companies seen today.

Moreover, one of the main characteristics of the concentration of enterprises in the latter half of the 1920s was trust among already combined enterprises, as seen in the heavy and chemical industries; the significance of this was great. In other words, according to the product in the final process sector (typical in the steel industry), the rolling sector allocated the production capacity of various products to specific plants. Furthermore, the production capacity was allocated to the processes that preceded the rolling sector, namely the iron production and steelmaking sectors. Therefore, compared to a consolidation of companies that did not combine such successively related processes, the concentration and specialization of production by product sorts could be conducted more thoroughly, and the reorganization of the entire trust's production organization could be promoted more drastically. Major enterprise concentrations were not the simple consolidation of two capitals but the concentration of more capitals or the same kind of production department into one large capital in the concerned industrial sector regarding the degree of production concentration and market share, such as in the iron, steel, and chemical industries. This situation created an important foundation for drastic rationalization.

Promoting industrial rationalization through the concentration of enterprises in a trust was a preparatory stage for the full-scale development of rationalization at the individual enterprise level. It was intended to create the conditions for mass production of specific products. For example, in IG Farben, reducing excessive production capacity and specialization of production using trust should create the possibility of providing financial support for research and development in new business fields through improving the profitability of the dye department as a core business until then.

Thus, enterprise concentration in Germany during the 1920s significantly contributed to the development of rationalization. However, in the case of Vereinigte Stahlwerke AG, the closing and intermission of plants and production equipment did not always progress in terms of the concentration of production on better plants and equipment, the division of labor, and specialization due to competition between centralization and decentralization. Rationalization measures, partly implemented during the Great Depression, were continued in 1933. These were strongly pursued by dissolving complicated capital relations based on interlocking interest and excessive capital with consolidation and return to private ownership (Kudo 1977, pp.116–118).

In the 1920s, trusts played a significant role; however, the number of cartels remarkably increased despite monopoly regulation measurement by the Cartel Ordinance (the Cartel Law) in 1923. Cartel policy was significant in coping with the high market risk of specialization and its role in improving the premise for specialization (standardization, reduction of type, and industrial concentration) by mitigating such risk.

Based on discussions in this book, including those in this section, Table 15.1 visualizes the conditions surrounding business management changes in Germany until the end of World War II in the field of enterprise concentration.

Table 15.1 German business management until the end of World War II (enterprise concentration)

Management phenomenon	Enterprise concentration	
Period	Period of the Second Reich	Period of the Weimar Republic
Socioeconomic backgrounds	• Change in the structure of capitalism due to the tendency of productive forces over the scale of markets, such as seen in chronic crises occurring at approximately 10-year intervals • Monopolization as an important foundation for export dumping due to the relatively small domestic market • Shift to a conservative customs system in 1879 that made it easy to build cartels by decreasing the number of enterprises in competition and accelerated the establishment of such monopolistic organizations • Development of production technology and growth of industries based on it, where the scale of required invested capital was immense • Diffusion of the joint-stock company system, which was helpful as a means of concentrating massive capital • Role of banks as organizers of industrial enterprise concentration that strongly promoted enterprise concentration	• The much narrower domestic market due to hyperinflation • Disappearance of the competitiveness of German enterprises in exports utilizing the dumping effect caused by the decline in the currency exchange rate with the end of inflation and the stabilization of the German Mark • The stringent export market conditions • The loss of production capacity and demolition of the division of labor in industrial regions such as the Rheine–Westfalen district due to the alienation of territories, as seen in heavy industry, consisting of the mining and iron and steel industries • The significant change in the situation surrounding the German chemical industry with World War I due to the growth of the chemical industry in foreign countries such as the United States, the United Kingdom, and France • The inevitable and urgent necessity to reduce excess production capacity due to significant changes in market conditions and the existence of production equipment with no technologically organic relation to the entire production process that was created aiming at the inflation effect • An important foundation for promoting consolidation created by the aid of the state in terms of tax (Case of merger leading the creation of Vereinigte Stahlwerke AG)
Actual conditions of the management phenomenon	• Cartels or syndicates as the dominant form of enterprise concentration • Cartel as "one of the foundations of the whole of economic life" • Relatively easy building of agreement between enterprises and prevalence of cartels and syndicates in the mining industry in which products were the equality of products, the commonality of interests and similarity of mining costs determined by the geographical conditions of coal production, and the limited value of products concerning transportation costs	• Vertical concentration with raw material departments to cope with shortages of goods until the end of inflation after World War I • Horizontal concentration to achieve the advantages of mass production and mass selling of certain products in a relatively stable period • Trusts, such as Vereinigte Stahlwerke AG, as a change in the order of competitive dynamics of the whole iron and steel industry

(continued)

Table 15.1 (continued)

Management phenomenon	Enterprise concentration	
Period	Period of the Second Reich	Period of the Weimar Republic
	• Great differences between industries in the ratio of the production of cartel member enterprises to total production • Great differences in the formation of cartels and syndicates and the effects of price regulations by cartels or syndicates among products in the same industry, such as in the iron and steel industry • Tendency in which cartels in the raw material industries promoted the formation of cartels and vertical concentration in the processing industries • Attempts to regulate production volume by production allotment cartel rather than trust that played a significant role as a rationalization function in the United States • Predominance of mixed enterprises combining mining and iron and steel sectors in the production allotment cartel • Promotion of exports at low prices by cartels and export dumping in German industries based on price controls in the domestic market through cartels • Delay in consolidations such as trusts and mergers compared with the United States • Progress of trust in industries, such as the electrical industry, in which the production process was complicated, many kinds of products were manufactured, and new products would be developed in a relatively short term • Many cases in which enterprises in the raw materials and semifinished product sectors were acquired to cope with changes in product prices in these sectors by cartels and syndicates • Formation of a community of interests and its dominant form of enterprise concentration in the chemical industry due to limitations caused by the large number and variety of products	• Enterprise concentration aimed at the reorganization of industry • Great increase in the number of cartels in the 1920s despite monopoly regulation measurement by the Cartel Ordinance (the Cartel Law) in 1923 • Multiple ties and webs through cartels to complement the effects of trust • Remarkable differences in the conditions of the concentration movement and the integration capacity between industries and between individual enterprises due to technical reasons or in terms of capital and purchasing equipment and other economic reasons

(continued)

Table 15.1 (continued)

Management phenomenon	Enterprise concentration	
Period	Period of the Second Reich	Period of the Weimar Republic
German characteristics of the management phenomenon	• Premature birth of cartels and syndicates • Delay in the formation of trusts compared with the United States • Building of cartels or syndicates combined with a conservative custom system • Broad existence of a cartel in the form of a syndicate • Significance of the formation of cartels based on cooperation in the field of techniques, including license pool agreements in the electrical industry due to factors such as the importance of technology and the rapid tempo of technological progress • Progress of forward integration of manufacturing enterprises through syndicates as a means of integrating the sales function without establishing their own sales organization	• Specialization of production implemented by mutual allotment of production according to the specialties of individual companies and plants in certain products • Trust-based specialization of fusion aimed at pursuing locational and production technological advantages • Fusion of vertically integrated enterprises enabling a more thorough implementation of production concentration and specialization, such as typically seen in the iron and steel industry • Not the simple consolidation of two capitals but the concentration of more capitals or the same kind of production department into one significant capital in the iron and steel and chemical industries that occupied overwhelming weight in the concerned industrial sector in terms of both the degree of production concentration and market share
Factors determining the German development of the management phenomenon	• Promotion of dumping exports due to relatively small domestic market and competitive pressure from other capitalistic nations such as the UK and the US and the necessity to intercept price decline under the repetition of crisis and to maintain high prices for covering profit losses caused by such dumping • Promotion of broad diffusion of cartels and syndicates due to state policy that approved cartels from the perspective of industrial and trade policies under a tendency to regard the cartel as an appropriate means of easing cyclical fluctuations	• Overcoming the delay in consolidations such as trusts and mergers compared with the United States • Strong necessity to pursue the thorough rationalization effects in terms of reduction of excessive production capacity and the division of labor in the production of various products due to the significant gap between production capacity and demand compared with the United States • Possibility to attempt a drastic reorganization of the production organization based on the existence of enterprises that have already integrated different yet related production processes

(continued)

Table 15.1 (continued)

Management phenomenon	Enterprise concentration	
Period	Period of the Second Reich	Period of the Weimar Republic
Significance of the management phenomenon	• Coping with structural changes in capitalism due to the tendency of productive forces over the scale of markets by creating market control institutions such as cartels and syndicates • Early shift to monopolistic capitalism and the birth of monopolistic large enterprises • Formation of the system of price control and production allotment by monopolies • Establishing an important basis for export dumping through price controls in the domestic market by cartels • Significant role of syndicates as a means of forward integration into the sales function instead of building the company's own sales organization	• Providing the possibility to help the concerned industry match production with demand by thoroughly eliminating excess production capacity using trust • Trusts, such as Vereinigte Stahlwerke AG, as a change in the order of competitive dynamics of the whole iron and steel industry from that based on cartel-centered industry • Creating a more effective foundation of production and sales and an important basis for the rationalization at the level of individual enterprises by enabling large enterprises formed by trusts to eliminate excessive production capacity and achieve the division of labor in production based on product type within a company • Providing financial support for research and development in new business fields through improvement of the profitability of the dye department as a core business until then by the thorough reduction of excessive production capacity and specialization of production using trust in the chemical industry • Great significance of the development of trust for acquiring urgently needed foreign loans, such as seen in the case of the merger that created Vereinigte Stahlwerke AG • Great contribution to the regrouping of production organization and program using trust to improve productivity and realizing economies of scale • Cartel policy as a measure to cope with the high market risk of specialization and its role in improving the premise for specialization (standardization, reduction of type, and industrial concentration) by mitigating such risk

(continued)

Table 15.1 (continued)

Management phenomenon	Enterprise concentration	
Period	Period of the Second Reich	Period of the Weimar Republic
Limitations of the management phenomenon	• Limitation in continuance in a relatively short term and insufficient effects of cartels or syndicates in industrial sectors in which the production process was complicated; many kinds of products were manufactured, and new products would be developed • Cases in which the production allotment volume was increased despite production volume restrictions • Limitation of cartels in decreasing overproduction and controlling the members' desire to expand production • The less effective the cartels due to the existence of mixed enterprises through self-consumption problems in such types of enterprises • Opposition between coal mining companies and companies integrating ironworks caused by the existence of mixed enterprises • Limitation in forming cartels and restriction of their effects in the electrical industry due to the diversity of product types and the rapid cycle of technological change • The most significant difficulties in cartelization in the mechanical engineering industry due to the great variety of products required for countering the customer's specifications • Insufficient attempts to pursue rationalization functions due to a delay in the formation of trusts enabling the reduction of excess production capacity and concentration of production on the most advantageous plants in terms of technology and locating conditions among all manufacturing establishments of an enterprise included in a merger • The high-cost structures of German enterprises created by long-term imbalances between demand and supply due to maintaining excess production capacity and the decline of operating rates • Limitations of coordinating production capacity and demand using the production allotment function of cartels and creating the differences in competitive power between Germany and the US	• Small effects of attempts to reduce product types • A compromise and a "half consolidation" of enterprises with the same product programs in the heavy industry (Vereinigte Stahlwerke AG) due to the situation that some leading companies such as Krupp, Mannesmann, Hoesch, and Gutehoffnung did not participate in the merger and the existence of powerful outsiders continued • Inconsistent progress of closing and intermission of plants and production equipment in terms of the concentration of production on better plants and equipment and the division of labor and specialization among them due to competition between orientations toward centralization and decentralization despite pursuing such attempts in the case of Vereinigte Stahlwerke AG

(continued)

Table 15.1 (continued)

Management phenomenon	Enterprise concentration	
Period	Period of the Second Reich	Period of the Weimar Republic
	• Maintaining excess production capacity and decreasing operating rates due to the limitation of the function of the production allotment cartel • Higher price setting in cartels combining enterprises of very different sizes, including smaller and weaker firms that have higher production costs than those of large-scale plants due to the necessity to guarantee a sure profit to even the weakest firms • Delay in achieving balance between demand and supply through market mechanisms and obstruction to market recovery by maintaining high prices through cartels or syndicates • Many cases in which the acquisition of enterprises was implemented to increase allotments in cartels and syndicates • Restriction on the competitiveness of German processing enterprises by export dumping of raw materials and semifinished goods based on special profits in the domestic market controlled by cartels or syndicates • Great limitations in the function of coordinating demand and supply through membership in syndicates due to no company's own sales organization enabling us to directly gain information regarding market	

Source This table was compiled by the author, based on discussions in this book

15.1.2 The Taylor System, the REFA System, and Labor Management

From the end of the nineteenth century, the necessity to reduce costs increased under the trend of long-term depression. Moreover, the possibility of production cost reduction by replacing machinery and equipment was restricted due to the burden of fixed costs arising from the existing production equipment under the lower operating rate. In the period, in the face of fierce international competition, especially with American firms, management reform was undertaken to overcome the limitations of management under the internal contracting system. In this system, each workshop could be only separately managed by the different internal contracting foremen, and laborers could only be indirectly managed from the viewpoint of the enterprise.

Two directions of labor management reforms can be observed. On the one hand, an attempt was made to deploy the Taylor system, which was born in the US. On the other hand, German companies tried to separate planning and execution functions by dividing the former supervisor function; however, such efforts did not progress sufficiently and smoothly. In many cases, individual attempts to introduce only a particular element or plural elements of the Taylor system were pursued instead of deploying the entire system. Such limitations occurred due to (1) the existence of relatively abundant skilled workers and the relatively low labor cost compared with the US, (2) the way German capitalism was created and developed decreased the domestic market, leading to an underdeveloped consumer goods market, and (3) the trend toward opposition of the labor side to the Taylor system. Management reforms were attempted only by a few large companies in the electrical engineering and machinery industries, characterized by labor-intensive production processes and an orientation to making strong inroads into export markets. Moreover, even among firms in these industries, in many cases, such reforms were not seriously pursued; instead, the introduction of individual components of the Taylor system was observed. The separation between planning and execution (the core of the Taylor system's management method) and the direct control over work by enterprises (based on leadership's movement in decisions regarding the speed of work from workers to management) was hardly achieved.

During World War I, conditions changed. Under the massive demand for munitions, the necessity to increase munition production and the possibility of implementing the mass production of related products proliferated with the shift to a war economy. Furthermore, unlike the preceding period, with the cooperation policy of the Social Democratic Party in the war effort, changes in industrial relationships occurred, and the Taylor system was considered an effective means of increasing productive forces. Labor unions' cooperative policy with the national task of achieving the enlargement of munitions production and the entire abandonment of strikes helped improve the foundation for the deployment of the Taylor system during World War I.

The situation changed dramatically after World War I, especially during relative stability in the 1920s. In the revolutionary period after World War I, with the participation of the Social Democratic Party in the Weimar government, the Free Trade Unions were also faced with restoring and developing the German economy. This task coincided with the socialization problem, and the deployment of the Taylor system was crucial. During the inflationary period, the shift in the standard of work output from money to time became an important issue, which prompted research on the labor process, as seen in studies by the Committee for Time Study (Ausschuβ für Zeitstudien).

Subsequently, under the development of the rationalization movement during the relatively stable 1920s, the deployment of the Taylor system made significant progress, bringing about changes in labor organization and management in many industries. Changes in historical conditions during this period can be seen in the following points. The first is the change in market conditions, where the domestic market became narrower due to hyperinflation, and the necessity and significance of expanding exports increased decisively. Furthermore, with the end of inflation and the stabilization of the "Mark," the competitiveness of German enterprises using the effect of foreign exchange dumping was lost. A thorough reduction of production costs to promote exports became a decisively important issue for the entire industrial level. Second, the economic concessions made by capital to avert the systemic crisis caused by the German Revolution (including an eight-hour workday, improved wage system, recognition of trade unions, and contractual wages) led to a trend of rigidity in wage decline, and reducing labor costs became an even more important issue. Third, concerning labor relations, the defeat of the revolutionary forces in the fall of 1923 eliminated the premise of "socialization," and the line of labor-capital cooperation took root. As a new ideology in place of the previous "socialization," rationalization was emphasized and regarded as a potent means of achieving the American high standard of social life that they had set as their goal in their "Economic Democracy Theory" based on the idea of the free labor unions emphasizing the productive forces. In this context, the Taylor system was considered one of the most important rationalization measures. Furthermore, in the financial markets, the shortage of capital under the constant shortage of credit and the burden of capital costs determined by the shortage of capital restricted the development of technological rationalization. The Taylor system became critical as a rationalization measure that did not necessarily require capital expenditures.

Nonetheless, the rationalization movement was also undertaken from a national economic perspective, and opposition and resistance to the Taylor system from the labor side remained. This situation led to modifying the system to a unique "REFA system," which could be regarded as the German version of the Taylor system. Two difference points exist between the Taylor system and the REFA system. (1) The task standard was modified from "maximum output" based on the fastest time of a first-class worker in the Taylor system to "normal output" based on the average time of a mean worker in the REFA system. (2) A wage system was adopted in which the relationship between wages and output changed not progressively (in the Taylor system) but proportionally (REFA).

The prevalence of time and work studies based on the REFA system progressed, and the full-scale deployment of the Taylor system realized the separation of planning and execution functions through setting tasks and management based on it. This environment shifted the initiative in determining the speed of work from the workers' side to the company's side, laying the foundation for direct management and control by the company over the process of labor power expenditure. Therefore, for German companies, the introduction of the REFA system represented a major step forward in introducing the Taylor system that had been attempted since before World War I. Thus, the reorganization of the labor organization of industrial enterprises was carried out through the REFA system, and the modernization of the labor management system, which had lagged behind that of the US, was realized. The introduction of the REFA system made the labor process a "black box" for workers, and despite the change in the standard of work from "maximum performances" (the Taylor system) to "normal performance" (the REFA system), as seen in the reduction of piecework rates through "re-inspection," the difference in the influence on workers between the two systems was not substantial and was only relative. The introduction of the REFA system facilitated the spread of time studies, and in the Ford system, the time study was used as the basis for organizing the production line in the flow work system and was an important foundation for the development of the Ford system.

In the deployment of the Taylor system, the transformation of the Taylor system into the REFA system, and the introduction of the latter in Germany during the 1920s, one prominent characteristic can be seen. This characteristic is apparent in the roles of the rationalization sciences, such as management science (*Betriebswissenschaft*)—which played a prominent role in introducing the Taylor system at the beginning of the twentieth century—and labor science (*Arbeitswissenschaft*). The study of fatigue in enterprises based on psycho-technology was emphasized, and German labor science (psycho-engineering or management science) attempted to contribute to mitigating distrust in scientific management. Despite its development during this period, these sciences were still only in the first stage of development. Furthermore, labor unions tended to be friendly with studies in these fields; however, labor science could not understand labor as capitalistic labor processes, which indicated the limitations of this science.

The Taylor system prevailed as the REFA system in many industries; however, differences remained in adoption among industrial sectors, for example, between the metal, machinery, and electrical engineering and the iron and steel, mining, and chemical. REFA was essential in training work time and piece wage calculators through education courses.

In the US during the 1920s, the adoption of the management system was broadly expanded to scientific management, including the study results of H L. Gantt and the Gilbreths over the Taylor system. Frank Bunker Gilbreth undertook his important work in the German industry (Drury 1922, p.171), and the separation between planning and execution could be realized; however, the deployment of the Taylor system and its principle in itself was an indispensable task and did not still arrive at the higher stage seen in the US.

In the 1920s, in the US, cooperation between management and labor in the labor union movement took root; the involvement of labor unions in management through concession and trade played a role in the development of scientific management. In Germany, the Works Council Act enacted in 1920 allowed labor participation in management, and collaboration between management and labor was emphasized in the rationalization movement. However, labor unions' attempts to influence management and regulative power were minimal, and relationships between management and labor did not reach the level seen in the US.

In the period of National Socialism, the REFA system, created under special conditions in Germany during the 1920s, was further developed under the strong involvement of the state, and its introduction into companies proceeded. The REFA system was promoted by the necessity to increase production (including munitions) and promote time economies under the planning framework of the entire Nazi state economy, the lack of skilled workers, and the expectation of the role of REFA activity in decisive contribution to "scientific" solutions. Further incentives included the mitigation of social conflicts within enterprises and the realization of a socially harmonious "community within a company" ("industrial piece") by "scientificity" and "objectivity" of the REFA system and implementation of wage payments suitable to worker performance. However, troubles with using stopwatches and calculators occurred frequently in parallel with the diffusion of the REFA system despite eliminating workers' ability to repress output.

Cooperation was established between REFA and other institutions concerned with problems in the labor science field (i.e., state and quasi-state institutions, such as the German Technical Labor Education Institute [Dinta] and The Agency of Professional Training and Corporate Leadership [Amt für Betriebsführung und Berufserziehung]) within the German Labor Front (Deutsche Arbeitfront). The importance of REFA activity and the expansion of its activities were possible through the involvement of state institutions in promoting rationalization and their initiatives. The rapid expansion of the REFA system was based on the support and involvement of quasi-state institutions, such as the German Labor Front.

The REFA system spread, expanding its scope from the study of time to the study of work. The REFA in training work study staff through the expansion of implementing education played a significant role in training personnel for work study and time measurement through education courses. The number of participants in its courses also significantly increased; thus, the fundamental modernization of labor organizations progressed through promotion by REFA and the Agency of Professional Training and Corporate Leadership in many enterprises broadly belonging to the metal processing industry, such as metal, electrical, and machine. However, the number of REFA training courses and participants decreased after 1943 due to the difficulty and impossibility of observing production-related economic principles and implementing time economy measures under constant changes in the war economy. Moreover, the use of the work study declined due to the burden caused by the war.

In this way, the REFA system proliferated due to the need to increase munitions production and the labor shortage; thus, the system was considered vital in munitions-related industries. However, because the Nazi state's control of economic policy concentrated on the munitions industry sector, other less emphasized industrial sectors, especially the shipbuilding industry and the consumer goods industry, were left behind, despite the existence of departments in which the diffusion of the REFA system further progressed.

Furthermore, the involvement of state and quasi-state institutions in the activities of the REFA significantly contributed to the further expansion and diffusion of the REFA system. However, institutions like the REFA became a part of complex state and party organizations for their continuance through cooperative relationships between the REFA and the state or quasi-state institutions. In stark contrast to the Weimar period, the REFA system was influenced by the state to control workers and strengthen Nazi ideology. As a result, the involvement of quasi-state organizations such as the German Labor Front led to a significant deviation from the original goal of the REFA, which was to ensure "neutrality" and "objectivity."

Based on the discussions in this book, including those in Sect. 15.1.2, Table 15.2 displays the conditions surrounding business management changes in Germany before the end of World War II in the field of labor management.

15.1.3 The Ford System and Mass Production

The necessity of thorough cost reduction based on mass production under the intense competitive pressure in domestic and export markets from US enterprises made deploying the Ford system and mass production indispensable for German enterprises. Regarding the evaluation of the Ford system, the relatively positive attitude of labor unions tended to occur due to the expected economic effects, such as the decline of costs and product prices, high wages, and promotion of consumer society. "White socialism" was based on the effectiveness and possibility of developing a society that mass production could create. The positive evaluation of the Free Trade Union to the Ford system was based on the Economic Democratic Theory, emphasizing the significance of developing productive forces. Meanwhile, the aspect of the labor management system of the Ford system tended to be negatively evaluated due to the significant increase in labor intensity and monotone in the flow production system. However, criticism from the labor side regarding the Ford system's influence on workers was inconsistent despite its function of increasing labor intensity at the flow production method compared with the Taylor system. Therefore, it is important to distinguish these two aspects when evaluating the Ford system.

Regarding the deployment of the Ford system, the standardization of production was vital for efficiency improvement as an effective rationalization measure without capital expenditures under the conditions that rationalization in the technology field encountered limitations due to a lack of capital and the burdensome capital costs required. It was also an important basis for introducing the flow production method. Furthermore, unlike the US (where standardization of consumption progressed), in

Table 15.2 German business management until the end of World War II (The Taylor system, the REFA system, and labor management)

Management phenomena	The Taylor system, the REFA system, and Labor management		
Period	Period of the Second Reich	Period of the Weimar Republic	Period of National Socialism
Socioeconomic backgrounds	• Change in the structure of capitalism due to the tendency of productive forces over the scale of markets, such as seen in chronic crises occurring at approximately 10-year intervals • Strong necessity to reduce costs under the circumstances in which possibilities of production cost reduction by replacing machinery and equipment were restricted due to the burden of fixed costs arising from existing production equipment under the lower operating rate brought by the longtime depression • Competitive pressure from the US due to the technological gap between Germany and the US • Limitations of the internal contracting system in which each workshop could not be managed in a centralized form, and workers were managed only indirectly through internal contracting foremen from the enterprise perspective • Necessity to cope with the management problem brought about by breaking up the control power of all-around skilled supervisors in workshops that were a foundation of worker resistance	• Increasing necessity and significance of transforming the standard of work output from money to time with unprecedented inflation after World War I and promotion of the study of the labor process based on such changes • The narrower domestic market due to hyperinflation and the increase in the necessity and significance of expanding exports • Decisive increase of necessity to reduce costs for enlarging exports in the relatively stable period with the disappearance of competitiveness of German enterprises utilizing the dumping effect caused by the decline in the currency exchange rate under the inflation • A trend of rigidity in wage decline brought about by the economic concessions to the working class in the revolutionary period after World War I as a significant restrictive factor to cost reduction and increased necessity to improve productivity • Changes in labor relations based on the Economic Democratic Theory of the Free Trade Union emphasizing the idea of productivity and trade unions' cooperative policy with the Rationalization movement	• The necessity and significance of the REFA system's "scientific" work and time studies due to the further increase in the importance of production and time economies under the planning framework of the entire Nazi state economy • Expectation of the role of REFA activity in decisive contribution to "scientific" solutions, mitigation of social conflicts within enterprises, and realization of a socially harmonious "community within a company" ("industrial piece") by "scientificness" and "objectivity" of the REFA system and implementing wage payments suitable to worker performance • Increased significance and role of the work-study further to expand munitions production and address the issue of lack of skilled workers during World War II • Lack of workers and greater necessity to increase the intensity of labor and replace skilled workers with semi-skilled workers • Necessity to improve productivity for enlargement munitions production

(continued)

Table 15.2 (continued)

Management phenomena	The Taylor system, the REFA system, and Labor management		
Period	Period of the Second Reich	Period of the Weimar Republic	Period of National Socialism
	• The necessity to increase the production of munitions and the possibility to implement the mass production of products related to munitions with the outbreak of war and the shift to a war economy	• Restriction to the development of technological rationalization that needed capital expenditure due to the financial market conditions in the relatively stable period, such as the shortage of capital under the constant shortage of credit and the burden of capital costs and increases in the deployment of the Taylor system that did not necessarily need capital expenditure	
Actual conditions of management phenomenon	• Two directions of labor management reforms: (1) deployment of the Taylor system as an American management system and (2) Germany's original efforts to separate the planning and execution functions by dividing the former foreman function • The electrical and machine industries as the main sectors in which labor management system reforms were attempted due to their industrial characteristics: (1) the existence of workers taking charge of various kinds of machines and many types of jobs, (2) one of the most important sectors in terms of the number of enterprises and workers and industrial export products, and (3) intense competition with the UK and the US companies • Significant delay in the introduction of the Taylor system compared with the United States	• Modifying the Taylor system to the REFA system due to worker influence and opposition and Germany's specific conditions and diffusion as the "German" Taylor system or the revised Taylor system in companies • Two difference points between the Taylor system and the REFA system: (1) modification of the task standard from "maximum output" based on the fastest time of a first-class worker in the Taylor system to "normal output" based on the average time of a mean worker in the REFA system and (2) adoption of the wage system in which the relationship between wages and output changed not progressively (case of the Taylor system) but proportionally • Using the concept of "normal output" in the task standard as a tactical concession on the side of capital to drive rationalization for German entrepreneurs	• Expansion of the field of REFA activity from time study to all work studies, such as setting standard time, job design, job evaluation, and work guidance • Diffusion of motion study • Rapid expansion of the REFA system after the assumption of power by the Nazis • Progress of the fundamental modernization of labor organizations promoted by REFA and the Agency of Professional Training and Corporate Leadership in many enterprises belonging to the metal processing industry in a broad sense, such as the metal, electrical, and machine

(continued)

Table 15.2 (continued)

Management phenomena	The Taylor system, the REFA system, and Labor management		
Period	Period of the Second Reich	Period of the Weimar Republic	Period of National Socialism
	• Tendency to introduce each element of the Taylor system and delay in adopting time study as an important basis for the separation between planning and execution through setting tasks (exception case of Robert Bosch) • The trend of more progress in plant management reform in the electrical industry than in the machine industry, in particular, the machine tool industry • Due to characteristics of production processes, a requirement of the technical department that should play an important role in management reform, in the machinery industry where mass production was still not developed • No necessity for a technical department in mass production plants, such as steel plants, rolling mill plants, and bicycle or furnace plants	• Acceptance of the REFA system by trade unions due to expectation of accurate and objective calculation of peace work time using this system as well as modification of the abovementioned two points • Prevalence of time and work studies based on the REFA system • Prevalence of the REFA system in many industries with differences among industrial sectors, for example, between the metal, machinery, and electrical engineering and the iron and steel, mining, and chemical • Many cases in which the piece rate was lowered shapely by changes in the standard of calculation, motion study, and measurement of the shortest time of elements of motions for the reason of "re-examination" when workers achieved piece wage at a certain level • Great role of the REFA in training work time calculators and piece wage calculators through holding education courses	• Existence of industrial sectors in which systematic work and time studies encountered many difficulties or were not heavily pursued, such as the shipbuilding industry, the chemical industry, and consumer goods industries, despite the existence of departments in which the diffusion of the REFA system further progressed • The significant role of the REFA in training work-study staff through the expansion of implementing education courses and the increase in participants that reached a peak in 1943

(continued)

Table 15.2 (continued)

Management phenomena	The Taylor system, the REFA system, and Labor management		
Period	Period of the Second Reich	Period of the Weimar Republic	Period of National Socialism
German characteristics of management phenomenon	• Germany's independent attempts to separate the planning and execution functions by dividing the former foreman function that was composed of two trends: (1) the division into the general foreman with well-versed knowledge in theoretical calculations and taking charge of setting piece wages with production engineers, and the lower foreman responsible only for assigning and supervising work and (2) moving decisions of calculable piece wages to the technical department • Individual attempts to introduce only a specific element or plural elements of the Taylor system instead of the deployment of the entire system	• Emphasis on a social perspective applicable to various fields of enterprise or the entire industry in attempts at standardization of task norms • Trend toward placing importance on finding the "righteous" and "fair" wage and decision of objective and fair standard work volume in discussions on the REFA system by management, labor scientists, and labor side • Diffusion of REFA's wage payment system instead of the differential piece wage system • Major Roles of the rationalization sciences such as management science (Betriebswissenschaft) and labor science (Arbeitswissenschaft), progress of the systematization, concentration, and unification of the German rationalization science in the Weimar period, and contribution to the REFA system • Unlike the Taylor school, the role of the German post-Taylor school in the study of fatigue in enterprises based on psycho-technology and attempts of German labor science (psycho-engineering or management science) to mitigate distrust in "the scientific management." • Case in which time studies were a means of implementing managerial social policy	• Cooperation between REFA and other institutions concerned with problems in the labor science field, in particular, state and quasi-state institutions, such as the German Technical Labor Education Institute (Dinta) and the Agency of Professional Training and Corporate Leadership (Amt für Betriebsführung und Berufserziehung) within the German Labor Front (Deutsche Arbeitfront) • Increase in the importance of REFA activity and expansion of its activities through the involvement of state institutions in promoting rationalization and their initiatives • Rapid expansion of the REFA system with the support and involvement of quasi-state institutions, such as the German Labor Front • Support for rationalization by the Agency of Professional Training and Corporate Leadership that was usually implemented with the mediation of the state industrial group • Complete loss of the independence of REFA under the Nazi acquisition of administrative power and the German Labor Front's enforcement of labor control

(continued)

Table 15.2 (continued)

Management phenomena	The Taylor system, the REFA system, and Labor management		
Period	Period of the Second Reich	Period of the Weimar Republic	Period of National Socialism
			• The Nazi regime's attempt to apply scientific management in a way consistent with its ideology and to combine scientific management with its idea of "community" and "leadership." • Broad REFA activity, including work studies such as setting standard time, job design, job evaluation, and work guidance, as well as time study • Like in the 1920s, the significant role of the scientific study of labor in the rationalization sciences, such as seen in the use and diffusion of psychological results
Factors determining German development of management phenomenon	• The low need for many German companies to broadly and thoroughly introduce elements of the Taylor system • Three primary factors determining the delay of diffusion of the Taylor system: (1) the narrow domestic market due to the underdeveloped consumer goods market, (2) the existence of relatively abundant skilled workers and low labor costs compared with the United States, and (3) the trend toward opposition of the labor side to the Taylor system • Promotion of the deployment of the Taylor system based on the expansion of the munitions market and changes in industrial relationships based on labor unions' cooperative policy with the national task of achieving the enlargement of munitions production and the entire abandonment of strikes during World War I	• Modification of the task standard from "maximum output" to "normal output" based on the great significance of the arrangement of miscellaneous processes, consequently unifying them at a certain standard due to the situation in which the standardization of task norms did not progress in Germany • The necessity and meaning of standardization from a social perspective, including the entire enterprise and industry based on the rather average, normal conditions, unlike the case of the Taylor system	• Influences of labor control by the Nazi state • Influences of two ideologies as an important theoretical foundation for fascist labor management: (1) "the managerial community theory" that eliminated class discrimination between capitalists and laborers and (2) "the leader's principle" that viewed both parties as having a relationship between direction and obedience • Involvement of state institutions in REFA and their initiatives focusing on increasing munitions production and improving its productivity

(continued)

Table 15.2 (continued)

Management phenomena	The Taylor system, the REFA system, and Labor management		
Period	Period of the Second Reich	Period of the Weimar Republic	Period of National Socialism
Significance of management phenomenon	• Beginning and progress of modernization of management to a certain degree through the application of principles of the Taylor system, such as the centralization of management • Implementation of piece wages based on tasks and the standardization of work execution based on time-saving principles prevailed in many industries • Expansion of modern management thought	• Realizing the separation between planning and execution and direct control over work by enterprises by moving the leadership in decisions regarding the speed of work from workers to management • Progress of concentration of knowledge regarding the labor process from workers to management, making all expertise for planning functions such as calculation of standard time and determination of peace rate "black box" for workers by implementing the REFA system • Significance of the diffusion of the REFA system for the deployment of the Ford system, such as seen in building the base for organizing production line of flow production method by time study • Overcoming the delay in the development of a modern labor management system compared with that of the United States	• Importance of the role of the REFA system as an effective means of work-study and for the rationalization of work preparation, work management, and work design • Importance of REFA activities in attempts to realize rational methods of human work as one of the emphases of the National Committee for Production Increase and committees thereunder • Contribution of the improvement and modernization of labor organizations based on the REFA system to the transformation of declining productivity trends until the 1932–1934/35 period • Contribution of tables and standard values created by REFA and their use for making complex plans punctually beforehand without any loss of time, calculations in advance, and using the remaining room to increase output for the war economy on the basis of accurate time measurements • Existence of cases in which realizing requests for an increase in armament production depended decisively on the success of REFA activity • Role of staff trained by the REFA system in coping with wage problems, such as the regrouping of wages throughout the industry

(continued)

Table 15.2 (continued)

Management phenomena	The Taylor system, the REFA system, and Labor management		
Period	Period of the Second Reich	Period of the Weimar Republic	Period of National Socialism
			• Setting narrow limits on workers' own "piece wage policy" by gaining more accurate knowledge about workers' operative capabilities and performance possibilities and eliminating workers' ability to repress output
Limitations of management phenomenon	• Delay in scientification of the piece wage system based on the methods of F. W. Taylor or work and time studies • Except for companies strongly oriented toward the expansion of exports and mass production in the electrical and machine industries, the low need to broadly and thoroughly introduce elements of the Taylor system • No realization of the separation between planning and execution as the core of the management method of the Taylor system and no direct control over work by enterprises based on the movement of the leadership in decisions regarding the speed of work from workers to management	• Delay in the development of scientific management in a broad sense that included the study results of H L. Gantt and the Gilbreths over the Taylor system compared with the United States • Unlike the United States, where a line of cooperation between management and labor in the labor union movement took root, and the involvement of trade unions in management was approved and promoted, and played a significant role in labor relations, the very limited regulative power of labor unions in Germany and the low involvement of trade unions in management despite the possibility of union participation based on the Works Council Act of 1920	• Underlying the increase in community consciousness and the loyalty of workers to the state without emphasizing problems such as the pursuit of the most suitable worker efficiency performed by managers and labor scientists after the introduction of scientific management due to the involvement of the state • Becoming institutions such as REFA part of complex state and party organizations for their continuance • Great difficulties in achieving essential goals of REFA, such as securing "neutrality" and "objectivity" due to the involvement of quasi-state institutions, such as the German Labor Front and the labor control by the Nazi state, even though educational REFA courses were implemented at its own expense and did not receive support from the German Labor Front

(continued)

Table 15.2 (continued)

Management phenomena	The Taylor system, the REFA system, and Labor management		
Period	Period of the Second Reich	Period of the Weimar Republic	Period of National Socialism
			• Decrease in REFA activity in terms of decline of the number of REFA training courses and participants after 1943 due to much more difficulty and impossibility in observing production-related economic principles and implementing time economy measures under constant changes in the war economy • Decline of the use of the work-study on account of the increase of the burden caused by the war • Stopping REFA activity at the end of the Nazi rule • The frequent occurrence of troubles over the use of the stopwatch and calculator occurred in parallel with the diffusion of the REFA system despite eliminating workers' ability to repress output

Source This table was compiled by the author, based on discussions in this book

some situations, consumer individualism was an obstacle to enlarging the production volume of the same products, making standardization a more important task.

Standardization attempts had already systematically begun in the 1910s. The Bureau of Standards was founded to create standards for munitions production during World War I, and the German Industrial Standards Committee (Normenausschuß der deutschen Industrie) was established in 1917, tasked with creating and establishing uniform industrial standards. However, it was not until the 1920s that the process took off. In 1926, the German Standards Committee (Deutscher Normenausschuß) was established, and efforts were systematically promoted under the involvement of the Committee as the "standardization movement." Thus, the idea of standardization penetrated large corporations and military companies and broadly affected the level of small and medium enterprises. One of the most important characteristics of standardization in Germany can be seen in more systematic development than in other countries. The "standardization movement" was pursued as a line in the chain of the rationalization movement during the relatively stable period of the 1920s.

The standardization of production was particularly advanced in the processing and assembly industries, such as electrical, automobile, and machinery. In the electrical industry, the progress of standardization tended to be more prominent than in other industries due to the high concentration of Siemens and AEG. However, the differences between the industrial sectors and between the product departments in the same industry were remarkable. For instance, differences in the development of standardization existed between consumer goods products, which progressed relatively quickly, and producer goods or products, in which the tempo of innovation was early, and product innovation was rapidly implemented.

In the 1920s, many factors restricted the standardization of production. Contributing factors included consumer individualism, insufficient understanding of the merits of standardization and no interest in it by enterprises, and the existence of many small and medium firms due to delays in concentration in industrial sectors such as the machinery industry. Furthermore, helping consumers recognize the benefits of mass-producing standardized products was challenging because in Germany (unlike the US, where production and consumption were standardized), the reduction in product prices was not sufficiently implemented, corresponding to the reduction in production costs enabled by the development of standardization and mass production. As a result, the intense individualism of consumers in Germany continued to be a decisive factor restricting the progress of standardization. Even in the late 1920s, the standardization of production and consumption lagged that of the US, limiting mass production development.

Later, during the Nazi period, efforts to overcome the limitations in the progress of standardization were developed through state involvement and coercion under the challenge of increasing munitions production. Standardization and reduction of type became new goals of the economic policy of fascism. Systematic efforts appeared in compulsion under the goals and direction of the state and the standardization based on the remarkably increasing norms set by the German Standards Committee (DINs norm lists), the cooperation of manufacturers integrated in organizations (such as the industrial associations and the circle organization or special committees), and working committees organized to advance more rapid and intense standardization.

However, even in the automobile industry (where such efforts were most strongly implemented under state direction), limits to the progress of standardization remained, hindering mass production. Frequent changes in the type of munitions to be produced and the transformation of production goals due to modifications or fundamental changes in the plans for the munition preparation also significantly restricted the progress of standardization and its effect. The diversity of standardized munitions products was an important factor limiting mass production's development and effectiveness based on the flow production method. Furthermore, as seen typically in the machinery industry, in industrial sectors where there were many very small enterprises and the concentration level was low, standardization efforts were forced to be greatly restricted. Differences in the standardization progress between industrial sectors and enterprises or product departments in the same industry were also significant.

Standardization efforts were promoted even more strongly during World War II as a national policy. Standardization tended to encounter limitations regarding capitalistic competition and restrict technical advances, particularly during the years of war production. Cases arose in which the reduction of product types was not always suitable for mass production and where the constant change in a few existing types was implemented under wartime production. The capital goods industry trended toward avoiding specialization to secure competitiveness in the export market. Moreover, cases occurred in which a strict decrease in type restricted the possibility of a new design.

In this way, standardization lagged behind that of the US, where the market has long been more homogeneous than in other countries (Chandler 1977, p.498) and where standardization of production and consumption has made significant progress.

Next, considering the introduction of the flow production system in the 1920s for German enterprises, it was decisively necessary to thoroughly reduce costs under the intense competition pressure from foreign companies, especially US companies. It was pursued mainly in the processing and assembly industries, such as the electrical engineering, automobile, and machinery sectors; however, there were differences among the industrial and product sectors in the Weimar period. Under the strict market conditions of a narrow domestic market and difficulties in export markets, some progress in introducing such American production and management methods was made only in a few enterprises in these industrial sectors or their advanced factories, specific process sectors, or product sectors.

In many cases, the introduction of American production and management methods, such as the Ford system, was limited to a few companies in these industrial sectors. The belt conveyors tended to be arranged primarily in pre-assembly, final assembly, and packaging. Cases in which transformation to the flow production system was performed in all casting and forging processes, mechanical processing, and assembly, and a high-level transportation system between processes was introduced were very rare. In many cases, variant forms other than "the conveyor system," such as the method called the "conveyor type of tact system," the "changeable flow production" (die wechselnde Fliessarbeit), and the "standstill work type of flow production" were adopted. In particular, in the entire machinery industry (excluding partial product sectors), the overwhelming rate of the flow production system was organized without the conveyor. Despite various efforts, the flow production system's development can be regarded as a primitive rather than a "complete" form. Even in the automobile industry, where the deployment of the Ford system was decisive and strongly pursued, the system combining the flow of work and conveyors was dominant, and the rate of employees working directly on the conveyor in the automobile industry was very low. Eliminating skilled workers by introducing the flow production system did not progress as smoothly in Germany as in the US. Despite various efforts to introduce the flow production system, a significant difference appeared in the production structure based on the Ford system between German and American automobile companies.

Attempts were made to introduce production systems that were not "rigid" concerning market fluctuations—such as the Ford system—and could achieve the effects of mass production with smaller quantities than in the US. Such systems could ensure a certain degree of "flexibility" concerning the diversity of products and market fluctuations. Such a production system was developed on the basis of a shift in the principle of organizing production from "specialization" in the Ford system to "generalization" of production. This approach attempted to supplement the realization of "economy of scale" through "economy of scope." Meanwhile, attempts at building the flow production system as a "flexible production concept with an emphasis on quality" relying on workers' skills—such as seen in Daimler-Benz AG—indicate one of the German characteristics in deploying the Ford system. In most cases, the Ford system itself remained the very "ideal model" that was the goal in Germany at the time.

When the piecework was adopted under the flow production system in Germany, compelling workers to follow the faster work tempo functioned more strongly. The piecework that was applied to workers at the group unit could further strengthen such a function. In such cases, the task standard was set on the basis of the fastest time of a first-class worker instead of "normal output" based on the average time of a mean worker in the REFA system. This time was established by measuring the highest speed of the most skilled and fastest workers with stopwatches to set the tempo of the belt conveyor.

The delay of mass production in the automobile industry that should have taken leadership of the development of mass production in many industrial sectors restricted the development of the national economy. The major factors determining such restrictions included the completion of the freight railroad network and passenger transportation, the state transportation policy that emphasized railways, insufficient road construction, and the heavy tax burden of automobile ownership and use due to state tax policies and customs that restricted demand on production volume. Such situations significantly differed under the motorization policy of the Nazi state.

In the Nazi period, under the remarkable expansion of the munitions market, the possibility of mass production was given, and almost "American" sales conditions for Ford-like mass production were created, as seen in the industries related to munitions, such as the electrical industry. Differences existed in the progress and type of the flow production system between industrial sectors, between companies in the same industry, between product departments of the company, and between production processes. Nonetheless, such a production method was expanded on a scale not previously observed after 1936 when the Second Four-Year Plan started.

The special conditions of the munitions market, such as the diversity of munitions formulas, short delivery times, and the need for design changes due to frequent changes in military plans and drastic fluctuations in demand, led to the key issue of how flexibility could be secured to adapt production to such various market requirements. German enterprises were forced to implement flow production methods, considering production flexibility to adapt to specific munitions market conditions and acquire orders from the states, instead of implementing the American mass production method represented by the Ford system. As a result, the attempt to introduce the Ford system was an extension of the restrictive conditions of the 1920s in Germany. In this respect, how the mass production system was developed differed significantly from that in the US, where production could be expanded on the basis of the expanding domestic market, especially the consumer goods market.

The German way of developing the Ford system as a mass production system and its limitations also led to substantial restrictions in terms of the spread of the economic effects of mass production to related industries and the national economy in general. During the Weimar period, the automobile industry should have taken the lead in mass production; however, the narrowness of the domestic market, the intensifying competition from foreign (especially American) firms in the domestic market, and various export market difficulties severely delayed the industry. The delay in mass production in the automobile industry failed to generate sufficient growth in demand for many related industries ahead in the production process, which significantly restricted the development of mass production in those industries and the economic development based on it. At the same time, the constraints on mass production in related industries also limited the automobile industry's ability to lower its production costs due to a limitation in the declining costs of raw materials and semifinished goods and equipment. This situation also applied to the machinery industry, where the automobile industry's lag constrained its mass production and made it more expensive to manufacture machinery. This condition was also a limiting factor for rationalization in sectors such as the electrical industry, which was moving toward mass production using machine tools for processing. Germany (which faced market conditions at home and abroad) could not realize development where the pursuit of capital accumulation through rationalization simultaneously created and shaped the market demand due to the significant delay in the expansion of the automobile industry. The limitations of Germany during this period can be seen in this point, as well as the restrictions brought about by the intertwining of these industrial linkages.

During the Nazi period, the effects of mass production were limited to a specific "narrow" range of military demand. Unlike the mass production of consumer goods, especially durable consumer goods, the economic spreading effects from the creation of demand in other industries had to be relatively small in terms of the breadth of the related industries. The economic ripple effect of mass production of consumer goods, especially durable consumer goods such as automobiles, was considerable in the US. In contrast, mass production in the German military industry rarely reached the national economy. After World War II, the consumer goods market was fully expanded and developed, and the development and diffusion of such modern mass production in Germany proceeded in earnest, resolving the differences with the US.

Based on the discussions in this book, including those in Sect. 15.1.3, Table 15.3 illustrates the conditions surrounding business management changes in Germany until the end of World War II in the deployment of the Ford system and mass production.

15.1.4 Corporate Structure and Organizational Structure

Next, considering changes in corporate structure and organizational structure from the late nineteenth century to the beginning of World War I, we saw changes in corporate structure and organizational reforms that are the prototypes of today's big business. In Germany, modern business enterprises with multiple business units and managerial hierarchy (Chandler 1977, p.1) were also created and developed under corporate scale expansion, vertical integration progress, and partial diversification from the late nineteenth century onward.

Regarding changes in corporate structure, prominent progress of concentration occurred in capital-intensive industries, such as the iron, metal smelting, electrical engineering, and chemical sectors. The trend toward vertical integration appeared in almost the same period as when modern business enterprises rose in the US. Sales integration became a usual strategy in enterprises of many industrial sectors without limitation to industries like iron and steel, electrical, and chemical. The main form of the forward integration toward sales changed from membership in syndicates from 1887 to 1907 to establishing a company's own sales organization after 1907. Meanwhile, backward integration toward raw materials as a defensive policy progressed relatively strongly in the coal, iron and steel, and chemical industries, where securing raw materials became an important issue (Kocka 1981, S.48–50). The movement toward backward integration tended to be less active compared with forward integration. This situation differed from the period after World War I until the end of inflation when purchasing raw materials and consolidating companies in such sectors became significant as a countermeasure due to the tremendous price increase for raw materials. Furthermore, the existence of many enterprises that integrated all of the various stages of production from coal and iron mining or via the production of pig iron and steel through many stages of metal processing and occasionally even heavy machinery indicates a prominent characteristic of vertical integration in German firms.

The early diversification of the largest 100 manufacturing and mining firms was also important. Diversification was an attractive and effective means for companies to use capital-intensive equipment and existing valuable know-how. However,

Table 15.3 German business management until the end of World War II (deployment of the Ford system and mass production)

Management phenomenon	Ford system and mass production			
Period	Period of the Weimar Republic		Period of National Socialism	
	Standardization of production	Flow production system	Standardization of production	Flow production system
Socioeconomic backgrounds	• Strong competitive pressure in domestic and export markets from US enterprises • Necessity of thorough cost reduction based on mass production • Relatively positive attitude of labor unions to the Ford system due to its economic effect based on mass production, such as the low price based on cost reduction and high-wage cost • Positive evaluation of the Free Trade Union to the Ford system based on the Economic Democratic Theory emphasizing the significance of the development of productive forces • Insufficient criticism of the Ford system by the labor side despite its function of increasing labor intensity at the flow production method compared with the Taylor system		• Great market condition changes based on the expansion of munitions demands due to the militarization of the economy and the war economy • Serious shortage of labor force and a further lack of skilled workers due to the exodus to the military • Policy to promote motorization and benefits from the regime's favorable policies for German automobile enterprises, such as tax incentives, allowing roadside parking, simplifying drivers' licensing, and lowering insurance and registration fees	
	• Standardization is an important issue of efficiency improvement and an important basis for the introduction of the flow production method • The necessity to implement standardization as an effective rationalization measure without capital expenditures under the conditions that rationalization in the field of technology encountered limitations due to a lack of capital and the burdensome capital costs it required	• Decisive necessity to thoroughly reduce costs under the strong competition pressure from foreign companies, especially US companies • Necessity for enterprises to cope with a trend of rigidity in wage decline brought about by the economic concessions through the mass production system and changes in the way of labor management	• Position of standardization and reduction of type as new goals of the economic policy of Fascism • The progress of standardization due to the involvement of the state in promoting rationalization under the militarization of the economy • Standardization activity as a central task decided in the urgent plan of the Ministry for the Economy in May 1939 • The low degree of capital concentration and the extremely small production lots of any product in the German automobile industry	• The tremendous expansion of the munitions market under the militarization of the economy • Necessity to cope with a severe lack of a labor force, particularly skilled workers • The further serious shortage of skilled workers due to the exodus of them to the military during wartime

(continued)

Table 15.3 (continued)

Management phenomenon	Ford system and mass production			
Period	Period of the Weimar Republic		Period of National Socialism	
	Standardization of production	Flow production system	Standardization of production	Flow production system
	• Unlike the US, where the standardization of consumption had progressed, an obstacle to standardization due to consumer individualism • Necessity to pursue cost reduction by the production of a unified type in large lots due to competition in foreign markets		• High cost of raw materials for the German automobile due to the delay in parts standardization • The necessity to reduce the types of passenger cars for civil demand to a minimum for the German market from the national economic perspective after the outbreak of World War II, unlike truck production	
Actual conditions of management phenomenon	• First systematic attempts to reduce product type and standardization as a movement during World War I • Systematic efforts toward standardization by agencies that took charge of establishing norms, such as organizations formed during World War I and the German Standards Committee of Industry (Normenausschuß der Deutschen Industrie) founded in 1917, and the German Standards Committee (Deutscher Normenausschuß, “DNA”) founded in 1926	• Trend to the arrangement of belt conveyors primarily in pre-assembly, final assembly, and packaging • Great difference in diffusion of the flow production system between individual industrial sectors and between product departments in the same industry and among production processes • The sporadic cases in which transformation to the flow production system was performed in all casting and forging processes, mechanical processing, and assembly, and a high-level transportation system between processes was introduced	• Efforts of standardization based on the remarkably increasing norms set by the German Standards Committee (DIN norm lists) • Beginning of compulsory application of standardization by order of the minister of the economy with the Second Four-Year Plan in 1936 • More urgent and systematic development of standardization efforts with the outbreak of World War II • Standardization and the reduction of product types strongly and systematically driven by the state in the processing and assembly industries and industrial sectors related to munitions under the task of realizing the mass production of munitions	• Expansion of the flow production after 1936 on a scale not previously observed • The eager introduction of belt conveyors that were not observed in very small enterprises until 1933 • Attempts to complete the flow production system and install the partially or completely automatic machines under the conveyor much more effectively in the metal processing industry • Methods such as flow production that were not very developed in the consumer goods industries

(continued)

Table 15.3 (continued)

Management phenomenon	Ford system and mass production			
Period	Period of the Weimar Republic		Period of National Socialism	
	Standardization of production	Flow production system	Standardization of production	Flow production system
	• The most aggressive pursuit of the standardization of production in the automobile and electrical engineering industries • Progress of standardization in the electrical engineering industry due to a high degree of concentration by Siemens and AEG • Differences in the development of standardization between consumer goods products, in which it progressed relatively easily, and producer goods or products, in which the cycle of innovation was short and product innovation was rapidly implemented	• Even in product sectors and production processes in which the flow production system using the conveyor was introduced, many existences of other variant forms different from "the conveyor system" in which each task was performed with moving forms according to conveyor movement • Attempts to adopt various methods of flow production • Efforts to organize the flow production system characterized as a sort of "elastic flow production" that enabled to cope with the possibility of much smaller sales compared with the United States, change in demand, and relatively many types of products • Overwhelming rate of the flow production system organized without the conveyor in the entire machinery industry, excluding the partial product sectors • Actual condition in which the Ford system itself was "an ideal type" that was regarded as a goal in Germany at the time • Momentary end of the expansion of the flow production system with the world economic crisis	• Differences in the progress of standardization between industrial sectors, such as seen, for example, between the electrical engineering industry, where such changes were prominent, and the machine tool industry, where thorough standardization was difficult because standard machines had to adapt to the structure and volume of parts to be produced and between enterprises or product departments in the same industry	• Two different types of development of mass production systems in the automobile industry, such as the cases of Adam Opel pursuing American mass production and Daimler-Benz pursuing "the flexible production concept with an emphasis on quality" • Differences in the progress and type of the flow production system between industrial sectors, between companies in the same industry, between product departments of the company, and between production processes • Many cases in which attempts to secure production flexibility in the development of the flow production system were implemented

(continued)

Table 15.3 (continued)

Management phenomenon	Ford system and mass production			
Period	Period of the Weimar Republic		Period of National Socialism	
	Standardization of production	Flow production system	Standardization of production	Flow production system
German characteristics of management phenomenon	• Development of the "Standardization movement" pursued as a line in the chain of the rationalization movement during the relatively stable period of the 1920s (1924–1929) • More systematic development in Germany than in other countries • Significant role of the German Standards Committee, such as seen in the increase in the number of norms (standards) set by this committee • Cases in which standardization was implemented being led by the core institutions of the company, such as the central norm department	• Development of the flow production system as a primitive form rather than the "complete" form • Many attempts at the introduction of the flow production system aimed at obtaining some of the benefits of mass production, even with decreased production output, and securing a certain level of flexibility for dealing with demand fluctuations between products • Cases in which variant forms of the flow production system using a conveyor other than the conveyor system, such as the "standstill work type of flow production," the method called the "conveyor type of tact system," and the "changeable flow production" (die wechselnde Flieβarbeit) • A decisive role of "the changeable flow production" as an attempt to organize flow production to flexibly change large volumes and diverse types in efforts to pursue more suitable methods for German conditions • Cases in which the adoption of piece work, including those applied to workers at the group unit under the flow production system, compelled workers to have a faster work tempo in the dual manners by combining the conveyor work with peace work	• Systematic efforts of standardization and reduction of type that were driven by the compulsion of the state • Stronger involvement and compulsion by the state in the efforts of standardization during wartime • Great significance of introducing standards developed at the plant level • Role of state forces in coping with the high market risk of specialization in a few types of products through enforcing such rationalization measures, unlike cartel policy as a measure to cope with such problems in the Weimar period • Significant role of cartel organizations in driving standardization • Cases in which good effects of standardization were achieved by the cooperation of manufacturers integrated into organizations such as the industrial associations and the circle organization or special committees and working committees organized to advance more rapid and intense type reduction • Cases in which standardization was pursued by using "the unit system" that enabled model variety and economically viable production volumes	• Attempts to organize the flow production system to secure a certain level of flexibility for dealing with demand fluctuations between products rather than the American model of mass production fundamentally to manufacture the same types of products in massive numbers • "The flexible production concept with an emphasis on quality" aimed to adapt to changes in demand thoroughly to secure the labor process flexibility and the interchangeability of the product variations to be manufactured and to produce products of a much higher quality than American competitors as an important basis for avoiding competition with them

(continued)

Table 15.3 (continued)

Management phenomenon	Ford system and mass production			
Period	Period of the Weimar Republic		Period of National Socialism	
	Standardization of production	Flow production system	Standardization of production	Flow production system
		• Attempts at building the flow production system characterized as a "flexible production concept with an emphasis on quality," such as that seen in Daimler-Benz AG • Cases where the task standard was set on the basis of the fastest time of a first-class worker instead of "normal output" based on the average time of a mean worker in the REFA system by measuring the highest speed of the most skilled and fastest workers with stop watches at setting the tempo of the belt conveyor • Endeavors to implement more effective production methods in the machinery industry: (1) production by product type, (2) how production for both smaller and larger series was performed with the same workers and at the same conveyor, and (3) the "mixed production" in which series production was performed in mechanical processing and flow production was implemented in the assembly process • Transformation of the principle for forming the flow production from "specialization" in the Ford system to "universalization"		

(continued)

Table 15.3 (continued)

Management phenomenon	Ford system and mass production			
Period	Period of the Weimar Republic		Period of National Socialism	
	Standardization of production	Flow production system	Standardization of production	Flow production system
Factors determining German development of management phenomenon	• Urgent and decisive challenge of rationalization for rebuilding enterprises, industries, and the economy • Influence of the development of rationalization as a national movement • Shortage of capital and burden of capital costs • Influences of consumer individualism	• Influence of the narrow and intensely changing domestic market and the necessity for production in small lots and to secure production flexibility • The original characteristics of the German and European markets, such as demand preferring specific modes and changeable liking of customers • Trend of diversity of products in Germany compared with the United States due to the delay in standardization of consumption • Standardization degree determined by the market characteristics and conditions of each product as one of the essential factors of difference in the development of the flow production system between products • Influences of the lower ratio of wages to total production costs and the higher ratio of material costs to total production costs in the automobile industry compared with the United States	• Necessity to create the important foundation for the mass production of munitions • Frequent changes in the type of munitions to be produced and the transformation of production goals due to modifications or fundamental changes in the plans for the munition preparation • Influence of the existence of many very small enterprises employing 100 workers at most and a low level of concentration on the delays and limitations in the efforts of standardization in the machinery industry	• Necessity to realize the mass production of munitions • Characteristics of the munition market such as varieties of munitions, the frequently changing demand with modifications or fundamental changes in the plans for the munition preparation, the rapidity of technological innovation, short delivery times, and the necessity for companies to make the flow production method adapt to such unique market characteristics

(continued)

Table 15.3 (continued)

Management phenomenon	Ford system and mass production			
Period	Period of the Weimar Republic		Period of National Socialism	
	Standardization of production	Flow production system	Standardization of production	Flow production system
		• Influences of factors restricting demand for automobiles on production volumes, such as the completion of the freight railroad network and passenger transportation, state transportation policy emphasizing railways, insufficient road construction, and the heavy tax burden of automobile ownership and use due to state tax policy and customs • Existence of excessive production capacity and its influence on the possibility of expanding productive forces by thorough investment		
Significance of management phenomenon	• Cost reduction effects of standardization • The role of standardization of production in cost reduction as the prerequisite condition for strengthening competitiveness • Significance of standardization of production as an important measure of rationalization that needed no capital expenditure • Standardization as an important basis of mass production based on the flow production system	• Establishment of compulsory work time at the flow production • Realization of the particular effects of cost reduction brought about by mass production • Increase in the ability to adapt production to markets and their changes by organizing production according to the principle of "generalization" and flexibility based on it	• Contribution of standardization efforts, such as extensive reductions in the types of products to the continued increase of production until the late of World War II despite the striking loss of plant facilities by bombing in wartime • More effective progress of standardization during wartime and many beneficial results	• Contribution of efforts to realize mass production based on the development of the flow production system to increase the capacity to supply munitions products for the army, such as seen in a truck known as "Opel Britz" produced at the Brandenburg plant in Adam Opel • Significance of attempts to build the flow production system that enabled us to secure production flexibility for adapting to the changing munitions markets and acquiring orders from the states

(continued)

Table 15.3 (continued)

Management phenomenon	Ford system and mass production			
Period	Period of the Weimar Republic		Period of National Socialism	
	Standardization of production	Flow production system	Standardization of production	Flow production system
Limitations of management phenomenon	• Obstacle to the standardization of production due to consumer individualism • Insufficient understanding of the merits of standardization • Restriction of the progress of standardization by difficulty for consumers to sufficiently recognize the benefits of mass-producing standardized products due to rare cases in which the amount that product prices declined equaled the cut in production costs enabled by standardization • Insufficient reduction of the number of car types, the very small effect of standardization of parts due to delays in such effort and product type reduction, and delay in the specialization of production within the company on account of the insufficient progress of parts standardization in the automobile industry	• Great delay of mass production in many industries in which the introduction of the Ford system was implemented • Great difference in the level of the production structure based on the Ford system between German automobile companies and the Ford Motor Co. despite various efforts to introduce the flow production system • Dominance of the system combining the flow of work and work conveyors and the very low rate of the employees working directly under conveyors in the automobile industry • Delay in the elimination of skilled workers by the introduction of the flow production system compared with the United States • Creating excess production capacity through introducing the flow production system and the decline of the operating rate brought about it • Great restriction of the delay of mass production in the automobile industry on the development of the related industrial sectors and national economy	• General conditions in which the contribution of standards to rationalization was not as significant as considered and further making norms compulsory was needed to enlarge their effect significantly • Trend in which standardization not only encountered limitations regarding capitalistic competition but also restricted technical advances, particularly during the years of war production • Restriction by strict reduction of type to the possibility of new design and the arrangement of special-purpose machines, which should significantly contribute to the improvement of productivity • Cases of reduction of product type that was not always suitable for mass production • Existence of cases where the constant change in the few existing types was implemented under wartime production	• Restrictive situation in which German enterprises were forced to implement flow production methods considering production flexibility to adapt to specific munitions market conditions, instead of the implementation of the American mass production method represented by the Ford system • Cases in which the production structure seldom reached that of the Ford Motor Co. despite efforts to realize the effects of mass production, such as seen in the case of Daimler-Benz • Insufficient adoption of mass production methods in the capital goods industry due to supplying a large variety of products under its individualistic and highly competitive nature and delay in specialization despite the tremendous expansion of the munitions market caused by the militarization of the economy and the war economy

(continued)

Table 15.3 (continued)

Management phenomenon	Ford system and mass production			
Period	Period of the Weimar Republic		Period of National Socialism	
	Standardization of production	Flow production system	Standardization of production	Flow production system
	• Delays and limitations in the reduction of product types and parts and the production specialization in the machinery industry due to three factors: (1) the existence of many small and medium firms, (2) the trend toward insufficient understanding of the merits of standardization or no interest in standardization activity, and (3) delays in concentration • Cases in which efforts to reduce the number of specifications and types of products were hindered by new product structures, such as those seen in the electrical industry • Cases where the design department that should play an important role in attempts to reduce type repeatedly encountered dilemmas between standardization efforts and endeavors to improve products		• A transitional phenomenon of standardization in which the types chosen in the introductory stage were added to existing standards during the war • Even in the case that once systematic goals such as the Schell program were established, existence of the phenomenon in which enterprises were forced to cope with excessive requests of this plan • Insufficient progress in the reduction of the type of electric motor due to failure in an attempt to limit manufactures to one or two suppliers • Limitations such as those seen in cases in which attempts to achieve the use of common parts between motor vehicles for military and civilian use based on interchangeability in truck production did not always succeed due to the dispersion of production • Trend to avoid specialization in the capital goods industry to secure competitiveness in the export market	• Delay in the mass production of machine tools based on the flow production system due to the existence of unused excessive production capacity and lack of production volume of machine tools enabling the implementation of genuine flow production as observed in the automobile industry despite the increase of the entire demand for machine tools for an enlarged economic sphere in Europe • Delay in the transformation into an economic structure in which the expansion of mass production's effects could reach many related industrial sectors by generating demand for many other industrial sectors of the entire national economy due to the underdevelopment of the consumer goods industries, in particular, durable consumer goods industries • Influence of delay in the development of the automobile industry, such as seen in the condition that the leading role of this industrial sector was forced to be limited to the technical field, unlike the United States, where this industry already became a leading sector not only technically but also economically

Source This table was compiled by the author, based on discussions in this book

the specific conditions, such as the relatively underdeveloped small-scale and low, transparent domestic market and the delay in the progress of the social division of labor, were concerned with such a trend. Among various industrial sectors, diversification was a much more limited phenomenon in the less capital-intensive and consumer goods industries than in the capital-intensive industries. Concentration on economies of scale and speed was emphasized in the US. In contrast, German enterprises emphasized economies of scope and vertical integration.

Concerning changes in organizational structure and management style, in many cases, as in the US, a centralized functional departmental structure was formed as a response to the management problems associated with the development of vertical integration. In enterprises where the company scale increased and business units were regionally dispersed, people employed for delegated tasks tended to take charge of management. Generally, the degree of the division of labor and decentralization depended on the number of business units and the business scale. In Germany, bureaucracy influenced changes in the organizational structure at the middle and lower levels of management. This situation can be seen in the emphasis on written procedures, regulations, and systematic job descriptions. However, the limitations of bureaucracy, such as slow responses, organizational bottlenecks, and excessive formalization, had become prominent due to the company's market dependence and particular achievement orientation and the importance of private property as a major source of legitimate power. Furthermore, the number of nonmanual employees as a new class within the company increased with the building of the middle and lower layers in management.

In Germany at the time, although diversification tended to be more advanced than in the US, adopting an organization-like divisional structure did not progress. In most cases, diversification was in the form of expansion into related products within existing business fields. Diversification from the formation of monopolies to World War I was not the same as that seen in the 1920s, where companies diversified into fields outside their main businesses, nor was it often pursued as a clear growth strategy. Therefore, the companies rarely dealt with multiple product lines under very different conditions regarding production, sales, purchasing, etc., which did not cause as many problems in corporate management as in the 1920s. As a result, organizational structures such as decentralized divisional organizations did not need to be created in most cases. One important exception was Siemens's case in the electrical industry, where diversification was high, ranging from the heavy- and light–current fields.

Furthermore, various measures for institutions of the central office were implemented. Some large firms established organizations such as executive committees within the board of directors to represent the firm's business operations and various committees to perform staff functions to support the executive committees. A trend toward functional separation of the directors' duties occurred, such as in manufacturing, commercial management, and overall management, with the establishment of a central office. Reform of the accounting system was implemented through the foundation of departments, such as the calculation and inspection departments, to strengthen the central office function. The creation of the executive's representative organization as the core top management organ and the creation of committee organizations as staff institutions for support and advice to top management also progressed.

In Germany and the US, there was a trend toward the retreat of the owner executives and the rise of the salaried managers. The family's roles were important in solving industrial business management problems at the early stage of the development of capitalism because of its economic functionality and the lack of effective alternatives. However, the need to provide a driving force in the development of industrial capitalism around the outbreak of World War I tended to decline compared with the period in the middle of the nineteenth century. The establishment of many corporations in the form of joint-stock companies and their rapid diffusion and vertical expansion accelerated the rise of managerial enterprises. However, managerial enterprises only had a relatively minor existence, and entrepreneurial and owner enterprises were still predominant even in the 100 largest enterprises despite an apparent increase in the former. Significant growth of managerial enterprises did not occur until after World War I when rationalization and mergers and acquisitions became a prominent phenomenon. Even then, many entrepreneurial firms remained among the largest 100 firms, and the influence of owner executives was still stronger in Germany than in the US. However, considering the issue of the type of company and its management reveals that the development of an oligopolistic market inevitably led to more and more similar strategies, as seen in Siemens and AEG in the electrical industry, compared to companies managed by family and proprietors. Therefore, it is important to understand how companies respond to growth challenges in the context of their managerial behavior.

Regarding managerial background, professional managers were more likely than owner-managers to have had secondary or higher education; however, the tendency for secondary and higher education to replace capital ownership as a prerequisite for managerial positions has been a slow and prolonged process. In this respect, there was a significant difference compared to the US, where advanced professional education at universities and graduate schools (business schools) played a major role in training professional managers.

In terms of the behavioral pattern of salaried managers, they tended to emphasize long-term planning, preserving, and expanding the company, preferring future profits to short-term opportunities to maximize profits and regarding the company's continuance as their primary purpose. They also tended to emphasize reinvestment rather than dividend payments, which was deeply connected with their professional characteristics.

Furthermore, changes in corporate and organizational structures appeared after World War I. Corporate structure changes were caused by enterprise concentration aimed at effectively reorganizing business units and diversification. At the beginning of the relatively stable period in the 1920s, reducing excessive production capacity and pursuing rationalization focusing on the concentration and specialization of production based on product type became a decisive task. Enterprise concentration in the form of trust had great significance as an effective countermeasure. The corporate structure changed regarding the composition of business units dispersed according to product or region by considering regional conditions and merits of the division of labor. Such reorganization built an important basis for promoting active initiatives of each operating unit and competition among similar business units. Furthermore, diversification changed the corporate structure by adding and reorganizing business fields, giving the potential to cope with the business cycle by leveling the differences in the trade cycle among business fields. However, some new business areas did not always produce satisfactory results and profitability. These limitations were due to difficulties in markets (such as the narrow, changeable, and only insufficiently expanding domestic market) and stringent circumstances in the export markets, such as strict competition with foreign companies and the accumulation of excess production capacities despite diversification into promising new business fields.

Moreover, organizational reforms were undertaken with the full-scale development of enterprise concentration in the form of trusts and the pioneering development of diversification. IG Farben AG and Vereinigte Stahlwerke AG are representative examples from this period; this book focuses on IG Farben.

The organizational changes in these companies were a response to the management problems associated with the development of concentration and rationalization (concentration and specialization of production by product) in the mid-1920s.

In the first stage, managerial problems caused by enterprise concentration and the production concentration and specialization based on product type were the background of IG Farben's organizational reform. Organizational reform was required to cope with management problems with the dispersion of each plant without being closed according to product or region. As a result of the concentration of enterprises on an industrial scale, it became important to reorganize many companies, factories, and sales organizations to efficiently manage, control, and coordinate the various activities of these massive enterprises and rationalize the entire corporate organization.

The concentration and specialization of production (according to product types among the many factories) was a kind of "contractual division of labor" within the trust, dividing the market by product and allocating production to each. The remaining factories that were not closed were dispersed by product sort or region, creating clusters of factories producing a particular product or related products in the primary regions. The main task of each factory was to formulate their production plans and produce a specific product group under the most favorable conditions, which required them to reorganize their production organizations under the principle of "decentralized centralization."

Based on this principle, the regionally divided groups called "the Operating Community" ("Betriebsgemeinschaft") were formed. In each group, routine factory problems were relayed to one of these subsidiary managerial groups, and each plant was primarily responsible for its technical direction and labor. The "centralized, vertically formed organizational structure according to product management" and "regional, horizontal management of individual production locations" were created. This reform aimed to provide a foundation for securing maximum flexibility and to actively increase the initiative of different plants in various places by decentralizing management to regional factory groups that would form a cohesive management unit. Promotion of ideal competition among the operating communities under the central office's control was pursued.

Meanwhile, centralization of the sales department was attempted, and five sales groups organized according to product (called the "sales community" [Verkaufsgemeinschaft]) were built. This change aimed to make the best use of the very abundant experience of marketing of merged enterprises. The concentration of sales and marketing control in the hands of the sales community contributed to the significant simplification of the whole commercial end and the reduction of marketing costs.

Creating various committee organizations at the top management and operational levels was an important characteristic of organizational structure reform in IG Farben. The Working Committee (Arbeitsausschβ) was established to improve the efficiency of top management's business execution as a representative execution organization within the managing board. The Technical Committee (Technicher Ausschuβ) was established as the highest organization concerning technical affairs, and the Commercial Committee (Kaufmännischer Ausschuβ) was established as the highest institution concerned with fundamental and important commercial matters for all sales group issues. The Technical Committee enabled managers to understand accurate outlines of production and costs in various factories, and the committee's activities provided the central source of information for the board of directors. These organizations were a very elaborate structure of committees aimed at creating the necessary flexibility within the company before making decisions.

Furthermore, a series of central departments were founded to deal with the problems of the entire enterprise as staff organizations, such as central finance, national economy, economic policy, central purchasing, and press departments. Various committees were also set up as staff organizations to improve the headquarters management structure and help the Working Committee.

In this way, in the first stage of organizational reform, a system for reinforcing management functions at both the top management and operational levels was built. Moreover, the improvement of initiatives and the promotion of ideal competition at the level of the operating departments by management decentralization were pursued. However, efforts to create an organizational structure to cope with management diversification issues were implemented in organizational reform at the first stage despite the development of diversification after the merger. Therefore, the second stage of organizational structure reform was needed.

IG Farben faced two serious, unforeseen management problems as the company diversified its business. Under the centralized functional structure, the heads of departments confronted difficulties in dealing with diverse product fields in which the operating conditions for fundamental functions, such as production, sales, and purchasing, differed significantly. These middle- and lower-level operational management limitations made it challenging for top management to focus on entrepreneurial or executive decisions, such as allocating business resources from the perspective of long-term administration and the entire enterprise. As an organizational response, a new organizational structure was created. It comprised three product divisions (consolidated according to the technologically or chemically related products) and the Central Committee (Zenralausschuβ), a smaller representative body of the board of directors than the Working Committee. The Central Committee's most important duties were decisions regarding the fundamental principles of business policy and the selection of managers. This top decision-making institution primarily aimed to make organization members concentrate on strategic decision-making by separating tasks from day-to-day operational duties and achieving the division of labor in general management functions with the Working Committee. One important characteristic can be seen in the high rate of chemists among members of the Central Committee and the significant roles of chemists in the three divisions and operating communities.

IG Farben was a prime example of organizational innovation in German companies during this period; however, in contrast to the success of Du Pont in the US, such organizational reforms had significant limitations. The number of product-specific business units (divisions), which were important in separating the top management from the actual business operations, was small regarding the overall business area and the differences among the business areas. Therefore, it was impossible to fully overcome the management problems when multiple product lines with different production, sales, and purchasing conditions were handled in a functional division organization. Furthermore, the divisions did not function as profit centers with independent profitability. Not adopting the self-supporting accounting system as a core element of decentralized management in the divisional structure became a primary factor in determining limitations in such organizational reforms. Furthermore, the lack of an organization that could function as a general staff to assist management in strategic decision-making was another factor that limited organizational innovation. In contrast to Du Pont (IG Farben's largest competitor), the success or failure of these organizational changes affected its investment decisions in diversified business areas and significantly affected the company's subsequent development through investment decisions (Yamazaki 1997, Chapter 9).

Based on the discussions in this book, including those in Sect. 15.1.4, Table 15.4 visualizes the conditions surrounding business management changes in Germany before the end of World War II in the field of corporate and organizational structure.

15.2 "Continuity" in Business Management Before and After World War II and Its Significance

Based on the examinations in Sect. 15.1, this section examines how "continuity" can be seen in business management before and after World War II. The special character of the development of German capitalism until the end of the war presented business management with restrictions caused by market conditions and competitive structure. How was the progress of business management development in this period, and how did it influence and contribute to business management in the postwar period? These

Table 15.4 German business management until the end of World War II (corporate and organizational structures)

Management phenomenon	Corporate and organizational structures			
Period	Period of the Second Reich		Period of the Weimar Republic	
	Corporate structure	Organizational structure	Corporate structure	Organizational structure (Case of IG Farbenindustrie AG)
Socio economic backgrounds	• The development of modern industrial capitalism based on technological progress and the integrated domestic market in the second half of the nineteenth century • Five major factors of the rise of the modern business enterprise: (1) the process of expansion, integration, and diversification; (2) the emergence of cartels and associations; (3) changes in the relationship between industry and banks; (4) the rise of managerial capitalism with its tendency toward the separation of ownership and control and the appearance of salaried entrepreneurs; and (5) the increasing importance of science and systems in production, distribution, and management • The enterprise's expansion, integration, and diversification process as the most important factor in the birth of the modern business enterprise		• Necessity to reduce excessive production capacity and to develop rationalization focusing on the concentration and specialization of production based on product type and great significance of enterprise concentration in the form of trust as an effective means of countermeasure • Necessity to find new prospective business fields and enter into various fields in the chemical industry, such as synthetic ammonia, synthetic methanol, artificial oil, synthetic rubber, light metal, artificial and staple fiber, and synthetic resin	• Managerial problems caused by enterprise concentration and the concentration and specialization of production based on product type from the perspective of the "division of labor based on contracts" as the background of the organizational reform of IG Farben AG in the first stage • Managerial problems that appeared with the dispersion of each plant without being closed according to product or region and the birth of groups of plants in primary regions that produced specific products or related products as a factor determining organizational reform of IG Farben AG in the first stage • Managerial problems with changes in the structure of business fields caused by diversification under the centralized functional structure, such as seen in two major points in the organizational reform of IG Farben AG in the second stage: (1) difficulties in which the heads of departments confronted in dealing with diverse product fields in which operating conditions for fundamental functions such as production, sales, and purchasing differed significantly and (2) difficulty in concentration by top management on entrepreneurial or executive decisions such as allocating business resources from the perspective of long-term administration and the entire enterprise due to limitation in middle- and lower-level operational management

(continued)

Table 15.4 (continued)

Management phenomenon	Corporate and organizational structures			
Period	Period of the Second Reich		Period of the Weimar Republic	
	Corporate structure	Organizational structure	Corporate structure	Organizational structure (Case of IG Farbenindustrie AG)
Actual conditions of the management phenomenon	• Prominent progress of concentration in capital-intensive industries, such as the iron, metal smelting, electrical engineering, and chemical sector • Trend toward vertical integration in almost the same period as the rise of modern business enterprises in the United States • Trend in which sales integration was a usual strategy in enterprises of many industrial sectors without limitation to industries like the electrical, chemical, and distillation industries • Changes in the main form of integration from membership in syndicates from 1887 to 1907 to the establishment of a company's sales organization after 1907 • Relatively substantial progress of backward integration toward raw materials as a defensive policy in the coal, iron, steel, and chemical industries • Trend to the appearance of early diversification in the largest 100 manufacturing and mining firms	• Appearance of enterprises in which management was increasingly controlled by people employed for delegated tasks with regional dispersion of business units brought about by the enlargement of enterprise scale • Dependence of the degree of the division of labor and decentralization on the number of business units and the scale of business and top managers in individual enterprises • Centralized functional structure as the dominant form of organizational structure due to the progress of vertical integration by internalization of different functions such as sales and purchase, as in the cases in the United States • Exceptional case of organization similar to the divisional structure due to conditions that managerial problems with diversification under the functional structure: (1) the difficulty encountered by each department's head manager in keeping pace with basic functions such as the production, sales, and procurement of a division where multiple and vastly different product lines are managed together and (2) the top management's frustration with making administrative decisions rather than executive decisions, such as allocating corporate or long-term business resources, were still not decisively caused unlike the 1920s • Trend of functional separation of the duties of directors into three fields of manufacturing, commercial management, and the entire management, with the establishment of a central office	• Corporate structure change in terms of the composition of business units that were dispersed according to product or region • A definite tendency toward diversification into the production of products outside the department and change in corporate structure in terms of the business structure in the 1920s	**<Organizational reform of IG Farbenindustrie AG in the first stage>** • Attempt to promote initiatives of different plants located in various places by management decentralization as the central responsibility of management • The "centralized, vertically formed organizational structure according to product management" and "regional, horizontal management of individual production locations" as the dominant forms of organizational structure • Formation of the regionally divided groups called "the Operating Community" ("die Betriebsgemeinschaft"), based on the principle of "decentralized centralization," in which all routine factory problems were relayed to one of these subsidiary managerial groups, and each plant was primarily responsible for its technical direction, labor • Foundation of five sales groups, organized according to a product called the "Sales Community," and centralization of the sales department to best use the abundant marketing experience of merged enterprises [The five sales groups were (1) dye, (2) chemicals, (3) pharmaceuticals, (4) photography and artificial silk, and (5) nitrogen]

(continued)

Table 15.4 (continued)

Management phenomenon	Corporate and organizational structures			
Period	Period of the Second Reich		Period of the Weimar Republic	
	Corporate structure	Organizational structure	Corporate structure	Organizational structure (Case of IG Farbenindustrie AG)
	• A much more limited phenomenon of diversification in less capital-intensive industries and the consumer-goods industries in general • Diversification as an attractive and more effective strategy for companies to use capital-intensive equipment and existing valuable know-how	• Progress of reform of the accounting system through the foundation of departments, such as the calculation department and the calculation inspection departments, for strengthening the central office function • Establishment of the executive's representative organization as the core top management organ • Creating committee organizations as staff institutions for support and advice to top management • Increase in the number of nonmanual employees as a new class within the company by building the middle and lower layers of organization in management • Progress of separation to a certain degree between capital ownership and the administration of enterprises during the late Second Reich as well as the Weimar period • A relatively minor existence of managerial enterprises and the majority of entrepreneurial enterprises and owner-enterprises in the 100 largest corporations despite an apparent increase in the former • Rare cases of managerial enterprises among the smaller companies compared with the 100 largest corporations • Tendency for salaried managers to emphasize long-term planning, preserving, and expanding the company and preferring future profits to short-term opportunities to maximize profits and regard the continuance of the company as their primary purpose • Trend of salaried managers to emphasize reinvestment rather than dividend payments		• Creation of various committee organizations at the level of top management and operational fields, such as the Working Committee (Arbeitsausschβ) as a representative execution organization within the managing board, the Technical Committee (Technicher Ausschuβ) as the highest organization concerning technical affairs, and the Commercial Committee (Kaufmännischer Ausschuβ) as the highest institution concerned with fundamental and important commercial matters for all sales group issues • Foundation of a series of central departments to deal with problems of the entire enterprise as staff organizations, such as the central finance, national economy, economic policy, central purchasing, and press departments **<Organizational reform of IG Farbenindustrie AG in the second stage>** • Creation of a divisional organizational structure composed of three divisions consolidated according to the technologically or chemically related products in the organizational reform of IG Farben AG in the second stage • Responsibilities of the general manager as the chairman of the division to the managing board for R&D programs, all problems relating to salaried staff, and technical matters of his division • Establishment of the Central Committee (Zenralausschuβ), whose most important duties were decisions regarding fundamental principles of business policy and the selection of managers, as the top decision-making institution composed of fewer members than the Working Committee to enable members of the new committee to devote themselves to strategic decision-making

(continued)

Table 15.4 (continued)

Management phenomenon	Corporate and organizational structures			
Period	Period of the Second Reich		Period of the Weimar Republic	
	Corporate structure	Organizational structure	Corporate structure	Organizational structure (Case of IG Farbenindustrie AG)
German characteristics of the management phenomenon	• Predominance of the producer goods industries over the consumer-goods industries in transformations to the joint-stock company and the expansion of enterprise scale as a different trend from that in the United States • Membership in cartels or syndicates as a means for a firm to integrate forward without establishing its own sales organization • The existence of many enterprises that integrated all production stages, from the mining of coal and iron or via the production of pig iron and steel through many stages of metal processing and occasionally heavy machinery	• Influence of bureaucracy on changes in organizational structure at the middle and lower levels of management (Emphasis on written procedures and regulations and systematic job descriptions) • Organizational structure similar to divisional structures in the early stage at Siemens • Stronger influence of owner-managers in German firms than in American firms as a general trend • Use and roles of family resources in solving industrial business management problems and decline of necessity to provide a driving force in the development of industrial capitalism around the outbreak of World War I as they did in the middle of the nineteenth century	• The thorough pursuit of building the division of labor based on concentration and specialization of production according to product type compared with other countries considering regional conditions due to the serious excess production capacity at the beginning of the relatively stable period • Stronger diversification into the broader product areas in IG Farben, even compared with US enterprises	**<Organizational reform of IG Farbenindustrie AG in the first stage>** • Organizational reform based on the "decentralized centralism" principle of IG Farben AG in the first stage • A broad delegation of authorities regarding autonomous management activities as an effective means for making plans according to products and executing production • Horizontal integration as the main principle guiding decentralized management to offer a foundation for securing maximum flexibility and individual initiative in the management of the separate plants • Arrangement of managers to combine competent functional fields such as science, production, technical affairs, wages and salaries, and accounting and calculation with each plant within the operating community

(continued)

Table 15.4 (continued)

Management phenomenon	Corporate and organizational structures			
Period	Period of the Second Reich		Period of the Weimar Republic	
	Corporate structure	Organizational structure	Corporate structure	Organizational structure (Case of IG Farbenindustrie AG)
	• Trend of the stagnant movement toward backward integration after 1907, with an exception in the period after World War I until the end of inflation when the price of raw materials rose tremendously • Unlike the United States, where concentration on economies of scale and speed was emphasized, trend of German enterprises to attach great importance to economies of scope and vertical integration • Progress of integration and diversification at almost the same time (despite the slightly earlier appearance of the former)	• Differences in recruitment and career patterns of salaried managers at top management levels between managerial enterprises and owner-enterprises (tendency of salaried managers to have received more secondary and university-level education than owner-entrepreneurs) • Gradual and long-term movement toward the decline in the meaning of capital ownership as a premise for engaging in top management positions and the tendency for capital ownership to be replaced by general secondary education and secondary professional training		• Building accounting, statistics, and legal departments and committee organizations, taking charge of advice in each sales group (the "Sales Community") • A very elaborate structure of committees that created the necessary flexibility before making decisions **<Organizational reform of IG Farbenindustrie AG in the second stage>** • Creation of divisions suitable for managing the company's technical aspects • No adoption of a system in which the chairpersons of the division had responsibility for the profit and loss account of their product groups, unlike the case of Du Pont • The high rate of chemists among members of the Central Committee and the significant roles of chemists in the three divisions and operating communities

(continued)

Table 15.4 (continued)

Management phenomenon	Corporate and organizational structures			
Period	Period of the Second Reich		Period of the Weimar Republic	
	Corporate structure	Organizational structure	Corporate structure	Organizational structure (Case of IG Farbenindustrie AG)
Factors determining the German development of the management phenomenon	• State policy that approved cartels and syndicates • Delay in the development of the social division of labor and the characteristics of the domestic market, such as small scale and low transparency, as factors determining the trend of early appearance of diversification • Trend in which some factors bringing about diversification and integration became less powerful with the further development of the economy and the formation of a more elaborate overall division of labor and more transparent or predictable markets	• Necessity to cope with the limits of management based on the board majority system and realize quick decision-making by founding committee systems built departmentally and functionally in the managing board to secure uniform operation execution to deal with various forms of business created by diversification and functional integration and expansion of the business scale • Factors that determined the early appearance of organizational structures similar to divisional structures in Siemens: (1) high diversification ranging from the heavy- and light–current fields as the most important factor, (2) the role of tradition of family-ism in promoting top managers to display paternalistic leadership in organizational reforms, and (3) the bureaucratic tradition	• The necessity and importance of "negative rationalization" using enterprise concentration in old fields (such as dyes) and to reorganize production emphasizing the principle of the division of labor due to the broad existence of excessive production capacity with low operating rates and profitability in the relatively stable 1920s • Strong necessity to rapidly and broadly expand new production areas for the German chemical industry due to their high weight and the promising markets and business opportunities	**<Organizational reform of IG Farbenindustrie AG in the first stage>** • Enterprise concentration in the form of trust • Development of rationalization via trust focusing on production concentration and specialization based on product type and the regrouping of production organizations **<Organizational reform of IG Farbenindustrie AG in the second stage>** • Strong orientation toward committee organizations • The relative delay in the decentralization of management such as seen in divisional structure until then compared with the United States

(continued)

Table 15.4 (continued)

Management phenomenon	Corporate and organizational structures			
Period	Period of the Second Reich		Period of the Weimar Republic	
	Corporate structure	Organizational structure	Corporate structure	Organizational structure (Case of IG Farbenindustrie AG)
Significance of the management phenomenon	• Possibility to coordinate business processes by forward and backward integration in manufacturing companies • Expansion of room to pursue market opportunities and cope with economic cyclical change by coordinating the allocation of business resources among business fields • Possibility of coordinating production and market (consumption) by understanding market conditions and achieving throughput via integrating functions, such as sales and purchasing	• Modernization and improvement of the efficiency of management based on organizational structures • Beginning of managerial coordination among business processes such as purchasing, production, and sales • Progress to some degree of professionalization of management	• Building a foundation for cost reduction through the optimal allocation of production capacity based on product type among various plants • Building a basis for promoting active initiatives of each operating unit and competition among similar business units by further specialization • Possibility to pursue business opportunities through diversification • Potentiality to cope with the business cycle through leveling the difference in the trade cycle among business fields	**<Organizational reform of IG Farbenindustrie AG in the first stage>** • Improvement of initiatives on the level of the operating departments by management decentralization for each plant, scattered in regions, to formulate its manufacturing plan for each region and analyze the most favorable production conditions • Building an organizational structure aimed at achieving savings in various fields, such as avoiding unnecessary duplication, facilitating improvements in technological aspects, administration, and holding and managing inventory • Promotion of ideal competition among the Operating Communities under central office control • Great simplification of the entire commercial end of the chemical industry and reduction of marketing costs by the concentration of sales and marketing control in the hands of the Sales Community • Realizing company managers' better understanding of accurate outlines of production and costs in various factories and providing the central source of information for the board of directors through the activities of the Technical Committee

(continued)

Table 15.4 (continued)

Management phenomenon	Corporate and organizational structures			
Period	Period of the Second Reich		Period of the Weimar Republic	
	Corporate structure	Organizational structure	Corporate structure	Organizational structure (Case of IG Farbenindustrie AG)
				<Organizational reform of IG Farbenindustrie AG in the second stage> • Attempts to establish organizational structure enabling them to effectively cope with changes in business structure brought about by diversification • Efforts to make members of the Central Committee devote themselves to essential top management functions such as allocating business resources from the long-term perspective of the entire enterprise by separating their tasks from day-to-day operational duties and achieving the division of labor in general management functions with the Working Committee
Limitations of the management phenomenon	• Progress of diversification that was not always pursued as a definite growth strategy • Great limitations in the function of demand and supply coordination through membership in syndicates due to companies' sales organizations being unable to directly gain information regarding the market	• Limitations of bureaucracy in terms of slow responses, organizational bottlenecks, and excessive formalization due to the company's market dependence and particular achievement orientation, and private property as a significant source of legitimate power in the company	• Conditions that many new business areas did not always bring about satisfactory results and profitability due to the strict competition with foreign companies, the insufficiently expanding markets, and the accumulation of excess production capacities under such market circumstances despite diversification into some new promising business fields	• Difficulty in efficiently monitoring costs due to the system in which the proceeds from the sales after deducting expenses were credited to the concern's central financial administration • No efforts to create an organizational structure to cope with management problems with diversification in organizational reform at the first stage despite the development of diversification after the merger • Decrease in the influence of the Central Committee and increase in the importance of the administration of divisions and products departments in decision-making within IG Farben with the shift of Carl Bosch from managing board to supervisory board in 1935

(continued)

Table 15.4 (continued)

Management phenomenon	Corporate and organizational structures			
Period	Period of the Second Reich		Period of the Weimar Republic	
	Corporate structure	Organizational structure	Corporate structure	Organizational structure (Case of IG Farbenindustrie AG)
				• Unlike Du Pont, the failure of IG Farben in creating an organizational structure enabling members of the Central Committee to devote their efforts and time to allocating business resources from the perspective of long-term company growth and the whole enterprise due to three factors: (1) lack of a system in which each division dealt with only one product line in which conditions of fundamental functions, such as production, sales, and purchasing did not differ; (2) lack of a profit center system based on the self-supporting accounting of the divisions; and (3) disestablishment of organizations that should function as general staff

Source This table was compiled by the author, based on discussions in this book

problems are concerned with "continuity" or "discontinuity" in business management between the end of World War II and the postwar period.

In productive force, American technology and management methods were important bases of Germany's postwar development in Europe. Technical assistance under the framework of the Marshall Plan created more favorable conditions for learning and deploying technology and management methods from the US. The productivity movement led by the US promoted the introduction of American methods to increase productive forces (Yamazaki 2013, Chapter 2).

Furthermore, market conditions significantly changed in three aspects: expanding the domestic market based on the progress of equality of rights between the capital and labor sides, building a free trade system led by the US, and creating and enlarging common markets in Western Europe. Realizing the capital-labor equality of rights tended to be observed in other European advanced countries, greatly expanding the export market. The fact that the US forced numerous nations that received the Marshall Plan aid to open their markets to free trade significantly contributed to the promotion of free trade. Such changes in market conditions provided an important foundation for the progress of Americanization in business management and technology.

Thus, in postwar Germany, the full-scale introduction of the productive force was driven on the basis of American technology and management methods. Some parts of the primary management methods were already introduced during the period before the end of World War II and "continuity" with the postwar period can be understood. It is important to understand the development of business management in Germany until the end of the war as not only a "limitation" but also accurately interpret its positive significance. How did elements of business management in the period until the end of World War II succeed after the war and influence and contribute to postwar development? The points to be evaluated relative to postwar development are clarified through the following analysis.

First, the influence of REFA activities in the study of labor processes and the introduction of the REFA system to German enterprises in the deployment of industrial engineering (IE) after World War II is considered (Yamazaki 2013, Chapter 7). In Germany, there was a history of institutions such as REFA taking charge of the study of labor processes since the 1920s. The fields of REFA activity were expanded from primarily time studies to work studies, and job design and the methods developed by this organization were broadly introduced in various enterprises in many industries during the Nazi era. This became an important factor in the deployment of IE based on these experiences and the development of a hybrid form of IE combining German and American elements. Konrad Schlaich noted that, from an operational perspective, it was only natural that the spread of IE was attributed to REFA (Schlaich 1969, S.234). REFA was strongly involved in the introduction of IE and took the initiative in its development by holding training courses. Indeed, there were certainly efforts to reduce production times by partially adopting new IE methods on the basis of US practice, but these methods would not have succeeded without their incorporation into REFA's methods (Hämmerling 1960, S.127). REFA researched and examined various predetermined time methods including Methods-Time Measurement (MTM) and work factor (WF) for a long time and as a result decided to support WF, obtaining a license to use and disseminate the method (Jaeckel 1961, S.223; Pilz 1961, S.124). However, REFA did not, for the most part, deprioritize its own systems in promoting WF. As a result, these US methods were not widely adopted by German industry, unlike in countries such as Sweden where the creator of MTM, Harold Bright Maynard and his consulting firm, was highly successful in selling the method to corporations (Kipping 2004, p.36). The German industry created work studies on the basis of REFA thinking over several decades after World War II (Schwartmann 1975, S.205). The dissemination of IE was related to REFA activities and was greatly affected by US-based IE. Thus, the deployment and dissemination of American-style methods continued with the help of REFA's leadership in work studies and their activities in the 1920s, along with attempts to apply these methods to German circumstances under REFA's strong influence.

In the deployment of the Ford system, German elements during the prewar period succeeded and had positive significance. During the Weimar Republic, the introduction of the flow production system was aimed at obtaining some of the benefits of mass production, even with decreased production output, and securing a certain level of flexibility for dealing with demand fluctuations between products was attempted in many enterprises or plants instead of using methods without production elasticity such as the Ford system. The methods observed in Germany aimed at increasing the operating rate and realizing the economies of scale of mass production by securing lots based on the production of multiple products in the same manufacturing line and having the flexibility to deal with demand fluctuations by engaging production on the basis of the "universalization" rather than the "specialization" principle. Although market conditions significantly changed and the foundation of full-scale mass production was established after World War II, the experience of German enterprises until the end of the war made the most of and had a large significance in realizing an effective mass production system under a smaller market volume than the US.

Before the end of World War II, German enterprises pursued their own path that emphasized avoiding intense competition as much as possible by focusing on the quality market segment. After World War I, the promising markets for the German economy bust, capital for innovative new development was lacking, and limitations can be seen in the sale of high-innovative products and the belt conveyor production of mass products. Under the restricted possibility of developing the American path of Fordism, markets for diversified quality products in which the German economy could exhibit relative strength became vital (Abelshauser 2001, S.520). The "quality and a flexible production concept" aimed to secure competition in the niche, upper market segment as a specific method of responding to market limits. In rationalizing German enterprises during the 1920s, skilled workers were generally vital to the German variety of capitalistic production and manufacturing of higher-quality products (Meskill 2010, pp.125, 128). David Meskill points out (2010, p.134) that when the influences of restriction after World War I were mitigated and inflation ceased, many German industrialists became more convinced of the importance of the skilled worker as "an irreplaceable part of a policy of flexible rationalization"

(Meskill 2010, p.134). He stresses "in almost all cases, companies chose or learned from experience, to adopt mixed strategies that integrated improvements to physical and human capital" (Meskill 2010, p.123).

The basic principles of this production concept could also be observed in postwar Germany; that is, one can identify German characteristics in production methods and systems based on product design concepts such as avoiding price competition, positioning, and specific niche strategies in postwar international market expansion. Although work organization was based on a flow production system that may have been founded on a US model and these enterprises pursued economies of scale in mass production, the elements of high quality, knowledge-intensive production relying on skilled labor, and German-specific vocational education systems and specialist qualifications, such as the Meister system, were quite significant. The principle and idea of "quality and a flexible production concept" in the prewar period succeeded in causing production emphasizing to secure product quality in terms of functionality and labor flexibility and make the best use of worker skill and "diversified quality production" focused on niche market segments. The width of supply indicates a differentiation strategy of the German export economy oriented toward relatively strong specialized high productive sectors and especially resistant to competition and cyclical fluctuation (Abelshauser 2001, S.523). The diversified quality production contributed to establishing the foundation of Germany's international competitiveness in European markets.

Afterward, the limitations of the mass production system modeled after American methods represented by the Ford system became prominent under structural changes in capitalism that occurred after the 1970s and production system reforms consequently became an important management problem (Yamazaki 2024, Chapter 13). The production of numerous product types using the American mass production method was not easy given the problems with equipment investment and fixed cost amortization. Moreover, these efforts were not cost effective and proved inflexible in the face of changing demand. As a result, to realize the mass production of various products while satisfying demand fluctuations between different types of products became an important issue for business management. Indeed, market conditions during the 1920s in Germany in which realizing mass production of single product types using a specialized flow production line was not possible differed greatly from the period after the 1970s. But the German variant of mass production methods until the end of World War II included many effective elements for implementing flexible mass production and contributed to such development in the 1970s and the 1980s.

When examining such production developments in relation to the characteristics of the European prewar market, it is important to consider the differences in market character between Europe and the US and the commonalities between European markets before and after World War II. As abovementioned, the American market has been more homogeneous than other countries for many years (Chandler 1977, p.498) and therefore its standardization of consumption advanced. Considering these market and consumption characteristics, mass production and market competition aimed at fully standardizing production and such production premised mass market and mass consumption. American management styles and methods based on the principle of "efficiency improvement" were therefore created to reflect free competition and were compatible with those conditions in these markets. In the period after World War I, the US also introduced the newest, best, and most profitable means of production and production methods as the only victorious nation in this war. All European countries were already indebted during and after World War I (Weiss 1926, S.23–24), which greatly contributed to the high competitiveness of US enterprises and the economic predominance of this country.

In contrast, Germany did not experience the same advancement in consumption standardization as the US. Consumer individualism was dominant in Europe, including Germany, which became an obstacle to standardization. Even in the 1950s, many Europeans perceived mass-produced products as standardized and mass production contrary to individualism (Schröter 2005, p122). In the 1920s, whereas in the US, the effective use of labor forces and the standardization of production and consumption were characteristic (Rauecker 1925, S.743), consumer individualism was dominant in Germany. Even in the emergent period of World War I and in the first years after the war, consumer individualism hindered the production and sales standardization of necessities of life such as food and clothing (Rauecker 1925, S.744). Indeed, the enterprise concentration that occurred at the beginning of the rationalization movement in the 1920s built the foundation for standardization activities. Furthermore, the restriction of competition and the influence of consumer individualism made it easy for German enterprises to specialize in producing a few products through enterprise concentration (Bauer 1931, S.136–137). However, consumer individualism remained dominant, which became an obstacle to standardization and mass production. Moreover, during the 1920s, while the cartelized sector urgently needed consolidation, eliminating unproductive plans and enterprises with difficulty continuing to exist did not progress. Furthermore, the benefits of rationalization were wasted by monopolistic price policy, and the increasing displacement of labor forces brought about hollowing out the consumer goods market (Hagemann 1984, S.115).

In Germany, there were markets of various products for civil demand and intermediate goods reflecting this consumption pattern. The characteristics of such markets were an important factor in determining German-specific development of the Ford system in the period until the end of World War II as well as the narrowness of the German market and export difficulties. For instance, the orientation toward the "German flow work" in the German electrical industry's production in the interwar period was determined by the original factors of the German product market for both civil and industrial use such as changeable liking and temporal restrictions. It was a device to develop appropriate "mass production" for such market characteristics and attempt to create a unique, new model taking flexibility and varieties of production into consideration according to German changes in living and consumption patterns. The development of such flow production was determined by the original characteristics of the German market such as narrower markets at home than the US, demand preferring specific modes, and changeable liking of customers. Such conditions can be observed not only before World War II but also in the postwar period (Imakubo 2001, pp.19, 21). Therefore, the experience and practice of introducing the flow production system in the period before the end of World War II were significant in the development of mass production to adapt to German- or European-specific market conditions after the war.

The difference in market characteristics between Germany and the US is one of the most important and decisive factors determining the development of business management and corporate expansion peculiar to Germany. Bernd Dornseifer (1995, pp.197, 226) stressed the specific nature of the German market and its influence on the selection of competitive and corporate strategies and the evolution of peculiar managerial capitalism in this country. He pointed out the existence of two groups of industries that achieved a prominent level of international competitive power in Germany during the second phase of industrialization: the chemical industry and broad branches of the electrical and non-electrical machinery, equipment, and instruments industries (Dornseifer 1995, pp.197, 226). In the period from the late nineteenth century to the middle of the twentieth century, while being a remarkable strength to innovate in low-volume, high-value-added capital goods sectors with high international competitiveness, the retarded development of high-volume consumer goods markets restricted the innovation opportunities for German enterprises (compared with the US) (Dornseifer 1995, pp.201, 206, 225). Ulrich Wengenroth also emphasizes that despite the universal Americanization of the consumer goods market and the management style after World War II, the traditional dominance of the producer goods industry in West Germany was reinforced rather than weakened because of the new competitive advantage pattern among postwar European manufacturers (Wengenroth 1997, p.161). In contrast to the weak performance of innovation in the high-volume consumer goods industries, niches of the capital goods sectors could attain a high level of international competitiveness due to a threefold comparative advantage. This advantage included (1) a cost advantage in wages, (2) a broad supply of skilled labor, and (3) the existence of and access to a dense research infrastructure financed mainly by the state (universities and numerous research institutions supported by the state) (Dornseifer 1995, pp.206–208, 225–226). According to Dornseifer (1995, pp.208), the particular configuration of competitive advantages and disadvantages that occurred in the last third of the nineteenth century built the background for firms' strategic choice and organizational evolution. The strategic outcome was threefold: (1) "a continuing move into high-value-added, low-volume segments and niches," (2) "a preference for product differentiation," and (3) "rapid diversification mainly through internal product development." Such a particular configuration in Germany led to the development of "a type of technical managerial capitalism" (Dornseifer 1995, pp.212, 226). The heterogeneous characteristics of the German market, which differ from the homogeneous characteristics of the US market, became an important factor in determining the specific development of German enterprises (Plumpe 2018, S.38–39, 65, 89, 122; Plumpe 2006, S.72).

Thus, attempts to implement German enterprises' own flow production methods succeeded in production system development and German manufacturing appropriate for market structures in Europe emphasizing product technology, quality, and functionality. After World War II, the market characteristics and consumer behavior trended toward emphasizing technology, quality, and functionality and focus was put on competition in terms of quality. These market characteristics are not only seen in Germany but also in Europe, the core market for German exports. Thus, under market characteristics that differed from those in the US such as seen in aggressive price competition (Streeck 1997, pp.39–40), German enterprises tended to emphasize on product differentiation based on technology, quality, and functionality. Of course, the terms for a technological and qualitative competitive advantage differ vastly depending on the product and in product groups in which differentiation is difficult, the American method has more significance. However, the divergence of American and European market conditions is a generally important factor that defined the nature of business management in Germany.

In comparing Germany's business management until the end of World War II with that after the war, despite various attempts by German enterprises to adapt to the European markets an overall business management system suitable for this regional market as a core of export, as they did after World War II, could not be achieved sufficiently. In this sense, German business management before the end of Worl War II can be characterized as "unfinished management tailored to European markets." However, such experiences during this period laid the groundwork for attempts to establish a management system or style well-suited to European markets after the war.

Efforts to improve organizational structures before the end of World War II also succeeded in reform after the war. Indeed, organizational reforms at IG Farben between the 1920s and 1930s ended in failure in contrast to Du Pont's success. However, elements of German reform succeeded and were made use of. For instance, at Hoechst, one of largest chemical companies, committee organization at IG Farben was modeled on the adoption of a divisional structure (Winnacker 1971, S.184). In addition, experiences such as "the decentralized centralization" for building divisional structures during the period until the end of World War II influenced the pursuit of a German system in the deployment of American-style divisional structures after the war that reflected the management value and business traditions which were concerned with the authority-responsibility relations based on the highly centralized hierarchies as a cornerstone in German companies in the first few years after the war (Yamazaki 2024, Chapter 9; Dyas and Thanheiser 1976, p.128).

Endeavors to concentrate and specialize production according to product type among plants using trust as a type of enterprise concentration in the 1920s succeeded in the reorganization of corporate groups after World War II. In heavy industries, particularly, the iron and steel industry combined with coal mining, some large enterprises were forced to encounter the dissolution and their business units were divided into some succeeding enterprises according to the postwar occupation policy of victorious nations. The reconcentration of monopolies and reorganization of corporate group systems progressed apace after the mid-1950s. Enterprise concentration was driven considering the benefits of the division of labor between enterprises within a corporate group and between corporate groups. Each company chose to expand and integrate its production capacity in separate domains, seeking profit through a division of labor complementary to each product. This type of restructuring of industrial organizations helped create a system that exhibited economies of scale through the benefits of specialization and the division of labor. Such complementary product-based division of labor between companies was observed between corporate groups (Yamazaki 2013, Chapter 5. Also see Herrigel 2000; Dyas and Thanheiser 1976, p.92). Experience of production concentration and specialization according to product type among plants using trusts in the 1920s was applied to the reorganization of corporate groups that aimed at the benefits of the division of labor between enterprises after World War II. The principle of "a division of labor based on contract," such as observed at Vereinigte Stahlwerke and IG Farben, was successfully applied to the postwar system for the division of labor within corporate groups.

Thus, the prewar structure of domestic markets was replaced by an oligopolistic structure by means of a policy of deconcentrating and restructuring corporate groups after World War II. New developments in large corporate groups were created by reorganizing business structures that were adaptive to oligopolistic competition, which differed from the assumptions of the prewar German industrial organization and market structure (Yamazaki 2013, Chapter 5).

In this way, the original elements of business management in Germany until the end of World War II were used in the development of the management system and postwar organizational structure. In Germany, until the end of World War II, business management limits were under restrictive conditions of the domestic and export markets due to the lack of an international cooperative system. However, despite such limitations, the positive significance of business management during this period must be accurately evaluated by considering historical "continuity" as a foundation for the development of enterprises and management after the war.

Based on the discussions in this book, including those in Sects. 15.1 and 15.2, Table 15.5 visualizes the conditions regarding the continuity of business management in Germany until the end of World War II with the period after the war.

15.3 Pursuit of Economic Rationality in Germany: Origins of the Nature of Enterprise as a "Social Community"

Business management and enterprise development in Germany are inextricably linked to the characteristics of economic rationality it emphasizes. In Germany, managers, industrialists, and workers tended not to believe in the effectiveness of the market mechanism as those in the US and the UK did (Locke 1996, p.57). Under such circumstances, "social rationality" rather than "rationality for capital" has been emphasized. Economic prudence is centered on coordinating various stakeholders' interests, including workers. Such ideologies emphasize the importance of long-term profit rather than short-term profit in business and the nature of enterprise as a "social community" (Albert 1991, pp.105, 137, 231–232, 275). While labor relations such as the codetermination system highlight regal labor participation at the plant and corporate levels and the collective agreement system, German-style management has emphasized such social rationality. The transformation of "rationality for capital" to "social rationality" in pursuit of economic rationality has been highlighted in German

Table 15.5 Continuity of business management in Germany until the end of World War II with the period after the war

Management phenomenon	Enterprise concentration	The REFA system and labor management	The Ford system and mass production	Corporate and organizational structures
Continuity of business management until the end of World War II with the period after the war	•Application of experience of production concentration and specialization according to product type among plants using trusts in the 1920s to the reconcentration of monopolies and reorganization of corporate group systems, emphasizing the benefits of the complementary product-based division of labor between companies after the mid-1950s	• Deployment of Industrial engineering (IE) after World War II based on these experiences through expansion of the fields of REFA from primarily time and work studies; job design and the methods during the Nazi era and broad introduction of measures of this organization in various enterprises in many industries and the development of a hybrid form of IE combining German and American elements • Strong involvement and initiative of REFA in the introduction of IE by holding training courses and with the incorporation of IE methods into REFA's methods after World War II • Trend toward prioritizing its systems in promoting the work factor (WF) despite REFA's decision to support WF after research and examination of various predetermined time methods and influence of it on no wide adoption of these US methods by German industry after World War II due to experiences of REFA activities and the REFA system before the end of the war • The deployment and dissemination of IE with the help of REFA's leadership in work studies and their activities in the 1920s, along with attempts to apply these methods to German circumstances under REFA's strong influence	• Succeeding of German elements, such as seen in the introduction of the flow production system aimed at obtaining some of the benefits of mass production, even with decreased production output, and securing a certain level of flexibility for dealing with demand fluctuations between products until the end of World War II in the deployment of the Ford system and the full-scale development of mass production after the war • Succession of experiment in the transformation of the principle for organizing the flow production system from "specialization" to "universalization" to cope with the necessity to achieve the economies of scale of mass production under a smaller market compared with the United States and secure the flexibility to deal with demand fluctuations • Accession of the principle and idea of "a flexible production concept with an emphasis on quality" in the period before the end of World War II to the postwar development of production to secure product quality in terms of functionality and labor flexibility and make the best use of worker skill and "diversified quality production" focused on niche market segments • Using many practical elements of the German variant of mass production methods until the end of World War II in necessity to implement flexible mass production, enabling to secure economy of scale under smaller production lots and flexibility for coping with demand change among products kind in the 1970 and the 1980s • Applying the "unit system" as a principle that enabled model variety and economically viable production volumes to achieve economies of scale easily after World War II	• Succeeding of elements of German reform at IG Farben between the 1920s and 1930s, namely the committee organization system and its fundamental principle to adopting a divisional structure at Hoechst, one of largest chemical companies after World War II • The influence of experiences such as "the decentralized centralization" for building divisional structures in the period before the end of World War II on the deployment of American-style divisional structures after the war reflecting German management values and business traditions, which were concerned with authority–responsibility relations based on highly centralized hierarchies as a cornerstone in German companies in the first few years after the war

Source This table was compiled by the author, based on discussions in this book

management. The stress of such rationality has been an important determining characteristic of business management in Germany and an ideological foundation for an economic system known as a "coordinated market economy" (Hall and Soskice 2001).

Such German management values and the characteristics of economic rationality to be emphasized differ from those in the US, where the pursuit and realization of economic rationality through improving efficiency under free competition has been stressed as the basic principle of business management. Such thinking is based on a belief in market functions such as market mechanisms and emphasizes the benefits of creativity and merit brought about by competition. In Germany, the market should be the sole judge, and whether a company succeeds or fails in acquiring a market is the basis for a high position (Hampden-Turner and Trompenaars 1993, p.169). Pragmatism as a social ideology is an important background for prioritizing such rationality. In the American pursuit of economic rationality, "rationality for capital" is emphasized in business and management as an important element of management value for enterprises, which is deeply concerned with the profit orientation of the US enterprises. According to this way of thinking, a company is regarded as "the nexus of contract" and is thus regarded as an objective to be sold and purchased to improve economic efficiency regardless of the interests of labor forces and society. Companies' freedom to engage in merger-acquisition-takeover business maneuvers is fundamental in such a scheme of thinking, consistent with the dominance of equity financing, short-termism, and the priority given to shareholder value (Barsoux and Lawrence 1991, p.199). Thus, "US companies are managed toward the maximization of profits and the short-term satisfaction of shareholders: managers are rewarded mainly on profitability targets and strategies are designed to improve return on investments" (Calori 1994, p.13).

Nonetheless, management values and business management culture are not simply matters of general culture; they are inextricably linked with the structural characteristics of the target markets of corporations. For example, comparing the German market conditions after World War II with those of the US (where standardization was very advanced) reveals differences in market conditions, such as a consumer emphasis on quality or functionality. Conversely, the American pragmatic management value emphasizing the efficiency principle has reflected the characteristics of the US in which the standardization of consumption has progressed compared with other nations. Management values emphasizing technology, quality, and production in Germany after World War II reflected characteristics of the European market, the core market for German exports.

The value norms emphasized in the rationalization movements in Germany until the end of World War II or the productivity movement after the war were, by nature, "efficiency" or "productivity." They have characteristics as the concept of results in fields such as production rather than the whole economic society. Even when rationalization was developed as a "systematic movement," its main sphere stage was the enterprise. Therefore, the concept and value norm indicated by "efficiency" or "productivity" focused on the enterprise. In this sense, they greatly reflect the perspective of "rationality of capital." However, the viewpoint of "social rationality" in Germany means an emphasis on "economic efficiency" ("Wirtschaftlichkeit") that is not limited to spheres such as production and enterprise, namely efficiency-oriented toward the whole economic society. This perspective was deeply concerned with the fact that the concept of economic efficiency was emphasized as the direction toward the rebuilding of economic society after World War I in the rationalization movement in the 1920s. Rationalization to be pursued at the enterprise level by nature was understood as an issue at a dimension of the whole industry and national economy exceeding the improvement of efficiency or productivity of an individual enterprise. As representative researchers in German business economics (Betriebswirtschaftslehre), Heinrich Nickrisch (1922a, b) and Eugen Schmalenbach (1926, 1928) introduced the "economic efficiency" or "socioeconomic efficiency" principles ("Gemeinschaftliche Wirtschaftlichkeit") as the guiding principle of management, which was closely connected with "the economic rationality" oriented at the time (Nickrisch 1922a, b; Schmalenbach 1926; Schmalenbach 1928).

The fact that rationalities like "economic efficiency" or "socioeconomic efficiency" became important was determined by the specific conditions during World War I and changes after the war. The concept that regarded enterprise and management as a community was created under the birth of the conception of the labor community regarding wage agreement during World War I, recognition of labor unions, and the central labor community agreement between the labor union and employer association that was created with the German Revolution, and approval of labor rights by the Weimar Constitution (Nakamura 1982, pp.168, 238).

Heinrich Nikrisch (1922b, S.58–59) points out that the intention of the community existed not as the mere sum of the intentions of members but as the same intention and purpose; it was supposed to be a community (Nickrisch 1922b, S.58–59). He also insisted on economic efficiency as "the law of formation and maintenance in business economic production process" instead of the profitability principle on which he placed the highest priority until then (Nickrisch 1922a, S.81). Economic efficiency was regarded as the "criterion" for profit (Nickrisch 1922a, S.83). Thus, the dominance of profitability principle in terms of the profitability of capital was denied entirely. The principle of economic efficiency was considered the sole and primary fundamental prop of all systems (Schönpflug 1954, S.161).

Meanwhile, Eugen Schmalenbach (1928, S.258) advocated not the whole private profit of enterprise but "socioeconomic efficiency" as the whole profit under the political and economic circumstances that reflected the crisis of the capitalistic system brought about by the German Revolution (Schmalenbach 1928, S.258). He regarded the enterprise as an institution for the socioeconomy and emphasized how business economic actions were productive, and enterprise should behave like socioeconomic profit and private economic profit was ordinarily accorded (Schmalenbach 1928, S.94–95). His study focused on socioeconomic efficiency concerning profit. His view that only profit that could realize the principle of economic optimum in the meaning of the whole could be approved attempted to indicate the direction of German capitalism and enterprises under the political and economic conditions in which unreserved pursuit of profit by enterprise could not be supported (Nakamura 1982, pp.238, 268).

Unlike the economic rationality in management based on the thorough efficiency principle in the US, the German characteristic can be typically seen in the rationalization movement in the relatively stable period in the 1920s. The National Center for Economic Effectiveness [*Reichskuratorium für Wirtschaftlichkeit* (RKW)] occupied an important position as an institution for guiding and supervising rationalization and attempted to grasp rationalization at the dimension of "economic efficiency" (Yoshida 1976, p.91). Unlike the US, in which issues of standardization, simplification, simple implementation, and management were emphasized in the national movement whose goal was "elimination of waste in industry," in Europe, these problems and issues of the whole economy exceeding them were summarized with the concept of "rationalization" (Reichskuratorium für Wirtschaftlichkeit 1930, S.96–97). This situation is true for Germany, where economic efficiency exceeded "efficiency," and "productivity" was emphasized as an industrial and national economic issue.

In Germany, relationships based on orientation toward the community between management and labor in which the company aims at increasing workers' welfare and considers improving their lives had been established in the development of German capitalism. Such a system based on the idea of public welfare (das Gemeinwohl) was developed into a socialized system in the process of the labor movement through building various legal measures for labor protection after World War I (Tanaka 2001, pp.23, 445–446, 451, 454). Under the political and economic situations in which the approval of the pursuit of profit by the enterprise on the labor side became an important issue, such a traditional view on the relationships between management and labor provided an important foundation for the emphasis on the existence of a company as "a social community" by focusing on the interests of the whole economy.

American ideology regards companies as a "nexus of contracts" and considers them the objective of buying or selling. In contrast, in Germany, the view of a company not as a "money-making machine" but as a place where products are designed, produced, and eventually sold has been dominant and is connected with a greater emphasis on production objectives over financial ones. This crucial factor makes shareholder value maximization less important for top managers (Fiss and Zajac 2004, p.505). In such management value, a company tends to be considered where workers cooperate, which is deeply concerned with an important foundation for the concept that considers a company "social community." Supported by the safety net functions in the form of social and wage security of the codetermination system (Yamazaki 2013, Chapter 4), this concept can be regarded as harmonious with the principle of the social market economy aiming at the correction of social inequality.

Emphasis on the perspective of such economic efficiency was an important characteristic in German economic society that can be observed since the period before World War II. It has been successful and is a factor determining the characteristics of business management in this country. The origin of an entity as a "social community" that is deeply concerned with the unique nature of German capitalism called "Rhenish capitalism" (Albert 1991) can be seen in the view of the company as a community in the confusing period after World War I, the emphasis of economic efficiency or socioeconomic efficiency, and the orientation toward socioeconomic efficiency as a whole during the relatively stable period in the 1920s. Continuity in management value and pursuit of economic rationality before and after World War II is deeply concerned with the characteristics of German enterprises as a "social community" and has been an important foundation for their behavioral mode.

References

Abelshauser W (2001) Umbruch und Persistenz: Das deutsche Produktionsregime in historischer Perspektive. In: Geschichte und Gesellschaft 27(4):503–523

Albert M (1991) Capitalisme contre capitalisme. Éditions du Seuil, Paris

Barsoux J-L, Lawrence P (1991) Countries, cultures and constraints. In: Calori R, Lawrence P (eds) The business of Europe. Managing change. Sage, London, pp 198–217

Bauer O (1931) Rationalisierung und Fehlrationalisierung. Wiener Volksbuchhandlung.

Calori R (1994) The Diversity of Management Systems. In: Calori R, Woot P de (eds) A European Management Model. Beyond Diversity. Prentice Hall, New York, Tokyo, pp. 11–30

Chandler AD Jr (1977) The visible hand: Managerial revolution in American business. Harvard University Press, Cambridge, Massachusetts

Dornseifer B (1995) Strategy, technological capability, and innovation: German enterprises in comparative perspective. In: Caron F, Erker P, Fischer W (eds) Innovations in the European economy between the wars. Walter de Gruyter, Berlin, pp 197–226

Drury HB (1922) Scientific management. A history and criticism, 2nd edn. Columbia University, New York

Dyas GP, Thanheiser TH (1976) The emerging European enterprise. Strategy and structure in French and German industry. The Macmillan Press, London

Fiss PC, Zajac EJ (2004) The diffusion of ideas over contested terrain: The (non) adoption of a shareholder value orientation among German firms. In: Admin Sci Q 49(4):501–534

Hagemann H (1984) Lohnsenkungen als Mittel der Karisenbekämpfung? Überlegungen zum Beitrag der ,Kieler Schule' in der beschäftigungspolitischen Diskussion am Ende der Weimarer Republik. In: Hagemann H, Kurz HO (Hrsg) *Beschäftigung, Verteilung und Konjunktur. Zur Politischen Ökonomik der modernen Gesellschaft. Festschrift für Adolph Lowe.* Universität Bremen, Press- und Informationsamt, Bremen, S97–129

Hämmerling F (1960) Die Mechanisierung von Montagen in der Elektroindustrie. In: Brandt L, Gardellini R, King A et al. (Hrsg) *Industrielle Rationalisierung 1960.* Verkehrs- und Wirtschafts-Verlag, Dortmund, S127–129

Hall PA, Soskice D (eds) (2001) Varieties of capitalism: The institutional foundations of comparative advantage. Oxford University Press, Oxford

Hampden-Turner C, Trompenaars A (1993) The seven cultures of capitalism: value systems for creating wealth in the United States, Japan, Germany, France, Britain, Sweden, and the Netherlands. Currency and Doubleday, New York

Herrigel G (2000) American occupation, market order, and democracy: Reconfiguring the steel industry in Japan and German after the Second World War. In: Zeitlin J, Herrigel G (eds) Americanization and its limits. Reworking US technology and management in post-war Europe and Japan. Oxford University Press, Oxford, pp 340–399

Imakubo S (2001) Taisenkanki Doitsu denki kogyo ni okeru nagare sagyo hoshiki no donyu to tenkai (Introduction and development of the flow production system in the German electrotechnical industry in interwar period). In: Keizai Ronso (Econ Rev) 167(3):1–22

Jaeckel B (1961) 10 Jahre REFA-Bundesverband. In: REFA-Nachrichten 14(6):221–226
Kipping M (2004) 'Importing' American ideas to West Germany, 1940s to 1970s. In: Kudo A, Kipping M, Schröter HG (eds) German and Japanese business in the boom years. Transforming American management and technology models. Routledge, London, New York, pp 30–53
Kocka J (1981) Groβunternehmen und der Aufstieg der Manager-Kapitalismus im späten 19. und frühen 20.Jahrhundert, Deutschland im internationalen Vergleich. In: Histrische Zeitschrift 232: 39–60
Kudo A (1977) Nachisu taisei ka no tekko shihon (Iron and steel capital under the Nazi system). In: Institute of Social Science, University of Tokyo (ed) Nachisu keizai to nyu deal (The Nazi Economy and the New Deal). Tokyo daigaku shuppankai, Tokyo, pp 87–134
Locke RR (1996) The collapse of the American management mystique. Oxford University Press, New York
Meskill D (2010) Optimizing the German workforce. Labor Administration from Bismarck to the Economic Miracle. Berghahn Books, New York
Nakamura T (1982) Doitsu keiei keizaigaku (German business economics). Tokyo daigaku shuppankai, Tokyo
Nakata M (1983) Genda kigyon kozo to kanri kno (Structure of contemporary enterprise and functions of management) Chuo keizaisha, Tokyo
Nicklisch H (1922a) Wirtschaftliche Betriebslehre. 6. Auflage von "Der Allgemeine kaufmännischen Betriebslehre." C. E. Poeschel, Stuttgart
Nicklisch H (1922b) Der Weg Aufwärts! Organisation. Versuch einer Grundlegung. C. E. Poeschel, Stuttgart
Pilz HE (1961) Die Einfürung des Work-Factor-System in Deutschland. In: REFA-Nachrichten 14(4):124–125
Plumpe W (2006) Unternehmen. In: Ambrosius G, Petzina D, Plumpe W (Hrsg) Moderne Wirtschaftsgeschichte. Eine Einführung für Historiker und Ökonomen, 2., überarbeitete und erweiterte Auflage, R. Oldenbpurg, München, S61–94
Plumpe W (2018) Unternehmensgeschichte im 19. und 20. Jahrhundert. De Gruyter Oldenbourg, Berlin
Rauecker B (1925) Wege und Möglichkeiten der Rationalisierung. In: Die Arbeit 2(12):743–751
Reichskuratorium für Wirtschaftlichkeit (1930) *Handbuch der Rationalisierung*. Zweite, unveränderte Auflage. Spaeth & Linde, Berlin
Schlaich K (1969) Die Anpassung der Aufgaben und Methoden des Arbeitsstudiums an die wirtschaftliche und technische Entwicklung. In: REFA-Nachrichten 22(4):229–234
Schmalenbach E (1926) Dynamische Bilanz. G. A. Gloeckner Verlagsbuchhandlung, Leipzig
Schmalenbach E (1928) Selbstkostenrechnung. I. In: Zeitschrift für handelswissenschaftliche Forschung 13 (9/10): 257-299
Schönpflug F (1954) Betriebswirtschaftslehre. Methoden und Hauptströmungen. 2.erweiterte Auflage von "Methodenproblem in der Einzelwirtschaftslehre." C. E. Poeschel, Stuttgart
Schröter HG (2005) Americanization of the European economy. A compact survey of American economic influence in Europe since the 1880s. Springer, Dordrecht
Schwartmann J (1975) Praktische Arbeitsgestaltung in der Automobilindustrie. In: REFA-Nachrichten 28(4): 205–207
Streeck W (1997) German capitalism: Do it exist? Can it survive? In: Crouch C, Streeck W (eds) Political economy of modern capitalism: Mapping convergence and diversity. Sage, London, pp 33–54
Taguchi N (2018) Book review: Kigyo keiei no nichi doku hikaku (Comparison of business management in Japan and Germany, Book review). Hikaku Keiie Kenkyu (Comparative Management Study) 42:139–147
Tanaka Y (2001) Doitsu kigyo shakai no keisei to heny (Formation and changes in German company society). Minerva shobo, Kyoto
Weiss H (1926) Rationalisierung und Arbeiterklasse:Zur Rationalisierung der deutschen Industrie. Führer-Verlag, Berlin

Wengenroth U (1997) Germany: competition abroad—cooperation at home, 1870–1990. In: Chandler AD Jr, Amatori F, Hikino T (eds) Big business and the wealth of nations. Cambridge University Press, Cambridge, pp 139–175
Winnacker K (1971) Nie den Mut verlieren. Erinnerungen an Schicksalsjahre der deutschen Chemie. Econ Verlag, Düsseldorf
Yamazaki T (1997) Doitsu kigyo kanrishi kenkyu (History of management in German enterprises). Moriyama shoten, Tokyo
Yamazaki T (2013) German business management: a Japanese perspective on regional development factors. Springer, Tokyo
Yamazaki T (2024) Japanese and German enterprises: Comparison of industrial concentration system and business management. Springer Nature, Singapore
Yoshida K (1976) Doitsu gorika undou ron (The Rationalization movement in Germany). Mineruva Shobo, Kyoto

Archival Sources

1. **Historisches Archiv Krupp, Essen**
   WA41/2-105, WA41/2-108, WA41/6-207
2. **Thyssenkrupp Corporate Archives, Duisburg**
   A596/2, VST/590, VST/1588, VST/3844
3. **Bayer Archiv, Leverkusen**
   004/B-14-3-6, 004/C-19, 010-003-001, 010-004, 1/6-6-25
4. **BASF Archiv, Ludwigshafen**
   I.G.C0/2, IG C0/3, Vogtländer-Tetzner V, Ohne Signatur (Der Mensch in der BASF. 1865–1939)
5. **Hoechst Archiv, Frankfurt am Main**
   IG 194, IG200, IG214, IG234, IG235
6. **Siemens Archiv, Berlin**
   11/Lf494, 15/Lg562, 15/Lc815, 15/Lc816, 64/Lc511, 68/Li180, Ls101
7. **Mercedes-Benz Classic Archiv, Stuttgart**
   Kissel Protokolle, I/1, Kissel Protokolle, I/2, Kissel Protokolle, I/3, Kissel Protokolle, I/4, Kissel Protokolle, I/5, Kissel Protokolle, I/8, Kissel Protokolle, I/9, Kissel Protokolle, I/10, Kissel Protokolle, I/11, Kissel Protokolle, I/12, Kissel Protokolle, I/13, Kissel Protokolle, I/14, Kissel Protokolle, I/15, Kissel Protokolle, I/22, Kissel Protokolle, I/23, Kissel Technische Protokolle, 1.22, Kissel Technische Protokolle, 1.23., Kissel Technische Protokolle, 1.29, Kissel Technische Protokolle, 1.30, Kissel, Werk Untertürkheim, Kissel, Werk Gaggenau
8. **MAN Archiv, Augsburg**
   1.3.3.5, Akt 17, 2.3, Nr.19, 2.3, Nr.23, 2.3, Nr.24, 2.3, Nr.26, 2.3, Nr.27, 2.3, Nr.28, 2.3, Nr.29, 2.3, Nr.31
9. **National Archives, Washington D.C.**
   RG59, RG469
10. **Bundesarchiv Berlin, Berlin**
    R43-1/1201, R1501/107158, R1501/107163, R/3001/7921, R/3101/12361, R/3101/12362, R8119F

T. Yamazaki, *A History of German Business*, https://doi.org/10.1007/978-981-96-8476-2

11. **Historisches Archiv des Deutschen Technikmuseum, Berlin**
I. 2.032 0007, GS6385

Index

T. Yamazaki, *A History of German Business*, https://doi.org/10.1007/978-981-96-8476-2

T

www.ingramcontent.com/pod-product-compliance
Ingram Content Group UK Ltd.
Pitfield, Milton Keynes, MK11 3LW, UK
UKHW020630260926
475829UK00003BA/13
* 9 7 8 9 8 1 9 6 8 4 7 5 5 *